תשנ"ה 5755

LEARN TORAH WITH...

1994-1995 TORAH ANNUAL

A COLLECTION OF THE YEAR'S BEST TORAH

EDITED BY RABBI STUART KELMAN
AND JOEL LURIE GRISHAVER

ALEF DESIGN GROUP

ISBN# 1-881283-13-5

ALEF DESIGN GROUP • 4423 FRUITLAND AVENUE, LOS ANGELES, CA 90058

(800) 845–0662 • (213) 582-1200 • (213) 585–0327 FAX

E-MAIL <MISRAD@TORAHAURA.COM>

MANUFACTURED IN THE UNITED STATES OF AMERICA

Learn Torah With...

Welcome to **Learn Torah With....** It has been our distinct pleasure to bring these gems of Torah to you each week. Truth to tell, it has been exhilarating to be in communication with so many of our authors and exciting to look forward to each week's new commentaries. Over the course of this, our first year of **Learn Torah With...,** we have been guided by three Rabbinic phrases:

Le-hag'del Torah u-le'ha'adera: "To enhance the Torah and make it precious" goes the often quoted Rabbinic phrase. It is an apt background to this project, for that is exactly what we, as editors, set out to accomplish. Making the Torah come alive in our modern world meant securing fine scholars, rabbis, and teachers and asking them to comment on a specific parashah.

Le-hafeetz Torah b'rabim: "To spread Torah among the masses." We wanted to take the weekly parashah and make it accessible to the layperson. This was not to be a commentary for the Jewish professional, but rather for the intelligent Jew who is searching for depth rather than breadth in struggling with our tradition. We assumed that our audience was capable of handling a sophisticated rendering of the text. We also learned that many of you would go on to make copies for friends! To our surprise and delight, many of you have told us how much these weekly studies have influenced your thinking. We should note that this is particularly true of people living in far-flung places throughout the world.

Ha-fokh ba, ve-hafokh ba dekulei bah: "Turn it and turn it yet again, for all is in it (Torah)". This meant not watering down the content; to the contrary, we wished to empower every reader not only to read the text but react to it as well. Our "Third Page" of comments from readers has been steadily growing as a location for exchange of views as seen through the lens of the weekly readings. It is this unique feature of fax and e-mail that we wish to stimulate even further.

Hadran alekha: "We shall return to You." Finally, a note of gratitude to the Almighty who made all this possible in the first place. We shall return.

Rabbi Stuart Kelman
Rosh ha-Shanah, 5757

Learn Torah With... may not make your whites whiter, but it might remove the waxy build-up from your soul. It will not assure fewer cavities, but it might connect you to a sense of the Eternal.

Any fax on the weekly Torah portion promises to bring directly into your life the peiodic cycle of every Jew's quest for wisdom. The reality of studying a piece of Torah each and every week is Judaism's way of keeping Judaism from becoming only *für de kinder*, from being reduced to only pediatric truths. Our friends Gail Dorph and Vicky Kelman love to quote their teacher, Rabbi Joseph Lukinsky, who is fond of saying, "Every week Jews should put on their *parashat ha-Shavua* (weekly Torah portion) spectacles." In other words, each week the *sidrah* (the portion) is supposed to—like a time-release capsule—release some of the wisdom we need to get through that week. And, every week, our own life experience is supposed to rub against the words of the biblical text and release some truth we would never have seen otherwise.

We believe that any Torah fax would do that but we think **Learn Torah With...** will also do something else—something more.

Frederic Brenner is a Fench Jew who is presently shooting forty images of Jewish America for an issue of *Life* magazine. In order to capture who we are, he is asking two questions: (1) In what ways is the American diaspora a kind of Egypt? and, (2) What *midah* (measure) will be added to the *tikkun* (the future redemption) of the Jewish people because of their time in America? For us the answer begins with "democracy," which creates a sense of "individualism" unique in the Jewish experience which, in turn, gives rise to the "pluralistic" truths and visions of American Jews. The Torah of "America" (the culture, not the country) is a three-dimensional Torah. It is a Torah which pops off the page because it is etched and cross-hatched by complementary and contradictory understandings. It is rich in harmony, made richer through contrasting textures and even sporadic dissonances.

Every week, **Learn Torah With...** offers you the chance to bask in and celebrate the diversity of American Torah. Our teachers are poets and scholars, spiritual teachers and academics, rabbis, working-class writers, storytellers, teachers and secular professionals with deep Jewish souls. We will simultaneously offer rabbinical insight and archeological truths; we will look concretely at the Torah as literature and soar on the magical carpet of midrashic fantasy. Our Torah teachers are traditionalists and radicals, spiritual seekers and methodical researchers—and at the same time, parents who go to *shul*, just like you do. We promise Women's Torah and Feminist Torah, Orthodox Torah and Radical Torah, Scientific Torah and Spiritual Torah, Renewed Torah, Reconstructed Torah, and even Deconstructed Torah. (Yes, we will be Reform and Conservative—and lots of other flavors, too.) And, perhaps most importantly, we promise Your Torah as well.

Learn Torah With... is not just for rabbis. It is an invitation to every Jew to sit down once a week, with a cup of coffee or tea, and give your soul and your mind fifteen or twenty minutes of seeking the Eternal. It is an invitation to put on *parashat ha-Shavua* spectacles and see the wisdom of our people in three dimensions. Perhaps it will even make your whites whiter.

Joel Lurie Grishaver
Rosh ha-Shanah, 5757

To receive **Learn Torah With...** weekly
by fax, by e-mail or by mail,
call 800-BE-TORAH (800-238-6724)
fax 213-585-0327 or
e-mail <misrad@torahaura.com>.

To participate in our free electronic Torah dialogue,
send a posting to <misrad@torahaura.com>.

Table of Contents

Devarim/Deuteronomy 329

בראשית
Bereshit

The first parashah of the Torah has the dual role of conveying its own story and setting the context of the entire Torah. The Torah's stories have been observed to be rich in background, as opposed to, for example, Homer's stories. In Homer, each episode of the epic is self-contained; all the information that the reader needs is provided then and there, and all action is in the foreground. That is fine, but it is not the way of the Torah. To read the Torah at any level beyond

Bereshit
Genesis 1.1–6.8
Professor Richard E. Friedman

RICHARD ELLIOTT FRIEDMAN IS KATZIN PROFESSOR OF JEWISH CIVILIZATION AT THE UNIVERSITY OF CALIFORNIA, SAN DIEGO. HE RECEIVED A DOCTORATE IN HEBREW BIBLE AT HARVARD, HELD VISITING POSTS AT OXFORD AND CAMBRIDGE, AND JOINED IN THE EXCAVATIONS OF BIBLICAL JERUSALEM. HE IS AUTHOR OF *WHO WROTE THE BIBLE?* AND OF *THE DISAPPEARANCE OF GOD*.

"Sunday school," one must have sense of the whole when one reads the parts. To comprehend what happens in the exodus and in the revelation at Sinai, you have to know what has happened in Genesis 1.

Like some films that begin with a sweeping shot that then narrows—think of Hitchcock's famous opening of *Psycho* that moves from a view of a city, to a building, to a window, and into a room with a man and woman in it—so the first chapter of Genesis gradually moves from a picture of the heavens and earth to the first man and woman. The story's focus will continue to narrow: from the universe to the earth, to humankind, to specific lands and peoples, to a single family. (It will expand back out to nations in Exodus.) But, the wider concern with heavens and earth that is established here in the first parashah will remain. When the

דָּבָר אַחֵר **DAVAR AHER (Another Insight). IN THE BEGINNING GOD CREATED... [GEN. 1.1].** Sunday morning, just like the *New York Times*, I was delighted to receive **Learn Torah With....** I think we need *Bereshit* after facing the end of things during Sukkot. Between *Koheleth* and looking at my dying tomato plants, I feel a melancholy amidst the harvest... **Malka Drucker <MalkaD@aol.com>**

דָּבָר אַחֵר **DAVAR AHER. IN THE BEGINNING GOD CREATED... [GEN. 1.1].** In addition to fourteen letters on each half of the first verse, the first verse has seven words, including each "אֵת" (*et*) as a word. The second verse has fourteen words. The emphasis on seven and its multiples is obvious. It is explicit in the Torah in terms of time, i.e., the seventh day, the seventh month, the seventh year and the Jubilee (7x7+1). There

בראשית ברא אלהים את ז

story narrows to a singular divine relationship with Abraham, it will still be with the ultimate aim that this will be "A BLESSING TO ALL THE FAMILIES OF THE EARTH. [Gen. 12.3]" Every biblical scene will be laden—artistically, theologically, psychologically, spiritually—with all that has come before. So when we read later of a man and his son going up a mountain to perform a fearful sacrifice, that moment in the history of a family is set in a cosmic context of the creation of the universe and the nature of the relationship between the Creator and humans. You *can* read the account of the sacrifice of Isaac without being aware of the account of the creation or the account of the covenant between God and Abraham, but you lose something. The something that you lose—depth—is one of the essential qualities of the Torah.

The first parashah initiates the historical flow of the Torah (and of the entire *Tanakh*). It establishes that this is to be a related, linear sequence of events through generations. That may seem so natural to us now that we regard this point as obvious and banal. But the texts of the Torah are the first texts on earth known to do this. The ancient world did not write history prior to these accounts. The Torah's accounts are the first human attempts to recount history. Whether one believes all or part or none of its history to be true is a separate matter. The literary point is that this had the effect of producing a text that was rich in background: every event carries the weight of everything that comes before it; and the historical point is that this was a new way to conceive of time and human destiny.

It was also a new way to conceive of a God. The difference between the Torah's conception of God and the pagan world's conception is not

Synopsis: The Torah begins with God's acts of creation. In seven days the reality we know is brought step-by-step into existence. We begin in chaos, climax with the creation of people, and end creation with the first Shabbat. Then we begin our study of Toldot, "family-histories," first of heaven and earth, then of Adam and Eve, then of Cain and Abel, and then of the next ten generations. In a series of ten rapid "cross-dissolves" we go from Adam to Noah. The sidrah ends with the coming attractions for "Parashat Noah." We learn that God is comfortable with Noah (whose name means "comfort") but uncomfortable with the rest of creation. What happens—is next week's story.

---

is a more subtle use of seven in the genealogy, which appears in chapter 5, at the end of *Bereshit*. The use of seven is obvious in Lamech's age, 777 total years, but U. Cassuto finds additional uses of seven as he explains in his book, *A Commentary on the Book of Genesis*. He notes that all the ages in the chapter 5 genealogy, prior to the birth of the firstborn and following, are divisible by five. The only exceptions have the number seven added to a number divisible by five. There is also an explanation for the age of the earth based on a sexagesimal system augmented by the number seven. Returning to the number of letters and words in the opening verses, one might hypothesize that from the very beginning of the Torah, there is a subtle emphasis on the number seven. **Rabbi Allen Juda, Brith Sholom, Bethlehem, PA**

דָּבָר אַחֵר **DAVAR AHER. AND THE EARTH WAS** *TOHU VA-VOHU* **(in chaos)… [Gen. 1.2].** Each of us as we leave the old year, face newness, the life ahead we can't yet see. Each of us, each year face the primeval תֹהוּ וָבֹהוּ *tohu va-vohu*. As we walk fresh from the Days of Awe, fresh from the sukkah, and into the year, *Bereshit* offers wisdom to guide us on our way to meet and shape the as of yet unknown that the new year will gift.

merely arithmetic: one versus many. The pagan deities were known through their functions in nature: the sun god, *Shamash*, was the sun. If one wanted to know the essence of *Shamash*, the thing to do was to contemplate the sun. If you wanted to know the essence of the grain deity *Dagon*, you contemplated wheat. To know *Yamm*, contemplate the sea. But the God of the Torah was different, creating all of nature and therefore not knowable or identifiable through any one element of nature. You could learn no more about this God by contemplating the sea than you could by contemplating grain, sky, or anything else. The essence of this God remains hidden. One does not know God through nature but by the divine acts in history. One never finds out what God *is*, but rather what God *does*––and what God *says*. This conception, which informs all of biblical narrative, did not necessarily have to be developed at the very beginning of the story, but it was. *Parashat Bereshit* establishes this by beginning with accounts of creation and by then flowing through the first ten generations of humankind. (Those "begat" lists are thus more important than people generally think.)

The Torah's theology is, thus, inseparable from its history and from its literary character. Ultimately there is no such thing as "The Bible as Literature" or "The Bible as History" or "The Bible as…anything." There is only the Bible, and one can barely enumerate all the other strands of the biblical fabric that are set out prominently in the first parashah, from the psychological element to *gematria*.

PSYCHOLOGICALLY: The first stories of the Torah are a Freudian's bread and butter. *The sexes*: A naked man and woman who choose knowledge of good and bad, even at the risk of death, for the sake of becoming "LIKE GOD." "THEREFORE A MAN SHALL LEAVE HIS

Bereshit

Just as the Holy One, about to create, was not alone, so too are we not alone, as we are about to walk forward. *Ha-Yotzer*, according to midrash, was accompanied by angels and Torah. So these escort us as well as we enter our new year.

Teachings from the Acts of Creation as we face *tohu va-vohu*: (1) TEXT: THE FIRST DAY: The earth was unformed and void, darkness was upon the face of the deep. "LET THERE BE LIGHT (אוֹר *or*)"; Dividing the light from the darkness (day, night). INTERPRETATION: The first act is facing our *tohu va-vohu* of darkness, the unknown, and consciously opening the light of our heart, allowing our heart to open and to be receptive, to be soft. For from an open and soft heart light flows. (2) TEXT: THE SECOND DAY: Firmament (רְקִיעַ *rakiah*) divided the waters under, waters above (שָׁמַיִם

בראשית ברא אלהים את השמים ואת הארץ

FATHER AND HIS MOTHER AND SHALL CLEAVE TO HIS WIFE, AND THE TWO OF THEM SHALL BECOME ONE FLESH [Gen. 2.24]"—give me another 200 pages, and I'll analyze that. *Sibling rivalry*: The first siblings compete and end in fratricide (which will become a continuing biblical theme: Jacob and Esau, Joseph and his brothers, Absalom and Amnon, Solomon and Adonijah).

DIALOGUE: The conversation between God and the two humans in the garden is a masterpiece. The Deity says, "WHERE ARE YOU? [Gen. 3.9]"—which is a strange thing for a deity to say. The man says, "I HID BECAUSE I WAS NAKED, [Gen. 3.10]" and his Creator pounces like an attorney who has caught a witness in a stupid mistake on the stand: "WHO TOLD YOU THAT YOU WERE NAKED?! HAVE YOU EATEN FROM THE TREE…?" [Gen. 3.11] To which the man replies, unchivalrously: "THE WOMAN" and ungratefully: "WHICH YOU PUT WITH ME," and trying to escape responsibility for his own actions: "SHE GAVE ME FROM THE TREE, AND I ATE." [Gen. 3.12] The Creator

turns to the woman, who also tries to pass the responsibility down the line: "THE SNAKE DECEIVED ME. [Gen. 3.13]" God pronounces a curse on the snake (and on all snakes)—no dialogue, there's no one left for the snake to blame—but then God turns back to the woman and pronounces a painful fate for her (and all women) as well. During this pronouncement one should consider the tension in the man, who does not know if the pendulum of recompense will swing all the way back to him. He soon learns that it will, as his Creator pronounces a hard fate for him (and all men) as well. This first divine-human dialogue in the Torah is remarkable—at times humorous and at times fearfully serious—but my point is not merely a literary one; it is a psychological and spiritual one as well. This exchange is a powerful introduction to the coming account of the relationship between God and humans in the Torah.

DIVINE-HUMAN RELATIONS: Humans are created in the divine

image. We argue but truly do not know what is meant: physical image, spiritual, intellectual. Whatever it means, though, it implies that humans are understood here to share in the divine in a way that a lion or tiger or bear does not. That is crucial to all that will follow. The paradox, inherent in the divine-human relationship, is that only humans have some element of the divine, only humans would, by their very nature, aspire to the divine, yet the Deity regularly communicates with them by means of *commands;* they are subordinates. In biblical terms that would not bother a camel or a dove; it will bother humans a great deal. Thus the snake's argument to attract the humans to the tree is, "IN THE DAY YOU EAT OF IT…*YOU WILL BE LIKE GOD.* [Gen.3.5]" The first parashah, thus, sets up and develops the tension between God and humans that will persist throughout the Torah and be a powerful element within it.

MALE-FEMALE RELATIONS: Woman is usually understood to be created as

---

shamayim). INTERPRETATION: Being aware of the waters of our past below us, and of the waters of our future hopes and desires and expectations above, and separating them out, is the second act toward walking into the newness. (3) TEXT: THE THIRD DAY: Gathering waters under heaven, letting dry land (אֶרֶץ *eretz*) appear; gatherings of water, seas (יַמִּים *yamim*); from the earth: grass, herb yielding seed, fruit tree bearing fruit with

seeds. INTERPRETATION: Seeing the waters, the thoughts and experiences from the past and the waters of desires and hopes for the future, we next attempt to let the dry land of being in the present come forth from in between the two. Then, being in the present, from that place, all kinds of seeds can then emerge. (4) TEXT: THE FOURTH DAY: Lights dividing day from night, signs, seasons, days and years; two great lights, stars. INTER-

PRETATION: When living in the present, we become aware of and move in concert with the natural cycles. The lights and seasons mirror our very bodies and souls, are filled with teachings and gifts. Through their movements, we become aware of and alive to our days and our years. (5) TEXT: THE FIFTH DAY: Waters swarm with living creatures, fowl fly: "BE FRUITFUL AND MULTIPLY." INTERPRETATION: As we enter the present we will learn

a suitable "helper," (עֵזֶר) *eizer*, to man in this parashah. The Hebrew root, however, can also mean "strength." (See cases of it in parallel with (עֹז) *oz*, as, for example, Ps. 46.2; see also Azariah [2 Kgs. 14.21] and Uzziah [2 Chr. 26.1] as alternative names of the same king.) The Hebrew phrase (עֵזֶר כְּנֶגְדּוֹ) *eizer k'negdo*, therefore, may very well mean "a corresponding strength." If so, it is a different picture from what people have thought, and a more welcome one in terms of current sensitivities concerning the sexes and how they are pictured in the Torah. In Genesis 1, man and woman are both created in the image of God; in Genesis 2, they are corresponding strengths. However one interprets subsequent stories and laws in the Torah, this essential equality of worth and standing introduces them.

The opening parashah of the Torah is so phenomenally rich that the limitations of size of this commentary make it barely possible even to list all the areas in which to look for these riches, much less to describe or even summarize them. But, it is a beginning.•

Bereshit

from the creatures from the waters, our unconscious, as well as from those that fly, our intuition. Both enable us to be fruitful and live well. (6) TEXT: THE SIXTH DAY: Earth brings forth living creatures, cattle, creeping things: "ADAM" first human being: "BE FRUITFUL AND MULTIPLY." INTERPRETATION: With intuition and the subconscious alive, then the life force can spring up from the earth. We can become male-female, integrated, grounded. A whole creation, we can then be fruitful and from that place can create newness. (7) TEXT: THE SEVENTH DAY: Rest. INTERPRETATION: To create and live freshly, fruitfully, requires time to rest from creating. A time to enjoy, to enjoy being, and to enjoy the creations, and to fill up with our Creator. **Rabbi Vicki Hollander, Seattle, WA**

דָּבָר אַחֵר **DAVAR AHER. …FROM ALL THE WORK WHICH ELOKIM HAD CREATED TO MAKE. [Gen. 2.3].** Passing over the issue of evolution vs. the creation story, there are four major morals in the creation story: (1) That the Creator of this wonderful universe is *Elokim*. All we have been given on earth is from G-d—thus sacred….(2) That everything is good, even by our Creator's judgment. (3) That the climax of creation is man/woman. They are now the recipients of the gifts of creation and then placed in charge of them all…. The crowns of creation are obligated to care for all of their gifts from the Creator. (4) The ultimate of creation is G-d's supreme gift of Shabbat…in these accounts of creation one finds the very essence of Judaism. **Rabbi Morris A. Kipper, Coral Gables, FL**

דְּבָר אַחֵר **DAVAR AHER. THIS IS THE FAMILY-HISTORY OF THE HEAVENS AND EARTH…[Gen. 2.1].** The first chapter of the Torah is a study of the tension between order and chaos. Einstein looked at the created universe and said, "God doesn't play dice with the universe." In other words, "There is order and purpose." Rabbi Nachman of Bretzlav looked at that same universe and said, "The world is a tumbling die." He said, "Paradigms and realities keep shifting. There is an order, but we can't chart it. There is a purpose, but it is not a straight line." Joseph Ford (a mathematician interested in chaos) said, "God plays dice with the universe, but the dice are loaded." Simply put, there is no order, but there is a pattern to the chaos. He also says, "Evolution is chaos with feedback." I suggest, in that feedback we find God's footprint.

Edward Lorenz is a chaotician. Originally he was a meteorologist who sought the secret of why weather seems to have a pattern but can never be predicted. Ultimately, he found a thing he called a "strange attractor"—a graphic pattern, not a formula. "The map displayed a kind of infinite complexity. It always stayed within certain bounds, never running off the page, but never repeating itself, either. It traced a strange, distinctive shape…the shape signaled pure disorder, since no point or pattern of points ever recurred. Yet it also signaled a new kind of order." (*Chaos, Making a New Science*, James Gleick, Penguin, New York, 1987)

When I read the day-by-day account of creation in Genesis 1, the reality is that none of the days are alike, that no poetic pattern exists which all days share, yet a rhythm emerges and an echo of what a created day should be—remains; I see "strange attractors." In the idiosyncratic numbering of each day, the nonlinear placement of names, blessings, and the perception of "good," the number of things created each day, etc. I find a pattern, not a formula. Here are harmonic possibilities—not anything that is linear. My heart says, "Life is just like that."

"Nature forms patterns. Some are orderly in space but disorderly in time, others are orderly in time but disorderly in space. Some patterns are fractal, exhibiting structures self-similar in scale. Others give rise to steady states or oscillating ones. Pattern formation has become a branch of physics and of material science, allowing scientists to model the aggregation of particles into clusters." [Ibid.] I will suggest that "pattern formation" is also the work of the soul. We live in a world where we feel the strange attraction of a greater purpose hidden in chaos. Genesis 1: "LET THERE BE LIGHT," begins our journey to gather divine sparks into clusters. The missing, "GOD SAW THAT IT WAS GOOD" on the second day reminds us that the dice are spinning. **Joel Lurie Grishaver <gris@torahaura.com>**

דְּבָר אַחֵר **DAVAR AHER. THIS IS THE FAMILY-HISTORY OF THE HEAVENS AND EARTH…[Gen. 2.1].** The *gematria* idea sparked a *drash* which is echoed in Joel's chaos/order discussion: The division of the first sentence…could indicate that from the start of the creative process there was a tension between dichotomies—between fulfillment and boredom, between destruction and redesign. This tension also seems mirrored in *Kohelet*'s "TIME FOR EVERYTHING [Ecc. 3.1]," which we just finished reviewing during Sukkot. Our job as fixers of the world is to return to and maintain the original positive tensions through which the world was created in such a way as to allow for continued growth. Isn't it nice that we picked (had picked for us) a job description almost guaranteeing 100% employment? **Larry Moldo, Beth El Synagogue, Omaha, NE**

דְּבָר אַחֵר **DAVAR AHER. THIS IS THE FAMILY-HISTORY OF THE HEAVENS AND EARTH…[Gen. 2.1].** *Chaos And Creation: A Review Essay*: (*Creation and the Persistence of Evil*), Jon Levenson, Harper & Row, and *Chaos: Making New Science*, James Gleick, Penguin. According to the nineteenth-century philosopher and mathematician Laplace, a supreme intelligence, knowing the place of every particle in the universe, would be able to predict the future and present the past with total accuracy. In this view, reality is a series of logical causal events. Indeed, by the late nineteenth century, it was assumed that the complete set of natural laws was within the grasp of humanity, and that all that was needed was to clear up some minor problems.

…Life is more complex than any theory or theology. We look out at the marvels of nature and we see also the cruelty of life. We behold the lofty achievements of humanity and we cringe at the same time at the depths to which it can sink. Sometimes the world is ablaze with God's glory; other times it seems filled with the stink of death and evil. Underneath the neat lawns of our ordered existence lies the hidden chaos, the disorder that can overwhelm us.

In Judaism there has always been, in addition to the tradition that sees evil as something nonexistent or abstract, a tradition that sees evil as real, as part of the fabric of the world. In the Kabbalah especially, chaos is an inevitable part of the process of creation, the result of a glitch in the divine machinery, so to speak…Levenson shows that creation *ex nihilo* (something from nothing) is not an accurate portrayal of creation in the Bible. There is a primeval "world" of disordered nature, although the Bible is more concerned with God's mastery over it and the subsequent creation of "an environment ordered for peaceful human habitation against the onslaughts of chaos and anarchy."

The initial creation of this order, according to the analysis advanced by Levenson, was not a peaceful process but rather a massive struggle between God and the forces of chaos as represented by a primordial sea (often called Leviathan). While some biblical texts see this combat as taking place only in the past, some relegate it to the future: a final decisive victory over Leviathan…Chaos survives in the various sources of evil in the world, including the evil or material drive within the human self—the *yetzer harah*…How may humanity participate in the control of evil?…The Temple was meant to be an earthly microcosm of the divine process of control. The building of the Temple, the festivals, the Sabbath ritual are

Bereshit

echoed in the Genesis 1 account. Thus, "God functions like an Israelite priest, making distinctions, assigning things to their proper category, and assessing their fitness, and hallowing the Sabbath." The sacrificial system is, therefore, "an order-maintaining system," a means for humanity to deal with chaos and evil. It "transforms chaos into creation, ennobles humanity, and realizes the kingship of the God who ordained the cult and commanded that it be guarded and practiced." This is how God's "good world" is created and realized. Levenson also points out that not only the covenant itself and Israel's maintenance of it are necessary to create and maintain order, but also that God relies upon people as partners and witnesses in creation so that God can be actualized in the world….

Chaos theory may be defined briefly as a universal theory of deterministic disorder. The term was first coined by mathematician James Yorke in 1975. Gleick points out that, in traditional science, chaos was ignored because scientists assumed that "simple systems behave in simple ways." Chaos was thought to be the result of inaccurate measurements or "noise." Laplace's determinism was the ideal that scientists sought to achieve, an ideal that they thought was attainable if they could only solve the problem of inexact measurements. Chaos was usually dealt with by assuming that the approximate behavior of a system was a sufficient description to make accurate predictions of the future behavior of that system. With the advent of computers, scientists began to try to make more and more accurate computer models of systems in order to make more accurate predictions. It just did not turn out the way they thought it would….

Gleick's first, and perhaps best, example of the theory and practice of chaos science is *The Butterfly Effect*. This was first elucidated by meteorologist Edward Lorenz in the 1960s. It is a half-humorous term referring to the eventual effects of small local weather fluctuations on larger weather systems. Tiny differences in input can create large differences in output, or "a butterfly stirring the air today in Peking can transform storm systems at the end of next month in New York." The new discipline soon acquired a name, conferences began to be called on chaos theory, journals sprang up and, in more and more areas, scientists began to see chaos. Einstein once said that God does not play dice with the universe. Physicist Joseph Ford is quoted by Gleick as saying that God does play dice with the universe, but they are loaded dice.

In their presentations, Levenson and Gleick have given us new perceptions of the role of chaos in the biblical and scientific views of the universe. God is not all-powerful. God plays loaded dice with the universe. These are difficult ideas for us to accept, considering the long history of Western scientific and religious thought. We have looked at God as a kind of linear religious equation: *God is all-powerful + God is all-good + God should be all-knowing = perfect world.* Since we know this is not true, what is evil?

Most of the traditional answers to this problem tried to retain the old equation. Science, for its part, tried to see nature as a series of linear equations. If anything failed to fit, it was dismissed as unimportant or a result of improper measurements. Now scientists realize that the non-linear problems reveal nature to be a dialectical combination of order and chaos. Today many religious thinkers grapple with the idea of a limited or a self-limiting God evolving alongside of an imperfect but perfectible universe. Now that it is also possible to see a religious source for a view of reality that corresponds to our scientific world view, what kind of theology emerges?

In order to accommodate this new world view, however, we must integrate change and chaos. There is, for example, the Rabbinic idea that we can serve God with both of our impulses, our *yetzer ha-tov*, our altruistic impulse, and our *yetzer ha-ra*, our egoistic impulse. In Rabbinic anthropology, it is the *yetzer ha-ra* that is the source of chaos and evil in humanity. It is, however, a necessary component of the human psyche, a human parallel to the dance of chaos and order that is reality. Excerpted from *The Reconstructionist*, Autumn, 1991. **Lawrence Troster, Oheb Shalom Congregation, South Orange, NJ**

דָּבָר אַחֵר **DAVAR AHER. AND THE ETERNAL, GOD, FORMED ADAM OF THE DUST OF THE GROUND, AND BLEW INTO HIS NOSTRILS THE SOUL OF LIFE…[Gen. 2.7].** I am dismayed by Richard Friedman's statement that in the Torah we don't come to know God through nature, but only through divine action in history. If God is the Creator of nature, as is so clearly and succinctly spelled out in Genesis 1, then it should be possible to know God through contemplating various aspects of nature. The theological imbalance which over-emphasizes God's action in history and under-emphasizes the wonders of God's creation has caused humanity to create a very unbalanced situation in nature, thus endangering creation and all its inhabitants. It is time to reexamine this story to find the God who not only created nature, but is made manifest through nature, AND to look for clues as to who or what God IS in addition to what God does.

Rabbi Ted Falcon has translated the tetragrammation YHVH as BEING ITSELF….We can also get a sense of the divine essence in Genesis 2.7 where God breathes the breath of life into Adam's nostrils and Adam then becomes a living thing. From this we can surmise that God is the Life Force, the Enlivener of creation. (It is interesting to note that the breath is an important focus in the meditative experience.) Thus God's essence as "Enlivening Principle" and God's action as "Enlivener" and perhaps "Ensouler" are intimately connected. One of the challenges of our time is to find balance and wholeness—balance between the polarities of Being and Doing, Creation/Nature and History, the Masculine and the Feminine, Israel and the Nations, etc., and to hallow both poles. There is much in the creation story that can help us move in this direction. **Debra Cohn-Levine, RJE, Tulsa, OK**

תמים היה בדרתיו

Bereshit

דָּבָר אַחֵר **DAVAR AHER. AND THE ETERNAL, GOD, FORMED ADAM OF THE DUST OF THE GROUND, AND BLEW INTO HIS NOSTRILS THE SOUL OF LIFE… [Gen. 2.7].** (1) The name of God in the Bible, YHWH (not YHVH!), is a verb and therefore should never be translated as "being itself," which is incorrect and misleading. (2) The notion that the essence of God cannot be known through nature is a common and basic understanding in biblical scholarship. It is not at all meant to "under-emphasize the wonders of God's creation." It means only that God in the Bible remains a "HIDDEN GOD" [Isaiah 45.15] and does not make known the divine essence through the elements of nature in the way that pagan gods do. For further reading see Frankfort, *The Intellectual Adventure of Ancient Man*, and G.E. Wright, *The Old Testament Against Its Environment.* (3) On the root [עזר] *AZR* as denoting strength, see cases of it in parallel with [עז] *OZ*, as, for example, Ps 46.2; see also עֲזַרְיָה *Azariah* [2 Kings 14.21] and עֻזִּיָּהוּ *Uzziah* [2 Chr 26.1] as alternative names of the same king. **A Response by Richard E. Friedman**

דָּבָר אַחֵר **DAVAR AHER. AND SHE TOOK THE FRUIT AND ATE…[Gen. 3.6].** In *Parables and Portraits,* Stephen Mitchell, Harper & Row, 1990, Eve bites into the fruit. Suddenly she realizes that she is naked. She begins to cry. The kindly serpent picks up a handkerchief, gives it to her. "It's all right," he says. "The first moment is always the hardest." "But I thought knowledge would be so wonderful," Eve says, sniffling. "Knowledge?!" laughs the serpent. "This fruit is from the Tree of *Life.*" **Rabbi Elias J. Lieberman, Falmouth, MA**

דָּבָר אַחֵר **DAVAR AHER. AND SHE TOOK THE FRUIT AND ATE…**Why did God create people with the capacity to do evil? To complete things—otherwise it would be like making spaghetti without adding the tomato sauce. **Scott Moskowitz, Agoura, California, age 11**

DAVAR AHER.
TEHILAH L'MALKAH
O shelter of the world, I long to find
My face in your mirror, for only then
Will I know who I am. From time to time
You have let me know you.

After I gave birth my body knew
You on the seventh day, empty and resting.
When I nursed my sons my breasts were Moses
And Aaron, giving your milky words
To your beloved children.

When the day turns dark and I am cold
To the bone, clutching my sides and rocking,
Mute with grief, suddenly I glimpse you. Your hand
Is my mother's, breaking my fall and joining
My severed heart. Sweet Shekhinah
You make the world bearable.

You are transcendent and unimaginable. Yet
The part of you that aches and rejoices
With me is close. At dawn your fragrance and
Your dewy touch on my skin awaken me
To sing my song to you, drink
From your stream of delights, and live with you
Forever.

Malka Drucker

NOAH:
A Modern Midrash

Noah

Genesis 6.9–11.32

Professor Burton L. Visotzky

PROFESSOR BURTON L. VISOTZKY HOLDS THE APPLEMAN CHAIR IN MIDRASH AND INTERRELIGIOUS STUDIES AT THE JEWISH THEOLOGICAL SEMINARY OF AMERICA. HE WAS ORDAINED AT JTS AND SERVED AS THE FIRST RABBI OF ITS EGALITARIAN SYNAGOGUE. RABBI VISOTZKY IS THE AUTHOR OF *READING THE BOOK: MAKING THE BIBLE A TIMELESS TEXT*, PUBLISHED BY ANCHOR/DOUBLEDAY.

HAM, FATHER OF CANAAN, SAW HIS FATHER'S NAKED BODY, THEN HE TOLD HIS TWO BROTHERS OUTSIDE [Gen. 9.22].

This past July, I attended the International Council of Christians and Jews in Warsaw, Poland. The day following our moving visit to Treblinka, one of the diocesan priests who were serving as our hosts took me aside to relate the following story.

In the 1960's, when Poland was heavily Communist and it was very difficult to find suitable candidates for the priesthood, a novice, on the verge of taking his vows, revealed something to him in confession. Now that thirty years had passed and that novice had died, the priest was eager to unburden himself of the confession he had been forced to carry as a secret for three decades.

"Forgive me Father, for I have sinned," the novice confessed. "I was born a Jew and it seemed that I, like my neighbors, was destined to die in the Warsaw Ghetto. My father, a brewmaster, had found some favor with certain Nazi officers for his talents at filling a bottle and so arranged to have me 'apprenticed' to one of them for the duration of the war. Thus it came to pass that I was spared while my fellow Jews perished either in the camps or in the uprising.

I do not know to this day if my father actually understood the terms of my apprenticeship—it is hard to believe that

דָּבָר אַחֵר **DAVAR AHER....AND THE EARTH WAS FILLED WITH** חָמָס **(***HAMAS***)** [Gen. 6.11]. Heard from Professor Michael Chernick, HUC-JIR, NY: The word חָמָס "*Hamas*" is usually rendered "INJUSTICE" or "VIOLENCE" or "LAWLESSNESS." Tracing it back to its roots, it has a special nature which may explain why it was sufficient to justify the flood. It is the act by which the strong approaches the weaker and says, "I want that 'thing' that you have. It is worth five dollars. Here is five dollars."

And he takes it from the weak who is unable to say no or defend it. The violence is done to the self-esteem and dignity of the weak; he sees himself as one who is exploitable, vulnerable, easily humiliated—a special kind of violence, lawlessness and injustice which does both material and spiritual injury. **Harry Danziger, Rabbi, Temple Israel, Memphis, TN <danziger@baste. magibox.net>**

a father might curse his son to a life of slavery and prostitution, even with the best of lifesaving intentions. I was pretty and slim, and that was enough to keep me alive, being passed from one SS officer to another for his perverse pleasures. I endured, I survived, but I cannot say that I ever forgot or forgave my father for having thus 'spared me.'

After the war, I remained here in Poland where I continued to ply my trade, first among the soldiers, later among the communist appa-ratchiks—all of whom amply rewarded me as much for my discretion as for my 'talents.' I became known in certain low-life circles as one who would endure almost anything—and the reward for my endurance was the opportunity to endure the drunken imprecations of my clients. There was, of course, no hiding my Jewishness under those circumstances—but it seemed to provide an added pleasure to the perverse sport of the anti-Semitic louts who made up my specialized trade. In an era of starvation brought on by a planned economy, I grew wealthy. I was proud of my talent as a survivor.

Once, an older client was particularly abusive. Under the circumstances, I unsheathed a stiletto which I kept beneath my mattress and slashed the very tool with which he was abusing me. He bled profusely, vomited and keeled over. In my frantic attempts to revive him, I rolled him on his back and was astonished to see that he, too, was circumcised. On his beefy forearm I saw where the numbers were tattooed. He died and that same night I fled to the local monastery. I thought I'd simply lie low until the trouble blew over. Instead, I cursed the God of the Jews who brought me to my lowly state. I finally found my peace with Christ."

The priest who had related this sat silent while I struggled to discern why I had been chosen to hear this particular tale. The priest was not a

Noah

דָּבָר אַחֵר **DAVAR AHER. AND GOD SAW THE EARTH, AND BEHOLD, IT WAS CORRUPT. [Gen. 6.12]**. As heard from Cantor Ida Rae Cahana, Temple Shomer Emunim, Toledo, OH. Even the t'amin (cantillation notes) reinforce the idea that the flood is the opposite of creation. The first time God looks at an element of creation, light, God declares it good: וַיַּרְא אֱלֹהִים אֶת-הָאוֹר כִּי-טוֹב *va-yar Elohim et ha-or, ki tov*, AND GOD SAW THE LIGHT, THAT IT WAS GOOD [Gen. 1.4]. When God looks down during the story of the flood, these words are echoed with a twist: וַיַּרְא אֱלֹהִים אֶת-הָאָרֶץ וְהִנֵּה נִשְׁחָתָה *va-yar Elohim et ha-aretz, v'hienei nish-hatah*, "AND GOD SAW THE EARTH, AND BEHOLD, IT WAS CORRUPT" [Gen. 6.12]. Just in case you missed the point when reading it, both verses are chanted with the same melody. **Rabbi Michael Cahana, Toledo, OH** <ha6465@aol.com>

participant in the Council, and surely this story did not seem to advance the cause of Jewish-Christian dialogue. Yet just before I turned to press the priest he quietly told me, "Rejecting the God of the Old Testament is a heresy—it's one of the oldest heresies, called Marcionism. The story of Noah and his sons, indeed, the story of Lot and his daughters, is the story of our times. We've all survived the Flood—and it seems we'll survive it no matter how many times God brings it upon us. Alas, we've learned the secret of survival—we

build our smokestacks higher than the raging waters."

WHEN NOAH AWOKE FROM HIS DRUNKEN-NESS HE KNEW WHAT HIS YOUNGEST SON HAD DONE TO HIM [Gen. 9.24].

Rav and Shmuel disagreed about the meaning of this verse. One said that he had castrated him, the other said he had raped him. [*Babylonian Talmud, Sanhedrin 70a].•*

Synopsis: The flood story is the opposite of the creation. The world is essentially corrupt and Noah is called upon to carry out God's plan. The catastrophic destruction of almost everything created in the first parashah is complete; the dove finds dry land, and history begins again. Noah builds an altar to God who then promises never to destroy every living being again. The בְּרִית *brit (covenant) in the form of the rainbow symbolizes both God's promise and the beginning of a new social order, starting with Noah and his own family. His three sons people the world and give rise to the "Table of Nations." The Tower of Babel marks the transition point before the patriarchal narratives.*

דְּבָר אַחֵר **DAVAR AHER. HAM, THE FATHER OF CANAAN, SAW HIS FATHER'S NAKEDNESS AND TOLD HIS TWO BROTHERS OUTSIDE…[Gen. 9.23].** When I teach this section I see a warning against לְשׁוֹן הָרַע l'shon ha-ra. What Ham did was gossip about his father's condition. He also passed up the opportunity to do a mitzvah by simply covering his father and treating him with dignity despite his drunkenness…Noah, the most righteous man of his generation, was not given this respect by his son, Ham. How easily we, too, forget to give basic respect. **Donna L. Halper, High School of Jewish Studies, Boston, MA**

דְּבָר אַחֵר **DAVAR AHER. HAM, THE FATHER OF CANAAN, SAW HIS FATHER'S NAKEDNESS…[Gen. 9.23].** Long before I saw "True Lies" or read Rabbi Manis Friedman, I felt that complete openness about everything was not desir-

able: God, Himself, changes the story for the sake of שְׁלוֹם בַּיִת Sh'lom Bayit. And it's not even enough to keep one's feelings to oneself; loyalty and faithfulness demand, as Rabbi Friedman writes, that "You have to be like the sons of Noah and not see them." That's why I'm worried about creating the impression that the best way to deal with feelings is to communicate them. We must cultivate alternative models of healing such as that of Dr. Stephens, recognizing the power of the soul to heal itself, not by penning up feelings inside, but through spiritual purification/meditative practices which allow those feelings to slowly flow out…Only when we learn to appreciate the healing power of silence for body and soul, as R. Shimon b. Gamaliel says [*Avot* 1.17], will we cure the leprosy of l'shon ha-ra. **Hazan Ira Rohde, Shearith Israel, NYC <75610.1722@compuserve. com>**

דְּבָר אַחֵר **DAVAR AHER. AND NOAH, A MAN OF THE GROUND, BEGAN AND PLANTED A VINEYARD [Gen. 9.20].** After receiving the promise of ha-Shem that the world would not be destroyed again, seeing the rainbow, and receiving the seven laws, Noah's first act was to plant a vineyard. Noah could have planted a fig tree or any other vegetation that he wanted, but NO-AWE decided to plant a vineyard so that he could get drunk. He wanted to celebrate his coming through the flood and/or he wanted to escape. How many times have many of us come home and decided that we needed a reward of a drink, just to get the edge off, to celebrate another day of work done, the weekend, etc. or so that we could tune out the children, the spouse, the parents, etc…. AND HE DRANK OF THE WINE AND WAS DRUNKEN; AND HE WAS UNCOVERED WITHIN HIS TENT. [Gen. 9.21]. Noah got drunk and then was immodest. He drank of the vine, not as

Dr. Peter Pitzele

PETER PITZELE IS A PSYCHOTHERA-
PIST AND AN ADJUNCT FACULTY
MEMBER AT THE HEBREW UNION
COLLEGE-JEWISH INSTITUTE OF
RELIGION, THE JEWISH THEOLOGICAL
SEMINARY, AND UNION
THEOLOGICAL SEMINARY. HE IS THE
AUTHOR OF *OUR FATHERS' WELLS*.

Noah

I Am Noah

I am Noah. It is not important how I found out the secret of the grape, its strange intoxicating power. All you need to know is that this alchemy became my chief preoccupation after the flood had passed, after my other "undertakings" had been concluded. These researches did not keep me sane; no, I would never say that. I lost my sanity in the course of forty days.

No, rather my vineyards and my studies of the grape were the methods of my mania, the ceaseless experiments in which I sought for something that could anesthetize my soul.

Is there a greater force in man than the desire for escape? Is there a more potent genius? I think not. In making wine I made a god, and in the almost endless twilight of my life—my blood became the servant of this god, for the God who had me build an ark never spoke to me again.

A list perhaps. A list will be enough. Small things first, almost comical, like the ridicule of friends who saw me building a boat in the middle of dry land. Painful domestic moments, the insolence of sons, their sullen cooperation. More painful things, the mother and father who thought I was mad. And at first, of course, my own doubts growing as the project grew, the monumental idiocy of

a sanctification, not as a holy act, but until he was drunken! Noah, the man chosen to start the world over again, gave in to the temptation of the fruit of the vine. After this, we learn that he was uncovered. He was in his tent, alone or not, passed out or awake, and was uncovered so that his sons could see him in his immorality and immodesty. And through his example, *ha-Shem* teaches us that it would be better for

us to do otherwise. **Mark Borowitz, Director of Outreach, Beit T'shuvah, Los Angeles.**

דָּבָר אַחֵר **DAVAR AHER. AND SHEM AND JAPHETH TOOK THE GARMENT AND LAID IT [Gen. 9.23].** (A question) I read in *The Pentateuch and Rashi's Commentary* by Rabbis Abraham Ben Isaiah and Benjamin Sharfman, S.S. & R. Publishing Co., Brooklyn, NY, 1949, page 85, the commentary made by

this enterprise, the gnawing fear that the voice I heard was the voice of God and that a man like me was to be the savior of the world. No one can keep balance among those dizzying perspectives. Yet hard work is an antidote. I cut lumber; I built like a demon on that ark.

Then the rains began. Gentle at first, a relief to the dry land. But after two days all dust was mud. He slung the dark rain down like pitch. As if guided by a fear, the animals arrived, mud-mired, fur-drenched, wing-weary. It gave me some joy to give them shelter. Overnight it seemed, by the third day, it was already too late. The houses were islands. The roads were streams, the streams were rivers, and the water had covered every field. Some few of the friends of my sons, strong young men pad-dled makeshift rafts to us and pounded on the ark's sides, asking for entry. But we had already begun to rise on the lake that was our field. From the deck I could see my father's house. Already the way between us was an impassable current, uprooted trees, the bodies of the cattle floating bloated on the stream. Once, just before we battened down, in the screaming wind I thought I heard my mother's scream.

And then the world was swallowed up in night as we closed the shutters down. Never mind the reeking pitching timeless passage, the howls and bellows of the animals. The desolate empty calm. The silence worse than noise. All through the nights and days I only heard that scream, and it seemed in my mother's scream, in the wind's scream, in the banshee's scream, in the scream of birds I heard the whole world scream, the cries of mothers, infants, lovers and beloved. That scream was fire. It roasted my brains. It made my soul a cinder.

And then when we came out upon the land, there was a world to bury. That task I took as mine. While my sons sowed and reaped and built and fathered, I went about digging holes. The world was a corpse, and I was its undertaker. I found the seeds. I planted them. Grapes grew. I tasted, and in the taste I dreamed of an escape. Patiently, season after season, I tried, until gradually I perfected wine. And then I drank. Pity the men that old God chooses. I found another god. Naked I feel no shame.●

Rashi concerning the third person singular of the verb to take, namely, וַיִּקַּח שֵׁם וָיֶפֶת אֶת-הַשִּׂמְלָה וַיָּשִׂמוּ *va-yikah Shem veYafet et ha-simla va-yasimu*…Translated: "AND SHEM AND JAPHETH TOOK THE GARMENT AND LAID IT…" Rashi was puzzled by the singular form of the verb "take" (וַיִּקַּח *va-yikah*) when two people are mentioned; indeed the verb "lay" is in the plural (וַיָּשִׂמוּ *va-yasimu*). Rashi interprets it as an indication that Shem was the more eager of the two to act in favor of his father and his sons were rewarded more honorably with the טַלִּית שֶׁל צִיצִית *talit shel tzitzit* (the future opportunity to receive the mitz-vah of wearing *tzitzit* (fringes) on their four-cornered garments). I propose a linguistic DAVAR AHER. In Arabic when a verb precedes its subjects it has to be used in the singular; it is the only grammatical form allowed. On the other hand, if a verb follows its many subjects it is used in the plural. The plural is also used when the subjects are implicit, not directly associated with the verb. Thus, using the Arabic form, we would say וַיִּקַּח שֵׁם וָיֶפֶת "*va-yikah shem ve-yafet*" or וְשֵׁם וָיֶפֶת יִקְחוּ "*ve-Shem ve-Yafet yikhu.*" The plural וַיָּשִׂמוּ *va-yasimu* would also be correct because the subjects for this verb are implicit. Although the Hebrew language does not have such a rule, influences from the region could possibly creep in from time to time, as one senses sometimes in parts of the Bible.

Ed Cohen <cohen@admin1. njit.edu>

The Shekhinah as Psychological Healer

The *Shekhinah* is synonymous with the divine presence. Literally it means "indwelling," from the Hebrew root [שכן] *shakhan.* In Rabbinic literature it refers most often to the presence or immanence of God in the world, the aspect of the divine which can be experienced in the human order....

Up until the 12th century the *Shekhinah* image was quite abstract, not personified. It was "a radiance, a blinding light,"...in the 12th century the *Shekhinah* underwent a major transformation. The image became less abstract and the face was seen. It was the face of a woman. She is called daughter, princess, the feminine principle of the divine.... She is often envisioned as a young woman, beautifully gowned and radiant, but who speaks to the sufferer in a maternal way using such phrases as: "My son...." Here is where the significance of the *Shekhinah* as a psychological healer begins to emerge. She is not an esoteric philosophical concept. She has a body, hand, face, words. She comforts. It is her voice that is most commonly experienced with or without an accompanying image. Language gains her entry into the human psyche and her image fixes the meaning of the

Dr. Barbara D. Stephens

BARBARA D. STEPHENS, PHD., A CLINICAL PSYCHOLOGIST AFFILIATED WITH THE C.G. JUNG INSTITUTE OF LOS ANGELES, WRITES AND LECTURES ON RELIGIOUS AND SPIRITUAL THEMES IN PSYCHOTHERAPY.

Noah

דָּבָר אַחֵר **DAVAR AHER. AND AS FOR ME,** *HINEI,* **I CUT MY COVENANT WITH YOU...[Gen 9.8].** What follows is the *drash* I gave at my *aufruf.* The Noahide laws are seven laws deemed to be the minimum in moral behavior. While observance of the entire Torah was incumbent upon Jew alone, the laws of Noah were perceived to be required of everybody. In that sense, God has a covenant with all mankind and all of us are *"B'nei Noah."* What are the seven laws and what is their origin? There is no biblical "text" that contains the Noahide laws. They are exegetically derived from several verses in *Bereshit,* mostly from the flood story, with some from the story of Adam. These verses are *Bereshit* 2.16 and 9.1-8 and the derivation of the seven laws is in *Genesis Rabbah* 16.6 and 34.8. Early Talmudic sources contain the first

16—נֹחַ

words. She challenges, guides and soothes. She comes at a time of suffering which is so profound that it connects the person to something deeply within but at the same time reaches beyond, into the divine. At that moment a *conjunction* has occurred, a sacred marriage of *myself* and *I*, and *I* with *other*, which comforts and transforms the sufferer....

In 1913, Carl Jung encountered a *Shekhinah* image who guided him to unconscious discoveries which resulted in the first psychological theory to take the spiritual seriously. The encounter came during a period of "inner uncertainty" following the break with Freud. In his autobiography he writes that she emerged as the face of a woman (Salome).... At the time Salome/*Shekhinah* may have been communicating a message Jung was not yet prepared to hear,

thus causing his initial discomfort. He labeled the image *anima* (soul) and says he felt "a little awed by her...it was like the feeling of an invisible presence in the room."

In clinical work we have not given much credibility to the healing power of the unconscious. Its devouring aspect captures the focus of our inquiries and gains most of our respect as a professional community. Its healing power seems oddly to have been given over to the religious practitioners of society, the priests and rabbis. Almost the entire body of psychoanalytic literature focuses on the pathology of the unconscious. Lately, however, object relations theorists and others have spoken for the positive healing aspects of the unconscious. They speak of internal objects, self-objects, or object relations units which fuel our affects and

actions. If one digs at these concepts theoretically and moves towards their inner core, it is possible that the "radiance" of the *Shekhinah* and the blinding light of the collective unconscious realm that she represents will begin to emerge.

Novik considers this generation a "midwife for the rebirth of the *Shekhinah*." I disagree. The *Shekhinah* doesn't need to be reborn. She has always been with her people in exile [Deut. 30.3]. We must relearn how to look at her when she is seen. Whether we will see her as a whole, as healer *and* devourer, is intimately tied to our desire and ability to enter with awe the whole of our own world within.

•

Excerpted from: *The Journal of Psychology and Judaism*, Vol 15, No. 1, Spring 1991

mention of the laws, in particular the *Tosefta*, attributed to Ḥiyyua ben Abba, circa 160 CE. That text gives the seven laws as prohibitions of (1) idol worship, (2) incest, (3) murder, (4) blasphemy, (5) theft, (6) eating flesh from a living animal, and (7) injustice to other men, Not all Tannaitic sources agree on the laws: another adds sorcery and magical practices while *Sanhedrin 56a* includes crossbreeding, an extra biblical source, the Book of Jubilees [7.20] has a substantially different set of the laws of Noah and includes only six: (1) observe

righteousness, (2) practice modesty, (3) bless the Creator, (4) honor parents, (5) love one's neighbors, (6) guard against fornication and uncleanness. There is not much overlap between these laws and what is taken to be the usual set of Noahide laws.

If the laws are derived partly from text dealing with Adam, why are they called the Noahide laws, rather than the Adamite or Adamic or whatever laws? Particularly, why is this so in light of the Midrash that the seven laws were revealed to Adam? The

answer to this lies in the nature of the flood story and the circumstances of the revelation to Noah by God. God's first covenant with man is after the flood, when He uses the rainbow as a symbol of that relationship and makes some explicit moral/behavioral demands, The Noaḥide laws, in fact, are biblical mitzvot and are the first step in a framework that will be expanded later. Without the covenant to provide a legal basis, there is no point in speaking of "laws"; it is for this reason that these are the Noaḥide laws...After the Hasmonean

Noah

revolt, their influence increased even more. Noahide laws were held to be applicable to non-Jews living under Jewish authority, as can be seen in the fact that the Talmudic sources treat them as an enforceable and consistent body of law.

The Rabbis ping-ponged over the authority for the Noahide laws, between revelation to the Noahites and alternately acceptance of them by the Noahites. Maimonides wrote about the seven laws in *Melakhim*, a section of his Code. He states that the only basis for acceptance of the seven laws is divine revelation, and that one who believes in them due to intellectual persuasion alone is not among the righteous of the world. Rambam held that belief in a divinity and revelation is an unstated eighth law, in the same sense that he said this is the 614th mitzvah. Maimonides also used the seven laws to universalize Judaism by expanding its view of the other monotheistic religions, Christianity and Islam. Noahites, which would include Christians and Muslims, according to the Rambam, held a share in the world to come, thereby, in effect, creating an equality of sorts among the three religions.

In their usual fashion, the Talmudic authorities and commentators considerably expanded the scope of the seven laws and in fact managed to subsume about 100 of 613 mitzvot into the seven Noahide laws. One of the seven laws is a simple prohibition against theft. That category was expanded to include overcharging, dishonest weights and measures, kidnapping, shifting a land-mark and forcible robbery. In this manner, one can see the exegetical mind at work, expanding the Noahide laws to the point where they resembled the mitzvot of the Torah. However, because they did not adhere to all of Torah, Noahites were not required to perform *Kiddush ha-Shem* rather than commit idolatrous acts, as was a Jew. On the other hand, in the universal spirit of the laws, forced shedding of human blood was grounds for martyrdom, even for a Noahite.

Sometimes the Noahide laws were perceived as the basis for a rational ethical system without revelation or divine beings, although as we have seen, the Rambam strongly disagreed. Jews were obligated to attempt to establish the seven laws wherever possible; sort of like spreading the good news. In the 17th century the legal scholar Hugo Grotius used the seven laws to establish a rudimentary system of international law. There were a number of "converts" to Judaism who accepted the Noahide laws but who never actually converted halakhically. The most famous of these were Aime Palliere and his teacher, an Italian, Rabbi Elijah Ben-Amozegh, both of whom lived into this century. In a series of letters, Ben-Amozegh attempted to develop Noahism into a universal religion.

I'd like to personalize this and draw some connections, however tenuous, between the story of Noah and my marriage. God makes his first covenant with man after the flood and, for the first time, reveals laws. After the flood, man has a new set of obligations and their relationship with God and between themselves is permanently altered. With our marriage, Sheila's and my relationship will be changed; as with the post-flood man, we assume new obligations and responsibilities to each other.

God makes specific commandments to Noah and also makes a covenant with him, spelling out His requirements for human behavior. Judaism partially treats marriage in the same sense. The *ketubah* is a contract, an analog of a covenant, which contains very specific language on what is expected of the marriage partners. There are no surprises for either party to the arrangement as the responsibilities are clearly detailed; this is true for both of the *ketubah* and the covenants of God with man. Drawing upon the notion of the flood's marking the revelation to man of divine commandments, marriage itself is a mitzvah and an analog for many Jewish experiences. Both the Sinai revelation and Shabbat are often described in terms of a bride and groom.

The flood provided a new beginning to the earth, a new creation for both man and the world. Noah and his children were a bridge between the antediluvians and the time of the patriarchs. They were the means of repopulating the earth. In the same sense, marriage is the bridge to children and fulfillment of one of the specific commandments to Noah: "BE FERTILE, THEN, AND INCREASE [Gen. 8.17]."
Gregory Bearman, Jet Propulsion Laboratory, Pasadena, CA

דָּבָר אַחֵר **DAVAR AHER.** Epilogue. Oh boy, Noah. Visotsky's piece caused me to weep, and maybe you know I've read many Holocaust stories by now. Somehow, though, this one, tied to the horror of Noah, unable to bear his life after the flood, destroyed me. It reminded me of an interview we had with Sofia Baniecka, a Polish woman (the one who spoke at the Washington, D.C. Holocaust Museum's inaugural). She was a maid who saved a family of brothers and had married one, but only after he agreed to convert to Catholicism. This chilled me, and she was the only rescuer of 105 that I couldn't warm to. After the interview in Brookline, MA, we went downstairs to meet her husband, Joe, a dentist. He had the saddest eyes I'd ever seen. He said, "You know, they killed six million during the war, but they killed many more than that. Do you think after you've witnessed your eight-year-old daughter raped and murdered, that you are still alive?" I thought of those two survivors, both dead men, and poor Noah, trying to find a temporary escape from the third world in which he lived: the first before the flood; the second—the flood; and the third—being violated by his son. I'm a writer, but I can't find words for this kind of death….Barbara Stephens' excerpt was a balm. **Malka Drucker <MalkaD@aol.com>**

Lekh Lekha

Genesis 12.1–13.18

Savina J. Teubal

SAVINA J. TEUBAL IS THE AUTHOR OF *SARAH THE PRIESTESS: THE FIRST MATRIARCH OF GENESIS, HAGAR THE EGYPTIAN: THE LOST TRADITIONS OF THE MATRIARCHS*, "SIMCHAT HOCHMAH" ("JOY OF WISDOM," A CRONE RITUAL) WITH DRORAH SETEL, AND THE WORDS TO ITS THEME SONG "L'KHI LAKH" WITH DEBBIE FRIEDMAN.

How many words does it take to say something meaningful or profound? Very few, if we take the Bible as our guide. Take, for instance, the first sentence in Genesis 12 that says:

לֶךְ-לְךָ *LEKH LEKHA* (fem. *LEKHI LAKH*) GO, TAKE YOURSELF FROM YOUR NATIVE LAND AND FROM YOUR FATHER'S HOUSE TO THE LAND THAT I WILL SHOW YOU. These are the words of the oracle received by Abram while still in his homeland in Haran (N. Mesopotamia).

GO! (לֶךְ *lekh*) This first pronouncement by the oracle is a call to action; an act of separation. To go is to leave one situation behind and begin another. However, the directive does not come from a subjective voice. This voice comes from one in authority. It lets us know immediately that someone is being told to do something by someone else. It takes only this very small word for us to know that the protagonist is in a subordinate position. We already have an insight into the social structure of the scene: it is hierarchical. We also know that the authority figure is that of a deity (the first words of this sentence having been, "The Lord said to Abram"): the act of separation will be divinely guided.

TAKE YOURSELF (לְךָ *lekha*), you, and that which completes you as a human being: the woman who shares your life. We learn from Genesis that Man and Woman are

דָּבָר אַחֵר **DAVAR AHER. (A Prologue)…**TERAH DIED IN HARAN [Gen. 11.32]. There's more to the story than all that. Terah is a lost character, a pre-Jew, the last pre-Jew in fact, who nonetheless is among those who were taken into paradise alive. We "lose" Terah because his first and final appearance in Torah is in *maftir Noah*—the coming attractions for the week afterwards (and the rabbis, we assume, knew what they were doing when they cut the *parashot* that way).

Suddenly I see in Terah something that I have never seen before. He leaves behind part of the family in Haran. He is a divider, a severer of sons from each other, a worthy grandfather to Ishmael and Isaac, and great-grandfather to Esau and Jacob, and great-great-grandfather to Joseph and his brothers. One brother wins the covenant, the other/others lose out.

At some point they are tempted to point back to Terah and say: It

לך לך מארצך ממולדך

made of the same substance: "THEREFORE A MAN LEAVES HIS FATHER AND MOTHER AND CLINGS TO HIS WIFE, SO THAT THEY BECOME ONE FLESH." [Gen. 2.24] Abram is not called upon to leave alone but with SARAI.

FROM YOUR NATIVE LAND, a deceivingly simple phrase with the impact of a sledge-hammer. The protagonists are being asked to wrench themselves from everything that is familiar to them: the sights and sounds of their native land, the streets they walk, the people they meet, the shrines or temples they worship at. Sarai, too, is leaving her native land (Ur), her kin and all that she loves and knows.

FROM YOUR FATHER'S HOUSE, not your own separate residence, rather the home you share with your kin. We know from the previous chapter that Abram and Sarai's extended family in Haran consisted of their father Terah (they had the same father but different mothers),

Abram's brother Nahor, Nahor's wife Milcah, daughter of Sarai's brother Haran (who had died in Ur, Sarai's birthplace), and Iscah, Milcah's sister. Not only were Sarai and Abram summoned to leave their physical surroundings, they were asked to abandon their blood ties as well. So far, this is an exercise in letting go.

Interestingly, Sarah means "princess" in Hebrew and Malcah means "queen." However, the language of our ancestors was not Hebrew but Babylonian; in Babylonian the meanings are reversed: *sarratu* being the queen and *malkatu* the princess. It can hardly be coincidence that these two names belong to deities in the pantheon of Haran and Ur, where *sarratu* was a title of the moon-goddess *Ningal* and *malkatu* a title of *Inanna/Ishtar*. Both goddesses were worshipped in Ur and Haran.

TO A LAND THAT I WILL SHOW YOU. Here we have perhaps the

Synopsis: The stories of the patriarchs begin here with Abram. Without any introduction, God tells him to take his entire family and go to a foreign land. In return, he is promised land and progeny. Together with Lot, Abram lands in Shekhem and builds an altar. A famine ensues and Abram travels to Egypt, whereupon his wife, Sarai, is taken to the Egyptian palace. Plagues break out, the true identity of Sarai is revealed and Abram, once again, journeys—this time back to Beth El. Lot, by virtue of his association with Sodom, is taken captive and Abram rescues him. The "Covenant Between the Pieces" seals the dual promises of land and children. Hagar, Sarai's servant, gives birth to Ishmael. Sarai's and Abram's names are changed and Abraham undergoes a circumcision (another covenant).

started there on the outskirts of Haran. Nahor wanted to come along, but didn't. Neither, for that matter, did Terah. Don't blame us. That's the way family patterns go. They are learned and re-learned, taught and retaught, until someone (Ephraim and Menasseh, who share but a single blessing) is able to break the chain of pain and say: We can begin again. **Rabbi Jeff Salkin, Central Synagogue of Nassau County, Rockville Center, NY <JEFFSALK@aol.com>**

דָּבָר אַחֵר **DAVAR AHER. ...YOUR FATHER'S HOME...**[Gen. 12.1]. While I was discussing the parashah with my sixteen-year-old son, he had an insight which I had never before considered. He commented that it is interesting that when God told Abram to leave his country, the land of his birth and his father's home, the text specifically states, בֵּית אָבִיךָ "*BEIT AVIKHA*: YOUR FATHER'S HOME." Pointedly, God does not tell Abram to leave his father, but his father's house. The

command was to leave his father's home, not his father. What a wonderful thing to hear from a son! **Rabbi Stuart Weinblatt, Congregation B'nai Tzedek Potomac, MD**

most dramatic part of the sentence: You are to give up everything that is familiar and dear to you…but for what? The oracle did help just a little with this question:

I WILL MAKE OF YOU A GREAT NATION
AND I WILL BLESS YOU;
I WILL MAKE YOUR NAME GREAT,
AND YOU SHALL BE A BLESSING:
I WILL BLESS THOSE WHO BLESS YOU,
AND CURSE THOSE WHO CURSE YOU;
ALL THE FAMILIES OF THE EARTH
SHALL BLESS THEMSELVES BY YOU.

לֶךְ-לְךָ *LEKH LEKHA*/לְכִי-לָךְ *LEKHI LAKH* is a query as well as a directive. An oracle tells you what will happen if you accept its bidding, it does not compel you to do what it suggests. In this case God says: "If you go, without knowing where I am leading you, I will do all these things for you." In other words, the ancestors had a choice either to follow the suggestion and possibly be rewarded for it, or decide not to heed the oracle and accept whatever consequences that decision may have brought. That they accepted the challenge already tells us something about the character of the protagonists: they were not satisfied with the status quo.

Most important of all, these words are the words of a divinity; a god, it would seem, who was different from the deities of the region with whom our ancestors were brought up. It is conceivable that the god of the oracle was operating in foreign territory (in those days deities were restricted to their own locales) and would have been unable to fulfill any promises in Mesopotamia. Whatever the reason, it is the god Yahweh who sets these people on their journey into the unknown, "TO THE LAND THAT I WILL SHOW YOU." It is no small decision that faces Sarai and Abram: Make a commitment to an unfamiliar god who promises renown in a foreign land! Our ancestors are being asked to radically change their lives; if they accept, it is purely an act of faith.

TO A PLACE YOU DO NOT KNOW. The oracle of לֶךְ-לְךָ *LEKH*

Lekh Lekha

דְּבָר אַחֵר **DAVAR AHER. …YOUR FATHER'S HOME… [Gen. 12.1].**
As always, I was taken with Savina Teubal's comments on *Lekh-Lekha*. However, with regard to a spiritual journey occurring only in old age. I have to take some issue. True, in later years, we frequently have the luxury of time to reflect and ruminate on our relationship with the divinity. But it is this very relationship with our God that guides us in our actions and deeds all through our lives. I realize that in our youth and years of family-centered concerns we have little time, or rather take little or no time, to cogitate about our relationship with God. Yet, perhaps, if we would take a few moments to actually "contemplate our navels" we would not have to leave the spiritual quest to our later years. I heard on the radio this morning that when 4,000 people

לֶךְ לְךָ מֵאַרְצְךָ מִמּוֹלַדְתְּךָ מִבֵּית אָבִיךָ

LEKHA/לְכִי-לָךְ *L'KHI LAKH* is not yet fulfilled. Go, take yourself...to a place you do not know. The second part of the directive (a place) is not the same as the first (a land). A LAND THAT I WILL SHOW YOU has the connotation of life and descendants; a glimpse of immortality throughout the generations. 'A Place you do not know,' is something beyond life, after the lifespan. This Place is not connected to the Land, rather it is a fusion with divinity...an unknown Place that is the destination of לֶךְ-לְךָ *LEKH LEKHA*/לְכִי-לָךְ *LEKHI LAKH*.

That the mission has other than merely human connotations is insin-

uated at the very beginning of the episode. Immediately after the oracle, Abram's age is given: he is seventy-five years old. Sarai is sixty-five. This is not the story of a young couple going off on an exciting pilgrimage with their whole life before them; rather, it is a quest into the unknown in the last phase of human life. Metaphorically speaking, Abram and Sarai are embarking on a journey of the spirit, a last journey that will reunite them with the supernatural. In a sense, Sarai and Abram are being told that they will glimpse the hereafter; they will experience divine presence while still on earth on faith

alone, if they take the path that is being offered to them.

We, the Children of Israel, will be their reward. And our reward, if we follow in their footsteps, is to perpetuate their heritage. לֶךְ-לְךָ *LEKH LEKHA*/לְכִי-לָךְ *LEKHI LAKH* is a summons to our ancestors (and therefore to us as well) to embark on a spiritual journey in the last phase of our lives (our old age) with confidence and faith, in the knowledge that the guiding spirit of divinity is with and within us. •

---

descended on Washington, D.C. last year in order to meditate, there was a drop in the crime rate of 40%. That should tell us something. **Janice Alper, Jewish Education Services, Atlanta, GA**

דָּבָר אַחֵר **DAVAR AHER.** *LEKH LEKHA* TO A LAND THAT I WILL SHOW YOU. [Gen. 12.1]. So Abraham began the first Jewish journey. Since then each Jew has been on a journey. To begin a journey people need to know where they are, their starting point. Abraham was quite aware of where he was at the beginning of his journey and what he was leaving; it was his destination that held the mystery. Each Jewish journey today is imbued with the power of the history of our ancestors and each of their journeys, yet our personal destinations are still a mystery. The Baal Shem Tov said "Know where you come from and where you are going." Our destinations may be made clearer

by looking at qualities attributed to the four directions much like the Plains Indians used their Medicine Wheel. A journey takes place in space and time and it moves in a direction. Let us look at the characteristics of the four directions and what they may hold for us:

In the 1500's, the Kabbalists of Safed celebrated *Tu b'Shvat*, the New Year of the Trees, with a ritual seder to honor all nature. Their seder was a four-part ceremony with readings, blessings, fruit and wine to honor the four worlds (see graph below).

Borrowing from the Kabbalists who attributed not only names to the four worlds but also characteristics, elements and a season, we can begin to explore the four directions with a new understanding of what we may find there.

The midrashic story of four angels surrounding the throne of God gives us another way to understand the four directions. The story tells us that four angels surround God: Uriel, behind, reflects the vision of God; Raphael, in front, reflects the healing power of God; Michael, on the right, reflects the

	NORTH	SOUTH	EAST	WEST
Element:	Fire	Water	Earth	Air
Season:	Fall	Spring	Winter	Summer
Character:	Spiritual	Emotional	Physical	Cerebral
World:	Atzilut	Yetzirah	Assiayah	B'riyah
Angel:	Uriel/	Rafael/	Gabriel/	Michael/
	Vision	Healing	Strength	Godliness

Rabbi Manuel Gold

RABBI MANUEL GOLD IS A DIRECTOR OF THE PRINCIPAL'S CENTER OF THE BOARD OF JEWISH EDUCATION OF GREATER NEW YORK AND THE AUTHOR OF A FORTHCOMING BOOK ON THE ORIGIN AND DEVELOPMENT OF THE JEWISH FESTIVALS FOR THE UNION OF AMERICAN HEBREW CONGREGATIONS.

Lekh Lekha

Abram and God: The Questions and the Answers

Human nature has not changed dramatically in the last 3,000 years. The first step in finding the answers to the problems we face in life is still dependent on how we formulate our questions, how we formulate our dreams and hopes, and where we choose to direct those questions. Without our probing and searching for meaning and direction, we will not find the answers to who and what we are. If we adopt *others'* questions, we will uncover only *their* answers, not our own. Our questions are the beginning of finding our answers. This is the story of Genesis 12.

We are prisoners of our expectations, especially when we study our past. *Lekh Lekha* is a powerful demonstration for this axiom. Our prior expectations present us with the usual questions. Paraphrasing the line from *Casablanca* we could say, "Round up the usual questions" and then add, "Round up the usual answers." We expect:

(1)   Q: Why did Abram go to Canaan?

     A: God told him to go.

(2)   Q: How did God communicate with Abram?

     A: God "said," that is, God "spoke" to him.

---

godliness of God; and Gabriel, on the left, reflects the strength of God. Each night when we face our vulnerability at sleep time we can ask God to change places with us so that we can be surrounded and protected by the attributes of the angels while God sleeps in our bed. By placing Angels in the four directions we may also be able to learn from their qualities on our journey.

Like Abraham (if we are lucky) we know where we begin on our journeys, but not where we will arrive. Through exploring the four directions, we can develop a better idea of where we are going. Jewish journeys continue to be a part of our Jewish identity and can help us understand ourselves and our Jewishness more fully. **Deborah Newbrun**

Our early education has prepared us with the *correct* questions and the *correct* answers. They are: God initiated the command to go to Canaan, selected the words for the command, and spoke them in a manner very much like human speech. To Abram, God's words come as it were from "out of the blue." However, there is much more to this story than the usual oversimplified readings. To get a deeper understanding we need to ask more probing questions:

Q: Who first came to the conclusion that Abram and company should set out for Canaan?

A: Surprise! It was neither God nor Abram. It was Terah! In Genesis 11.31-32, it says clearly, "Terah took his son Abram, his grandson Lot,...and with them he left the city of Ur...to go to the Land of Canaan. But when they reached Haran, they stayed there. Terah died there at the age of...." Terah decided to go to Canaan on his own. No command from God is mentioned. No purpose or reason is given. But, Canaan is clearly his goal. Unfortunately, not having gotten very far (Ur was probably located in the north, near Haran), Terah dies.

That much is clear from the text. An awareness of those verses should lead us to new questions.

Q: Why did God order Abram to go to Canaan? How did Abram receive this communication?

A: The text of the Torah was better understood by those who lived in the period closest to its writing or redaction. They did not have to have every last detail spelled out. Much of what they understood as normal did not need to be stated in the text. For them, it was redundant. They all knew that one of the ways that God communicated with people was by means of oracles.

Oracles worked this way. If a person had a problem or troubling question, s/he would visit a local "oracle shrine." The priest at the shrine would help the petitioner rephrase the problem into two questions. (To check out this pattern, see 1 Samuel 14.36-45, particularly that part of verse 41 which is missing from the Masoretic Hebrew text but found in the Septuagint, see the footnote in JPS 1962 or most non-Jewish translations.) There, the questions asked of the *urim v'tumim* (the oracle) took the form of these two questions: **Q1:** "Shall I go ahead and fight the Philistines?" And, **Q2:** "Will I be victorious?" [1 Sam. 14.37]

Applying this understanding of oracles to the story of Abram, we can then visualize the story through this reconstruction. *(Italics indicate information not found in the biblical text.)* (1) Terah decides to take his whole family, which included his son Abram, to Canaan *for business reasons.* (2) They leave the city of Ur *in what is today Northern Syria* and

travel to the *nearby* city of Haran, *the major commercial center in the region.* (3) Terah dies there. *Abram is distraught. He does what any person of his day would do. He goes to a local shrine and consults the oracle to ask his god for the answer to his questions. Abram faces this dilemma: Was my father's premature death an omen or a message that his god was displeased with him (a) for failing to complete the journey to Canaan? or (b) for leaving Ur in the first place? or (c) for stopping in Haran?*

Abram formulates his concerns into two question which he asks the "oracle."

Q1: "Shall I continue on to Canaan?" and **Q2:** "Will I be successful?"

The answers to these questions are preserved in Genesis 12.

A1: "Leave your native land and your family holdings and go forward!" [12.1]. And,

A2: "I will make of you a great nation and I will bless you." [12.2-3]

In this as in many other biblical instances where God speaks, God's answers are presented in the texts while the questions asked of God through the oracle are lost. For Abram's contemporaries in the biblical world, God's answers were much more important than the questions.

This insight into the use of oracles has the potential to completely revise our thinking about Abram and his way of communicating with God. We no longer need view God as appearing abruptly to the biblical personages from Abram to David. Rather, the message from God comes through an oracle, and only after the individual perceives the need to seek divine guidance about the dilemmas and vicissitudes of life. Potentially, every time that the biblical text presents two answers from God, we can see them as the responses to the two questions that can be reconstructed. Like ours, our ancestors' relationships with God were driven by their questions, problems, hopes, visions, and, indeed, their personalities. They were struggling to understand

what to do in the face of life's obstacles; to understand their God's guidance. When we are able to envision the questions posed by the biblical personalities, we begin to discover the deeper dimension of their personalities. By recovering their questions, their dilemmas, searchings and yearnings, we can relate them to our own questions and dreams. •

Lekh Lekha

וירא אליו יהוה באלני ממר

Early in the portion, (Genesis, chapter 18), three angels come to visit Abraham and Sarah. At the time, the Patriarch is ninety-nine and his wife, ninety; throughout their marriage they have been childless. At one point (verse 9), the angels ask Abraham, "WHERE IS YOUR WIFE SARAH?" and Abraham replies "IN THE TENT." One of the angels then offers a prophesy, "I WILL RETURN TO YOU NEXT YEAR, AND YOUR WIFE SARAH SHALL HAVE A SON."

According to the text, Sarah was listening to the conversation, and when she heard the angel's prophesy, she "LAUGHED TO HERSELF, SAYING, 'NOW THAT I AM WITHERED, AM I TO HAVE ENJOYMENT— WITH MY HUSBAND SO OLD?'" (verse 12).

A verse later, God appears to Abraham, and asks, "WHY DID SARAH LAUGH, SAYING, 'SHALL I IN TRUTH BEAR A CHILD, OLD AS I AM'?" (verse 13)

Compare the two verses, and you find that God conveyed to Abraham part, *but not all*, of Sarah's original statement. God left out Sarah's concluding thought, "WITH MY HUSBAND SO OLD." Why? Apparently, either God feared that Abraham would be hurt by these words, or would be infuriated at his wife. The Rabbis of the Talmud deduce from this omission an important moral insight, "Great is peace, seeing that for its sake even God modified the truth [*Yevamot* 65b]."

Jewish law, attached as it normally is to truthfulness (e.g., "STAY FAR AWAY FROM FALSEHOOD" Ex. 23.7), nonetheless allows

Va-Yera

Genesis 18:1–22.24

Rabbi Joseph Telushkin

RABBI JOSEPH TELUSHKIN IS THE AUTHOR OF *JEWISH LITERACY, JEWISH WISDOM, JEWISH HUMOR* AND *WORDS THAT HURT, WORDS THAT HEAL.*

דָּבָר אַחֵר **DAVAR AHER. THEY WILL KEEP THE WAY OF THE ETERNAL, DOING** *TZEDAKAH* AND *MISHPAT.* **[Gen. 18.19].** The Torah tells us that Avram and his nephew Lot have a conflict because "THEIR POSSESSIONS WERE SO GREAT THAT THEY COULD NOT REMAIN TOGETHER" [Gen. 13.6]. Avram offers a resolution to the conflict: He lets Lot choose any part of the country he wants, and they separate from each other.

I have long been bothered by the concept that Avram was a *tzadik* because he gave

the choice to Lot. I do not believe that he gave that choice to Lot at all. Imagine the two men looking to the East and to the West. When Lot looks to the East he sees fertile pastures for his flocks; when Avram looks to the East, he sees the cities of Sodom and Gemorrah where immorality is rife. When Lot looks to the west he sees barren land; when Avram looks to the west he sees the potential for a new, safe environment to be created for his family. In essence, Avram had already made his

truth to be modified where other people's feelings are at stake. Indeed, as Jewish law rules, if you are speaking to someone and the person asks what somebody else said about him or her, you should leave out any negative observations that were made. If the person continues to press you, "Is that all he/she said? Did he/she say anything bad?" you are permitted to lie, and say "No." The only instance in which you should tell the truth is if there is a pressing reason for the person to whom you are speaking to know what is being said about him (e.g., if somebody is going around calling an honest person a thief, the person should be apprised). But most of the time when people say hurtful things about others, it is something not nearly so shocking. Very often, many of us say somewhat nasty things even about people for whom we deeply care. Some three centuries, ago, the French Catholic philosopher, Blaise Pascal, noted

that if everybody knew precisely what everybody else said about them, there would not be four friends left in the world.

In this Torah portion, God reminds us that we should be careful with our tongues, and not be quick to pass on comments that could hurt others. God's example is one that all of us, particularly those of us who are quick to pass on gossip and hurtful words, should try and emulate.

The same chapter, Genesis 18, goes on to raise a profound moral issue. At a later point in the chapter, God informs Abraham that He intends to destroy the evil cities of Sodom and Gemorrah. Abraham protests the decision, and challenges God with forceful words, "SHALL NOT THE JUDGE OF ALL THE EARTH ACT WITH JUSTICE?" (verse 25). Abraham then bargains with God, asking the Lord to save the cities if first fifty, then forty-five, forty, thirty, twenty or even ten righteous people can be found within them. God expresses no rage

Va-Yera

choice, but he created the illusion of giving Lot his choice. They both got exactly what they wanted. **Rabbi Rick Sherwin, Beth El Congregation, Phoenix, AZ**

דָּבָר אַחֵר **DAVAR AḤER. SHALL NOT THE JUDGE OF ALL THE EARTH ACT WITH JUSTICE? [Gen. 18.25].** (There are) two perspectives that I think Joe Telushkin left out from his otherwise interesting *drash*. When he credited

his anonymous friend who noted that Abraham demanded justice for all the people of Sodom and Gemorrah, righteous and wicked (a wonderful point, by the way), it wasn't mentioned that Abraham is the one who "molds" God by demanding (via his rhetorical question: "SHALL NOT THE JUDGE OF ALL THE EARTH ACT WITH JUSTICE?") that God be, in fact, a God of justice. No one had ever mandated that divine personality trait before.

at Abraham's provocatively phrased question, and even enters into negotiations with him. Each time Abraham makes an offer, God accepts it. He then checks and reports that the requisite number of righteous people have not been found. Finally, when it becomes apparent that with the exception of Abraham's nephew Lot and his family, the entire populace is evil, God goes ahead and destroys the cities.

Several things become apparent from this episode.

(1) Despite God's obvious superiority to human beings, people are permitted to argue with God, even to challenge God. As Jews living in the post-Holocaust age, we should reflect as well on the issue of when we too are entitled to ask God, "Shall the judge of all the earth not act with justice?"

(2) The chapter leaves open an important philosophical issue. Is something good because God

demands it, or does a standard of good exist independently of God? There is evidence for both positions in the Torah, indeed in *Va-Yera*. In chapter 22, God asks Abraham to sacrifice his son, Isaac, and the Patriarch sets out with Isaac to do so. Only at the end of the chapter does God send an angel to stop Abraham from sacrificing his son. Prior to that, however, the Patriarch assumes that anything that God wants is, by definition, right. On the other hand, Abraham's question to God, "SHALL NOT THE JUDGE OF ALL THE EARTH ACT WITH JUSTICE?" implies a standard of justice to which God Himself is bound (otherwise, the mere fact that God wanted to destroy Sodom and Gemorrah would make this act morally right, and there would be no reason for Abraham to argue with Him).

The fact that God feels the need to show Abraham that there are no righteous people in the city likewise

Synopsis: Three "angels" visit Abraham and Sarah at Mamre during the heat of the day. Abraham and Sarah are wonderful hosts and, at the conclusion of their brief stay, the "angels" tell Sarah of the future birth of a child. God then reveals the plan to destroy Sodom and Gemorrah which leads to the powerful negotiation with God about the future of these cities. Events develop quickly, and the story of Lot and his family precedes the actual destruction of the cities in chapter 19. Lot's daughters give birth, by their father, to two sons who later become the heads of the kingdoms of Moab and Ammon. Abraham continues his journey, and, once again, Sarah is taken by a foreign king, this time by Avimelekh. Once again, Abraham assists in the resolution of this dilemma. The parashah concludes with the birth of Isaac, the expulsion of Hagar and Ishmael, an accounting of the relations between Abraham and Avimelekh, and the binding of Isaac.

Which brings me to the second point. If it is Abraham, and not God, who carries the Banner of Justice in this parashah, why doesn't he demand justice for his own son, Ishmael, and the boy's mother Hagar, when Sarah expels them from the camp (and God validates Sarah's decision)? And, *al ahat kama v'khama*, how much the more so, why doesn't he demand justice for Isaac when God demands him as a human sacrifice? The tradition

says that the *Akedah*, the Binding of Isaac, is only one in a series of tests that were given by God to Abraham. Perhaps after Sodom and Gemorrah, God wanted to see if Abraham would argue as forcefully for his own children as he would for strangers. Apparently he couldn't. As a result, the mantel of leadership soon passes to Isaac. But we will have to wait one more generation for the kind of leader God was looking for, Jacob, a

God-wrestler. **Rabbi Neil Comess-Daniels, Beth Shir Sholom, Santa Monica, CA**

דָּבָר אַחֵר **DAVAR AHER. AND THE ETERNAL DEPARTED...[Gen. 18.33].** In Rabbi Joseph Telushkin's commentary on *Va-Yera*, he refers three times to God's reporting to Abraham that there are not even ten righteous people to be found in Sodom and Gemorrah. The "shortfall" is clearly to be inferred

indicates that God does not want people to think something is right or wrong just because God says so. He wants to show mankind that His decrees are not arbitrary; that if he inflicts such severe punishment on these cities, it is because their inhabitants truly deserve it.

(3) Many years ago, a friend—I unfortunately have forgotten who it was—challenged one of my most basic assumptions about the story of Sodom and Gemorrah. I had always assumed that Abraham's concern was with saving the righteous people of the two towns (that's why he pleaded with God not to destroy the cities if at least ten righteous people could be found within them). But my friend noted that if that was Abraham's concern, he could simply have pleaded with God to spare the righteous, and to lead them out of the cities before destroying them. Instead, Abraham asks God to spare all the people of Sodom and Gemorrah if ten righteous people can be found within them. Abraham is arguing, therefore, on behalf of the wicked even more than the righteous.

By the way, why does Abraham stop at ten? When God reports to him that there are not even ten righteous people in the cities, Abraham falls silent, and pleads no more. I suspect that ten constitutes a minimum quorum necessary to influence the rest of the citizenry. If ten righteous people live within the city, they can establish a small community, and that community can, in turn, influence others. But at a certain point, less than ten, the forces of good are too weak to have any hope of transforming the broader community. That's why, as long as ten righteous people exist within Sodom and Gemorrah, it would be wrong for God to give up on them. Those ten people could still have an impact, one that could ultimately transform the moral landscape of these towns. But when God reports to Abraham that

Va-Yera

from what happens next in the story, namely the angels' going to rescue Lot and his family before the cities are destroyed. However, the text does not record another interchange between God and Abraham after the end of the negotiation session until well after the destruction has occurred. Thus, if God does report to Abraham on the failure to find ten righteous people before proceeding with the cities' destruction, it is in a midrash (and if so, I'd appreciate the citation so I can look it up)—or in the subconscious midrash that the reader is almost forced to create in order to have the text make ethical sense. This is a wonderful example of the "filling in" that one cannot help doing when reading the sparse but richly suggestive narratives of Genesis. **Rabbi Suzanne Griffel, Chicago, IL <sbgriffe@midway.uchicago.edu>**

וירא אליו יהוה באלני ממרא

Sodom and Gemorrah don't have even ten righteous people, he understands that there is no course from which the evil people can be influenced. The cities are evil and will remain evil.

There's a lesson in this for us. Unlikely as it is that we are living in cities quite as depraved as Sodom and Gemorrah, it reminds us of the need to live in the midst of a community of people who are striving to be righteous. To be one good, yet totally alone, family is not enough (for one thing, the likelihood that the majority will influence you is far greater than the likelihood that you will influence the majority). That is why it is impor-

tant to try and set up small communities of good people, and to live amongst those who share with you a desire לְתַקֵּן עוֹלָם בְּמַלְכוּת שַׁדַּי *l'taken olam be'malkhut Shaddai,* to perfect the world under the rule of God. •

דְּבָר אַחֵר **DAVAR AHER. BUT WHERE IS THE SHEEP FOR THE SACRIFICE?** [Gen. 22.7]. *The Tulsa Institute for Adult Jewish Studies Monday night Parashat ha-Shavuah class came up with the following:* What prompted the usually speechless Isaac to ask "BUT WHERE IS THE SHEEP FOR THE SACRIFICE?" He knew his father was getting on in age and at times was a little *farklempt.* He saw the firestone and wood, and wondered whether old Abraham had just been a bit forgetful. But why did it take him three days to ask? **Davar Aher:** Isaac knew what was going on and was really trying to suggest going back for the sheep to forestall things. **Debra Cohn-Levine, RJE, Temple Israel, Tulsa, OK**

דְּבָר אַחֵר **DAVAR AHER. DO NOT SEND YOUR HAND AGAINST THE BOY…**[Gen. 22.12]. While facing the *Akedah* in Torah time, we are also engaged in learning all about *The Cross and the Rose* and *The Order of the Solar Temple* (A cult whose members committed suicide in both Canada and France simultaneously) in real time. Holy blood is on the floor; blood not covered with dirt. Blood not rendered kosher. Deja vu: Jonestown. Deja vu: Waco. Deja vu:

Baruch Goldstein. We live with a secret knowledge that religion has its shadow and that faith can be very toxic. The haunting fear of the *Akedah*–the haunting fear of this week–is that madness can come with deep faith. Despite all of our "rationalizations" and P.C. *drashot* which say that this story teaches that "God doesn't want child sacrifice," we can recognize the madness. Kierkegaard saw the madness and wrote this monologue for Abraham: "Stupid boy, do you think that I am your father? I am an idolater. Do you think that God wants this? No, it is what I desire…" But Abraham said in a low voice to himself, "O God in heaven, I thank You. It is better for him to believe that I am a monster than to lose faith in You." Rashi sees the madness, too. His Abraham says, [Gen. 22.12] "If this be so, I have come up here for nothing. Let me at least inflict a wound on him and draw some blood from him…" When we are honest, we know that piety and madness are linked. Religion brings its light and kindness and compassion– and its compulsions, too. This week, *Akedah* in hand, this week, newspaper in hand, we learn about the meanings of faith. The *Akedah* is not only a test of faith, it is also an acid test for our sanity

as well. Every year, it forces us to define the best and the worst of our sense of being religious. **Joel Lurie Grishaver** <gris@torahaura.com>

דְּבָר אַחֵר **DAVAR AHER. DO NOT SEND YOUR HAND AGAINST THE BOY…**[Gen. 22.12]. Ever read the *Kol Eliyahu* (the Vilna Gaon) on the *Akedah*? The gist of it is that Abraham, whose natural tendency was to serve the Lord through kindness and goodness, had to prove himself by incorporating the opposite trait of cruelty in his Divine Service. The person who is truly *shalem* or spiritually whole is he who possesses all of the opposite traits of character, "good" and "bad," in due proportion, and stands ready to summon them for the Divine Service. Only showing that he could be cruel allows Abraham's kindness to be interpreted as coming out of his spiritual devotion and not because he was Mr. Nice Guy. The Gaon extends this to the Jewish people as a whole, saying that there are mitzvot, such as that of sending away the mother bird when taking the chicks, whose purpose is to teach us cruelty. (You thought that mitzvah teaches mercifulness towards animals? Ha!, says the Gaon, just the opposite! The *Zohar* writes that the mother bird would rather drown in the sea than go on living

A Ram Caught In The Thicket
[Genesis 22]

I watched horrified as he bound the boy
and lay him on the altar.
I watched as he shoved the child's head back
with his left hand under his chin,
and took the knife in his right hand
as my horns got caught in the thicket.
I bleated and struggled
as the Voice called out from Heaven,
Do not lay your hand on the boy
and do not do anything to him;
for now I know that you fear me;
you did not withhold your beloved son.
And I struggled and he saw me
his face aglow his son unbound
and he came to release me on this joyous day.
But he took the cord and bound me and lay me on the altar
and he shoved my head back
with his left hand under my chin,
and he took the knife in his right hand.
I bleated and struggled
awaiting the Voice from Heaven
but it did not come.
His face was aglow as he brought down the knife
And his son watched...

SAVINA J. TEUBAL IS THE AUTHOR OF SARAH THE PRIESTESS: THE FIRST MATRIARCH OF GENESIS, HAGAR THE EGYPTIAN: THE LOST TRADITIONS OF THE MATRIARCHS, "SIMCHAT HOCHMAH" ("JOY OF WISDOM," A CRONE RITUAL) WITH DRORAH SETEL, AND THE WORDS TO ITS THEME SONG "L'KHI LAKH" WITH DEBBIE FRIEDMAN.

Va-Yera

a life separated from her young.) Taken to the extreme, this Torah is dangerous. But Abraham never had to execute, only show that he was ready to. **Hazan Ira Rohde, Cong. Shearith Israel, New York, NY**

דְּבָר אַחֵר **DAVAR AHER. DO NOT SEND YOUR HAND AGAINST THE BOY...[Gen. 22.12].** I am a Chagall painting with a cloud of images swirling around my head. My desktop is covered with open windows. I click from one to another. The open window is brighter; the inactive ones are dimmed, but still there. This parashah is not transparent. There's more here than the beginning of animal rights. The Holy One knew this particular riddle would be difficult, so we have it to ponder twice each time around. It has borne a lot of turning over, and bears it still.

I saw a few moments of Nahshon Waxman's videotaped ransom plea, and heard a terribly abject plea, and wondered whether I would be able to announce to the world, "I regret that I have but one life to give for my country," or if I would try to smuggle something out in code—that I had graduated proudly from Nathan Hale High School, or would have if we hadn't moved. But there would be talk; he was after all, a spy. What kind of God is this that bids us put our brothers and sons in harm's way, to sacrifice real lives for ideas, for language about metaphors of metaphors?

…I can't find the only book by Soloveichik I've read, and I don't recall the title, but he talked about the two Adams: the technologist, master of the earth, and the other one, the one who wants to be in relation, to use your borrowed metaphor, the one looking for the missing part, the one who longs for the indwelling *Shekhinah*. They are always both Adams; both windows are open. They have multi-finder; they run two applications simultaneously. Our transcendence comes out of immanence. *Asher kidshanu b'mitzvotav* (Who makes us holy with the commandments). The Torah teaches us how to live with each other, not how to get out of here. And the communitarian quality of Judaism serves to tether the otherwise too-free flights of fancy to which we as isolated individuals are prone….

What can we do when we find ourselves still here after some part of Chaos and/or Evil has swept through

again and moved on? We can pretend it never happened, the real madness, or we can pick up our Torah, dust it off, and together, start turning it over, again. **David Keene <DHKeene@aol.com>**

דָּבָר אַחֵר **DAVAR AHER. AND THE TWO OF THEM WALKED TOGETHER. [Gen. 22.6.8].** I have recently been intrigued by lines 6 and 8 of Genesis 22. In both of these settings we find the phrase וַיֵּלְכוּ שְׁנֵיהֶם יַחְדָּו "*va-yel'khu sh'neihem yah-dav.*" And the most common understanding of the phrase "AND THE TWO OF THEM WALKED TOGETHER," is that it refers *in both instances to Abraham and Isaac.* I offer you a davar aher. I suggest that the first instance of "*va-yel'khu sh'neihem yah-dav*" refers to the present and past relationship of Abraham and God; i.e., that "THE TWO OF THEM WALKED TOGETHER" from the time of *Lekh Lekha* and until this moment in their shared history. They shared a mutual past and present. Because they walked together, implying a deep faith on the part of both God and Abraham, the second rendering of "*va-yel'khu sh'neihem yah-dav*" now takes on a new meaning. Abraham, by his very being, can reassure Isaac that "EVERYTHING WILL BE ALL RIGHT." In other words, I am suggesting that because Abraham had already walked with God (implying trust, faith, assurance of purpose), he knew that God would ultimately provide the appropriate sacrificial lamb. In fact, he knew it so deeply and with such assurance that he could say to his "favorite" son: "GOD WILL SEE THAT THE APPROPRIATE LAMB IS PROVIDED." **Albert Micah Lewis, Rabbi, Temple Emanuel, Grand Rapids, MI**

דָּבָר אַחֵר **DAVAR AHER. On Rams in Thickets.** The binding of Isaac is important to Judaism in so many ways and on so many levels. If nothing else, it teaches us about Abraham's deep commitment to G-d. Beyond that, it gives us a view of Isaac that is necessary if we want to understand his life better: Love of G-d or not; love of Abraham or not—imagine the psychological toll that act had on the rest of his life! I have always found the *Akedah* to be inspirational. Since when does Judaism encourage the humanization of animals? Does this mean that we should go back and reevaluate our feelings about the priests? Weren't they responsible for all of those sacrifices? Instead of reading a poem that's meant to make one feel bad about such a seminal event in our history, I would rather read one that has the ram thanking G-d for the opportunity to serve Him in a holy way. For, instead of being just another animal that we never would have known or cared about, this animal is now a part of our history. **Barry H. Davis (co-signed by Marty Moskowitz) <BarryhD@aol.com>**

דָּבָר אַחֵר **DAVAR AHER. On Rams in Thickets.** Savina J. Teubal's poem, *"A Ram Caught in the Thicket"* is one of the most wonderful *drashot* I have ever seen on the *Akedah*. I haven't been this "positively disturbed" since I first heard Leonard Cohen's, "The Story of Isaac." **Rabbi Neil Comess-Daniels, Beth Shir Sholom, Santa Monica, CA**

Hayyei Sarah

Genesis 23.1–25.18

Professor Carol Meyers

CAROL MEYERS, AUTHOR OF *DISCOVERING EVE: ANCIENT ISRAELITE WOMEN IN CONTEXT*, IS PROFESSOR OF BIBLICAL STUDIES AND ARCHAEOLOGY AT DUKE UNIVERSITY. SHE CO-DIRECTS DUKE'S SEPPHORIS REGIONAL PROJECT, A DIG IN ISRAEL NEAR NAZARETH; AND SHE IS ASSOCIATE DIRECTOR OF THE WOMEN'S STUDIES PROGRAM AT DUKE.

This parashah bears the name of a woman, the matriarch Sarah. But the centerpiece of the Torah portion for this week is really another woman, Rebekah. The entirety of Genesis 24, which happens to be the longest chapter in the Book of Genesis, contains the endearing tale of how Rebekah became the wife of Isaac. The very fact that such an extensive narrative is devoted to a female character alerts us to the special role that she plays in the unfolding drama of the ancestors in the Promised Land.

The Rebekah story, which is sometimes dubbed the "Courtship of Rebekah" or the "Wooing of Rebekah," tells us about the journey of the trusted, yet unnamed, servant of Abraham to the city of Nahor, in Mesopotamia. There he identifies Rebekah as an appropriate mate for his master's heir (Isaac), makes the nuptial arrangements, and brings the bride-to-be back to Palestine, where Isaac is waiting for her.

This charming tale, although it does depend to a certain extent on our knowing something about Abraham and his designated heir, in fact, stands rather well on its own. It has its own complex plot, which is developed through a series of dialogues and speeches. Indeed, it can be classified as a novella, one as compelling as any in the Bible. Furthermore, many aspects of the narrative make it a woman's story, one of only a handful of biblical

דָּבָר אַחֵר **DAVAR AHER.** SARAH'S LIFETIME WAS ONE HUNDRED AND TWENTY AND SEVEN YEARS...[Gen. 23.1]. I loved the counterpoint between Meyers and Finkelman. I am uncomfortable with Meyers' blanket assertion that Rebekah is much more active and autonomous than the other "mothers." She certainly does not have Sarah's "freedom of expression." Genesis 24.65, where Rebekah dons the veil, is a foreshadowing that her

greatest accomplishment (the shifting of the birth blessing) will be achieved through stealth. Mother Sarah, on the other hand, is able to confront her husband openly over the Isaac/Ishmael succession, and win. It appears to me that Rebekah's generation has regressed in this important regard, and had she challenged Isaac directly over the fitness of a particular child to succeed, she may have been vetoed. It is not only Isaac who

וִיהיו חיי שרה מאה שנה

passages that feature a female character in her own right.

Just what are the aspects of the Rebekah tale that give it that female perspective?

For one thing, especially in comparison with the other "mothers" of Genesis, Rebekah is a much more active and autonomous individual. The very language of this parashah contains a far more dynamic vocabulary than does the language associated with her mother-in-law (Sarah) or her daughters-in-law (Rachel and Leah). Notice how Rebekah "CAME OUT" [24.15], "WENT DOWN" [24.16], "LET DOWN HER JAR" [24.18], "RAN" [24.28], "AROSE, AND RODE UPON THE CAMELS" [24.61]. A similar vocabulary of activity appears in the birthright story of Genesis 27, which recounts her collusion with her favored son, Jacob, to secure the inheritance for him.

Rebekah clearly outshines the other matriarchs in the way she is portrayed as the agent of several critical moments in the saga of the ancestors. In addition, she is, in a sense, equated with none other than the foremost of the patriarchs, Abraham. Because of the language of 24.4 and 38, we know that when Rebekah finally heads for the Promised Land, she is leaving her "COUNTRY," "KINDRED," and "FATHER'S HOUSE," just as her father-in-law did at the momentous opening of the patriarchal epoch in *Lekh Lekha*, Genesis 12.1. The Rebekah story thus echoes the language of God's call to Abraham.

Similarly, Abraham's dramatic departure from the land of his birth, which is signified by the verb [הלך] *HLK* (לֵךְ *Lekh* "GO FORTH"; see Genesis 12.1, 4], is mirrored and intensified by Rebekah's departure from that same foreign land. The key verb "GO" appears seven times in the Rebekah story. Because seven is a highly symbolic number

Synopsis: Although this week's parashah is entitled "The life of Sarah," the opening verses and the rest of chapter 23 deal with Sarah's death and the negotiated purchase of the cave of Makhpelah. Our attention turns now to the rather well-known and dramatic story of the betrothal of Isaac, placing the next generation, Isaac and Rebekah, on history's stage as the next link in God's original promise to Abraham. As a thematic unit, the last verse of chapter 24 has Isaac bringing Rebekah into the tent of his mother—and, by so doing, finding comfort after the death of Sarah. Abraham takes another wife, Keturah, dies at the age of 175 and is buried in the cave of Makhpelah by his sons Isaac and Ishmael. The genealogy of Ishmael, and his death and burial at age 137, conclude this week's parashah.

---

appears passive compared to Abraham; Rebekah is tough, but in comparison does not have Sarah's "moxie." **Simcha Prombaum, Sons of Abraham Congregation, La Crosse, WI <KPROMBAU@UWLAX.EDU>**

דָּבָר אַחֵר **DAVAR AHER. SARAH'S LIFETIME WAS ONE HUNDRED AND TWENTY AND SEVEN YEARS...[Gen. 23.1].** In studying *Hayyei Sarah*, I always have trouble getting past the first line. The

treatment of 100+20+7 years has always intrigued me. Or maybe I try harder to understand because I want to bring myself—as a male—closer to our matriarch Sarah. So there each year I get stuck. This year was no different and Carol Meyer's piece—while quite informative—still didn't help me. So I turned to the *Sefas Emes* to get me out of the jam. He claims—expanding on Rashi—that Sarah's days are all called good because she

(applying *Brakhot* 6.5) blesses the good and bad. Even the worst days were good in her view. So I drag myself back to the Talmud and other sources. No one wants to deal with that challenge: blessing good and bad. Rabbi Norman Cohen translates "BLESSING" as "ACCEPTING." That helps him, but I don't think the Rabbis would agree so readily. It isn't until I come to the end of the *Sifre* comment on this passage [*Piska* 41] that I find

in the Torah, the sevenfold use of "GO" emphasizes that the shift in Rebekah's life course is every bit as significant as is the earlier relocation of Abraham.

One other Rebekah-Abraham parallelism occurs in the way Rebekah is blessed, as the future "MOTHER OF TENS OF THOUSANDS [GEN. 24.60]," whose "SEED (WILL) POSSESS THE GATE OF THOSE THAT HATE THEM." Like Abraham, she is viewed as the ancestor of multitudes who will inherit the land of God's promise.

Another noteworthy feature of the Rebekah story is the appearance of a very unusual phrase, בֵּית אֵם Bet Em ("MOTHER'S HOUSE" or "MOTHER'S HOUSEHOLD") in 24.28. In only three other places in the Hebrew Bible does such a term occur: once in Ruth [1.8], and twice in the Song of Songs [3.4 and 8.2]. It is no accident that those other uses of the term are in passages that can properly be called women's texts. In all these instances, Bet Em ("MOTHER'S HOUSE") replaces the much more common term Bet Av ("FATHER'S HOUSE") as the technical designation for the family household. In other words, when viewed from the perspective of a woman's text, the vocabulary used to denote the most important unit of society—the family—is a female term, "mother's household." This startling fact makes us aware that many more women's ways of viewing the world are probably masked by the male perspective of most of scripture.

But getting back to Rebekah herself, it is important now to note that, even though it is reported in a passage that is outside today's parashah, she is the only one of the foremothers who receives an oracle directly from God [Gen. 25.23]. And, as already noted, she is the initiating agent, in another text, in the plot to secure the birthright for Jacob.

Why is it that Rebekah emerges so prominently in Genesis 24 as well as in other texts? The clue perhaps

<u>H</u>ayyei Sarah

any relief. There, the Rabbis teach, "Whatever you do should be done out of love for God." OK. If that's the case, I can accept the bad—however unjustified it seems—as long as it is in the context of my relationship with the Holy One of Blessing. **Rabbi Kerry Olitzky, Director of School of Education HUC-JIR, New York, NY <Olitzky@huc.edu>**

דָּבָר אַחֵר **DAVAR A<u>H</u>ER. The ETERNAL HAD BLESSED ABRAHAM WITH EVERYTHING. [Gen. 24.1].** What I have always found striking about this parashah is the incongruity of the description of Abraham as a man whom God had blessed in all things [Gen. 24.1]. Abraham had driven one son (Ishmael) out into the wilderness; his second son (Isaac) he had nearly sacrificed on Mt. Moriah. He lost his argument with God to

resides in how she is positioned in this very parashah. _Hayyei Sarah_ begins with the death and burial of Sarah—the procuring of a burial place in Hebron and Sarah's interment there [Gen. 23]. And the parashah ends with the death and burial of Abraham in the same place. That is, the end of the first generation of ancestors encircles the story of a representative of the second generation. That representative is Rebekah, rather than her husband Isaac. Indeed, there is no independent narrative about Isaac in Genesis; and when he does appear, his characterization is rather weak and passive. Clearly Rebekah is the stronger member of the second ancestral pair. Her portrayal as an active individual overshadows the sparse accountings of Isaac.

For the transition between the first father, Abraham, and the third father, Jacob (= _all Israel_), Rebekah's role as mother of nations looms larger than that of her husband as father of nations. This parashah showcases the matriarch who dominates the second generation of the ancestry sequence of Genesis. Rebekah is the one who supplies the vitality of the lineage. This fact makes us wonder whether we ought to replace the familiar sequence "Abraham, Isaac and Jacob" with a more accurate "Abraham, Rebekah and Jacob" in referring to the leading figures of this period of the ancestors. ●

save Sodom and Gemorrah on behalf of the few righteous inhabitants of those cities—instead he "HURRIED TO THE PLACE WHERE HE HAD STOOD BEFORE THE LORD, AND, LOOKING DOWN TOWARD SODOM AND GEMORRAH AND ALL THE LAND OF THE PLAIN, HE SAW THE SMOKE OF THE LAND RISING LIKE THE SMOKE OF A KILN" [Gen. 19. 27-8]. In _Hayyei Sarah_, Abraham has been forced by circumstance into humiliating negotiations with the local Hittites, who are identified several times as "THE PEOPLE OF THE LAND," i.e., of the land that Abraham himself had been promised! And he is also in the position of practically begging a servant to find a wife now for Isaac. The future of his whole lifelong monotheistic endeavor hangs in this delicate, almost pathetic balance. Yet Abraham is "BLESSED IN ALL THINGS"—perhaps to teach us something about the radical nature of true blessing. That blessing is not defined by material well-being, that all of us can accept. But that blessing might not reside either in warm human relationships or in family harmony—that is a dangerous and challenging concept. **Rabbi Michael L. Joseph, Temple B'nai B'rith, Kingston, PA**

Rabbi Eliezer Finkelman

ELIEZER FINKELMAN IS RABBI OF CONGREGATION BETH ISRAEL, AN ORTHODOX CONGREGATION IN BERKELEY, CA.

Hayyei Sarah

Carol Meyers tells us that Isaac is presented in the sacred record as "rather weak and passive." The real hero, Rebekah, is vital, active, and let me add, decisive. Poor Isaac. Perhaps we ought to reconsider his role as a patriarch, even if we are not changing the classical structures of Jewish prayer (see *Berakhot* 40b). How does Isaac measure up? Poor Isaac, our forefather.

The young Rebekah is decisive when Abraham's servant first meets her: She says but two words, "DRINK, MY SIR" [Gen. 24.18], then a whole sentence in which she takes responsibility for watering all ten camels [24.19]. Offered a choice, she is decisive about leaving with the servant: "I WILL GO" [24.58]. Offered a nurse as company [24.59], she takes several servants [24.61]. Years later, when she overhears that Isaac will give his blessing to the son whom she does not love, she is again decisive. She plans Jacob's deception of his father and talks Jacob into carrying it out. Their plan has negative consequences: When Esau finds out, he is ready to kill Jacob, but resourceful Rebekah is wise enough to send Jacob away to her family, ostensibly to find a wife. Once again, she takes decisive action. On second reading, the whole deception might not be necessary, for Isaac may have intended to give the blessing of Abraham to Jacob all

דָּבָר אַחֵר **DAVAR AHER. ISAAC WENT OUT TO SUPPLICATE IN THE FIELD...** [Gen. 24.63]. Eliezer Finkelman asks: "What virtues can a passive man have?" In addition to all those he enumerates, Isaac is also the "middle child," the one who wants only to please his parents (and, by extension, to please the rest of the world where he lives). Is he a *"gibbor"* (hero) in Kabbalistic terms or is he a wimp? Can we see this generation of North American Jews as the "Isaac" of contemporary Jewish history, coming as we do after Abraham, the "first child" of Destruction\Redemption and Jacob, the "youngest child," not yet born? At the risk of upsetting the delicate balance created by our move to the "New World" after the Shoah, we have given in and given up our Jewish identity far too easily, and therefore our people are

ויהיו חיי שרה מאה שנה ועשרים שנה ושבע שנים

along. Isaac does not give that blessing to Jacob disguised as Esau [27.28-29], nor to Esau himself [27.39-40], but only to Jacob when he comes in his own name [28.3-4]. Perhaps Rebekah is in such a hurry to take matters into her own hands that she does not have time to check out Isaac's intentions.

Meanwhile, what can we say about Isaac? What virtues can a passive man have? After his heroic moment, when he passively endures being bound for sacrifice (chapter 22), Isaac's virtues are moderate. He meditates in the field [24.63]. He loves his wife [24.67], and makes love with his wife [24.67]. He mourns for his mother [24.67]. He, together with his brother, buries their father [25.9]; apparently Isaac has managed to make peace with his outcast brother. He prays for his wife [25.21]. He loves his son [25.28]. He works to earn a living [26.12]. When he is old and blind [27.1], he remembers to bless his son, or, I think, each of his sons

with a different appropriate blessing. That is Isaac at home. What ordinary virtues! Any man could aspire to such virtues, if he values his family; if he wants to become a patriarch.

Isaac abroad, dealing with powerful strangers, prefers to avoid conflict by moving a short way on, or by agreeing to peaceful terms. Only once does he engage in deception, the traditional deception of calling his wife his sister as they enter the Philistine city of Gerar [26.7]; even when the deception is discovered, Isaac remains in that land. When the envious king orders him to leave Gerar [26.16], Isaac moves, but only as far as Naḥal Gerar [26.17]. When the local Philistines challenge his rights to his inherited wells, he has his shepherds move and dig new wells, until the Philistines leave him alone [26.16-22]. Even so, he moves on [26.23]. Better to avoid a fight. When the king of Gerar comes back to negotiate with Isaac, after having driven Isaac out of his territory, Isaac challenges his

motives [26.27]; when the king says that he comes in peace, Isaac celebrates a treaty with him [26.28-31]. Let bygones be bygones. That is how Isaac deals with strangers. He is a man of peace, ready to accept an offer of peace, ready to move on.

Though Isaac never leaves the holy land [28.1-5], his peace-loving, self-effacing virtues are a model of how his descendants have endured life in exile. Isaac's virtues are the millennial virtues of Jewish men. If these seem weak to us, perhaps it is because we, Americans or Israelis, are used to admiring only men of action. But consider how close these virtues are to what the Arabs call *summud*, steadfastness; sometimes the steadfast have proven harder to overcome than the violent. I refer to these as non-heroic virtues, but, oddly enough, the word which the Kabbalists use to describe this character of Isaac is *gevurah*, heroism: heroism of a peculiar kind. ●

far too apathetic, intermarried and uneducated (to paraphrase a famous *Akedah* midrash, maybe we were slaughtered on Moriah....). And so now we wait for Jacob, the "new generation," who will doubtless be, we hope, a product of our efforts at Jewish continuity. I hope Jacob comes soon, before it is too late. How long can Rebekah wait at the well this time? **Rabbi Melvin J. Glazer, Congregation Olam Tikvah, Fairfax, VA**

What Did Isaac Know?

I

This parashah begins with a contradiction. It says at the beginning that it will concentrate on Isaac, but in fact it begins the story of Jacob.

Of Isaac we learn very little, and clearly the Torah focuses on Jacob—the man after whom our people have been named ever since. We are called either the House of Jacob or the House of Israel

(Jacob's other name), and the Jewish state is called after him as well. There is every reason to ask just why it is that he became our chief ancestor rather than Abraham. The parashah gives us no answer, in fact it compounds the difficulty of answering this question.

Just who was Jacob? His Hebrew name, *Ya'akov*, is explained as "holding onto the heel" of his first-emerging twin brother Esau. The Hebrew עָקַב *akav* has many additional meanings in biblical and modern Hebrew: to cheat, supplant, cancel. Jeremiah said that "THE HEART IS DECEITFUL עָקֹב (*akov*) ABOVE ALL THINGS." A derivative form (עָקֵב *ikkev*) means to hinder, prevent, keep back, hold up, delay.

What kind of an ancestor is this whose name is related to so many negatives? For the positives are very few. None is really found in the Torah, only modern Hebrew has

Toldot

Genesis 25.19–28.9

Rabbi W. Gunther Plaut

RABBI PLAUT IS THE EDITOR AND PRINCIPAL AUTHOR OF *THE TORAH— A MODERN COMMENTARY*.

דָּבָר אַחֵר **DAVAR AHER. THE CHILDREN STRUGGLED WITHIN HER...[Gen. 25.22].** This year the Torah portion *Toldot* coincides with the distribution of report cards. We read here about the struggles of the twins, Esav and Ya'akov, for primacy and blessing in their parents' household. Esav, as we know, was the rough and tumble brother, an אִישׁ שָׂדֶה *ish sadeh*, a man of the field. Ya'akov, was an אִישׁ תָּם *ish tam*, a mild man, described as

יֹשֵׁב אֹהָלִים *yoshev ohalim*, that is, as "SITTING IN THE TENTS." (Tradition tells us that these tents were a *yeshivah*!) Much has been made of the contrast between Ya'akov, making his way through life by his brains, as opposed to Esav, who got through life by brawn. Ya'akov, of course, became Yisrael, our forefather, from whom we are told to take example! The most important distinction between the brothers, I believe, is

ואלה תולדות יצחק בן א

latched onto a meaning which it must have discovered buried somewhere in the nature of the root. Today, יַעֲקוּב yikkuv indicates something raised to the third power (like the number 8 which is 2 x 2 x 2) and עָקִיב akiv means logical or consistent. All of which may indicate that hidden within the name יַעֲקֹב Ya'akov was a power with varied potential.

This did not show itself at the beginning. Trying to hold onto his brother's heel, perhaps trying to prevent him from being born first, gave him the name, a beginning which a few years later was followed by the incident of Esau's sale of the birthright: the older brother, coming home thirsty and hungry, finds his younger brother cooking a tasty meal and asks him to share it. No, says Jacob, not until you sell me your birthright. Esau is too tired and hungry to argue about this unbrotherly bargain; the Torah adds

that he thus despised his birthright, but it says nothing about the morality of Jacob's way of attaining it, which to the naked eye appears very far from having been ethical.

The Torah [Gen. 25.27] also describes this very Jacob as an אִישׁ תָּם ish tam, which the Jewish Publication Society translation renders as "a mild man." We have met the Hebrew word before in the description of Noah [Gen. 6.9], where it appears in its expanded form, tamim, and is rendered as "blameless." Tam can also mean simple, and that is the way it is used in the Haggadah in the description of the third son.

But how does that fit Jacob? He was many things, but not simple in the way we use the word, and certainly not straightforward. The best way we can understand the use of tam as applied to Jacob is that it appears as a contrast to his brother Esau who is depicted as a skillful hunter, the strong, muscular, out-

Synopsis: Isaac's family now becomes the center of attention. Rebekah gives birth to twins—Esau and Jacob—and the famous story of the birthright gives us insight into the character of these two men. Once again in the patriarchal narrative, there is a famine and Isaac, in his travels, stops at Gerar. Here, the covenant is reaffirmed and an encounter with the local king, Avimelekh (similar to the one between Abraham and Pharaoh) occurs. Isaac is blessed with wealth—and this richness causes him to be asked to move to another nearby location. In that place, too, he is the cause of local discontent and so Isaac moves to Beer Sheva whereupon Avimelekh, king of Gerar, seeing that God has made Isaac prosper, cuts a treaty with him. Two short verses describe the bitterness between the wives of Esau and his parents which sets the stage for the famous story of the stealing of the blessing by Jacob. The four main characters—Jacob, Esau, Rebekah and Isaac—play out the scenes of this drama and, at the end of our parashah, Jacob listens to his parents' voices and flees to Padam Aram.

not one of native brain power, but one of "application" and "motivation." This is why the story of selling the birthright for a mess of pottage determines who will ultimately get the fuller blessing. In this story, Ya'akov demonstrates his resourcefulness and drive to get ahead. Esav demonstrates his apathy and lack of initiative. The Torah puts it disdainfully, "AND HE ATE, AND HE DRANK, AND HE GOT UP, AND HE WENT, AND HE, ESAV, WASTED HIS

BIRTHRIGHT. [Gen. 25.34]" So, too, with us today! Application and motivation are the path to report cards of which you can be proud! **Dr. Zvi Schoenburg, Solomon Schechter Day School of Memphis, Memphis, TN**

דָּבָר אַחֵר **DAVAR AHER. Two NATIONS ARE IN YOUR WOMB...[Gen. 25.22].** The narrative of the Torah utilizes the theme of sibling rivalry—Cain and Abel, Ishmael and Isaac, Esau

and Jacob, and Joseph and his brothers—to illustrate the inherent dangers of brotherly jealousy, mistrust and hate for one another. Each brother sought to become either their parent's or G-d's chosen one. Jacob's platform of deception was no secret as he frequently is depicted in the realm of art as pulling his brother Esau's heel back so he could be the firstborn. Jacob would find out the hard way that those you deceive will

doorsman—and we must not forget that in those days this was a quality which above all made a man worth his salt. Measured on that scale, Jacob was *tam*, a description of few skills rather than of character. For the boy's character was far from simple, it was, in fact, highly complicated.

II

That brings us to the center of the parashah, the blessing that Isaac bestows on his son. The story is one of cunning and deception and not at all "nice."

Isaac is old, he can no longer see very well, and he thinks that death is approaching. Therefore, he prepares to give the customary fatherly blessing to his firstborn son, vesting him with all the privileges that primogeniture implied in those days. So he calls Esau, tells him to hunt for some venison, which Isaac loves to eat, and after the festive meal he will pronounce his blessing.

What the blind man does not know is that his wife Rebekah has overheard this and is highly displeased with the plan. Rebekah, we already learn from an earlier chapter of the Torah (chapter 24), was not only beautiful but also imaginative, and she shows it to perfection in what is now going to happen. (Maurice Samuel wrote a delightful little volume entitled, *Certain People of the Book*, in which he calls Rebekah "The Manager." She managed her husband, he tells us, and certainly does so in the parashah before us.)

She calls her favorite son Jacob and makes him dress up in skins to smell like his brother, and asks him to pretend that he is, in fact, Esau, so that while his brother is out hunting Jacob can obtain the blessing. Never mind the deceit, she seems to imply, as long as Father blesses you, it cannot be reversed. Jacob goes along and the ruse succeeds. Jacob is blessed, and when Esau returns he finds out that he

Toldot

ultimately trick you, proving the cliche "What goes around, comes around." In a world where the conflict between brothers rages on, we turn to the Middle East for a modern illustration in the religious realm. Greek Orthodox, Roman Catholic, Armenian and Christianity are the rival "siblings" in a contemporary analogy of the Jacob and Esau conflict. The Church of the Holy Sepulcher in Jerusalem, where

many traditional Christian sects believe Christ was buried, is in itself a study of the rivalry between brothers leading to mutual suspicion. Under the rules adopted by the Ottomans more than a century ago, patriarchs for the three major sects—Greek Orthodox, Roman Catholic, and Armenian take turns cleaning the tomb and the anointment stone. The minority Assyrians and Ethiopians have their own set

has been cheated and that he must be satisfied with a secondary benediction.

But how can a blessing issued to the wrong person have any effect?

III

To begin with, a blessing is not a legal contract but a prayer. Yet, when issued by a father it was believed to have special power, for God is involved when a father gives his blessing to his son. A blessing is not like a piece of merchandise that can be taken back when it is seen to be flawed. Once given, it is in God's hands.

May we then draw the conclusion that the whole of Jacob's future (and thereby our own) rests on a mistaken blessing? It would appear so, yet, in fact, Isaac was not deceived at all.

The deception was undertaken by Rebekah and agreed to by Jacob. But Isaac, himself, was never taken in. Ironically, Jacob and Rebekah involved themselves in moral turpi-

tude in order to achieve what Isaac wanted all along.

A close reading of the text will show that Isaac, blind but not senile, knew precisely who Jacob was. When Esau first comes into the room and his father asks him who he is [27.1], he says a single word, הִנֵּנִי *Hineni,* "HERE I AM"—and his father knows at once that he is Esau.

Now note: when Jacob enters [27.18] he greets his father and says, "FATHER," to which Isaac replies, "YES, WHICH OF MY SONS ARE YOU?" When Esau identified himself there was no question in Isaac's mind; when Jacob does the same the father appears dubious. The fact is, he knew very well that this was not Esau. His was a rhetorical question. No amount of play acting, false skins, and goat disguised as venison could really deceive him. Why?

Because he wanted to be misled. In his heart he had known all along that Esau was not the one who could bear the responsibilities of the blessing, that despite his faults, Jacob was

the one that had to be chosen. Isaac knew it—and tradition says that this was the way God planned it.

However, Isaac was a weak person, managed by his wife, and though he should never have let Esau believe that he would obtain the blessing, Isaac did not dare face his son with the truth. Rebekah helped him do it through the deception, which turned out to be no deception at all. Isaac—we may assume—was glad it happened this way.

It is therefore not surprising that the Torah records no reprimand to Jacob when the deception is uncovered. How could Isaac be angry at deceit when he welcomed it in his heart? He knew that Jacob was the one to be chosen.

But that, of course, explains only one part of the problem. It does not tell us how Jacob—who believed that he was deceiving—was morally worthy of what he received. The Torah helps us out. In its concept, God was the guide of the ancestors' lives. Being human they were imperfect, and God

---

of tasks, zealously guarded. Scaffolding to repair the ceiling has remained in place for decades because the sects can't agree on the design of the dome today. They trust one another so little that the keys to the church have been entrusted to the Muslims. The message of *Toldot* (generations), the story of Esau and Jacob, remind us to rethink and consider the consequences of these continual acts of deception, suspicion and mistrust

which link the generations past, present and future. Can we dare echo the words of Psalm 133.1: *Hinei mah tov u-mah na'im shevet ahim gam yahad*– "HOW WONDERFUL IT IS FOR BROTHERS TO DWELL TOGETHER!" Have we learned a lesson from the Jacob and Esau episode? **Rabbi Barry Blum, Congregation Ner Tamid, Broomall, PA**

דָּבָר אַחֵר **DAVAR AHER. Two NATIONS ARE IN YOUR WOMB…[Gen. 25.22].** *A Forum from the Torah Aura Newsletter. Toldot* is essentially a series of "Isaac is cool" stories woven among a series of Jacob vs. Esau struggles. The subtext, especially the midrashic subtext of the story, is the "war" between Jewish culture and Greco-Roman culture (because midrashically Esau, who forms Edom, is the symbol of Rome). The stories

had to choose imperfect persons to carry the divine message to an imperfect humanity. Noa<u>h</u> was righteous in his age, but tradition points out that he was far from perfect. Abraham committed a grave sin (as Nachmanides emphasizes) when he distrusted God's promise and left the land in a moment of crisis for the bread of Egypt. Isaac was weak though steady. Now we come to Jacob, who will have to do a lot of maturing before he wrestles with the angel, and is renamed Israel. Tragedy follows him, but as he matures his spirituality is broadened. The young Jacob is left behind and the ancestor of the Jewish people emerges.

This, then, is the beginning of Jacob's biography. It starts on a dubious note. But one has to read on to get the full story. •

Toldot

try to prove that, despite (or maybe because of) the cunning Jacob uses, he deserves to be the future of God's chosen faith, even though Esau was legally next in line. These stories say quite profoundly: "Judaism is better."

Last night, Jon Harris, a 10th grade Hebrew High School student, asked me: "Do you think Judaism is better than Christianity? Why?" After I gave him a short answer: "Yes" (with explanations), he asked me a 90's question I would never have anticipated: "In what ways do you think Christianity is better than Judaism?" He wasn't being obsequious. It's a good question.

This week, as Jacob and Esau struggle their politically incorrect struggle, as Judaism fights its demographic fight with Edom over our students' dating habits and future offspring, Jon's Torah is a powerful lesson to those of us who teach. Try his questions on your kids. The lesson learned from my *Parashat ha-Shavua* bifocals is that we have to acknowledge the gifts of Esau and still affirm (as difficult as it may be) the superiority of Jacob. That is our birthright that was hard won this week. **Joel Grishaver <gris@tora-haura.com>**

דָּבָר אַחֵר **DAVAR A<u>H</u>ER.** I believe it is wrong for any religious school teacher to assert that Judaism is better than Christianity or any other religion. We *should* start with the assumption that all religions *are* created equal," since each group feels that way. Jewish school teachers can respond that Judaism is the better religion for them, but in a world all too often fractured by social and religious divisiveness, I don't see the need for theo- or religio-centrism. I tell my students that Judaism has wonderful, unique and admirable characteristics, but saying that it is better than other religions is dangerous and misguided. **Steve Friedman, Brandeis Hillel Day School, San Francisco, CA**

דָּבָר אַחֵר **DAVAR A<u>H</u>ER.** I understand where this letter is coming from, but Judaism is hard enough— and there is no immediate benefit, because Judaism is not an "immediate-benefit" religion. If Judaism isn't better, we all might as well switch to Christianity, or some "immediate-benefit" religion. Public schools can equivocate about "equal value systems." That's not our job. **David Barany, B'nai Joshua Beth Elohim, Glenview, IL**

דָּבָר אַחֵר **DAVAR AHER.** I stayed up most of the night thinking about this question. I think I agree with Steve. I've tried to think about it from the point of view of a teacher, a communal person, and a parent—because I am all of those things. Each religion thinks it's the best one. We have to teach that Judaism is unique, powerful and special, and make the education so intense that Judaism can answer all our children's questions, but not dishonor any other religion as we do so. **Carol Starin, Executive Director of the Jewish Education Council, Seattle, WA**

דָּבָר אַחֵר **DAVAR AHER.** We are not dealing with whether or not it is true that Judaism is better than other religions—but with a dialectic that the Torah presents. The Torah emphasizes choice. To say that people make choices without valences is absurd. My response: It is a question of how you deal with *Or la-Goyim* (Light to the Nations) without saying we're better. It's an interesting problem, but to say all religions are created equal is *Narishkeit.* **Kyla Epstein, Fairmont Temple, Cleveland, OH**

דָּבָר אַחֵר **DAVAR AHER.** I think that it is nice to be politically correct, but I am a Jew because I believe in Judaism. It is what drives me into the future, and I will take along on the

journey anyone who is willing to come. When I find something from the Christian culture that has something to teach, I transform it in order to call it our own. **Rabbi Kerry Olitzky, Director of School of Education HUC-JIR, New York, NY <Olitzky@huc.edu>**

דָּבָר אַחֵר **DAVAR AHER.** I am in a *gam zeh v'gam zeh* situation. We sometimes soft-pedal to our children the particular joy and power of what it means to be a Jew. But we've struggled hard to be a people, and as a group of survivors, we have to acknowledge that we have in Judaism something that is *not only* as good, but something worth dying for. That means that it is *more than* "as good as." On the other hand, given the post-modern pluralistic world, we have to be careful to define who and what we are in relationship to, and not as opposed to. The message of living in America is that somehow we can live with mutual respect for each other's ideas and each other's chosen path of worship. **Rabbi Keith Stern, Congregation Beth Shalom, Arlington, TX**

דָּבָר אַחֵר **DAVAR AHER.** I disagree with both positions. Both of you think in a very Aristotelian manner. Your assumption is: if you are right, someone else must be wrong. If you are better, someone else must be worse. And, the opposite of equal is unequal in a measurable way. Being right doesn't mean that they're wrong. I don't believe it is right to teach kids that "Judaism is better," because they don't understand "better" without believing that others are "worse." I

prefer to say "unique." No one has the challenge that the Jews do from God. Without our challenge, the world in which we live would be out of balance. Would the world be a worse place without Jews? Yes! Does that mean that Judaism is better than other religions? No! Why do we pray "the whole world shall come to serve You" stuff? Do we really want the whole world to be Jewish (because that must mean we are "better")? No. We'd like the outcome if the whole world were Jewish. The real issue is not about better and worse, but about particular and universal, and our Aristotelian background teaches us that "particular" is supposed to be "better." I am a big-time particularist; I'm just not big on thinking about better and worse. **Rabbi Elliot Kleinman, Temple Sholom, Chicago, IL**

דָּבָר אַחֵר **DAVAR AHER.** I didn't read it that way initially. I saw the positiveness about being Jewish. Teachers have to present the positive truths about Judaism. If they don't, then kids begin to question. We need to take a strong stand about how we feel about Judaism, and why we have made certain choices. I don't see that as putting down another religion. **Patti Kroll, Beth Shalom Synagogue, Kansas City, KS**

דָּבָר אַחֵר **DAVAR AHER.** It is a struggle I am in personally and as an educator. If Judaism isn't ultimately critical as a "truth," it doesn't have value. On the other hand, one doesn't want to impose it. Personally, when I say the *kiddush* or an *aliyah*, I change the words to אֲשֶׁר בָּחַר בָּנוּ עִם כָּל הָעַמִּים *"Asher bahar banu im kol ha-amim"*—we were chosen *"with* all the people" not *from* them; but I keep the "*Asher natan lanu,*" because Torah is our special gift. I think each people has been chosen, but Torah is *our* special gift. *This came out at our faculty meeting last week. Teachers raised this question, and they, too, have problems with the idea of chosenness. It is a big issue.* **Shoshana Silberman, Jewish Center, Princeton, NJ**

דָּבָר אַחֵר **DAVAR AHER.** I think Carol (Starin) put it best. Each religion is unique and special, as each child is unique and special. None is "better." They all are different. I would always choose my own child or my own religion because of the special qualities I love within each. **Sharon Morton, Am Shalom, Glencoe, IL**

דָּבָר אַחֵר **DAVAR AHER.** The only problem in teaching that Judaism is better is the implied permission it gives students to denigrate other religions. Inward pride is not the problem. Outward hate is the problem. Is there no room for a benign chauvinism that allows us to accept our own heritage as better without feeling the need to ridicule others? That is the source of true Jewish pride: to be so secure in our own "betterness" that we are unconcerned with and passive to the claims and actions of other religions. **Rabbi Larry Freedman, Roslyn Heights, NY**

דָּבָר אַחֵר **DAVAR AHER.** My friend since childhood, Kinky Friedman, once responded to the challenge of why he wore his Judaism on his sleeve by noting that when one had been around 5,000 plus years like we had, it was OK to sit back with some degree of pride. If there is going to be anyone in the future to claim Jewish heritage as their own, it is most likely going to be because they find it the best tradition for them. Telling our kids that Judaism is the best is a statement of pride in our choice and is the kind of message we need to pass on. Do we want them to think we are into a second-rate covenant?! Are we to acquiesce to the old anti-Jewish label of being the ultimate pariah damned to wander the world?! Teaching our kids that Judaism is the best has nothing to do with other traditions. It is a statement of what we think of ourselves. It is a declaration of our pride in who and what we are. Once attained, the issue becomes how we use that pride and that belief in and about Judaism, not should we have it or foster it? Perhaps it is the way the issue is joined that causes the problems. It should not be the belief. That should be a given! **Rabbi Jimmy Kessler, Galveston, TX**

דָּבָר אַחֵר **DAVAR AHER.** Every person who belongs to any cohesive group needs to feel that that group is unique, special and best for them. Otherwise, why should one choose to belong? This point was made clear to me at our interfaith Thanksgiving Service that takes place each year between our synagogue and the local Methodist Church….At the (combined) youth program that follows the service, teenagers from both congregations get together in a formal program to learn about one another's religion.

Toldot

What invariably happens is that each teenage participant's own religious beliefs and commitments get reinforced. When our kids hear their rabbi express ideas that are inherent in Judaism and familiar to them, they nod their heads. The Christian youth members do the same thing when their pastor speaks. I have learned through this experience that it is important for Jews to get together with people from other faith traditions…not only to learn about another religion…it is also an opportunity for Jews to express their pride in the tradition in which we were raised. **Eliot Fein, Temple Eilat, Mission Viejo, CA**

דָּבָר אַחֵר **DAVAR AHER. Two NATIONS ARE IN YOUR WOMB…[Gen. 25.22].** Still not ready to let go of the Isaac, Jacob and Esau saga—with the comparison of Esau and Jacob, we wonder what role justice played in it all. From all indications, except for the intervention of Rebekah, Isaac would have complied with the concept of primogeniture—first born son takes it all…. My question is—where is justice in all of this? We are known as the people of justice; G-d guides us to dispense and to live a life based on justice. Yet we are told that Jacob lived most of his life ridden with fear, guilt and pain because of his compliance with his mother's plan to get him the birthright that his older (by seconds) brother was entitled to…. When we see this, we wonder what is the true meaning of "entitled"—the unworthy but firstborn son getting it all vs. the second, but more worthy son losing the blessing that would eventually guide his entire life. I see "entitled" as

truly unjust. I am delighted with the conclusion whereby, as we all know, Rebekah took it upon herself to intervene, resulting in Jacob's receiving the proper birthright—but suffering throughout the remainder of his life for compliance with his mother's plan. If it had gone according to habit—with Isaac giving the birthright to Esau, his first born—that truly would have been an injustice. **Elayne Meir Breslaw, Hebrew Union College, Los Angeles, CA**

דָּבָר אַחֵר **DAVAR AHER. …JACOB WAS AN *ISH TAM* (simple man). [Gen. 25.27].** Seemingly trapped by the expectation that Esau will become the next patriarch after Isaac, Rebekah determines to find a way to block his ascension. Her rejection of Esau is not personal so much as it reflects her concern over the responsibility for the fulfillment of the promise and covenant began between God and Abraham. She cannot accept that Esau can or will care enough to lead his family and people on to the next stage…. One gets the impression that Isaac went along with the deception because he needed it in order to accomplish another goal. Upon his return Esau discovers that Jacob 'THE SIMPLE' has again taken from him. He swears to kill him after Isaac dies. What follows seems to compromise the actions of both Isaac and Rebekah. Instead of facing Esau with the truth of his inappropriateness to be patriarch and insuring that Jacob not marry non-Hebrews as Esau had, they council Jacob to flee from his brother to their original homeland to find himself

Is the purpose of this transparent charade only to remove Esau and replace him with Jacob? While the focus appears to be on the character of Esau, we know little of Jacob except that he is A SIMPLE MAN; אִישׁ תָּם *ish tam* who blindly obeys his mother's orders to lie to his father and cheat his brother. The תָּם *tam*, the simple son of the Passover Seder, is not pictured as retarded or stupid. The *tam* is the child who is yet untaught and untried in the events of life. He has not yet faced the challenges of life to know what he is made of. The *tam* is the unknown quantity whose untapped potential lies hidden, especially from himself. One cannot be forced in achieving potential, it must arise from the person's own need to respond to life. Learning must come from coping with one's own experience.

The reason for the transparent deception becomes clear. As long as Jacob sat in his mother's tent he would never know what he might or had to become. His maturity could not be forced on him by expelling him from the safety of his home and yet if he were to prove himself capable of the great task of being the patriarch he had to leave. Not that alone—he had to leave bereft of all hope to return. He had to be totally dependent on his own potential to survive. He had to be tested to ascertain if he could learn to rise to his own occasion. Since it was his task to assume the stature of his grandfather, Abraham, and be the founder of the great nation, he had to re-enact the same experience. "God said to Abram—לֶךְ לְךָ *Lekh L'kha*—'GET OUT OF THE LAND, OUT OF THE PLACE OF YOUR BIRTH, OUT OF YOUR FATHER'S HOUSE

Toldot

AND GO TO A PLACE I WILL SHOW YOU." [Gen. 12.1] Just as Abraham had to leave the safety of his home to find the potential that awaited him, so did Jacob have to be totally dependent on his own resources to discover the true self locked deep inside his passivity.

The collusion of Isaac and Rebekah in the deception of the blessing was in fact a deception played upon Jacob that forced him to leave his safety net so he could find his potential to serve God as Patriarch. The deception made Jacob confront his own passivity and indifference to his life and the future of his father's faith. Jacob ran not just in fear of Esau, but in fear of himself and the truth of his being. Cut loose from family, he was removed from unproductive conflict with Esau and set on the road to resolve the conflict of his own soul. Jacob found his רְחוֹבוֹת *rehovot*—his space to live and grow in his wilderness trek to a new life. Isaac and Rebekah had fulfilled their responsibility both as parents and Patriarch/Matriarch. They set free the untried spirit of their son so that he could grasp the future that awaited him and his descendants.

The message of the portion is now clear—conflicts demand their own resolution regardless of our desire to avoid them. The role of a conflict is to push us toward the spiritual/psychological maturity implicit in our character but unacknowledged in our consciousness. Since growth is both risky and challenging, we frequently avoid it, preferring the 'safety of the tent' as did Jacob. Yet events circle around us, conspiring to drive us to resolve those issues we seek to avoid. At birth, it is clear that Jacob was no *ish tam*—no quiet passive person-ality. He struggled with Esau over who would emerge first and so have the right to the leadership of the family and faith. Though he lost the battle, he emerged grasping Esau's heel (עָקֵב *akeiv*), showing his determination not to be left behind. But as he grows he retreats into passivity. He buries his potential. He is resigned to his status. But he cannot remain so. The reality of Esau's deficiencies forces Rebekah and Isaac to devise a conflict resolution that will push Jacob into the role for which he was born. Jacob is jerked from the external conflicts with his brother by the deception of the blessing, and is forced into a journey that will resolve the inner conflict of his soul. Only by resolving the inner conflicts can he become Israel, the father of our people. So, too, all of us are frequently pushed forward on the path of growth by such conflicts and are forced to realize the truth of our potential hidden within. So our inner conflicts must be embraced not avoided. They are the dramatic themes of our lives and show the path we are yet to travel. **Rabbi Stephen Robbins, Congregation N'vay Shalom, Los Angeles, CA**

דָּבָר אַחֵר **DAVAR AHER. WHEN ESAU WAS FORTY YEARS OLD, HE TOOK AS WIVES JUDITH...AND BASEMATH...[Gen. 26.34].** Rebekah and Isaac fear that Esau, in his anger and hurt, will bring harm to Jacob, so they send Jacob away. Esau, seeing what has transpired, marries women from within the family of Abraham. Some commentators point to this with the comment, "Nice try, Esau, but it is too late!" I see the situation a bit differently; Esau understands the implication of his flippancy and arrogance and he does *t'shuvah*. Twenty years from now Jacob will come home, worried about what Esau will do to him. The text already shows us that Jacob does not have any need for worry, as Esau understands only too well the respect he must show for the Covenant which is to be passed on not through him, but through his younger brother, Jacob. **Rabbi Rick Sherwin, Beth El Congregation, Phoenix, AZ**

דָּבָר אַחֵר **DAVAR AHER. YOUR CURSE, MY SON, WILL BE ON ME...[Gen. 27.13].** At a CLAL session on women recently, a large segment of discussion was focused on Rebekah as a model for "active, manipulating woman." Comments kept cropping up how Rebekah did her best to make sure that her son received what was due to him. The strongest comments against Rebekah were that she was a schemer and slightly fraudulent. Usual discussion of the dysfunctional nature of that family focuses on the seeming lack of communication between Rebekah and Isaac. There seems to me to be a darker side to this scenario which might be worth exploring. Full exploration of this darker side might explain and/or redeem certain actions taken recently which have received wide play in the media.

To start, I have a question. I can understand Sarah's opinions and action with Hagar and Ishmael. She thought she could handle an open adoption/surrogate mother situation, and she couldn't. I can understand Sarah, but I'm having trouble understanding Rebekah's animosity toward Esau. Esau is also her son. All the scheming which she did for the sake of Jacob, her son, had to deprive Esau, her son, of these things he had reason to expect. Where's the "motherly love?" Talk about emotional abuse! And child abuse is the issue. Every defense of Rebekah I have seen is based on the endpoint of Jacob's being the best prospect for Patriarch. To attain that desirable goal, anything seems allowable. Deceiving Isaac, depriving Esau, placing a deep enmity between Esau and Jacob, and banishing Jacob.

To put this in a modern context, if somebody believes that quiet in the home is God's command, that would seem to give them the right and responsibility to maintain that quiet, even going to the extremes of punishing those who make noise (crying children) or putting tape across the mouths of anybody who wasn't up to par. We can all come up with other, more disturbing scenarios. You can argue about the importance of the endpoint (quiet in the house seems petty compared to God's blessing). Yet it doesn't seem to matter in the long run; abuse is still abuse.

And Rebekah, in essence, is giving up on Esau. She is relinquishing her right to parent that child—without having any idea of what to do with him, or who will raise him properly. She certainly doesn't think Isaac can do the job right. So is Rebekah the management flunky or the stressed-out abuser? Or can some people, in some situations, be both? **Larry Moldo, Beth El, Omaha, NE**

דָּבָר אַחֵר **DAVAR AHER. WHICH ARE YOU, MY SON? [Gen. 27.18].** I enjoyed Rabbi Plaut's assertion that Isaac knew full well that he was blessing Jacob and not Esau and was not deceived at all. Still, a question remains. If Isaac intended all along to hand the mantle of leadership to Jacob and not Esau, why did he not do it openly, instead of appearing to be deceived? The answer may be Isaac's desire not to rupture his relationship with his favorite son Esau. He knew that if he denied him the blessing, he would hurt Esau terribly. Isaac, the one who knew what it felt like to be hurt by his father, wanted to avoid inflicting the same pain on his own son. So he played along with the deception, even to the point of acting shocked and dismayed when Esau appears after Jacob has already been blessed [27.33]. The real deception in the story was of Esau, not Isaac, for he never really knew his father's real intentions. **Rabbi Mark Cooper, Temple Beth Ahm, Aberdeen, NJ**

דָּבָר אַחֵר **DAVAR AHER. WHICH ARE YOU, MY SON? [Gen. 27.18].** My esteemed colleague W. Gunther Plaut could have answered the questions he raised, had he been permitted to move into the next parashah. After a life of deception and being treated in kind by Laban, Jacob faces his life at the lowest moment. After placing even his wives and dear ones in front as a defense against his brother Esau, Jacob confronts himself in the middle of the night. And he does not desist until he becomes a new person, Yisrael. No longer the עֵקֶב *ekev*, but the יָשָׁר אֵל Yasher El—one who now walks upright with God, or (שַׂר אֵל) Sar El) Prince of God. And then he walks with a limp thereafter. After such a profound experience, it is most natural for one's physical posture to also be altered. And that is a name worthy to all of us. Not born of complacent aristocracy, but struggling to become Yasher El. A name to be earned by each of us as did Ya'akov. **Rabbi Dr. Morris A Kipper, Coral Gables, FL**

דָּבָר אַחֵר **DAVAR AHER. WHICH ARE YOU, MY SON?** [Gen. 27.18]. Rabbi Plaut, in his comments on the blessing of Jacob and Esau, offers an interesting insight into Isaac's thinking. But I disagree that the text has to indicate that Isaac knew with certainty that Jacob was deceiving him.

Rabbi Plaut notes that "when Esau first comes into the room and his father asks him who he is [27.1], he says a single word, הִנֵּנִי Hineni, 'HERE I AM'—and his father knows at once that he is Esau." But in that instance, Isaac had specifically called for Esau and there was no reason to suspect that anyone else would appear. But following Jacob's deception, when Esau arrives with food for his father, Esau announces [27.31] "LET MY FATHER ARISE, AND EAT OF HIS SON'S VENISON, THAT THY SOUL MAY BLESS ME." If Isaac had known for a certainty that Jacob had once again supplanted his brother, why was it necessary for Isaac to ascertain Esau's identity [27.32] and why did Isaac tremble exceedingly [27.33]? More importantly, if Isaac was a willing partner to the deception, why did he wait until chapter 28, verses 1-4, to give

Jacob the crucial "BLESSING OF ABRAHAM?" I believe that Rabbi Plaut is right when he indicates Isaac knew all along that Jacob had been chosen as the next leader of the "tribe." And therefore, Isaac never intended to give that blessing to Esau, as shown by chapter 28. For me, the story of deception emphasizes that Isaac was weak, not only with his eyesight, but also with his insight. (Perhaps he was permanently traumatized by the Akedah.) He should have realized that Jacob was tricking him, suspected as much, but was not strong enough to force the issue. As for Jacob, his deception had no purpose. He received the Abrahamic blessing anyway. But the story does play a significant role in Jacob's personal development, as well as in the Genesis narrative, as it is the initial link in the chain of deceptions in Jacob's life (midah keneged midah) which ultimately include Leah and Rachel and Joseph. **Rabbi Allen Judah, Brith Shalom, Bethlehem, PA**

דָּבָר אַחֵר **DAVAR AHER. WHICH ARE YOU, MY SON?** [Gen. 27.18]. If Isaac knew he was being deceived, why did he break out in violent trembling when he asked who the second son was [27.33]? Why does he tell Esau that Jacob came "WITH GUILE [27.35]?" I think he really was deceived. Isaac is a תָּם tam, so he is unsuspecting and trusting, especially of his children at a moment when his own life is ending and his sons' lives as adults are about to begin. Wouldn't he as a parent want to think that he had raised his children to do right and therefore

Toldot

would never have suspected them of deceiving him? The only answer I can come up with is that he really was deceived.

However, believing this leaves me with more questions than answers. Should we learn from this that although Rebekah was right in what she did that justifies her coming up with this deception? Or that no matter what old and infirm parents want children should assert themselves and do what they think is best? I think not. Perhaps the answer is hidden in what comes next. Isaac sends Jacob off to live with Laban, Isaac's brother-in-law. Later [29.24ff] we learn what a conniving, scheming guy Laban is. Isaac must have known what kind of person his brother-in-law was. Perhaps Isaac accepts Rebekah's excuse to send Jacob to Laban because he knows in his heart that in the end Jacob will get what he deserves as retribution for what he has done. Therefore, the lesson is that even in the Torah what goes around comes around, although it takes a couple of *parashot* to find that out. **Michael Raileanu, Beth Haverim, Agoura Hills, CA**

דָּבָר אַחֵר **DAVAR AHER. An Epilogue.** One late September afternoon, Rebekah sat placidly outside her tent and waited for the sun's intense heat to give way to the relief offered by the cooling breezes of the evening. Her marriage to Isaac had not been an unhappy one, yet, as in every marriage, she thought there were issues unresolved; question marks raised along the way fraught with doubts about one's very identity and resulting decisions one makes, for better or

worse, whose consequences form the story of our lives.

The signs were surely there from the beginning, but how could she, as a young woman, inexperienced in such matters, have possibly understood those signs? Time after time, Isaac's weakness as a father and his favoring of Esau forced Rebekah to assume a role as both mother and father to Jacob. Jacob's skills as a cook could surely be attributed to the hours he spent in the company of his mother, observing Rebekah's culinary skill and later improving on what he had learned.

She had done her best to raise her sons to be the men she hoped they would be. It was no easy task raising these boys to manhood. For models she turned to the only real men she had known in her life: her father, Bethuel, and her brother, Laban. Indeed, Rebekah was well suited for the task of raising her sons. Although her husband was, in her sight, a weak man (and she certainly did not want her sons to grow up to be like their father), growing up with her own father and brother had indeed taught Rebekah a thing or two about life and Rebekah had been a most astute pupil....

She thought back to that day at the well when she encountered her future father-in-law's servant, Eliezer. Little had she known what could lie ahead beyond the long journey from her father's home to her new life as Isaac's wife in Canaan. How could she have been so eager to go with Eliezer, leaving all that was familiar behind? Why did she so readily agree to marry a man whom she had never

seen, one whose reputation and character were totally unknown to her, solely on the recommendation of the persuasive Eliezer and the security of blood-ties?

Perhaps it had been a romantic notion that obsessed her at the time: the promises of wealth as inheritance from Abraham that would be hers as Isaac's wife, perhaps an even stronger desire to get away from the very home to which she later turned for inspiration and guidance, to break the bonds of an overbearing brother and father who took little interest in Rebekah who, as a woman, could do so little to carry on the family name and business.

Rebekah knew she could do more—so much more. And the promise of a new life—a secure one, at that—as Isaac's wife, as part of Abraham's household, may have been the chance she needed to prove to everyone just who she was. Most of all, she needed to prove her abilities to herself. Little could she have known then, so long ago as she began her journey with Eliezer, just how fruitful the opportunities would be. Unfortunately, though, they came to her, as a woman, due only to the ineptness of her husband, Isaac. She found him to be handsome and she thought, a bit shy. While the initial meeting had been awkward, Rebekah was readily accepted and welcomed by Abraham who saw in his new daughter-in-law, Rebekah, a woman who could serve as the heiress to the family that God had promised him, a strong woman to head the household which had not been the same since his beloved wife, Sarah, had died.

Toldot

Rebekah would have loved Sarah, at least so she thought from the stories that Abraham would tell. There had been other women in the camp for company and companionship. Abraham's young wife, Keturah, was not unfriendly, but, as far as the others, a proper distance had to be observed between the female servants and concubines in the household and herself as Isaac's wife, heiress to the position of Sarah as mother of Abraham's growing clan. When her father-in-law passed on, she deeply mourned his loss. Next to Abraham's magnetism, his vision, his intellect, Isaac seemed a lost young man and Rebekah found herself easily able to wrest control from him. He almost willingly allowed Rebekah free hand in raising the children and running the household. His thoughts seemed to be elsewhere—his attentions were not focused on his wife and sons. Not that he had been an unloving father (at least to his son, Esau) but his attentions were often diverted in other directions and he chose not to share those with Rebekah, his wife.

How strange was this man she had married, how mystical he often seemed to her and how frustrated was she because of it. On one hand, coupled with his physical attributes, it made Rebekah want him and to be with him even more; on the other hand, she found it difficult to communicate with her husband on matters of importance regarding the upbringing of their sons and running of their household. How could she have understood this man, this husband? He had been an enigma to her and the sense of mystery was, initially in their marriage, fascinating and attractive to her. As the years went by, she found it simply frustrating. How could she, or anyone for that matter, have understood what pain and anguish he must have felt—the recurrent nightmares that plagued him throughout his life—of being tied to the altar with knife poised to take his life away and by none other than the man who had given him life. How could she help him forget? How could she comfort him as he awoke night after night with these visions of horror? Her initial love of her father-in-law turned to abhorrence once she realized the full impact of what he had done and how many lives he had changed. She now understood how knowledge of Isaac's ordeal had killed not only Sarah but Isaac in a sense as well. Yes, it had been up to her to ensure that her sons would be raised without the fears their father had experienced, and would have to search for new ways of confronting their God. When Isaac lost his sight later in life, Rebekah realized that he was blind in another way as well—to the truths of his family and to his retreat from life.

In her son, Jacob, Rebekah's hopes and fears were realized, and it would be through Jacob and because of her, that God's promise to Abraham would be fulfilled. **Bonnie Morris, Director of Education, Temple Solel, Paradise Valley, AZ**

ויצא יעקב מבאר שבע וילך

Va-Yetze

**Genesis
28.10–32.3**

Rabbi Jack
Riemer

RABBI JACK RIEMER IS THE SPIRI-
TUAL LEADER OF CONGREGATION
BETH TIKVAH IN WEST BOCA
RATON, FLORIDA. HIS NEW BOOK,
WRESTLING WITH THE ANGEL, HAS
JUST BEEN PUBLISHED BY
SCHOCKEN BOOKS, AND HE IS THE
CO-EDITOR OF *SO THAT YOUR
VALUES LIVE ON*, PUBLISHED BY
JEWISH LIGHTS, ANDTHE EDITOR
OF VOLUMES 1 AND 2 OF *THE
WORLD OF THE HIGH HOLY DAYS*.
RABBI REIMER IS THE FOUNDER OF
THE NATIONAL RABBINIC
NETWORK, AND IS A MEMBER OF
THE COMMITTEE THAT IS AT WORK
ON THE NEW TORAH
COMMENTARY FOR THE
CONSERVATIVE MOVEMENT.

Why Did Jacob
Decide to Leave?

 want to share with you
four stories that I think
make the very same point.
One comes from this
week's Torah portion. One
comes from one of the
great Orthodox rabbis of
the last generation; one
comes from one of the
great Reform rabbis of the
last generation; and one
comes from one of the best
storytellers that we have
in this generation.

Story One: Near the end of the Sidrah,
Jacob gathers his wives and his children and says to them, "I think it is time
to go home because your father,
Laban's face is not the same to me as it
used to be." What does that phrase
mean—your father's face is not the same
to me as it used to be? Most of the commentators think that it refers to his attitude. He no longer looks on me with
favor; now he looks on me with hostil-
ity and envy.

But is that true? When did Laban ever
look upon Jacob with kindness? He was
always manipulative, cunning and cruel
toward him.

Story Two: Rav Kook, the first Chief
(Orthodox) Rabbi of Israel, offers a different explanation. He says that Jacob
said, "We have to leave this place
because when I first came here, I
looked at this man, Laban, and saw
how he lived, and how devious he was,
and I abhorred him; I was repelled. I
couldn't stand the sight of him and I
hated the way he did business. But now

דָּבָר אַחֵר **DAVAR AHER. …TAKING ONE
OF THE STONES OF THE PLACE, HE PUT IT UNDER
HIS HEAD AND LAY DOWN IN THAT PLACE, HE
DREAMED… [Gen. 28.11-12].** *For Shaye
Horwitz.* Once, God made this rock which
helped people remember their dreams.
God put it in a place in the Land of Israel,
almost between the tribe of Benjamin
and the tribe of Ephraim, and it stayed
there a long time. Near there was an
ancient city called Luz. Once, Jacob went
by this place, he slept on that rock, and

called it "Beth El," God's house. He said,
"God's house is a good place to dream."

Jacob's son, Joseph, loved that rock.
When he was feeling left out, and no
one wanted to be with him (because he
was the only son of the favorite wife,
except for his baby brother) he would
often go and look at the stars, leaning
on that rock. It was on this rock that he
had his two famous dreams, the one of
the sun, moon, and stars bowing down,
and the one of the sheaves of grain

that I have been here for twenty years, I have gotten used to him. I have reached the point where I think what he does is what you are supposed to do, that it is normal and proper to be devious. I look at him and I am no longer shocked or offended. Therefore, we better leave this place quick. Because, if we stay much longer, I will get so accustomed to him and to his ways of doing business that I will eventually become like him."

Story Three: Rabbi Stephen S. Wise was one of the leaders of Reform Judaism in the last generation. I don't know if Rav Kook and Rabbi Wise ever met. If they did, I am sure that they had very little in common, for one was a mystic and the other was a social activist; one was meticulously observant and the other was not; one believed in the centrality and the holiness of the Land of Israel; the other, while a passionate Zionist, nevertheless saw his own place here in America. These two men had very different backgrounds, very different temperaments and very different outlooks of life; and yet Rabbi Wise tells a story that I think parallels the comment of Rav Kook.

He once told the story of his first visit to China. When he got there he found out that the only available means of transportation was by rickshaw, and many of these rick-

Va-Yetze

bowing down. Joseph chipped off a piece of this rock and kept it in his pocket as a rubbing stone. He took it to Egypt when he was sent there, and continued to have wonderful dreams of a promising future. For the 400 years the Jewish people were slaves in Egypt, they continued to rub the rock and remember their dreams of the land that God had promised them, of a time that would be better. Hundreds of years passed.

When Joshua brings the Jewish people back from Egypt, the second place he camps is near Beth El. He sleeps on the rock and again wakes up in the morning and writes the song we now sing before *Birkat ha-Mazon* on Shabbat, *Shir Ha-Ma'alot*: "WHEN GOD BROUGHT US BACK TO ISRAEL WE WERE LIKE DREAMERS…[PS. 126.1]."

Many Jews remembered many dreams on or near, or even just by telling the story of, that rock.

When Jeroboam dreamed of a country of his own, he led a revolt against Rehoboam and split Israel from Judah. He built one of his two Temples over that rock, and for a short while (until the people began to ignore their dreams because they were too difficult) Israel was filled with dreams. Then the Assyrians came and destroyed and conquered and drove many Israelites down to hide in Judah, down to hide in Jerusalem. They brought a big chunk of the dream-remembering rock with them.

When Hezekiah held back the Assyrians, he started the Jewish religion anew. He went from place to

ויצא יעקב מבאר שבע וילך חרנה

shaws were pulled by weak, old feeble people who would cough as they dragged the wagons through the streets. At first, he said, he couldn't stand the sound of their coughing and their groaning. It gave him a guilty conscience every time he hired one to take him around. Then, after he had been there for a while, he realized a shocking thing. He realized that he had gotten so accustomed to their coughing that he no longer heard it. At this point, he said to himself, it's time to leave.

Story Four: From Elie Wiesel, who is surely the storyteller of our generation. It is a story that he tells about the time of the Bible, but I am

sure that when he tells it he has our generation in mind, too.

He says that once a *tzadik*, a truly righteous person, came to the wicked city of Sodom. He was horrified by what he saw—the corruption, the cruelty, the brutality, the chicanery that he witnessed sickened him. So, he picketed and he protested and cried out against injustice. He stood outside their stores, their homes, their offices and their country clubs and lifted up his voice against what they were doing. Everyone ignored him. This went on for many years.

Finally, someone took pity on him and said to him, "Don't you see that you are wasting your time? Don't

Synopsis: Jacob sets out from Be'er Sheva and travels to Haran. At Beth El, Jacob has a dream of a ladder with angels of God ascending and descending. Once again, the blessings of children and protection are offered to Jacob as they were to the other patriarchs, and in return, Jacob offers a tithe. In return for his labor (and after some deception), Jacob acquires as wives the two daughters of Laban, Leah and Rachel. The births of Jacob's children to Leah (7), Bilhah (2), Zilpa (2), and Rachel (1) are then recorded. Jacob cuts a deal with Laban and prospers. But the enmity between the two festers and Jacob starts out on his journey to return to Canaan. Laban chases after him accusing him of theft. Again, a pact is drawn and a mound of stones is erected at Galed in witness to that event.

place where the Jews had worshipped idols and done wrong, and destroyed everything. He made them one people again. When he came to Beth El, he took the dream rock and smashed it into thousands of pieces. He gave one to everyone in his army, and to everyone who was with his army. Many dreams were remembered.

Those slivers of rock have been passed from hand to hand, from place to place. Every time that Joseph Caro dreamed of the *Shekhinah*, a piece of rock was near. Every time Rashi understood a piece of Torah in one of his dreams, a sliver of rock was on the spot. For thousands of years, people have been remembering their best dreams of what they and the world could be, just because

of a sliver of rock. Herzl had his big dream, the *Im Tirtzu*—IF YOU WILL IT, IT IS NO DREAM—dream, near a big hunk of Jacob's dream-remembering rock. And someday, when we get all the pieces of this rock back together again, all of our best dreams will come true. That is no dream. So, where do you keep you sliver of dream-remembering rock hid`den? **Joel Lurie Grishaver <gris@ tora-haura.com>**

דָּבָר אַחֵר **DAVAR AHER. ANGELS ASCENDING AND DESCENDING…[Gen. 28. 12].** One of the images from this parashah that has long intrigued me is that of the angels ascending and descending the ladder in Jacob's dream. The Rashi on the verse—that the guardian angels that accompanied Jacob in the Holy Land could not

leave with him and had to be replaced by "diaspora angels"—is one of my favorite commentaries. At times I have been amused by the idea of angels whose domain is proscribed by political borders. I picture these geopolitical angels taking out their passports and being turned away by border control. This time, while thinking about the verse, I had a different interpretation. What if the borders the angels can't transcend are our physical and psychological ones? As we move in life from health to illness, from depression to joy, from life to death, our needs differ. As we cross over these borders, it makes sense that our guardian angels change as well. The things that provide comfort and strength in one situation doesn't work for every situation we face. As I reflect on many different

Va-Yetze—55

you see that no one is listening?" He said to the man who took pity on him, "You don't understand. When I started, I picketed and protested in order to change them. Now, I picket and I protest...in order that they shouldn't change me."

I think that these stories belong together, for they make the same basic moral point, which is that we must not, we dare not, ever get so hardened, so callous, so accustomed to evil that we take it for granted and think—that's the way it is and that's the way it always was and that's the way it is always going to be. Because when that happens, then we are spiritually numb and morally dead. It is all right to live with Laban, provided that you do not become so accustomed to his ways that you begin to think they are right. It is all right to take a rickshaw if that is the only means of transportation avail-

able, even if that means that your convenience is gained at the cost of the pain of weak, feeble old men. But it is not all right to get so used to the coughing and the wheezing of the old men that you no longer hear it. When you begin to take their pain for granted, when you get so used to it that it no longer bothers you, then it is time to leave.

Perhaps we can't change the world, but we can at least strive and fight to try to make sure that the world doesn't change us. That, at least, according to Rav Kook, was the reason Jacob finally decided to pick up stakes and move from the house of Laban. He wanted to move and go back home from the house of Laban before it was too late, before he came like him. ●

Va-Yetze

psychological or physical states, I can picture ladders with angels going up and others coming down. The message of the dream becomes a strong comfort as well. God is always with us, no matter what our circumstances, we just need to become aware of God's presence. **Rabbi Julie Wolkoff, Congregation Berith Sholom, Troy, NY**

דָּבָר אַחֵר **DAVAR AHER. AND IN THE MORNING BEHOLD IT WAS LEAH...[Gen. 29.25].** When I read the story of Jacob, I found out that...the Torah was going BACKwards! First, Jacob tricks Isaac. Then, Laban tricks HIM! This is really weird. Jacob doesn't want to be tricked BACK. When the Torah is going forward, that is the time when Jacob tricks Isaac. Then it goes backwards with Laban and Jacob! If Jacob didn't listen to

Rabbi Dov Peretz Elkins

RABBI DOV PERETZ ELKINS OF THE JEWISH CENTER, PRINCETON, NJ, IS EDITOR OF THE TWO-VOLUME HIGH HOLIDAY ANTHOLOGY, *MOMENTS OF TRANSCENDENCE* (JASON ARONSON, 1992), AND A NEW VOLUME OF SERMONS, *PRESCRIPTION FOR A LONG AND HAPPY LIFE: AGE-OLD WISDOM FOR THE NEW AGE* (GROWTH ASSOCIATES, 1993). HE IS NOW COMPILING AN ANTHOLOGY OF ESSAYS ON SHABBAT.

Va-Yetze

Jack Riemer's point is powerful (as any point Jack Riemer makes always is), and I want to piggy-back (is there a Jewish-sensitive, p.c. substitute for that term?) on his idea.

I want to emphasize that bad habits develop gradually, and become sick parts of our *neshamah* (soul) when we let them. Dysfunctional behavior patterns have a way of creeping up on us, and we don't notice them. That's what makes them so dangerous.

It's like the old nasty joke (which you should only tell mature students) about the man who is asked if he would compromise himself sexually for $100 million. It's a lot of money, and a hard decision, and he finally says, "Eh, yes, I guess so." Next question: Would you do it for $100. Answer: What do you think I am? Whereupon the questioner responds: We already know that, right now we're only talking about the price.

Let me translate that into an ethical generalization. Our conscience protects us from blatant evil, but when we are tempted by some appealing weakness, or when our defenses are down, we give in. All of Jack Riemer's four stories have to do with people who had their defenses down—through habit. Living with Laban for a short while, we are strong enough to maintain our normal standards of morality. After repeated experience, our resistance weakens. Sometimes we call it compassion fatigue, or morality failure. Any healthy trait, like a pair of shoes, can get worn out.

Rebekah, then the Torah wouldn't go in the other direction. What I mean is if Jacob didn't trick Isaac, Laban wouldn't trick him. But that wasn't what Jacob did. Instead, Laban knew that he had tricked his father (well, almost—maybe Isaac really knew because Esau never talked about God and Jacob did), and he tricked Jacob back. It should have gone the right way, so that everything would be normal and Laban wouldn't trick Jacob. My dad says that if the story of Laban and Jacob had happened first, maybe Jacob wouldn't have tricked his father. **Shaye Horwitz , 6 years old, <RABBIDANNY@aol.com>**

דָּבָר אַחֵר **DAVAR AHER. GOD IS IN THIS PLACE AND I DON'T KNOW. [Gen. 28.26].** What did Jacob take from this dream? Jacob said, "GOD IS IN THIS PLACE AND I DON'T KNOW. I DON'T KNOW *anything*" that I used to know—I'm overwhelmed by what I feel now." What did he feel? Jacob's words are a way of describing the paradox of God

In Rav Kook's interpretation, Jacob is sensitive enough to catch himself just before sinking into the ugly habits of his father-in-law. Rabbi Wise became guilty of sensitivity-fatigue, but he recognized it, and pulled himself out of the situation before getting in too deep. Elie Wiesel makes the same point by recognizing that it takes proactive, defensive behavior to prevent oneself from falling into the habit of corruption and cruelty. Even just sitting passively and watching it is sometimes enough to make us fall into the trap of aping the crowd (and who knows about that better than Survivor Wiesel)?

I want to add a fifth example to Jack Riemer's four stories, this one from the world of nature. If you place a frog in boiling water, it jumps out. Its instincts protect it from the danger of self-destruction. But you can deceive its natural instincts by putting the frog in cold water, and slowly warming the water. If you do that, the frog will remain in the water and it will eventually permit itself to boil to death.

Every tyrant from Pharaoh to Hitler who has tried to destroy the Jewish people has used the same tactics of breaking down their defenses. In these cases, the decay was not evil

Va-Yetze

everywhere, all the time, and a child dying, a war happening, an earthquake, a disease, a famine, a curse, it's a way of authenticating the whole grand scheme—it is what it is, and it is still full of God. Not either/or but both. All of the above. Don't I know this about life? I do know it, but I don't have words for it. Neither did Jacob, so he said "GOD IS IN THIS PLACE, AND I DON'T KNOW *a darn thing*," a feeling so expansive it drives everything else out, all the contradictions, gone. God is in this place, this moment God, the rocks God, the ground God too, you me God, the light the darkness God. The dream? God. The night terror God, too. No place empty of God. When Jacob felt that, all the illusions collapsed into one long affirmative embrace that pushed all his prior notions out of him, and he said, "SURELY GOD IS IN THIS

PLACE, AND I DON'T KNOW *a thing*." "THIS IS THE BEGINNING OF WISDOM [Proverbs 4.7]" "*I DON'T KNOW*." Now he is free to be taught the truth of the world. (**An e-mail file whose authorship was accidentally deleted. Sorry!**)

דָּבָר אַחֵר **DAVAR AHER. On "piggyback".** A "Jewish sensitive, p.c." replacement for "PIGGYBACK" is "BUILD ON," a phrase commonly used in business school classrooms and other learning environments as well. Not only does the phrase avoid the *treif*, it has the benefit of alluding to the teaching "not to read *'your children*,' but rather *'your builders*,'" i.e. those who follow in the way of your ideas build up both your name and Torah itself. **Sharon Silverstein, San Diego, CA**

דָּבָר אַחֵר **DAVAR AHER. On "piggybacking".** In Yiddish a *davar aher*

ויצא יעקב מבאר שבע וילך חרנה

behavior, but becoming callous to oppression—a subtle kind of evil in itself. The tyrant is too smart to make a sudden and total attack. First Pharaoh took away some of their rights, so gradually that they didn't realize it until they found themselves slaves. When they realized that they were beginning to accept their oppressed status, it was time to leave Egypt.

Hitler did the same. First the Nuremberg Laws. Then they lost their jobs. Next the yellow badge of shame. Then they couldn't run for office, or be in the army. Hitler heated up the water very gradually, and before they knew what hap-

pened, our brothers and sisters were on the way to the "showers."

Jack Riemer's entry point about Jacob is that the Patriarch is beginning to slide down the slippery slope of immoral behavior. I am pointing out that the same slippery slope permits someone to oppress us, and we become partners in their evil. They both have to do with the gradual and imperceptible shifting of our moral compass. It's like trying to watch grass grow, or our kids mature. We don't see it from day to day, but after a year or two or three, there is this sudden paradigm shift, and then a radical change. In the same way, we

slowly and unknowingly compromise our moral standards.

The Talmud puts it very succinctly: Sin dulls the heart [*Yoma 39a*]. The Zohar sums up the whole message: A sin leaves its mark; repeated, it deepens; when committed a third time, the mark becomes a stain. I guess Jacob left Laban because he didn't want a bad mark to become a stain. ●

---

is the word for pig so piggyback would be a synonym BUT better מוּסָף *Mussaf*, הוֹסָפָה *Hosafah*. Another Yiddish usage had the word עוֹדְךָ *Odkha*-for עוֹד *Od* (and this is from Hallel where in we repeat אוֹדְךָ כִּי עֲנִיתָנִי *Odkha Ki Anitani*)." A *DA* can also be read דֶּרֶךְ אַחֶרֶת *Derekh Aheret* and I like that better than דָּבָר אַחֵר *Davar Aher*. I feel there must be more words and if they show, I will send them as a further דְּרֹשׁ וְקַבֵּל שָׂכָר *D'rosh v'Kabbel S'khar*. (Interpret and be rewarded.) **Zalman Hiyya S-S <Zalmans@aol. com>**

דָּבָר אַחֵר **DAVAR AHER.** RACHEL… SAID TO JACOB, GIVE ME SOME CHILDREN— OTHERWISE I AM DEAD…[Gen. 30.2]. The film *Raise the Red Lantern* (available on video) tells the story of a 19th century family in rural China in which one man has four wives. Conjugal duties

are rotated at the husband's whim. A red lantern hung by a wife's doorstep in the morning means it's "her turn" that night. This "privilege" confers upon her a special status and extra benefits (such as a foot massage by the servants), so the wives compete with each other ruthlessly to win the husband's favor. Being pregnant automatically raises one's status and confers conjugal rights. What's more, in this story, one of the wives develops a bitter rivalry with a maidservant for the attention of the husband. The wife tortures her own servant who, in turn, believes her mistress (who had been imported from the outside) has ruined her chances to become wife #4. What's especially interesting in this portrayal is the way in which a wife can be lowered or raised in the esteem of her entire household depending on how her husband

looks at her. No wonder Sarah blames Abraham when Hagar "regards her lightly." And no wonder Rachel explodes at Jacob when after the birth of Judah he apparently, finally, begins to pay some attention to Leah. This is a must-see movie for anyone who wants to understand the story of the Matriarchs in cultural context. **Rabbi Jay Rosenbloom, Congregation Beth Israel, Worcester, MA**

Va-Yetze—59

Va-Yishla<u>h</u>

**Genesis
32.4–36.43**

Professor
Barry W. Holtz

BARRY W. HOLTZ IS ASSOCIATE
PROFESSOR OF JEWISH EDUCATION AT
THE JEWISH THEOLOGICAL SEMINARY OF
AMERICA. CURRENTLY, HE IS ON LEAVE
FROM THE SEMINARY, SERVING AS SENIOR
EDUCATION OFFICER AND DIRECTOR OF
THE BEST PRACTICES PROJECT OF THE
COUNCIL FOR INITIATIVES IN JEWISH
EDUCATION (CIJE). HIS BOOKS INCLUDE:
*BACK TO THE SOURCES: READING THE
CLASSIC JEWISH TEXTS* (SIMON AND
SCHUSTER, 1984), *FINDING OUR WAY:
JEWISH TEXTS AND THE LIVES WE LEAD
TODAY* (SCHOCKEN BOOKS, 1990), AND,
MOST RECENTLY, *THE SCHOCKEN GUIDE TO
JEWISH BOOKS* (1992). HIS FIRST BOOK
(WRITTEN WITH ARTHUR GREEN), *YOUR
WORD IS FIRE: THE HASIDIC MASTERS ON
CONTEMPLATIVE PRAYER*, HAS RECENTLY
BEEN REPRINTED IN A REVISED EDITION BY
JEWISH LIGHTS PRESS.

The mysterious tale of Jacob's wrestling with the angel is one of those biblical texts that seems to expand before our eyes into something more than a mere story. Although this interlude plays an important role in the saga of Jacob's life, the encounter with the angelic opponent also takes on its own particular life, standing out on its own—part of Jacob's "history" and yet separate from it. The characters lose their identity as individuals, as mortals on the biblical stage, until

we, the readers, are, like Jacob, "left alone" with the story.

In other words, the story of Jacob's wrestling becomes not one episode among many in the biography of the Patriarch Jacob, but rather a self-contained myth that has a life of its own. Perhaps it is even a kind of allegory.

But of what?

This tale, with its elusive quality, seems to open endlessly, seems to accommodate virtually any reading. There is little surprise, then, that these ten (!) verses (more or less, depending on where you see the narrative starting) have occasioned so much ingenious interpretation throughout our Jewish past.

Of one thing there is little doubt. It is here, in this parashah, in the moment of the wrestling, that the Jacob story comes to its climax. Here the wanderer ceases wandering and the story itself starts to

דְּבָר אַחֵר **DAVAR A<u>H</u>ER. J**ACOB WAS LEFT ALONE AND HE WRESTLED WITH A MAN…[Gen. 32.25]. In this parashah, we have the famous wrestling with the angel, whom some call a man, some call Satan, some call Yaakov's *yetzer ha-ra*. In verse 8 of this chapter, the Hebrew is translated as "Jacob was greatly afraid and distressed." Can it also be read as "Jacob felt great awe/trembling and his *yetzer* fell/was low?"

Here we can see another place where Jacob was still unsure of *haShem*'s guarantee, where he could only see Esau as coming to get him, not to greet him. Jacob was not entertaining the idea that Esau could have found a way to forgive him. Jacob petitions G-d after this and then starts sending gifts to Esau, all good ideas and ways to insure his good fortune.

move homeward. After all, that is Jacob's destination, back to the land that he fled so many years before.

The Jacob story is a remarkable example of what modern literary critics call a *bildungsroman*, a story of human growth and learning. Jacob the deceiver, the crooked one (for so the name יעקב *Ya'akov* suggests: a literal "heel") begins as a kind of hard-dealing operator. He bamboozles his brother with a pot of beans and, more dramatically, tricks his father and brother at once by an act of brazen deception—stealing the blessing meant for Esau.

Note how *indirectly* Jacob acts. Nothing is done head on; nothing means what it seems to mean: "COME EAT THE FOOD I AM COOKING," for instance, really *means* "SELL ME YOUR BIRTHRIGHT." When the deception of father Isaac is complete, Jacob does not confront his brother directly. Instead he flees. Nothing happens, as it were, "face to face." For the image of "face" haunts

this tale from its very beginning: the lack of confrontation, the blind man Isaac unable to see his son's face, and later, when Jacob is far from home, the face of the bride hidden from view, so much so that Leah is given instead of Rachel, and the trickster Jacob is undone by a master deceiver, his uncle Laban.

Therefore, in this parashah we are struck by the way indirection turns to confrontation, indeed to *wrestling,* for what metaphor could express directness better? The mysterious being whom Jacob confronts will not let him escape. Perhaps it is that very fact which results in the blessing of a new name for Jacob. He has, for the first time in his life, refused to run away or dissemble and for that, as a reward, he is now Israel. In the Bible a name signifies the essence of the being. Jacob's transformation is complete. His very character has turned with the change of name from "heel/deceiver" to Yisrael, explained

Synopsis: In this parashah, Jacob and Esau meet again. In anticipation, Jacob prays and prepares a lavish gift. Taking his entire family, Jacob crosses the Yabok river and there, at Peniel, encounters a mysterious assailant with whom he wrestles. In the morning, Jacob prevails, though injured, and his name is changed from Jacob to Israel. Esau finally appears and rushes to embrace Jacob. At the conclusion of the dialogue, Jacob and Esau go their separate ways—Esau returns to Seir and Jacob to Canaan. There, Jacob's only daughter, Dinah, is raped by Shekhem, the son of a local tribal chief. When Shekhem then asks to marry Dinah, Jacob's sons agree, on the condition that all the men of the tribe become circumcised. Three days after they comply, Dinah's brothers take their revenge— killing and plundering. After this bloody episode, God tells Jacob to travel to Bethel, where he is again blessed, but his beloved Rachel dies giving birth to Benjamin and is buried on the road. The parashah closes with a genealogical summary of the line of Isaac, enumerating both Jacob's sons and the descendants of Esau.

The wrestling scene is one that has been debated greatly. My question is, was the wrestling with the *yetzer ha-ra* or the *yetzer tov*? In other words, could the match have been between Jacob and the *yetzer tov*, where he needed to see how strong the good inclination really was and that it could fight with the evil urges and at least get a draw? Maybe Jacob had to learn that the good inclination was the first line of defense and action,

not the pushover. Since Jacob did indeed wrestle with G-d, and saw G-d face to face (verse 31), maybe what Jacob was fighting was his own good inclination. Possibly that is where he faced the spiritual damage that he had suffered by being in Laban's presence and he became convinced that the *yetzer tov* and *ha-Shem* were the path to follow. Esau greets him with kindness and love and seems to be looking for a way to live with his

brother. **Mark Borowitz, Beit Tshuvah, Los Angeles, CA**

דָּבָר אַחֵר **DAVAR AHER. NO LONGER WILL YOUR NAME BE CALLED JACOB, BUT ISRAEL…THEN JACOB ASKED…[Gen. 32.29-30].** Jacob's name is changed to Israel, but the text immediately reverts to Jacob (unlike Abraham and Sarah, whose name change is permanent). This tells us that Jacob remains essentially who he is, but he has

in the biblical etymology in our parashah, as "ONE WHO STRIVES WITH GOD." This internal gloss, offered by the text on itself, differs from a modern scientific etymology (which is considerably less clear about the meaning of the word "Yisrael"), but it expresses the heart of what the story is about: the move from the old Jacob to the new "STRIVER"—Israel.

With the wrestling completed, Jacob/Israel is able to "*face*" his brother, to end the years of disconnection. With great insight, Rabbinic sources identified the mysterious angelic figure as the heavenly representative of Esau. It is that very demon of the past, that guilt about what he did to his brother, that Jacob must confront. Thus, it is no accident that the place of the wrestling is called פְּנִיאֵל *Peniel*, literally "GOD'S FACE," and that Jacob reflects on his experience by saying in 32.31 "I HAVE SEEN A DIVINE BEING *FACE TO FACE*, YET MY LIFE HAS BEEN PRESERVED." And in Chapter 33.10, in one of the most remarkable verses in the entire Torah, Jacob unites the themes of brother and God, wrestling and reconciliation, making it clear if it hasn't already been

---

discovered a new dimension in his life. He has found it possible to say *Thou* to life—he has just had a literal *I-Thou* encounter ("I HAVE SEEN GOD FACE TO FACE [GEN. 32.30]")—and now, whenever he says *Thou*, he will be *Yisrael*, the one who struggles to find God in everyday life. **Samuel G. Broude, Rabbi Emeritus, Sinai, Oakland, CA, Interim Rabbi, Beth El, Berkeley, CA**

דְּבָר אַחֵר **DAVAR AHER. JACOB ARRIVED WHOLE TO THE CITY OF SHEKHEM...DINAH, THE DAUGHTER OF LEAH WENT OUT...[Gen. 33.18, 34.1].** Why does the parashah take a journey to Dinah and not talk more about the reunion with Jacob's father? Maybe Isaac did not forgive his son Jacob for his trickery, for there is no mention of any intimacy between them before Isaac died. Jacob hadn't seen his father for so many years, it seems strange that he would not have gone directly to him upon meeting and making peace with Esau. Another interesting point, maybe, is why Esau is listed first in Chapter 35.29 when it speaks of burying Isaac. Was Esau the son who showed proper honor to his father while Jacob did not? Isaac was mentioned before Ishmael when Abraham was buried. **Mark Borowitz, Beit Tshuvah, Los Angeles, CA**

דְּבָר אַחֵר **DAVAR AHER. DINAH WENT OUT TO VISIT THE DAUGHTERS OF THE LAND...[Gen. 34. 1].** Daily I see in my mind the hour that I "WENT OUT TO VISIT THE DAUGHTERS OF THE LAND [Gen. 34.1]." It was then that Shekhem came to me whispering honeyed words. When my heart did not answer, he proclaimed his desire with such force that instead

Va-Yishlah

so, that we the readers must view them as connected—when he says to Esau "TO SEE YOUR FACE IS LIKE SEEING THE FACE OF GOD!"

Earlier I said that the story is so evocative it calls out to be read as an allegory, one that reaches across time with remarkable clarity. It's hard not to notice the way that certain features of this story strike home with particular immediacy in our times. I think, in this light, that the name change from Jacob to Israel carries special weight. For us today, Israel is not only *B'nei Yisrael*—the children of Israel, or even *Am Yisrael*—the people Israel, but just as surely it is *Eretz Yisrael* and *Medinat Yisrael*—the land of Israel and the State of Israel.

It is in this direction that the allegory pushes us. We see a familiar scenario: Israel locked in mortal combat with an enemy, groping in the confusion of a moral or spiritual "night." One speaks; the other speaks, yet so unclear, so dark is the scene, we can hardly tell which is which, if at all.

Even the name of our foe is uncertain—today we speak of Arabs and Palestinians, of terrorists, of intifada-fighters. What is the real name? Perhaps, we wonder, the combatant is ourselves, as shocking events in recent times have shown us. We are, as well, the reconciler and the peacemaker. The confusion that all of us feel in thinking about the contemporary struggles of Israel echoes in the sacred and timeless text of this week's parashah.

Yet there is light here, too; the sun rises upon Jacob, as he limps along his way. What does it mean for Israel to limp, and to hold that limp in memory, ritualized into prohibition on eating a certain type of food? The limping Israel is not a tragic picture. It is not the limp of a defeated man. Rather it is that of one who has found triumph in meeting an enemy "*face to face*" and seeing the enemy as a representative of God. Jacob becomes Israel when he understands the essential divinity of the "other," when, in other words, the enemy

turns into an angel. Israel limps because he has learned that there is no perfection without some imperfection. The sun rises upon Israel when Israel learns that every vision means losing something too, in the world of necessary compromises in which we all live. ●

---

of being filled, my heart broke. No love was created and the world drew further away from God and all that was left was shattered glass.

Tears run down my cheeks as I cry out to God. Can the world ever be made whole when all that I see is fragments that amass? What can I do or, better yet, what is my choice? I ask these questions as I ponder the realities of blessing and curse. But in a moment of silence I hear a very small

voice, that echoes in my mind, an answer from God. It's then that I know what path I must choose, so slowly I rise and respond to the call. Cautiously, but with new resolve, I begin to gather and paste together the bits of broken glass. **Marjorie Hodges, Shreveport, LA**

דָּבָר אַחֵר **DAVAR AHER....AND HE HUMBLED/OVERPOWERED HER. [Gen. 34.2].** *In a discussion in the Torah Aura Bulletin Board, it was suggested that the p'shat*

(plain meaning) actually implies Dinah was seduced, not raped. The following two responses answer that assertion. Dinah was raped. I am invoking Rabbi Yishmael's *"G'zerah Shava"* in support of the argument. The only other exact usage of the key verb וַיְעַנֶּהָ *"ya-yeh-ah-neh-ha"* ("and he HUMBLED/OVERPOWERED her.") [Gen. 34.2] is II Samuel 13.14, where Tamar is "HUMBLED" by Amnon by forced sex. Note also that the humbling, in both cases, is directly related to "LAYING DOWN"

Rabbi Laura Geller

RABBI LAURA GELLER SERVES AS THE SENIOR RABBI OF TEMPLE EMANUEL IN BEVERLY HILLS. BEFORE COMING TO TEMPLE EMANUEL, SHE SERVED AS THE EXECUTIVE DIRECTOR OF THE AMERICAN JEWISH CONGRESS, PACIFIC SOUTHWEST REGION, AND AS HILLEL DIRECTOR AT THE UNIVERSITY OF SOUTHERN CALIFORNIA.

Va-Yishlah

The Jacob story does indeed come to its climax in *Parashat Va-Yishlah*. The story does not end with the nocturnal wrestling, however. After the powerful scene of reconciliation between brothers, we confront a painful story about a different kind of wrestling: NOW DINAH, THE DAUGHTER WHOM LEAH HAD BORNE TO JACOB, WENT OUT TO VISIT THE DAUGHTERS OF THE LAND...Like Jacob, Dinah goes out alone, seeking some kind of connection. For Jacob turned Israel, it was reconciliation and wholeness; for Dinah, daughter of Jacob, it was the daughters of the land.

What was she looking for? Some commentaries suggest she was looking for nothing good—an experience of idolatry, or even for sexual trouble, dressed, as they suppose, in revealing clothes and gaudy jewelry. Some commentaries imply she got what she deserved. Perhaps she was really looking to visit the daughters of the land...perhaps she was just lonely, looking for some women friends. She apparently never found them.

Of Jacob's wrestling match we know a great deal. Jacob confronts his adversary face to face, refusing to run away. He is wounded in the struggle, but ultimately he is blessed. Of Dinah's wrestling, we know little. Her adversary sees her and rapes her; then falls in love with her and speaks tenderly to her. How does she feel? Our text is

(*intercourse*). However, in Sam II, the humbling occurs after Tamar verbally indicates that she has no interest in his proposition...before he lays with her. That is, through inversion of the key verbs, Tamar's rape occurs before Amnon lays a hand on her. She knows the ramifications of the act he advocates, IN ADVANCE. In the Genesis usage, Dinah may not have known that she was raped until after the event had occurred. This is analogous to the girl who is sexually abused during her youth and later realizes what has happened to her. If that isn't rape, what is? **Cantor Simcha Prombaum, Sons of Abraham, LaCrosse, WI**

וישלח יעקב מלאכים לפניו אל עשו אחיו

silent. We know only what her father and brothers think—she has been defiled, she has been treated as a whore. No one asks her what she wants, what she needs, how she can be comforted and made to feel whole again.

Through Jacob's wrestling, he confronts his brother and transforms his past. Dinah's wrestling leads to a confrontation with her brothers—but of a very different kind. They want to avenge her disgrace, and they do it with guile (מִרְמָה mirmah), the very same word used to describe how Dinah's father stole the blessing from his brother. Jacob might have

learned through his wrestling to turn indirection to confrontation, but his sons revert to their father's old ways. Jacob learned, as Barry Holtz describes, to meet his enemy face to face and to see his enemy as a representative of God. But his sons seem schooled in the old ways of their father. Jacob himself seems to have forgotten some of what he has learned; his response to his daughter's ordeal is strange. First he is silent, waiting for his sons. Then, after learning about Simeon and Levi's act of retribution, he seems only concerned with the safety of his

household and what people will say to him.

What about Dinah? Could she see in her adversary the face of God, or was her wound so terrible that there could be no blessing? Did she hope her brothers would rescue her from Shekhem's house and his bed or was she drawn to him as he was to her? We do not know. Her story is never fully told. Two wrestlings in the same parashah: Jacob's name is changed, but we never hear from Dinah again. ●

דָּבָר אַחֵר **DAVAR AHER. AND HE HUMBLED/OVERPOWERED HER...[Gen. 34.2].** The word עִנָּה inna in certain contexts means rape [cf. Judg. 19.24; 20.5; 2 Sam. 13.12, 14, 22, 32; Ezek. 22.11; Lam. 5.11] according to Ariella Deem in an article she wrote in 1978. However, Moshe Weinfeld (1972) disagrees, writing that inna in piel form in the passages cited above may denote sexual intercourse rather than rape. He concedes in a footnote that

inna might refer to sexual intercourse which involves an element of imposition upon the woman. It might then still refer to seduction. I think it is a legitimate reading to see what happened to Dinah as rape; even if in the context of the times it was considered to be a way of getting a wife—and then the objection of the brothers would have been to intermarriage. Actually it would have been mind-boggling if the marriage would have

taken place—peace with our neighbors in Shekhem back in biblical times; think of all the early converts to Judaism. It was a veritable missed window of opportunity because of Dinah's hot-headed brothers who were bent on revenge and nationalism. **Naomi Graetz >graetz@bgumail. bgu.ac.il>**

Professor Marc Bregman

FOR THE LAST 17 YEARS, MARC BREGMAN HAS BEEN TEACHING AT THE JERUSALEM CAMPUS OF THE HEBREW UNION COLLEGE, WHERE HE IS PRESENTLY ASSOCIATE PROFESSOR OF RABBINIC LITERATURE. DURING 1996, BREGMAN SERVED AS THE STROUM PROFESSOR OF JEWISH STUDIES AT THE UNIVERSITY OF WASHINGTON IN SEATTLE. HE HAS PUBLISHED ACADEMIC RESEARCH AND BELLES LETTRES ON A WIDE VARIETY OF TOPICS IN BOTH SCHOLARLY AND POPULAR JOURNALS, MOST RECENTLY AN INTRODUCTION AND THEMATIC COMMENTARY TO THE NOVELLA BY HOWARD SCHWARTZM THE FOUR WHO ENTERED PARADISE, PUBLISHED IN 1995 BY JASON ARONSON, INC.

Va-Yishlah

The Torah reading this Shabbat continues the great saga of Jacob and his family. In last week's portion, fleeing from the anger of his brother, Jacob had one of his mysterious encounters with the Divine. Alone, at night, in a dream, Jacob saw God standing at the top of a ladder. In this dream, God promised Jacob that he would return with many descendants to his homeland under divine protection. In this week's parashah, we read of Jacob's return.

Now, many years later, Jacob is indeed not only a husband and a father, but also a very wealthy and powerful man. Yet, he is most definitely still in need of God's protection. For his brother Esau is still alive, and quite likely still nurturing his anger. So Jacob fords the river under cover of night with all his family. But then, surprisingly, he separates himself from his camp. And now Jacob has another of his mysterious meetings with the divine. The scene for this eerie encounter is set with just three words: וַיִּוָּתֵר יַעֲקֹב לְבַדּוֹ *va'yivater Ya'akov levado*— JACOB REMAINED ALONE [Gen. 32.24]. Here, it almost seems as if a hush falls over the ongoing flow of the biblical narrative. Jacob remains alone, by himself, at night. And immediately the verse continues with a most enigmatic statement: וַיֵּאָבֵק אִישׁ עִמּוֹ עַד עֲלוֹת הַשָּׁחַר *va-yeavek ish imo ad alot ha-sha-*

דָּבָר אַחֵר **DAVAR AHER.** JACOB'S SONS ANSWERED SHEKHEM AND HIS FATHER HAMOR DECEITFULLY... [Gen. 34.13]. The rape of Dinah is an extremely powerful piece of text. When we read it, we cringe with embarrassment for at least two reasons. First, how could Jacob's sons speak בְּמִרְמָה "b'mirmah"—WITH GUILE—and insist that for Shekhem to marry Dinah they would be required to be circumcised knowing

full well that they had no intention of "BECOMING ONE PEOPLE?" And second, the barbarity of Simeon's and Levi's reaction to this "THING WHICH IS NOT DONE IN ISRAEL." Adding insult to injury, after the slaughter of all the newly circumcised men on the third day, they took their "FLOCKS, HERDS, AND ASSES AND ALL THAT WAS IN THE HOUSES" as booty. Did the sons not know how this would impugn their

וישלח יעקב מלאכים לפניו אל עשו אחיו

har—"And a man struggled with him until the break of dawn."

Who is this אִישׁ "*ish*," this "MAN," whom Jacob encounters in such a lonely setting? It is only further on in the story that we get some inkling of whom this mysterious being might be-only after Jacob has overcome him and he has been forced to give Jacob a blessing. For it is in the puzzling language of this blessing that we are given another clue as to the identity of this so-called "MAN": "He said: "YOUR NAME SHALL NO LONGER BE יַעֲקֹב *YA'AKOV*, BUT יִשְׂרָאֵל *YISRAEL*—FOR YOU HAVE STRIVEN WITH GOD AND MEN AND YOU HAVE PROVEN YOURSELF ABLE."

Scripture seems to hint here that the spectral being with whom Jacob has been struggling is not any mere "MAN," but rather some human reflection of God. The enigmatic language of this passage has led some commentators to suggest that the man-God whom Jacob encountered by night and with whom he struggled until the dawn was, in fact, the divine aspect of his own self.

But even if we accept this interpretation, what are we to make of the startling phrase: "FOR YOU HAVE STRIVEN WITH GOD" כִּי שָׂרִיתָ עִם אֱלֹהִים *ki sarita im Elohim*. How can a mere mortal—even our Patriarch Jacob—be said to have struggled physically with God? And this phrase cannot be dismissed as mere Biblical hyperbole. For it contains the etymology of Jacob's new name: *Yisrael*-THE ONE WHO STRIVES WITH GOD. And the name Israel, bequeathed to us as Jacob's descendants, remains an eternal memorial to that fateful struggle with the Divine.

In a more rationalistic age, this mythopoeic story of Jacob's physical struggle with God could no longer be accepted at face value. Later Jewish thinkers felt free to look beyond the biblical etymology of the new name given to Jacob. In the first century, the Jewish philosopher Philo proposed an alternative explanation of the name Israel. *Yisrael—Ish Ra'ah El*—"A MAN WHO SAW GOD." And we must admit that this alternative etymology makes very

good sense in light of the continuation of the biblical story.

AND HE blessed Jacob there. AND JACOB CALLED THE NAME OF THE PLACE PENIEL, FOR I HAVE SEEN GOD FACE TO FACE AND I HAVE SURVIVED. AND THE SUN ROSE UPON HIM AS HE PASSED PENUEL....

Now this last phrase-

וַיִּזְרַח-לוֹ הַשֶּׁמֶשׁ כַּאֲשֶׁר עָבַר אֶת פְּנוּאֵל

vayizrakh lo ha-shemesh ka'asher avar et Penuel—"AND THE SUN ROSE UPON HIM AS HE PASSED PENUEL."—also raises questions. Rabbi Akiba, in the second century, is said to have asked with his own brand of Socratic irony: "Does this mean to say that the sun only rose upon Jacob on that day?!" And this question was still being addressed hundreds of years later, by the most famous of medieval Bible commentators, Rashi. He explains that the expression "AND THE SUN ROSE UPON HIM" can be understood simply as a turn of phrase, for people are given to saying when they arrive at a new place in their lives, that it was as if "a new day dawned for me."

---

reputation? Did they give no forethought to its ramifications?

The Torah tells us that when Jacob's sons answered Hamor's and Shekhem's request for the bride price so that Dinah might be married to Shekhem and began to put into motion this barbaric plan, they said, "WE CANNOT DO THIS THING, TO GIVE OUR SISTER TO A MAN WHO IS UNCIRCUMCISED, FOR THAT IS A DISGRACE AMONG US." Indeed, when they said "THAT IS A DISGRACE

AMONG US" they were being prophetic about themselves and their family and did not even know it at the time. The real disgrace was not that Shekhem and Hamor and the men of the city were עָרְלָה *orlah* but rather that the sons made the offer in guile and massacred them on the third day.

This episode is, in fact, disgraceful, though our sages are not sure who is to blame. Some blame Dinah who

"WENT OUT" of the city "adorned like a harlot" [*Bereshit Rabbah* 80.1]. This is a classic example of blaming the victim; an affliction we still have to this very day. Other sages try to exonerate Simeon and Levi. Maimonides, for instance, say that they went out seeking revenge (which may have been acceptable), but then justifies their slaughtering the town because "they saw and knew and did not punish him (Shekhem)." Whether we try to

And by struggling with the Divine, Jacob has indeed arrived at a new place, not just geographically, but spiritually. Having dared to encounter God face to face—Jacob has been transformed. He has been blessed with a new and highly significant name, *Yisrael*. But let us not forget that, though he has survived this confrontation with the Divine Self, he has not come away unscathed: "AND JACOB CALLED THE NAME OF THE PLACE PENIEL, FOR I HAVE SEEN GOD FACE TO FACE AND I HAVE SURVIVED." But Scripture goes on to say: "…HE PASSED PENIEL, LIMPING…."

Jacob has seen God face to face. He has seen not only God's benign, healing face, but has also confronted the dangerous, threatening, shadowy aspect of the Divine—what Christian theologians would later call the *mysterium*

tremendum, and the medieval Jewish mystics would refer to as the *sitra aḥra*—the "other side."

Not surprisingly, the notion of Jacob's spiritual transformation was seized upon by these more esoterically inclined Jewish thinkers. In the magnum opus of medieval Jewish mysticism, the *Zohar* [I, 144b], we find the following interpretation: "YOUR NAME SHALL NO LONGER BE YAAKOV, BUT YISRAEL, FOR YOU HAVE STRIVEN WITH GOD AND MEN—*Yisrael*: כִּי שָׂרִיתָ עִם אֱלֹהִים וְעִם אֲנָשִׁים *ki sarita im Elohim ve-im anashim*." Note that Scripture does not say "שָׂרִיתָ עַל אֱלֹהִים *sarita al Elohim*." It does not imply that Jacob prevailed over any being, Divine or human. Rather it says: עִם אֱלֹהִים וְעִם אֲנָשִׁים *Im Elohim ve-im anashim*—"WITH GOD AND WITH MEN." Jacob, now transformed as

Va-Yishlaḥ

blame the victim or the innocent civilian witnesses of this crime there remains an uneasiness within us that cannot be explained away by either the midrash or Rambam. Rather, we should face the *p'shat* of the text—its obvious and simple meaning head on and say, as did Nachmanides, "(Rambam's commentary) is completely unacceptable in my eyes."

This seems to be father Jacob's response, as well. When he is administering his deathbed blessing to his sons Levi and Simeon he says, "CURSED BE THEIR ANGER…[Gen. 49.8]." That should be our response, too. The lesson we learn from Jacob

(and Nachmanides) is this: Whether an injustice is done by Jews or Gentiles, it is incumbent upon us to speak out and publicly condemn it. Whether the injustice be sexual harassment or other sexual crimes like rape and child molestation (in which the victim is often blamed) or excesses in times of war (such as My Lai) or the various contemporary manifestations of McCarthyism, it is our task to seek justice whether or not the perpetrator is a Jew. To explain away the actions based on "present political realities" or perceived improprieties obfuscates the real injustices. The rape of Dinah is our wake-up call to vocally, force-

וישלח יעקב מלאכים לפניו אל עשו אחיו

Israel, does not strive to overcome God or even any other man. Rather, Yisrael has become the one who now strives to unite the human with the Divine.

Such daring and imaginative plays on the language of scripture, found in the ancient midrashic and mystical writings, admittedly may seem far from our contemporary sensibilities. So what possible meaning can such an enigmatic and downright primitive tale as the story of Jacob's wrestling with God still have for modern people like ourselves? The answer to this question is, I think, disclosed when we return to the beginning of the story: וַיִּוָּתֵר יַעֲקֹב לְבַדּוֹ *va-yivater Ya'akov levado*—"JACOB REMAINED ALONE." It is when one remains alone—in spirit-ual solitude—that one just may encounter the Divine. And this very individual encounter is not necessarily pleasant. It may well be—as it was for Jacob—a kind of wrestling match with some unknown self. And there is risk involved; we—like Jacob—may well be wounded in the encounter. But if we are found able, we, too, receive a blessing. Like Jacob, we, too, may just glimpse the human face of God and the God-like face of Man. We, too, may arrive at a some new place of spiritual transformation. And—having survived this struggle—like Jacob our forefather, then we, too, will truly deserve to be blessed with the name *Yisrael*. ●

---

fully, and publicly resist the temptation to ignore real pain. **Rabbi Cy Stanway, Temple Beth El, Las Cruces, NM**

דָּבָר אַחֵר **DAVAR AHER. AND THESE ARE THE** תּוֹלְדֹת *TOLEDOT* **OF ISAAC, ABRAHAM'S SON. ABRAHAM FATHERED ISAAC.** [Gen. 35.19]. That is how Isaac authenticates his life; he is Abraham's son. This is how Abraham authenticates his life; he is the father of Isaac. Generations—תּוֹלְדֹת *toldot*—is written half *haser*, half *malei*. (*Haser* and *malei* are styles of Hebrew spelling where consonants are used (malei/full) or not used (haser/missing) to indicate the vowels which are not being printed.) Was it not enough that each of them, father and son, could derive his worth from the other? When one of them was *haser*, could not the other find the fullness that authenticates itself from the other? Is it not healing to receive that kind of love? "I love you enough," Abraham said, "I love you enough to give you the gift of my love; when you cannot find it in yourself, I give it to you. I love you that much." "I love you enough," Isaac said, "I love you enough to give you the gift of my love; when you cannot find it in yourself, I give it to you. I love you that much." *Haser malei, malei haser*… I love you that much, my child, that whenever you cannot find it in yourself, you may fill that emptiness from me. I love you that much. **Reb Stavisker <Stavisker @aol.com>**

דָּבָר אַחֵר **DAVAR AHER. AND HE CALLED HIS NAME *BEN-YAMIN*…** [Gen. 35.18]. Jacob's supposed transformation from cheater to *tzaddik*, which took place while he wrestled with a man (Esav's alter ego, his own conscience, etc.) was hardly a transformation at all. His lack of sensitivity at the slaughter of the men of Shekhem at the hands of his own sons, together with his open favoritism for Joseph, demonstrated that he had not really matured at all. He was the same petty, self-serving creature as when he cheated his brother years before. Did he do anything in his lifetime of redeeming value? Scanning the passages about his life, I come up with this sole example: He renamed his son after Rachel's death [35.18]. In her anguish, Rachel called the boy *Ben-Oni*, son of my pain. Perhaps not wanting to risk burdening his son for a lifetime with the guilt of causing his mother's death, he changed his name to *Ben-Yamin*, son of my strength and vigor. That was truly an act of a *tzaddik*. **Rabbi Mark Cooper, Temple Beth Ahm, Aberdeen, NJ**

Va-Yeshev

Genesis 37.1–40.23

Robert Alter

ROBERT ALTER IS THE CLASS OF 1937 PROFESSOR OF HEBREW AND COMPARATIVE LITERATURE AT THE UNIVERSITY OF CALIFORNIA AT BERKELEY. HE IS AUTHOR OF *THE ART OF BIBLICAL NARRATIVE, THE WORLD OF BIBLICAL LITERATURE*, AND NUMEROUS OTHER WORKS.

Why does Joseph dream two different dreams, evidently to the same purpose? Later in the story, when Pharaoh, too, has a doubled dream, Joseph himself offers a simple explanation that appears to address, as well, his own repeated dreams: "AND AS FOR THE REPETITION OF THE DREAM TWICE TO PHARAOH, THAT MEANS THE MATTER HAS BEEN FIXED BY GOD AND GOD IS HASTENING TO DO IT [Gen. 41.32]." But Joseph's explanation of the repetition as an indication of the certitude of the prediction by no means exhausts the role of ostensible doublings in this narrative.

In fact, pairing—of both incidents and motifs—is a formal key to the Joseph story. In addition to Joseph's and Pharaoh's doubled dream, we have the paired dreams of the chief steward and the chief baker. Then, various narrative elements from the early part of the story find twins in the later part of the story: Joseph is cast into a pit by his brothers, and into the prison house by Potiphar; he is separated from his brothers, and loses his freedom in Egypt, and that is the temporary fate he imposes on Simeon; the silver given the brothers by the Ishmaelites for the sale of Joseph reappears in their saddle packs as they return from Egypt many years later; Joseph is virtually autonomous major domo in the prison house as he was in Potiphar's house (and, of course, as he will be in the governing of

---

דָּבָר אַחֵר **DAVAR AHER. JOSEPH WOULD BRING EVIL REPORTS OF THEM...[Gen. 37.2].** Don't you think Joseph's problem is that he had to learn how to direct his gifts? In the beginning, he simply brags and struts, but all that time alone in the prison let him remember the source of the gifts, and then he acts with wisdom and compassion. I'm a writer. What should I write about? How do I know where to focus my attention? I know Joseph's showing off only too well. **Malka Drucker <MalkaD@aol.com>**

דָּבָר אַחֵר **DAVAR AHER. JOSEPH DREAMED A DREAM...[Gen. 37.5].** Robert Alter's column on the double dreams of the Joseph narratives argues for a presumptiveness "on the part of the young Joseph." While this is the intent the narratives wish to convey in a first reading of

וישב יעקב בארץ מגרי א

Egypt). Even in regard to procreation, Joseph produces exactly two sons, who exchange positions at the end.

The dreams of the steward and the baker are an instructive limit-case in this system of pairs: they appear to be entirely parallel, as the baker erroneously assumes, but, in fact, they are opposite in meaning. A general principle is intimated here: repetitions may reflect virtual identity of meaning and so confirm one another; they may intimate some sort of narrative and thematic development; they may signal an approximate or qualified analogy; and they may even prove, as in the two prison dreams, to be a spurious repetition that actually points to a polar difference.

The predictive power of Joseph's two dreams should not distract our attention from the naïveté of the language in which he reports them (quite unlike the choreographed descriptive prose of Pharaoh's dreams): the

authority of Joseph's election is not allowed to mitigate the representation of his adolescent narcissism. First he says to his brothers, "Listen to this dream that I dreamt," as though all the world ought to be fascinated by what has been playing inside his head in the midst of sleep. His account of both dreams is very brief, perhaps breathless, and quite without descriptive elaboration. The prominent word in both reports is וְהִנֵּה *ve-hinneh*, "AND LOOK," the so-called presentative, which here functions as a repeated exclamation of excitement: "AND LOOK WE WERE BINDING SHEAVES IN THE FIELD, AND, LOOK, MY SHEAF ROSE AND IT ACTUALLY (וְגַם *ve-gam*) STOOD UP, AND, LOOK, YOUR SHEAVES TURNED ROUND AND BOWED TO MY SHEAF" [37.7]. Joseph's language here is very far from the assured speech he will adapt when he addresses Pharaoh. The brothers scarcely have to be told the point of the dream: they immediately spell it out in another kind of

Synopsis: From this parashah through the end of Genesis, the Torah tells the story of Joseph beginning with the favoritism shown him by his father. Joseph dreams about sheaves and the sun, moon and stars—all bowing. The story continues with his journey to the brothers who plot his sale. Saved by Reuven, he is thrown into the pit, his coat is taken and he is sold to the caravan of Ishmaelites who happen by. News reaches Jacob who mourns the loss. At the same time, Joseph is sold to Potiphar. The narrative is interrupted with the story in which Judah, through deception, sleeps with Tamar who gives birth to twins. The Joseph narrative continues with his life in Potiphar's palace. The often-told sequence of stories of Potiphar's wife's attempt to seduce Joseph, the subsequent imprisonment, the encounter with the cupbearer and baker and their dreams and interpretations provide a suitable conclusion to this piece of the pre-Exodus story.

Joseph, who initially appears as an obnoxious, favored twerp whose bravado offends the sensibility of the modern reader, the modern reader is often so taken by her/his own cultural biases that the narrative is not understood on its merits.

When the reader first encounters Joseph, s/he is offended with an intolerable display of braggadocio, but the initial presentation of the Joseph story is belied by the subsequent narra-

tional development. Just as the Joseph narrative consists of three double dream sequences, the Torah juxtaposes, for the reader's consideration, the actual behavior of Judah, who sold Joseph into slavery, and Joseph, the object of his unbrotherly act.

Upon the death of his wife, Judah consorts with Tamar, whom he takes to be a *kadesha*, a cult prostitute, who in turn exploits Judah's lust in return for his identifying staff and signet

ring. At the same narrational moment, Joseph is successfully resisting the unwelcome but threatening advances of Potiphar's wife. By juxtaposing these two narratives, the reader learns that from Scripture's perspective, Tamar *and* Joseph are more righteous (*tzaddikim*) than Judah and than the initial impressions that the narrative gives us.

Joseph's success in Egypt is testimony to the rightness of Joseph's earlier

doubling, the parallelistic repetition of a line of formal poetry. Their words, here rendered literally to indicate the repetition within repetition in each half of the line, are: "REIGN, WOULD YOU REIGN OVER US,/RULE, WOULD YOU RULE US?" [37.8]. This response does not deter Joseph from reporting his second dream in a manner that is stylistically continuous with the report of the first dream, though the dream-imagery has changed: "LOOK, I DREAMED ANOTHER DREAM, AND LOOK, THE SUN AND THE MOON AND ELEVEN STARS WERE BOWING DOWN TO ME" [37.9].

What is the difference between the two dreams, and does the transformation from the first version to the second tell us anything about the subsequent course of the narrative? In two ways, the first dream begins in the real life setting inhabited by Joseph and his brothers at the beginning of this story. Its framework is an actual agricultural activity they would have been accustomed to perform as a routine

matter, and before the dream turns fantastic with the bowing of the sheaves of grain, its first brief clause is perfectly realistic: "AND LOOK, WE WERE BINDING SHEAVES IN THE FIELD." Since sheaves of grain would be approximately the same size and shape, they serve to represent different members of the same class—siblings—as the brothers are quick to see, and parents do not figure in this dream.

In contrast to all this, the second dream does not begin with a realistic setting but with a full-blown fantasy: the sun and the moon and the stars, immediately seen by the dreamer as bowing down. In this dream, the brothers are not explicitly indicated (as in "WE WERE BINDING," "YOUR SHEAVES"), and a human agent enters the dream only in the last Hebrew word of the report, לִי *li,* "to me." The interpreter of the dream in this case is not the brothers but the father, who recognizes in the sun and the moon figures for himself and Joseph's mother (Rachel, in fact,

Va-Yeshev

self-evaluation, as well as his father's halting, half-hearted and embarrassed realization that Joseph was a man of many moral and material talents. It seems that the Torah teaches that judgments should be suspended until one sees all of the facts. And ultimately, only God has all the facts. Just as God was willing to engage Abraham in conversation regarding the salvation of Sodom on the contingency

of finding ten righteous people, we soon learn that Lot's house was surrounded by the entire population of Sodom which was unified in immoral resolve to gang-rape Lot's guests. While the Torah does discourage people from making critical judgments, the Torah *is* teaching that our judgments should be more restrained and equivocal, especially when evaluating the narrative intent of the Hebrew Bible.

וישב יעקב בארץ מגרי אביו בארץ כנען

is already dead) and expresses indignation at the notion that father and mother and brothers will come to bow before Joseph.

Now, it is clear that the second dream is more grandiose than the first, and it is a grandiosity that has implications both for the characterization of Joseph and the development of the plot. The sheaves of grain of the first dream point forward as a concrete term to the means Joseph will use to exercise power over Egypt: storing up grain in huge silos to dispense to all the inhabitants, for the price of their land and their freedom. But the *setting* of the first dream is the agricultural scene of rural Canaan of the beginning of the story whereas the setting of the second dream is—metaphorically—the imperial court of Egypt where the last act of the story will unfold. Joseph surrounded by the celestial bodies is Joseph in the grandeur of Pharaoh's court. It surely would not have escaped the ancient audience that Pharaoh himself was associated

with the sun-god, and so the bowing of the sun as well as the moon and stars to Joseph would suggest something quite audacious about Joseph's future career in the Pharaonic sphere. In the event, Pharaoh, of course, does not bow to him, though he effectively takes over the practical exercise of power from Pharaoh. Finally, the setting of the first dream is daytime, the setting of the second, by implication, nighttime (despite the sun), because of the presence of the moon and stars. In any case, the celestial bodies take us into the nocturnal realm of dreams in which Joseph the interpreter will wield his uncanny gift of knowledge and thus make his way to preeminence.

But if the second dream is predictively true, it also points up more strikingly than the first the presumptuousness of the young Joseph. Instead of a mere bowing down of sheaves, it is the celestial luminaries (compare Gen. 1.16] that prostrate themselves before him. The ultimate implication of the image is

equally heretical from an Egyptian point of view (the sun-god bowing to Joseph) and from a monotheistic one. And, in the familial perspective, even doting Jacob understands that the son he has so extravagantly favored dreams of setting himself up over his own parents as well as over his brothers. At the end of the story Joseph, the regent of Egypt, will actually treat his father with great deference, and there is no question of Jacob's literally bowing down before him, yet we can scarcely forget that Joseph has become immeasurably his father's superior in power. The prophecy of the second dream is not without its human ambiguities.

Joseph's two dreams, then, are a kind of formal prelude to the themes and events of the subsequent story. What may be most interesting about them, however, is that they present the reader with an explicit model for how to read the story. Look carefully, they tell us, at everything that occurs in twos: two-ness itself is an index of

---

Rabbi Alan J. Yuter, Congregation Israel, Springfield, NJ. Rabbi Yuter teaches Bible and Jewish Heritage at Touro College, Brooklyn, NY

דָּבָר אַחֵר **DAVAR AHER. THE PIT WAS EMPTY; NO WATER. [Gen. 37.24].** The first of Rashi's comments on a biblical text that I remember learning in rabbinical school is on a verse in this week's parashah, *Va-Yeshev*. When Joseph's brothers cast him into the pit

we read, "THE PIT WAS EMPTY; THERE WAS NO WATER IN IT." Rashi asks if the pit is empty, why does the text add that there is no water in it? The phrase is there, he writes, to teach us that although there was no water in the pit, it was full of snakes and scorpions. This was my introduction to Rashi. I have never forgotten this comment because it struck me as such a farfetched conclusion.

Recently I was reading an article by Rabbi Richard Israel on giving a *D'var Torah*. One of his suggestions for gaining insight into the text is to read Rashi. He writes, "Rashi is mainly interested in answers to questions he finds in the text, questions you probably didn't even notice." Rabbi Israel goes on to say, "his answers are almost never useful for a contemporary *D'var Torah*, but his questions are." This comment caused me to go

narrative significance. But look as well for the differences in the seeming repetition, for they will often provide finely instructive measures of how the meanings of the story are complicated, of how providential design and the imperfections of individual character together make a strange chemistry. ●

Va-Yeshev

back to this first Rashi that I learned.

Rashi raises a good question on this verse. Why *does* it add that there is no water in the pit after first telling us that the pit is empty? This time I asked myself a question as well. What does water symbolize? Water, cross-culturally, is a symbol of life and birth. When the Israelites travel through the desert after the exodus from Egypt, they are accompanied by Miriam's well. It sustains them on their journey. The search for water is a theme that runs through their travels. In our tradition, we also speak of מַיִם חַיִּים *mayim ḥayim*, living waters. It is one of the metaphors we use for the Torah.

When Joseph is thrown into a place with no water, he is taken away from all that nourishes his life. Not only is the pit empty of the physical things needed for life, it is also bare of the spiritual and psychological underpinnings of life. There is no food, no water, no ornamental clothes, no family in the pit. God's plan is also hidden from Joseph. By telling us that the pit is empty, with no water in it, the Torah is telling us that at this moment Joseph is completely, utterly alone. All the familiar things of his life are gone. He has entered the dark night of the soul with no apparent suste-

nance to help him through it. These three simple words, אֵין בּוֹ מָיִם *ain bo mayim*, teach us of Joseph's hopelessness and despair as he is sold into Egypt. **Rabbi Julie Wolkoff, Congregation Berith Shalom, Troy, NY** Permission to reprint given by *The Jewish World*, Annual Chanukah Edition, November 24, 1994.

דָּבָר אַחֵר **DAVAR AḤER. BUT ONAN KNEW THAT THE OFFSPRING WOULD NOT BE HIS...** [Gen. 38.9]. The Torah portion *Va-Yeshev* has many interpretations. However, the interpretation that comes to my mind is different from others I have heard. Onan was obligated to marry his brother's widow, Tamar, and to father a child with her under his brother's name. Onan did marry Tamar, but he died without her conceiving. Onan died in sin because he took advantage of Tamar. Onan had no intention of conceiving children with Tamar, but he still slept with her. He should not have married her and lied to her if he knew what his intentions were. His major sin was sexually taking advantage of Tamar. <Rebgiraffe@aol.com> **Marcy Churgel, Confirmation Class, Congregation B'nai Tzedek, Fountain Valley, CA**

וישב יעקב בארץ מגרי אביו בארץ כנען

Navah Kelman

NAVAH KELMAN IS THE ASSISTANT DIRECTOR OF CAMP RAMAH IN OJAI, CALIFORNIA

This week's parashah contains the first of two Tamar narratives found in the Bible. A frustrated daughter-in-law tricks her father-in-law into sleeping with her so that his line can continue. She is "rewarded" with not one child but twins—and not just twins but the ancestors of kings. Years later, her lineage continues with the second Tamar [II Sam. 13]. Tricked and raped by one brother, the second Tamar lives out her days silenced and hidden by another. Why two Tamar narratives?

Are they connected by more than just the name Tamar?

The first Tamar appears in chapter 38 of Va-Yeshev. There is a clear philological emphasis throughout this chapter on sight and perception identifiable in the Hebrew text through the use of the verb רָאָה "ra'ah" (to see) and the noun עַיִן "ayin" (eye). In the beginning of the chapter we are told that Judah *sees* Bat-Shua and takes her as a wife (v. 2). In contrast, when it comes time to take a wife for his oldest son, Er, he simply takes Tamar without seeing her—a fore-shadowing of things to come.

Keeping a watchful eye on the situation unfolding around her, Tamar *sees* that Shelah is old enough to be given to her in marriage (v. 14). When Judah finally *sees* Tamar וַיִּרְאֶהָ (*vayir'eha*, v. 15) it isn't even Tamar he sees but a harlot standing before him (the whole scene, of course, taking place at the entrance to עֵינַיִם *einayim*, meaning "eyes"). Judah doesn't see Tamar when he

---

דָּבָר אַחֵר **DAVAR AHER. SHE THEN SAT BY THE CROSSROADS...**[Gen. 38.14]. I have never been particularly fond of flying. I try to bury myself in a book or a magazine and try not to come up for air before it is time to "deplane." Still, whenever I fly into my hometown of Toronto, there is always some urge to look down upon the city and identify major landmarks. Though the city has changed each time, there are still enough identifiable areas that take me back to years

ago and, as I recognize the intersections of the streets below, I am also identifying the intersections of my youth, and for a moment, the circumstances, incidents, and choices I made are both symbolically and actually represented for me 25,000 feet below where I sit. To be aware of life is to wander upon intersections every day. Some intersections have a more lasting effect than others. Some give your life added depth or meaning and some give that added meaning to

chooses her for Er and he doesn't see through her disguise at *Einayim*.

In the second Tamar narrative [II Sam. 13], we are introduced to a lovesick Amnon, lusting for Tamar in his heart but knowing in his *eyes* (וַיִּפָּלֵא בְּעֵינָי *va-yipaleh b'einey*) [*Amnon* v. 2] that he cannot act on his feelings. Amnon's cousin, Yonadav, concocts a scheme involving Amnon and Tamar's father, King David, coming to *see* an "AILING" Amnon (v. 6) in order for Amnon to request from him that Tamar help him get better by "PREPARING THE FOOD IN (HIS) *SIGHT* SO THAT (HE) MAY *SEE* IT" (v. 5). Once she arrives at his house (v. 8), Tamar proceeds to prepare the cakes for Amnon לְעֵינָיו *l'eiynav* (lit. in front of his eyes).

The reader, too, is drawn into what can and cannot be seen. In both narratives, while Tamar herself is present, her name disappears at the time of sexual interplay. The first Tamar is told in 38.13 that Judah has gone up to Timnah to shear sheep. As her veil goes on, her name disappears from the text until Judah is told she is pregnant [38.24]. The second Tamar is last "seen" going into Amnon's chamber to give him the cakes she had prepared [II Sam. 13.10]. The next time her name appears in the text it is after the rape as she rips her virgin's clothing from her body [13.19]. In both stories, as the shady sexual dealings unfold, the reader (like the characters in the story) must also strain to see.

The names repeat, the themes of sight, trickery, and deception repeat, and the stories mirror each other. One Tamar stands at the beginning of the Davidic dynasty, while the second marks the beginning of the end of that same dynasty. The first Tamar sees, the second doesn't. The first Tamar is active, the second, a victim. The stories of these women become even further connected by yet a second name that appears in both

Va-Yeshev

others. How many countless lives have been changed by chance meetings at the "intersections" of our lives—both real and metaphorically.... Tamar, knowing her responsibility to her dead husband's name, and seeing that Shelah "WAS NOT GIVEN TO HER AS A HUSBAND" finds an intersection on the road to Timnah where Judah, her father-in-law, will soon pass on the way to the sheep shearing station. Tamar dresses like a prostitute and entices Judah to have intercourse with her so that she may conceive and, in doing so, have Judah essentially perform the mitzvah of לְבִיר *levir* though he himself is not aware of it. The rabbis praise Tamar, and do not fault her for deceiving Judah or "PLAYING THE HARLOT." In fact, the rabbis tell us that God's spirit was upon her and it was that spirit that led her to cover her face with a veil.

stories—Bat-Shua. In Genesis 38, she is Judah's wife [38.2]. In II Samuel 12 (the chapter immediately preceding that of Tamar and Amnon), she is the object of King David's voyeurism (although here she is referred to as Bat-Sheva, in I Chronicles 3.5 she is referred to as Bat-Shua). The plot thickens. The repetition of yet a second woman's name in the same two narratives can only be a signal to the reader to look even deeper into the similarities and differences between these four women and their stories.

In Genesis 38, Bat-Shua marries Judah, has three sons, and dies. In contrast, her daughter-in-law Tamar realizes that she won't be able to have children unless she takes matters into her own hands. The Bat-Sheva of II Samuel must also take action as her own story unfolds (see I Kings 1.11-31], while the Tamar of II Samuel 13 becomes the victim of her own brother. An active Tamar, an

active Bat-Sheva, a passive Tamar and a passive Bat-Shua. The balance these women create within the text plays their respective stories one off the other. The heroism of the Genesis Tamar is emphasized by the tragedy of the second. The character of the second Bat-Sheva is enhanced by the subtlety of the first. It is through this balance that the Tamar/Bat-Sheva stories stand, as they should, as a study in Biblical women, literary balance, and historical symmetry.

One final historical footnote. At first glance, the Tamar stories appear to conclude at the end of II Samuel 13 when, after the rape, Avshalom (Tamar's brother) comforts her, asks for her silence, and hides her away. There is, however, yet a third Tamar. II Samuel 14.27 tells us about Avshalom's children—three sons and a daughter, Tamar. Avshalom, the brother who came to his sister's aid, gave his own daughter the name of

the sister he hid. The verse continues, adding one last interesting piece of information about her—
הִיא הָיְתָה אִשָּׁה יְפַת מַרְאֶה "*Hi haytah eishah y'fat mar'eh*" ("SHE WAS A WOMAN OF BEAUTIFUL APPEARANCE"). The name Tamar repeats and the theme of sight returns.

What legacy does this third Tamar carry with her? Will she possess the character of her distant grandmother or repeat the tragedy of her aunt? Perhaps the end of verse 27 should be read with an ellipsis:
הִיא הָיְתָה אִשָּׁה יְפַת מַרְאֶה "*Hi haytah eishah y'fat mar'eh* ...." And the story continues. ●

When Judah walked by, he sought to turn away from what he rightly supposed was a prostitute. The rabbis tell us that he gave this woman a second thought when he could not figure out why a prostitute should be wearing a veil. Knowing that there was something else to this woman, he accepted her advances. The progeny of that union included King David and, in time to come, the Messiah, as well. One never knows who is standing at the next intersection. **Rabbi Cy Stanway, Temple Beth El, Las Cruces, NM**

דָּבָר אַחֵר **DAVAR AHER. BUT HE ADAMANTLY REFUSED, HE SAID TO HIS MASTER'S WIFE...** [Gen. 39.8]. In the *sidrah* of *Va-Yeshev*, Joseph refused the temptation to lie down with Potiphar's wife. The Torah trope offers the reader a unique insight into Joseph's future. In Chapter 39.8, above the Hebrew word וַיְמָאֵן *va-yima'ain*, meaning "HE REFUSED," the reader finds the rare trope, or Torah cantillation note, of *shalshelet*, meaning chain. Joseph refused Potiphar's wife's offer and he would bear the consequences of becoming incarcer-

ated or *chained* in prison. Joseph's righteous refusal marked a new chain of events as his character was transformed into one of greater integrity. **Rabbi Barry Blum, Congregation Beth El-Ner Tamid, Broomall, PA**

n *Miketz*, Joseph's ability and skill at dream interpretation come to the fore again. The young dreamer, the lad who dreamt of glory and importance, has now matured into a dream interpreter and analyst. The chief cup-bearer can now repay his debt to Joseph by mentioning him to Pharaoh and thereby freeing Joseph from prison.

Pharaoh's dreams are well known. Seven handsome and sturdy cows are consumed by seven ugly gaunt cows.

Seven healthy and solid ears of corn are swallowed up by seven thin and scorched ears of corn. No one can be found—not one magician or wise man—who can interpret them for Pharaoh. At that point, the cupbearer mentions Joseph, Pharaoh sends for Joseph, the dreams are interpreted, and we know the rest—Joseph's appointment to the office of Viceroy of Egypt and the reunion with his brothers and father.

However, the story of the dream analysis still remains mysterious and problematic. The dreams do not seem that difficult to interpret—after all, seven of something bad related to the land or flocks will destroy or overcome seven of something good. Evil will consume good. Is it possible that with all of Pharaoh's resources, all the wise men who counseled and advised him, all the magicians of his powerful empire, not one person could interpret these

Miketz

Genesis 41.1–44.17

Rabbi Sheldon Zimmerman

RABBI SHELDON ZIMMERMAN SERVES AS THE RABBI OF TEMPLE EMANU-EL IN DALLAS, TEXAS, AND IS PRESIDENT OF THE CENTRAL CONFERENCE OF AMERICAN RABBIS. IN ADDITION, RABBI ZIMMERMAN IS AN ADJUNCT PROFESSOR AT PERKINS THEOLOGICAL SEMINARY AT SOUTHERN METHODIST UNIVERSITY. SINCE WRITING THIS PIECE, HE HAS BEEN ELECTED THE PRESIDENT OF THE HEBREW UNION COLLEGE—JEWISH INSTITUTE OF RELIGION.

דָּבָר אַחֵר **DAVAR AHER. BUT HE ADAMANTLY REFUSED, HE SAID TO HIS MASTER'S WIFE...[Gen. 39.8].** Astro Rabbi Barry Blum's note on the *shalshelet* above the word "AND HE REFUSED" in *Parashat Vayeshev*. I read it a bit differently. The *shalshelet* is read up and down, up and down, and then up and down a third time. It reminds me of going back and forth, "Should I or shouldn't I? Well—maybe yes...no, I think not."

The note sounds like a person ambivalent and wavering. This is Joseph's greatness in refusing Potiphar's wife. Like any of us in a tempting moment, he wonders, "Gee, nobody will see me, nobody will know...." He vacillates. He wants to! But he doesn't. It is at this moment that Joseph has finally grown up from the kid who wants to and then does: tell his dreams, wear the coat, tattle on his broth-

וידי מקץ שנתים ימים וׁפ

Synopsis: Our parashah begins with Pharaoh's dream. The cupbearer remembers the Hebrew lad who had correctly interpreted his dream. Joseph is called to provide an interpretation and offers some practical suggestions regarding the future food shortage. Joseph becomes vizier, marries Asnat, fathers two sons, Menasheh and Efraim, and the famine begins. Jacob sends the brothers to procure food in Egypt. The well-known story of the encounter in the palace between Joseph and his brothers follows: the deception, the leaving behind of Shimon, the return to Jacob with the request for Benjamin, the return to Egypt, the placing of the goblet in Benjamin's sack, the return encounter with Joseph—and the concluding verse in which Joseph asserts that he will hold in Egypt just he in whose possession the goblet was found.

dreams? Pharaoh was surrounded by the wisest counselors of the world—an extraordinary empire. Could no one be found?

Rashi suggests that there were interpreters but none who could satisfy Pharaoh [Gen. 41.8]. All their interpretations did not satisfy him or still his agitation. Pharaoh knew that the message was important and he was not privy to its fullness and meaning. Sforno suggests that their interpretations were beyond rational acceptance because they did not realize that it was one dream [Gen. 41.8].

So Pharaoh received many interpretations, but in each one something was missing—a basic understanding and a plan. He knew that he had received a message, a divine revelation, and that his empire, his reign and his very being depended on a correct analysis. But how would he know if it was correct? It seemed that Pharaoh understood

more of the dreams than we are led to believe—he had a sense of what they were about—he needed someone to help him connect them, and move forward with a plan. Intuitively, he rejected all interpretations—he was ready for Joseph.

Joseph displayed a unified understanding. Pharaoh's two dreams were really one dream—one repeated the other for emphasis, to demand attention, to create a sense of urgency. They were the same dream.

So many of us see differences—we are so often overwhelmed by what is different that we lose a sense of the unity, the commonalties that lie beneath the surface. To be able to see unity among the fragmentation is a precious gift and Joseph possessed it. Pharaoh's dreams are one dream—there is one message here. Just as one malady can have many symptoms, and just as one basic problem can manifest itself in dif-

ers—to the adult who thinks before he acts, who wants to but doesn't.
Rabbi Elyse Goldstein, Director of Kolel: A Centre for Liberal Jewish Learning, Toronto, CANADA
<Baruch_Sienna@mail.magic. com>

דָּבָר אַחֵר **DAVAR AḤER. JOSEPH HAD TWO SONS...[Gen. 41.50].** It is incredible to me how Joseph's portrait emerges in *Miketz* as that of the most ancient post-modern Jew. To wit: (1) His chil-

dren's names are Ephraim and Menasseh. Ephraim means "I HAVE BEEN FRUITFUL" and Menasseh means "GOD HAS CAUSED ME TO FORGET THE TRIBULATIONS OF MY FATHER'S HOUSE." They are really named, therefore, Success and Amnesia. (2) Joseph's name is changed—an often overlooked facet of the story. He is not the first person whose name is changed in the Torah. Abram becomes Abraham, Sarai is Sarah, Jacob is Israel. But Joseph

becomes צָפְנַת פַּעְנֵחַ *Tzafnat-Paneaḥ*—an Egyptian name. This time, however, the name change comes not from God, but from Pharaoh—a pseudo-god, as it were. Joseph is the first Jew who gets his "name" (read: essence, identity) from the dominant culture. (3) It will eventually play itself out as Jacob lies on his deathbed. "Who are these kids?" says Jacob of his grandchildren. He can't recognize himself in them. Scary stuff. One

ferent ways, to truly understand we have to get to the base, to the root. The greatest thinkers, scientists, doctors and researchers possess the skill to find the unity. Real differences remain—but superficial differences vanish under their analysis.

Joseph could perceive the basic and unified message and thus would be able to move to the second step. Joseph understood that in these dreams Pharaoh received the message of a major threat to Egypt and Pharaoh himself. Perhaps Joseph saw even more. In times of drought and famine, all the neighboring lands and their people needed Egypt's steady supply of produce which the Nile provided as a reliable source of water. If Egypt were consumed with drought, so, too, would Joseph's brothers and father be consumed and die. Jacob's life and his sons' lives all depended on a correct, unified understanding. Had Joseph not understood, all would have been

lost. So essential is the person of understanding when crisis threatens, that without him there would be no future. Rather than *shrai gevalt*, as we are so prone to do, Joseph perceived the danger and was ready to move forward.

Joseph does not wait to be asked. He proceeds from interpretation to a plan of action [Gen. 41.33 ff] for Pharaoh and Egypt. Pharaoh has to appoint someone who can oversee a 20% tax on land and produce during the good years. Someone who can come up with a system of storage and a system of apportioning food during the years of famine. Pharaoh and his advisors react favorably immediately. "Could we find another like him, a man in whom is the spirit of God? [41.38]." In verse 39, the Torah tells us that Joseph is נָבוֹן *navon* (discerning) and חָכָם *ẖakham* (wise). Rashbam comments and tells us that this means that Joseph can foresee the future and use the experience of what he has seen and heard.

Miketz

more thing: Joseph's brothers describe themselves as being בְּנֵי אִישׁ אֶחָד *benei ish eẖad*, the sons of a certain man. Or: the sons of a man who is אֶחָד *eẖad*, one, newly whole after the battles of his life. So may we all be אֶחָד *eẖad* and whole, as God is אֶחָד *eẖad* and whole.
Rabbi Jeffrey K. Salkin, Central Synagogue of Nassau County Rockville Centre, NY

דָּבָר אַחֵר **DAVAR AHER. Joseph had two sons…[Gen. 41.50].** This parashah is significant to the importance, encouragement and vitality of Outreach. Joseph finds himself successful, wealthy, and apparently totally assimilated into Egyptian life. He is in an "interfaith" marriage with no consideration of his wife's converting to Judaism. They have two sons and do not seem to have any more than Joseph's personal iden-

Joseph has come up with the ultimate marketable plan. It is in everyone's interest. Food will be available and the challenge of the famine will be met. In addition, Pharaoh gains—his coffers will be filled with grain sold and he will have control over one-fifth of the land. He and his officials will be in charge (almost total charge) of Egypt. Eventually, as the story unfolds, grain is sold to foreigners (more money for the treasury)—and when the people have no more funds to buy food, Joseph will take control of their flocks in Pharaoh's name, for Pharaoh's purse, in payment for food. Not being an Egyptian, Joseph will have authority only as given by Pharaoh and will not be a threat. In fact, Joseph lives "so close" to Pharaoh, and under such surveillance, that whatever occurs in Joseph's home is immediately heard in Pharaoh's palace. Thus, Pharaoh gains in many ways—no wonder he moves quickly to place Joseph in charge.

Yes, Joseph gains as well. Unknown to Pharaoh, Joseph will be able to save his family and continue the unfolding of God's plans as revealed to Abraham. Jacob and his family would be permitted to live in Egypt only because of Joseph's position and eminence. Surely we can understand Joseph's statement later to his brothers, "GOD HAS SENT ME HERE לְמִחְיָה L'MIHYAH—TO SAVE AND PRESERVE LIFE" [45.5]. "God has sent me ahead of you to insure your survival upon earth, and to save your lives in an extraordinary deliverance." Joseph not only understood the message of the dreams, he was able to dig deeper and understand the message for himself, his family and the future of the Jewish people who would emerge in Egypt.

So often we can see the danger signs—what is coming down the pike—and we know that there will be very real problems. Sometimes it is intuitive, or we "see" something, or we put the signs together in our minds. But what do we do? Here emerges the true challenge. Joseph could see, "This is what God is going to do. Now this is what we need to do." Surely this is a test of leadership and of human capacity—to face crises and respond with a plan that is לְמִחְיָה l'mihyah—lifesaving, sustaining and preserving.

Joseph perceived this imminent crisis. He defined the problem and came up with a unified, comprehensive answer and a plan of action. He persuaded and convinced those in power that it was in their best interest, as well as the common good, to accept and use this plan of action. Joseph then was able and willing to undertake the task and to act on it. Ultimately, Joseph could succeed because, as he perceived so extraordinarily, it was a plan לְמִחְיָה l'mihyah—to preserve, affirm and sustain life. God's will becomes actualized through Joseph's life, skill, vision and action. Through human understanding, vision and behavior, we, too, can actualize God's will. This is what God is challenging us with and this is

---

tity as a link to Judaism. The kids have Jewish names but we do not know if they've had a Jewish upbringing. Except by the Reform Movement's 1983 acceptance of patrilineal descent (which requires a Jewish upbringing and identity, in addition to a Jewish father), there is no way that we know that these children are Jewish.

Jacob not only recognizes them fully as his family and heirs to a major lineage, but gives them the distinction of the special blessing of the children, regardless of the other issue of birth order. He shows that rather than rejecting interfaith couples and their children, we should go out of our way to help them to learn about Judaism and to make Jewish choices.

The special recognition of Ephraim and Menasseh helps reawaken or strengthen Joseph's Jewishness. The parallel today is the Jewish partner's reawakening and reeducation about Judaism and that partner's heightened Jewish identity while the interfaith couple explores Judaism. **Dennis and Linda Krauss, Co-Chairs of OUTREACH, Temple Society of Concord, Syracuse, NY**

what we need to do. Through Joseph's life, even through his own loneliness, sense of personal betrayal, frustration and pain, came a growing maturity, so that when this crucial time arrived he was able to respond. Then, when confronted with his brothers, he was able to struggle with and overcome the desire for revenge, and eventually reveal himself to them.

לְמִחְיָה *L'miḥyah*—we too become agents for life, for its preservation and sustenance through our struggles, insights, painful transformations and what we do with the crises we face. The common cliché, "When given lemons in life, make lemonade" is all too true and challenging. No one escapes pain, no life is totally free from challenges. It is what we see and understand, and then what we do that makes all the difference—*l'miḥyah.*

Miketz

דְּבָר אַחֵר **DAVAR AḤER. Now THEY DID NOT KNOW THAT JOSEPH UNDERSTOOD, BECAUSE THERE WAS AN INTERPRETER BETWEEN THEM...**[Gen. 42.23]. In studying this parashah, I came across two things I hadn't known or thought about before. One has to do with Joseph's brothers speaking among themselves and thinking that Joseph could not understand them, assuming Joseph did not understand Hebrew. The interpreter has been identified as Joseph's son, Menasseh, so it's great to think that Joseph would have taught his son Hebrew and also that he maintained his Jewish identity as well during his time in Egypt. At this time of year when some Jews feel the pull of the "December Dilemma," Joseph is a good example. Also, for those of us who live outside of urban settings, it is a good lesson for our kids to know that not only can they maintain their Jewish identity, being in a small minority, but that they have Joseph to look up to as an example. **Mina Cohen, Mendocino Jewish Community, Mendocino, CA <mcohen@tcsgi.mhs.mendocino. k12.ca.us>**

דְּבָר אַחֵר **DAVAR AḤER. HE TURNED AWAY FROM THEM AND CRIED...[Gen. 42.24].** Rereading the story of Joseph, I have discovered how much I like our biblical forefather. Despite his sometimes questionable behavior and his deceit, Joseph is the most human character in *Bereshit*. He cries more often than any other character in the Bible. It's no accident that the term וַיֵּבְךְ *va-yevk*, "and he cried" appears seven times in this narrative. Joseph turns away and cries twice when he witnesses his brothers' personal turmoil and remorse [Gen. 42.24, 43.30]. He cries when he reveals his true identity to his family—first with his brother Benjamin [Gen. 45.14],

ויהי מקץ שנתים ימים ופרעה חלם

When we read and reread in Leviticus and Deuteronomy "A PERSON SHALL LIVE BY THEM" [Lev. 28.5] and "CHOOSE LIFE" [Deu. 30.19] we reflect more and more upon Joseph and his ultimate understanding *l'miḥyah*, for only when he gained that understanding could he serve as the pivotal agent in God's unfolding drama of our birth as a nation. In our personal familial and communal lives, as well as our lives as a people, we have to see the unity in the many, to come up with a vision, concrete goals and direction that are life-affirming. We need to develop the ability and possess the will to pursue action. By persuading others to join with us and in doing so, carry out the most ancient mandate לְמִחְיָה *l'mi-ḥyah*—to preserve and sustain life. ●

---

then with his other brothers [Gen. 45.55], and, finally, when he reunites with his father [46.29]. Joseph cries when his father dies [Gen. 50.1], and when his brothers demean themselves by lying to protect themselves from Joseph's vengeance [Gen. 50.17]. We find in this narrative tears of anger and self-pity, tears of catharsis and reconciliation, and tears of sorrow and loss. We ought to ask ourselves when and why we cry as we encounter Joseph's tears. Our tears are a measure of our humanity. Are we big enough to cry? Are we brave enough to share our tears with others? **Rabbi Mark Greenspan, Beth El Temple, Harrisburg, PA**

דָּבָר אַחֵר **DAVAR AḤER.** HE TURNED AWAY FROM THEM AND CRIED... [Gen. 42.24]. Rabbi Greenspan points out Joseph's crying and his humanity. It is not hard to imagine that he would cry at the emotional reunion with his brothers and later his father. But the Torah's description of each encounter is slightly different. The first time he cries [42.24] the Torah says he turns away from them and weeps. It is as if he has a lump in his throat, and is able to cry silently (behind their backs, as it were). The second time [43.30] when he sees Benjamin, he loses his composure and must leave the room and wash his face before returning. The third time, he is "no longer able to control himself" and can only command his attendants to depart before revealing himself. **Rabbi Elyse Goldstein, Director of Kolel: A Centre for Liberal Jewish Learning, Toronto, CANADA <Baruch_Sienna@mail.magic. com>**

Va-Yigash

Genesis 44.18–47.27

Rabbi Lawrence Kushner

Lawrence Kushner is rabbi at Congregation Beth El of the Sudbury River Valley, Sudbury, MA. He serves as an adjunct member of the faculty of the Hebrew Union College–Jewish Institute of Religion in New York. He has lectured widely on Jewish spirituality, and has written several books—*Honey from the Rock*, *God was in This Place* and *The Book of Words*, among others. All have been published by Jewish Lights, Woodstock, Vermont.

"Not You, But God"

The Joseph novella may be the first modern story: God (apparently) does nothing. Throughout the preceding hero narratives of Genesis and subsequent national miracle legends of Exodus, God is everywhere, telling people what to do, intervening in their affairs, suspending the laws of nature, klutzing up the plot.

But from Genesis 37 (two weeks ago) until the end of Genesis at chapter 50 (one week from now) God seems to be nowhere. God talks to no one, apparently lets folks do pretty much whatever they please, tolerates the caprice of natural law; literally, *does* nothing. And, in this week's parashah (surely the emotional zenith of the story if not of the Hebrew Bible itself), the secret is given. Indeed, only one character figures it out. He even tells everyone, but they, like most of us, are too caught up in the drama to realize what, as the kids say, "is coming down."

If we switch to a wide angle lens, we realize that the Joseph saga (the last thirteen chapters which constitute the final four parashiot of Genesis) functions as a kind of transition piece joining Genesis with Exodus. Its job is to get us down to Egypt. At the beginning of the

דְּבָר אַחֵר **DAVAR AHER. Then Judah approached him...** [Gen. 44.18]. Last Shabbat at services we were doing Peter Pitzele's thing, another adventure in Living Torah. All of a sudden, the Joseph story became an Agatha Christie moment. Standing at the border of Egypt, with the guards stopping us and finding the silver and the stolen cup, doubts began to surface. Most of the brothers suspected that Benjamin (the spoiled brat) had stolen it. After all, he was a Rachel kid, just like Joseph. Benjamin began guessing which of the brothers hated him most. By the time we got to the denouement, Judah's big speech, we were sure he was lying through his teeth. We have selfish, angry, double-crossing brothers—a real family—who manage to get it together and cry as one, anyway. The real miracle of the Joseph fam-

novella, when Jacob gives Joseph that beautiful coat, the Jews are a bunch of recalcitrant nomads living in the Promised Land in daily communication with God. By the first chapter of Exodus, they have become an enslaved nation of 600,000 souls, living in exile, who haven't had so much as a postcard from God in 400 years! Something seems to have happened.

And what has happened is "Joseph"—his agonizing descent into Egypt, his astonishing rise to power, his reconciliation with his family and finally their subsequent resettlement in Goshen. The characters in the tale are so consumed with trying to manipulate their fortunes that they all (like most of us, also) fail to notice what is really happening, not only around them but—and here is the key idea—through them and despite them. Nobody gets it. Nobody, that is, but Joseph. He even tells everyone

(several times), but they are too preoccupied to appreciate his discovery.

All the players remain stuck in their own convictions that no one is running anything but themselves. Joseph's brothers think they can get away with either killing or selling him. Reuben figures he can outwit them. Judah figures he can skip town without penalty. Potiphar's wife thinks she can have or destroy whomever she pleases. Even Joseph has been trying to manipulate his whole family (albeit by giving them all a second chance, this time by selling out his only remaining full brother, Benjamin, for the benign purpose of ascertaining if they have, indeed, made repentance). All of them are busy trying to manipulate the outcome of this (apparently) Godless plot, and they are all literally dumbfounded. This week, Joseph figures it out.

Synopsis: The Joseph story has now reached its climax with Judah's plea on behalf of his father. Joseph can no longer conceal his identity, and with Pharaoh's invitation, sends the brothers back to their father with instructions to return to Egypt with the entire family. Jacob sets off on the journey. A census is conducted. Jacob and Joseph reunite. Joseph instructs the brothers and his father about what to say when they meet Pharaoh. Joseph presents his agrarian policies.

---

ily is not his continued success—that often happens—but the reconciliation after the inevitable explosion. At the end, when Hercule Poirot does his big expose, the answer to the mystery came out "God did it." **From the Junior Congregation at Temple Israel in Orlando, FL**

דָּבָר אַחֵר **DAVAR AHER. I AM JOSEPH! IS MY FATHER STILL ALIVE?** [Gen. 45.3]. Although the *p'shat* is clear when Joseph asks "DOES MY FATHER STILL LIVE?," I suggested another reading of these three Hebrew words "עוֹד אָבִי חָי" *"od avi chai"* to a Bar Mitzvah. Joseph is telling his brothers that God (אָבִי *Avi*) still lives within him. Despite being away from his family and his home, Joseph has been able to thrive because God still

lives within him. When Joseph identifies himself to his brothers, he tells them the two most important things, his name, and the fact that he remains faithful to God, even while being isolated in Egypt for so many years. **Rabbi Bruce Greenbaum, Congregation Beth Israel**

Joseph sits there up on his throne (not just a political power, but also the power that comes from watching events from a high enough plane of vision). He watches his brothers, remembers his dreams, his father's dotage, Mrs. Potiphar, the dungeon. He listens as Judah (finally) "draws near," and realizes that something else has been going on all along. Suddenly the whole thing is clear: "IT WAS NOT YOU," he tells them, "WHO SENT ME HERE, BUT GOD! [Gen. 45.8]." He, in effect, says, "This is just the way things were meant to be from the very beginning. Now I understand that everything has to be just the way God had intended it all along. It's all been set up." But what could this mean?

Surely most of us believe in free will and in the importance of taking responsibility for our actions. Unfortunately, for logical consistency, most of us have also known moments when we felt as if we were permitted to survey our lives from such a high place that our freedom was revealed to be illusory. Such moments are as fleeting as they are awesome. They often coincide with the great religious passages of life, like Bar or Bat Mitzvah, marriage, or, God forbid, death. We realize that we were part of something much larger than our daily decisions. With or without our consent we, too, were players in a kind of divine scheme. Of course, it is preposterous, and it makes no rational sense, but for just a moment or two it is as if we rise to encounter our destiny. "IT WAS NOT YOU WHO SENT ME HERE, BUT GOD!"

God is to the world as our unconscious is to our everyday lives—quietly, invisibly, secretly guiding our steps, feeding us our lines, moving us into position, unifying everything we do. We are chastened to realize that what we thought an accident was, in truth, the hand of God. Most of the time we are simply unaware. Awareness takes too

Va-Yigash

דָּבָר אַחֵר **DAVAR AHER. I AM JOSEPH YOUR BROTHER WHOM YOU SOLD OUT INTO EGYPT. [Gen. 45.5].** Wisdom begins with the tale told truthfully: This is what happened ("I AM JOSEPH YOUR BROTHER WHOM YOU SOLD OUT INTO EGYPT." [Gen. 45.5]). In the telling of his own tale, Joseph rises above the events, above his own anger and hurt...he says, "DO NOT BE DISTRESSED OR REPROACH YOURSELVES BECAUSE YOU SOLD ME OUT, IT WAS TO SAVE LIFE THAT GOD SENT ME AHEAD OF YOU". The verb changes from "SOLD OUT" to "SENT" and the entire series of events is reconstrued for a higher purpose...Until he told his own story and squeezed it for its hidden Godliness, the higher truth of his own life had eluded him. Joseph is known in the Kabbalah as "the harvester," he is the one who harvests events to reap Truth. It is a surprise even to him. **Reb Stavisker** <Stavisker@aol.com>

much effort and, besides, it's more fun to pretend we are running the show. But every now and then we understand, for just a moment, that God has all along been involved in everything. Rabbi Zaddok HaKohen of Lublin taught that: "The first premise of faith is to believe with perfect faith that there is no such thing as happenstance...Every detail, small or great, they are all from the Holy One." Everything is organically, seamlessly joined to everything else and run by God, or perhaps simply *is* God.

Nowadays, the sacred usually masquerades as "coincidence." We become aware of some greater network of which we suddenly seem to have always been a part all along. We glimpse why we were created. The coincidences can take myriad forms. We can have the strange sensation of knowing why we were where we were years ago. We can suddenly sense the presence of a network of mutual interdependence binding us to others. Or, we can sim-

ply be shocked to discover that what we have been doing fits into some larger purpose. Coincidence is God's way of remaining anonymous. Among those of my generation, there is even a melody that we jokingly hum as a way of saying, "Something very big is happening and we have just had a glimpse." It is the theme song from the old television program *The Twilight Zone*.

Menahem Mendl of Kotzk offered the following misreading of another passage later on in this week's parashah, where, after having revealed his identity to his brothers and learning that his father was still alive, he dispatches them to Canaan to fetch the old man. The text says, "AND AS THEY LEFT HE SAID TO THEM, 'DON'T QUARREL ON THE WAY.'" The Hebrew for "ON THE WAY," is בַּדָּרֶךְ *ba-derekh*. But the preposition *ba*, in addition to "on" can also mean "with." "For this reason Joseph said to them, (suggests Kotzk) 'the hour of your arrival at your destination has been appointed by Heaven. If you hurry on

the way, you will only be delayed by some other reason. So don't quarrel *with* the way that has been appointed for you.'"

This does not mean that we give in and simply "go with the flow." Indeed, frequently, what is "set before us" to accomplish requires stubborn, solitary, courageous and "seemingly" autonomous action. But now we feel less fragmented than before. Now we understand the strange Talmudic maxim: "All is in the hands of Heaven, save the fear of Heaven." The only thing truly within our power, and our power alone, is whether or not we will behave each moment with arrogance or reverence. Beyond that, life goes on as before. The only difference is that now we do what we do with *yirat shamayim*, which I would translate as "grateful reverence" or perhaps even "amazing grace."

In this way, we begin to resolve the paradox created by our modern insistence that neither God nor any *deus ex machina* be allowed in the plot

---

דָּבָר אַחֵר **DAVAR AHER. AND (YOSEF) FELL ON THE NECK OF BINYAMIN HIS BROTHER AND CRIED. AND BINYAMIN CRIED ON (YOSEF'S) NECK.** [GEN. 45.14]. In observance of the Tenth of Teves here is one of my favorite thoughts. "AND HE FELL ON THE NECK OF BINYAMIN HIS BROTHER AND CRIED. AND BINYAMIN CRIED ON HIS NECK." Rashi comments that this joyful reunion was marked with tears because of future not-so-joyful historical events. Yosef "FELL ON THE NECK" and

"CRIED" two actions symbolic of the destruction of the two Holy Temples that were to be built in the land inherited by Binyamin. In turn, Binyamin "CRIED," one gesture symbolizing the destruction of the *Mishkan* (Tabernacle) in Shilo that was to be erected in land inherited by Ephraim. The *Me'am Loez* comments that Binyamin's tears were not over the destruction of the *Mishkan*, a temporary structure, but rather for the loss

of Jewish lives in connection with its destruction. One should always be reminded of these sad events even in the most joyful times...and it is for this reason that a glass...is broken in the *hupah*. **Dr. Jeffrey C. Ratz, Brooklyn, NY**

and our fleeting religious hunch that God may actually be running everything. In the final analysis, that may be the only difference between life and literature. For "In life," as Professor Uriel Simon of Bar Ilan University has taught, "unlike in literature, we cannot discern the hand of God." And in this week's parashah it is Joseph who now teaches his family and anyone else who cares to listen: "It was not you who sent me here, but the Holy One!"

Alas, there is one more curve ball. Not even Joseph understands how big this thing really is. He thinks God has used him to help his family win the lottery. But we (who have read the story since we were children) know better. We've already seen the movie. We know that his joyous "living in condos in the land of Goshen" is, alas, only the first chapter of what will yet become a tale of great oppression and agony before it is done, and ends "IN THE MIDST OF THE [RED] SEA ON DRY GROUND." As another theologian once observed: "It ain't all over 'til it's all over." ●

Va-Yigash

דָּבָר אַחֵר DAVAR AHER. THEY CAME TO EGYPT, JACOB AND ALL HIS OFFSPRING WITH HIM... [GEN. 46.6]. In this week's Torah portion, Joseph is reunited with his brother and father. The encounter is an emotional one, as they have not seen each other for 22 years. The rabbis criticize Joseph for not having made an effort to contact his father during these many years. They believe that he could have and should have made an effort to let him know that he was still alive, especially once he had risen to a position of prominence and means in Egypt. The reasons offered by our traditional commentators are rather unsatisfactory and really do not offer us any acceptable explanation or help us understand Joseph's silence. So let us further examine what happened to Joseph...Joseph was a victim of his brother's cruelty toward him. We know that victims are often ashamed and fear that in some way they may have been responsible for what was done to them. Perhaps this may help us to better understand Joseph. He knew that his boastfulness about his dreams was partly responsible for the antagonism felt by his brothers toward him. Like today's victims of abuse and harassment, he was embarrassed and could not speak about his fate. Yet Joseph's silence brought pain and loneliness to his father and caused him to remain cut off from his family. Perhaps one of the lessons we can learn from this week's Torah portion is how important it is for victims to reach out and not carry the burden of their shame by themselves. **Rabbi Stuart Weinblatt, Congregation B'nai Tzedek, Rockville, MD**

THE VISIT

December 25, 1974:
Parashat Va-Ye<u>h</u>i

In memory of my grandfather
Sholom Dovid ben Avrom Abba,
5648–5736

Va-Ye<u>h</u>i

Genesis
47.28—50.26

Marcia Falk

MARCIA FALK'S RECENT BOOKS
INCLUDE *THE SONG OF SONGS:*
A NEW TRANSLATION AND
INTERPRETATION (HARPER, SAN
FRANCISCO, 1990) AND *WITH*
TEETH IN THE EARTH, A TRANSLATION
OF YIDDISH POETRY OF MALKA
HEIFETZ TUSSMAN (WAYNE STATE
UNIVERSITY PRESS, 1992). HER
LATEST BOOK, *THE BOOK OF*
BLESSINGS: A RE-CREATION OF JEWISH
PRAYER FOR THE WEEKDAYS, THE
SABBATH, AND THE NEW MOON
FESTIVAL, WAS PUBLISHED BY
HARPER, SAN FRANCISCO IN 1995.

We park the car on Findlay
Avenue
and lock it,
take our bundles with us,
leave the suburbs behind.
We're back
at the doors beneath the sign:
Home of the Daughters of Jacob.
I enter and become
a daughter again.
Here, in the Bronx of my infancy,
the Bronx you never left, Grandpa,
Jacob is murmuring.
It's Christmas Day, and here
it's any Wednesday,
you're sitting at the desk,
expecting no one,
studying the portion for Shabbos—

Jacob lived in the land of Egypt sev-
enteen years
(I have been in exile twenty-seven of
my years)
so the whole age of Jacob
was one hundred forty-seven years
("I'm not old," you tell me)
"What are you reading, Grandpa?"
"<u>H</u>umesh. How's by you, Mama-leh?"
(You always called me that. Even now
when I stand a head taller than you,
I'm still your little mama, k'neyne-hore,
I should grow up to be a mother)
And the time grew near for Jacob to
die
"I'm not old, just my head is old"—
you pat the sores on your hairless skull
beneath the huge black yarmulke.
and he called his son Joseph
and said to him:
If I have found favor in your sight,
please, I pray you,
put your hand beneath my thigh,
and deal kindly
and truly
with me

דְּבַר אַחֵר **DAVAR A<u>H</u>ER. WHEN JACOB**
FINISHED INSTRUCTING HIS SONS, HE DREW HIS
FEET ONTO THE BED…[Gen. 49.33]. *Midrash*
Tan<u>h</u>uma introduces the *Shema* as
Jacob's children's response to him when
he worries about their loyalty to God.
Their response is an interesting one.
Why do they say, שְׁמַע יִשְׂרָאֵל *"Shema*
Yisrael?" After all, they are talking to their
father. Why not say, שְׁמַע אַבָּא *"Sh'ma*
Aba?" **T'shuvah**: After they told
Ya'acov/Yisrael that Yosef was still alive,

he realized that they had been lying to
him for 22 years, and that their story
about Yosef having been killed by an
animal was not true. This caused a dis-
tancing between him and his children—
hence they called him after that by his
formal name, and not the more loving
אַבָּא *"Aba."* There is also the question of
why does Ya'acov/Yisrael answer,
בָּרוּךְ שֵׁם *"Barukh Shem …"* quietly?
T'shuvah: In our discussion of this past
Shabbat, Al Rubin explained that

Samuel slides his hand
beneath the sheets,
throws me a look:
no one's changed the bed today.
"How're things, Grandpa?"
   Now what
will we say?
Should we speak the Yiddish
of your youth,
of the village—now dead—
that I never knew?
Or the Yiddish-English of the old
   Bronx
I've almost forgotten?
I would speak to you in street-
   corner Hebrew
but you've never walked the stones
that have burnt my feet,
and for you, it's a holy tongue.
At the desk in this tiny room
(suddenly I'm overgrown)
Jacob is talking to Joseph—
   Bury me not in Egypt,
   let me lie with my fathers—
   Swear to me!
(I swear it, Grandpa,
the Bronx was my home once,
but where are your fathers buried?

Do their bones ache like mine for
   Jerusalem?)
It's the end of Genesis, Joseph will
   die too
(What do you see in our faces?)
and Jacob tells the future of his
   sons:
Of the first-born Reuben, unstable
   as water,
of Simeon and Levi, whose swords
   were bitter,
and Judah, the lion's cub—
those white teeth and dark eyes
(I have my father's eyes, everyone
   says).
And of Zebulun who will dwell at
   the sea,
and Issachar, lover of the land,
and Dan, the serpent, who will
   judge.
And of Gad, who defeats the
   raiders,
and Asher, who will prosper,
and wild Naftali, the hind.
And Joseph, whose arms are made
   supple at the bow,
and Benjamin, the youngest, the
   wolf,

Va-Yehi

Ya'acov/Yisrael couldn't say it out loud since in Egypt the Pharaoh was considered the King. Had Ya'akov/Yisrael said it out loud he might have put himself and his children, including Yosef, in danger. In worrying about how his family will do when confronted by the foreign culture in which they found themselves, Ya'akov/Yisrael also tipped his hat to the reality of that experience. Have we not done that throughout the

centuries, and in what ways do we still do the same today? **Rabbi Michael Cohen, Israel Congregation, Manchester Center, VT**

דָּבָר אַחֵר **DAVAR AHER. YOUR FATHER GAVE ORDERS BEFORE HIS DEATH…[Gen. 50.16].** This last chapter in *Sidrat Va-Yehi*, and the entire book of Genesis, tells of the possible renewal of hostile relations between Joseph and his brothers. After Jacob

who devours his prey in the morning
and distributes the spoils at night.
It's almost dusk, and churchbells
from the street
penetrate the silence of the room.
"Tell me a story, Grandpa."
When will we hear of Jacob's
daughters?
Is this the history I must carve
with my life, with my hands
inscribe my own books,
prophesy my own fate?
"Azoy iz."
Daughter today, I would mother
and heal your sores if I could,

make supple your fingers, arched
like tiny bows
above the words in the Humesh
like the perfect silver pointers
they used in the old shul on
Shabbos.
Grandpa, what can I promise you?
Samuel looks at his watch: it's time.
You go down to shul for the afternoon prayers
and we leave for the street,
our coats wrapped around us,
and Jacob calling after us
as we descend into the darkening
Bronx. ●

Synopsis: Jacob is dying. Menasheh and Efraim are brought to Jacob who, in this blessing, switches hands. Joseph protests—but Jacob continues and blesses Efraim before Menasheh and finally, Joseph. Jacob gathers his sons to his side and offers what has been called Birkat Yaacov—the Blessing of Jacob. Jacob wants to be buried in the cave of Makhpelah—and after his death and appropriate mourning, Joseph, with Pharaoh's permission, returns to bury Jacob as he had been instructed. Again, the brothers engage in a display of complicated sibling behavior. Joseph lives 110 years and is buried in Egypt.

dies, Joseph seems to put distance between himself and them. The brothers are so afraid of Joseph that, to protect themselves, they lie about some last words of Jacob (see 50.16-17). Joseph's response (verses 19-20) is lukewarm at best. Rashi implies that, despite the family's new circumstances, all the brothers persist in behavior modes that they displayed in their youths. This scenario and commentary demonstrate how siblings often bring heavy baggage from their youth into so-called maturity, affecting their relationships throughout their lives. We're only kidding ourselves if we think these issues will simply disappear; only when we work at their resolution can true reconciliation take place. **Rabbi James R. Michaels, Temple Israel, Wilkes-Barre, PA**

Rabbi Stephen Robbins

Stephen Robbins serves as the rabbi of Congregation N'vay Shalom in Los Angeles, CA

Va-Ye<u>h</u>i

"God Meant It for Good"

In this week's Torah portion, the Book of Genesis (*Bereshit*) draws to a close and so does the first stage in the development of the religion and people of Israel. In the bulk of Genesis, the story of the birth of Judaism is told in stories of specific individuals and limited to a small group of families. It seems an unstable relationship at best for the presence of God and the future of Judaism to be in the hands of a few Patriarchs and Matriarchs. As the book ends, so does the patriarchal period. In this week's portion, we are being prepared for a fundamental change to take place in the nature of the leadership, faith and peoplehood of Israel.

This change is foreshadowed in Joseph. His personae and relationship to God defines the skills needed in the next stage—the Exodus. Joseph is not a patriarch. He never dialogues with God. He understands God's will by interpreting dreams and finding meaning in the significance of events and the direction by his own human struggle. And yet of all the personae in Genesis, he is the one most sure of himself, his faith and his God. While all of the Patriarchs and Matriarchs are conflicted with doubts about their relationship to God, Joseph's conflict is not with God but with himself and his inability to fulfill God's purpose.

After Jacob's death, Joseph's brothers fear that he will seek revenge. They plead forgiveness. Joseph weeps at their words, "AM I A SUBSTITUTE FOR GOD? ALTHOUGH YOU MEANT ME EVIL, GOD MEANT IT FOR GOOD...THE SURVIVAL OF MANY PEOPLE" [Gen. 50.17-20]. Once again they hurt him, doubting his integrity. He weeps not at his pain but theirs. Their fear comes from their inability to forgive themselves. In weeping for their continued pain and guilt, he seeks to remove their fear that he will use his power against them. Instead he uses it to heal them—"YOU MEANT IT FOR EVIL, GOD MEANT IT FOR GOOD." In the simplicity of these poignant words Joseph teaches us that a person of real faith is not trapped in bitterness by the past. He knows now his suffering was necessary for his growth. His faith is strengthened by his confidence that it was in God's service. Joseph's faith and devotion were forged from suffering and hardship that led ultimately to wisdom and understanding—true spiritual maturity.

Joseph learns the lesson of יִסוּרִין שֶׁל אַהֲבָה *Yisurin shel Ahavah*—"visitation of Divine love " [*Ber*, 5a] "WHOM THE LORD LOVES, HE REBUKES" [Prov. 3.12]. We usually see our sufferings as punishment, our pain the affirmation of our guilt. The more we suffer the more we cleanse the sin. Not so; it is not suffering that is required but that we learn by the pain what it is that is required of us. Pain shakes us from our self-delusions and denials so we see the real truths that await us. By our response to the suffering we are taught what we are made of. Those who run are beaten. Those who embrace the suf-

fering and rise above it find the message. God leaves messages about the purpose of our lives in His service. God seeks not to control and punish but to support and educate—both done by love. *Y'shurin shel Ahavah* teaches us that spiritual maturity comes through confrontation with the real hard issues of living. Joseph's faith was purchased with his pain. He crafted it out of the shell of his own suffering. It was not a faith of escape from his life but the faith that made his life worth living.

So the Joseph story closes Genesis. Unlike the Patriarchs and Matriarchs, who are larger than life, Joseph is someone we can all identify with. Each of us can learn from and aspire to be a Joseph. Joseph is no distant hero. He is "everyman" and "everywoman" upon whom God must rely to fulfill the partnership of faith—the *brit*—the covenant. ●

חֲזַק, חֲזַק, וְנִתְחַזֵּק
Hazak Hazak v'nit-Hazek

שמות

Shemot

DNA Analysts

The average height of young Chileans has increased by 6 inches in the past 50 years." (Dr. Fernando Monckeberg) *The Toronto Star*, March 21, 1992.

BUT MOSES SAID TO THE LORD, "PLEASE, O GOD, I HAVE NEVER BEEN A MAN OF WORDS, EITHER IN TIMES PAST OR NOW THAT YOU HAVE SPOKEN TO YOUR SERVANT; I AM SLOW OF SPEECH AND SLOW OF TONGUE." [NJPS Ex. 4.10] "THEY WON'T BELIEVE ME; THEY WON'T LISTEN TO MY VOICE. THEY WILL SAY, 'GOD DIDN'T APPEAR TO YOU.'" [Ex. 4.1]

Shemot
Exodus 1.1–6.1

Danny Siegel

DANNY SIEGEL IS A FREE-LANCE TEACHER, POET AND AUTHOR, AND TZEDAKAH ACTIVIST LIVING IN ROCKVILLE, MD. HE IS THE FOUNDER AND CHAIRMAN OF ZIV TZEDAKAH FUND, INC. AMONG HIS LATEST PUBLICATIONS ARE *TELL ME A MITZVAH*, CHILDREN'S TZEDAKAH STORIES AND *A HEARING HEART*, A VOLUME OF POETRY.

Of course the Children of Israel wouldn't believe Moses. The people would wonder why anyone with a stutter, slur or mumbling pattern of speech—or whose words came so slowly that it was agony to listen—would be chosen as Leader and Teacher רַבִּי [*Rabbi*]. What kind of diplomat could possibly succeed if he or she couldn't put a sentence together without visible strain? The people would whisper in their hovels and justifiably so—"This must be some kind of joke."

Here are some answers that students have given as to why Moses, of all people, should have a speech impediment:

(1) It is a constant reminder to Moses and the people that no one is perfect, so that there is no danger of mistaking Moses for some supernatural or divine being. By the same midrashic line, it teaches the lesson that humility is an absolutely essential quality for leaders. As the Torah

דָּבָר אַחֵר **DAVAR AHER. AND THESE ARE THE NAMES...[EX. 1.1].** The conjunction of Winter Solstice and the Book of Exodus is startling. It makes perfect sense to face a new Pharaoh, the one who does not remember, on the shortest day of the year. It feels very Greek, very mythic, very Persephone. We've eaten our six pomegranate seeds. The Death of Joseph feels like the end of autumn. The last leaf falls

from the trees. We get our tribal blessing and cocoon our way through the coming cold. Spring feels a long way away.

Amid the end-of-school parties, vacation plans, the slow unwinding of our schedules of learning, the deconstruction of our weekly rhythms of Torah, we know that the period of darkness is coming. Torah tells its story of the winter of the human soul as the weather

states later on, "MOSES WAS VERY HUM-BLE, MORE HUMBLE THAN ANY PERSON ON EARTH." [Num. 12.30].

(2) One must listen much more carefully to catch the meaning of the words. (Someone once told me—though I can't say for sure it is true—that Chaim Weizmann always spoke very softly, so people would have to pay closer attention.)

(3) No one could accuse the Jews of accepting the Torah because Moses was a dazzling speaker. On the contrary, Moses' inarticulate mumblings prove it was *the content* of the Torah, not the mode of delivery, that moved them to say, "WE WILL DO AND WE WILL LISTEN." [Ex. 24.7] (Professor Saul Lieberman ז"ל)

(4) This would cause Moses and his brother, Aaron, to become particularly close, since Aaron would actually speak Moses' words to Pharaoh.

Reply: Not always true. Imagine Moses, alone, coming down the mountain, proclaiming just one phrase of the Ten Commandments.

Reply #2: Danger of pathological dependency. As students of Torah, we must review all cases where Moses did it himself, spoke God's words and his own himself, did what he had to do without using Aaron. That is one reason why blind people should own their own automobiles.

(5) It is living proof of the ability of disabled individuals to succeed.

Reply: This can sound patronizing.

Reply #2: True, but only sometimes. Not *everyone* has a success story. We never read about the others in the newspapers. Still, there is much to learn from the winners.

Our job in life is: (1) to question diagnoses, and (2) to try *all* methods, *absolutely all* methods to differentiate between genetically-caused or trauma-induced limitations and false or temporary

Synopsis: "And these are the names of the children of Israel" is how the book of Exodus begins, linking God's promises to the ancestors to the oppression and slavery in Egypt. A new king arises who has no link to the Jewish past—but perceives the Jewish people as a threat to national security. Forced labor is decreed and when that proves inadequate, the killing of male infants is demanded. Shifrah and Puah save many infants. Moses is born and the famous story of his saving by the daughter of Pharaoh leads us to a full appreciation, by various stories, of the person Moses. Moses marries Tziporah and she gives birth to Gershon. While shepherding, Moses encounters God at the burning bush and he is called upon to lead the people out of slavery. Three signs are offered and finally, Moses accepts his role and the first frustrating encounter with Pharaoh takes place.

forecasters do blizzard projections, as our institutions rig for silent running, as our institutional selves are getting dressed in our winter clothes. It will be a long time before we teach Passover. In the meantime, a lot of kids will miss school for many skiing trips. That, too, is Egypt. Exodus is the time of the night light. It is the time of repressing our night terror because a still, small light continues to burn, pushing back the darkness, reminding us that our parents are still close, that we, too, have within an eternal light.
Joel Lurie Grishaver <gris@tora-haura.com>

דְּבַר אַחֵר **DAVAR AHER.** THEY (THE MIDWIVES) FEARED (REVERED) G-D [EX. 1.17]. A member of my congregation recently described to me the question posed by her young grandson after he had visited Yad va-Shem. "Why didn't they help the Jews?" he plaintively asked. His grandmother's reply, in my opinion, was too dark, too absolute. "Because they were Jews," she said, "no one would help."

While rabbinic sources are of different minds as to the nationality of the heroic midwives, Shifra and Puah, I prefer to think of them as being non-Israelites. For this enables me to see them as prototypes of "righteous gentiles." "THEY FEARED (REVERED) G-D" the Torah teaches us [1.17]—which might

disabilities that can be eliminated through (a) the mitzvah of *tzedakah*, i.e., what is just and right, (b) love and care, (c) creative therapeutic techniques, and (d) constant reminders to ourselves that a certain percentage of the irreversible (17%?, 29%?, 68%?) is not irreversible.

I owe this insight to a very sensitive and bright 13-year-old young man, president of his day school student body, who described visits to the local residence for elders. They visit, they talk, they listen, they sing and entertain, but underneath it all, as he described it, is that most of them are "gone," irrevocably condemned to a zombie-like state. He is wrong. Until everyone involved in the lives of those elders reassesses which ones are absolutely irreparably *biologically* damaged, the 13-year old's job is to discover and develop any and all methods to bring out the best, most glorious, most noble aspects of their beings back into the light of day.

We need to find out what is caused by weak or damaged genes, cellular degeneration, poor nutrition, and depression, loneliness or uselessness, so we can proceed accordingly with the appropriate acts of *Tikkun olam*—fixing things. That's our job, no less than the physician's or the psychologist's.

Three Well-Known Examples:

Helen Keller and Annie Sullivan.

The Special Olympics.

Wilma Rudolph, world record holder in the 1960s of the 100 and 200 meter dash…despite having a leg damaged in childhood, a leg supported by orthopedic braces. Her childhood reality included polio, scarlet fever, and double pneumonia.

We would do well to apply the First Rule of Special Education to all education and human interrelationships, namely: Look at the other person fairly and lovingly, discover by any and all methods what the person's abilities and talents are, and use any and all methods to

Shemot

mean they had that precious ability to see the image of G-d in every human being and so were unable to obey the dictates of power.

I think that a young boy would have been better served, after his Yad va-Shem initiation into Jewish reality, by being told that some, albeit not enough, non-Jews responded appropriately. This is a message kept alive in the opening chapter of *Shemot*. It is a message

which can help keep despair at bay and that can help us as we struggle to see ourselves as potential "MID-WIVES," alert to opportunities to serve others by "FEARING G-D." **Rabbi Elias J. Lieberman, Falmouth, MA**

דְּבָר אַחֵר **DAVAR AHER.** SHE SENT HER MAIDSERVANTS AND SHE TOOK IT…[Ex. 2.5]. A hearty *yashir koah* to Danny Siegel on his beautiful Midrash via the work of Dr.

actualize those abilities and talents. That is, always seek out the glorious soul within, the נוטע נשמה, *gutte neshumah*, the good, sweet, divinely-given soul of which all human grace and poetry spring.

We should buck the trend of complicating terminology. On resumés, on tax forms, on applications, and when referring to ourselves, we should write and say, "teacher." There is really no need for the word "educator" or "pedagogic specialist." Making it longer doesn't help. Think of the medical term P.I.E.—pyrexia of indeterminate etiology—compared to F.U.O.—fever of unknown origin. If it was good enough for Moses to be called רַבֵּנוּ *Rabbenu*, Our Teacher, it should be good enough for us. Indeed, we would do well to consider that, of all the descriptive titles the Talmud and Midrash could have given Moses—Our Leader, Our Prophet, Our Liberator—they chose רַבֵּנוּ *Rabbenu*, Our Teacher.

And so, it would seem that what we might want to be when we grow up is a teacher, the one who reveals all that is hidden in the human soul, reveals the grandeur and glory to the person himself or herself and to all others who would meet that human being in the course of a natural lifetime.

Why young Chileans are 6 inches taller than they were in the 1950s:

Suppose you and a friend are traveling through Scandinavia. At some point, perhaps while savoring the herring in Reykjavik or Oslo, you might remark on the striking height and build of the Icelanders or Norwegians. Finishing the meal with some unusually tasty flatbread, you might add, "What marvelous genes these folks have!" Suppose you and a friend are on vacation, strolling around Santiago or Valparaiso or Antofagasta. You might never remark, "How short the children are compared to ours in America!"

…because Dr. Fernando Monckeberg set up infant nutrition centers throughout Chile.

…because Dr. Fernando Monckeberg established a system of intensive treatment centers for infants throughout the country.

דָּבָר אַחֵר **DAVAR AHER.** Another statistic: Whereas in the 1950s more than two-thirds of Chile's children age 6 and younger were undernourished and mentally damaged, today, about 8% are undernourished, most of them to a mild degree.

דָּבָר אַחֵר **DAVAR AHER.** Another statistic: In the 1950s, the infant mortality rate in Chile was more than 130 deaths/1,000 live births. Today it is less than 16/1,000.

Let us, then, consider, all those Chileans in their early and mid-childhood, their teens, 20s, 30s and 40s who are bright, active, animated citizens, because of the good Dr. Monckeberg. Let us, then, consider all those Chileans in their early and mid-childhood, teens, 20s, 30s, and 40s who might not be alive today at all were it not for the wise Dr. Monckeberg who suspected all along it wasn't in the genes at all. And so,

Monckeberg in Chile! By way of adding *hizuk* to this illustration, allow me to share the following midrash on the narrative where Pharaoh's daughter discovers the reed basket containing the Hebrew infant.

The *p'shat* of the text relates that the princess sent forth her אֲמָתָהּ (*amah-tah*) "HANDMAID" to fetch the basket from the water. Rashi, however, in a discussion in Tractate *Sotah, drashes*

the Hebrew אֲמָתָהּ to mean not a separate person, but rather the princess' own hand—by means of a miracle, her hand was elongated by several אַמּוֹת (*amot*) "HANDBREATHS"—and thus she rescued the child herself. The Kotzker Rebbe adds to this elucidation a touching moral: Even though we as mortals are "shorthanded" in our respective abilities to achieve great things, we are nonetheless obliged to stretch forth our hands

and, with God's help, our endeavors of *hesed* will not be denied their fulfillment. **Rabbi Bernard Gerson, Cong. Rodef Shalom, Denver, CO**

דָּבָר אַחֵר **DAVAR AHER.** SHE SENT HER MAIDSERVANTS AND SHE TOOK IT…[EX. 2.5]. For almost three decades, I have worked in developing countries on questions of health, nutrition and education. So, you can imagine how thrilled I was to see Danny Siegel's

what we might want to be when we grow up is a Fernando Monckeberg.

דָּבָר אַחֵר **DAVAR AḤER.** Rachel, according to those who knew her, died at age 100. Born in Kurdistan, she came to Jerusalem many years before she died, perhaps in the late 1940s or early 1950s. In her old age, for reasons unknown to me, she became one of Jerusalem's street beggars. Into her 80s she sat there, hand extended, rattling her coins to get the attention of passers-by. Sometime during this period, Myriam Mendilow, God rest her awesome soul, came along and put Rachel to work at *LifeLine for the Old*. She made ceramic beads that became beautiful jewelry. Hundreds, perhaps thousands, of Jerusalemites and tourists from around the world wear jewelry fashioned by her ancient hands. This is what Mrs. Mendilow wrote to me a number of years ago, "I regret to inform you that we lost Rachel, from Ceramics. She was 100 years old when she died—she just lay down and fell asleep forever. For me, she represented the story of *LifeLine*. I shall always remember her. From a beggar in the streets, we made of her an honourable and beautiful citizen." She might have lived her last years and died a nobody, just another beggar whose body was found one day in her room by some neighbor. No one would have noticed. No one would have missed her. That is why, when we grow up, we might want to become a Myriam Mendilow.

When our young Moses's voice says, "THEY WON'T BELIEVE ME; THEY WON'T LISTEN TO MY VOICE" [Ex. 4.1] the good Dr. Monckeberg and Myriam provide us with our answer! ●

Shemot

reference to Dr. Monckeberg and the dramatic nutritional improvement that has been achieved in Chile. However, I'd like to offer a somewhat different interpretation of events there, the one that prevails in the professional literature…simply put, it is that the impressive gains in the nutritional status of Chilean children are not the work of one great man acting alone. Instead, it is the product of partnership and self-help among everyday Chileans whose individual sparks joined together to usher in a better future for their children. To be sure, Dr. Monckeberg is a worthy leader; but his accomplishment was to create coalition, consensus, and connectedness on behalf of a worthy goal. He knew, in other words, that true *tikkun olam* can only occur when we enter into partnership both with God and our fellow planet-dwellers. **Beryl Levinger, Senior Director for International Programs, Education Development Center < BerylL@edc.org >**

אלה שמות בני ישראל הבאים מצרימה

Debbie Friedman

DEBBIE FRIEDMAN IS AN INTERNA-
TIONALLY ACCLAIMED SINGER AND
SONGWRITER ACTIVE IN VARIOUS
AREAS OF JEWISH EDUCATION AND
SYNAGOGUE LIFE.

Shemot

Dear Mom,

You won't believe this but the other day while I was working with the sheep, I came upon a bush that was consumed in flames. For as long as I was watching, nothing happened to that bush. Then I heard my name being called. All the other shepherds had the day off, so I knew that it was not one of them calling me, and it wasn't the sheep, because sheep don't talk. I came closer to the bush and turned to stare at it and the voice called again and said, "MOSES, MOSES." [Ex. 3.4]

I answered, "I AM HERE." [ibid]

TAKE OFF YOUR SHOES, YOU ARE STANDING ON HOLY GROUND! I AM THE G-D OF ABRAHAM AND SARAH, THE G-D OF ISAAC AND REBECCA, AND THE G-D OF JACOB, RACHEL AND LEAH. [Ex. 3.6]

Mom, I was so embarrassed that I was not aware that this was G-d talking to me, that I hid my face. G-d told me that even though I had been a stranger in a strange land, I was not a stranger to G-d. G-d said, "I've been watching you and the Israelites as well. I know how miserable they are. This bondage is really a problem. You must lead them to their freedom, Moses."

I said, "G-d, why is it that you want me to do this job.? What makes you think that I can do it? And furthermore, how can I explain who sent me?" [Ex. 3.13]

G-d said, "Look, MOSES, MY NAME IS 'I AM THAT I AM.' YOU TELL THE ISRAELITES THAT 'I AM' SENT YOU." [Ex. 3.14]

Then G-d said, "I AM THAT I AM" is about Me and only Me. I am all that there is and can be. I exist in every living thing, I am present in all places and at all times. I have revealed a part of Me as a

דָּבָר אַחֵר **DAVAR AHER. SHE SENT HER MAIDSERVANTS AND SHE TOOK IT… [Ex. 2.5].** Danny Siegel's piece was a boost for those of us who tilt towards the behavioristic/behavior modification end of the psychological spectrum. And I cannot help but think how appropriate Moses is as the example of one who has a disability to overcome. I always felt that despite the need to be sensitive to the needs and *natures* of each individual, it is our duty

as educators to stress the pre-eminence of the *nurture* side of the equation—that what matters most is what we do now; how students can make the most of the opportunities to learn that are right in front of them. We behavior modification people often get a bad rap for trying to force everyone into a set form or mold, but there is a spir-itual truth to us as well—the truth of transcending confining limitations, of transformation.

model for humans. That is the "I AM" piece of Me. The part that allows each human being to acknowledge their intrinsic compassion and understanding, gentleness and kindness, and all like qualities which cannot be seen, bought or pretended in this life.

And, "Moses," G-d said, "I AM" is a state of being. It is knowing that there is good and bad. "I AM" fills the space of "I AM HERE" by giving a quality of substance and meaning. "I am" is what fills the "I am here" with awareness and consciousness and otherness. It is what pushes our minds and hearts to recognize what exists beyond human limitations. It is the "I am here" that sees that we are in *Mitzrayim*. It is the "I am" that gives us the courage to move out of bondage and into freedom."

Mom, G-d wants me for this job. G-d believes we all have the capacity to reach inside of ourselves to find the resources to fill our presence with *kedushah*. We will know that we are on the right track when we begin our experience in moments of beyondness and otherness in our lives. Then we will taste our freedom and we will learn to see that miracles are not some distant fantasy, but ever present in our every day lives.

I must go now. Stay in touch. I will speak with you after I get them out of Egypt. I'll call you when I get there, or maybe you'd like to go with us?

Love, Mo ●

Shemot

I often find this spirituality represented in the Torah-centered outlook of the leaders of the *Misnaggedim*, the great "halakhic men." What one author I read remembered most about Slobodka Yeshiva was that it was an atmosphere that encouraged all its students to aspire to greatness, to fulfill their potential. R. Soloveichik writes that the essence of *teshuvah* is the assumption of a totally new identity: The *grace of repentance* allows the 'old me' to die and be left behind so that the 'new me' is no longer bound by past hindrances.'

This is 180 degrees from the Hasidic view of the first Lubavitcher Rebbe, which is that *teshuvah* is a return to oneself, to one's true inner spiritual identity, and that in study and changing behavior one is simply shedding the external masks and costumes that obscure it, clothing it instead in proper forms and behaviors which bring out its true colors. The Hasidic view is represented in Debbie Friedman's article, in the reaching inside ourselves to find the "I am" (I enjoyed the contrast!). Of course, in this as well as other "arguments for the sake of Heaven," the real truth lies in the unity of the bipolar dialectic. *Tayku*!

Hazan Ira Rohde, Cong. Shearith Israel, NewYork, NY <75610.1722@compuserve.com>

אלה שמות בני ישראל הבאים מצרימה

דָּבָר אַחֵר. DAVAR AHER. AND SHE BORE HIM A SON AND HE CALLED HIS NAME GERSHOM: FOR HE SAID, I HAVE BEEN A STRANGER IN A STRANGE LAND. [Ex. 2.22]. A beautiful *davar* was told to me by a patient named Rabbi Elimelech Laufer concerning Moshe's two sons. He taught: We are not told the name of Moshe's second son until *parashat Yitro* when once again the Torah [18.3] writes about Gershom and in 18.4 the Torah writes "AND THE NAME OF THE OTHER WAS ELIEZER; FOR 'THE G-D OF MY FATHERS, SAID HE, WAS MINE AND DELIVERED ME FROM THE SWORD OF PHARAOH.'" Rabbi Laufer asks two questions. The first: Why was it necessary for the Torah to repeat the name and purpose of Gershom twice and Eliezer just once? And the second question: If we follow the proper order of events, doesn't it seem that Moshe's two sons were named out of order?

Rabbi Laufer's answer to both questions first alludes to the fact that after Ya'akov wrestled with the angel, the Torah says "AND AS HE PASSED OVER PENUEL THE SUN ROSE UPON HIM, AND HE HALTED UPON HIS THIGH." [Gen. 32.31] In the literal sense Rabbi Laufer comments that in good times we, the Jewish people, see the extent of our injuries. It's during the good times "WHEN THE SUN RISES" that assimilation is rampant and we forget our roots. But during the dark times—the times of slavery in Egypt, pogroms in Europe, the Warsaw ghetto and the Holocaust—we Jews band together, remembering our roots and heritage and focusing on the right purpose.

Rabbi Laufer concludes that Moshe understood these lessons in naming his sons. Without Torah we Jews are "STRANGERS IN A STRANGE LAND" [Ex. 2.22]. We must always remember the dark periods during the good times and focus on what makes our religion special. Once we accomplish this feat, only then will the G-d of our fathers save us from our enemies. **Dr. Jeffrey C. Ratz, Brooklyn, NY**

דָּבָר אַחֵר. DAVAR AHER. GOD HEARD THEIR MOANING…[Ex. 2.24]. At a weekly Torah study session on *Shemot*, a congregant offered a beautiful insight on Exodus 5.6-23, where Pharaoh responds to Moses by denying straw to the Israelite slaves, thus making their work even more difficult. In one current Reform Haggadah, we are taught that when "GOD HEARD THEIR MOANING" [2.24], God actually was responding to their silence: "When the Israelites had grown accustomed to their tasks, when the Hebrews began to labor without complaint, then God knew it was time to be liberated" (CCAR, *A Passover Haggadah*). The first step toward redemption, therefore, was for God to cause Pharaoh to increase their labor so that the Israelites would again cry out. In other words, God decided to rescue us when slavery began to be tolerable. The first step was to teach us, again, that slavery is never tolerable. **Rabbi Michael Joseph, with thanks to Mr. Leon Saslaw**

דָּבָר אַחֵר. DAVAR AHER. I WILL TURN AWAY AND SEE THIS GREAT SIGHT, WHY THE BUSH IS NOT CONSUMED. [Ex. 3.3]. It is said that the Ba'al Shem Tov derived a lesson in *teshuvah* from the episode of the burning bush. In Exodus 3.3, Moses says, "I WILL TURN AWAY AND SEE THIS GREAT SIGHT, WHY THE BUSH IS NOT CONSUMED." Moses has an audience with God and turns away? Unusual word "TURN AWAY"—(check out Rashi!). Rashi writes "turn away here and come close there." This is what *teshuvah* is, said the Baal Shem Tov, getting unstuck. It's about movement and transformation, it's not about arriving, but about approaching; it's not about destinations but about journeys; not about arrivals at all, but about roads; not about achieving, but about being; not about performance, but about effort; to move from here and come close to there. It's not even about sin, it's about change. We celebrate the journey when we make *teshuvah*. When we lose our way, we are taught that the right path calls us back, when we lose our way the roads go into mourning. This is especially true of the hard case scenario, of every difficult transformation, every startling *teshuvah*. One moment to the next might conceal the transformation that is possible for everyone. We tend to think of *teshuvah* like the Rambam and Rabbeinu Yona, as deep and methodical and sequential, but the Zohar tells us it can happen "in a moment." This means that you never give up on anyone. This means that the possibilities for repair and reconciliation, transformation and reclamation, *teshuvah*, are always present. You never give up on anyone. Especially the hard case stories. I am such a story. If I could get it, anybody could get it. **Reb Stavisker (James Stone Goodman) <Stavisker@aol.com>**

Shemot

דָּבָר אַחֵר **DAVAR AHER. I AM** *KAVED* (heavy/hard) OF MOUTH AND *KAVED* OF SPEECH. [Ex. 4.10]. Danny Siegel comments regarding Moses' speech impediment, i.e., his being כְּבַד פֶּה *k'vad peh,* and he offers several conjectures as to the function of this disability. Siegel then argues that the commandment of *tzedakah* is the covenantal instrument by which individuals and societies might overcome unfortunate disabilities. However, one might also conjecture that the entire Torah may be taken as the Divinely-approved ordering instrument by which the primordial chaos might be overcome. Siegel also cites the late Prof. Saul Lieberman, ז"ל, who contends that Moses' imperfect speech forces the listener to address the content rather than the mode of delivery. It is this insight that best illustrates Exodus' narrative intent.

Pharaoh ruled his society as an autocrat. Pharaohs could, according to the Biblical account, take women as they willed, condemn children to death, and even stand on water. According to the ancient Egyptian belief, Pharaoh was, in life, the incarnation of the god Horus. (His power is premised upon his charisma.) In Israel, Moses is the transmitter of the Law, not the Giver of the Law. Moses is the most modest of men, not the favored elect of God. Moses was chosen because he sought right rather than might, and as a consequence, he emerged as the most appropriate transmitter of the divine law that explicitly denies authority to charismatics who impute divine sanction to selfish, subjective inventions and intentions. *Tzedakah* is one important command among many, and is an instrument whereby humankind may fix that which is broken in the world. But, just as no human being possesses divinely-authorized charisma, no commandment possesses magical qualities which raises it above other commands. **Rabbi Alan J. Yuter, Congregation Israel, Springfield, NJ and Assistant Professor, Judaic Studies, Touro College, NY**

דָּבָר אַחֵר **DAVAR AHER. AND IT CAME TO PASS ON THE WAY AT THE LODGING-PLACE, THAT THE LORD MET HIM, AND SOUGHT TO KILL HIM. THEN ZIPPORAH TOOK A FLINT AND CUT OFF HER SON'S FORESKIN, AND TOUCHED MOSES' FEET WITH IT, AND SAID, "SURELY YOU ARE A BRIDEGROOM OF BLOOD TO ME!" [Ex. 4.24-6].** The man was walking at a faster pace than the beast that was all but buried under its load: the woman, the two children, and the most minimal necessities for travel. They were two days on the way and he was still out in front, traveling as if alone, placing his staff firmly onto the sandy ground before his feet, with no more regard for the sheep that occasionally brushed against his legs than he had for the woman trailing behind him on the ass. Looking at him, Zipporah was as tired as she had ever been in her life.

She did not want to complain. Moses was indefatigable, that she knew. He would keep on marching toward his goal without ever stopping to rest, without ever stopping to think that nursing two babies and keeping them pacified on a clumsy-gaited donkey was also a challenge. He kept his eyes straight ahead, scanning the now dimly lit horizon for dangers, whether to him or to all she was not sure. She wondered what she was doing, trudging through the Wilderness of Paran like a nomad when she might still have been lazing in her father's comfortable courtyard in Midian, had he not, in one of the outbursts of excessive hospitality by which he demonstrated his importance, given her to the courtly Egyptian who was now her husband.

Courtly Egyptian, indeed, she laughed to herself. Courtly Egyptians don't give up the luxuries of gilded palaces for the desolation of Midian simply for the pleasure of tending sheep in a strange land! Had her father invited her opinion, she would have told him a thing or two. She was not taken in by the handsome good looks, the royal demeanor. There was more to this Moses than met the eye, she would have said. He had an intensity that had startled her, yes, and pleased her too the first time that he spoke to her, but she had seen something strange about him long before he started disappearing into the mountains for days on end. To "get instruction from God," he said. The man was a zealot. What was she doing trailing behind him?

"Moses," she called out. "Have some mercy on me. I ache all over. In case you have forgotten, let me remind you that it was just before the new moon that I gave birth to a child. We are near the well-place. Let us stop and seek lodging for the night."

"There is no stopping now," he countered, turning his head to face her and falling into pace with the animal. "If you were not up to making this journey, you should have remained back. This is no idle mission on my part, you know, that I can perform or not as the mood strikes me. I have given God my word to go back to Egypt, to redeem my people out of slavery, and to do so in haste. The schedule is not mine to alter. We must keep going."

She felt herself becoming angry. "It will be no credit to you to arrive in Egypt with a donkey laden with corpses."

Her voice rose and her temper flared. "Could you perhaps think of me for a change, and this baby that you have barely seen? He is yours, you know, and yours to name, even though you found it necessary to be on one of your excursions onto the mountain when my time came to deliver, and have since barely found a moment to look at him. Stop now for an instant and look at him, you single-minded, hard-hearted, self-appointed...."

She fell into silence as she saw him stop suddenly, his hand clutching his chest.

"What is it," she cried. "What ails you, my husband?"

He fell to the ground. She slipped quickly down from her mount and bent over his body. He was pale and shivering. "The covenant," he muttered. His face was twisted with pain as he spoke. "I ignored the covenant God made with Abraham. The new one has not been circumcised, and I must die."

"You are a fool!" She screamed, jumping to her feet. "One does not ignore babies, or the commands of gods!"

In a series of swift motions, she laid the infant on the ground, unwrapped his swaddling clothes, and, with a deftness inspired by her rising emotions, withdrew a flintstone from a bag tied around her waist and used it to remove the tender foreskin of her infant son.

"There! Take that for your God!" She hurled the tiny piece of bloody flesh at his feet. "Is that too much for you to handle? Can you do that much for your son? To protect his safety?" She was shrieking. "Pay attention to me. For surely you are now a bridegroom of blood to me."

Silent still, Moses held the speck of flesh aloft and rose to his feet. She saw that his face was glowing again, that he was well again, and her anger subsided. When she spoke again, she was calm.

"My calling you a bridegroom of blood is just a way of speaking, my husband, a way of saying we are now linked by blood, by means of the circumcision. You can see now that I am as good as a blood relative, that I will always be bound to you by blood. You cannot get away from that, and neither can I."

He faced her now, looked into her eyes. "Nor would I want to. You have saved me, and set me on the right path. I will not forget that. But I can delay no longer."

She watched as Moses resumed his interrupted trek to Egypt, then turned back to Midian to allow the baby to heal in the comfort of her father's household. **Miriam Raskin, Central Reform Congregation, St. Louis, MO**

Va-Era

Exodus 6.2–9.35

Rabbi Harold S. Kushner

RABBI HAROLD S. KUSHNER IS RABBI LAUREATE OF TEMPLE ISRAEL OF NATICK, MA, AND THE AUTHOR OF *WHEN BAD THINGS HAPPEN TO GOOD PEOPLE, WHEN CHILDREN ASK ABOUT GOD,* AND *WHEN EVERYTHING YOU'VE ALWAYS WANTED ISN'T ENOUGH.* HIS LATEST BOOK IS *HOW GOOD DO WE HAVE TO BE? A NEW UNDERSTAING OF GUILT AND FORGIVENESS,* PUBLISHED BY LITTLE, BROWN AND CO.

MIRACLES AND MAGIC

The confrontation between Moses and Pharaoh in parashat Va-Era is more than a confrontation between two strong-willed men, more than a showdown between two ways of life, the Egyptian commitment to a society based on slavery and the Israelites yearning for freedom. It is a confrontation between two kinds of religion, two ways of understanding the human being's relationship to God.

A century ago, Sir James Frazer offered the classic definition of the distinction between religion and magic. Religion, he taught, was serving God; magic was using God. When Moses turns the water of the Nile into blood, he is obeying God's command as he does so. When Pharaoh's magicians turn water into blood, they are manipulating God/the gods to obey *their* command. The purpose of the Ten Plagues was to demonstrate God's power over humanity. The purpose of the magical acts performed by Pharaoh's courtiers was to demonstrate the power of clever men over the gods. (Indeed, why else would they take some of the small supply of potable water remaining in Egypt and render it undrinkable? Why would they respond to Moses' summoning up a plague of frogs by producing more frogs, when more frogs was the last thing Egypt needed, except to demonstrate their ability

---

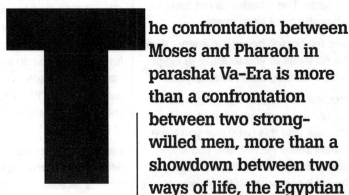

דָּבָר אַחֵר **DAVAR AHER. THEY WOULD NOT LISTEN TO MOSES BECAUSE OF AN IMPATIENT SPIRIT** *(mi-kotzer ruah)* **AND FROM HEAVY BONDAGE...[Ex. 6.9].** The portion *Va-Era* is dominated by the story of the plagues on Egypt and the great confrontation between Moses and Pharaoh. This contest of power over the fate of the Hebrew slaves was, in fact, no test of God's power; its ending was a foregone

conclusion. Pharaoh is not the problem. It is the Israelites themselves, who are unable to hear Moses' message. When Moses spoke, "THEY WOULD NOT LISTEN TO MOSES BECAUSE OF AN IMPATIENT SPIRIT *(mikotzer ruah)* AND FROM HEAVY BONDAGE" [Ex. 6.9]. The phrase מִקֹּצֶר רוּחַ *"mikotzer ruah,"* impatient spirit, described their spiritual bondage prior to their physical bondage. The word *"katzar"* in this

to make the gods do what they wanted?)

We know the outcome of the confrontation between Moses and Pharaoh. God's will prevailed, the Israelites went free, and Pharaoh, who began by saying, "I DO NOT KNOW THE LORD; WHY SHOULD I HEED HIM? [Ex. 5.2]" had to give in. But the confrontation between two competing understandings of religion, symbolized by the Biblical narrative, continues to this day. Does religion teach us to serve God, or does it teach us to use and manipulate God?

One of the forms magic-based religion takes is the assumption that the future has already been determined, that God knows the future, and that if we are clever enough, if we know the tricks, we can compel God to share that secret knowledge with us. When my hometown newspaper, most of whose pages reflect a liberal-intellectual approach to life, prints a daily horoscope, it is paying

homage to a magic-based view of religion: clever people can read God's mind and compel Him to reveal His secrets.

Many superstitions are rooted in the belief that there are forces more powerful than God, forces which God Himself is obliged to obey. If we know how to pronounce the right spells and perform the right rituals, we can compel God to do our will and give us the results we desire. More significantly, when people assume that because they have been ethically upright and ritually observant, God *owes* them good health and good fortune, their understanding of what it means to be religious veers dangerously in the direction of magic, doing what religion asks of us not out of love and loyalty, but as a way of controlling God's actions in response.

A colleague of mine, prompted by the statement in Deuteronomy 10.17 that God cannot be bribed, suggests that

Synopsis: *Starting with a reminder of the covenantal promises to our ancestors, God continues to promise to bring the people of Israel out of Egyptian slavery. After a bit of protest about a speech impediment, Moses, accompanied by Aaron, is to appear before Pharaoh. God foretells the outcome of these encounters. Moses and Aaron perform signs in Pharaoh's presence—but to no avail. The plagues begin. In this week's parashah: blood, frogs, vermin, swarms, pestilence, boils, and hail.*

case means to be cut off, shortened or limited. *"Ruah"* is a name for God and the word for spirit. They could not hear Moses' message because they were spiritually "cut off" from God. They did not recognize the ancient name of God as Moses called to them. It had been lost to them in their assimilation into the life and religion of Egypt. To them, their suffering slavery only validated the power of the Egyptian deities. They lost the attach-

ment with the God of Israel that could have sustained them. Worst of all, they had become idolators themselves, worshipping the Egyptian deities and acknowledging Pharaoh as divine.

The Midrash teaches us that they responded to Moses: "How can we serve two masters?Pharaoh will punish us." Tied to Pharaoh and in collusion with their spiritual slavery, they could not accept the God who would

free them. This was a greater bondage than the weight of their physical servitude. The problem facing Moses was how to reawaken and refocus the spiritual resources of his people so they could participate in their own liberation. They could not become free until they were willing to be free in body and spirit. The spiritual liberation was the prerequisite for the physical.

many religious people operate on the assumption that God can, indeed, be bribed. He recalls being invited to officiate at the wedding of the daughter of a prominent congregant in the backyard of the congregant's home. The wedding would be held outdoors, weather permitting, and would be moved indoors to a less comfortable setting if the weather turned unsuitable. About an hour before the ceremony, dark clouds gathered ominously overhead. The mother of the bride took a twenty dollar bill out of her purse, gave it to her husband and told him "Here, put this in the *pushke* (charity box) that it shouldn't rain." Forty-five minutes later, as the guests were being seated and the wedding party lined up, the clouds were even darker and more threatening. The bride's mother gave her husband another twenty dollars for charity. The wedding went off without a single raindrop to mar it. I am sure that woman believes it

was her *tzedakah* that controlled the weather, and will continue to believe it until someone she loves is seriously ill, when she will give a thousand dollars to charity and be very upset when God changes the rules on her.

It is very tempting to believe that our bribes, our behavior, can give us power over God, but there are two things wrong with that attitude. First, it doesn't work; God is not controlled to do our bidding, no matter what we do. And secondly, it is bad religion. To *use* God—to shore up our flagging self-esteem, to bring about a desired result, whether a boyfriend or a winning lottery ticket—is to make ourselves and our wishes primary and God secondary. Just as authentic Jewish prayer involves listening to God more than talking to Him, authentic Jewish religious behavior means trying to discern what God wants us to do, rather than trying to get God to do what we want Him to.

Va-Era

Moses does not understand his role. It is not Pharaoh whom he must convince. It is the people of Israel who must be taught that Pharaoh is no good, that all the Egyptian deities are lifeless stone and that their slavery is political oppression, not Pharaoh's divine will. The plagues serve as the device to teach that Pharaoh is only a man willing to sacrifice anything to keep up the charade of his own divinity. Moses

must become a god to dethrone a god. "SEE, I HAVE SET YOU AS A GOD BEFORE PHARAOH..." [Ex. 7.1]. Now we understand the enormity of Moses' role. In this strange verse God tells Moses that he must appear as God instead of Pharaoh, even replace Pharaoh as God. In their poverty of spirit the slaves could never understand the invisible God of *ruah* (spirit) Who called to them. They had become subservient to the

וארא אל אברהם אל יצחק ואל יעקב באל שדי

This is what bothers me about that loosely defined philosophy known as New Age thought. My problem is not that it imports elements of Buddhist theology and other Eastern thought. Its concept of karma is not that different from my grandmother's notion of *beshert*. My problem with New Age thought is that, though it tries to sound religious, it is all about *using* God, not serving God. It tends to see God as a kind of universal energy into which we can tap if we know the technique. Just as chemistry can cure your headache and physics can cook your dinner, divinity can help you be more cheerful and productive.

I miss the notion of a God who commands and demands. I believe that the essential feature of the God of the Torah, that which distinguishes Him from the pagan gods, is that He takes humanity seriously enough to enter into a covenant with us, to expect us to uphold our share of the agreement by meeting His expectations, rather than treating humanity as infants whose needs have to be met whenever they cry. And we respond to that summons because at some level, we *want* to be taken seriously as moral beings. It is not that we want to be told what to do. We want to be summoned to be fully and authentically human. A religion which only serves us and never makes demands of us, cheats us.

I believe God works miracles in people's lives. But I don't believe that we have the right or the power to summon up a miracle to suit our needs or our convenience. If sick people recovered every time we prayed and gave charity on their behalf, life might be more pleasant, but that would presuppose a world in which *we* would be God and God would be our servant. We cannot command a miracle; when one happens, we can only bow our heads at the wonder of it.

Pharaoh's courtiers worked miracles to show that they had power over the gods. As a result, when they reached the limits of their power, they had nowhere else to turn for help. Moses worked miracles as manifestations of God's power. As a result, when he reached the limits of his power, he could turn to God for aid. Twentieth century man has come to believe that he possesses the ultimate power. As a result, when he confronts a problem he cannot solve, he despairs. Would that he realized that the answer, a three-thousand-year-old answer, was not that far away.●

---

power of the physical world, their spiritual sense eclipsed by the visual. They were so blinded by the shining splendor of Pharaoh that they could not see the spiritual deception below the surface. Only the contest laid out between Moses and Pharaoh could raise them to a new level of spiritual growth. Moses had to win by Egyptian rules so that the slaves would realize the truth on their own. Forcing them to acknowledge the true God would be no liberation, only a replacement of one idol for another.

It was the slaves' self-realization of the truth that God required. He could become their God only if they needed it and willed it. The liberation was not just freedom of the body but freedom of spirit. It is not the miracle of the plagues that is important but that the nature of divine power is redefined. "NOT BY MIGHT AND NOT BY POWER BUT BY MY SPIRIT" [Zech. 4.6]—Moses teaches us of a God who teaches, supports and empowers us to act as the expression of the divine in the world. As Moses was transformed to enact the image of God, so must each of us stand forth for the image of the divine in our souls to teach the truth of God's presence. Our freedom of spiritual power used in the service of God is the tool by which God's presence is shared by all and liberates all.
Rabbi Stephen Robbins, Congregation N'vay Shalom, Beverly Hills, CA

דָּבָר אַחֵר **DAVAR AHER. AND I WILL HARDEN PHARAOH'S HEART AND I WILL MULTIPLY MY SIGNS AND WONDERS IN THE LAND OF EGYPT. [EX. 7.3].** This is an interesting use of the root [קשה], *KShH* (HARDEN). In the following chapters we read frequently of the "HARDENING HEART." The Hebrew usually is either from the root [כבד] *KVD* (HEAVY, BURDEN) or [חזק] *HZK* (STRONG, HARD), but here [קשה] is used. An obvious connection is with the use of the word in 6.9, when it refers to עֲבוֹדָה קָשָׁה *AVODAH KASHAH* (HARD/DIFFICULT WORK). What is interesting to me is that we know about the difficult work from the straw story. And specifically in 5.12 we're told: "SO THAT THE PEOPLE

Jody Hirsch

JODY HIRSCH IS THE PROGRAMMER
FOR THE JEWISH COMMUNITY
CENTER OF HONG KONG.

Va-Era

It was the first plague that should have tipped me off. I, Moses, did what I was told. "LET MY PEOPLE GO" [Ex. 5.1], I told him. "That's what the Lord told me. Let them go or else." "Or else what?" he asked with that smug smile of his. "Or else what...?" I stuttered. "Why, the Nile. Your Nile. Your precious sacred Nile will turn to blood." He didn't believe me, of course. Who could? Even my people, they didn't listen to me.

I suspect that even my brother, Aaron, thought I was crazy. No one believed...I mean really believed. I myself never thought about the poetry of it. The rightness of it.

Water, of course, was the main thing. Oh, I know there were others—fire for instance. But it was mostly the water. Over and over again, the God of our father Abraham controlled the water. I should have thought about the water. At every stage, the water controlled history. Only God controlled the water. I remember the dim days of my childhood—before I was set in my basket in the water of the very Nile that later turned to blood. My mother told me about our God who created the world in six days. The water came first—before light, before the world, before grandfather Adam. "IN THE BEGINNING," my mother said, "THE SPIRIT OF GOD HOVERED OVER THE FACE OF THE

SPREAD OUT THROUGH THE WHOLE LAND OF EGYPT לְקֹשֵׁשׁ קַשׁ לַתֶּבֶן *L'KOSHESH KASH LA-TEVEN* (TO GATHER STRAW FOR STUBBLE)." What an ironic Hebrew word play! Just as the Children of Israel suffered by קַשׁ *kash* (STRAW), so too, will Pharaoh suffer by [קשה] *KShH* (A HARDENED HEART). **Arnie Draiman, Director of Jewish Education, Leo Yassenoff Jewish Community Center, Columbus, OH**

דָּבָר אַחֵר **DAVAR AHER. AND I WILL HARDEN PHARAOH'S HEART. [Ex. 7.3].** The question as to how to reconcile God's justice with His "HARDENING OF PHARAOH'S HEART" clearly has tremendous religious implications.Consider, for example, a situation in which an adolescent wants something from a parent. Let us further assume that the parent is relatively insecure and immature—given, say, to rash emotional reac-

WATERS" [Gen. 1.1-2]. Even then, God controlled the waters. He subdued them. He divided them. None of us were around back then to be impressed. Later, He let them take over. Grandfather Noah knew their power.

The Egyptians worshipped the water...or at least they worshipped the Nile part of the water. When Pharaoh wanted to wipe us out, he ordered all the boy babies thrown into the Nile. It was a sort of sacrifice, I guess, to their gods. The irony, of course, is that I *was* thrown into the Nile...by my mother in that awful reed basket. But still...it was the water that manipulated history. If I

hadn't been put into it...if the Pharaoh's daughter hadn't come down to bathe in it. The water manipulated history—and who manipulated the water?

Water saved us again. We sang at the shore of the Red Sea with the cries of the Egyptian soldiers ringing in our ears. Our eyes had witnessed the splitting of the sea. Over and over again, though, no one really believed. I accused them of being stiff-necked people. But I...I was as guilty as they. "SPEAK TO THE ROCK, [Ex. Num. 20.8]" He said at that cursed place Meribah. "SPEAK TO THE ROCK THAT IT GIVE FORTH ITS WATER." But did I speak? No, I struck it. Yes...we got

the water. Where did it get me? I should have spoken. Spoken quietly even. I didn't and now I sit here alone. Looking at my people crossing yet another river into the promised land that I'll never enter after this interminable forty years.

I didn't get it. It was that first plague that should have tipped me off. It is the water, more than anything, that divides our history—my history—into nice neat sections. The Nile...the Nile turning to blood was the midpoint. It was a not very subtle hint that the water was God's force in history. ●

tions and not being particularly introspective or self-disciplined (unfortunately, not all that uncommon a situation). Given that the adolescent has had the benefit of several years of experience in dealing with this parent, is there any doubt that the adolescent, by saying the "right" thing or doing the "right" chore—in other words, by "pushing the right button"—can effectively manipulate that parent into giving whatever permission he desires? Of course, the parent certainly has the power to say "no." It is just that, by recognizing the parent's weaknesses and tendencies, the adolescent can render that power ineffective.

I think it is certainly fair to characterize Pharaoh as being at least as weak

as this parent. Having been worshipped as a god, used to having his every whim followed instantly, never having to consider the possible consequences of any binge or tantrum—I would think he would make an easy target for such a master psychologist as God. Indeed, this approach makes God's behavior throughout the entire story all the more sensible. After all, considering the wide variety of options at His disposal for saving the Jews and defeating the Egyptians, this tactic of sending two coarse shepherds—one a stammerer!—to deliver His message would not appear very efficient. On the other hand, if the goal is not simply to save the Jews and defeat the Egyptians, but also to make God's superiority and Pharaoh's human fallibility clear to everyone

concerned, then the tactic is as brilliant as it is effective. After all, it would be one thing to be challenged by some tremendous military power or, better yet, by the thunderbolts of a god. There was no way that Pharaoh could bring himself to concede to two such uncouth individuals. That is how "GOD HARDENED HIS HEART."

Ultimately, it is Pharaoh's own pride that paves the way for his downfall. As the Rabbis have said, "All is in the power of heaven except for the fear of heaven." The power of that "fear," however, should not be underestimated. Seen in this light, then, there is no moral/ethical problem of God's "HARDENING PHARAOH'S HEART." Now, if one wants to think about the injunction against "placing an obstacle before the blind," *that* may be a real problem. **Arthur Yavelberg, Principal, Solomon Schecter Middle School in Nassau County, Long Island, NY**

*EDITOR'S NOTE: The discussion of the hardening of Pharaoh's heart continues in **Parashat Bo**.*

דָּבָר אַחֵר **DAVAR AḤER. AND I SHALL MULTIPLY MY SIGNS AND MY WONDERS IN THE LAND OF EGYPT… [EX. 7.3].** Rabbi Kushner's interpretation provoked a spirited discussion in our junior congregation this past Shabbat. Our talk was continued on Sunday morning and tape recorded. Topics included: the difference between magic and miracles; why G-d needed ten plagues to free the Israelites; and honest grappling by the children about their own relationships with G-d. ON MIRACLES: "There's always a trick to magic—something you can figure out—there's no trick to miracles." "A miracle is just G-d's power." "A lot of things G-d does, we don't understand; maybe G-d likes it that way." ON PHARAOH AND THE PLAGUES: "G-d needed all those plagues to show how powerful He was. First He showed them smaller plagues and built things up. Then finally He did the last plague and G-d knew that Pharaoh wouldn't want to find out what the eleventh plague would be." "When G-d sent plagues and Pharaoh couldn't do anything about them, he figured out he had no real power." "When G-d actually gets down to His real stuff like throwing plagues instead of snake-rods, it

shows He's more powerful than any person." **Tamara Fleischer, age 10, Judy Herbstman, 10, Ted Herbstman, 7, Alex Reich, 6, Rachel Reich, 9, Elana Sitrin,12, Bari Wolf, 8. Risa Graff, Congregation Am Echad, Park Forest, IL <RisaJoy@aol.com>**

דָּבָר אַחֵר **DAVAR AḤER. AND EGYPT SHALL KNOW THAT I AM THE ETERNAL…. [EX. 7.5].** Rabbi Kushner, indeed, is correct in pointing out that the confrontation between God and Pharaoh is about KNOWING God. As Kushner mentions, Pharaoh begins by saying, "I DO NOT KNOW THE ETERNAL…" [EX. 5.2]. Then, in each plague (for a total of ten times), the phrase "to know the Eternal" appears [7.5, 7.17, 8.6…14.18]. By creating this "number/theme word" (*leiterworter/leading word*) of [ידע] *"yada"* (know), the Torah is sending the message that the plagues were a pedagogic tool to teach Pharaoh a difficult lesson. **Rabbi Elyse Goldstein, Director of Kolel: A Centre for Liberal Jewish Learning, Toronto, CANADA <Baruch_Sienna@mail.magic.com>**

Va-Era

בא אל פרעה כי אני הכבד

THEN THE ETERNAL SAID TO MOSES, "GO TO PHARAOH. FOR I HAVE HARDENED HIS HEART AND THE HEARTS OF HIS COURTIERS, IN ORDER THAT I MAY DISPLAY THESE MY SIGNS AMONG THEM." [Ex. 10.1]

Studying the *sidrah* each week and searching for something new is both exciting and challenging. But it is just as rewarding to revisit a midrash when one is at a different stage of life. Textures and contexts DO change.

I first learned this midrash to Bo as a student at the Jewish Theological Seminary.

Then, at the very beginning of a career, I could easily apply this text (or many of them, for that matter) as a piece of midrashic advice, challenging both my colleagues and myself to "start off on the right foot." There was every indication that these first tentative, hesitant steps would be the format for straight linear choices (or non-choices) in life. And I, with a great degree of respect and a little chutzpah, could even chide my teachers for being too set in their ways (remember, this was the early '60s)! At JTS, the intellect ruled—and so the patterning I often thought about (anxiously) was to be found through logical processing, not emotions. My understanding, then, was theoretical rather than practical, but rooted in the optimistic potential of the '60s. The heart, in biblical times, was, after all, the seat of the intellect, not the emotions.

The heart of Pharaoh and the actions of God became linked through what may be the most famous locus for the age-

Bo

Exodus 10:1-13:16

Rabbi Stuart Kelman

RABBI STUART KELMAN IS THE RABBI OF CONGREGATION NETIVOT SHALOM IN BERKELEY, CALIFORNIA. RABBI KELMAN IS THE EDITOR OF *WHAT WE KNOW ABOUT...JEWISH EDUCATION* AND THE CO-EDITOR OF *LEARN TORAH WITH...*

דָּבָר אַחֵר **DAVAR AHER.** THE ETERNAL SAID TO MOSES, "COME TO PHARAOH...I SHALL BRING A LOCUST-SWARM... [Ex. 10.1,4]. Suggested by the question of R. Levi Yitzhak of Berditchev. Abravanel answers the question. "Why does *Bo* begin where it does?" Because this plague, locusts, begins the negotiations that ultimately end with the Exodus. Here as elsewhere, I love the question more than the answer. "Why mark the beginning of freedom?" To introduce the

question. "When does liberation begin?" Does it begin with being hauled by our ears out of Egypt? No—it does not begin there. It begins earlier, back beyond that. Does it begin with the eighth plague, locusts? No—it begins earlier than that. Does it begin with a meeting with God at a bush full of fire [Ex. 3.3]? No—it begins earlier than that. Does it begin with a single act of spontaneous defiance against Egyptian oppression [Ex. 2.11]? No—earlier than that. Freedom is infi-

old problem of freewill and predestination. It is to be found in this week's parashah (and earlier) where God hardens Pharaoh's heart. Even the early midrash [*Exodus Rabbah* 13.4] picks up and amplifies the apparent contradiction: "How can one be free to choose, yet believe that God has already chosen or at least, determined the answer?" The rabbis phrased this as: "How can anyone be prevented from doing *teshuvah*—even Pharaoh?" How can God remove the possibility of change from anyone? The midrash:

R. Yochanan says: "Doesn't this provide an opportunity for heretics to claim that Pharaoh had no possibility to repent, since the verse in Exodus states: "… FOR I HAVE HARDENED HIS HEART" [10.1]?

R. Shimon ben Lakish replied: "LET THE MOUTHS OF THE HERETICS ('*minim*') BE STILL." There is a verse from Proverbs 3.34 that says: "AT SCOFFERS, GOD SCOFFS.…" God warns a person once, twice, even three times—at that point the individual locks his/her own heart from the possibility of doing *teshuvah*—in order for God to exact vengeance for one's sin. So, here, in the case of the wicked Pharaoh. God sent five messages to him and still he did not change his words. God said. "YOU HAVE STIFFENED YOUR NECK AND HARDENED YOUR HEART, NOW I WILL ADD MORE UNCLEANNESS ONTO WHAT YOU HAVE ALREADY MADE UNCLEAN." That is the meaning of the verse in Exodus which reads. "FOR I HAVE HARDENED HIS HEART."

In other words, the first five times that Pharaoh and Moses engage, Pharaoh hardens his own heart and refuses to release the people of Israel. But for the next five plagues, the words in the Torah change. Until now, the Hebrew has read. וַיֶּחֱזַק לֵב פַּרְעֹה *va-yeḥezak lev Paroh* (Pharaoh hardened his own heart). From here on, the Hebrew changes to. וַיְחַזֵּק ה׳ אֶת חֵב פַּרְעֹה *va-yeḥezek ha-Shem et lev Paroh* (God hardened Pharaoh's heart)

Bo

nitely regressible. Each act in the chain of behavior which leads to freedom is built on a previous act. You may never know when it begins. Every act contributes in some small way to freedom. No deed is done, no thought is thought, no dream is dreamed for nothing. Everything contributes in some inscrutable way to freedom. When does freedom begin? It may begin today, with this thought. This thought was preceded by the events of yesterday, which may have been preceded by the dream the day before. Back beyond today, every act, every thought may be a gesture for freedom. Every act has a liberating potential of which we may be unaware. No deed is wasted, no thought for nothing. When did we get free? When we stopped, when we resisted, when we dreamed it, when we listened,

Synopsis: The plagues continue: locusts, darkness and finally, the announcement of the final plague. The beginning of the year with the month of Nisan, the details of the pascal offering in Egypt and the establishment of the festival of matzot and instructions regarding the placing of blood on the doorposts precede the enactment of the final plague. The exodus begins. The laws pertaining to the firstborn, matzot and tefillin are institu-ted as reminders that God brought the Jews out of Egypt.

(Rashi on Ex. 7:3). Pharaoh's behavioral pattern has become imprinted, allowing what appears to be only limited free will (which, according to David Winston, was what the ancients believed anyway). Habit replaces free will. Five times Pharaoh had the opportunity to change his behavior—but to no avail. Up until now, his actions were the logical consequences of thoughtful (but clearly wrong) beliefs. Finally, there came a point, after the first five plagues, when he acted automatically. Try as he might, because of conflicting commitments, he could no longer control himself, and so it was here that God hardened his heart.

Change is hard. We all have experienced that; but, according to our midrash, change may also be impossible. Even though we like to believe that there is always hope, sometimes it can be too late. Are there limits to change? Maybe Freud was right? Maybe organizations, institutions and even countries become immune to the possibility of change, or, in the

language of our midrash, get to the point where God takes over and hardens our (collective) hearts.

Now, relearning this midrash a quarter of a century later, what has changed? The world certainly has become more complicated—so did life and so did this midrash. The map now looks very different, the words of the midrash have obtained expanded and often conflictual meaning, and I, too, have aged and changed. What has remained constant is my struggle with this midrash.

Whereas the classic reading taught that heart (read. head) was in control, Pharaoh could not have been immune to the cumulative impact of the plagues. In spite of the seemingly simple and repetitive linguistic rejection by Pharaoh of all his promises, we are led to believe that they were all logical recantations of purposeful actions. But perhaps that is precisely the point. the irony is that the emotions have been isolated or negated. What was Pharaoh feeling each time

back beyond, way beyond, before it came to be. **Reb Stavisker** <Stavisker@aol.com>

דְּבָר אַחֵר **DAVAR AHER. FOR I HAVE HARDENED HIS HEART AND THE HEARTS OF HIS COURTIERS…[Ex. 10.1].** Like many who have confronted the text, I, too, have been troubled by the phrase "AND GOD HARDENED PHARAOH'S HEART." The rabbis tackled the problem by suggesting that God had given

Pharaoh plenty of opportunities for repentance and when he did not do his *teshuvah*, God simply got fed up with him and sent plague upon plague to prove how powerful He was. Though I can understand this explanation and even agree with it up to a certain point, it is hardly the Deity for Whom "the gates of repentance are always open." I would like to suggest another explanation.

In an ancient Greek history written by

Philostratus, there is described a wonder worker, demon exorciser and cult reformer named Appollonius. According to Philostratus, he was especially adept at manipulating nature in order to heal. Since nature was seen by the common folk as cause and effect originating in heaven with the gods, "reverse influence" by a magician from earth to heaven, engendering a more desired outcome would be welcome, espe-

he was tested? The silence of the text in Exodus invites speculation. Is logic the sole path to change? It's just too simple to believe that the Ninevites changed as a result of Jonah's message! Today, we know better (think diet)!

The midrash asks us to place ourselves in Pharaoh's place. It says that we, too, have our plagues. diabetes, cancer, AIDS, heart disease. For some of us, those plagues are merely warnings intended to frighten us into action or reaction. For many of us, those plagues are chronic illnesses that we live with moment to moment. Sometimes, we are offered warnings; often not. Sometimes, there are early stages during which we may be able to reverse the process; often not. Sometimes there is a turning point beyond which nothing curative can be done—only the spiritual can provide comfort and relief. The process, however, is far from linear and far from clear. It certainly doesn't happen after five warnings.

Often, there are absolute rights and absolute wrongs. We do have choices—albeit limited ones. If this holds for serious illness, how much the more so for habits.

So, can Pharaoh do *teshuvah*? Can we? Is *teshuvah* the antidote to the slippery slope argument? The *Etz Yosef* tries to smooth over the problem by stating that had Pharaoh done real *teshuvah*, it would not have been rejected at any time. In effect, he claims, there are no time limits to doing *teshuvah*. As proof, he points to the famous verses in Amos that begin "FOR THREE TRANSGRESSIONS OF... FOR FOUR I WILL NOT REVOKE IT." From this the rabbis in *Yoma* deduce that three times one must ask for forgiveness. Yet here, the *Etz Yosef* claims, Pharaoh had five opportunities and even an additional four more—and still God would have accepted his repentance. A nice, liberal tradition—but it clashes with the reality of disease and with life. Life itself is a limit. Maybe the only way to

Bo

cially if a ruler held the magician's pursestrings. Fooling around with nature to make it serve the needs of the magician was merely a tool, but it was a tool that could be utilized to prove one's control over nature and, consequently, over life itself.

Pharaoh had in his court sufficient magicians like the aforementioned Appollonius. When confronted by Moses and Aaron, it is no wonder

that Pharaoh would be confident enough to say "WHO IS THIS GOD THAT I SHOULD LET YOU GO?" He knew that his magicians would and could perform for him and that any nature-miracle by Moses and Aaron could be duplicated by them. When God acted through Moses and Aaron with His own nature-miracles, He was speaking Pharaoh's language, for Pharaoh understood that whoever had the magic had the power.

understand this is by listening to the words of Larry Kushner (*God was in This Place & I, i Did Not Know*). "The rate at which Pharaoh's heart becomes sclerotic is precisely the rate at which Israel's heart begins to lighten. Pharaoh does not lose his freedom, he merely lives out the consequences of his own arrogance and ambition" (p. 145).

Maybe the whole scenario is simply drama. After all, what happens in negotiation is a play—with actors knowing full well the outcome, often before the curtain rises. Take the negotiation between management and labor, for example. In most negotiations there is a ritual containing steps and sequential interactions, a definite rhythm and momentum that determine the pace. There are only a certain number of steps that can possibly happen until the game is over (see Francis Quittel, *Fire Power*, Berkeley, CA 10 Speed Press, 1995). Are we, like Pharaoh, simply obligated to play out our roles on the historical stage? Or does the contin-

ual engaging in patterned behavior turn that behavior into evil itself— into the most subtle type of evil? Evil begets evil, turning its owner into evil. The midrash's use of the word "moseef" ("adding") suggests that because you (Pharaoh) fixed your actions, I (God) will make it worse. What about the victim(s)? (See Rabbi Dov Peretz Elkins' comments on *Va-Yetze*). Or, as Rabbi Harold Shulweis claims in *For Those Who Can't Believe*. "Habits instilled in themselves by human beings may create a second nature that distorts the capacity to choose." Can we tell this with foresight or are we consigned to live only in retrospect?

How do we overcome and change anyway? The paradox in the midrash is that only through some sort of Divine *hesed* can we change. It may be a profound truth that "everything is in the hand of heaven except for the awe of heaven." As long as Pharaoh is trying to unharden his own heart with his own hands, he fails. The second that he invites God

into his heart, it softens. That's why 12-step programs work. That is the essence of recovery and *teshuvah*. Now it is clear why *teshuvah* was invented before creation. It may be impossible for Pharaoh (or us) to change his (or our) heart, but it is possible for God to change it. What we have the potential to do, is to invite God to make that change.

The hardened heart is a fantasy that it is we who are in control of our emotions and our souls.●

But why should this succession of miracles harden Pharaoh's heart? The answer is simple. The heart was considered to be the seat of wisdom, knowledge, and the mind. Pharaoh had been brought up convinced that he was a direct descendant of the gods, that he was all-powerful, and that through his magicians, nature would bend to his will. Imagine his shock at finding out that he was a mortal, was not at all descended from any gods, and controlled nature not

one whit. His mind was frozen—simply another way of saying "HIS HEART WAS HARDENED." Indeed, God hardened his heart but that was only a result of the miracles, not one of the miracles.

I submit then that the phrase "GOD HARDENED PHARAOH'S HEART" should not be seen as a characteristic of a callous and vengeful God. Rather to harden Pharaoh's heart means that Pharaoh's psychological defenses were activated by the obvious mira-

cles before him. Indeed, the rabbis were right. Pharaoh could have repented at any time before his "HEART WAS HARDENED." But it was impossible to repent after witnessing so many other miracles, for to do so would have sent Pharaoh into such a depression that it is quite possible that all of Jewish history might have been different, and that we might never actually have escaped Egyptian bondage. **Rabbi Cy Stanway, Temple Beth El, Las Cruces, NM**

Rabbi Leonard Matanky

RABBI LEONARD MATANKY IS THE ASSISTANT SUPERINTENDENT OF THE ASSOCIATED TALMUD TORAHS OF CHICAGO AND THE RABBI OF CONGREGATION K.I.N.S.

Bo

YOU WILL THEN BE ABLE TO CONFIDE TO YOUR CHILDREN AND GRANDCHILDREN HOW I DID FEARSOME ACTS WITH THE EGYPTIANS AND HOW I PERFORMED MIRACULOUS SIGNS AMONG THEM—YOU WILL THEN FULLY REALIZE THAT I AM GOD."
[Ex. 10:1-2]

It took ten plagues to teach Pharaoh a lesson. But the last three taught us something as well. And what did they teach us? A lot of things.

But this week, there are two lessons in particular.

Both began in a midrash, and both were later taught to us by the greatest Biblical commentator, Rashi.

It was during the ninth plague, the plague of darkness, that the Egyptians finally began to understand the power of God. The darkness was palpable, so much so that people were afraid to even move. They were literally paralyzed from fear—"no one left his place for three days" yet, as terrible as this plague was for the Egyptians, it was far worse for the Jews. For the darkness that was created was part of a Divine plan to conceal the deaths of four out of five of all the Jews in Egypt.

Or to put it more bluntly—and to use a little bit of math—if two to three million Jews survived this plague and ultimately left Egypt, then during the plague of darkness eight to ten million Jews died! During the plague of darkness more Jews died

---

דָּבָר אַחֵר **DAVAR AHER.** FOR I HAVE HARDENED HIS HEART [Ex. 10.1]. In Egyptian culture, their mythology taught that after death the heart was weighed. You can see this on tomb paintings. If the heart was heavier than a feather, the afterlife was denied. The Egyptian ideal was to have a weightless heart. When Pharaoh hardens his own heart, he is condemning himself to miss eternity. It is as if he is saying, "My anger is more important to me than my soul." When God adds weight to the heart, it is hardened in its heaviness, God is saying, "You have chosen your own fate." **Regina Silver, Los Angeles, CA**

דָּבָר אַחֵר **DAVAR AHER.** FOR I HAVE HARDENED HIS HEART [Ex. 10.1]. Rabbi Kelman discusses the perplexing problem of the heart of Pharaoh, the actions of God, and free will. I wish to add three perspectives: the

בא אל פרעה כי אני הכבדתי את לבו

than in the Holocaust! And why did they die? It was a punishment from God, explains the midrash. Because four out of five Jews refused to leave Egypt. They had become too assimilated, too comfortable, too unwilling to accept or participate in the reality and responsibility of Jewish life.

That's lesson number one.

And lesson number two? Well, let's start with Cecil B. DeMille. Why Cecil B. DeMille? Because for most people, and maybe even most Jews, most of what they know about the ten plagues and the Exodus from Egypt goes back to him and his movie *The Ten Commandments*.

Before the tenth and final plague, the death of the firstborn, God told Moses to tell the Jews to take the blood of the paschal lamb and smear it on the doorways of their homes. Why? As a protection from the plague. But where exactly did they smear the blood? According to DeMille, on the outside. According to our Rabbis, on the inside. And what's the proof? It's a verse in this week's Torah portion—"THE BLOOD WILL BE A SIGN FOR *YOU* ON THE HOUSES WHERE YOU ARE STAYING" [Ex. 12:13]. Not a sign for anybody

else—but for you! (Cecil, I'm sorry, but you're wrong, again.)

That's lesson number two.

And what's the connection between these two lessons?

Simple. It's an article by Professor Steven M. Cohen in the December issue of Moment Magazine. It's an article that asserts that many of the statistics of the 1991 National Jewish Population Survey are wrong. Not that our Jewish community is growing—it's not. Intermarriage, while not 52%, is still, according to Cohen, 41%. But, "what we are really witnessing is a transformation to, using the current argot, a 'leaner and meaner' American Jewish community, a somewhat pared down version that is, in many ways, stronger, more committed and more observant." Why? Well, the Jews who are intermarrying tend to be more assimilated to begin with, while the Jews who remain are studying more (day school enrollment continues to climb); observing more (Jews in their mid-30s to 40s are 50% more likely to observe Shabbat and six times more likely to fast on the Fast of Esther than Jews in the 55-64 age

group); and having more children (about 6% of American Jews in their 50s are Orthodox, while 12% of children under ten years old are Orthodox).

So what happened in exile in Egypt? Basically the same thing that is happening in the exile of America today.

Millions of Jews disappeared in the dark. Vanished-because they were too assimilated, too uncommitted to survive. But those who did remain—the strong and committed minority, the 'leaner and meaner' Jews—they were the ones who took the lessons of Judaism into their homes. They marked the doorposts of their homes, not on the outside, but on the inside. To them, and to us, Judaism was something that one lives and not just observes. Judaism was family and children and teaching and learning. So they survived the plagues, and they were redeemed. They survived the plagues, and we are their descendants.

Those are two of the lessons of this portion. Lessons that we would do well to learn ourselves. *Originally published in the Chicago Jewish News.* ●

---

approaches of Plaut, Schaalman and Goldman.

Plaut points out that, "The focus of the Torah was not on the problem of free will but on its main intent, to praise the absolute power and unsurpassable glory of God." A variation of the theme identified by Plaut is per-

ceptively and splendidly described by Rabbi Herman E. Schaalman. Rabbi Schaalman reminds us that the whole story is a contest between God and Pharaoh, who is a pseudo-god to the Egyptians and to himself. Repeated plagues acted to humble him and cause him to understand how far he had overreached himself when

brought face to face with the real God. Schaalman notes, "This does not come easily; this takes time. It takes a whole series of blows and humiliation to drive out of Pharaoh's mind the notion of his omnipotence."

Rabbi Solomon Goldman published a dramatically different explanation.

Bo

When faced with this question of free will, he noted, "Neither apologetics, nor the supercilious attitude of some scholars toward the God of the Old Testament has contributed to its clarification. Now the truth is that the Bible, from Genesis to Revelations, is a product of distant ages. It is therefore inevitable that if should contain a whole body of opinions and ideas that strike us as strange, revolting and unacceptable. We doubt whether in recent years anyone was prepared to say that God had arbitrarily hardened the heart or softened the brain of the Nazi chancellor. We just do not seem to think the way the ancients did. Mental processes and methods of communication have changed radically, whether or not sentiments and emotions have remained unaltered. Certainly conceptualist thinking was not our narrator's 'metier.' He was not troubled by metaphysical abstractions, by the problems of predestination and freedom of the will. Having known little or nothing about natural causes, whether primary or secondary, and having, as a result, formed a habit of attributing everything that was or happened, including the depraved heart of tyrannical rulers, to God, he stumbled into the contradiction of making a just God impel an evildoer to greater evil, with the intent of punishing him more. To his way of thinking, the persistent stubbornness of Pharaoh and his long refusal to let Israel go was in itself a plague, a creation, that is, an act of God." **Alfred Soffer, MD, Master Fellow ACCP, Glenview, IL**

דְּבָר אַחֵר **DAVAR AHER. FOR I HAVE HARDENED HIS HEART [EX. 10.1].** *A Tale of the Academy. Part I:* **Yoni Reznik** asked: "What does it really mean that God hardened or strengthened Pharoah's heart?" The teacher's response was to bring in Rabbi Stuart Kelman's article on *Shemot Rabbah* 13.3. In the midst of the explanation, Yoni then asked, "But doesn't Pharaoh harden his own heart?" (It was his bar mitzvah-yet-to-come portion). The teacher said: "Let's look it up." A dozen kids (12-14), eleven *humashim* and one lap top with *Bibleworks* on it, went to work. They discovered a pattern. Nahum Sarna tells us (*JPS Commentary on Exodus,* page 23) "Pharaoh's heart runs through the entire Exodus story; it appears exactly 20 times. Half the references are to Pharaaoh doing the hardening, half are due to God's intervention." He then, in the footnotes, lists the citations.

Looking at a different matrix, here is what we found. When Pharaoh hardens his own heart, the root is always [כבד] *KBD* (made heavy). When the heart is passively hard/strong/heavy, it is sometimes [כבד] *KBD* and sometimes [חזק] *HZK* (made strong). When God is effecting the affect, it is usually [חזק] *HZK* (made strong), except for one use of [קשה] *KShH* [7.3] (difficult) and one use of [כבד] *KBD* [10.1]. *Now it was time to drash.*

Iris Ahronowitz: The root [כבד] *KBD* can mean one of three things: heavy, liver, or to honor, (i.e. *likhvod*) as in a holiday. The root [חזק] *HZK* means "strong," (i.e. physical strength), and the root [קשה] *KShH*, which is used only twice, means hard (like a seal of metal), or inflexible. The root [כבד] *KBD* is used solely by Pharaoh, when he is doing the hardening, with the exception of in verse 10.1. So, when it is done by Pharaoh, it can be interpreted as him, swollen with pride, feeling "above" the Israelites and being ignorant of their plight, honoring himself. In all other instances, it is God who is doing the hardening, making Pharaoh's heart even harder than it already is, i.e. helping it along. It can be "justified" by saying that God isn't making much of a difference, because Pharaoh started the hardening.

Jeremy Oberstein: Each word is a synonym but is in a way different stages of hardening.

Benjamin Vorspan: They are not very different at all. We might find that God had a good thesaurus when He was writing the Torah. I don't think that He/She really meant anything by it.

Margo Lurie: I think that the difference between the words is just that [כבד] *KBD* is a stronger verb—I think that Pharaoh is making his heart heavy, but G-d just strengthens that decision, not the heart itself, until the end. This could mean that G-d is not forcing anything on Pharaoh, and what G-d does to Pharaoh is totally Pharaoh's decision. I think that Pharaoh had control of the situation, even though he did not realize it.

Rachel Resnick: [כבד] *KBD* has a double meaning. While "honor" and "heavy" may appear to be two very different things, I do not believe that they are. If Pharaoh were to make his heart *heavy*, in the dense, interesting sense of the word, he would *honor* himself by believing that he was all-powerful. This would make him conceited forcing him to honor and worship himself. So [כבד] *KBD* has much to do with both but can be used for both reasons separately at the same time. *Then the bell rang.*

A Tale of the Academy. Part II: In the next session we found the twenty passages which talk about Pharaoh's heart being hardened. The first, Exodus 4.21, uses [חזק] *HZK*—God makes an overall prediction of what will happen: "I WILL BE 'STRENGTHENING' PHARAOH'S HEART." The second, which uses [קשה] *KShH*, (made difficult/problematic) [7.3] is also an overall statement. God seems to be saying, "THE END RESULT WILL BE A HEART THAT HAS SHORT-CIRCUITED." Next, there are three passive hardenings (7.13–[כבד] *KBD*) (7.22–[חזק] *HZK*) (8.11–[כבד] *KBD*). Now, finally in 8.15, we have the first active hardening which is attributed to a source: Pharaoh hardens his own heart [כבד] *KBD*. This is repeated in 8.28, and again later in 9.34. In between there are two more passive hardenings (9.7–[כבד] *KBD* and 9.12–[חזק] *HZK*). Finally, in Exodus 10.1, the twelfth occurrence of hardening of the heart, the tenth "real-time" event, after Pharaoh actively hardened [כבד] *KBD* his heart and God reinforced this process [חזק] *HZK*. God says to Moses, "I HAVE CAUSED PHARAOH'S HEART TO BECOME HARDENED" [כבד] *KBD*. This is the turning point: six more times God strenghens Pharaoh's resolve (six in the past tense [10.20, 10.27, 11.10, 14.4, 14.8] once in the predictive future [14.17]).

Then the entire sequence is bracketed by the second and final usage of [קשה] *KShH* 13.15, the confounded heart that allows—despite all evidence—the firstborn to die.

In *Shemot Rabbah*, the rabbis explain [9.8] that [כבד] *KBD* is making a heart like a liver—stubborn and angry, and [8.1] "heavy" like a lead weight which drags you down. No comment is made on [חזק] *HZK* or [קשה] *KShH*. Based on all of this, this is what we theorized:

Bobby Pezeshki: [כבד] *KBD* means to make harder. Pharaoh made his own heart hard [כבד] *KBD* and became extremely stubborn. [חזק] *HZK* means strong. God was making Pharaoh's hardening even stronger. It was sort of in a way serving as a punishment for continuing to keep the Jews as slaves. [קשה] *KShH*—God was making the conflict of whether to free the Jews or keep them as slaves even harder and more fierce and difficult. In other words, God was putting a great deal of stress on Pharaoh, bringing it to a crisis.

Karen Weise: [חזק] *HZK* was used much more as a punishment than anything else. It's like if you heat Cream of Wheat for too long: all of a sudden "poof"—it's all over your microwave. [כבד] *KBD* seemed to be Pharaoh's attempt to punish G-d, and almost describes Pharaoh's stupidity. Pharaoh tries to say "Ha ha" to G-d. "I'm not going to move. What are you going to do?" And G-d just goes "Duah." [קשה] *KShH* is used in "cahoots" with a miracle or great event done by G-d, and sums up the epitome of it all. It's like the grand "Harden."

Yoni Reznik: Pharaoh uses [כבד] *KBD* instead of [חזק] *HZK* or [קשה] *KShH* because you can make your own heart heavy, but you can't strengthen or harden your own heart, only God can. When you make your heart heavy, you decide to be worse, but when God strengthens your heart, you can't decide to be better anymore, and the same thing when He hardens your heart, you can't decide to soften it.

Sepideh Pezeshki: The reason why G-d kept taking control of Pharaoh and kept changing his mind after every single plague...He made it so hard that Pharaoh couldn't turn back or change.

Rebecca Olch: I don't think that any of these three words have any specific reason for being in a certain place. I think that the man who wrote the Bible just didn't want to repeat the words over and over again. I do not agree with Rashi that every word in the Torah is there for a reason. I believe the Torah was written like any other book and not meant to be broken and studied word for word. These words are just three different synonyms for "heavy" used in the Torah to keep it from being repetitive.

When we started, we thought we had discovered something new in the Torah's use of these three verbs. Now, we think we have just uncovered and charted the linguistics which underpinned the rabbinic insight in the midrash Stuart Kelman cited [13.3]: That God sets Pharaoh up (and manipulates him),

but doesn't directly control him. That is the contrast in the usage of [חזק] *HZK* and [קשה] *KShH.* God makes sure that Pharaoh's worst tendencies come through. The end result is [קשה] *KShH,* a heart that is so confused and so confounded that it cannot act. **Iris Ahronowitz, Meredith Askuvich, Oren Lazar, Margo Lurie, Jeremy Oberstein, Rebecca Olch, Bobby Pezeshki, Sepideh Pezeshki, Rachel Resnick, Yoni Reznik, Devin Schiff, Benjamin Vorspan, Karen Weise—students at the Los Angeles Hebrew High School**

דָּבָר אַחֵר **DAVAR AHER. THIS MONTH SHALL BE FOR YOU...[Ex. 12.2].** Why wait until *Bo*, 15 Torah portions into Torah, to begin in earnest a comprehensive list of positive and negative mitzvot? (Three mitzvot appear in *Bereshit* and *Shemot* up to this point.) And why does that listing of mitzvot (20 according to the Rambam) begin with a commandment about a calendar, about keeping time? A close look at the internal structure of Torah reveals something quite amazing. From *parashat Bo* until Passover, there are 14 weeks. From *Bereshit* until *parashat Bo*, there are 14 weeks, 14 weekly Torah portions. The mitzvot of Passover, of counting time, appear exactly midway between the beginning of Torah and the time when Passover is actually observed and re-lived. An important teaching of Torah is hidden in its very structure.

Now, in mid-winter, with the blooming of spring not yet noticeable, is the time to begin preparing to once

Bo

בא אל פרעה כי אני הכבדתי את לבו

again leave *mitzrayim*. Now is the time to look at where we are in relationship to where we want to be in 14 weeks. Now is the time to enter into a more concrete and active relationship with mitzvot and in particular the mitzvah of time, of orienting ourselves to the Jewish calendar and a most extraordinary moment in our people's history. **Rabbi Marc Sirinsky, Temple Emek Shalom, Ashland, OR**

דָּבָר אַחֵר **DAVAR AHER. AND IT SHALL BE WHEN YOUR CHILD ASKS YOU…[Ex. 13.14].** Both the beginning [Ex. 10.2] and end [13.14] of *Parashat Bo* instruct and remind us to tell it to our children. The canonizers of this Torah *sidrah* clearly understood that the passing down, from parent to child, *dor vador*, of Jewish history, Torah teachings and Jewish values was essential to Jewish continuity and Jewish survival.

There can be no argument that Jews have differing concepts of God and Judaism. Some Jews will always try to adhere to all 613 mitzvot, others less. But Jews have a common history, culture and a belief in *ha-Shem* that somehow must transcend these differences. In this period of time, we may not agree about aspects of halakhah and some of us will always feel others have erroneous beliefs about true Judaism…this is nothing new. The growing schism between Orthodox, Conservative and Reform movements is clearly a dangerous threat to American Jewish survival. We are not three different religions, despite our differences…we are all Jews and we are commanded to love our fellow Jews and strive for *tikkun olam*…and this is what we must tell our children. **Lawrence J. Deutsch**

ולא נחם אלהים

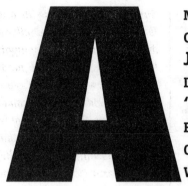

AND MOSES TOOK THE BONES OF JOSEPH WITH HIM, FOR JOSEPH HAD MADE THE CHILDREN OF ISRAEL SWEAR, 'GOD WILL SURELY REMEMBER YOU, AND YOU SHALL CARRY UP MY BONES HENCE WITH YOU.' [Ex. 13.19]

"What do you want to do with these old prayer books?" our synagogue administrator asked me.

"Which old prayer books?" I answered.

"The ones that the Cohens brought in for us. They're moving to Santa Fe, and they say that they have no room for these old prayer books that have been lying around their house for years. Are they of any value?"

Beshallah

Exodus 13.17–17.16

Rabbi Jeffrey K. Salkin

JEFFREY K. SALKIN IS THE RABBI OF CENTRAL SYNAGOGUE OF NASSAU COUNTY IN ROCKVILLE CENTRE, NEW YORK. HE IS THE AUTHOR OF *PUTTING GOD ON THE GUEST LIST: HOW TO RECLAIM THE SPIRITUAL MEANING OF YOUR CHILD'S BAR/BAT MITZVAH* AND *BEING GOD'S PARTNER: HOW TO FIND THE HIDDEN LINK BETWEEN SPIRITUALITY AND YOUR WORK*, BOTH PUBLISHED BY JEWISH LIGHTS, WOODSTOCK, VT.

דָּבָר אַחֵר **DAVAR AHER. FOR JOSEPH HAD MADE THE CHILDREN OF ISRAEL SWEAR, 'GOD WILL SURELY REMEMBER YOU, AND YOU SHALL CARRY UP MY BONES HENCE WITH YOU.'" [Ex. 13.19].** Rabbi Jeffrey Salkin touched a tender spot. Two years ago, at age 55, I became a Bar Mitzvah. I looked and looked for the *tefillin* that were in the box on top of the closet

I quickly perused the old, dusty, tattered siddurim. In my hands were several copies of *Siddur Tikkun Meir*—a standard issue traditional siddur. But when I opened two of them up, I realized that glued to the inside cover of each volume was a *brit milah* certificate—one for Mr. Cohen and one for his younger brother. Each certificate listed the name of the child, the parents, the *sandek*, the *kvatter*, the name of the rabbi, both in English and in Hebrew. On the opposite page, there was a guest list of everyone who had attended each of the *brit* ceremonies. Fanny and Sylvia and Henry, their names inscribed in fountain pen ink, along with the signature of the family rabbi, a Brooklyn rabbi of no small reputation, a man who spiritually led his people through the good times of the 1940s and 1950s, and retired several years after the neighborhood started to go bad in the 1960s.

"What should we do with these prayer books?" the administrator repeated. "And not only prayer books," she continued. "Look! They

when I was a kid growing up in Mississippi. Our parents and grandparents and my generation tried to look American, and in Mississippi tried to be Jews, but tried to look white. We put the things in the top of the closet that made us think or appear different. I keep looking for the *tefillin* and for the other bones of my ancestors. If

also left several sets of *tefillin*."

The fantasy goes like this: "Hello, Bekins. We're moving to Santa Fe. How much to move six rooms of furniture, our stereo system, our computers, our art work—and do you have a 'We're leaving the Jewish stuff behind' discount?"

I thought of all the excess baggage that we Jews have shed along the path.

In the passage from Europe to the new world of America, our ancestors cast off their excess baggage. In my wildest imaginings, I suspect that if skin divers dove into New York harbor, they could dredge up an underwater mountain of *tefillin*. As the boats carrying our great-grandfathers passed by the Statue of Liberty, they literally kissed their *tefillin* goodbye. Religious observance was for another land and another place.

From the Lower East Side to Brooklyn, Bubbe and Zeyde cast off their excess baggage. Yiddish went, not at once, but slowly. The Mike Meyers character, Linda Richman, on *Saturday Night Live's* "Coffee

Talk" gets *shpilkes* in her *genechtegezoit*. She often gets *farklempt*, and then she assigns us a topic and asks us to *discuss*. What irony: most of her Yiddish is not Yiddish. Come to think of it, she (Mike Meyers) is not even really Jewish (his mother-in-law is Jewish). Come to think of it, she's not even a *she*.

And then, from Brooklyn to the manicured lawns of Long Island, Mom-Mom and Pop-Pop (read Bubbe and Zeyde) cast off their excess baggage. Goodbye to the old neighborhood, the culture of stoops and handball, the culture where the policeman, the storekeeper, the woman down the street all had claims upon you.

And now, forty years later, from Long Island to the great unbounded Southwest. Get rid of the siddur. As *The Wiz* put it years ago: "Don't cha carry nothin' that might be a load, as you ease on down, ease on down the road." Or as the poet Adrienne Rich might choose to put it, a little more elegantly, we carry "the invisible luggage of fifty years.

Synopsis: Pharaoh lets the people of Israel go. God leads in a pillar of cloud by day and a pillar of fire by night. Pharaoh has a change of heart and pursues. At the shore of the sea. the people panic. Moses is told by God to hold his hand high and the sea splits. The children of Israel pass safely through but the Egyptians drown. Shirat ha-Yam, the Song at the Sea, provides a poetic closure to this initial stage of wanderings. Miriam rejoices. The journey continues with the crises in the desert: the bitter waters at Mara, the mana and quail (leading to a section about the Sabbath), and the events at Massa and Meriva. The parashah concludes with the battle of Amalek.

I can find the bones and make them live for me then perhaps they will also for my children and my grandchildren. Study of Torah makes the bones live. **Herman Solomon, Wichita, KS**

דָּבָר אַחֵר **DAVAR AHER. YOU SHALL CARRY UP MY BONES HENCE WITH YOU… [Ex. 13.19].** I love the metaphor and I would just like to take it a bit further. Eventually, Joseph's bones were buried along with others from our founding mothers and fathers. In that way, bones are not like siddurim and/or *tefillin*. The former are "buried away"

and interacted with only rarely and completely symbolically . On the other hand, siddurim, *tefillin* and the other accoutrements of Jewish spiritual behavior are supposed to be our partners, equipment that enables us to "do Jewish." Bones are to be buried. Old prayer books should be given new life. Ours is one of the many synagogues

It goes around on the airport carousel, and you wait for it, and you wonder if your luggage simply looks like everyone else's."

What should we do with the old siddurim and *tefillin* sets?

Suddenly I remembered the Exodus from Egypt.

On the night that we left Egypt, God told Moses to instruct the Israelites to borrow objects of gold and silver from their Egyptian neighbors. As the Israelites grabbed the booty of Egypt, Moses suddenly remembered that they couldn't leave yet. He remembered the story of his ancestor Joseph. When Joseph lay upon his deathbed, he told his brothers, "GOD WILL SURELY REMEMBER YOU. WHEN YOU LEAVE, BRING MY BONES UP OUT OF THIS PLACE." [Gen. 50.24] Moses suddenly remembered that he had to carry the bones of Joseph with him. And Moses did not know where the bones of Joseph were buried. Moses suddenly knew that we could not leave Egypt without them.

The midrash [*Mekhilta, Beshallah,* paralleled in *BT, Sotah* 13a] teaches that Moses looked for three days and nights for the coffin of Joseph, but he looked in vain. Serah, the daughter of Asher, the niece of Joseph, a survivor of that generation, told Moses where Joseph was buried. The midrash assigns this task to the already-ancient Serah because she is listed in Gen. 46.17 as being among those who accompanied Jacob and his sons to Egypt, and she is mentioned again in the census in Num. 26.46. From this double mention, it is no great leap to imagine that she was still alive on the eve of our entry into the Land. (There are even those who teach that Serah was among those who entered Paradise alive, among those over whom the Angel of Death had no apparent power.)

Serah took Moses to the banks of the Nile, and she told him that the Egyptians had sunk Joseph's lead coffin in the Nile so that its waters

Beshallah

that is privileged to have one of the Czech memorial scrolls in its possession. Fortunately, we have one that is usable enough that it is not "on display"; it is actively used and interacted with within the context of our Jewish community. It is a member of our community. There is an aura about it. The souls who touched it, carried it, danced with it and wrestled with its teachings surround its worn parchment and faded calligra-

phy. It is an amazing experience, a great honor and responsibility whenever a *hakafah* brings it into our midst and we read from its sometimes wrinkled and mildewed columns. I think Rabbi Salkin admonishes us to do the same with our old siddurim, *tefillin* and *tallitot* that have attained a permanent kashrut despite their holes and tatters (Jewish "Velveteen Rabbits"). We are too quick to carry them off to be

ויהי בשלח פרעה את העם ולא נחם אלהים

would be blessed. Moses stood on the banks of the Nile and cried out to the waters. "Joseph, Joseph, the time has come, Joseph," he cried. "The time has come to redeem the oath that you exacted from your brothers. It's time to go home." The coffin floated to the surface, and Moses placed it on his shoulders and he walked off into the wilderness. A generation later, after our entry into the Land, Joseph's bones were buried in Shekhem, in the shadow of the place where Joseph had been sold into slavery [Jos. 24.32]. The bones could only be buried after Joshua died, and right before Eleazar, the son of Aaron, dies, which teaches us that an entire generation must sometimes pass on

before we can completely deal with that which is left over from the past. To carry the bones is to possess the sacred; to bury the bones means getting on with life.

The forlorn siddurim in the hands of our synagogue administrator were the bones of Joseph. All of Jewish life in our time is a quest for the bones of Joseph. Sometimes those bones come in the form of text, or ritual, or stories, or holy places, or holy people.

Rabbi Meir suggests that Moses was not alone in redeeming the bones of Joseph. Each tribe had to take the bones of their own tribal parents with them. For it is only through our families that we redeem the bones of Joseph. I looked at the siddurim and

the *tefillin*, and I was seized by an almost uncontrollable sadness. I told my secretary, Peggy, to call the siddur donors, and to say this: "We are not accepting your prayer books. We're sorry that you cannot take them with you. Send them to your children. They need them more than we do." ●

buried in a cemetery. Each Jewish household should have a *geniza* of all these old tools of our peoplehood, not merely to gather dust, but rather to frequently come off the shelves. **Rabbi Neil Comess-Daniels, Beth Shir Sholom, Santa Monica, CA**

דָּבָר אַחֵר **DAVAR AHER. AND MOSES SPREAD HIS ARMS OVER THE WATERS... [Ex. 14.17].** In *Parashat Beshallah* the phrase used "to split the Sea of Reeds (the Red Sea)" and "to return the waters to their normal flow" is עַל הַיָּם וַיֵּט מֹשֶׁה אֶת יָדוֹ *va-yait Moshe et yado al ha-yam* "AND MOSES SPREAD HIS ARMS OVER THE SEA (or waters)." It is interesting to note that the act and the words used, (a) for splitting the sea and, (b) for returning the water, are identical. We are able to interpret the text

through the study of the trope (cantillation). In the first instance, the tropes are: *"pashta munakh zarka segol."* When chanted, it should be done without hesitation or pause, with a sense of urgency and danger. After all, the Egyptians were hard on the heels of the Israelites, so it was necessary for Moses to act in all haste to allow the Israelites to cross in safety, thus saving themselves. When it came to returning the sea to its normal flow, thus causing the death of the Egyptians, the trope is as follows: *"t'lishah k'tanah kadmah v'azlah r'vi."* When it is chanted, there is a pause between each of the words, and it is done with a sense of hesitancy. Moses, being the great humanist that he was, and being concerned with

the lives of people, in his hesitation was probably hoping that the Egyptians would see the danger that they faced, turn around, and go back onto the shores of the sea, thus saving their lives. They followed their Pharaoh, who displayed a hardness of the heart throughout all of the negotiations with Moses and, as we know, drowned. To me, this is an excellent example of the importance the trope plays in enlightening us on the text. **Rev. William Finer, retired Hazan Sheyne of Congregation Beth-El, Quebec, Canada**

Beshalla<u>h</u>

דָּבָר אַחֵר DAVAR A<u>H</u>ER. AND MOSES SPREAD HIS ARMS OVER THE WATERS… [Ex. 14.17].

From Shaye to Joel: How did the Red Sea split?

From Joel to Shaye: This is a hard answer. Actually, it is easy for me to understand, but hard to tell other people. The Red Sea split because my mother remembered that it did, and because she told me about it. I don't care about the mechanics. Some

people think that God just thought and there was just a forcefield that did it. Other people talk about winds blowing in just the right way, at the place where the tide was lowest, at the moment when the pull of the moon was just the strongest. The midrash (those great rabbinic stories which make sense out of the Torah) suggests, but doesn't say, that God stuck His two hands—the outstretched arm and the mighty hand—into the water and held back the waves. Israel walked out of Egypt by walking between God's (invisible) hands. Sometimes, I like to think it happened because at just the right moment, two seven-year-old kids were playing at a stream in the middle of Africa (near Mt. Kilimanjaro) and made a dam. That dam stopped up the river when it was still a little stream. They swam and played in the little pool which they had made. Meanwhile, hours or days later, the little water they stopped for their swimming hole became a big stoppage—and Israel crossed on dry land. Then they went home, and an elephant stepped on the dam. You know the rest of the story. To me, it doesn't

matter how God did it. It could have been a force field, a wind, giant invisible hands, or two little kids building a swimming hole. What matters is that God did do it. And what matters more, is that we remember, tell the story, and ask big questions like, "How did God do it?" "What do you think?" "What do you think it would have been like to cross the Red Sea?" "What do you remember about going out of Egypt—when you got to escape?" **Joel Lurie Grishaver <gris@ torahaura.com>**

דָּבָר אַחֵר DAVAR A<u>H</u>ER. THERE REMAINED NOT ONE OF THEM… [Ex. 14.28]. I can understand the movement from slavery to freedom and the Exodus from Egypt. What I can't understand is why God chose to kill off all the firstborn of Egypt *and* the entire Egyptian army so that we could get out of Egypt. I understand that God was flexing God's Divine muscles, *kiv'yakhol*; nevertheless, I would think that there should have been another way. I guess it's part of my *hutzpah klappei malah* posture. Yes, I do hold God responsible for lots of things in the world. It's all part of my relationship with the Divine. **Rabbi Kerry Olitzky, Director of School of Education HUC-JIR, New York, NY <Olitzky@huc.edu>**

Torah Changes: Leaving Our Wilderness— Coming to Our Sinai

Yitro

Exodus 18.1–20.23

Rabbi Kerry M. Olitzky

RABBI KERRY M. OLITZKY, D.H.L., IS DIRECTOR OF THE SCHOOL OF EDUCATION AT HEBREW UNION COLLEGE-JEWISH INSTITUTE OF RELIGION IN NEW YORK WHERE HE ALSO DIRECTS ITS GRADUATE STUDIES PROGRAM. AMONG HIS NUMEROUS TITLES, HE IS THE AUTHOR OF THE LEADING CONTRIBUTION TO JEWISH TWELVE STEP SPIRITUALITY: *TWELVE JEWISH STEPS TO RECOVERY*. HE IS CURRENTLY COMPLETING A BOOK ON JEWISH SPIRITUAL GUIDANCE WITH DR. CAROL OCHS.

Parashat Yitro, containing the Ten Commandments or, more literally, *Aseret ha-Dibrot*, the Ten Utterances (of God), is a portion rich with spiritual opportunity. This *sidrah* is named for Jethro, Moses' father-in-law. According to some, Jethro (whose name and function in the Torah narrative are debated by many scholars) seems to have taught Moses about the personal challenges implicit in living with one God way back when Moses took shelter in Midian.

You'll remember that Moses hurriedly left Egypt following the slaying of the Egyptian taskmaster, waiting in Midian until things settled down somewhat at Pharaoh's palace in Egypt. Through Jethro, Moses learned a lesson that many of us have also come to understand in the spiritual journey of our own lives: it often takes someone else to open us up to a potential relationship with God.

With the flame of the bush burning in his soul, Moses readied himself for religious leadership. As the most significant element, Jethro advised him to be responsive to revelation and the responsibility it implies. In our portion, Jethro once again emerges in the continuing saga of Moses' evolving journey of faith. In this segment of the Exodus story, Jethro teaches Moses the proper way to govern the people. Through the experience at Sinai, Moses later comes to understand for himself something that we must learn as well: our relationship with people should mirror the one we establish with the Divine, what theologian Eugene Borowitz often calls the "covenantal relationship."

דָּבָר אַחֵר **DAVAR AHER.** JETHRO, THE PRIEST OF MIDIAN, MOSES' FATHER-IN-LAW, HEARD ALL THAT GOD HAD DONE. [EX. 19.1]. Kerry Olitzky is absolutely right when he suggests that "it often takes someone else to open us up to a relationship with God," and that is just what Jethro did. I believe that in addition to that message, this one from Jethro is also appropriate: we Jews can always learn from non-Jews. Other religions have their truths which we should not ignore. Being God's Chosen People does not release us from the obligation to learn from, and perhaps even experiment with, the ways that other religions worship. I am envious, for example, of monks and nuns who use extended silence as a gateway to hearing and speaking to God. (We Jews like to talk, sing and responsively read, and the "silent" *Amidah* never really is.) Or the Baptists who encourage

Moses' often difficult encounters with the world around him actually strengthened his faith. Similarly, Egyptian slavery forged the disparate Israelite masses into a people, preparing them for the possibility of revelation and ultimate redemption. Some teachers even dare to suggest that the wilderness journey and the ascent to Canaan would not have been possible without the descent of our people into Egyptian bondage. After experiencing the miracles and wonders of the Exodus itself, traveling only three months in the desert, the Jewish people met their God. In reality, we had travelled a long distance since slavery. It seemed like we had been in the desert a long time, but that's the way life-changing journeys are. And, then, when we do have intimate contact with the Divine, our lives are radically changed forever. It's as simple as that. When we allow God to touch our lives, we gain an entirely different perspective on time and space—and on ourselves.

Because such critical encounters in the modern world seem elusive and rare, we look to that nearly inexplicable moment at Sinai for inspiration and insight. The encounter at Sinai collectively transformed the Jewish people, but changed each individual on a personal basis. While the exact location of the sacred mountain is unknown, we have all strained to reach its peaks in our own lives, in our own journeys—if only to stand on its summit for a moment. For those of us who constantly struggle for a glimpse of the Divine in our daily lives, we actually carry Sinai with us each time we encounter the sacred text through study, each time we reenact revelation through the public reading of Torah. Amid thunder and lightning and then suddenly in awesome silence, the Sinai experience was shared by all those who surrounded the foot of the mountain—as well as by those among us who claim the experi-

Yitro

their preacher with cries of "Amen" during the sermon. When I deliver my sermon I have absolutely no idea who (if anybody) is listening. After guest sermons I have given in the past in Catholic and Baptist churches, I have received standing ovations. Contrast that to the response I get after my sermon in the synagogue! If indeed there are "seventy faces to Torah," it is good to know that Jethro had one of

them. Even without thunder and lightning, lots of people in our world are talking to God. Jethro teaches us that we need to listen better to all of them. **Rabbi Melvin J. Glazer, Congregation Olam Tikvah, Fairfax, VA**

דָּבָר אַחֵר **DAVAR AHER. GOD SPOKE THESE WORDS...** [Ex. 20.1]. What did the People of Israel hear at Sinai? Did they hear God pronounce

ence as our own. What makes it so extraordinary, perhaps, is that God's voice still echoes from that mountain top. In order to hear it clearly, we have to be willing to listen for God's voice, to get rid of all the unnecessary noise that gets in our way. In essence, we have to actually become Torah: receptacles for God's revelation. Abraham Joshua Heschel taught it to us this way: "Only when we are able to share in the spirit of awe that fills the world are we able to understand what happened to Israel at Sinai."

We were there with Moses, with the people, in a mystical, metaphysical sort of way. Regardless of our individual ways of interpreting what happened, Sinai is the common experience that unites generations of Jews. Some say that each of our souls is connected to one of 600,000 primordial souls who actually witnessed *mattan Torah* (the giving of Torah). And in that part of our soul, we carry a vivid recollection of the event. Indeed, the mem-

ory of Sinai lives with each of us, particularly in the sacred relationship we constantly strive to maintain between ourselves and God.

In one form or another, the revelation of Torah took place at Sinai, but Torah only exists in our dynamic relationship with it. For me, Torah cannot abide merely in the form of a written scroll. That is just one interpretation of Torah fixed in a given point in time, from the perspective of the generation of the desert. In fact, this week's Torah portion teaches us that the revelation of Torah filled the world with limitless potential for holiness and personal spiritual growth. Thus, each time we enter into a relationship with the text, Torah changes as a result of that relationship. Similarly, we change as a consequence of our encounter with it. The Torah transcends the limitations of any written text. Thus, for me, the essential message of revelation is in the dialogue. The real meaning of living our lives as Jews

Synopsis: *Jethro, Moses' father-in-law, hears about Moses and all that God has done for the people of Israel and takes Zipporah, Moses' wife, as well as Gershon and Eliezer, his sons, to see Moses in the desert. Jethro comes to the camp, offers a sacrifice, organizes the courts and judiciary system and then leaves. In the third month after leaving Egypt, the people come to Sinai where they are charged to become "a kingdom of priests and a holy people." Moses gathers the people together and charges them to prepare three days for the theophany. On the third day, there is thunder and lightning and a dense cloud on the mountain. The people are afraid—but Moses reassures them that they will not perish. God then speaks all the "words" (the Ten Commandments) and the parashah concludes with the reaction of the people to this event and verses about the making of a proper altar in order to worship God.*

all ten commandments or only two? In Exodus, it is only after all ten of the edicts are spoken by God that the people ask Moses to stand between them and the Almighty. In Deuteronomy, however, Moses suggests that he was playing the role of intermediary from the outset. Building on these two traditions, Judah Halevi and the Rambam also come to different conclusions regarding the events that transpired at Sinai. Halevi,

accepting the maximalist view of *Mattan Torah,* holds that though the people were frightened by the power of the encounter with God, they had the innate capacity to achieve a direct prophetic experience. Rambam, holding with the minimalist tradition, believes that, due to his unique prophetic capability, only Moses was able to sustain a direct relationship with God. Perhaps there is truth in both approaches. There are moments

when we readily can hear the voice of God reverberating in the world around us, and we have a sense of spiritual exhilaration and illumination as we share a moment of intimacy with the *Shekhinah.* There are other moments when God's presence seems nowhere to be found, and in our spiritual loneliness we seek the assistance of others to help us find God. **Rabbi Joel Rembaum, Temple Beth Am, Los Angeles, CA**

is in the interaction, the unfolding process of our religious growth, as we try to live a holy life reflective of the covenant entered into by our ancestors and by us.

The core of the covenant is in the Decalogue, providing us, within the context of revelation, ten general parameters for sacred living. These ten commandments provide us with the means to hold onto Torah once we have discovered her wisdom. By guiding our interactions with God and others, they provide us with an entry point for living a life filled with the Divine presence. Yet, they represent only the primary ingredients; there is much more to living a holy life than observing the Ten Commandments. There are numerous additional mitzvot brimming with opportunities to make our lives a blessing. Martin Buber suggested that we should joyfully choose to observe all those mitzvot that we feel

addressed by—not just ten, but all those that bring us closer to God and self. Regardless of our personal conception of mitzvot, they have the potential to place a holy order on our lives. In fact, that's the essential claim mitzvot have on us.

To fully understand our relationship with God through mitzvot and enter Torah's spiritual realm, we have to let go of all the heady stuff in the material world that drags us down, preventing us from reaching heavenward. It's easy to be critical, to intellectualize. There is a place for such criticism and analysis in the classroom, but not when we are trying to find a holy place for ourselves in the world. According to rabbinic tradition, one has to be like a wilderness (to journey in the desert like our ancestors) in order to receive Torah.

Ever since Sinai, we have expected our lives to be filled with peak spiritual experiences. However, we will

Yitro

דָּבָר אַחֵר **DAVAR AHER.** GOD SPOKE THESE WORDS... [Ex. 20.1]. What did God's voice sound like? It was night. God came down on Mt. Sinai in a ball of fire. The Earth quaked. There was thunder and lightning. The families of Israel heard the sound of the shofar becoming louder and louder, until it almost broke their eardrums. *Mekhilta, Yitro: 1.57a.* God's voice was a big booming sound. God had great bass reproduction. **Shane Liebling.** God's

voice sounded like my father's. **Andy Ortner, Temple Beth El, San Pedro, CA**

דָּבָר אַחֵר **DAVAR AHER.** I AM THE ETERNAL, YOUR GOD... [Ex. 20.2]. This epochal moment in history begins with the great opening statement, "I AM THE ETERNAL YOUR GOD—אָנֹכִי ANOKHI—and ends with the word, רֵעֶךָ RE'EKHA—"Your neighbor's." We begin with the understanding of our relationship to God, and end on a

וישמע יתרו כהן מדין חתן משה

undoubtedly encounter both hills and valleys in our journey through life. In fact, most of our lives will be spent rambling down a bumpy road, struggling to make sense out of daily living. So we keep on going because the journey is never really over. And that's the point. Once we have discerned the holy, we no longer mind how long the trip takes. There is so much more to learn along the way.

There are many among us who have felt God in our midst, acknowledging the Divine presence in the journey of our lives. Torah and its study presents us with the essential opportunity to shape the raw poetry of that profound awareness for others. Yet, what do we do about expressing our own gratitude to God, the source of all that is, for joining with us in this covenant? As might be expected, our Torah portion offers us some insight and direction. *Parashat Yitro* concludes with an introduction to the next portion—*Mishpatim*—as a sort of preamble to how God should be worshiped by teaching us to assume a prayerful posture to all that we see, all that we do, all that we are. So in those early morning waking moments, as we wipe sleep from our weary eyes, that's what should be on our mind as well: what can we do today to change our lives and make room for God? We may not be able to discover all the answers in one day, but won't you join me in an effort to spend the day trying?●

societal level in relationship to our neighbor. Thus the decalogue is the basis of our relationship with both God and people. We root the first commandment, the commandment of belief, in our people's historical experience—in Egyptian slavery. Observing the mitzvot is in response to the historical event of the Exodus. In some ways, as a student once explained, "Following the mitzvot is our way of saying thanks to God for all God does for us." Certainly our ancestors at Sinai felt that this was part of the bargain, having been freed from the torturous slavery of Egypt. The experience of Sinai draws the line of Torah from God to Egypt to our neighborhoods. It goes from God's "I" to our "We." **Rabbi Morley Feinstein, Temple Beth El, South Bend, IN**

Rabbi Janet R. Marder

RABBI JANET R. MARDER IS THE ASSOCIATE DIRECTOR, PACIFIC SOUTHWEST COUNCIL OF THE UAHC.

Yitro

Rabbi Olitzky refers to the Talmudic teaching *[Eruvin 54a]* that only those who make themselves like the wilderness are worthy to receive Torah. The Talmud explains "wilderness" as a symbol of humility, for "everyone tramples on it." And it makes sense to say that we can receive Torah—we can achieve genuine religious insight—only if we are humble, rather than puffed up with who we are and what we already know.

But I want to argue that there's more to the idea of "becoming like the wilderness" than humility alone.

Take Moses, for example. Consider the young man who grows up fatherless in Pharaoh's court. He gets into trouble because he can't control his violent impulses, so he flees to Midian. As if sensing the need for some structure and discipline in his life, he immediately forms an attachment to Jethro, the hero of this week's parashah: an older man, a wise and stable father-figure whose counsel he'll come to depend on. Not long after, he enters into an even more profound relationship that will provide all the "fathering" he will ever need; he responds to the Voice in the burning bush and becomes "THE SERVANT OF THE LORD."

Moses' inner wilderness—his state of emptiness and deprivation, his need for connection with a strong, loving Father—makes him receptive to the Voice when it calls out. The same might be said of the Israelites, who are not able to hear the Voice at Sinai until they, too, have "made themselves like the wilderness"—suffering abasement and experiencing absolute dependence as they wander forlorn in the desert.

Understood in this way, "the wilderness" represents a state of psychological or spiritual neediness, of inner barrenness and desolation, which may be a precursor to genuine connection with God. Religious experience, after all, comes not to the complacent, but to hungry and thirsty souls who do not feel complete in themselves and yearn for something more.

Perhaps that's why our tradition strives so hard to keep our memories of slavery and wandering alive, evoking them throughout the *Tanakh* and the liturgy. Jews of all

וישמע יתרו כהן מדין חתן משה

time—even those who live amidst prosperity rather than pograms—are asked constantly to remind ourselves of times when we were despised outsiders whom "everyone trampled on." This is more than an exercise in masochism. It's a way of making ourselves like the wilderness—maintaining an awareness of our own vulnerability and inadequacy, our own need for connection with something greater.

It is not pleasant to admit to ourselves that neediness and dependence are at the root of religious feelings. But *Parashat Yitro* reminds us that encountering God and receiving Torah are more than joyous "peak experiences." They're "wilderness experiences"—experiences that come out of harsh and painful emotions: loneliness, fear, awareness of our terrible vulnerability and transience in the world. We open ourselves to God and God's teaching only when we recognize the pain of living without them.•

One Mitzvah: Do Not Curse a Judge

Mishpatim
Exodus 21.1–24.18

Rabbi Daniel Pressman

RABBI DANIEL PRESSMAN SERVES CONGREGATION BETH DAVID IN SARATOGA, CALIFORNIA. HE IS THE CREATOR OF *TORAH SPARKS*, A PARASHAT HA-SHAVUA PROJECT OF THE UNITED SYNAGOGUE OF CONSERVATIVE JUDAISM, AND THE EDITOR OF *THE ORCHARD*, PUBLISHED BY THE RABBINIC CABINET OF THE UNITED JEWISH APPEAL.

One less well-known mitzvah is found in Chapter 22, verse 27, which states,

אֱלֹהִים לֹא תְקַלֵּל
וְנָשִׂיא בְעַמְּךָ לֹא תָאֹר

YOU SHALL NOT CURSE *ELOHIM*, NOR PUT A CURSE UPON A RULER AMONG YOUR PEOPLE. Rabbinic tradition derives three different mitzvot from these words: (1) Not to curse a judge, (2) not to curse God, and (3) not to curse a ruler. Our focus will be the prohibition of cursing a judge.

First of all, how did the judge get into the picture? Rabbinic tradition sometimes interprets the word *Elohim* as referring to judges. This is most clear in 22.8: "ONE WHOM *ELOHIM* DECLARES GUILTY SHALL PAY DOUBLE TO THE OTHER." Obviously, God is not directly judging every case of law. Furthermore, the word יְרְשִׁיעֻן *yarshi-un*, "DECLARES GUILTY," is in the plural, which is never the case when the Torah uses *Elohim* to refer to God. So it must refer to judges.

What is the reason for this prohibition? In *Midrash Shemot Rabbah* 31.8, a telling story explains: "It once happened that a man had a lawsuit and came before a judge who pronounced the verdict in his favor. He then went about saying: 'There is no judge like this in the whole world.' In the course of time, he had another case and came before the same judge, who this time gave the verdict against him, so he went about saying: 'There is no greater idiot of a judge than this one.' People then said to him:

דָּבָר אַחֵר **DAVAR AHER. YOU KNOW THE HEART OF THE STRANGER. [Ex. 22.20].** When so many groups and individuals seek "victim status" to claim special prerogatives or special justification for actions otherwise seen as immoral (the Menendez brothers come to mind), Ex. 22.20 and 23.9 forbid wronging the stranger precisely because "YOU KNOW THE HEART OF THE STRANGER" and "YOU WERE STRANGERS IN THE LAND OF EGYPT." Thus the experience of being a victim demands greater sensitivity and response to needs of others; it is not a reason why others should cater to us. Elie Wiesel's consistent call for the Holocaust to sensitize us to the current pain of others because of our familiarity with pain is a modern echo of *Mishpatim* as it applies to the

אלה המשפטים אשר תשיב

'Yesterday he was splendid, and today he is an idiot?'" This seems familiar, doesn't it? Whenever a decision goes against us, it is a natural human tendency to cry out, "I was robbed! That judge (umpire, mediator, principal, boss or rabbi) is an idiot!" This mitzvah commands us to suppress that impulse. Such behavior harms the judge, the law and ourselves.

It harms the judge by undermining authority. The curse is a rejection of the judge's decision, but it is more than rejection—it is a hostile act. The Talmud took curses very seriously, leading the *Sefer ha-Hinukh* to state, "The basic purpose of the mitzvah is to remove from judges the fear of a person on trial and his curse, so that they can reach a true verdict." Even if we don't believe literally in the power of a curse, we don't want the losing defendant or litigant's anger to hamper the judge's work.

Cursing the judge harms the law because "the law" only exists as

Synopsis: Parashat Mishpatim follows the giving of the Ten Commandments at Mount Sinai. In the Mekhilta, the earliest rabbinic commentary on Exodus, Rabbi Ishmael says: "These [commandments] are added to the preceding ones. Just as those preceding were given from Sinai, so also those following were given from Sinai." This juxtaposition tells us that the other mitzvot are as significant as the Ten Commandments. Furthermore, toward the end of the parashah (24.12), it says, "Adonai said to Moses, 'Come up to Me on the mountain and wait there, and I will give you the stone tablets with the Torah and commandments which I have inscribed to instruct them.'" This verse seems to say that the entire Torah was written on the tablets, which does not fit with the rest of the narrative. Therefore, Rashi explains, "All the 613 commandments are implicitly contained in the Ten Commandments." In other words, each section of the Decalogue is a heading or general statement which is then fleshed out by other mitzvot of the Torah. Parashat Mishpatim begins this task.

The opening words of this parashah, "These are the rules [מִשְׁפָּטִים—mishpatim] that you shall set before them," begin the first extensive collection of laws in the Torah. Sefer ha-Hinukh (an annotated list of the 613 commandments) lists 52 mitzvot in this parashah. They cover the full range of biblical law, including criminal law (capital punishment for murder); civil law (laws of personal injury, property damage and negligence); ethical injunctions (laws forbidding the oppression of the powerless; the mitzvah of lending to the poor); and ritual law (laws of the sabbatical year, Shabbat and festivals). All the mitzvot are covenant obligations. The parashah emphasizes this by concluding with a formal ceremony of ratification in God's presence by Moses, Aaron and the seventy elders, who accept the covenant on behalf of the entire people: "All that Adonai has spoken we will faithfully do!" Moses then ascends Mt. Sinai alone to receive the stone tablets, remaining there forty days and nights.

---

responsibility of one who has been a victim. **Rabbi Harry K. Danziger, Temple Israel, Memphis, TN**

דָּבָר אַחֵר **DAVAR AHER.** IF A MAN GRAZES HIS LIVESTOCK IN A FIELD OR VINE-YARD AND LETS IT STRAY AND GRAZE IN ANOTHER MAN'S FIELD, HE MUST MAKE RESTI-TUTION. [Ex. 22.4]. The word here for "livestock" is not the usual word *bakar*

(בָּקָר) or *b'heymah* בְּהֵמָה but a rather somewhat rare word *b'ir* בְּאִיר. It is used only 3 times in the Torah. It probably is derived from *bo-er* בּוֹעֵר meaning "to burn" or "to consume." Thus these are "consumers." Not only does Torah consider "consumers" as cattle, but we, living in modern American society, can see that the mass media ad campaigners also

regard consumers as cattle. I believe these "beasts" represent our consumptive (selfish) side. Unlike cattle, these beasts provide neither milk nor meat. Torah often makes nouns out of verbs and hence in the "nounifying" of this word, it teaches us that we are what we do. If we merely selfishly consume, then we truly are these: "beasts" or "consumers." Ultimately,

embodied in a system of justice. If no one accepts a verdict, if there is no final resolution of any dispute or indictment, then society boils in constant turmoil, conflict and discontent. This is discussed in Pirkei Avot [1.8]: "Yehudah ben Tabbai says: When the parties in a lawsuit stand before you, regard them as wicked; but when they leave, regard them as innocent once they have accepted the judgment."

Yalkut Me'Am Lo'ez comments, "The most important thing is not how both parties argued, but how both accepted your judgment after the case was concluded. In every such case, there is bound to be a winner and a loser. When both parties accept your verdict graciously, they must both be considered righteous. This is especially true when the loser in the case shows absolutely no resentment toward the judge." This assent is necessary to an orderly, civil society.

Finally, the impulse to curse the judge harms the complainer, because, as Sforno writes, "Even if you think that the judge has miscarried justice, do not curse him, for no person can find fault with himself." Civil disputes and criminal accusations are decided by trained, objective third parties because people are true geniuses at rationalizing and justifying their own behavior.

Rabbi Israel Salanter, the great moral teacher, once wrote, "The first time a person commits a transgression, he knows he did wrong. The second time he does it, he thinks it's permitted. By the third time, he thinks it's a mitzvah!"

If we look around at today's society, we see "cursing the judge" on the increase, and peaceful acceptance of a decision in decline. If a defendant has the means, an adverse verdict is appealed endlessly. We routinely see high-profile cases tried in the media. The result is that prominent people (or corporations) in trouble turn first

Mishpatim

someone more responsible than us will have to pay for our consumption. **Michael Kaminski, Price, UT**

דָּבָר אַחֵר **DAVAR AḤER.**
Epilogue. *On the Discontinuity of the Torah's Narrative.* Here is where the Torah feels like someone had the typed manuscript, dropped it, and then put the pages back in the wrong order. Here is the way the story goes. Moses goes up Mt. Sinai to get the Ten Commandments and never comes back [*Yitro*, Ex. 20]. Next, in *Mishpatim*, we go off on a multi-chapter tangent listing slave rules, torts, and all kinds of other practical stuff. We write the entire MISHNAH (or at least the proto-text for *Nezekin*, Damages) in chapters 21-23. Then Moses leaves to go up on the mountain again [Ex. 24]. Then Chapter 25 (*Trumah, Tetzaveh,*) and forward involves us in building

not to the legal process, but to public relations firms to put the proper "spin" on events. Umpires and referees in every sport are subject to verbal abuse by players and fans, even death threats. In such a social climate, where no decision is ever accepted as final, where people nurse grievances forever, we lose a vital element of social cohesion. Conflicts and disputes simmer unceasingly, and personal reconciliation and societal peace become ever more elusive. Underlying all of this is the fundamental disrespect for the legal process and self-serving egotism that this mitzvah addresses.

This insight is challenging to those of us who are automatically suspicious of authority (there are right-wing and left-wing versions of this libertarian, anti-authoritarian trend). Jewish law is very aware of the temptations of power. In the *Mishneh Torah* (*Laws of Sanhedrin*, chapters 25 and 26), Maimonides summarizes the laws commanding the judge against arbitrary and arrogant abuse of authority before the prohibition of cursing judges. There are many safeguards to protect litigants and defendants, but ultimately there must be an authority that makes decisions, and the parties involved must respect that ruling. It is true that some officials earn our distrust, but if we revile every authority figure, the buck stops nowhere, and nothing is ever resolved.

There is also a spiritual dimension to this prohibition. Rabbenu Yonah, commenting on *Pirkei Avot* "When they leave, regard them as innocent once they have accepted the judgment," explains, "Once he has accepted the sentence, it is not right to continue treating him with suspicion, even though he has been found guilty. One is rather to assume that he repented, that he intends never to behave this way again."

Those who scream, "I was robbed! The judge is an idiot!" are captive to the egocentric rationalizations that Sforno and Salanter described. They won't do *teshuvah* because they have constructed an elaborate defense of their own righteousness, and placed responsibility for their plight outside themselves.

Sforno comments on the book of Genesis where the Torah describes the people God condemned with the Flood: "THE ETERNAL SAW HOW GREAT WAS HUMANITY'S WICKEDNESS ON EARTH, AND HOW EVERY PLAN DEVISED BY THEIR MINDS WAS NOTHING BUT EVIL ALL THE TIME." [Gen. 6.5] He taught: "HOW GREAT WAS HUMANITY'S WICKEDNESS—in the past; how EVERY PLAN DEVISED BY THEIR MINDS—in the future, for they did not listen to the rebuker, and there was no hope that they would repent."

This helps us relate this legal and social text to our personal lives and issues. It is easy to condemn the litigant who curses the judge or the accused who fights back through public relations manipulation. It is harder to look at ourselves and ask how often we demonstrate this behavior in our lives, through spurning criticism and rejecting authority, even when part of our soul knows

---

the Tabernacle. Finally, in Chapter 31 (the middle *of Ki Tissa)*, Moses comes down the mountain and encounters the Golden Calf.

Yesterday's Hebrew High class explained this passage to me. Not through words, but through actions. I was teaching the *sidrah*: "EVERY PARENT MUST TELL HIS CHILD ABOUT THE EXODUS" when Yoni asked, "Here is something we debated in *shul* this Shabbat: if you were a rabbi, would you perform an intermarriage?" Before I could answer him, I stopped my lesson to deal with Adam and Michael who were messing around. As soon as I had done my evil eye stare, before I could answer Yoni, Lindsey asked me if I had read this "feminist" novel about a woman in some Arab land and her struggle for rights. I wrote down the name of her novel. Then, I turned back to Yoni, who should be answered before I returned to our Torah text. And, per usual, the bell rang.

This is the message of *Mishpatim— Torah Interruptus*. We are always going up and down Mt. Sinai. Halfway up, we are called on to apply a mishnah to Adam and Michael's classroom behavior or to answer Yoni's inquiry about congregational policy. The moment always makes its demands and teaches Torah in its own pragmatic way.

that we are wrong. Biblical law is religious law—our covenant obligations to God. The laws of jurisprudence are concerned about justice, not about winners and losers. They are also interested in the moral rehabilitation and repentance of the offen-der. Resentment and denial which lead to cursing the judge interfere with both.

Parashat Mishpatim's wide range of concerns teaches us that for Judaism, law is not just a means of assuring social order, but a tool for moral education. As Ibn Ezra put it:

עִקַּר כָּל הַמִּצְוֹת לְיַשֵּׁר הַלֵּב (*Ikar kol ha-mitzvot l'yasher ha-lev*) "The essential purpose of the commandments is to make the heart upright." The mitzvah against cursing the judge helps create the atmosphere of respect and receptivity which allows the Torah and mitzvot to do their work of refining the human heart and creating a society which follows God's ways.•

Mishpatim

Then, eventu-ally, we continue to tell the story, continue the ascent up the mountain to meet in spirit and intellect the God we already know through practice and application. That is what I learned about *Mishpatim* this week. **Joel Lurie Grishaver, <gris@torahaura.com>**

דָּבָר אַחֵר **DAVAR AḤER. On Torah Interruptus.** Your comment on *Torah Interruptus* was a real scream, and a golden nugget of truth. My take on it, of course, comes from the perspective of one who deals with synagogue leadership, usually very good leadership in our case. They get the mission all worked out, then stop to deal with a family crisis, or someone else's family crisis, then we get some anti-Semitic graffiti or spend some time writing a grant proposal, then we get a small fire in the building (last July, for real) and everything in the building gets moved around. Yet they keep at it, going into the sea, up the mountain, whatever it takes. (And people ask why I stay in Kansas City!) **Rabbi Daniel Horwitz, Congregation Ohev Shalom, Prairie Village, KS**

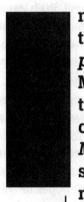

n *Parashat Terumah* and the following two *parashiyot*, God gives Moses detailed instructions for the design and construction of the *Mishkan*, the portable sanctuary that accompanied the Israelites on their journey from Mount Sinai to the Promised Land.

At the heart of the *Mishkan* was the Holy of Holies, the chamber containing the Ark. The Ark was a chest containing the two Tablets of the Covenant. It was covered with a lid adorned with two three-dimensional figures of cherubs.

Terumah

Exodus 25.1–27.19

Professor Jeffrey H. Tigay

JEFFREY H. TIGAY IS ELLIS PROFESSOR OF HEBREW AND SEMITIC LANGUAGES AND LITERATURE AT THE UNIVERSITY OF PENNSYLVANIA AND AUTHOR OF THE JPS COMMENTARY ON DEUTERONOMY.

What did the Ark signify to our ancestors? What did it resemble in their experience? Prof. Nahum Sarna, in his book *Exploring Exodus*, observes that scholars have found the greatest similarity to the Ark, and to the entire portable sanctuary, in the *Utfah* and the *Qubbah*, two Arabic artifacts used as far back as Biblical times.

The *Utfah* is "a tentlike structure made of thin wooden boards and having a domed top. It is fastened on the baggage saddle of a camel...Allah is believed to reside in it and supernatural properties are attributed to it. When the camel carrying it begins to move, the entire tribe follows suit, and where it kneels is where the camp is pitched. At critical moments in battle the *Utfah* is brought out to ensure victory," just as the Ark was in the days of Samuel [1 Samuel 4.3ff.].

Even older than the *Utfah*, Prof. Sarna reports, "is the pre-Islamic *Qubbah*, which was a small portable tent shrine constructed of red leather...[It] con-

דָּבָר אַחֵר **DAVAR AHER. TELL THE ISRAELITE PEOPLE TO BRING ME GIFTS. [EX. 25.1-9].** At an education Shabbat, I will be reading from Exodus Chapter 25.1-9. "THE LORD SPOKE TO MOSES, SAYING: TELL THE ISRAELITE PEOPLE TO BRING ME GIFTS; YOU SHALL ACCEPT GIFTS FOR ME FROM EVERY PERSON WHOSE HEART SO MOVES HIM.... EXACTLY AS I SHOW YOU—THE PATTERN OF THE TABERNACLE AND THE PATTERN OF ALL ITS FURNISHINGS—SO SHALL YOU MAKE IT." As we see from these verses, it took a variety of gifts to build the Tabernacle. The Israelites gave these gifts willingly, thereby building the Tabernacle and causing God's presence to dwell among them. Our students are faced with a task much more daunting and overwhelming than that of building a Tabernacle. They must create a future by working toward finding solutions to the many problems that face our planet. Like the Israelites, our students bring a variety of gifts. Unlike the gifts of the Israelites who brought specific material

tained the idols and cult objects of the tribe and was often mounted on the back of a camel. When the tribe pitched camp, the tent shrine was unloaded and set up beside the tent of the sheik. People would come to it seeking oracles," as was regularly done at the Ark of Israel.[1]

These parallels suggest that the Ark was similar to a small, portable shrine, which in contemporary nomadic culture was used to house the idol representing the deity. But there was a crucial difference: in the Israelite Ark was no idol, but instead the two Tablets of the Covenant containing the first statement of God's law, the Ten Commandments. In Judaism this implies that the Ten Commandments, and later the entire Torah, take the place of idols as the representatives of God's presence. Representations of God's person are banned and replaced by texts containing statements of His will. With the giving of the Torah and the prohibition of idols, the study of the Torah and its commandments becomes the means of access to God.

This distinction is dramatically represented by the way we treat the Torah scroll in the synagogue. It is given the treatment which in other cultures is reserved for monarchs, or popes or, le-havdil, for icons and idols. Like all of these, the Torah is carried in procession when it is taken out of the Ark and when it is returned there after the reading. Like a monarch, an Ashkenazi Torah is dressed up in a mantle, belt, and crown, and even has a hand (the Torah pointer). The Torah is housed in an Ark that, in traditional Jewish sources, is called the heikhal, the "palace," and we pray facing this Ark. In Japan, there are temples constructed exactly like synagogues, with an ark at the front—the difference being that the

Terumah

items, the gifts our students bring are often intangible. Among these gifts are many skills and talents, perhaps the greatest of which is imagination. May we, their teachers, have the wisdom to recognize and nurture the gifts of our students. May we create contexts in which our students can give their gifts willingly and joyfully. May we help them respect and value each other's unique contributions. Let this be our way of building the kind of world that causes God's presence to dwell among us. **Debra Cohn-Levine, RJE, Temple Israel, Tulsa, OK**

דָּבָר אַחֵר **DAVAR AHER. TELL THE ISRAELITE PEOPLE TO BRING ME GIFTS [EX. 25.1-9].** I mentioned to my daughter-in-law that I was giving the d'var Torah on Terumah and her response was "my favorite parashah—I love all the details about the Tabernacle

דבר אל בני ישראל ויקחו לי תרומה

Japanese ark contains an idol. The similar treatment of the Torah and statues is even more obvious in the case of oriental Torah scrolls, those of Jewish communities from the Middle East and further east, which resemble portable Japanese shrines. An oriental Torah scroll is mounted in a hard case resembling a building. When the Torah is read, it stands vertically on the reading table, with the two sections of the front opening sideways on hinges to expose the scroll. The portable Japanese shrines are virtually identical to these Torah cases, but inside is not a scroll, but an idol. The Ark and oriental Torah cases are thus an artistic denial of idolatry in favor of the Torah. Ashkenazi and oriental Torahs signify what the biblical Ark indicates: access to God is not gained by means of idols but through the Torah and its commandments. In other words, the Torah and its commandments are

more than a book and a series of rules and customs; they are a way of establishing a relationship with God and coming to know the Deity.

These inferences are supported by statements in Talmudic literature that speak of the role of the Torah as God's representative. According to *Pirkei Avot* 3.2, "If two sit together and exchange words of Torah, the Divine Presence abides between them." In the *Sifrei*, the rabbinic commentary on Deuteronomy, Rabbi Meir explains the meaning of *v'Ahavta* in the following way: Why does *v'Ahavta* begin with "You shall love the Lord" and then add: "And these words which I command you today shall be on your heart..." Because "you shall love" by itself does not tell us *how* to love God; therefore the Torah adds: "These words shall be on your heart," meaning: take to heart these words—God's commandments and actions described in the Torah—for

Synopsis: The parashah begins with instructions about the gathering of materials needed to outfit the sanctuary. These gifts are to come from public contributions. Detailed instructions follow about: the ark (אָרוֹן *aron); the covering (כַּפֹּרֶת *kapporet); the cherubs (כְּרוּבִים *keruvim); the table (שֻׁלְחָן *shulḥan); the lampstand (מְנוֹרָה *menorah); the coverings; the boards (קְרָשִׁים *kerashim); the inner curtain (פָּרֹכֶת *parokhet); the outer curtain (מָסָךְ *masakh); the altar (מִזְבֵּחַ *mizbeaḥ); and finally, the court (חָצֵר *hatzer).

and the furnishings." What else could I have expected from an artist! Then I looked closer, asked a few questions, checked a few sources and found there were a number of interesting facets to this seemingly obscure parashah.

We all know that the Torah can not be taken too literally with regard to numbers: how many people left *Mitzrayim*, how old people were at various times in the stories. An aside—

even had there been available this current medical procedure allowing women past menopause to bear children, 99 years old is still suspect! So too, sometimes the chronology is not to be taken too literally.

According to Nachama Leibovitz who quotes the Rambam, *Terumah* should come after *Ki Tissa*, the golden calf incident, not before. There are two midrashim which bring out this idea: The first midrash says that the com-

mandment to build the Tabernacle marked the Israelites' reconciliation with God after their estrangement—the golden calf story.

The second midrash says the Tabernacle was a consequence of the golden calf—that it must be reckoned as a concession to human frailty—a healing for their wounds. This was a very young people (not in age, but regarding religion, spirituality). We "enlightened" 20th century people

Terumah—143

that is how you come to know the Creator and adhere to His ways.[2] The point is clarified further by the *Sifrei*'s comment on the command to "CLING TO GOD" [Deut. 11.22]: "How is it possible for a human to ascend to heaven and cling to God, Who is like fire? What the Torah means is: cling to the scholars of the Torah and their students. Interpreters of *aggadot* say: If you want to know The Creator, learn *aggadah*, that is, the non-*halakhic* Bible interpretations of the rabbis—for that is how you get to know God."[3] By referring to scholars of the Torah and *aggadic* interpreters, these comments tell us that Torah, as a means of knowing God, means all of Torah—the Talmudic interpretation of the Torah as well as the original text.

The Torah is not regarded as the only way to learn about God. Maimonides, for example, held that studying God's works of creation—in other words, studying science—was another avenue for knowing

God.[4] But the Torah and the mitzvot are the most explicit and indispensable method we have.

How does this work? How do we come to know God through the Torah and the commandments?

(1) On the simplest level we learn about God's qualities and His will from the way they are depicted in the Torah. The story of creation teaches that God is beyond nature, from which we learn that we are not to deify and worship anything within nature. From the same story we learn of God's great solicitude for humanity, from which we learn that He is not indifferent to humanity and its aspirations. From His anger at human sinfulness we learn of His passionate involvement in the life of people. From God's discussion with Abraham about Sodom, we learn that He does not invoke power or authority to exempt Himself from objective standards of justice. From His willingness to forgive the penitent we learn that His aim is not to punish

Terumah

have trouble relating to an abstract principle, God. Imagine a people who were slaves in *Mitzrayim* who saw pagan practices of idol worship and are now expected to believe in something "other." No doubt a difficult situation.

Fifteenth century Biblical scholar Abravanel finds parallels between the building of the tabernacle and the creation story. Speaking of creation, did you know that God cre-

ated the world, plants, animals, man, and Shabbat in 34 verses? This parashah about the building of the Tabernacle is 96 verses long, almost three times as long, and many more in subsequent parshiot detailing the construction and decoration of the Tabernacle. At first I thought it must be because in creation God did it all Himself—here He had delegated the work to people and perhaps

wrongdoers but to reform them. From the story of Moses at the burning bush we learn of His patience and His willingness to adjust God's own plans to the weaknesses of His human partners. From the laws of the Torah we learn of God's love of justice. From the prophets' condemnation of the sacrifices of those who oppress the poor we learn that God hates religious hypocrisy. From the story of the Exodus, and from our annual reenactment of that story at the Seder, we learn of His aim that people be free.

The branch of Jewish learning that excels at learning about God's qualities from the Bible is *aggadah*. A lovely example is provided in an *aggadah* quoted by Rashi in his commentary on the story about the three angels that visited Abraham [Gen. 18.1ff.]. The Torah says that God appeared to Abraham when Abraham was sitting at the entrance to his tent at the hot time of the day. Rabbi Hama bar Hanina noted that in the previous chapter Abraham had

been circumcised, and so he reconstructed the following sequence of events: This was the third day following Abraham's circumcision, and God's visit was an act of *Bikkur Holim*, the mitzvah of visiting the sick. The reason for the heat was as follows: God knew that Abraham loved to perform the mitzvah of *Hakhnasat Orhim*, welcoming guests, and He feared that if guests came by while Abraham was still sore, he would cause himself great discomfort providing hospitality. So God removed the sun from its sheath so that it would blaze hotter than usual and prevent travelers from going out on the road and passing by Abraham's tent. But the plan backfired and Abraham was grieved because he had no guests. Therefore God sent three angels to him, disguised as persons, so that Abraham could have the pleasure of performing the mitzvah. The story, of course, is sheer fiction, but it expresses a perception of God's tenderness that is a genuine outgrowth of the Torah,

and it shows how the rabbis used the text of the Torah as a vehicle for teaching the nature of God.

(2) This story also hints at another way in which the Torah and the commandments teach us about God. The rabbis view the commandments as emulations of God's qualities. Just as He visits the sick Abraham, so are we commanded to visit the sick. We are commanded to clothe the naked because He does so, to bury the dead, to comfort mourners, to give charity, to be merciful to those who offend, to be gracious, and to be just—all because He does so. In this way, too, the Torah and the commandments represent God to us. By studying and performing them, we learn about Him.[5]

The Torah is regarded as so effective a representative of God that the rabbis went so far as to say that if a choice had to be made between abandoning God and abandoning the Torah and commandments, God would prefer that Jews abandon Him and observe the Torah, since study-

---

felt he must be very, very specific so that it would be done correctly.

Then, after I discussed it with David, we decided that maybe the reason was to make the people feel a part of the whole thing. God certainly could have made the Tabernacle with but a flick of the wrist or a twitch of the nose. However, just as in Sisterhood, the more people who are involved, the stronger the organization becomes—because of the feeling that

"we are all in this together." God wanted the people to feel this kind of bond with each other.

Another thing jumped out at me while reading and re-reading this parashah. The people were asked for gold and jewels to decorate the Tabernacle. Now, where did all these precious stones come from? Remember, these people were slaves up until a few weeks ago. Well, if you remember, God told all the Israelite

women to ask for gold and jewels and fine cloth from their Egyptian neighbors before leaving. [Ex. 3.22]. That must have been the source of those items.

Here again, the chronology may be suspect. Here in *Terumah* the jewels, etc. were given up willingly. In the golden calf incident, according to midrash, the women refused to contribute their treasures and as a reward were given *Rosh Hodesh* as a special

ing the Torah and practicing its commandments would lead them back to Him.[6]

(3) There is yet another way in which the Torah represents God. It is a criterion by which to judge the claims of those who claim to speak on God's behalf. Since the cessation of prophecy at the end of the Biblical period, the highest authority in Judaism has been that of the *halakhic* scholars, the masters of Jewish law. The extent of their authority is indicated in the Talmudic story:

> Rabbi Eliezer once used all possible arguments to validate a legal opinion of his, but his colleagues would not agree with him. So he said to them: "If the law is as I say, this carob tree shall prove it." The carob tree then uprooted itself and jumped 150 feet! But Rabbi Eliezer's colleagues said to him: "We don't bring proof from a tree."

> So he said to them: "If the law is as I say, the canal will prove it." The waters of the canal then flowed backwards. But Rabbi Eliezer's colleagues said to him: "We don't bring proof from a canal."

> So he said to them: "If the law is as I say, the walls of the Academy shall prove it." Then the walls began to teeter, but Rabbi Joshua shouted at them: "If scholars debate the law, what has it to do with you?" So the walls didn't fall, out of respect to Rabbi Joshua, but they did not straighten up again, out of respect to Rabbi Eliezer. They remained tilted from that time on.

> Then Rabbi Eliezer said: "If the law is as I say, it shall be proven from heaven." Then a small voice from heaven declared: "What business have you arguing with Rabbi Eliezer? The law is always in accordance with his opinion!"

Terumah

holiday for women. However, if they had given up the jewels for the Tabernacle first, they would not have had them for the golden calf; but if *Terumah* came after *Ki Tissa*, it would be more understandable. So, once again, we see the women (read that Sisterhood), beautifying the Tabernacle (read that "Temple Israel"!).

Another interesting idea from Simcha Bunem of Przysucha notes that the Torah is very specific about the order in which the work is to be done. From that comes the conclusion that all things must be done in the proper sequence, at the proper time. We should not put at the end what should be at the beginning and what is supposed to be at the beginning should not be put at the end. This, too, can be relevant to our own times—first things first!

My final look into the parashah for

At this, Rabbi Joshua jumped to his feet and quoted the Biblical verse "IT IS NOT IN HEAVEN" [Deut. 30.12]. What is the meaning of 'IT IS NOT IN HEA-VEN'? Rabbi Jeremiah said: The Torah was already given to *us* at Mt. Sinai, and since that time we pay no attention to voices from heaven, for at Mt. Sinai it was written in the Torah: 'You are to make legal decisions by majority vote.'"

Afterwards, Rabbi Nathan met Elijah and asked him: "What did the Holy One, Blessed be He, do when that debate took place?" Elijah answered: "God smiled and said, 'My children have defeated me, my children have defeated me!'"[7]

In this story God acknowledges that man cannot live on the basis of continuing communications from heaven. God made a record of the basic principles of His will for the Jewish people in the Torah, and from then on decisions on how to conduct ourselves must be made in conformity with the Torah as interpreted by the majority vote of each generation's experts on its legal interpretation. It is very important to note the stress on the principle of decision by majority. No single authority, no matter how learned or charismatic, can carry the day on his own. There is no room for the extremist whose teachings are so inconsistent with the Torah's values, as interpreted in Jewish tradition, that they cannot command the assent of a majority of qualified halakhic scholars.

These three avenues illustrate how the Torah serves as God's representative to the Jews: through the study of its contents, the performance of its commandments, and as a repository of God's will guiding Jewish behavior and setting limits on what may be claimed as God's will.

Modern insights into the symbolism of the Ark help us to see that the physical decoration of the Torah and the way in which we treat it reflect its role in Judaism as our chief avenue to God. This symbolism is well worth remembering each time we see the Torah carried in procession. This role of the Torah is beautifully expressed in a prayer that forms part of the *Birkhot ha-Shaḥar*, the prayer known from its opening words as *ve-ha'arev-na*:

O Lord our God, please make the words of Your Torah pleasant in our mouths and in the mouths of Your people Israel, so that we and all our descendants may all come *to know Your name* [that is, to know Your nature] and to learn Your Torah for its own sake. Praiseworthy are You, O Lord, Who teaches the Torah to Your people Israel.●

1. Sarna, *Exploring Exodus* (New York: Schocken, 1986), pp. 198-99.
2. *Sifrei Deuteronomy* 33; thus interpreted by Maimonides, *Guide of the Perplexed*, 3.28, 52; *Sefer Ha-mitzvot*, positive no. 3; *Sefer Ha-Ḥinukh* sec. 118.
3. *Sifrei Deuteronomy* 49. Cf. also *Midrash Tehillim* 105.1.
4. *Hilkhot Yesodei Ha-Torah* 2.2.
5. Schechter, *Aspects of Rabbinic Judaism* (New York: Schocken, 1961), pp. 199ff.; *Mekhilta Shirta*, 3; *Sifrei Deuteronomy* 49; Maimonides, *Hilkhot De'ot* 1.6.
6. *Yerushalmi Ḥagigah* 1.7, p. 76c; *Eikhah Rabbati*, proem 2 (ed. Buber, pp. 2-3); *Pesikta de-Rav Kahana* 15 (ed. Mandelbaum, p. 254).
7. *Bavli, Bava Metsia* p. 59b.

---

this morning concerns the word *"Terumah"* which means to give and at the same time to take. Verse 2: "SPEAK UNTO THE CHILDREN OF ISRAEL, THAT THEY TAKE FOR ME AN OFFERING; OF EVERY MAN WHOSE HEART MAKES HIM WILLING YOU SHALL TAKE MY OFFERING." As is very often the case, we give of ourselves and gain much more in return. Volunteer work often means giving up our precious time as well as money and, more often than not, the rewards are returned to us many times over. **Fran Elovitz, Temple Israel, Natick, MA**

דָּבָר אַחֵר **DAVAR AḤER.** LET THEM MAKE ME A SANCTUARY SO THAT I MAY DWELL AMONG THEM. [Ex. 25.8]. The *Tzeida la-Derekh* (Rabbi Issachar ben Israel Lazar Parnas Eilenburg) observes that the Hebrew doesn't say God will dwell "IN IT," i.e., *the sanctuary*, but rather "IN THEM"—*the people.* God doesn't dwell in houses of God. God dwells in the hearts and minds of people. When we come to synagogue, it is we who bring God's presence with us. Alice Walker writes in *The Color Purple*, "Have you ever found God in church? I never did. I just found a bunch of folks hoping for Him to show. Any God I ever felt

אֵלֶיךָ שֶׁמֶן זַיִת זָךְ

in church I brought in with me. And I think all the other folks did too. They come to church to *share* God, not find God."

The *Malbim* (Rabbi Meir Yehudah Leibush ben Yekhiel) teaches that the physical sanctuary of God is just a reminder of what God really wants—that each person builds a sanctuary within his or her heart for God to dwell therein. Exodus 25.8

expresses God's hope that we will open ourselves up to the spirit—for prayer and meditation, for Torah study, for relationship with *ha-Kadosh Barukh Hu*. God has no need to dwell in buildings. What God desires more than anything is to dwell—to live—in each of us. **Rabbi Stuart Weinberg Gershon, Temple Sinai, Summit, NJ**

Terumah

ואתה תצוה את בני ישראל

Tetzaveh

Exodus 27.20–30.10

Tikvah Frymer-Kensky

TIKVAH FRYMER-KENSKY IS THE AUTHOR ON *IN THE WAKE OF THE GODDESSES* AND DIRECTOR OF BIBLICAL STUDIES AT THE RECONSTRUCTIONIST RABBINICAL COLLEGE.

We are now in the heart of the cult. We have journeyed from the great narrative of redemption from Egypt, to the covenant with God that gives this redemption its meaning. Israel has entered this covenant with thunder and fire and dread, in the frightening and compelling events at Sinai. We have read ideas of how people can live out the covenant through mundane laws of everyday living, laws about slaves being freed, people being injured, oxen that gore and people who steal, and we have read about how people must live out the covenant through mindfulness of their past oppression and kindness to those oppressed. And then, understanding these laws, we have seen Israel enact its covenant in the symbolism of blood and in the quiet fellowship of a communion meal.

We have then moved inwards, to the housing of the covenant, the sheltering and buffering of the relationship with God. In the sanctuary, and in the Temple of Israel, God's presence can rest in the midst of Israel, rest in continual and peaceful content with this people that God has known only sporadically and in the powerful context of overwhelming events.

But the sanctuary is only a place. God does not decree the Divine Presence in the house of God because God needs a place to rest, but in order to be in perpetual contact with the people of Israel. And this means that the sanctuary must also house *people*, the human interface with God. And so we come to *Tetzaveh*, which brings us Aaron and his sons, who are to serve in the sanctuary as priests of God. We have met Aaron before, and we shall see him and his sons again as the narratives of Israel resume. But *Tetzaveh* presents us Aaron and the priests as part of the sanctuary, as the bearers of its purpose.

Terumah gives us great detail of the Tabernacle and its furnishings. The detailed instructions are an integral part of its purpose, for the Tabernacle is a "containment field" which allows God's enormous energy to be safely in contact with people. It must be prescribed and built exactly, for any deviation could mean that God could not be safely contained there. And once the priests are within this power-area, they, too, must have a precise containment field to cover them. *Tetzaveh* minutely describes the garments that the priests

Tetzaveh

must wear, and cautions that they must be made by wise people into whom God's wisdom can enter. Despite the minutiae of the descriptions, it is difficult today to picture exactly what these vestments looked like. The ancient priests knew them better, but the rest of Israel may have strained, like us, to imagine exactly how the *ephod*, the shoulder bars and the breastplate looked. But their purpose is very clear: these garments make it possible for Aaron to be holy, to bear his mission and come into contact with the holy.

The vestments were made with the finest of substances—gold and purple and scarlet, and upon the shoulders of the *ephod* were onyx stones engraved with the names of Israel. In this way, the priest carried the names of Israel before God. He also carried the names of Israel in to God on the most intricate breastplate, inlaid with fine precious stones engraved with the names of the twelve tribes. The breastplate is called "the breastplate of judgment"—but the only purpose mentioned here was to carry the names of Israel in to God. Israel—the people themselves—cannot come into the core of the sanctuary. But the priest carries their names in so that God can always be mindful of them. The breastplate also contains the *Urim* and *Tummim*, the great divination instrument that Israel would use to ascertain the will of God. In this

way, Aaron wears this instrument of contact with God as he himself comes before God.

Under the *ephod* is a blue shift that slips over the priest's head. This shift has a special hem, adorned with bells and pomegranates so that when the priest moves the bells sound. When Aaron, dressed in this outfit, goes into the sanctuary to minister to God, the bells ring and the sound can be heard.

Aaron cannot slip into the holy space casually or unobserved. The moment he begins the process and puts on the shift, the bells can be heard. On top of this he wears the heavy gold and jewel-encrusted *ephod*, with its breastplate and shoulder emblems, and on his head he wears a heavy mitre. With all this on, Aaron must walk slowly, in stately procession, clanging and ringing and announcing his presence with the noise, and with the words "Holy to the Lord" inscribed on his mitre. In this way he can go into the Holy of Holies safely, bringing in the names of Israel, and he can stand in the presence of the Holy and not die. This is Aaron's "holysuit"—like a space suit, it enables him to survive in an environment that an unprotected human cannot endure.

Unprotected contact with Holiness results in instant death, like the death of Uzziah, who reached out his hand to prevent the ark from falling [2 Sam. 6.6-7], or the death of the many people of Bethshemesh

ואתה תצוה את בני ישראל ויקחו אליך שמן זית זך

who went to greet the ark as it returned from the land of the Philistines [1 Sam. 6.19–21]. As the men of Bethshemesh learned, holiness is not sweetness and light; it is immense power: we must have God's holy presence to survive, but we must approach it only when it is contained in the precise manner God prescribes, and we come into the realm of holiness only in the holysuit God gives us.

In the modern world we have energy that can serve as a metaphor to model this divine power. Carefully contained nuclear power can fuel our cities, but if the plant has cracks, it will escape and destroy, and if an individual approaches without a radiation suit, that person is dead. The dilithium crystals that power the Starship Enterprise on its star trek are kept within a "containment field"; if the core is breached, no one can prevent the crystals from destroying the ship. The ancients had experience of the power of flood and fire; contained, they provide life; uncontained they destroy. Magnified above all these, in power and in danger, is holiness, the presence of God. •

SYNOPSIS: Continuing from last week, our parashah provides details of the Ner Tamid, preparation of the oil (shemen); the priestly vestments—both for the high priest and for the ordinary priests: the ephod, the breastplate, the robe, the headware, the tunic, the headdress, and the sash. The second part of the parashah describes the consecration of the priesthood. Lasting seven days, this ceremony contains instructions concerning the sacrifices, the offerings, the washing of the bodies of Aaron and his sons, their robing and anointing. The concluding verses describe the altar of incense.

דְּבָר אַחֵר **DAVAR AHER. AND THEY SHALL TAKE FOR YOU CLEAR OLIVE OIL… [EX. 27.20].** We are beating the olive into oil again. [Ex. 27.20] We are burning up those bullocks and rams and making a holy connecting. [Ex. 20.1ff] Aaron, the peace maker, Mr. *Middat ha-Rahamim*, is wearing the breastplate of judgment. I am left with an irony. Mr. Mercy, the chase-the-lost-little-lamb-and-bring-it-home guy is wearing the power suit and sprinkling blood everywhere. Yesterday in Poland, just before the anniversary of the liberation of Auschwitz, Jews and Poles played a round of "My Holocaust Was Worse than Your Holocaust." I am waiting for the pure light of beaten olive oil to burn eternally. I am wondering why we so often use sacrificial imagery for the Holocaust. **Joel Lurie Grishaver <gris@torahaura.com>**

דְּבָר אַחֵר **DAVAR AHER. AND YOU SHALL BRING CLOSE TO YOURSELF, AARON YOUR BROTHER AND HIS SON… [EX. 28.1].** I really enjoyed Tikvah Frymer-Kensky's analysis and wanted to add a quick footnote. She mentions the fatal outburst of holy energy that killed Uzziah [2 Sam. 6]. It is seemingly inexplicable why God would kill someone who sought to save the ark. Rav Kook offers a beautiful interpretation of the event: Notice, he says, that the text says the OXEN stumbled; yet Uzziah seeks to adjust the ark. That is a common sin; when the world goes awry, instead of changing the world, we seek to adjust the Torah. This was Uzziah's sin, according to Kook. It may not reconcile us to a profoundly disturbing episode, but it is by far the best try I've heard. **Rabbi David Wolpe, Jewish Theological Seminary, NY <DAJW@aol.com>**

Ari Kelman

ARI KELMAN IS A BAKER, A GUITAR PLAYER AND A HEBREW SCHOOL TEACHER.

This week's parashah opens with the prescription for the *Ner Tamid* which states that the lamp should stay lit from evening to morning, illuminating the entrance of the Tent of Meeting. Symbolically, this נֵר *ner* (light) can be understood as representative of God's omnipotence or of the eternal human spirit (the two letters נ *nun* and ר *resh* standing for נֶפֶשׁ רוּחַ *nefesh ruaḥ*). The lamp also serves a more practical function: providing light to the Israelites in the desert. In the narrative, the function of the lamp is much more clear. The commandment of the *Ner Tamid* bridges the description of the Temple (from last week's parashah) and the description of the priestly garments, which immediately follow in this week's parashah.

The lamp is a literal segue from the description of holy space (the *Mishkan*) to the description of holy people (who in turn serve to connect the sacred and the profane). As well, it signifies the importance of the Tent of Meeting, while also providing a safe, well-lit meeting place during the night. Thus, the *Ner Tamid* lies at the intersection of the sacred and the profane, the priestly and the common. If the *Ner Tamid* serves as a night light for the Israelites, it likewise begs the question: when can the morning officially begin with the ritual sacrifices?

The *Oraḥ Ḥayyim* [89.1] suggests that one would not begin to *daven Shaḥarit* until one can recognize a casual acquaintance at a distance of four cubits, thus establishing a vital relationship between social interaction and worship. I would take this one step further to suggest that not only must social interaction precede communal prayer, it is essential to it. Before one can begin the intense introspection of prayer, he or she must first recognize his or her own radical individuality in the face of another individual. This interaction disrupts our complacency, our self-sufficiency, by reminding us that we are continually an "other" to someone else. This act of mutual recognition and displacement must necessarily precede our entrance into prayer, as it is necessarily disrupting to our self-centeredness, and opens our minds to the transcendent or liberative potential of worship.

We return to the *Ner Tamid* via the prescription for daily sacrifice at the entrance to the Tent of Meeting. God commands "A REGULAR BURNT OFFERING (WILL BE OFFERED)...AT THE ENTRANCE OF THE TENT OF MEETING BEFORE THE LORD, FOR THERE I WILL MEET WITH YOU, AND IT SHALL BE SANCTIFIED BY MY PRESENCE." [39.42]. All night, the *Ner Tamid* has provided a safe place of meeting for the Israelites. If we extrapolate a bit, the *Ner Tamid* is nearly extinguished, and is returning the responsibility of illumination to the sun. Now, under the flickering *Ner Tamid* and the first hints of a rising sun, the people would begin to gather for the daily sacrifice, first recognizing one another following a long night's rest. As the people reacquaint themselves with each other, God's presence is among them, "AND THERE I WILL MEET WITH THE ISRAELITES, AND IT SHALL BE SANCTIFIED BY MY PRESENCE." [39.43]

God does not admit existence in the breastplate or the *Ner Tamid* or the details of ritual sacrifice; God's presence is only made explicit in the basic act of mutual human recognition. Sincere human interaction provides a site for experiencing the divine. God does not affirm God's existence at any other place in this parashah except outside the Tent of Meeting, where people first gather, look one another in the face, and say "good morning." •

Ki Tissa

**Exodus
30.11–34.35**

Professor Nahum M. Sarna

Nahum M. Sarna is Dora Golding Professor Emeritus of Biblical Studies at Brandeis University. He is General Editor of the *JPS Torah Commentary*, and author of the commentaries on Genesis and Exodus, and of *Understanding Genesis, Exploring Exodus, and Songs of the Heart: An Introduction to Psalms.*

Of the several topics that fill this parashah, the initial section dealing with the obligation to contribute to the upkeep of the Tabernacle in the wilderness [Ex. 30.11-16] has been singled out for special treatment. It is read once again on *Shabbat Shekalim,* the Shabbat immediately preceding the New Moon of Adar, and its precept was destined to play a special role in Jewish life and in the subsequent history of our people.

This portion of the Torah features many puzzling details. It obligates every Jewish male aged twenty and up, rich and poor alike, to pay to the Tabernacle exactly one half-shekel. As Maimonides formulated it, "even the indigent supported by charity" must make the contribution. Every Jew has an equal share in the Temple service. At first glance, the context would seem to require but a one-time contribution levied just for a specific occasion—the building of the mobile sanctuary to serve the spiritual needs of the Israelites in the course of their journeying in the Wilderness from Egypt to the promised land. However, it turned out that the injunction was really intended to prescribe a permanent, ongoing, annual imposition. Once the Temple was built in Jerusalem, every Israelite, wherever he resided, and whatever his status, had to pay the half-shekel every year. A story in II Kings 12. 5-16

דָּבָר אַחֵר **DAVAR AHER. Aaron said to them, "Take off your gold rings that are on the ears of your wives." [Ex. 32.2].** Upon reading Jeffrey Salkin's piece I wondered why the rabbis did not arrive at the same conclusion as U. Cassuto. To quote this master, "Aaron's intention when he made the calf, was only to fashion a vacant throne for the Godhead, like the throne of the cherubim...He made the calf in

order to satisfy the need of the multitude to see at least a tangible symbol of the deity's presence, the same need that the Torah sought to ratify when it permitted the cherubim...He (Aaron) thought that the prohibition of the decalogue referred only to prostrating oneself to idols and serving them, and he did not realize that the prohibition to make them...was a kind of 'protective fence' to prevent the general populace from

tells how King Jehoash ordered the donations to the Temple to be used to make repairs on the building. In the parallel account in II Chronicles 24.5-14, this money is called "THE TAX IMPOSED BY MOSES," an undoubted reference to the half-shekel.

When the Jews returned from the Babylonian exile, the reconstituted community once again obligated itself to make the annual payments [Nehemiah 10.33-34]. We have ample evidence that throughout the period of the Second Temple, diaspora Jewry continued the practice. No wonder this section of the Torah came to be read as the *maftir* on the Shabbat before Adar; it was a reminder to the people that the deadline for paying the tax was at hand [*Rosh Ha-Shanah* 7a]. Talmudic sources tell us that from the first of Nisan, the money raised was used for the purchase of the communal offerings in the Temple: the animal sacrifices, the meal

offerings, the wine libations, the incense, and so forth [*Mishnah Shekalim 4.1*]. It is a sad commentary on human nature that even in ancient times the Temple coffers into which the half-shekels were inserted had to be shaped like an inverted shofar—narrow at the top, and broad at the base—"on account of the crooks," so that one could not place one's hand inside, giving the appearance of contributing while actually stealing from it [*P. Shekalim 6.1*].

Following the capture of Jerusalem by the Romans and the destruction of the Temple, the imperial administration forced the Jews living within its borders to go on paying the half-shekel, but it was now officially dedicated to the pagan temple of the god Jupiter Capitolinus in Rome. This tax, known thenceforth as the fiscus judaicus, continued to be enforced until the first half of the third century C.E.

Synopsis: Each male, twenty and older, was required to pay a tax of one half-shekel to support the Tabernacle and as expiation (kofer). Description of the laver (kior), the aromatic anointing oil (shemen mischat kodesh), and the incense (ketoret) precede the appointment of Betzalel as the master craftsman. The last piece in this Tabernacle section is about Shabbat, and the text continues with Moses on Sinai— just before the making and worship of the Golden Calf. The familiar story includes two intercessions by Moses on behalf of the people, and Moses' unique relationship with God. Chapter 34 begins with the description of the second set of tablets. Appropriate worship, festival and ritual obligations to God precede the conclusion of the sidrah where the climax of the story of the tablets and Moses unfolds.

falling into error and being guilty of prostration to and worship of images...The Bible merely wishes to imply that Aaron sinned in that he did not take into account the need for a preventive measure and the possibility of error on the part of the masses." Aaron's innocence is the innocence of the Christians. Perhaps the rabbis did not have Cassuto's brilliance, or it may even be found someplace. More likely is that this would

be censored out for the sake of safety from the Christians, for then the Christians could not be superior when constructing images or likenesses of anything that "IS IN THE HEAVEN ABOVE OR THE EARTH BENEATH." Aaron was not replacing *Adonai* with the calf. He was replacing Moses. It was very dangerous for the rabbis to put the incident in the context of building an ark and then to explain that Aaron, destined to be the priest of the Lord's sanctu-

ary, did not commit the sin of idolatry. To add insult to injury, the *p'shat* of the story proves how dangerous it is to construct graven images, or likenesses, etc. How many plunders and pogroms would ensue with such a rabbinic commentary? **Dr. Morris A. Kipper, Rabbi, Coral Gables, FL**

דְּבָר אַחֵר **DAVAR AHER. TURN FROM YOUR BURNING ANGER...[Ex. 32.12].** Exodus 32.12-14 suggests that even

The original institution of the half-shekel payment is grounded by the Torah in a peculiar setting. The text ordains, "WHEN YOU TAKE A CENSUS OF THE ISRAELITE PEOPLE...EACH SHALL PAY THE LORD A RANSOM FOR HIMSELF...THAT NO PLAGUE MAY COME UPON THEM THROUGH THEIR BEING COUNTED." These stipulations raise many questions. What has the tax to do with census-taking, and why was a "census" thought to be hazardous to the public welfare? In order to clarify these enigmas, we have to know that throughout the ancient world, governments engaged in census-taking in order to levy new taxes and for purposes of military conscription. That is why the Latin word census passed into Hebrew with the derogatory meaning of "fine, penalty" (kenas). The announcement of an impending census was always ominous, foreboding evil. Here in the Torah we find a striking innovation. The census serves not war, but peace. Its purpose was not to supply the wherewithal of military operations, but the needs of the Tabernacle

and later of the Temple. The function of these institutions was to restore harmony between God and the people of Israel, to provide an effective instrument for satisfying human spiritual yearnings. According to the illustrious codifier of Jewish law, Jacob ben Asher (ca. 1270-1340), known as the Baal Ha-Turim, a hint of this understanding is seen to be embedded in the very language of the Torah if one utilizes the peculiarly Jewish version of mathematics or, more accurately, of numerology, known as gematria. This system is based on the notion of numbers as metaphysical potencies. Asher points out that the half-shekel tax is described in the Hebrew as being *kofer nefesh*, which term he renders "RANSOM FOR THE SOUL." He notes that the numerical value of the words נֶפֶשׁ *NeFeSh* and שֶׁקֶל *SheKeL* are identical. The contributions were to be utilized exclusively to enhance the soul-life of the community.

There are other, more sophisticated, reasons apart from those given

Ki Tissa

God does *teshuvah*; Moshe tells Him: SHUV, TURN FROM YOUR BLAZING ANGER, AND RENOUNCE THE PLAN TO PUNISH YOUR PEOPLE [for the sin of the golden calf]...AND THE LORD DID RENOUNCE THE PUNISHMENT HE HAD PLANNED TO BRING UPON HIS PEOPLE." The tradition makes a distinction between different kinds of *teshuvah* (see especially *Yoma* 86), primarily discussing *teshuvah* from fear and *teshuvah* from love. Moshe seems

to be pushing God to do *teshuvah* for both reasons! First: Don't give the Egyptians the satisfaction. This is fear; not of God, obviously, but of the consequences: You'll be undoing all You did in Egypt. Second: Remember the AVOT, the Patriarchs, and how much You loved them and what You promised them. Lessons: [1] If God repents of His anger, how can we not do so? [2] Whatever is true and motivates us to do

above as to why the census was thought to be a menace to society. It is recorded in 1 Chronicles 21 that a plague broke out following King David's census of the people of Israel, and that David reproached himself for having taken that step. He prayed, "I HAVE SINNED GRIEVOUSLY IN WHAT I HAVE DONE. PLEASE, O LORD, REMIT THE GUILT OF YOUR SERVANT, FOR I HAVE ACTED FOOLISHLY." The notion that counting Israel is sinful finds unambiguous expression in the Talmud [*Yoma* 22b]: "It is forbidden to count Israel, even for purposes of a mitzvah." Hence, it was the shekels that were counted, not the persons. To this day it is customary among traditional Jews, in ascertaining whether a *minyan* is present for holding a religious service, to use, not numbers, but a verse from the Bible which contains ten words, such as Psalm 28, verse 9. The "sin" of counting may be sought in the fact that assigning a number to a human being reduces that person to a cipher. It will be remembered that the first thing that the Germans did in World War II, when their victims

arrived at the gates of the concentration camps, was to brand each with a number on the arm as the beginning of the dehumanizing process. In the Bible, and in subsequent Jewish conception, a name signifies existence, individuality, even destiny, or at least the hopes and ambitions of parents for their children. It may have the function of preserving for the living the memory of dear ones now departed. To replace a name by a number is to destroy all this. It constitutes an assault on the dignity of a human being. That is why numbering may be a sinful activity which requires expiation, as the Torah lays down.

The great thirteenth century Bible exegete and kabbalist, Bahya ben Asher, pointed out that assigning a number to an individual can have the effect of destroying the consciousness of belonging to a community. The sixteenth century commentator from Safed, known as the Alshekh, further developed this idea by suggesting that the mitzvah to pay an annual tax of only one half-shekel, and not a full shekel, for the servic-

ing of the spiritual needs of the community was intended to teach the importance of Jewish unity and communal participation. An individual qua individual is an incomplete person. One can only realize one's full potential by contributing together with other individuals to the community as a whole.

To revert to the story of the plague that broke out on account of the census of Israel that King David took: we find that it was checked at "THE THRESHING FLOOR OF ARAUNAH THE JEBUSITE," and that David bought the site and built there an altar to the Lord. The author of Chronicles informs us that on this very spot King Solomon built the Temple and that it was none other than Mount Moriah [2 Chron. 3.1-2]. This was where Abraham was ordered to sacrifice his son Isaac. Was the Chronicler telling us by this midrash that the key to Jewish survival and continuity is to be found in individual sacrifice to enhance the spiritual welfare of the community? •

---

teshuvah and to correct our behavior—even if it isn't the highest motive—is acceptable, as we can learn from both Moshe and God. One would hope that God's repentance, and ours, would be of a high order...but as with a few other areas in life, we should, in the words of the late Rabbi Robert Gordis, "leave a little to God." **Rabbi Danny Horowitz, Prairie Village, MO <RABBIDANNY@aol.com>**

For more on the two kinds of t'shuvah, see Rabbi Harold Schulweis' d'var Torah on Nitzavim.

דְּבָר אַחֵר **DAVAR AHER. CUT FOR YOURSELF TWO TABLETS OF STONE…[EX. 34.1].** While reviewing last week's parashah, *Ki-Tissa,* I came across this beautiful *davar aher:* פְּסָל לְךָ שְׁנֵי לֻחֹת *Pesol lekha shney luhot.* G-d commanded Moshe to "ENGRAVE FOR YOURSELF" two tablets similar to the first

ones. The same words that are found in this verse, *pesal likha,* are also in Exodus 20.4. לֹא תַעֲשֶׂה לְךָ פֶסֶל *Lo ta'aseh lekhah fesel* "YOU SHALL NOT MAKE FOR YOURSELF A GRAVEN IMAGE." The difference between them is as follows: When the root [פסל *PSL*] signifies something sacred, then the word לְךָ *lekha* "FOR YOURSELF" comes after; but when the word לְךָ *lekha* "YOURSELF" comes before it, then it signifies something profane. Reb Yisrael of

Rabbi Jeffrey K. Salkin

RABBI JEFFREY SALKIN IS THE RABBI OF CENTRAL SYNAGOGUE OF NASSAU COUNTY ROCKVILLE CENTRE, NEW YORK. HE IS THE AUTHOR OF *PUTTING GOD ON THE GUEST LIST: HOW TO RECLAIM THE SPIRITUAL MEANING OF YOUR CHILD'S BAR/BAT MITZVAH* AND *BEING GOD'S PARTNER: HOW TO FIND THE HIDDEN LINK BETWEEN SPIRITUALITY AND YOUR WORK*, BOTH PUBLISHED BY JEWISH LIGHTS, WOODSTOCK, VT.

Ki Tissa

I was once complaining about a bar mitzvah family who left the synagogue right after the last verse (no, make it the second to last verse) of *Ein Keloheinu* at the ceremony. "How could they do this, in the immediate not-even-aftermath of their child's bar mitzvah moment?" I wailed to a friend. He wisely reminded me: "And how long after Sinai was the Calf?" The sin of the Golden Calf is a constant, ritualized, liturgized reminder of our massive failures and weaknesses.

No one looks good here. First, the Israelites. They wanted another god, or at the very least, they wanted another Moses to lead them. Second, Aaron. In a great moment of seeming vacillation, he gave in to the rabble. And finally, there is Moses. In a great moment of anger and frustration, an anger and frustration that perhaps we can understand, he shattered the tablets of the Covenant at the foot of the mountain.

But the subtle message of the midrashic tradition is that everyone and everything is redeemable. So, let's vindicate our ancestors—and by implication, ourselves.

Take the Israelites (or, as Moses might have added: "Please!"). This story of the Golden Calf has allowed anti-Semites to wreak all kinds of mischief upon the Jewish people. Pagan anti-Semites used to teach that the Jews worshiped an ass in the Temple. For this reason, the ancient Jewish historian Josephus deliberately eliminated any mention of the Calf in his account of the desert wanderings. The Church Fathers, the founders of Christianity,

---

Ruzhin comments that when a man does something positive with no thought of self interest—that is, when לְךָ *lekha* "YOURSELF" comes last—then he is indulging in a sacred activity. If, however, he does the same thing—but with his own benefit foremost—that is, putting לְךָ *lekha* "YOURSELF" first—then his otherwise positive deed becomes profane via transgressing the commandment "YOU SHALL NOT MAKE FOR YOURSELF A GRAVEN IMAGE." **Jeffrey C. Ratz, Brooklyn, NY**

taught that because of the sin of the Golden Calf, the people of Israel lost their right to the Covenant.

Here the defense will come from Moses himself. Moses will remind God that the Israelites had just come forth out of Egypt—a land of idolatry. We were "victims" of our environment. "Be tolerant," he says. "Know where this people has come from." As we must remember, too, where our people have come from.

Take Aaron. Some rabbis will say: "Yes, guilty—with an explanation." Rashi said that Aaron made the calf himself—to free the Jewish people from any guilt in the matter and to stall for Moses' return. Not only this, Aaron says that it is a "FESTIVAL TO THE LORD"—not to the Calf. The Midrash says that he was afraid that the people would kill him. Aaron was not only afraid for his own life. He was afraid that the people would incur terrible guilt upon themselves—both murder and idolatry. And so, says the Talmud in *Sanhedrin* 7a, he went for the lesser of two evils.

Therefore, Aaron stalled. He asked for the gold of the wives and daughters. He hoped that they would refuse to give up their jewelry. As it turns out, says the rabbinic tradition, the women did refuse—it was the men who brought their earrings.

Aaron is the ultimate humanitarian. In *Pirke Avot*, we read: "Be of the disciples of Aaron, pursuing peace and loving peace." Aaron went from person to person, getting them to make up with each other. When Aaron died, the people mourned more for him than for Moses. When Aaron died, the people had lost their best friend.

And then there is Moses. Moses' biggest problem is that he smashes the Tablets of the Covenant. What possible explanation will the rabbinic tradition offer us here? Yes, Moses really smashed them. He does it because the Israelites' sin would have made them liable for capital punishment. Therefore, he smashed the tablets so that they would not know that they weren't supposed to worship idols. If they didn't have the tablet before them that said, "DON'T BOW DOWN TO IDOLS," then they couldn't have known that they weren't supposed to bow down to idols.

The second opinion is that Moses didn't really smash them—he dropped them. When the letters saw what was going on, says a fanciful midrash, they flew off the tablets and they became too heavy for Moses to carry. Or, says another midrash, Moses and God were carrying the tablets together. When God saw what was going on, God retreated back up the mountain. Moses could not carry them by himself, and so he dropped them. Others say: they were both carrying the tablets—and they fought each other for them.

Perfect rabbis and educators and cantors and lay leaders get perfect congregations. Perfect congregations get perfect rabbis and educators and cantors and lay leaders. Everyone else has to make do. Even our imperfections are holy. Even our failings are sacred. Even our broken strivings are like the pieces of the broken tablets which, says the lore of our people, were borne with us in an ark next to the intact tablets of the covenant. •

f we made a secret list of Torah portions we are tempted to skip or listen to with half an ear, those about the construction and furnishing of the *Mishkan* would be jostling elbows with animal sacrifices and genealogies for first place. It's not that we are lazy or shallow, but rather that these parashiot make no sense to us. What we are receiving are the details of an encoded performance, and the less we understand the code, the less capable we are of organizing those particulars into a meaningful pattern. It is as if we were looking at a painting and seeing only a random spattering of paint blobs on a cloth-covered board, or attending a symphony and hearing only a cacaphony of twanging and honking. Unless we learn the code, none of it will make sense.

How, then, do we decode the *Mishkan*? The historian of religions, Mircea Eliade, says that a temple is a model of the cosmos [Eliade, *The Myth of the Eternal Return:* 1954]. If this is true, then it becomes clear why the Torah would dwell at such length upon the pettiest details of architecture and furnishing. Each of these details express symbolic

Va-Yak-hel

Exodus 35.1–38.20

Rachel Adler

RACHEL ADLER IS A THEOLOGIAN WHO HAS WRITTEN EXTENSIVELY ABOUT THE FULL INCLUSION OF WOMEN IN JUDAISM. HER BOOK *ENGENDERING JUDAISM* WILL BE ISSUED BY JEWISH PUBLICATION SOCIETY IN OCTOBER, 1997.

דָּבָר אַחֵר **DAVAR AHER. MOSES ASSEMBLED THE ENTIRE CONGREGATION OF THE FAMILIES-OF-ISRAEL. [EX. 35.1].** ITEM: The total number of people bowling in the United States is up 10% between 1980 and 1993, but bowling leagues are off by more than 40%. As a result of selling less beer and less pizza, lots of bowling alleys are closing. In *Democracy magazine*, Robert D. Putnam writes: "The broader social significance, however, lies in the social interaction and even occasionally civic conversations over beer and pizza that solo bowlers forgo. Whether or not bowling beats balloting in the eyes of most Americans, bowling teams illustrate yet another vanishing form of social capital." ITEM: Nachmanides teaches that this gathering which begins our Torah portion took place on the day after Yom Kippur when Moses returned

ויקהל משה את כל עדת

meanings about the nature of the cosmos as the Israelite people experience it. Rituals conducted in this sacred space are also freighted with symbolic meanings. These meanings are complex and multivocal. They cannot be flatly equated either with objects or abstract ideas, nor are they static. Rather, according to the anthropologist Victor Turner, ritual symbols are elements in ritual processes, which, like other human processes, are constantly being transformed [Turner, *The Ritual Process*: 1969]. *Va-Yak-hel* gives us the specifications for these encoded symbols, but it cannot tell all that they mean because it cannot depict how their meanings weave together, grow and are transmuted over the course of time.

The *Mishkan* itself exemplifies this. The *Mishkan* is a tent in the process of turning into a house. Constructed like a tent with supports and textile hangings, it is more massive than any tent. Its supports are mighty wooden beams covered with gold, which interlock for long-term stability. We sometimes imagine the Israelites wandering incessantly, but the narratives describe encampments for months or years. This ponderous structure of beams and heavy metals is not the kind of thing you dismantle daily and mosey on.

The *Mishkan* as a transitional structure mirrors the Israelites as a people in transition. The tent turning into a house parallels the nomads turning into a settled agrarian people. For post-exilic Jews, the transportable *Mishkan* reflects a transportable Judaism. It reminds us that wherever we go, we carry with us the power to create sacred space. For post-modern Jews, the *Mishkan* traveling through space evokes a Judaism traveling through time. Our very difficulty in decoding the *Mishkan* of our ancestors reminds us

Synopsis: Moses gathers the people to give instruction about the covenant and to begin work on the construction of the Tabernacle. Contributions are needed; the people respond; and the work of the construction begins. Details follow about the ark, the table, the menorah, the altar of incense, the anointing oil, the altar of burnt offering, the laver and the enclosure.

with the second set of Ten Commandments. Now the people were ready to build God's neighborhood, the *Mishkan*. ITEM: In *The Culture of Narcissism*, Christopher Lasch teaches: "(Post Modern-Man) extols cooperation and teamwork while harboring deeply anti-social impulses. He praises respect for rules and regulations in the secret belief that they do not apply to himself. Acquisitive in the sense that his cravings have no limits, he does not accumulate goods and provisions against the future, in the manner of the acquisitive individualist of the nineteenth century political economy, but demands immediate gratification and lives in a state of restlessness, a perpetually unsatisfied desire. The narcissist has no interest in the future because, in part, he has so little interest in the past...." That fits so well with what Thomas Moore teaches in *Care of the Soul*: "Loneliness can be the result of an attitude that community is something into which one is received. Many people wait for members of a community to invite them in, and until that happens they are lonely. There may be something of the child here who expects to be taken care of by the family. But a community is not a family. It is a group of people held together by feelings of belonging, and those feeling are not a birthright.

that there is not one timeless Judaism, but many Judaisms framed in specific social and historical contexts, and that even within those contexts, Judaisms are not static. As with the *Mishkan*, we are continually taking them apart and putting them back together.

Now let us consider a particular symbol in the *Mishkan*'s code, one with which we have some continuity, the *menorah*. What does it mean? The menorah's function is to give light, and light is an important element in our own ritual performances as well. We kindle lights for Shabbat, for *Yom Tov*, for Havdalah, for yahrzeit. The philosopher Ernst Cassirer says that the creation of light which begins so many creation myths represents the creation of consciousness [Cassirer, *Language and Myth*:1946]. Perhaps, when we ritually kindle light we reenact the dawning of consciousness which enables us both to know God and to be aware of ourselves.

The menorah is not just any lamp, however. It is a giant lamp of unusual design. First in Exodus 25 when the divine prototype is given, and then in Exodus 37 in our parashah when it is made by Bezalel, it is painstakingly described: a golden base, a tall shaft, six golden branches issuing from the two sides, each branch bearing three cups shaped like almond blossoms, detailed with calyx and petals, plus four more blossom-cups on the shaft itself. Atop these branches were seven golden lamps.

Clearly the menorah embodies some kind of metaphor. But metaphor has rules, just like tennis or Scrabble. One rule is that there has to be some link between the message or comparison and the concrete image that is its vehicle. What, then, is tall, has a *kaneh*, a stem, with *kanim*, branches, extending from it, *perahim*, flowers, intermixed with bud-like swellings that might be described as

Va-Yak-hel

'Belonging' is an active verb, something we do positively." ITEM: A midrash adapted from a folk tale found in *Corporate Cultures: The Rites and Rituals of Corporate Life* (Terrance E. Deal and Allan A. Kennedy). Solomon went in disguise to examine the work which was being done on the Holy Temple. He met with three workers and asked each what they were doing. The first responded: "I am cutting stones."

The second responded: "I am mixing the mortar to hold the stones in place." The third said, "I am working on the place where people will meet God." Solomon's favor fell on the third worker. And we can add: he then (still in disguise) joined the third worker's bowling team. In an age where community is falling apart (and you can list the reasons) we don't so much need programs and mailings, but real moments of

kaftorim? The menorah is a representation of an almond tree in flower! The almond blossoms beautifully and bears a sustaining fruit. It is also the emblem that justifies the legitimacy of the Aaronite priesthood. At the end of Kora<u>h</u>'s rebellion in Numbers 17, Moses deposits the staffs of all the Israelite chieftains in the Tent of Meeting, "AND THERE THE STAFF OF AARON OF THE HOUSE OF LEVI HAD SPROUTED: IT HAD BROUGHT FORTH SPROUTS, PRODUCED BLOSSOMS AND BORNE ALMONDS." [Num.17.23].

Now trees, as well as light, are associated with consciousness for Jews. Our moral consciousness comes from having eaten the fruit of a tree. The Torah is "A TREE OF LIFE TO ALL WHO HOLD FAST TO HER." [Prov. 3.17]. Trees are elders of the living earth. Their rootedness, their endurance, their capacity for renewal is a blessing extended to the righteous: "THE RIGHTEOUS SHALL BEAR FRUIT LIKE THE DATE PALM" [Psalms 92]; they are like "A TREE PLANTED BESIDE STREAMS OF WATER, WHICH YIELDS ITS FRUIT IN SEASON, WHOSE FOLIAGE NEVER FADES, AND WHATEVER IT PRODUCES THRIVES" [Ps.1].

But the menorah is yet a different sort of tree, because its branches are crowned with little bowls filled with oil and lighted. Whoever heard of a tree perpetually on fire? "HE GAZED AND THERE WAS A BUSH ALL AFLAME, YET THE BUSH WAS NOT CONSUMED. YHWH CALLED TO HIM OUT OF THE BUSH: 'MOSES! MOSES!' HE ANSWERED, 'HERE I AM.' AND HE SAID, 'DO NOT COME CLOSER. REMOVE YOUR SANDALS FROM YOUR FEET, FOR THE PLACE ON WHICH YOU STAND IS HOLY GROUND.'" [Ex. 3.2-4]

In his book, *Sinai and Zion*, Jon Levenson talks about the continuity in the transformation of the religion of Sinai into the religion of Zion [Levenson, *Sinai and Zion*:1985]. Just as Sinai, the wilderness mountain of the *s'neh*, thornbush, is cultically reproduced as Zion, the holy mountain of the Jerusalem Temple, the burning bush itself is reproduced as a golden tree lighted by priests. Levenson speculates that the emblem of the deity of Sinai was a tree of some sort. He points out that the blessing on the tribe of Joseph in Deuteronomy 33 identifies God as *Shokhni S'neh*, "THE ONE WHO DWELLS IN THE BUSH."

The feminist theologian Nelle Morton describes metaphor as an explosive process with a trajectory. "An image cannot become metaphoric until it is on its way—like a meteor. Where it explodes, when it burns out, how long or how far it journeys are unknowns" [Morton, *The Journey is Home*:1985]. The tree on fire that is not consumed is an image on an immense journey. It has traveled from Sinai to Zion, to Exile and beyond, and we have not even begun to exhaust its resonances.

A tree on fire embraces what we misperceive as antitheses: earth and heaven, matter and energy. All that we are accustomed to dichotomize, it reveals to us in blazing union. A tree on fire that is not consumed proclaims that what is material, temporal, perishable, can sustain what the Christian theologian Rudolf Otto calls

---

beer and pizza. It took the failure of the first ten commandments to get the community needed to build the *Mishkan*, once the second set was on site. It takes failures to build community, if there is anyone left to finish the pizza. **Joel Lurie Grishaver** <gris@torahaura.com>

דְּבָר אַחֵר **DAVAR AHER.** SEE, THE ETERNAL HAS SINGLED OUT BY NAME BEZALEL THE SON OF URI, SON OF HUR...[Ex. 35.30]. Listen to this sliver of *Gemara*: "Betzalel was thirteen years old when he built the Tabernacle...(his father) Kalev was forty years old when Moses sent him to spy out the land of Canaan [*Sanhedrin 74b*]." This seems backwards. The Torah tells us (last week) that Bezalel was wise-hearted and skilled. That doesn't sound like a bar mitzvah boy to me. Being an architect is more *Daedalus*. It is a *senex* (elder/wisdom) kind of thing. Spying, on the other hand, should be a young man's game. It is a *puer* (adolescent/heroic) act, it seems more *Icarus*. It takes young boys to fight wars. Spying, one would think, is all action adventure. But the Torah gets it backwards (and we know there must be a message in this apparent madness). What lesson is the Torah (and the Talmud) trying to teach, connecting bar mitzvah to the *Mishkan*, the "*mysterium tremendum et fascinans*," the "fearsome and fascinating mystery" of the presence of God [Otto, *The Idea of the Holy*: 1923]. If we were only able to see, the whole earth would appear to us like a tree on fire, and we would see a tree on fire in every human frame.

After Auschwitz the Jewish people itself is revealed to us as a tree, lightning-struck but living, bearing the stigmata of its encounters with the God who is a devouring fire and with the inferno of human evil. *And we cannot go on seeing all this, because it is unbearable.* Revelation is unbearable. T.S. Eliot was right when he wrote in "Burnt Norton," "humankind/cannot bear very much reality."

We cannot sustain our presence at the original moment when a startled shepherd sees a terrible and wonderful sight: a tree on fire, unconsumed. We can only make a memory-tree to remind us of that moment, an artifice-tree of ham-

mered gold, which we set afire, not abruptly, but with the choreography of ritual. Our reenactment distorts the story as it enriches it. The memory-tree is no humble wild thornbush, but the richly bearing fruit tree of the promised land, or the utterly stylized tree of modern ritual art. Other features have been tactfully muted. The memory-tree is a tree of wonder but not a tree of terror.

Nevertheless, we go on setting the memory-tree on fire. And the fire is not artificial, but real fire, with all its potential both for enlightenment and for danger. We go on taking the risk of reproducing the fire of God's presence. May "THE DWELLER IN THE BUSH" give us the courage to keep lighting our *Menorot* with real fire. •

Va-Yak-hel

and connecting the "age of understanding" (forty according to our favorite birthday mishnah in *Pirke Avot*) with spying? This is it: "Today I am a *Mishkan* (vs. a Bald James Bond)."

דָּבָר אַחֵר **DAVAR AHER.** Bezalel was thirteen years old when he built the tabernacle, yet wise and skilled according to the Torah. How can this be? The apparent contra-

diction of being thirteen (an age generally regarded as wisdomless) and being wise as well as skilled is similar in concept to the exceptional two or three-year-old who can read. Neither Bezalel nor that unusual toddler are the "source" of their gift. Though one may refine the gift with age, wisdom and skill are God-given. Bezalel could only build the tabernacle at age thirteen because God was actually the architect

Hazan Ira Rohde

HAZAN IRA ROHDE HOLDS BOTH A CANTORIAL DIPLOMA AND SMICHA FROM YESHIVA UNIVERSITY, AND HOLDS THE POST OF HAZAN AT CONGREGATION SHEARITH ISRAEL, THE SPANISH & PORTUGUESE SYNAGOGUE IN THE CITY OF NEW YORK, THE NATION'S OLDEST CONGREGATION. HE LIVES IN THE UPPER WEST SIDE OF MANHATTAN, WITH HIS WIFE LISA AND TWO CHILDREN, BARUKH AND RUTH MALKAH.

Va-Yak-hel

About four years ago, with Jeff, a bar mitzvah student from a non-observant background, I was discussing some of the traditional laws of the Sabbath. I got asked the "car" question, along with the usual objection that walking, which the halakhah permits, requires much more work. I gave my standard reply, that the types of labor which the halakhah prohibits are called *m'lakhah*—"creative labor," in imitation of God who rested from the work of Creation on the first Shabbat. Jeff began moving toward me waving his

arms wildly while making twisting motions with his torso. "What's that?" "Creative walking."

The question remains: what, from the standpoint of Sabbath law, defines labor, and what lessons can we learn from the categorizations of labor on the Sabbath to carry over the blessing of Shabbat into our workday week?

Moses assembles the people to give the go-ahead for commencing construction of the Tabernacle. But first he begins with the stern warning in 35.2-3. Rashi comments that the Sabbath prohibition of labor is reiterated here, preceding the command about the building of the Tabernacle, in order to emphasize that the construction, important though it is, doesn't supersede the Sabbath. Indeed, the 39 classifications of forbidden Sabbath labor are predicated upon the prohibition of building the Tabernacle on the Sabbath found here as well as in 31.13. Since work normally permitted

working through him. This apparent contradiction may come to teach us that we should be humble about our talents, for they really belong to God. **Rabbi Kathy Cohen of Temple Israel, Westport CT**

דָּבָר אַחֵר **DAVAR AHER.** It seems to me that, like a bar/bat mitzvah child, the *Mishkan* represents possibilities. It takes the vision of youth to be able to conceive of something as outrageous as a

house for God to live in—those of us who have reached forty and (supposedly) the age of understanding would be stymied by the mere thought that a building, no matter how beautiful, could contain God. That doesn't even touch how we'd react to everything that needs to be done to build a building. If we were organization-type people, we'd start creating committees; if we were lone geniuses, we'd be unlikely to react favorably to all the instructions and

in construction of the *Mishkan* was known to be prohibited on Shabbat, the types of labor involved in the construction of the *Mishkan* served as paradigms of forbidden labor.

The insight I derive from this is that the major focus of man's labor is the home. The Tabernacle applies the metaphor of man's home to God. I've never ceased to wonder at the degree of domestication of man in the Torah's portrayal. Man is discontinuous with nature; his equivalent of the Divine creativity in nature is the careful building of a home and the supplying and manufacture of its needs. Man is defined as a creature of civilization from the very outset. That is why the categories of forbidden labor are based upon the labors of the *Mishkan* rather than in imitation of the Divine creation. Man cannot exist in the wild as the animals do. He requires the building of forms, walls, and structures to sustain himself.

All of the traditional commentaries from the Talmud onward ask why the example of kindling a fire in the home on the Sabbath is specified here. One opinion in the Talmud held that the kindling of a fire was a separate admonition from the other prohibitions of labor, punishable not by death but in the same ordinary manner in which unspecified admonitions were punished: by lashes. After all, writes *Da'at Z'kenim*, kindling a fire in itself involves little effort and would not appear laborious. Indeed, writes Seforno, fire is more destructive than constructive. That is why an explicit prohibition is given.

When they had enough donations, "MOSES HAD THIS PROCLAMATION MADE THROUGHOUT THE CAMP: 'LET NO MAN OR WOMAN MAKE ANY FURTHER LABOR AS A GIFT FOR THE SANCTUARY!' AND THE WORK WAS ENOUGH TO DO ALL THE WORK AND LEAVE OVER SOME. AND THE PEOPLE STOPPED BRINGING" [36.6–7]. Rashi on 36.7: "The work of bringing was

Va-Yak-hel

restrictions God made concerning the *Mishkan*. I think Bezalel needed a rash streak to undertake and complete his work. He needed to be an "action-adventure-type" person. On the other hand, the main reason, as I understand it, for sending the spies was to bring a sense of reassurance and preparedness to the people before sending them into Canaan. Kalev was a reasonable man. He, like the other spies,

had seen the land and its richness, and the obstacles the Israelites would face in trying to conquer it. But rather than throwing up his hands and saying, "We can't do it," he understood that there would be obstacles that would take patience and perseverance. A bar/bat mitzvah rarely has those qualities, but the forty-year-olds (we understanding ones) would know how to organize those committees and wait for

enough for the workers at the Tabernacle for all the labor involved in the Tabernacle to make it and even to leave some over." *Siftey Hakhamim*: "That is to say, the first 'WORK' in the verse refers to the bringing of voluntary gifts and the second term 'WORK' refers to the labor in building the Tabernacle."

My *drashah*: We might relate this to the peculiar prohibition of "removing from one type of domain to another" on the Sabbath. After all, the only labor that the unskilled Israelites could contribute was their possessions, which they transferred from their own private domains to the public domain of the Tabernacle. Perhaps, too, we could see in this an anchor to the prophetic prohibition of buying and selling on Shabbat; i.e. transferring from one person's domain to another. •

---

long-term results! Kalev, at forty, would have know how to prepare the people for the long task ahead of them, while Bezalel, at thirteen, wouldn't have known they needed to be prepared. **Nancy Pryzant Picus, Director of Judaic Studies, Shlenker School, Houston, TX**

דָּבָר אַחֵר **DAVAR AHER.** Bezalel, as a thirteen-year-old, represents the task of all those leaving childhood and entering the adult community. He is becoming one of the community of Tabernacle Builders whose action causes God to "dwell among them"; i.e., by becoming a responsible, contributing member of the community and doing what is required to make the community *kadosh* (mitzvot), thirteen-year-olds contribute to bringing the presence of God into the community. On the other hand, it takes the wisdom and experience of a forty-year-old (like Caleb) to accurately assess a situation, to see the whole and not be intimidated by any given aspect of it. This was especially important in bringing back usable information to Moses who was preparing to lead the Israelites into the Promised Land. After all, is it a good land flowing with milk and honey? Or are we grasshoppers? It takes a wise person to understand a situation and how best to handle it, to know the strengths and weaknesses of the people s/he is dealing with, as we see the benefits and dangers involved in pursuing any given opportunity/challenge. **Debra Cohn-Levine of Temple Israel, Tulsa, OK**

דָּבָר אַחֵר **DAVAR AHER.** Since when was Torah intended to sit easily amidst our preconceptions and permit us to wallow in our own conclusions? First, Bezalel. Not the gangly, rebellious, feet-are-too-big, he's-still-too-short, loud-mouthed adolescent. Rather, the talented innocent who can still wonder at the world and feel he can make a significant contribution. Remember what it felt like to be certain that your elders had screwed it all up, but YOU, YOU would do things differently? Your motives would be pure; your intentions beyond reproach. It would be a different world when you and your peers got to it! Life itself was a form of worship. Awe was a part of the everyday. Let those who feel that love of life and optimism build a sanctuary! As for the spies, if, indeed, "it takes young boys to fight wars," let's make all spies over forty precisely because forty is the "age of understanding," that relationships, even among peoples, should be viewed as qualitative accommodation, not "action-adventure." The question is not "Can we win?" but rather, "How can we all truly survive?" **Sharon Halper of Westchester Reform Temple, Scarsdale, NY**

דָּבָר אַחֵר **DAVAR AHER.** Exactly a year from now my daughter Ilana will be thirteen and will mark becoming a bat mitzvah by chanting from this very parashah. On a literal level the Gemara you quoted does seem backwards. On a metaphorical level, however, I think its wisdom is brilliant. Each stage demands a distinctly different kind of "life-work," and each new "land" offers different kinds of adventures and possibilities. It's not the age of thirteen itself, but rather the years that follow which ask us to be like Bezalel—skilled, willing- hearted *"Mishkan* builders." The tasks of adolescence and young adulthood are tasks of construction. With the knowledge gained during this time in our lives, we gather skills, abilities, tools. We lay the foundation, working with what we are certain is a clear blueprint…. The age of forty (or thereabouts) marks an entry into another part of the journey…. He's more like James T. Kirk and the crew of the Starship Enterprise, daring to boldly go where no wo/man has gone before. He goes on a search and reconnaissance mission to check out the lay of the land and report back on the terrain, the risks, the fruits, the inhabitants, all the future possibilities. When he returns, he has the same information as the other spies, but instead of being driven by fear and resignation, he says "Let's go." By forty, we've lived, we've been bruised, our structures may have cracked, and we bring with us on this part of the journey greater awareness of life's twists and turns. We know enough to be afraid of things we didn't fear before. I think it's then that we need Kalev's will, inner strength and singular optimism to guide us in our sacred search for wisdom and understanding. **Joanne Glosser, Herzl-Ner Tamid, Seattle, WA** *From the Torah Aura Bulletin Board.*

דָּבָר אַחֵר **DAVAR AHER. THEN ALL THE WISE-HEARTED PEOPLE AMONG YOU SHALL COME AND MAKE EVERYTHING THAT THE ETERNAL HAS COMMANDED. [EX. 35.10].** I'm calling (as you suggested) with my "other" hat on. (I have a Ph.D. in comparative literature.) Many ancient cultures describe armaments and accouterments in exquisite detail (think of Homer's *Iliad* and *Odyssey*). We aren't so different, except in our case, God doesn't have armor, God has "houses." The people, who didn't have much of their own, have to be able to envision these "houses" on a grand and beautiful scale. God's Temples were magnificent beyond anything the people could conceive of. Our text devotes a great deal of space to detailing how beautiful these places were. **Jeff Kondritzer, Educator, Temple Chai, Long Grove, IL**

אלה פקודי הצשכן משכן

Who Will Bell the KaTZ (Kohen Tzedek)?

Pekudei

Exodus 38.21–40.38

Rabbi Daniel Landes

RABBI DANIEL LANDES IS DIRECTOR OF MACHON PARDES, A NON-DENOMINATIONAL CENTER FOR INTENSIVE STUDY OF JEWISH TEXTS AND THOUGHT LOCATED IN JERUSALEM.

Clothes do not fare well in the Beginning. The fig leaf reveals the first sin, a בֶּגֶד *BeGeD* (garment) covering בָּגַד *BaGaD* (rebellion). Yaakov, tutored by Rivkah, fools Yitzḥak with a hairy coat, a מְעִיל *Me'IL* signifying מָעַל *Ma'AL* (theft). Yaakov, in turn, can't see through Leah's lying veil, as his son Yehudah, much later, is likewise fooled by Tamar. *En passant*—we have the coat of פַּסִּים *passim*, evoking jealousy, and finally Yosef, robed in Egyptian royalty, is not recognized by his loving brothers.

Even in the legal section of שְׁמוֹת *SHeMoT* [sounds like *SHeMaTaH*?] a שִׂמְלָה *SiMLaH* (cloak) expresses the cruelty of one who wrests it away as a pledge and does not return it at nightfall.

Clothes thus hide the essence of humanity—or even distort it. At best they cover nakedness and offer a little protection from the night air. They both concede and are a concession to our frailty...until the latter part of Exodus. In *Pekudei,* we have the fulfillment of God's orders in *Tetzaveh* to make *bigdei kodesh*—holy garments—for Aaron and his priestly clan. These clothes actually create the priests. Rambam [1135-1204, Spain/Egypt] mandates that the regular *kohen* (who has four garments) as well as the *Kohen Gadol* (who has those four and four others), must be fully dressed to perform their service. If not, the penalty for dress code violation is severe: when their garments are upon them, their priesthood is upon them. If their garments are not upon them, their priesthood is not upon them. Rather, they are as strangers (*zarim*) and it says: "THE STRANGER THAT OFFERS A SACRIFICE SHALL BE PUT TO DEATH" [*Klei HaMikdash* 10.4].

דָּבָר אַחֵר **DAVAR AḤER. THESE ARE THE ACCOUNTS OF THE MISHKAN. [Ex. 38.1].** Rabbi Landes' drash on Aaron's vestments and the bells and pomegranates was itself so finely crafted that its double-entendres are still reverberating. And to think it all springs forth from a few words about a costume which hasn't actually been seen for a very long time, but whose meanings to us are still playing out as we join our forebears in study to hear its voice. Our Torah exists at once on so many independent and interrelated levels. If only we could teach our ears to hear its music. Or is it that our ears hear but our minds too rarely let us listen? "The temple bell stops, but the sound keeps coming out of the flowers." (Basho 1644-1694, Japan) **David Keene, M.D., Los Angeles, CA** <DHKeene@aol.com>

Do the *bigdei kodesh* so define the priest that they thereby eliminate his own personality? A small but unusual feature of the *kohen gadol*'s dress is instructive. In Exodus 28 the "WISE OF HEART" are told to create Aaron's robe:

"ON ITS HEM MAKE POMEGRANATES OF *TEHEILET* (BLUE), *ARGAMAN* (PURPLE) AND *TOLA'AT SHANI* (CRIMSON) YARNS, ALL AROUND THE HEM, WITH BELLS OF GOLD *B'TOKHAM* (AMONGST THEM), *PA'AMON ZAHAV* (A GOLDEN BELL) AND *RIMON* (POMEGRANATE) ALL AROUND THE HEM OF THE ROBE. AND IT SHALL BE UPON AARON FOR OFFICIATING; SO THAT THE SOUND OF IT IS HEARD WHEN HE COMES INTO THE SANCTUARY BEFORE THE LORD AND WHEN HE GOES OUT—SO THAT HE SHALL NOT DIE" [33-35].

The *Kohen Gadol* is ringed around with suspended bells and pomegranates. Commentators and codifiers differ on how this looks. A dominant view (Rashi, 1040-1105, France) is that the yarn pomegranates alternate with the golden bells, understanding "*b'tokham*" as "IN BETWEEN THEM." Rambam, in a

similar vein, codifies 36 bells on both hems; 72 in total, interposed among 72 pomegranates [*Klei HaMikdash* 9.4].

Given this view, the nature of the pomegranate must be understood. They were made of twined threads, eight each according to the Rambam, representing the dramatic colors of *Mishkan* use. *T'kheilet* (sky blue) is the covenantal color of the singular thread in the *tzitzit* penetrating into the infinite. The purplish *argaman* is a rich and royal color denoting majesty. The *tola'at shani* is scarlet red evoking the reality of sin that needs to be bleached white [Isaiah 1.18], the one missing but evoked color. The twined threads now twisted together inextricably link Covenant and Majesty with the eradication of sin.

The threads become a *rimon*— according to Rashi [based on *Z'vahim* 88b] an unopened, thus unripe pomegranate, with an elongated oval shape. The *rimon* is an

Pekudei

דָּבָר אַחֵר **DAVAR AHER. THE CHERUBIM SPREAD OUT THEIR WINGS ABOVE, OVERSHA-DOWING THE MERCY SEAT WITH THEIR WINGS, WITH THEIR FACES ONE TO ANOTHER; TOWARD THE MERCY SEAT WERE THE FACES OF THE CHERUBIM. [EX. 37.9].** I was very excited indeed to read Jo Milgrom's suggestion of the cherubim as ox-lion-eagle-human fusion and her connection of this with the four controlling signs of the Zodiac. Why

was I so excited? Because two *Shavuots* (*Shavu'otot?*) ago, in the all-night *tikkun*, when we read Ezekiel's vision of the Chariot, and I asked—"What WAS this anyway"— one of the people present (I'm sorry, I apologize for not redeeming the world by citing her name but it was about 4 a.m. and I was too woozy to remember more than the amaaaaaazing content)—said, calmly enough: "Oh, the four faces

unambiguous symbol of blessing—one of the seven fruits through which the land is blessed [Num. 20.5] and which exemplifies bounty as brought back by the twelve spies [Num. 13.23]. Here, these pomegranates adorn and describe the Kohen Gadol. The Kohen Gadol's mission/identity is unification of covenant, personal majesty and the battle against sin, hemming in his own space with Israel's blessing.

The pomegranate, however, causes a problem. The bells are there to ring out and as the Rashbam [d. 1174, Germany] points out, the rimonim interrupt the clanging of the bells against each other. The Hizkuni [13th century, France] settles this by stating that the "rimon is made so that the pa'amon can beat and hit against it in order to issue a voice." Evidently the threads were hard, giving resistance in order to produce the needed sound, "SO THAT HE SHALL NOT DIE."

The sound is needed to save Aaron. For many commentators this is tied to the Yom Kippur ritual of entering the Holy of Holies where many unprepared high priests did not survive. The p'amonim proclaim the Kohen Gadol to be the belle of this terrifying Yom Kippur ball as he negotiates the intricate dance of the avodah (service). The Tosafet Brakhah [R. Boruch Halevi Epstein, Lithuania, 1860-1942], however, convincingly demonstrates that this can't be the case, for the bells were attached only to the golden robe of the high priest which, because of associations with the golden calf, was not worn into the Holy of Holies on Yom Kippur. Therefore, a different explanation is needed.

Rabbenu Bakhya [Saragossa, 13th century] explains that the bells were there to protect the Kohen Gadol from the "holy angels," warning the latter that they should "open a space for the King's beloved ... in order that he might enter and serve there alone, and, further, that the Kohen should not be hurt as he enters there sud-denly. With this sign they would

Synopsis: All the metals are counted and the priests' vestments are made. The actual erecting of the Tabernacle, the anointing of the furnishings and the installation of the priests follows. The book of Exodus concludes with a description of the cloud covering and the presence of God which fills the Tabernacle.

Ezekiel saw—they were the four major faces of the Zodiac. Scorpio's higher symbol is the eagle, Aquarius is the human, Taurus is the ox, Leo..."Boom." In Ezekiel's chariot, the four faces are fully present and together make up one extraordinary Presence, with the Rainbow above the four faces, a kind of Keter/Crown (which the text says is the appearance of the likeness of the radiance of God—in case you were wondering what God looks like, kiv'yakhol).

At the time of this major revelation of what was (at least to me) new Torah, I was struck that this vision happened in Babylon, the home of the "Chaldean" astrologers. But Jo Milgrom's point is that the Zodiac influence goes back further. I think her point is reinforced by Ezekiel, and her point reinforces our Shavuot dis-

covery. Jo's point also makes a very interesting reconnection between Ezekiel and the cherubim of the (destroyed) Temple. Ezekiel evidently experiences not the cherubim themselves but a close relative from the same extraordinary family, one (or is it One?) who comes whirling all the way to Exile. So as Jo says, the cherubim and chariot become an even more wonderful focus for meditation. And I am left with a question: what

be pushed aside, emptying for him a space to serve the King. Upon his departure this would also be a sign as if the *Kohen* is calling them to return to serve Him as at first, for his own service has ended and he departs." Alternatively, the Ḥizkuni states that the sound of the bell's voice renders the *Kohen Gadol* "recognized and divided off in order that he might be the Separate of the Separate [*Kodesh ha-Kodashim*] of the rest of the *Kohanim* who therein serve."

For both Rabbenu Bakhya and the Ḥizkuni, the *Kohen Gadol* is separated from all others. The bells warn off all other competitors for God's attention. The *Mishkan* is depicted as an intersection of heaven and earth wherein all creatures—angelic and human—strive, out of an internal compulsion, to serve God. For this goal they are jealous, zealous and singleminded. The *Kohen Gadol's* bells are his way of cutting through this sea of creatures—they announce him not

as an individual but as the one chosen to represent the community of Israel, whose service in some mysterious way is demanded by God. As such he has no colleagues, or fellow travellers. The bells signal his separation, his cut-off status, his alienation from all others in order to create his unique position before the Lord. Indeed, even his own personality is a mystery—he serves without a name or individual style. He becomes the *Kohen Gadol* as he dons the robe, leaving his private identity behind.

Our parashah's recounting of the actual making of the garments cuts the priestly material differently: "AND THEY MADE BELLS OF PURE GOLD; AND THEY PUT THE BELLS *B'TOKH* THE POMEGRANATES, UPON THE HEMS OF THE ROBE *B'TOKH* THE POMEGRANATES" [39.25].

Commentators such as Saadia [Iraq, 882-942] and modern translators [old and new JPS] read בְּתוֹךְ *b'tokh* as "between" in keeping with Rashi's and Rambam's description that the bells alternated with the

Pekudei

does it mean for us that just as the Holy of Holies was guarded by the signs of Space and Time (and also of the Four Elements), so the Exile (or the whole whirling world?) were guarded by these same signs, the zodiac awhirl?

Blessed is the One Who gave me such a miracle of unexpected Torah today! **Arthur Waskow, Awaskow@aol.com**

דָּבָר אַחֵר **DAVAR AḤER. THE CHERUBIM SPREAD OUT THEIR WINGS ABOVE [Ex. 37.9].** The Tabernacle edges closer to idolatry than anything else in the Jewish tradition. Why the cherubim? Why in the attempt to keep God abstract and not make golden calves, do we make golden winged things? Ultimately I know no good answer to this one. It has bothered me for a long time. **Joel Lurie Grishaver <gris@torahaura.com>**

pomegranates along the hem. But the Ramban [1194-1270, Spain] discerning here repetitions of בְּתוֹךְ b'tokh reads it literally: EACH BELL IS WITHIN A POMEGRANATE! From this point of view and given the closed nature of an unripe pomegranate, each bell would then be tucked well inside the pomegranate, obscured from view and undoubtedly muffled in sound.

This would respond to the Netzib's [Naphtali Zevi Yehudah, Berlin Lithuania, 1817-1893] problem with loud bells—that as they herald the presence of the Kohen Gadol they also induce false pride in the Kohen Gadol as everyone scatters away. Nearly silent bells avoid that possibility, but what then is their purpose? Listen to the Ketav V'ha-Kabbalah [Jacob Zvi Meklenburg; Poznania, Koenigsberg, 1785-1865], for whom the bells are the hearing equivalent of the sight mitzvah of tzitzit: "through hearing the voice of the bells of the robe he shall awaken his consciousness and heart to before Whom he wears these garments and

Who commanded him to wear them, and to what purpose he alone is to be found within these garments ...." This insight answers perfectly the problem of the muffled voice. The bells are for the Kohen Gadol himself and for no other person. It is to remind him constantly of who he is and what his task is—as tzitzit remind the individual ("AND THOU SHALL SEE IT") of his personal religious responsibilities. Indeed, that is why some of the greatest Lithuanian authorities saw wearing tzitzit dangling out as forbidden yirah (overbearing pride)—it is not for others to see but only for you yourself to gaze upon and to remember. So, too, the muffled bells of the Kohen Gadol—they are his personal heart inspirer and consciousness raiser.

Thus, in accordance with the Meshekh Hokhmah [Meir Simcha of Dvinsk, Lithuania, 1843-1926], the term "TO SERVE" refers not to Aaron serving while wearing the bells, but rather indicates that the pomegranates and bells are present "TO SERVE

FOR AARON." These bells toll for him alone. •

דָּבָר אַחֵר DAVAR AHER. THE CHERUBIM SPREAD OUT THEIR WINGS ABOVE [Ex. 37.9]. You asked—why did God make the ark look so much like an idol if the people were supposed to forget idols? What's different about them is idols are something people think is a visible god. The ark is not on the idol's side. You don't pray to the ark. It's a good place to pray because it's a holy place; the Torah is in it. Torah is there so they will know what to pray

to (God). You need something to help you feel close to God. But we know it's not God. **Shaye Horwitz, 7 years old.**

דָּבָר אַחֵר DAVAR AHER. THE CHERUBIM SPREAD OUT THEIR WINGS ABOVE [Ex. 37.9]. A classic question, and, like many such classic questions, better than its attempted answers. But here are some:

(1) Sefer Hizkuni writes that this is not

in violation of the commandment against graven images, "for they were not made for worshipping or bowing down to, but rather for G-d to sit or dwell upon לִישְׁבָתוֹ (lishivato) in the likeness of the (Heavenly) angelic cherubim (under) the Throne of Glory." And we find many commandments like this in the Torah (where the Torah will permit in a special case or under certain circumstances that which it forbids in general), such as:

Dr. Jo Milgrom

JO MILGROM IS A POET AND ASSEMBLAGE ARTIST. DR. MILGROM LIVES AND TEACHES IN JERUSALEM. AMONG HER PUBLICATIONS ARE *THE AKEDAH: THE BINDING OF ISAAC, A PRIMARY SYMBOL IN JEWISH THOUGHT AND ART AND HANDMADE MIDRASH.*

Pekudei

About the Riddle of the Cherubim

In the course of teaching about sacred portals and the guardians of these gates I came across several images dating from the 9th and 8th centuries BCE. One of them, [*EJ*, vol. 5, col. 397] shows a sphinx-like cherub from King Ahab's ivory palace in Samaria. Another comes from the palace of Sargon II (8th century Assyrian conqueror of Northern Israel) at Khorsabad [*Views of the Biblical World*, vol. 3, p. 159].

The third is from the temple of Nimrod on the Tigris, where two cherubim are guarding the date palm tree of life. In each case the cherubim are composite mythic beasts. They have the wings of an eagle, face of a human, feet of an ox, and body of a lion. In each case they guard access to something eternal, either to the god/king or to the tree of life.

Later on I noticed that in Christian art there are many images of Jesus in a majestical setting, enthroned within an ellipse, and surrounded by the four evangelists, Matthew, Mark, Luke and John. Strangely, the composite beast of the Ancient Near East pictured at least a thousand years earlier as four-in-one, had come apart so to speak, and had become four separate entities. Each of the evangelists was associated with one of those four. Thus Matthew was the man; Mark, the lion; Luke, the bull; and John, the eagle. Of all the beasts of field why *davka* these four? And why the same ones a thousand years later?

Scripture states that all who do labor on (the Sabbath) shall be put to death, but commands us to perform the daily and additional sacrifices (which involve generally forbidden labor) as well as circumcision (on the Sabbath). We are (generally) forbidden to marry our brother's wife, but commanded concerning levirate marriage. We are forbidden to wear garments of mixed wool and linen, but commanded to make fringes (which usually contained *sha'atnez*).

(2) Eliyahu Munk translates *Akedat Yitzhak* as follows: the construction of [representations of] cherubs does not contradict the commandment not to make images, when in fact they [the angels themselves, previously defined

They seemed redolent of hidden symbol.

I was lost till I came upon *The Mythic Image* by Joseph Campbell. Campbell explains that Christian iconography adapted the four Chaldean zodiacal signs of the world quarters in order to convey visually how human time and space is related to God, to eternal time and space. This is how it works: Taurus, the bull, is the image of the eastern quarter, the vernal equinox i.e., spring. Leo, the lion, is the image of the summer solstice and the southern quarter. Scorpio, eagle or scorpion, is the image of the fall equinox and the western quarter. Finally, Aquarius, the water carrier, the man, is the image of the winter solstice, the north. In the ancient Near East these four beasts were combined and reduced to their mythic essence as cherubim and stood guard at the sacred portal. In other words, human time and space (the zodiacal/seasonal/directional) images flanked access to the divine beyond the portal, whether it was the tree of life or the god/king. Now, in Christian art, it

is the same. But here the four beasts are separated out. Each one is a direction/season, again (human space and time), and what do they flank? The Christian image of divinity.

But we have skipped the bottom line. We have gone from the 9–8th century BCE into medieval Christian art. What about the riddle of the cherubim and our *Mishkan*/Temple of the biblical period? Two things seem to be clear. They are associated with God and with the most sacred space. As two-dimensional images in the desert *Mishkan* they were woven into the inner curtains and the veil that closed off the Holy of Holies. As three-dimensional beings they were part of the covering of the ark within the Holy of Holies. In the Jerusalem temple they virtually filled the innermost chamber. They seemed to serve as God's resting place or throne. There are also images of the cherubim as God's high powered transportation. Their close connection to God is evident early on: they guard the gates to the Garden of Eden. Finally, the variations of their

appearance include the very four animals we have identified above: eagle, lion, bull, human.

It seems to me that the symbolism of the cherubim of the 9–8th centuries guarding access to the eternal One in the temples of Assyria and Samaria is identical to the symbolism of the evangelists flanking Jesus. And I submit that those very symbols work for our *Mishkan*/Temple as well. The cherubim are a visual image that says: we represent human time and space; we flank access to eternal time and space, the mysterious, transcendent reality beyond the portal.

I have no other academic support for this hypothesis than the visual forms cited, and their known historical earthly and celestial functions. For me it has the ring of authentic *p'shat* and besides, what a splendid image to meditate on! •

as 'spiritual beings who are close to God, and by means of whom inspiration is conferred upon man'] are not physical. Therefore, one does not violate the commandment not to reproduce a likeness, which presumably applies only to physical beings, when one fashions the cherubs. The Hizkuni's answer is not fully satisfactory to me, because it would seem to

make the prohibition or permissibility of things rather arbitrary. But he does state or imply two criteria: (A) They were not made for worship purposes; (B) You might infer from the comparison to sacrifices and levirite marriage that the special controlled circumstances in which such things were permitted would insure that the exemptions given here would be limited and

not be understood as applying elsewhere. Isaac Arama's answer (the *Akedat Yitzhak*) that the prohibition only applies to likenesses of physical beings, is more satisfying, but it, in turn, leads to another question: how could a spiritual being such as an angel have a likeness that can be represented physically? And further in the the question-within-a-question department: just what did a cherub look like, anyway? What was its purpose?

I long ago concluded that God isn't as abstracted from the physical world as some theologians may think. There may be "spiritual bodies" as well as physical ones. Perhaps they are like energy fields we may someday detect "scientifically." Even God partakes in some way of the qualities of a living organism. The representation of cherubs as winged children derives from the Talmud, which understands כְּרוּבִים *keruvim* as כְּרוּבִיַע *ke-rubia*: "LIKE A CHILD." But Rashi states that the face was like a child; the rest could have looked like some animal. The text describes them as having wings; on this basis, Sforno and the Ḥizkuni call them "A KIND OF BIRD." Ibn Ezra also quotes the "like a child's face" line, but alternatively interprets them as creatures with (strange) "forms (צוּרוֹת *tzurot*)," such as those found in Ezekiel 28, some of which are called חַיּוֹת *hayyot*" (wild creatures) and which partook of characteristics of several different animals in one. Rashi, on the Garden of Eden, doesn't call them "BABYFACE," calling them "ANGELS OF DESTRUCTION," whose purpose is to frighten off intruders. It's probable that he is alluding to similar weird (and hence scary) creatures (although I've seen plenty of babyfaced angels of destruction in my day).When I asked Akiva Silber about the purpose of the cherubs, he said that both here and in the Garden their function was to guard the Ark. I said I thought it might have been used like a kind of scarecrow. I like to think of them as really grotesque monsters, combined of various body parts from different animals—too hideous to be worshipped. My *Sifu*, Prof. H. I. Sober of Yeshiva U., told us that at Persepolis in Iran, the visitor to the palace had to pass through a whole series of bigger than life-size murals showing the vanquishing of various foes. By the time he got to King Darius, who was actually not that tall, the visitor was scared out of his wits. Something similar may be going on here. **Hazan Ira Rohde, The Congregation Shearith Israel, New York, NY**

דָּבָר אַחֵר **DAVAR AHER. WITH THEIR FACES ONE TO ANOTHER; TOWARD THE MERCY SEAT WERE THE FACES OF THE CHERUBIM. [Ex. 37.9].** Said in the name of Danny Landes (with whom I study *Parashat ha-Shavu'a*), the cherubim are standing face-to-face, showing where God can be found. Face-to-face in an I-Thou relationship with others. **Michael Tolkin, Los Angeles, CA**

Pekudei

חֲזַק, חֲזַק, וְנִתְחַזֵּק

Ḥazak Ḥazak v'nit-Ḥazek

ויקרא

Va-Yikra

On the Theory of Sacrifice

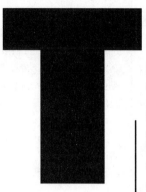

The sacrifices may be compared to a king's son who was addicted to carcasses and forbidden meats. Said the king, "Let him always eat at my table and he will get out of the habit" [*Midr. Lev. Rab.* 22.8]. This midrash clearly implies that the sacrifices were not ends in themselves but were divinely ordained in order to wean Israel from idolatry.

This approach was developed at length in a classic statement by Maimonides [*Guide* 3.32] and countered just as vigorously by Ramban (on Lev 1.9), who maintained that the sacrifices were inherently and eternally efficacious. In truth, the Ramban's rationalizations (mainly mystical) and those offered by other rabbis (e.g., *b. Menaḥ* 110a [bar.]; *B. Yoma* 86b; cf. Bekhor Shor on Exod. 30.1; Lev. 2.13; Abravanel, *Introduction*), no different from Maimonides', also betray uneasiness with this institution. Nonetheless, we must begin with the assumption that Israel believed that the sacrifices had intrinsic value. It is, therefore, incumbent upon us to probe deeper, if at all possible, into the psyche of early humankind to see if any of its purported motivations for sacrifice also hold for Israel.

Va-Yikra

Leviticus 1.1–5.26

Professor Jacob Milgrom

JACOB MILGROM IS PROFESSOR EMERITUS OF BIBLICAL STUDIES, UNIVERSITY OF CALIFORNIA, BERKELEY. HIE IS PRESENTLY WORKING ON VOLUME 2 OF A COMMENTARY ON LEVITICUS FOR THE ANCHOR BIBLE SERIES, DOUBLEDAY PUBLISHING.

דְּבָר אַחֵר **DAVAR AḤER. WHEN ONE OF YOU BRINGS AN OFFERING BEFORE THE ETERNAL [Lev. 1.1].** As a Jew conditioned into his Judaism within the Reform movement, I always cross the threshold into Leviticus with a little guilt and much trepidation. When I was fifteen, I was on my high school swim team. In working out, I made friends with a kid who went to Maimonides Day School that shared our high school pool. He invited me, in a step he would never reciprocate, to join him at his shul, The Bostoner Rebbe's, Hasidic Central, for *Kabbalat Shabbat*. I put my *tallit* in my raincoat pocket prepared for its first post-bar mitzvah usage. When I arrived and met him outside the shul, I was gently and politely chastised twice, once for thinking a tallit should be worn at night, and secondly for carrying it on Shabbat.

Researchers in primitive and comparative religions distinguish four possible purposes behind the institution of sacrifice: (1) to provide food for the god; (2) to assimilate the life force of the sacrificial animal; (3) to effect union with the deity; and (4) to induce the aid of the deity by means of a gift.

The first three purposes are not to be found in Israel. True, the first one is attested in Israel's environment, for example, in Egypt, in Mesopotamia, and in some sacrificial idioms of the Bible: "MY TABLE" [Ezek. 44.16], "THE FOOD OF HIS GOD" [Lev. 21.22; cf. v. 17]; "MY FOOD... MY PLEASANT AROMA" [Num. 28.2], and the like. Moreover, the original aim of the sacred furniture of the Tabernacle-Temple—the table for the bread of presence, the candelabrum, and the incense altar—was to provide food, light, and pleasant aroma for the Divine residence. Even the sacrificial procedure betrays this anthropomorphic background; for instance, God must receive his share of the sacrifice before man [cf. 1 Sam. 2.29 [LXX]]. Nonetheless, these words, objects, and mores are only fossilized vestiges from a dim past, which show no signs of life in the Bible.

The second purpose is found in animistic religions but not in the Bible. Nevertheless, its derivative—the animal, lies on the altar instead of its offerer—continues to find adherents to this day. Originated in the field of general religions by Westermarck and championed most recently by Girard, this motive was applied to Israel, among others, by James and, most recently, by Rodriguez and Janowski. Yet anthropologists have found primitive societies in which substitution plays no role (e.g., Middleton). And as for Israel, the main plank in the substitutionary platform, Lev. 17.11, is capable of another interpretation;

Synopsis: Our third book of the Torah, Leviticus, opens with a description of the sacrificial system. Addressed to the people of Israel (and not the kohanim) these offerings were intended to serve a variety of functions. Details are provided for the burnt offering (the עֹלָה olah), the grain offering (the מִנְחָה minhah), the sacred gift of greeting (the זֶבַח שְׁלָמִים zevah shelamim); the sin offering (חַטָּאת hattat), and the guilt offering (אָשָׁם asham)

It wasn't meant as a rebuke, but I felt bad. That is always how I feel on entering Leviticus, especially because for both Mr. Temple (7th grade) and Mr. Ruben (10th grade) I had to memorize the big Amos speech, "I HATE, I DESPISE YOUR FEASTS, AND I TAKE NO DELIGHT IN YOUR SOLEMN ASSEMBLIES. YEA, THOUGH YOU OFFER ME BURNT-OFFERINGS AND MEAL OFFERINGS, I WILL NOT ACCEPT THEM...BUT LET JUSTICE WELL UP AS WATERS, AND RIGHTEOUSNESS AS A MIGHTY STREAM." Leviticus scares me because I don't know what to do with it. In a certain inner place, I understand the synagogue I often condemned for doing six or seven consecutive weeks of the Holiness Code every Shabbat, rather than facing the vortex of the priesthood. Leviticus is hard.

We don't know whether to treat it as an ambivalent historic memory—a "we used to find meaning" kind of thing. My friend Gail Dorph taught Vicky Kelman and me the great educational question, "Tell me one thing you used to believe that you no longer believe." Why we don't believe in Leviticus is one kind of learning—the Torah of values clarification from the Torah of the Priests. Leviticus also invites "Make a Metaphor Out of Me." In other words, "How is giving up a first-born lamb as an acknowledgment of God's gifts like sitting on the bench and letting everyone on your

the purification offering purges the sanctuary but not the wrongdoer, and certainly does not substitute for him on the altar; and the scape-goat, which indeed carries off sin, does not even die or, for that matter, rate as a sacrifice.

The third purpose, union through commensality with the deity, has even less of a basis in Israel and elsewhere. For example, the shared meal that follows a Nuer sacrifice is purely a secular affair [Evans Pritchard]. In the Bible, union with the deity is expressly denied in sacrificial accounts (e.g., Jud. 6.18-21; 13.16; cf. Ps. 50.12-13). Moreover, as Ehrlich pointed out, the sacrifice is eaten "BEFORE THE LORD" not "with" Him (e.g., Exod. 18.12; Deut. 27.7; cf. 1 Sam. 2.13-16).

The fourth purpose, a gift to the deity to induce his aid, seems to be the only one that manifests validity in all sacrificial systems. To begin with, the word "sacrifice," in Latin, means "to make sacred" and existentially, not just etymologically,

the asseveration can be made that "In every sacrifice, an object passes from the common to the religious domain; it is consecrated" [Hubert and Mauss]. The quintessential sacrificial act, then, is the transference of property from the profane to the sacred realm, thus making a gift to the deity. That this notion is also basic to Israelite sacrifice is demonstrated by fundamental sacrificial terms that connote a gift, such as מַתָּנָה *mattanah* [Lev. 23.38; Deut. 16.17), קָרְבָּן *korban* (see the Note on 1.2), מִנְחָה *minhah*, and אִשֶּׁה *ishsheh*. Moreover, it would explain why game and fish were unacceptable as sacrifices: "I CANNOT SACRIFICE TO THE LORD MY GOD BURNT OFFERINGS THAT HAVE COST ME NOTHING" [2 Sam. 24.24].

The motivation of seeking Divine aid is attested in many texts, such as "OFFER TO GOD A THANKSGIVING OFFERING AND PAY YOUR VOWS TO THE MOST HIGH... I WILL DELIVER YOU, AND YOU SHALL GLORIFY ME" [Ps. 50.14-15]. The help requested of God stems

Va-Yikra

little league team have a quality two innings?" Then there are proto-ethical sacrifices. It goes like this: "The sacrifices taught *kashrut*. *Kashrut* gave birth to the humane society. Therefore, ultimately, animal sacrifices will eventually make everyone on earth a vegetarian again, the way we are really supposed to be." This year, I've made a personal commitment to try to look Leviticus in the eye—to take it on its

own terms. No rationalizations. No mutations. No metaphors. I'm going to look directly into the fire at the bottom of the altar, and without flinching tell it: "Go ahead, make my faith." Without ducking, I'm going to ask just what all of this really means. You are welcome to join me.

The big question, however, is really "When is Leviticus?" Rabbi Akiva and Rabbi Ishmael debate that

from two needs: (1) external aid, to secure fertility or victory, in other words, for blessing; and (2) internal aid, to ward off or forgive sin and impurity, that is, for expiation. Thus the עֹלָה *olah* and מִנְחָה *minhah* are gifts to God to obtain His blessing or forgiveness. The שְׁלָמִים *shelamim* also reveals this two-faceted gift, for its blood ransoms the life of the slaughterer, and its suet is a gift to God (אִשֶּׁה *ishsheh*, Lev. 3.5, 11, 14) for the meat. The אָשָׁם *asham*, though its purpose is solely expiatory, also labels its suet an אִשֶּׁה *ishsheh* [Lev. 7.6]. Yet, though the חַטָּאת *hattat* falls under the same heading as the *asham* as an exclusive expiatory sacrifice, it is never called an אִשֶּׁה *ishsheh*. Furthermore, it is explicitly distinguished from it: "FOR THEIR ERROR THEY HAD BROUGHT THEIR OFFERING, AN אִשֶּׁה *ISHSHEH* TO THE LORD AND THEIR PURIFICATION OFFERING BEFORE THE LORD" [Num. 15.25b]. This אִשֶּׁה *ishsheh* refers to the burnt offering prescribed by the ritual (v. 24) and, hence, excludes the purification

offering [cf. *Sifre* Num. 111]. The logic is clear: the Lord is surely pleased with the offering of the penitent wrong-doer, but it is not a gift: it is his humble expiation. Thus, even if the idea of gift is the dominant motivation for Israelite sacrifice, it is not the only one, and in the case of the חַטָּאת *hattat*, as demonstrated, it is not even present.

Recently, two studies on Greek religion have promulgated new theories on the origin of sacrifice: (5) the animal served as a substitute for human victims of aggression [Girard] and (6) killing the animal evoked feelings of guilt that could only be assuaged by dedicating the victim to the deity [Burkert]. Whereas the former is remote from explaining biblical sacrifice, the latter rings with clear associative echoes. The rationale invoked by the Priestly texts for a mandatory sacrifice (שְׁלָמִים *shelamim*) each time meat is desired for the diet [Lev. 17.10-12] is precisely the same: to expiate for the crime of taking the life of the animal. There is now evi-

dence that the identical etiology prevailed from earliest times in the ancient Near East. The Sumerian myth of Lugalbanda relates that its hero, heretofore a vegetarian, receives divine approval in a dream to sacrifice whatever animals he can trap. He invites the four principal deities of the Sumerian pantheon to partake of the ritual meal. "The slaughtering itself is carried out according to divinely inspired prescriptions, by a divinely chosen individual, with weapons of rare metals. Presumably, then, we are to understand it as sacred, not profane, slaughter, indeed as the etiology of the sacrificial cult" [Hallo].

In the long run, this theory may prove to have penetrated deepest into the mystery of sacrificial origins. At present, however, it leaves other essential aspects of sacrifice unexplained. For the Bible, it illumines the origins of the *shelamim* but leaves in the dark the *olah*, which, as shown, was comprehensive and more widely practiced than the *shelamim*. Nor

---

question in the Talmud [*Zevahim* 115b]. Ishmael said, "The advance organizer for Leviticus was at Sinai, the actual book got taught in the Tent of Meeting." Akiva said, "The advance organizer and the lesson were taught at Sinai, the review, application, and closure were accomplished by the Steps of Moab in the Tent of Meeting." Critical scholars also ask the same question. Generally they argue over: "Is Leviticus 'Hezekiah' or is it

really "Samuel?" For me, I want to be Jewish and answer the question with a question: "Can we make Leviticus now? Not reduce it to relevant, but make it now?" **Joel Lurie Grishaver** <gris@torahaura.com>

דָּבָר אַחֵר **DAVAR AHER. WHEN ONE OF YOU BRINGS AN OFFERING BEFORE THE ETERNAL... [Lev. 1.1].** I hold my breath as *Vayikra* comes rolling out over the Torah table... All this talk of suet and

guts and entrails and buckets of blood... *gevalt*! Do I dare ask where God is in all of this? Perhaps objectively I can relate to sacrifice in anthropological terms... *Otherwise*... it seems to me vaguely ironic that the destruction of the Second Temple paradoxically wiped out the sacrificial cult—and thus saved Judaism. **Rabbi Keith Stern, Congregation Beth Shalom, Arlington, TX** <Jazzman900@aol.com>

does it relate to the מִנְחָה minḥah, not to speak of other vegetable offerings, such as the בִּכּוּרִים bikkurim and רֵאשִׁית reishit [Num 18.12–13]. Finally, the recent attempt to base sacrifice on the anthropological distinction between roasted (allegedly illicit) and boiled meat is vitiated, among other things, by the fact that there is no prohibition against roasting sacrificial meat in Scripture and that the "GREAT SIN" of Eli's sons [1 Sam. 2.17] is not that they intended to roast the priestly portion but that they took it before God received his portion, the suet, on the altar [vv. 15aa, 29 [LXX]].

In sum, no single theory can encompass the sacrificial system of any society, even the most primitive. Evans-Pritchard, in fact, lists fourteen of the many motivations that underlie the Nuer sacrifice:

"communion, gift, apotropaic rite, bargain, exchange, ransom, elimination, expulsion, purification, expiation, propitiation, substitution, abnegation, homage, and others." Researchers have been far more successful by premising multiple purposes for Israel's sacrificial system. One cannot but agree with the general conclusion of the anthropologist Bourdillon: "Any general theory of sacrifice is bound to fail. The wide distribution of the institution of sacrifice among peoples of the world is not due to some fundamental trait which fulfills a fundamental human need. Sacrifice is a flexible symbol which can convey a rich variety of possible meanings."

*For bibliography and discussion, see J. Milgrom, Leviticus 1–16. Anchor Bible 3. New York: Doubleday Press.*n

Va-Yikra

דָּבָר אַחֵר **DAVAR AḤER. WHEN ONE OF YOU BRINGS AN OFFERING BEFORE THE ETERNAL… [Lev. 1.1].** If sacrifices were a lower form of devotion than prayer, then why does the Torah make the central focus of our religious devotion a slaughterhouse? It's been ten years since I resumed eating meat, after seven years of vegetarianism. I made a *"Hattarat Nedarim"* ceremony with my Rosh Yeshiva and classmates. Rabbi Yossi Groner from Chabad-Lubavitch of the Carolinas had told me that, having broken my desire for meat, I was now in an ideal position to raise the sparks of holiness from the lower

level of animal life-forms to a higher plane, when this is done for the sake of a mitzvah such as a Sabbath meal or for furtherance of the [nutritional] needs of Talmud Torah. May this discussion further that end.

A few years later, on May 7, 1987, I attended a lecture at Yeshiva U. on צַעַר בַּעֲלֵי חַיִּים *Tza`ar Ba`alei Hayyim*/Vegetarianism/*Shehitah*/Animal Experimentation given by the halakhist and ethicist Rabbi J. David Bleich. I am indebted to the compilation of sources made for that lecture, as well as to his article "Judaism and Animal Experimentation" in *Tradition*, Spring 1986.

Rabbi Kerry M. Olitzky

RABBI KERRY M. OLITZKY, D.H.L., IS DIRECTOR OF THE SCHOOL OF EDUCATION AT HEBREW UNION COLLEGE-JEWISH INSTITUTE OF RELIGION IN NEW YORK WHERE HE ALSO DIRECTS ITS GRADUATE STUDIES PROGRAM. AMONG HIS NUMEROUS TITLES, HE IS THE AUTHOR OF THE LEADING CONTRIBUTION TO JEWISH TWELVE STEP SPIRITUALITY: *TWELVE JEWISH STEPS TO RECOVERY*. HE IS CURRENTLY COMPLETING A BOOK ON JEWISH SPIRITUAL GUIDANCE WITH DR. CAROL OCHS.

Va-Yikra

Sacrifices. This is the topic which dominates the opening portion of the book of Leviticus, as well as the ancient Jewish world. All kinds of sacrifices. Imagine the scene. It is a total assault on the senses, inviting us to engage our entire body in worshipping God, something from which we moderns—who often feel compelled to remain passive in fixed sanctuary seats—can definitely learn. Throughout much of Jewish history, many seem uncomfortable with the notion of sacrifices, preferring instead to turn them into metaphor.

Yet, we continue to perpetuate the lingering memory of sacrifice. Perhaps it is the mystery of the Temple cult which intrigues us Jews. It would be a lot easier to simply reject the whole notion as some sort of primitive practice, long since abandoned by our people—particularly after the destruction of the Second Temple. After all, this Torah portion is the beginning of the *Torat Kohanim*, the priestly code, designed to transform us into a holy nation, a dominion of priests. Here, we learn to raise ourselves from the rest of the peoples, establishing a distinct standard of conduct for an entire community. We may never reach that optimal level of behavior, but it remains our goal. In fact, many of the positive *mitzvot* find their origin in this central book of the Torah. Even Maimonides who concedes that the sacrificial system was designed for the common folk argued that during *mashiach-zeit* the Temple would descend from the heavens and the sacrifices would once again find their place in our midst.

R. Bleich begins his article by quoting Arthur Schopenhauer's provocative [read "anti-Semitic"] remark that "the denial of rights to animals is a doctrine peculiar to Western civilization and reflects a barbarism which has its roots in Judaism." R. Bleich then takes Schopenhauer to task, showing that animals do indeed have rights in Judaism, although not equal to the rights of man. But Schopenhauer is wrong on another score, as well. In the Romantic fascination with and bias towards the Sanskrit-derived traditions of Hinduism and Buddhism among the orientalists and spiritualists which began in his day and has continued down to our own, Schopenhauer fails to leave room for the appreciation of the spiritual traditions of the many meat-eating cultures of the world, both Western and non-Western. Although native Chinese culture has been overlaid with Buddhist practice, Taoism doesn't, strictly speaking, require vegetarianism and Chinese

Taking it beyond an obvious political statement, the rabbis themselves sought to begin their young students' studies with Leviticus. This is the way R. Assi put it: "their souls are pure; therefore, let them study what is pure." Nachmanides had it right when he noted that the word for sacrifice (קָרְבָּן *korban*) is related to the Hebrew "to draw near (to God)" and that's what we certainly want to do. Therefore, rather than argue from the perspective of primitivism, I would like to believe with regard to sacrifices—like so many other things in our tradition—

we have not *yet* come to fully understand the profundity of the Levitical text. There is more than smoke that rises from the altar.

Thus, we should transcend this instruction manual for an elaborate family barbecue and focus on the multiple levels of meaning behind the text.

One approach is to consider sacrifices as an ancient form of כַּשְׁרוּת *kashrut*. As Rabbi Les Bronstein contends, through the animal sacrifice, in particular, we acknowledge the Creator of all life who has, in turn, given us the means to sustain

Va-Yikra

as well as Southeast Asian culture has remained predominantly meat-eating, when people can afford it. I'll never forget the dog my neighbor brought back from 'Nam to keep it from being eaten. And what about Native American spirituality, not to mention that of African cultures? The Egyptians may have worshipped sheep, but seem to have tolerated raising cattle, presumably for consumption. It is Judaism that has preserved the older carnivorous, sacrificial tradition which predominated in Asian civilization prior to the spread of Buddhism. How can we come to an appreciation of the spirituality of that tradition? For one thing, it is predominantly non-ascetic, even anti-ascetic in tendency. Denial of flesh is linked to denial of the flesh.

In my student position, I often used to go to a small, local butcher shop

to wash sides of meat and keep the blood from coagulating with a retired *shohet* and *mashgiah*, Rev. Joseph Fooks, who told me an old Yiddish joke that illustrates the hasidic attitude: A hasid returned to his rebbe from the "*treifene medina* [America]," saying that, although he was able to make a living, he couldn't find a trustworthy source of kosher meat, and in all his years there he had tasted "no meat of an animal [*kein bosor beheima*]." The rebbe replied: "*Kein bosor?– Beheima*!"; that is: "No meat?—[You] animal!" Lack of meat for celebrating a festival showed a lack of respect for the festival as well as a lack of respect for one's own needs, an asceticism which took away from the proper degree of joy.

Tilting the delicate scale and inclining to asceticism carried the risk that one might lose one's spiritual bal-

ויקרא אל משה וידבר יהוה אליו מאהל מועד

our life. Before we place the conse-crated morsels in our mouths, we thank God for providing them for us. It is an ancient Jewish statement against the cavalier way we humans have a tendency to treat the world. It was not given for us to use, abuse, and then throw away. The entire Temple cult is an argument against such an approach, falling apart (say the prophets) when it became com-monplace and rather matter of fact.

On another level, Rabbi Yaakov Zvi Mecklenburg in *Ha-ketav Ve-haka-balah* wrote: we offer sacrifices to "purify the self from the stain of sin."

This we understand! Each sacrifice represents a step in our intense yearning for personal transformation. In the sin offering, we express our regret for the wrongs we have com-mitted. Through the peace offering, we voice our genuine gratitude for living. Through the community offer-ing, we acknowledge the interde-pendence required to live in commu-nity. Finally, the burnt-offering represents our total surrender to the will of God. Truly, the Psalmist understood the simple meaning behind this elaborate process for repentance and personal renewal

when she suggested, "THE SACRIFICES OF GOD REFLECT A BROKEN SPIRIT" [Ps. 51. 19]. This is the place where God called the people—וַיִּקְרָא *Vayikra*—instructing them to soar above the ashes and become wholly separate.

•

---

ance entirely and end up lowering one's spiritual level rather than rais-ing it. R. Joseph Albo in his late medieval book *Sefer ha-Ikkarim*, Third Essay, Ch. 15, gives a lengthy inter-pretation of the attitides towards meat-eating in Genesis, including a lengthy analysis of the Cain and Abel story. He shows how Cain, who origi-nally thought that the slaughter of animals ought to have been prohib-ited through the equivalence he makes between the value of human and animal life, ends up sanctioning the murder of his brother through the same equivalence, after seeing his brother's offering accepted. Even Rav Kook, who was a vegetarian (accord-ing to R. Shear-Yashuv Cohen, the Chief Rabbi of Haifa), warns against those who take on a level of concern with animals that is far beyond them. He compares them to the pig who sticks his kosher feet forward, divert-ing attention from their negligence

when it comes to human concerns. This bias against asceticism and con-cern with balance and equilibrium is, I think, part of something larger.

I have often felt that we Jews have the most organic, the most wholistic, of the major religious traditions. We are a highly civilized religion which has nonetheless not severed its links to its tribalist past. Nowhere is this more in evidence than in *Vayikra*. The Book of Leviticus is the book of purifi-cation. Traditionally, children began their study of Torah with this book: "Let the pure [in spirit] study the laws of purity," went the old adage. When modern man thinks of purity, he thinks of sanitation, of sterilization. When he thinks of purity of spirit, he thinks of a state of being far removed from the affairs of this world, ele-vated above and beyond the possibil-ity of sin. Not so, says *Vayikra*. Cleanness is about dealing constantly

with blood and guts all over; purifica-tion of spirit is a continual process of dealing with sin and guilt. Body and spirit are part of an organic whole, and our task is to integrate them bet-ter, to restore the equilibrium, to pre-serve the delicate homeostasis. Purification of the person as a whole must start with purification of the soul from sin; hence *Vayikra* deals with sin-offerings. Conversely, we learn later on that the holiness of תִּהְיוּ קְדֹשִׁים *"kedoshim tih'yu"* is impossible without physical cleanliness as well.

What is to be learned from the sacrifi-cial rite itself? All of the commenta-tors remark upon the emotional effect that seeing an animal slaugh-tered, its blood poured out, its pieces cut up and burnt as a vicarious replacement for oneself must have had upon the worshipper. But is there anything else to be learned from the slaughter of animals? For this I must

זאת תורת העלה

refer to my study of *shehitah*. The traditional Ashkenazic Orthodox rabbinic education and ordination, especially in their watered-down form today, place primary emphasis upon the study of the laws of ritual slaughter and *kashruth*. Not that anyone really expects to get a question about a pin in the chicken's stomach anymore. It's just one of the ways rabbis have usurped the old role of *kohanim*, I guess: people expect them to be experts in ritual. Very few actually try *shehitah* themselves, as very few try their hand at *safrut* (scribal arts) or *hazzanut*, or any of the "traditional arts." At Yeshiva U.'s Rabbinical school lately, you can study *shehitah* (and *safrut* as well), but only for token credit, through the cantorial school, with a rabbi from Sephardic studies. (I guess only "artsy," backward types would be interested in actually doing anything with their hands!) Having been enrolled in both

schools (and being entitled, as *Hazan* at a Sephardic congregation, to a dig at Ashkenazic rabbis now and then), I decided that it would be a great *Misnagdisher Tikkun* of my soul (i.e., if you have a natural tendency towards something, do the opposite!) to try to learn. Needless to say, I didn't get very far, although I still take out my poultry knife and sharpening stones from time to time to show kids at school. I didn't learn to do *shehitah*, but the up-close exposure that we got to individual animals, away from the usual "meat factory" crunch that you get when you visit the highly-mechanized slaughterhouses of today, stirred my thinking on *shehitah*. **Hazan Ira Rohde, Cong. Shearith Israel, New York, NY <75610.1722@compuserve.com>**

Va-Yikra

צו את אהרן ואת בניו לאצ

Tzav
Leviticus 6.1–8.36

Rabbi Herbert Bronstein

RABBI HERBERT BRONSTEIN IS THE AUTHOR OF THE BEST-SELLING CCAR (REFORM) HAGGADAH AND OTHER LITURGICAL TEXTS. HE IS A WELL-KNOWN LECTURER ON SUBJECTS RANGING FROM LITURGY AND MODERN HEBREW POETRY TO SHAKESPEARE. HIS WRITINGS HAVE BEEN WIDELY PUBLISHED.

n the minds of most Jews "traditionalism" is associated with Orthodoxy; and in the minds of many, perhaps even most Jews, "tradition" is associated with conformism, with fixity and a blandly accepting, unquestioning attitude. The Jewish "folk story" along these lines is about the kid in the old time eder who asks his melamed, his teacher, "How could the world have been created in six days?"—and in response, he gets rapped on the knuckles!

But this understanding of our tradition may be skewed. On the contrary, maybe we could use a dose of the kind of daring attitude—the "in- your-face" confrontationalism provided so strikingly by "the Tradition" in the readings for this week's portion, *Tzav*.

The Torah readings are, after all, a part of so strong a tradition for so many centuries, that they can be taken as a prime example of the fixity of traditional Jewish life. Just a brief reminder: For each of the Shabbat Torah portions read in the synagogue over the course of the year, all over the world on the same week, tradition assigns an additional coordinate reading from one of the books of the prophets. We call it, of course, the Haftarah. Now usually the reading manifests a harmonious parallel with the Torah reading. For example, for the Torah reading which contains the Biblical sabbatical legislation concerning the release from indebtedness and servitude [*Mishpatim*, Exodus 21.21–6], the parallel choice that week is from Jeremiah who condemns failure to observe these very mitzvot [Jeremiah 34.8–22].

But choices emphasizing *agreement* are not always the case in our tradition. Once in a while tradition throws in a reading from the prophets which seems, at least directly, at odds with the Torah reading; or minimally, which raises a lot of questions about the meaning of the Torah reading; in short, a passage which, far from encouraging bland acceptance, instead seems to encourage a questioning, confrontational, challenging response.

Such is certainly the case in this week's reading from *Tzav*. No passages in the Torah are more clear than those in this week's readings on the importance, the centrality, the fundamental nature of *sacrifice*. In *Tzav*, we go down the line listing the sacrifices, as Divine commandment, in

Tzav

emphatic detail. "THIS IS THE LAW OF THE BURNT OFFERING… [LEV. 6.1] AND THIS IS THE LAW OF THE MEAL OFFERING. THE SONS OF AARON SHALL OFFER IT BEFORE THE LORD IN FRONT OF THE ALTAR…" [LEV, 6.7] and so on. But for the Haftarah following the Torah reading, this is what we get: THUS HAS SAID *HA-SHEM*, THE G–D OF ISRAEL: "I NEVER SPOKE TO YOU, NOR YOUR ANCESTORS, NOR EVER COMMANDED THEM AT THE TIME I BROUGHT THEM OUT OF THE LAND OF EGYPT, ABOUT MATTERS OF BURNT OFFERINGS OR SACRIFICES. ONLY THIS WAS THE MATTER I COMMANDED SAYING: "HEARKEN TO MY VOICE….THEN I WILL BE YOUR G–D AND YOU WILL BE MY PEOPLE. AND GO IN ALL THE WAYS I COMMAND YOU IN ORDER THAT IT MAY BE WELL WITH YOU…" [Jeremiah 8.21-23].

How could Jeremiah have more blatantly contradicted the message of the Torah reading in the *Sidrah Tzav?* In his commentary, Rabbi Joseph Hertz follows a well-known way of avoiding this direct contradiction. Jeremiah's words, he says, were not intended to *oppose* the sacrifices but rather were, a call to inwardness and sincerity in offering sacrifices, a denunciation "of mere mechanical performance of acts of worship." But the very fact that he must make this comment means that the reading raises questions in the minds of many people. He does admit, however, that Jeremiah's words *did* have the effect of infuriating both priests and people, and placed Jeremiah at an imminent risk of death!

On the other side it was a commonplace contention of liberal Jewish scholarship for the last century that some of the prophets at least (like Jeremiah) were in outright opposition to sacrifices, and even to ritual altogether.

But we, making a fresh start, can ask: What possible other values do we find in a tradition that puts these two apparently contradictory passages together? The least we can say is that this kind of juxtaposition has contributed a great deal to some of the best features of the Jewish mind and the Jewish outlook, to some of the best elements of Jewish character, for example, the tendency to question.

Questioning has become a part of our religion. One of the great strengths of the Jewish mind has been, at our best bravely, and without avoidance, to examine every issue and context critically. One thinks, for example, of the probing, questioning quality of mind which we value, beginning with Abraham himself, who in the instance of Sodom and Gemorrah questioned even G-d's equity and justice. Our children are taught to ask questions at the Seder. It is was what enabled the great Rabbi Akiva to accept and resolve the contradiction between Divine Providence and human free will. He said: "All is foreseen and yet free will is given." Only through facing contradiction, did he arrive at a brilliant conclusion: "Everything is in the hands of heaven except our reverence for heaven." It is a questioning attitude of mind that produced that masterpiece of the analysis of contradictory issues: the

צו את אהרן ואת בניו לאצר זאת תורת העלה

Talmud. And should we not add the philosophies of Maimonides, of Moses Mendelsohn, and yes, the work of Spinoza and Freud? All of those accomplishments were the result not only of intellectual brilliance, but perhaps even more of the character trait of facing contradictions courageously and honestly.

And there is another reason that the recognition of contradictions is part of our Judaic outlook. We ought to be *religiously* concerned about too easy and too comfortable an acceptance of whatever the current "normal" institutional patterns and dogmas may be at any given time. If I were to use what our tradition does with the *Tzav* readings as a model for current application, we might arrive at something like the following examples:

[1] For many years many of our Jewish communal and religious institutions accepted as dogma the Jerusalem platform of the World Zionist Organization that the State of Israel is the spiritual center of the Jewish people and therefore of Judaism itself. It is what is taught still to this day in many of our religious schools, as if it were doctrine from Sinai. But in the spirit of what we might call peremptory challenge, we might match right alongside of this view, the following response: "No, you have got it all wrong. The spiritual center of Jews everywhere throughout our history, the glue that has bound us together for millennia, and still does, the core of our identity, is not a geographical location, not a central

office, and certainly not a state or government but rather—Torah! Torah is the spiritual center of Judaism, and of Jews everywhere."

[2] From the time of the Enlightenment out of which Reform Judaism was born, the idea of personal autonomy, free choice, has been the central principle of all Jewish liberalism, that is, freedom from any authority whatsoever. With this statement we might match the following: "There can be no Judaism without *Halakhah*, a definitive, authoritative "Way"; perhaps not what Orthodoxy considers the fixed body of *Halakhah* but a sense of ought, of obligation, of binding religious duty, finally of Divine commands. Judaism, as the words "Torah" and "mitzvah" themselves indicate, is a religion that is *halakhically* structured. If there is no *Halakhah*, if there is no definitive Way, then there is no Judaism, not even Reform Judaism. And if we are Jews, we are automatically *ipso facto* under authority.

[3] Or let us consider the doctrine of American Jewish civil religion, of Jewish life structured and centralized around Jewish Federation fund raising and allocation: "Federation has been, is, and will be the tower of strength of the Jewish community and the bulwark of Jewish continuity in America." To match this, if we have the same strength and courage as the tradition that matched the Leviticus statutes on sacrifice and Jeremiah's challenge back to back, we might say the following: "Federation, which has

Synopsis: *Ritual instruction concerning the burnt offering (עוֹלָה olah), the grain offering (מִנְחָה minhah), the grain offering of Aaron and his sons, the sin offering (חַטָּאת hattat), the guilt offering (אָשָׁם asham), and the sacred gift of greeting (זֶבַח שְׁלָמִים zevah shelamim) begin our parashah. The second part details the consecration of the priests and the tabernacle which begins the institution of formal communal worship in ancient Israel.*

Tzav

been a tower of strength, may also in some ways have weakened Jewish life by draining leadership and funds from the synagogue and not giving, over many years, consistent major, central, or even adequate priority to Jewish education. Federation may have performed a big disservice to Jewish diaspora life in fact by substituting fund raising dinners and money raising rallies for Jewish participation in worship and study as a way of life.

Finally, in addition to encouraging a questioning frame of mind and the courage to raise questions about whatever the contemporaneous dogma, tradition may have done us a great favor in the instance of the *Tzav* readings by reminding us that because life itself is full of contradictions, we are a better and stronger people in being able to accept the daily contradictions of life. In the nineteenth century, a pompous intellectual arose at a public forum and cried out loudly: "I accept the Universe!" The writer and historian, Carlyle, is said to have whispered to a friend: "Egad! He'd better." Since life is full of contradictions and problems, we are better people if we are able to face up to them.

> Even while rejoicing in our
> festivals,
> even while dancing and singing
> our joy,
> our beings are burdened by
> knowledge of suffering.
> The glories of nature dazzle our
> eyes;

> yet, injustice and brute pain still
> daily confront us.

[The Five Scrolls, CCAR, p.8]

Sometimes we cannot resolve contradictions on the intellectual level. In fact, Judaism resolves them on another level entirely. For example, the Book of Ecclesiastes, the biblical book in which we find a veritable catalogue of life's contradictions, concludes not with any resolution on an intellectual or mind level, but on the level of mitzvot, action. Judaism says that the answer to life's contradictions is to *act* to better the world. "THE END OF THE MATTER, ALL HAVING BEEN HEARD, IS TO REVERE G-D AND TO DO THE MITZVOT [Ecclesiastes 12.13]."

So, on one level Jeremiah and Leviticus do, after all, meet and come to at least one accord. It is in the word "mitzvah," in the word "command," *Tzav*. They agree that somehow we have to come to some conclusion in actual practice and not in solving contradictions intellectually. That is the endeavor of Judaism: Not to discover the answer to every puzzling question of life, but to try to discover, even if incompletely, what exactly it is that G-d wants of us. That is why the Talmud itself deliberately poses contradictions, not always to resolve them to everybody's intellectual satisfaction but finally to point to a way of deeds. That is the way, as well, that our tradition and the probing, questing nature of the modern mind can come to accord someday as well.•

Simcha Prombaum

SIMCHA PROMBAUM IS THE SPIRI-
TUAL LEADER OF CONGREGATION
SONS OF ABRAHAM, LA CROSSE,
WISCONSIN.

Tzav

A PERPETUAL FIRE SHALL BE KEPT BURNING ON THE ALTAR, NOT TO GO OUT. [Lev. 6.6] *Parashat Tzav* is read as we are coming off Purim this year. Purim lingers and resonates through this Shabbat for me because it is set against the backdrop of the Temple's destruction. *Megillat Esther* asks us to consider the consequences of physical and spiritual exile. *Tsav* commands a priestly, Tabernacle-centered caste to maintain the perpetual fire of Jewish life. Without the Tabernacle or its altar, how is a perpetual fire even possible? And where does that leave contemporary Jewish functionaries in exile?

Beginning with the first question, while our tradition asks us to entertain the possibility of caste Judaism, we cannot rely on that system for out survival. With Lev 8.2 as a starting point, "TAKE AARON AND HIS SONS WITH HIM...,"

Yeshayahu Leibovitz points out that the priesthood given to Aaron and inherited by his sons is unique in all of Torah. Except for the case of Aaron and his sons, one does not automatically inherit the values of faith and worship of G-d belonging to one's parents. The sons of Moses, Samuel or Eli the high priest did not have a role in maintaining the fire of Jewish life. Instead, the doors were left open for many an "Esther" to come to the forefront of Jewish life throughout history.

In our second question, Pinchas HaCohen Peli, z"l was drawn to two occurrences of תּוּקַד בּוֹ "*Tukad bo*," once in 6.2 and again in 6.6, both of which refer to the fire kept aflame on the altar. In consulting the translation of these verses in the Authorized King James Bible, Peli noticed a faithfulness to the original Hebrew which clearly distinguished the fire burning on the altar (*al ha-mizbeah*) from the fire burning in it (*tukad bo*), "or if you wish, in him, namely in the officiating priest," says Peli.

Peli continues: "It is not enough to have a fire burning on the altar, says the hasidic interpretation pointedly, emphasizing that there must be 'a perpetual fire' of enthusiasm within us when we truly worship G-d."

This suggests that the inflaming, spiritual altar within each person is more important than an external, physical altar. When Mordecai charges Esther with her responsibility to save the Jewish people, she asks for three days in which to prepare and ignite her own altar which had long grown cold, possibly because her Jewish identity had been submerged in the pursuit of more pressing objectives.

אהרן ולבניו ולזקני ישראל

All who seriously labor for Jewish continuity in exile must take the words of Lev. 6.6 to the altars of their hearts. But in doing so, the preceding, introductory verses of our parashah contain valuable wisdom to protect the laborers from "burnout."

Beginning with Lev. 6.5 and working backwards, we learn that fire is produced and maintained when fuel is added. Toss on another log and get a bigger fire, right? Not necessarily. Lev. 6.4 suggests that the quality of today's fire is affected by the ashes of yesterday's efforts. A build-up of old ash will smother new fire. We must remove the choking remains of yesterday. As S.R. Hirsch z"l put it, "Woe to him who rests upon his laurels… who does not begin the work of each day with new, complete devotions as if it were the very first day of his life's work."

Lev. 6.3, however, functions as a boundary for verse four. Analysis of a core sample of the preceding day's ash (conducted in full priestly regalia) is the first order of business in the new day. Yesterday's efforts are not completely valueless. They cannot simply bethrown away.

And finally, Lev. 6.2. reflects on the quality of the ash which is produced in the first place. The torah of the altar service commands devotion and follow-through. Unless we keep the fire burning, "ALL NIGHT UNTIL MORNING" if necessary, we are in danger of "short hitting," of not sticking with a course of action long enough to get meaningful results.

A well maintained personal altar which balances yesterday's byproducts with today's potential is critical for Jewish continuity. Those we touch must see an enthusiasm which burns continuously within our hearts, and thus through our labors we may hope that some future Esther will discover (or rediscover) her own fire.•

Tzav

Shemini

Leviticus 9.11–11.47

Professor Jacob Neusner

JACOB NEUSNER IS DISTINGUISHED RESEARCH PROFESSOR OF RELIGIOUS STUDIES AT THE UNIVERSITY OF SOUTH FLORIDA, TAMPA; LIFE MEMBER OF CLARE HALL, CAMBRIDGE UNIVERSITY; AND A MEMBER OF THE INSTITUTE FOR ADVANCED STUDY, PRINCETON, NJ. HE HAS PUBLISHED MORE THAN FIVE HUNDRED BOOKS ON JUDAISM, AND HOLDS A MORE THAN A DOZEN HONORARY DEGREES AND ACADEMIC MEDALS.

Ambition, Yes; Careerism, No— "And Aaron held his peace" [Lev. 10.3]

This Sabbath celebrates humility over arrogance, the wisdom of age over the impetuosity of youth, above all, ambition over careerism. Youth dreams of splendid careers, old age reflects upon fulfilling long-held, worthy ambition. Youth values fame. Sagacity aspires to achievement. Youth possesses opinions. Age asks for evidence.

The Torah takes the side of ambition over careerism, because the Torah looks into the heart. That, after all, is the Talmud's own judgment of matters: above all, the All-Merciful wants the heart. And "heart," we understand, includes attitude, emotion, feeling, the virtues of soul.

This week the Torah tells how God respects the humility of ambition—a mark of modesty in aspiration—and punishes the arrogance of mere careerism—a sign of self-importance above all. And the whole story is told in the contrast between Aaron's and Aaron's sons' conduct on the day on which Israel's service of God gets underway: the consecration of the altar. What to notice in the narrative is simple: Aaron's offering and God's response, Aaron's sons' actions and God's response. God does the same thing in both chapters, but with vastly different results.

First come Aaron's actions, always responding to God's commands set forth

---

דָּבָר אַחֵר **DAVAR AHER.** NADAV AND AVIHU EACH TOOK HIS FIREPAN...AND THEY BROUGH A STRANGE FIRE BEFORE THE ETERNAL... [Lev. 10.1]. Every time I read about the deaths of Nadav and Abihu, I get angry. What justification could there be for God to take the lives of two young priests, however presumptuous they may have been? Sure, the midrashim gives a list of all the reasons (rationalizations!), but none of them are quite satisfying. One midrashic scenario always stuck in my mind. It seems that Nadav and Abihu used to follow Aaron and Moses conspiring to wrestle leadership away from them. Were they leaders of the community, they would do things differently. Perhaps we are all guilty of assuming such a posture (the struggle of the *yetzer ha-tov* and the *yetzer ha-ra* gaining control).

Then yesterday it hit me. My colleague and classmate, Rabbi Jeff Salkin and I were having lunch, reviewing the latest

by Moses: "AND IT CAME TO PASS ON THE EIGHTH DAY MOSES CALLED AARON AND HIS SONS AND THE ELDERS OF ISRAEL, AND HE SAID TO AARON, TAKE A BULL CALF FOR A SIN-OFFERING AND A RAM FOR A BURNT-OFFERING, BOTH WITHOUT BLEMISH, AND OFFER THEM BEFORE THE LORD. AND SAY TO THE PEOPLE OF ISRAEL, 'TAKE A MALE GOAT FOR A SIN-OFFERING AND A CALF AND A LAMB'... AND THEY BROUGHT WHAT MOSES COMMANDED BEFORE THE TENT OF MEETING; AND ALL THE CONGREGATION STOOD NEAR AND STOOD BEFORE THE LORD. AND MOSES SAID, 'THIS IS THE THING WHICH THE LORD COMMANDED YOU TO DO; AND THE GLORY OF THE LORD WILL APPEAR TO YOU.' THEN MOSES SAID TO AARON, 'DRAW NEAR TO THE ALTAR AND OFFER YOUR SIN-OFFERING AND YOUR BURNT-OFFERING AND MAKE ATONEMENT FOR YOUR-SELF AND FOR THE PEOPLE AND BRING THE OFFERING OF THE PEOPLE AND MAKE ATONE-MENT FOR THEM, AS THE LORD HAS COM-MANDED'." [Lev. 9.1-7]

"THEN AARON LIFTED UP HIS HANDS TOWARD THE PEOPLE AND BLESSED THEM; AND HE CAME DOWN FROM OFFERING THE SIN-OFFERING AND THE BURNT-OFFERING AND THE PEACE-OFFERINGS. AND MOSES AND AARON WENT INTO THE TENT OF MEET-ING; AND WHEN THE PEOPLE CAME OUT, THEY BLESSED THE PEOPLE, AND THE GLORY OF THE LORD APPEARED TO ALL THE PEOPLE. AND FIRE CAME FORTH FROM BEFORE THE LORD AND CONSUMED THE BURNT-OFFERING AND THE FAT UPON THE ALTAR; AND WHEN ALL THE PEOPLE SAW IT, THEY SHOUTED AND FELL ON THEIR FACES." [Lev. 9.22-24]

Here is the story of a humble man who does as he is told. Notice, no one tells Aaron to bring fire to the altar. So he doesn't. No one asks for incense, so he leaves it out. He is instructed only to present the ani-mals on the altar. But don't miss the serene faith of Aaron either: Having laid the meat on the cold altar, he asked for no sign that God would accept the offering—except the blessing that he as a priest would bestow. Nothing much hap-pens. So Aaron has ascended to the

Shemini

trends regarding rabbinic placement and retirement. The rabbis now in preparation for retirement were the same rabbis who interviewed us—what seemed to be only a short time ago—then to become their assistants. Now we will be replacing them. **Rabbi Kerry Olitzky <Olitzky@huc.edu>**

דָּבָר אַחֵר **DAVAR AHER. AND THEY BROUGH A STRANGE FIRE BEFORE THE ETERNAL [LEV. 10.1].** And is it possible that the אֵשׁ זָרָה *esh zarah* emerges *not* from the altar, but from within *us?* We've all felt those fires (of ambition) burning within. Only a sincere immersion in the waters of Torah can tame the flames. **Rabbi Jeff Salkin <JEFFSALK@aol.com>**

top of the altar, laid out the offering, raised his hands to bless the people, and then—and then he has climbed down off the high place. Not embarrassed or ashamed, he and Moses go into the tent of meeting. The lifeless altar left behind, they bless the people. Then, and only then, "THE GLORY OF THE LORD APPEARED," and this is its manifestation: Fire from Heaven consumes the burnt offering. The faith of Aaron confirmed, the trust of Aaron vindicated, the people respond. Humility signifies faith in God, God who vindicates, God who responds to our humility by an act of uncoerced grace (for that is what miracles are all about). God cannot command our love but only yearn for it; God cannot demand our faith, but only respond to it. God's act of uncoerced grace then responds to ours. Faith is natural to the condition of the virtuous person.

The next lines draw the contrast between careerism and ambition. Aaron brought no flame to the altar, but his sons did. Aaron did not embellish the offering with the spice of incense, but his sons did. Aaron did what God commanded: nothing less and nothing more than what God commanded. His sons did what God had not commanded, and that means, and can only mean, that they did what they felt like doing. They placed their sense of matters above that of God's commandments. That arrogance signalled the absence of faith: God cannot be relied upon to do things properly, but we can. Here is the written and then the oral Torah's statement of matters:

"NOW NADAV AND AVIHU, THE SONS OF AARON, EACH TOOK HIS CENSER AND PUT FIRE IN IT AND LAID INCENSE ON IT AND OFFERED UNHOLY FIRE BEFORE THE LORD, SUCH AS HE HAD NOT COMMANDED THEM. AND FIRE CAME FORTH FROM THE PRESENCE OF THE LORD AND DEVOURED THEM AND

Synopsis: On the eighth day, the first sacrifices are offered. The sons of Aaron, Nadav and Avihu, die having offered a sacrifice with alien fire. Details for proper behavior of the priests follow this story. Chapter 11 contains some of the laws of kashrut—which foods are permitted and which are forbidden.

דָּבָר אַחֵר **DAVAR AHER. AND THEY BROUGH A STRANGE FIRE BEFORE THE ETERNAL [LEV. 10.1].** First—another angle on the "STRANGE FIRE" of Nadav and Avihu: The kids went farther than the father, because like all children of famous parents, like many rabbis' kids, like children of parents always in the limelight, they felt they had to be more—more radical, more daring, more spectacular, anything different—just to be noticed on their own merits,

to be appreciated for themselves. Perhaps Nadav and Avihu realized they would never be recognized as authority figures on their own—forever "oh, those are Aaron's boys"—until they did something which set them apart, made them priests of a different type than their dad. Unfortunately, they went too far and got infamy instead—like lots of kids who "act out" in the shadow of their famous fathers or mothers.

Second—on Aaron's silence as "humble acceptance of the justice of the Divine decree." No way. If you have ever been at the *shiva* of parents who lost a child, you know that such silence is not humble acceptance at all. It is the mute shock of one who simply cannot find words. Such *shiva* houses are unbearably quiet. Aaron was silent because in that situation, all words end up sounding shallow. **Rabbi Elyse Goldstein <Baruch_Sienna @mail.magic.ca>**

THEY DIED BEFORE THE LORD. THEN MOSES SAID TO AARON, 'THIS IS WHAT THE LORD HAS SAID, I WILL SHOW MYSELF HOLY AMONG THOSE WHO ARE NEAR ME, AND BEFORE ALL THE PEOPLE I WILL BE GLORIFIED.' AND AARON HELD HIS PEACE. [Lev. 10.1-3]

When the sons of Aaron saw that all of the offerings had been presented and all the rites had been carried out, and yet the Presence of God had not come to rest upon Israel, said Nadav to Avihu, "How can anyone cook without fire?"

They forthwith took unholy fire and went in to the Holy of Holies, as it is said, "Now Nadav and Avihu, the sons of Aaron, each took his censer and put fire in it."

Said to them the Holy One blessed be He, "I shall honor you still more than you have honored me. You have brought in before me unclean fire. I shall burn you up with clean fire!" [*Sifra XCIX.III.5*]

The father seeks achievement and hopes for grace. The sons thirst after public recognition—"incense over and above the offering, my what a good idea!"—and implicitly make their own judgment on their father and uncle, who have left the ark cold and still. The glory of the Lord appeared to all the people. Fire came from Heaven and consumed the burnt offering that Aaron had set forth upon the altar. And then —

And then, Aaron's sons, Nadav and Avihu, added to the rite. Their father's offering of meat and cereal demanded the addition of their spices, the flavoring of the incense, so they thought. Not only so, but the fire from Heaven not having sufficed, they also add fire to the altar: alien flame, unholy fire. What made it unholy was that it was such as the Lord had not commanded. And that is why, once again, fire comes forth from God's presence. And this fire devoured not the offering but the priests. The holy fire accepted the sincere offering, the sacrifice of a humble and

Shemini

דְּבָר אַחֵר **DAVAR AHER. AND THEY BROUGH A STRANGE FIRE BEFORE THE ETERNAL [LEV. 10.1].** I have two questions for Jacob Neusner, and our community of readers: How would Dr. Neusner have written this *d'var Torah* in his twenties, or even his thirties? I do not object to the analysis but to the tone of denigration toward the young sons of Aaron. Is it possible that their upbringing did not prepare them for this responsibility? Is their careerism any different than one would expect from young men? (See the life stages literature; I believe that you will find that Nadav and Abihu reacted in a most predictable fashion.)

If, as Dr. Neusner postulates, humility, obedience and forbearance are what G-d wants from us, why are we not all working diligently toward the reestablishment of the Temple and the ritual of sacrifice? Why are

contrite, obedient heart. The unholy fire marked those who presented it as disobedient, arrogant, insolent, self-important and self-aggrandizing. And God explains: "I WILL SHOW MYSELF HOLY AMONG THOSE WHO ARE NEAR ME." To be near God is to obey, doing neither more nor less than God's stated will.

To see how our sages of blessed memory explain the events, let us turn to their greatest commentary on Leviticus, which is *Sifra*, a work of the third or fourth century of the Common Era, thus contemporary with the earlier stages of the Talmuds, and, like them, a work of tradition of Sinai. And let us now start back with the question, on what account did Nadav and Avihu suffer Divine punishment? The sages here contrast Aaron's offering with that of his two sons, Aaron's attitude toward Heaven with the sons' attitudes toward Aaron and Moses. Aaron rejoiced at God's mercy, blaming himself for the absence of a miracle. His humility rewarded, God performed the miracle that was neces-

sary. Nadav and Avihu looked on impatiently, seeing their uncle and father as obstacles to the high position to which they aspired. Their arrogance punished, God performed precisely the same miracle as before, but with the opposite effect. Here is how our sages set the matter out (in my translation of *Sifra XCIX.III.1–3*): "AND HE CAME DOWN FROM OFFERING THE SIN–OFFERING AND THE BURNT–OFFERING AND THE PEACE–OFFERINGS":

When he had completed making his offerings, he came down from the altar in great joy.

Here is a subtle point. The Torah does not say that the heavenly fire has consumed the offerings, but it does now say Aaron was filled with joy. But why—when nothing has happened? The reason cannot be that Heaven has carried out its miracle, there having been none. It can only be joy because Aaron himself has carried out his task. Ambition feeds on achievement. But ambition is so humble as to criticize its own achievement, and here is our sages'

reading of Aaron's heart:

"AND MOSES AND AARON WENT INTO THE TENT OF MEETING":When Aaron realized that all of the offerings had been presented and all the rites had been carried out, yet the Presence of God had not yet come down to rest upon Israel, Aaron was standing in distress, saying, "I know that the Omnipresent is angry with me. It is on my account that the Presence of God has not come to rest upon Israel. This is what my brother Moses has done to me! I went in and was humiliated, for the Presence of God has not come to rest upon Israel."

Forthwith Moses came in with him and sought mercy, so that the Presence of God came to rest upon Israel.

That is why Scripture says, "AND MOSES AND AARON WENT INTO THE TENT OF MEETING [AND WHEN THE PEOPLE CAME OUT, THEY BLESSED THE PEOPLE, AND THE GLORY OF THE LORD APPEARED TO ALL THE PEOPLE]."

So much for Aaron. Everything we noticed in the written Torah's narra-

---

we free, today, to ignore these mitzvot, to make our own decision about our role in relationship to G-d, as did the sons of Aaron? **Nancy Ferst**

דָּבָר אַחֵר **DAVAR AHER. AND THEY BROUGH A STRANGE FIRE BEFORE THE ETERNAL [LEV. 10.1].** Yes, there are some inherent problems in generational turnover. Ambition, selfishness, humility and arrogance are on two different axis. Age provides a third,

and Neusner ignores the fact that the old can also be arrogant, or selfishly interested in their job security.

Paradoxes abound in the *Tanakh*. Nadav, Avihu and Pinhas would seem to be the same in their actions. Their eventual fates were radically different. If it is careeristic arrogance to supply an action that you think is missing, Pinhas should also have been expunged from the community.

A bureaucratic frame of mind (I just do what I'm told and follow the rules) can be dangerous when flexibility is required. Ultimately, the difference may be more a matter of faith. If a sacrifice is for God's benefit, and you have faith in God, you will let God take care of any other details that have not been commanded. If a sacrifice is for the people's benefit, and you think God depends on you for all the details (do I have to tell you about

tive is made explicit: Aaron's obedience, humility, purity of heart. Now to his sons:

At that hour punishment overtook Nadav and Avihu.

…they saw Moses and Aaron walking along ahead, while they were coming after them, and all Israel following.

Nadav said to Avihu, "In yet a little while these two old men will die, and we shall lead the congregation."

Said the Holy One, blessed be He, "We shall see who will bury whom! They will bury you, and they will continue to lead the community."

We begin with a specific portrait of naked careerism. The two young men want the office held by the elders—not the responsibility, which they can scarcely envision, but only the office: "we shall lead—so strike up the band." When the parade ends, the work begins. Seeing only the trappings of power but grasping nothing of the tasks,

they are drawn into their little conspiracy: we on our own shall correct father's mistake, leaving a cold altar indeed! Here is how our sages justify their view of Aaron's sons as insolent and arrogant:

"Nadav and Avihu": Why does Scripture add, "the sons of Aaron"?

It is because they did not pay respect to Aaron. Nadav and Avihu did not take counsel with Moses. "each took his censer":

Each acted on his own, and did not take counsel with the other.

"…why is it said, 'such as he had not commanded them'?

"It was because they had not consulted Moses, their master."

R. Eliezer says, "Nadav and Avihu became liable for punishment only because they taught law in the presence of Moses, their master, for whoever teaches law in the presence of his master is liable to death."

Here is arrogance. Here is naked careerism. Here is youth humiliating

Shemini

the honey in the mead?) that are not mentioned as commands, you will do whatever you think is right.

The *p'shat* is obviously against whatever Nadav and Avihu did, but it does not indicate that they did not think they were correct in their actions. Selfish careerism, to me, involves a conscious undermining of others' abilities and authority. **Larry Moldo, Beth El Synagogue, Omaha, NE**

דָּבָר אַחֵר **DAVAR AHER. And Aaron was silent.** [Lev. 10.3]. Perhaps a silent, quiet type like Aaron might have been driven to drink by the death of his sons. Maybe that's why Moses warns against drinking and wants him back on the job as soon as possible, to avoid his trying to drown his troubles in a bottle! I don't know—did the Canaanites drink at funerals? **Hazan Ira Rohde, Cong. Shearith Israel, New York, NY**

age. Why did they do what they did? It was explicitly to correct the failure of their father, and sages follow the Torah's narrative when they point out that fact: the altar was loaded with cold meat and empty of flame, so they will provide what Aaron forgot—old age indeed! How now does Aaron respond? We ourselves can readily answer the question. A man of surpassing humility, he will blame himself. He must have sinned, for only in that way can he explain this catastrophe; he is punished for his own failing: "AND AARON HELD HIS PEACE." His silence marked that true act of sanctification, the acceptance of the justice of God's decree.

Aaron takes his place in that long line of Israel's holy saints, whose sanctity consists of their acknowledging that what God does is just, however difficult it is for us to say in what that justice consists. Here is the main proposition that our sages set forth, appealing to a sequence of well-established facts:

The righteous as a matter of fact are accustomed to acknowledge the justice of the Divine decree.

Abraham acknowledged the justice of the Divine decree, as it is said, "AND I AM BUT DUST AND ASHES" [Gen. 18.27].

Jacob acknowledged the justice of the Divine decree, as it is said, "I AM NOT WORTHY OF THE LEAST OF ALL THE STEADFAST LOVE AND ALL THE FAITHFULNESS WHICH YOU HAVE SHOWN TO YOUR SERVANT" [Gen. 32.10].

David acknowledged the justice of the Divine decree, as it is said, "MY WOUNDS GROW FOUL AND FESTER BECAUSE OF MY FOOLISHNESS" [Ps. 38.5].

They acknowledged the justice of the Divine decree and remained silent.

So much for the sanctification of God's name accomplished by Aaron and his surviving sons: humility, obedience, forbearance, above all, hope.

Aaron looks neither backward nor forward but only upward. He understands what counts. To Jews without Judaism, he has nothing to say, for his is the message of how faith sanctifies God's name. To those of us who fear and love God and receive the Torah day by day, standing always

at Sinai, the Torah's message is this: What you do not understand, accept with humility, in silence. God will justify God. Our task is to acknowledge God's decree, to let God be God.

With our obsession with the Holocaust to the exclusion of the Torah itself, and with our restrictive definition of the theological task into one solely of theodicy—justifying God's way to humanity—we do well to contemplate the example of the priest who inaugurated the holy altar and lost his sons in a single hour, and for a single reason. What we learn from Aaron, in the end, is the humility of holy Israel's holiest saints: They possessed the humility to acknowledge the justice of the Divine decree and remain silent. The worldly careerists lost their lives. Because of his ambition to serve God, Aaron held his peace. For those of us among whom God yet lives, that is the task of the hour—and of the century to come.•

דָּבָר אַחֵר **DAVAR AHER. THE ETERNAL SPOKE TO AARON AND HIS SONS....** Aaron taught us the merits of being silent, and he focused on *Avodat ha-Shem*, and he merited great reward as did his grandson Pinhas. The survivors of the Holocaust teach us the same lesson. We must be grateful to our past teachers that we can learn from their actions. **Dr. Jeffrey C. Ratz, Brooklyn, NY.**

THE PRIEST SHALL LOOK AT THE AFFLICTION IN THE SKIN OF HIS FLESH... [LEV 13.3]

THE PRIEST SHALL LOOK UPON HIM ON THE SEVENTH DAY... [13.15]

THE PRIEST SHALL LOOK UPON HIM, AND IF THE AFFLICTION HAS TURNED WHITE THE PRIEST SHALL PURIFY THE AFFLICTION, DECLARING IT PURE. [13.17]

All of these discussions of skin diseases and their care, including quarantine, in ancient times have been the bane of the Jewish preachers' lives for many generations.

Tazria

**Leviticus
12.1-13.59**

Rabbi Arthur Green

RABBI ARTHUR GREEN, A STUDENT OF JEWISH MYSTICISM AND HASIDISM, IS THE PHILIP W. LOWN PROFESSOR OF JEWISH THOUGHT AT BRANDEIS UNIVERSITY.

"What to say on *Parashat Tazria?*" has affected the calendars of congregations ("Let's invite the scholar-in-residence that week" or "My sensitive little Kimberly will not be Bat Mitzvah when the Torah reading is all about acne!") and the careers of rabbis ("How could you let them schedule the interview that weekend?) more than is sometimes realized.

Such is not the case, however, for the hasidic literature that I spend much of my time reading. From the days of the earliest of the Ba'al Shem Tov's followers, a transition was easily made from "priest" to "rebbe," and from physical afflictions to those of the soul. The priest's looking at the affliction becomes the hasidic master's ability to look into the heart of his disciples, to see who among them needs healing, how that healing is to be effected, and how the disciple's

דָּבָר אַחֵר **DAVAR AHER. WHEN A WOMAN GETS PREGNANT AND THEN BIRTHS A SON, SHE IS 'CONTAMINATED' FOR SEVEN DAYS, DAYS OF *NIDDAH*... [Lev.12.2].** *This forum on niddah comes from the Torah Aura Bulletin Board.* This week we are studying *Tazria-Metzora.* That means we are in trouble from the start. The coward's way out is to make a metaphor out of leprosy and apply it to *lashon ha-ra* (gossip). You know, loose lips sell Phisoderm®.

This is the way the text starts: GOD SPOKE TO MOSES SAYING: "TEACH THE FAMILIES OF ISRAEL THAT WHEN A WOMAN GETS PREGNANT AND THEN BIRTHS A SON, SHE IS 'CONTAMINATED' FOR SEVEN DAYS, DAYS OF *NIDDAH*. DURING THAT TIME, SHE IS IMPURE. AND ON THE EIGHTH DAY, THE FORESKIN OF THE SON SHALL BE CIRCUMCISED..." We are in lots of trouble from the start. (1) Women are impure. (2) Daughters make mothers "unclean" for fourteen days, sons

דבר אל בני ישראל לאמ

spiritual נֶגַע (naga "affliction") might be transformed by a mere reversal of letters into עֹנֶג (oneg "joy.") The rebbe is in many ways the new priest, and his purported powers of healing (including physical healing) made for a large part of the support that hasidic leaders received, especially from the common folk.

While the master's closer disciples saw him as a source of profound teaching and spiritual counsel, ordinary Jewish men and women came to seek the rebbe's powerful blessing, especially in times of illness. The Ba'al Shem Tov himself, after all, had been just that: a ba'al shem or "master of the name," or one who could write amulets containing the Divine name that were supposed, along with herbal and folk medicines he prescribed, to have healing power.

We modern Jews have a significantly more ambivalent attitude toward the healing powers of our own religious leaders. While visiting the sick and reciting prayers for healing from the bimah are still expected of a rabbi, few Jews place any real stock in the special efficacy of the rabbi's prayers or his/her special "merit" in the eyes of heaven. It is rabbis themselves, especially those of the younger generations, who most clearly tell their congregants that they do not want to be seen as priests. The contemporary American rabbi prefers to emphasize the democratic and lay-empowering aspects of Judaism, those claiming that every person's prayer comes equally before God. This view sees the rabbi as teacher and perhaps as example, but not as one endowed with any Divine gifts that would grant the rabbi special power to bless or to heal.

In some more innovative congregations, especially those shaped by the influence of the Havurah movement, it is congregations themselves, and

Synopsis: With the birth of a male child, a mother is considered impure for 7 days (14 for a daughter). After this initial period, she remains in the status of impurity for 33 days for a son (66 for a daughter). At the conclusion she brings a sin (hattat) offering. A description of the symptoms of skin diseases (tzara'at) followed by infections in fabrics and leather concludes our parashah.

---

only seven. (3) Circumcision. The problem: Remain true to the text, and yet do not consider women dirty. There are no easy answers. One of the most interesting comes from Tamar Frankiel. Tamar Frankiel is an orthodox feminist who strongly advocates woman's issues—not a "traditional" feminist. Her book, *The Voice of Sarah,* is an interesting attempt to find "liberation" in the context of rabbinic sources. Her work sometimes feels

insightful, sometimes apologetic. I am still working it through, but here is what she says about niddah.

A friend and early teacher once remarked to me, "Judaism is a feminine religion with a patriarchal veneer."… The female rhythms lay the foundation, the male brings forth the spark. On a human level, her rhythms are decisive; there is a time for union and a time for separation. While the descriptions of the time of niddah are usually

translated "impurity" or "uncleanness," they do not connote magical danger or pollution, let alone dirt. The time is viewed negatively only from the point of view that now creative union cannot properly take place. No other pollution is invited, no other relations are forbidden. The only things not permitted at this time are entering into sexual relations, and gestures between husband and wife that might lead to such relations….When we take additional time

not only the rabbi, who are seen as bearing the mitzvah of *bikkur ḥolim*, visiting the sick.

But I believe this is only half the story. Our democratization of Judaism and "demystification" of the rabbinate do not come without a price. Jews who affiliate with the synagogue, in the moments of great need, still want the rabbi to be able to "do something." Democracy is all well and good, but not when my child, God forbid, is sick or my mother is dying. Even a generation of Jews who knows rationally that the rabbi bears no special powers wants terribly for that rabbi to care and to demonstrate that caring by some act of

"doing." Any rabbi with experience in the pulpit knows that this sense of caring and the perception of whether the rabbi does or doesn't "care about me" is what most often makes or breaks rabbinic careers.

But just what is it that the rabbi can do? We rabbis, like other non-priestly clergy, have to rediscover that aspect of our traditions that empower us as healers. New definitions of both "affliction" and wellness" abound in our day. They often have much to do with wholeness, integration with reality, and what our tradition encapsulates within the word "shalom." And if a rabbi isn't a descendant of Aaron, surely he or she should be a disci-

Tazria

out for spiritual pursuits during the days of *niddah*, it can sometimes relieve emotional distress—the anxiety, deflated energy, or depression that many of us experience at this time. Some women find it a fortuitous time for dreams or visualizations that give us insights or comfort.

In other words, this *niddah* is a privilege which gives women a private time to revel in the emotions and experience of birth. And, in the case of birthing a daughter, mother and daughter are privileged with twice as much intimate time together. It is an interesting spin on the traditional practice. I am struggling. What do you think? Let's start with the core statement. "Judaism is a feminine religion with a patriarchal veneer." Try that one on your bat and bar mitzvah class. Let us know what they think.

דָּבָר אַחֵר **DAVAR AḤER.** "I thought that the idea of mothers and daughters having time to bond was a nice idea—a nice explanation of the days of *niddah*. But underneath it all was problematic. The problems have to do with applying something that some women experience as an ordinance for all women. If all women's sexual and emotional responses were similar (or uniform) during menstruation and the days after, then one could say that this was a gift to women, but they are not—we know that from research in sexuality. Some women do desire sexual contact in the days during and after menstruation. Therefore, to put a monolithic structure on women is unfair and wrong. There are different women's voices. I think Tamar Frankiel's interpretation is interesting, a nice

דבר אל בני ישראל לאמר אשה כי תזריע

ple of Aaron, one who pursued shalom wherever it could be found. True, only God is called an עוֹשֶׂה שָׁלוֹם (*Oseh shalom*—Maker of peace.) But a רוֹדֵף שָׁלוֹם (*rodef shalom*—"pursuer of shalom") is a pretty good title for the post-modern healing rabbi. Here I would translate that phrase as "seeking wholeness." The rabbi should be, in the words of Psalm 147, one who "HEALS BROKEN HEARTS," helping those whose lives are shattered to recover the wholeness that is their natural state. Of course, it may be the family as well as the sick or dying person who needs this sort of healing, but the rabbi should be able to minister to both. Spiritual healing is a gift for all who hurt, and that includes both the sick and those who love them. God's compassionate love abounds for all creatures. By reminding us of that love even when we most need it and least feel its presence, the rabbi can help to open a channel for Divine love to flow and be received.

Can only the rabbi do this? I s there some mystique about rabbinic ordination that gives one powers of inner healing? Of course not. The de-mystification that made for modernity stands, and we do not seek to deny it. But we moderns find, lo and behold, that we still have need for healing, and especially for the voice of wholeness and continuity in the face of adversity that speaks to us from the depths of our tradition. Such a voice for us Jews is a rabbinic voice, and neither rabbis nor congregants should be afraid of that. A rabbi who is secure within his or her community can then share that voice, letting the charismatic gift go out among "seventy elders" as Moses was able to do.

"THE PRIEST SHALL LOOK AT THE AFFLICTION." If we are going to have real spiritual leaders, let us not be afraid to show them our pain. And if we are going to be real spiritual leaders, let us learn to say with the full power of our being that we know, that we care, and that we join with the afflicted and suffering in praying for wholeness.●

---

interpretation, and I may even teach it, but it needs to be voiced with a lot of cautions. **Shoshana Silberman of The Jewish Center, Princeton NJ**

דָּבָר אַחֵר **DAVAR AḤER.** I strongly disagree with the statement that "Judaism is a feminine religion with a patriarchal veneer." If Judaism were truly a feminine religion, I don't believe there would be terminology like *niddah* or an image of God as basically male. Female characters in the Bible would be clear and accessible, not in need of extensive detective work to reconstruct them. Jewish women in history would be naturally included in books on Jewish history, rather than an afterthought or in books solely on Jewish women. Jewish women would be equally as obligated to observe mitzvot as men, rather than most mitzvot being optional for women, which has had the practical impact of Jewish women having a lower status in the community than men. I could go on and on.

To say that the patriarchal tone of Judaism is only a veneer assumes that underneath the veneer is the real way that Judaism is. I'm not sure that anyone has the real way, but I don't think it's obviously a feminine nature. Women's voices from the past, women's rituals and stories, etc., need us to be good detectives and creators in the present. Perhaps with this type of work continuing, more feminine aspects will come to light. **Rabbi Wendy Spears of Temple Beth Haverim, Woodland Hills, CA.**

דָּבָר אַחֵר **DAVAR AḤER. THE KOHEIN SHALL LOOK AT THE AFFLICTION…** [Lev. 13.3]. Rabbi Arthur Green in his moving *drash* on *Tazria* alluded to the fact that the legacy of Aaron con-sisted of both ritual functions and of healing of the soul and body. He showed that modern day rabbis should be natural descendants and disciples of Aaron. I would like to call attention to another dimension of this issue which I learned from Rabbi Harold Kushner of Natick, MA. Modern day physicians should also look upon themselves as inheritors of Aaron's legacy. They practice the art of healing of the human body. Their work is much more effective, however, when taking care of the body is combined with caring for the patient's soul. Regarding the patient as a whole human being, paying attention to both physical and spiritual needs are the earmarks of truly great heal-ers. **Dr. Peter Cukor, Prompt Action, Inc. 39 Foxhill Dr., Natick, MA <pcmail@bunny.gte.com>**

Tazria

דָּבָר אַחֵר DAVAR AḤER. THE KOHEIN SHALL LOOK AT THE AFFLICTION... [Lev. 13.3]. Far more than Art Green might wish to venture, *prayer does promote actual physical healing*, whether by rabbis or by the well-intentioned laity. When a person enters the room of someone who is sick, and says, for example, "We are all hoping for your quick recovery," our tradition tells us that such an encouraging visit can be part (1/60) of the cure. But more than that, we also know that for most, reassurance, comforting words and gestures such as hand-holding and hugs, have real physical effects on the promotion of health. These words and those gestures are our "prayers." They are effective prayers. And as human beings we have evolved in such a way as to make such prayers effective. So whether or not our prayer is traditional, we thank G-d that we have been created in such a way as to make such words and actions effective. Prayer promotes healing, not in a roundabout way but really and directly. **Rabbi Howard Apothaker, Temple Beth Shalom, Columbus, OH.**

דָּבָר אַחֵר DAVAR AḤER. THE KOHEIN SHALL LOOK AT THE AFFLICTION... [Lev. 13.3]. One does not practice medicine very long before the power of faith, the power of peace of mind, the רְפוּאָה שְׁלֵמָה "*refuah shleimah*" (healing), becomes obvious. In our complex, so-called sophisticated and all knowing society, more that 2/3 of the office patients we see are affected by the conflicts and anxieties of urban life. Practicing gastroenterology, I remember being puzzled by a patient with a peptic ulcer that would not heal with the usual therapy, Tagamet and Zantac, Mylanta, and bland diet failed to calm his epigastric burning. The patient was a post office employee, a black man, who, taking the civil service examinations, had opted for this type of life and intended to make the post office his career. Although his work was superior, others kept being promoted over him. He felt contempt from his superior, and believed the color of his skin had something to do with the issue. It wasn't until, on repeated questioning, he reluctantly told me "what was eating him" that I encouraged him to face his employer and confront him with that he felt was unfair practice. He did so! For the first time, he felt relief, and from that time on, the ulcer became insignificant. Furthermore, the superior looked at him in a different light. Contempt changed to respect, seeing his strength in facing him, and eventually this led to a promotion.

I recall the circus trapeze artist who, after days of high flying acts without a net, had such anxiety that uncontrolled hives recurred, and the itching could not be relieved even with the most powerful steroids or antibiotics. Eventually he left this occupation, and the skin cleared. Why were the physicians of yesteryear successful and so respected, when today's practitioners with all their subspecialization, incur skepticism and suspicion, often resulting in lawsuits and repeated questioning? What healed the pneumonia when yesterday's doctor made a house call and diagnosed correctly, but had no antibiotic or magic bullet to offer?

The healing power of faith and the emotional support given by sitting at the bedside long hours watching the patient and counting the pulse as the only treatment, seemed to make a difference. Nowadays, we see that success is often directly proportional to how little we interfere with nature's healing process.

The "refuah" or medicine only the rabbi can administer is every bit as potent in controlling the endorphins, the T-cells, and the immune mechanisms, if the patient is a believer, as anything we doctors have in our bags. As it is said, "THE LORD LAYETH BEFORE THEE LIFE OR DEATH, THEREFORE CHOOSETH LIFE!" We literally will ourselves to life and health, or to death and despondency! Not infrequently, the patient on his death-bed chooses to live until the long-lost relative arrives, or the Shabbat or High Holiday passes. When we chose to disobey the inner power (soul) we have, whether it be by overindulgence, or by creating inner turmoil through lying or cheating our fellow man, we literally will ourselves to death. The man or woman who wants to live longer looks forward to a comforting family and a meaningful work life. He has the greatest chance to recover.

Physicians from the time of Maimonides and rabbis are blood brothers, "Priests" if you will, applying a balm whose action inter-twined produces mental and physical healing, It may be hard at present to measure the chemical changes that result, but some day this will be all the more obvious. Just as enlightenment brings science and religion together, so should physician and rabbi work together supplementing each other for our people's betterment. **Dr. Leonard Breslaw, M.D., Los Angeles, Ca.**

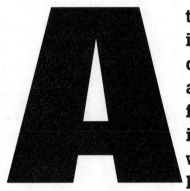

At times we are astonished by the Bible's closeness. The episodes and characters may step from the past, but they inhabit our emotional world. At other times, however, the Bible startles us with its strangeness. What lessons can we learn from a world whose time and beliefs are so far away? In *Parashat Metzora*, we find the Bible at its most impenetrably alien. How shall we understand the unrelenting and unedifying catalogue of sores and leprous spots?

Modern commentators often restrict themselves to a scientific investigation of these diseases. But the Bible is not a platform for science, it is a ladder for souls. How shall we use *Metzora* to aid our climb?

The first strategy is to extend the rabbinic idea of reinterpretation. The Rabbis midrashically recast the word מְצוֹרָע *Metzora* to mean מוֹצִיא שֵׁם רָע *Motsi Shem Ra*—one who blackens another's name. They argue that leprosy was the Divine punishment for evil talk. Judaism is a tradition that takes words very seriously. God creates the world through words—"LET THERE BE LIGHT." Words are the divine legacy to humanity through the Torah.

Just as words can create, the midrash is intended to remind us of the destructive power of speech. Like leprosy, gossip is an insidious destroyer of people's lives. The damage begins subtly and then

Metzora

Leviticus 14.1–15.33

Rabbi David Wolpe

RABBI DAVID WOLPE TEACHES AT THE JEWISH THEOLOGICAL SEMINARY, WHERE HE SERVES AS ASSISTANT TO THE CHANCELLOR. HE IS THE AUTHOR OF: *THE HEALER OF SHATTERED HEARTS: A JEWISH VIEW OF GOD; IN SPEECH AND IN SILENCE: THE JEWISH QUEST FOR GOD, TEACHING YOUR CHILDREN ABOUT GOD* AND MOST RECENTLY, *WHY BE JEWISH?*.

דָּבָר אַחֵר **DAVAR AHER. THIS SHALL BE THE LAW OF THE LEPER... [Lev. 14.1].** As we approach April 23, 1995, the 25th anniversary of Earth Day, I cannot help but wonder if the house in *Parashat Metzora* could represent our planet. I have always felt we are the guardians of the well-being of our planet. Perhaps all the floods, earthquakes, and mud slides are teling us to be more aware of how we treat this precious Earth. Just as we must care for a house with regular maintenance and cleaning, we must not take our beautiful trees, fields, beaches and waters for granted. They, too, must be maintained and cared for to avoid the "plague" of pollution. **Judy Miller, Director, Heritage Academy, Tulsa, OK**

דָּבָר אַחֵר **DAVAR AHER. THIS SHALL BE THE LAW OF THE LEPER... [Lev. 14.1].** Usually I do the מוֹצִיא שֵׁם רָע

becomes irrevocable. Like leprosy, it leads not only to private pain, but public humiliation. We can understand why the Rabbis sought to connect the two phenomenon. Moreover, there is a textual connection, For Moses' sister Miriam, who gossiped about Moses and his wife, was stricken by God with leprosy as a punishment [Num. 12].

A second strategy for dealing with *Metzora* is to find a modern analogy. The leprous individual is an outcast, and his disease is taken as a sign of moral taint. The problem is not simply medical, but also moral or spiritual. That is why he goes to the High Priest and sacrifices. Modern commentators have suggested many current analogies. The spread of AIDS is often interpreted more in moral than medical terms. Others have viewed homelessness as a modern leprosy, a visible plight that is often taken to denote some sort of moral failing. The analogy grows even more intriguing if we consider that *Metzora* talks about a "LEPROUS HOUSE." Apparently the plague does not only strike individuals, but families. Moreover, the house must be quarantined, because there is the conviction that such an infected house could spread.

The tremendous problems that bedevil modern families could be analogized to the leprous house. Families in crisis are often hidden and shame-filled. *Metzora* begins by giving directions for curing the leprous individual "AT THE TIME HE IS TO BE CLEANSED" [Lev. 14.2]. Some commentators understand this to teach that he cannot be cleansed until he is ready. Acknowledgement of the malady is a prelude to individual healing. The same is true of families. Families that are out of balance cannot be restored if they are unwilling—or if a single member is unwilling—to acknowledge a problem.

Synopsis: Our Torah reading this week is linked to last week's parashah whose topic was skin diseases (צָרַעַת *tzara'at*). Purification rites for those declard unclean are detailed. Chapter 14 concludes with a description of diseases found in building stones. Emissions from the sexual organs (both natural and abnormal) of both males and females conclude this larger section on impurity.

"*motzi shem ra*" thing, and jump right from these two *parashiot* (*Tazria* and *Metzora*) into their "moral truth." I follow the midrash and metaphorize מְצוֹרָע *metzora* (leprosy) as שֵׁם רָע מוֹצִיא *motzi shem ra* (gossip). This year I jumped out of the idea of the text and learned something from dealing with its immediacy. The access point was last week's ER. Amazingly, TV was brave enough to show an episode where an easy delivery falls apart and ends, despite the doctors' earnest efforts, in the mother's death.

Here is what I know. The Chinese name years after animals: the Year of the Dog, the Year of the Pig, the Year of the Horse, etc. Have gotten to be much more middle-aged, I now name my years after body defects. The year of the heart problem, the year of the jaw replacement surgery, the year of the hemorrhoid. I know all the nightmares. In my dreams, my house oozes pus, my guts pour out of my body, my skin flakes and peels away, I die giving birth. Decay and death, purity and life—go together.

In the terror of darkest night, living with my failures and my anticipated failures, I live the Torah of *Tazria* and *Metzora*, the world of pus and decay, of illness and stillbirth. The good news here is that impurity can be washed away. There is always new possibility. Sometimes, religion needs

That the leprous house threatens to infect other homes shows how intimate are the bonds that unite the Jewish community. No household exists in isolation. What goes on in families, even inside the soul of each individual, has implications for others. Perhaps the lesson of leprosy is paradoxical: This disease which so often results in isolation, is intended to teach us that community is indispensable.

Yet another approach comes to us from the Rabbis via the leprous house. For the Rabbis list the leprous house among the things "that never were and never will be." Why then does the Torah include it? "To study it so that you may receive reward." This rabbinic idea is that most of the Torah is studied for functional reasons: to apply the law. Yet certain portions of the Torah (the laws of the rebellious son is another) were not intended to be applied. Therefore, the Rabbis assert, one who studies it does so for the love of Torah alone. Such

study is pristine, untouched by any practical application. We receive a reward because it is done for its own sake.

Today we could approach the study of *Metzora* for a similarly "impractical" reason. The laws may not apply, but studying them will teach us how our ancestors saw the world. There is no practical application for laws of leprosy, but in exploring this realm, we draw closer, historically, to ancient Israel. We study it to receive reward of a special kind—intimacy with the past. However strange it may seem, this past is still our own, and in understanding it, we draw close to our ancestors.

There is one more possible approach to these peculiar rites and laws. The laws of leprosy are not about morality alone, and they are not ultimately about bodily health. They are about purity, which is *not* identical with cleanliness. Purity was central to the Bible, and to the Rabbis, and it is a

Metzora

to be a horror movie. **Joel Lurie Grishaver <gris@torahaura.com>**

דָּבָר אַחֵר **DAVAR AHER. This SHALL BE THE LAW OF THE LEPER… [Lev. 14.1].** He was accustomed to the close reading of texts, but on that day he sat with eyes that had never seen before and watched words on the page before him grow legs and dance, legs became wings, and words flew off the page like

pigeons off of cobblestones. Words so free, high–flying, and elusive that from that day on he fell under their spell and became a pursuer of words. Words, of course, were clues.

Words were clues. He turned them over slowly on his tongue. Some were elusive and soaring like birds, others were succulent and delicious like candy. Some he chased down and some he swallowed, digested and only from deep within his

realm we have lost. Modernity does not think of life in terms of pure and impure. But sanctity, purity and holiness are inextricably entwined in the world of the Bible and of the Rabbis. To a religious mind there is another dimension between space and time—there is the dimension of sanctity. In that world strange rules apply. To be pure, or sacred, you must be good. But goodness is not enough to achieve sanctity. There is a mysterious relationship between the individual and God that depends not only on ethics, but on cultic and ceremonial practices. In ways that are obscure, these practices help shape our souls. Like the emotion produced by certain ceremonies, we do not fully understand why cultic behavior aligns our souls with forces of purity and right, but that belief is central to the practice of Judaism.

Is there a tangible difference between the one who intones certain words each morning and the one who does not? Between the one who immerses him or herself in a rit-

ual bath and the one who does not? In other words, do practices with no immediate measurable benefit, practices such as are described in *Metzora* for the benefit of the leper, or practices such as observant Jews repeat today, make a difference in our lives? Judaism argues for the difference. It is not rational — it functions in a world where reason is no guide. Judaism has its realm of purity and mystery, beyond the reach of the grasping logician, beyond the categories of the analysts, and the sneers of the materialists. To a believer in dimension of the holy, a thoroughgoing rationalist is unreasonable, and one who sees only the visible is blind.

That realm of the pure and holy is the realm we reach towards not only with moral rules, but with ritual. It is that world we are reminded of in reading *Metzora*. The reminder is graphic and particular, speaking the language of scales and sores. But the concept is sublime: that there is an invisible order that we can touch,

and seek to arrange, but cannot truly understand. That we align ourselves with the wishes of God in mysterious ways; and that there are openings in the tradition that can be entered not by reason, not by ingenuity, not by learning, but only by *emunah*, trust in God, and in the mysterious world that God created.●

---

digestion did they yield their meaning. He was a reader of clues and a chaser of high–flying words. He was God's own detective.

On that day of his life, God's own detective sat in his fifth floor walk-up where he lived and worked, and there he read from the book of Leviticus. He read the clue words: זֹאת תִּהְיֶה תּוֹרַת הַמְּצֹרָע *Zot Tihye Torat ha-Me-tzora* —THIS IS THE LAW OF THE LEPER, and he stopped. The words

began to change for him. They grew legs and scampered over one another like mice. Then the words themselves separated like mitosis and he read: הַמּוֹצִיא רָע *ha-Motzi ra* instead of הַמְּצֹרָע *ha-Metzora*, he read the "REVEALER OF EVIL" instead of "leprosy," and he got no further that day than this one singularly devastating clue: the one word that had become two.

Ha-Motzi ta—the revealer of evil—the clue was a summons but it had yet to

be disclosed to him what it meant. He knew he was being sent—to where, he did not know.

In his hand he fingered an unlit, wilted Lucky; it wagged in his hand like a sixth finger. He was determined not to smoke that day. Outside the window of his office, a neon sign flashed on and off, twenty-four hours a day, He sat with his feet up on his desk, searching his experience for the dark irreducibility of his summons:

SOMETHING LIKE A PLAGUE

About two weeks ago after purchasing and moving into our first home, my wife and I left town for several days of vacation. Upon our return, we discovered to our alarm that the basement was flooded with water. It seems that a small, rubber washer in a downstairs bathroom finally wore out, coincidentally, while we were gone. Later, the home inspector confirmed the previous owner's claim that such an incident had never happened before.

Rabbi David J. Meyer

RABBI DAVID J. MEYER IS THE RABBI OF TEMPLE EMANU-EL IN MARBLEHEAD, MA.

The previous owner and his family had been the original builders, and had lived in the house for thirty years. Of course, we expected occasional repairs to become necessary, even though the house was in very fine condition. But within the first few weeks of moving in, it became almost eerie how many small things began to go wrong. First, it was the leak downstairs, then the control panel in the kitchen range, next a faucet, then the dryer. It seemed as if the house itself was trying to get accustomed to its new occupants.

I know now that our new-home experience was anything but exceptional. In his book on home repair, *The Walls Around Us*, David Owen explains that when a new family moves into a house, "the house suffers something like a nervous breakdown… The house is accustomed to being handled in certain ways… Familiar domestic rhythms are destroyed. While the house struggles to adjust, many expensive items—including, perhaps, the fur-

Metzora

the revealer of evil. He saw some wickedness, he saw great imperfection, he saw the casualties of dreams, but not evil.

He searched his experience of the world but found nothing that resonated like the evil he felt he had been called to reveal. It was at times like these that God's own detective demonstrated the powers of detection that set him apart from the guild detectives, who did not

recognize the holiness of the task for which they had been called. It was also at times like these that God's own detective was tempted to light that Lucky.

He saw not only the grandeur of his job, but the folly of it, the folly of his lone attempt to penetrate a reality beyond his ken and control. Partially because he had trained himself for nothing else, partially out of the presentiment of a life of

זאת תהיה תורת המצורע ביום טהרתו

nace—unexpectedly self-destruct. Then, gradually, new rhythms are established, the house resigns itself to the change of ownership, and a normal pace of deterioration is restored."

Is it really possible for a house made of wood, brick, plaster and nails to assume a personality of its own? Well, in a classic work of American fiction, such is certainly the case. Nathaniel Hawthorne's accursed House of the Seven Gables in colonial Salem takes on the features—the evil, the decay, the darkness and the illness—which emanate from the family history unfolding within. Throughout the novel, Hawthorne describes the house in human terms, as "a great human heart, with a life of its own, and full of rich and somber reminiscences." And we should bear in mind that Hawthorne's menacing house is not *haunted*—it is *sick*.

Perhaps this is the sort of condition envisioned in the Torah, which describes in *Parashat Metzorah* the condition of the leprous house. As we know from prevailing Jewish

interpretation, צָרַעַת *tzara'at* was a physical and clearly discernible affliction delivered by God as punishment for sinful speech or behavior. And whereas most of the *sidra* describes the detection, cure and purification rituals prescribed for persons afflicted with the plague, one curious section [Lev. 14.33-54] details how one recognizes a leprous house (נֶגַע צָרַעַת בַּבַּיִת "*nega tzara'at ba-bayit*") and what must be done to restore it to a habitable state of purity. In certain cases, such restoration was deemed impossible, and the house would be ordered destroyed to its very foundations.

The commentators of our tradition were rightfully perplexed by this mysterious and enigmatic portion. In *Vayikra Rabbah* 17.6, we find the assertion that God infected only the Israelite homes that had been previously occupied by Canaanite families, whose hidden gold and treasure would be discovered when the walls were torn down. On the other hand, we find in the Talmud [*Sanhedrin*

71a] an opinion that the leprous house described in our sidrah "*lo hayah, v'lo atid le-hiyyot*—never was and will never be." Thus, our passage is here classified with the assortment of strange and obsolete practices of the Torah, which only exist for the sake of the reward that comes from studying them.

We may not know for certain the full extent to which a house might take on the symptoms of a plague, or for that matter, if our homes might, in themselves, embody the ideal human qualities of love and holiness. The answer probably lies somewhere between the House of Seven Gables, and some unexpected leak—which always begins with a suspicious trickle! For even in our own day, and in our own homes, we must occasionally recognize when "something like a plague has appeared in the house." By our lives and by our actions, we might affect the cure that will transform a diseased home into a *mikdash me-at*, a small sanctuary, flooded with the spirit of God.●

---

an exceedingly noble variety, partially because he liked to live dangerously, he was willing to give himself to the task nonetheless.

He was good at it. Like every good detective, when the clues were especially impenetrable, he demonstrated the qualities of investigation with which he had been blessed. He saw the same clues as if with new eyes. "God may have given us the nuts," he would say, "but did not crack them."

God's own detective had learned to pull himself up by his own hair, turn himself inside out, as it were, and see the world with fresh vision. Only then would clues reveal their guarded secrets. He had trained himself to turn the world upside down by standing on his own head. It was his business.

Because he was willing to turn himself inside out or stand on his head if he had to, God's own detective often cracked clues that left the guild detec-

tives bewildered. "There are no simple answers—the answer can't be right if it's simple," he used to say.

In the great tradition of kabbalists and jazzmen who play the saxophone, God's own detective listened for the bustling textural and tonal variety beneath surfaces. It was the rhythms and tones lurking beneath the obvious he heard, "and once you hear that," he would say, "you never hear the same way again."

Rabbi
Lane
Steinger

RABBI STEINGER IS THE SPIRITUAL LEADER OF TEMPLE EMANU-EL, OAK PARK, MICHIGAN.

Metzora

The centerpiece of *Metzora* is the biblical prescription for a house in *Eretz Yisrael*, in which possible צָרַעַת *tzara'at* ("leprosy," perhaps actually some form of fungus or dry rot) has been noticed. The discovery of this malady was taken quite seriously in the Torah because the Land, its inhabitants, and even its structures were to be holy and ritually pure. For me, the house in *Metzora* represents a Jewish or a human institution, be it a home or a family, a congregation or a community, even a country.

Thus, *Metzora* instructs me that any or all of these institutions require constant care and vigilant attention as well as continual maintenance and support, and that they can be subject not only to external forces which threaten their well-being, but also to internal "plagues" which can be equally (if not more) damaging and destructive. Over time, I have likened the *tzara'at* in the house to *Gush Emunim* and Barukh Goldstein, to *Hamas* and *Hizbollah* and international terrorism, to David Koresh and the Branch Davidians and to corrupt tele-evangleists, and even to Jewish apathy, ignorance and indifference. ●

It was because of these highly developed methods of detection that God's own detective went searching for the evil he had been called to reveal within, in the dark well of self. There he descended.

In the darkest and most silent moment of his descent, God's own detective came to the blood-dark waters, from where arose the slow moving but methodical angels of destruction, creaking at the joints.

To a faintly beating drum in the distance, God's own detective locked himself in a death -wrestle with them. Just as they had nearly wrestled him into the waters from where they had arisen like night, he spoke the clue-words of the Psalmist, "SAVE ME, O GOD, FOR THE WATERS ARE COME INTO MY SOUL" [Psalm 69.2]. At that moment, the right arm of God was extended, and God's own detective found the courage to take hold of it.

He was pulled out as if from a well, from his death-wrestle with all that is fragmented, disintegrating, chaotic, but not evil. He felt closer to his summons but still not the revealer of evil for which he had been called. He understood the clue words of Rav Yossi in *Hagigiah* 12b, "alas for people that see, but know not what they see, they stand, but know not on what they stand." The earth rest on pillars, the pillars on waters, waters on mountains, mountains on wind, wind on the storm. The storm, the vertiginous and terminal, the blood-dark waters of dissolution, the storm is suspended on the arms of the Holy One, as it is written, "AND UNDERNEATH ARE THE EVERLASTING ARMS" [Deuteronomy 33.27].

He had descended into the storm of the dissolution of his own self, and lifted up by the everlasting arms, came back to tell the tale. For that he felt a gratitude without measure, and whenever God's own detective felt that way, he prayed.

He often prayed alone in his office. The old logo of a former tenant on the door, "East Asia Trading Co.", guarded him from interruption and mistaken callers. He began to recite the prayers. He felt the terrible weight of his summons being released, and by the time he reached the *Kedushah* prayer, he was filled with an overwhelming sense of awe and well-being.

He ascended to the top of the Throne of Glory. he saw the perspiration on the faces of the angels who were laboring before the Holy One. The angels spread their wings and under their sheltering protection he ducked the river of fire that emerged from God's Holy Throne.

He spread his own arms like wings, and in the language of the angels he whispered, "*Kadosh, Kadosh, Kadosh.*" He spoke the words over and over, "HOLY, HOLY, HOLY." He gobled them up like a handful of raisins and he felt himself released from the now oppressive summons to which he had been called.

Like all creations in Nature whose purposes are certain, like leaves pushing their way through leaves to sunlight, God's own detective surrendered, released himself from his unholy responsibility, הַמּוֹצִיא רָע *ha-Motzi ra*, the revealer of evil, and turned it over. He continued praying in an ecstasy unmatched in his prayer-life. He was off the case.

But like all good detectives, he couldn't quite give it up. In a posture of obvious eligibility, God's own detective sat in his office, waiting for the phone to ring and watching the sign flash on and of outside his window.

He saw her profile through the smoky glass door of his office. She paused to collect herself, she didn't bother knocking, she came in like fresh air. She asked for his help. She told him a story of such wickedness, deceit, and corruption that it made his ears tingle to listen to it.

"I'm off that case," said God's own detective. "I've been relieved of that awful summons," and he told her the story of the clue of the one word that had become two, and of the prayerful release after his descent into darkness. He tried to sound convincing.

But her story was raw, empty of mystery, it was only the brute facticity of evil acts of evil people. He saw in her story the irreducibility of evil that he could not find in his own experience.

These were the words that had ceased to be clues. His powers of detection were unnecessary, misleading Her story pointed to nothing beyond itself—the evil acts of evil people. No excuses, no motivation, evil not done out of ignorance or out of lack of self-consciousness, it was not evil done in the name of God or in the service of something else. This was evil for which there were no excuses left. He knew then that he was not free to relinquish the task.

"I'll take the case," he said, getting up and gathering his coat from the sofa on which he slept. "I know a nice little diner where I take most of my messages and business meetings. We can talk there."

He closed the door of the East Asia Trading Co. behind them, threw away the frayed Lucky, headed for the fire escape. Now part of a holy opposition of two, not yet in love (that would come later), but reaffirming his original summons, God's own detective, הַמּוֹצִיא רָע *ha-Motzi ra*, THE REVEALER OF EVIL, was back on the case.

A broken radiator was hissing steam in great billowing clouds into the hallway. God's own detective slung his coat over his shoulder, put his arm around her, and said out of the corner of his mouth, "You know, kid—this could be the beginning of a beautiful friendship." **James Stone Goodman** <76033.1157@compuserve.com>

מות בני אהרן

Aharei Mot

Leviticus 16.1–18.30

Rabbi Richard N. Levy

RABBI RICHARD N. LEVY IS THE
EXECUTIVE DIRECTOR OF LOS
ANGELES HILLEL COUNCIL.

When the rabbis divided up the Torah into 54 sections, each called a parashah, there is evidence that they tried to begin each section with a word or phrase that would give a clue to major theme in that parashah. If that is true, what were they trying to tell us with *Aharei Mot,* "After Death," or more literally, "After the Death of…?"

The simple answer comes in this portion's first sentence—the instructions about the rites of Aaron, the High Priest, are given to Moses "AFTER THE DEATH OF AARON'S TWO SONS, WHEN THEY DREW NEAR TO THE FACE OF GOD AND DIED."

But while this understanding locates the story of Aaron's upcoming atonement rites in time, our title has much more than chronological significance. Some commentaries read the cause of Nadav's and Avihu's death in this first verse—"THEIR DRAWING NEAR TO THE FACE OF GOD." But there are enough other interpretations of their sin to suggest that we can never know exactly what they did (see some of the commentary to *Parashat Shemini*).

In one verse of that parashah, Leviticus 10.3, God says, "MY HOLINESS WILL BE MANIFEST BY THOSE WHO ARE NEAR TO ME בְּקְרֹבַי *bikrovai*)," suggesting, by the play on the root [קרב *KRV*] that Nadav and Avihu's offering (קָרְבָּן *korban* "sacrifice," from the same root) led in some way to their deaths' becoming an offering. "AFTER THE DEATH OF" such valued human beings who were, after all, so close to God, our portion perhaps suggests that the whole

---

דָּבָר אַחֵר **DAVAR AHER. AND GOD SAID TO MOSES AFTER THE DEATH OF MOSES TWO SONS… [Lev. 16.1].** This past week I was asked to contribute to our services with a *D'var Torah*. I was able to utilize the most important point illustrated in last week's *LTW…* on *Aharei Mot*. A point made by the *Hazal* is that one should cry over the loss of Nadav and Avihu because even though they sinned, they were great

tzadikim. What if they would have lived out their days and contributed greatly to *K'lal Yisrael*? The fact is that "What if" questions arise every day of our lives. I believe the fact that the *Parashat Aharei Mot* is read the same week as Yom Ha-Shoah illustrates the same point of "What if." Not only a child of survivors, but all Jews must cry over the loss of six million possibilities. Aaron taught us the merits of

community needs to look at its own deeds, and seek atonement. This is clearly a parashah that tries to help us face some of the implications of our mortality.

The portion begins with actions necessary to protect the High Priest from death [16.2] because "I APPEAR IN THE CLOUD UPON THE ARK COVER." Aaron is first to avoid coming into the בְּכָל עֵת אֶל הַקֹּדֶשׁ v'khol eit el ha-Kodesh . What do these two Hebrew phrases mean? In one sense they are opposites— קֹדֶשׁ kodesh is usually understood here to mean the "HOLY PLACE," though it could be translated "HOLINESS." We thus find an ambiguity not possible in English: Aaron construes קֹדֶשׁ kodesh as an instruction not to enter the Holy Place בְּכָל עֵת v'khol eit, AT (JUST) ANY TIME. The Holy Place may not be entered at any old time—but the text does not specify at what time it may be entered. For subsequent generations the time is specified at the end of the chapter

(vs. 29ff.): the holy place may be entered only on what became Yom Kippur, the Day of Atonement.

But was it that day for Aaron? Was Aaron uniquely permitted to sense by himself what the proper time was to enter the קֹדֶשׁ Kodesh? And what does it mean for us who live after the Temple's destruction, who have no HOLY PLACE to enter at any time? קֹדֶשׁ Kodesh can also be translated "HOLINESS": You may not enter HOLINESS at any old time. For us, HOLINESS is present much less in space than in time, and so we must learn how to transform "ANY OLD TIME" into holy time, and when that has happened, enter it. After the death of the HOLY PLACE, for us there still is HOLY TIME. Aharei mot, Kedoshim (next week's parashah).

When Aaron does enter the קֹדֶשׁ Kodesh at the proper time, there are certain precautions he must take to prevent his death, since "I APPEAR IN THE CLOUD UPON THE ARK COVER." We recall God's earlier warning to

Synopsis: Purification of the sanctuary is the main topic of this week's parashah. Following the opening verses about the death of Aaron's two sons comes a portrayal of the role of the High Priest as he takes two he-goats—one for God, the other for Azazel—and carries out the elaborate ritual. The 10th day of the 7th month is designated as the occasion for atonement for priests and Israelites alike. Chapter 17, which is the beginning of the "Holiness Code", introduces the subject of incest and forbidden sexual unions that are inconsistent with holiness via a discussion of proper forms of worship.

being silent, and he focused on Avodat ha-Shem, and he merited great reward as did his grandson Pinhas. The survivors of the Holocaust teach us the same lesson. We must be grateful to our past teachers that we can learn from their actions. **Dr. Jeffrey C. Ratz, Brooklyn, NY**

דָּבָר אַחֵר **DAVAR AHER.** "AND WITH A MALE YOU SHALL NOT LIE (AS WITH) A LYING WITH WOMEN." [Lev. 18.22].

Nowhere in the discussion of Parashat Aharei Mot is there an acknowledgment that in our Torah, in our beloved Holy Book, is a verse that has caused so much pain. There is a discussion of the verse, but not about how these words have negatively affected on the lives of so many. "AND WITH A MALE YOU SHALL NOT LIE (AS WITH) A LYING WITH WOMEN." Rabbi Levy attributes these words to G-d when he says "Why should G-d have prohibited a

practice that flows from biological natures which God created?' Torah, with all the joy and light it brings into our lives, reflects the bias and prejudice of some of the people who wrote Torah. G-d could not have written words that would result in so much suffering for the gay community and their families—not my G-d. **Alan H. Rosenberg, Judaica teacher, Heschel Day School, Northridge, CA**

Moses, "NO ONE MAY SEE ME AND LIVE" [Exodus 33.20]. Aaron is to bring some animals with him which eventually will be offered up in smoke, enveloping him as God is enveloped in the cloud upon the ark cover. The smoke and the cloud permeate each other, protecting Aaron from the excessive nearness to God which was the downfall of Nadav and Avihu.

Perhaps it is this enveloping which explains the two things Aaron must take in with him: the animals, whose corporeality will be transformed into incorporeality through the fire on the altar, and the garments of natural vegetable fibers— בִּגְדֵי קֹדֶשׁ, big'dei kodesh garments reflecting God's holiness—which "COVER" Aaron's body along with the smoke. The Hebrew words for atonement (כַּפָּרָה/כִּפֻּרִים kapparah/kippurim) and the ark cover (כַּפּוֹרֶת kaporet) come from the Hebrew root [כפר] KFR. While there is much scholarly discussion as to whether [כפר] KFR really

means "COVER," all this emphasis on the garments and the smoke urge that "covering" is a major part of the atonement rite.

The body, after all, represents the corporeal part of us capable of sinning. God appearing in the cloud may represent the initial wind, or breath, which God breathed into the clay that had been Adam, breath which we later identify as our soul which is pure, sinless. The deaths of Nadav and Avihu were to remind Aaron of the inevitability of death— the demise of our corporeal parts. The smoke and linen garments "cover" his physical parts—protecting them, the white smoke and white linen symbolizing the purity, the eternality, of the soul. It is like the white garment, the *kittel*, we wear today on Yom Kippur. *After death,* the pure soul-breath still remains.

Some of the mysteries of sacrifice center around the root [קרב] KRV, "nearness." An offering in the Holy Place is intended to draw us near to God by turning a corporeal crea-

Aharei Mot

דָּבָר אַחֵר **DAVAR AHER.** "AND WITH A MALE YOU SHALL NOT LIE... [Lev. 18.22]. Alan H. Rosenberg of the Heschel School argues that "The Torah, with all the joy and light it brings into our lives, reflects the bias and prejudice of some of the people who wrote the Torah" in its ban on male homosexuality. By writing "G-d" instead of "God" (which has no basis in classical Jewish law, as English is not the language of the seven names whose

erasure is forbidden), the author sends a signal of piety while speaking impiously... By arguing that the Torah was written by authors rather than by God, Rosenberg also claims that he knows what is and what is not Divine intent in the Torah... In this age of political/theological correctness, those people who believe in the Author of the Torah regard those for whom instinct and passion overcomes them as instinctively challenged. I believe that

ture, as we are, into incorporeal smoke which "goes up" (the Hebrew word for burnt offering is עֹלָה Olah, meaning "going up")—entering the invisible realm of God. By placing our hands on the animal as Aaron did, we imply, "God, accept this creature as though it were I." If smoke represents the soul breath, it is as though in making offerings we were adding to the breath in the world, enriching the world with more of God's breath.

Perhaps the most controversial section of this parashah is its conclusion, Chapter 18, the traditional reading for Yom Kippur afternoon. The sexual prohibitions which comprise this chapter are introduced by a widely quoted verse [18.5]: "YOU SHALL KEEP MY STATUTES AND MY JUDGMENTS WHICH A PERSON SHALL DO IN ORDER TO LIVE BY THEM (חַי בָּהֶם hai bahem); I AM ADONAI." The purpose of the statutes which follow, regarding incest, adultery, homosexuality, and bestiality, seems from this context to be the preservation and enhancement of the life of the people, as well

as the preservation of the purity of the land [18.24ff]: "DO NOT BRING DEATH-RELATED, טֻמְאָה tumah [usually, and incorrectly, translated "IMPURITY"] THROUGH ANY OF THESE (ACTS)... FOR THROUGH ALL THESE THE NATIONS WERE MADE נִטְמְאוּ nitm'u, THE LAND BECAME וַתִּטְמָא vattitma...AND VOMITED OUT THEIR INHABITANTS." The prohibited sexual acts are each called תּוֹעֵבָה to-eyva, usually translated "ABOMINATION," but which in all contexts refers to pagan, polytheistic, orgiastic practices. The question has frequently been raised whether the Torah forbids these sexual crimes because they offended God or whether they offended God because they were part of the pagans' ritual practice.

But this passage raises another question as well. If these statutes are intended "IN ORDER THAT A PERSON MAY LIVE BY THEM," which a famous midrash says means 'and not die by them"—how are we especially to deal with the issue of homosexuality if we accept the growing scientific view that homosexuals do not choose their

sexual practice but find it determined by their biological or genetic makeup? Why should God have prohibited a practice that flows from biological natures which God created?

It is not only liberal Jews who find themselves facing conflicting mitzvot. The חַי בָּהֶם hai bahem verse introducing the laws on forbidden sexual practices is used in the tradition as a way of resolving some of those conflicts: if performing a certain mitzvah could cause one's death, one may violate the mitzvah, because the mitzvot are to enhance life, not end it. We might argue, then, that, particularly for those individuals whose biological nature has determined their homosexuality, the principle of חַי בָּהֶם hai bahem permits them to violate the mitzvah regarding homosexuality: to live means to love; to love, for some individuals, means to love a person of their own sex.

Why did God create the bodies of these individuals in such a way as to make this mitzvah so hard, perhaps impossible, to carry out? In The Way

---

Learn Torah With... should stick to its non-polemic format and explicate the Tradition rather than evaluate it. If we focus upon exegesis of p'shat rather than the isogesis of d'rash, we will strengthen our bonds to each other and to Torah rather than weakening them. **Alan J. Yuter, Touro College, Congregation Israel, Springfield, NJ**

דָּבָר אַחֵר **DAVAR AHER.** "AND WITH A MALE YOU SHALL NOT LIE... [LEV. 18.22] .

(A Response to Alan H. Rosenberg) Emanuel Levinas makes the good point, for those of us who want a leap into faith without denying evolution and the age of the universe—though better ethics follow a recent creation—that the Torah is no less divine for collective authorship than for being the word of G-d through Moses, and might, in fact, be the greater miracle for the divinely inspired revelation over time, across generations. Unless we see every word as written by the Creator,

we give up Adonai Ehad. Since Lev. 18.22 is as open to interpretation as any other compound sentence in the Torah, and open to interpretation in the time it is being read, which is the only path to new meaning, new revelation, there are ways of reading it to soften the harshest understanding, but as a general rule, it might be more courageous to say that it means exactly what we don't want it to mean. Better to defy the law, to stand in direct rebellion to G-d, in a heroic conversation with Him,

of God, Chaim David Luzzatto argues that each person's situation in life creates a unique challenge to serve God. Some people are born wealthy (there are laws against excessive wealth); others poor (some mitzvot require money to fulfill). Such people must discover the way to serve the God who has asked them to do mitzvot that their life situations seem to render impossible. The midrash says that God gives some people extra challenges in life (like Abraham, Sarah, and others) because God knows that, as the inner beauty of raw flax is brought out by beating it into linen, so there are people whose inner potential will be brought out through struggle. Perhaps this is why the High Priest was to wear linen garments on Yom Kippur.

Part of the struggle of those who are born homosexual, our text suggests, is to translate mere sexual acts into acts of love. Perhaps that is why homosexuality is described so crudely: "AND WITH A MALE YOU SHALL NOT LIE (AS WITH) A LYING WITH WOMEN [18.22]"—if such relationships are your destiny, relate with each other according to your uniqueness, with respect, and with love.

We may discern a similar message in the verses dealing with various kinds of incest. Forbidden sexual relationships are described as violent acts, uncovering that which since Eden was intended to be covered—one's nakedness (עֲרָיוֹת *ariyot*), basically one's genitals. This kind of sexual activity is introduced by a curious word, which we have seen elsewhere in this portion, and which may help to explain why this section was included. Verse 6 of Chapter 18 reads, "NO ONE MAY DRAW NEAR (תִּקְרְבוּ *tikravu*) TO UNCOVER THE NAKEDNESS OF THE FLESH OF ANYONE CLOSE TO THAT PERSON; I AM ADONAI." It was Nadav and Avihu's drawing near to God that initiated the expiatory rites of the High Priest on Yom Kippur; remember that Aaron was to be protected from drawing too near by being covered in linen garments and smoke. Perhaps his sons'

Aharei Mot

even at risk of our portions in the World To Come. Who knows but that such a commitment to Judaism in spite of the text might not mean that when we roll the Torah to that line next year, it won't be there? The Jewish laws that many of us don't follow don't stop being laws because we abandon them, but let's not pretend that in the disobedience there may not be a cost to our souls. For myself, the specific interpretation matters less than reasoning, method,

and rule, and I would pull my children from any day school where the teacher says, "This line is Divine, that line is human." That's not religion anymore, but the road to scholarship. Public school is cheaper. **Michael Tolkin, Los Angeles, CA.**

דָּבָר אַחֵר **DAVAR AHER. AND WITH A MALE YOU SHALL NOT LIE... [Lev. 18.22].** As a gay man, I appreciate the sentiments Mr. Rosenberg expresses about "a verse that has

וידבר יהוה אל משה אחרי מות בני אהרן

attempt to draw near to God was as heinous as our attempt to draw near sexually to someone related to us. Does sex itself have implications of an offering? As an offering enriches the universe, so does the sowing of seed in the act of making love—a new life may come into being as a result. One should draw near one's spouse for such an act of enrichment as reverently as one draws near to make an offering to God.

The sexual act, as Freud suggested, is the ultimate encounter of life and death: in the expulsion of seed, in the release of an egg, there is a momentary surrender of power, a momentary dying, even as we transcend death (our own mortality) by creating new life. With the world abounding in so many paths that lead to death, no wonder the God of mercy created so many acts and expiations to chase after death, *Aharei Mot*, with the powerful mitzvot that lead to life.•

---

caused so much pain." But his comment on Lev. 18.22 implies that he is able to distinguish between what "God could have written" and what actually is found in the Torah. It is a vastly inadequate response for those of us who believe that the acceptance of the Torah and the Covenant obligates us to deal with the text we have.

My view may be unconventional, but I do not find any proscription of homosexuality in the Torah. To read homosexuality into the passage quoted ("YOU SHALL NOT LIE WITH A MAN IN THE MANNER OF LYING WITH A WOMAN") is anachronistic: the very concept of homosexuality is a wholly recent one. The Torah must be read in its own language, and its language here clearly uses אִישׁ "*ish*" to talk about heterosexual men. The larger subject is the preservation of natural categories that is so important in this parashah: specifically, it forbids men who normally form relationships with women from having sex with men. It in no way considers or addresses a class of people who have a primary affectional and sexual attraction for people of the same sex.

Even the classic commentators see a loss of seed, and therefore a loss of potential life, as the major objection to this kind of sex. Of course, the same objection applies to masturbation or birth control. Yet contemporary opposition to homosexuality, allegedly founded on this *pasuk*, often is much more vehement than the disapproval of masturbation—because of individuals' prejudices, not because of Torah. People who cite this passage to support discrimination against gay people are forcing an extrinsic view upon the text. They have no more right to do that than Mr. Rosenberg does.

The *halakhah* of the future will, I believe, recognize homosexuals as a separate category created by God—a category whose boundaries are to be preserved in much the same way as with the categories about which the Torah is explicit. Meanwhile, our tradition has a great deal to say about how to treat one's neighbor, and how we deal with the marginal people in society. Any Jew who discriminates against gay people commits a serious *averah*. **Bob Goldfarb New York, NY** <rsgoldfarb@aol.com>

דָּבָר אַחֵר **DAVAR AHER**. "AND WITH A MALE YOU SHALL NOT LIE… [Lev. 18.22]. I've just read from the Torah, the holy scroll of the Jewish people. The Torah is composed of five books. It is read over the course of one Jewish year. The Torah is handwritten and flawless. It is the teachings of God revealed to the people at Sinai. When we interpret Torah we receive it as if we ourselves were at Sinai. My portion is found in Leviticus, Chapter 18, the laws of sexual offenses. This portion covers many aspects of sexual behavior. It begins with the people being told not to practice the ways of Egypt and Canaan. Egypt and Canaan had pagan rituals such as having temple prostitutes. God told the people that if they wanted to live long and be strong together they must not repeat the practices of where they had just been. I believe that my portion is an extremely important one because standards are important in dealing with sex. In modern society there are so many mixed messages about sexuality. In Judaism sex is thought of as such a wonderful and special gift but the beauty of a sexual relationship is lost when it is used in advertising for products or misusing the whole idea of sex for other reasons . Judaism is based on being a family, togetherness, and respecting other members of one's family. This Torah portion says do not practice incest and adultery, these were the

Larry Moldo

BETH EL SYNAGOGUE, OMAHA, NE

Aharei Mot

Based on the words "AFTER THE DEATH OF AARON'S SONS" in the first sentence I find that this parshah answers the question, "*After death—how do I go on?*" The work God prescribes for Aaron and his surviving sons is how to appropriately bring an atonement (כַּפָּרָה *kaparah*) for the people who are transgressors (חוֹטְאִים *hotim*). כְּפוֹרָה *Keporah* is related to כּוֹפֶר *kofer,* and per Brown, Driver and Briggs in their Lexicon, כְּפוֹרָה *keporah* and, כּוֹפֶר *kofer* can be defined as a way to hide something by covering it. In this case, a way to hide the sin (חֵטְא *het*) from being seen and punished and a way to keep the חֵטְא from dragging down the rest of the psyche.

What is the nature of this hidden חֵטְא *het*? Depression would most likely shape Aaron's days. Perhaps not clinical/pathological depression which requires treatment, but an ordinary depression which can affect any of us upon loss. Aaron was taught to מְכַפֵּר *mekhaper* his חֵטְא *het*, his household's חֵטְא *het*, and the people's חֵטְא *het*. Depression is a חֵטְא *het* because it keeps us from reconnecting. During our depressed state we are separated from others as well as ourselves. Like our bodies after a severe illness, our psyches need rest to process the new reality that grief brings. By symbolically sweeping our depression momentarily under the rug, the process of

ways of the tribes around you and shouldn't be your ways. The Torah says you don't have to be a part of what's going on around you, you can do what you know is right.

One interpretation of the passage referring to homosexuality: To understand this controversy I had to learn how to interpret Torah because there is deeper meaning than what is just written down. Tzvi Marx, an orthodox rabbi said "No matter how categorical scripture seems to be, though, one never assumes a subject is closed." Meaning nothing in the Torah is ever absolutely fixed. I spoke to different members of the Jewish Community about how they interpreted Torah and what they thought about the passage referring to homosexuality.

One person said he believed that the Torah and laws were written by people who reached so deep inside themselves that they touched a

כַּפָּרָה *kaparah* enables us to strengthen ourselves.

The parashah forbids private attempts at כַּפָּרָה *kaparah*. Everyone should try to be connected enough that they know where to go to find somebody who can help. Everyone should work to be a connected part of the community and the community needs to have central places and trained personnel to deal with these needs. If the community decides that some חֵטְא *het* is not worthy of recognition, then an individual feels cut off from the community.

The reconnections don't stop with your nearest and dearest. They extend to the land, which shows what we are becoming. When we can see trash along the highway and not feel discomfort at the disrespect, it is not much farther down the road of indifference before we can watch a stabbing or shooting and not feel anything.

The process of reconnection is almost complete when you can see what needs to be done to make your environment livable. The process is as complete as possible when you start doing something and follow through. What exists for the survivor after death of a dream, or a loved one? The struggle to reconnect with God and ourselves, which starts with the daily processes of life and living. May God grant comfort to us all.●

---

place where they met with God. This concept of Divinely inspired people writing the Torah came up in almost all of my discussions. As someone else put it, it is given to people by God because it comes from the part of us that is searching for an ethical way to live. But because the Torah came through imperfect human beings all the written words might not have been God's exact intent. Also the Torah cannot speak to all humans' experiences with God because women's voices are not yet included to the same degree as men's.

Several members of the community spoke of interpreting Torah through a historical perspective, remembering that the laws spoke directly to the ways of the tribal people wandering in the desert before becoming a nation. During that time, for the Jews to survive, reproduction was vital. Even the patriarchs had several wives. Homosexuality, at that time, could take away the energy from reproduction and that could account for the severe prohibition against it.

Another point that was frequently brought up was that you can be a good Jew without agreeing with all the historical interpretation of Torah. You can search deeply to find a new interpretation for today. But looking back on a different time period it is important not to criticize the standards of the people living then. Like us today, they were trying so hard to live life the right way.

In Torah today, a single word should never be changed, but while trying to make the Torah meaningful, we can look beyond the literal word so the Torah can speak to us. A level of reading Torah beyond the literal is to search for universal truth. In my portion this universal truth might be that it's very important who you get sexually involved with and you can't just go by your first impulse.

An even deeper level is to let the words sit long enough within you so you might actually experience the Divine meaning and get in touch with the right way for YOU to live. A community member I talked with had a lot of contact with gay men and said that through his work he has seen a lot of suffering and found that love is love and that all people go through the same things. For him the meaning of the "Do NOT LIE WITH A MALE AS ONE LIES WITH A WOMAN" passage might be saying, "Don't substitute the love of a man for the love of a woman," but that isn't what happens in homosexual relationships.

It was suggested to me that it takes generations to experience the whole Torah, that throughout one's life you should put your heart into different parts of the Torah and live that particular moment to its fullest rather than trying to live it all and never really get the wholeness of the experience. Parts go deep and you have to run them through your heart; you'll mature into different parts during different parts of your life. It is a blueprint for the long term survival of the Jewish people. Generations always emphasize or de-emphasize different parts. It is a lasting gift and teaching, almost too much for one lifetime. Who we are is part of God and God is inside all of us.

Now there is evidence that our sexuality is genetic and in the very core of

Rabbi Ellen Weinberg Dreyfus

ELLEN WEINBERG DREYFUS IS A RABBI AT CONGREGATION BETH SHALOM, PARK FOREST, IL.

Aharei Mot

The Torah portion for this week is called *Aharei Mot*—"after the death." The portion begins: "THE LORD SPOKE TO MOSES AFTER THE DEATH OF THE TWO SONS OF AARON WHO DIED WHEN THEY DREW TOO CLOSE TO THE PRESENCE OF THE LORD." This is a reference to the incident described in Leviticus, chapter 10, where we read about Nadav and Avihu, the sons of Aaron, who made an offering to God that was unacceptable in its form or content, and died as a result.

Mentioning their death again at this point may serve as a reminder to Aaron to be fastidious in his carrying out of his priestly duties, and to take care lest he make a similar fatal mistake.

Whenever I read the story in Leviticus 10, I am struck by one small phrase. Moses seems to attempt to explain their deaths by saying, "THIS IS WHAT THE LORD MEANT WHEN HE SAID, 'THOUGH THOSE NEAR TO ME I SHOW MYSELF HOLY, AND ASSERT MY AUTHORITY BEFORE ALL THE PEOPLE'." The next words are, "AND AARON WAS SILENT." Moses could have offered any explanation in the world, but it would not have given Aaron any words. He is in shock. His sons are dead, and he is silent. There are no words. Words cannot change the horrible reality that he must now face.

This week really feels like Aharei Mot. We all stand here, after the death... after the deaths of all those innocent

our being, not just a choice that someone makes. During one of my first meetings with Margaret, she told me about when she worked in a temple where many gays and lesbians came to pray. She told me of many times seeing people so sad and distraught because they knew the passage about homosexuals and couldn't understand why their holy book condemned them. They were created by God but were excluded from the example of what is good and holy. Some people today use this portion to condemn the actions of homosexuals. It is

painful to me to know that our holy book is interpreted to stigmatize people's loving relationships toward each other. In being used this way the beauty and wholeness of the Torah's light is dimmed. I wish everyone would try as hard as the people I talked to, to find meaning that brings people together rather than sets them apart. **Jenais Zarlin at her Bat Mitzvah, April 29, 1995.** *Jenais Zarlin lives in Comptche, CA. (pop. 300) and she is a member of Mendocino Coast Jewish Community. This Bat Mitzvah speech was submitted by Mina Cohen*

וידבר יהוה אל משה אחרי מות בני אהרן

children and women and men in Oklahoma City, after the deaths of those hundreds of thousands who died in Vietnam in an unpopular war that ended just twenty years ago this week. And after the death of six million Jews and millions of others at the hands of the Nazi murderers. This week we marked Yom Ha-Shoah, Holocaust Remembrance Day. We commemorated the day with solemn words and music. But like Aaron, we are stunned in silence. What can we say? We attempt to express our horror, our outrage, our deep sadness at such loss, such waste of lives, such unspeakable tragedy. And words fail us.

Since the bombing in Oklahoma, the airwaves have been full of news reports, analysis interviews, statistics and more reports and more analysis and more interviews, conjecture and theories, and politicians' blustering attempts to make things better by making speeches about them. And it is all words. And it only makes us more numb, and leaves us with nothing to say. How do we explain this to our children? How do we explain it to ourselves? The President approached the truth when he called it evil. But words are inadequate.

Since the war in Vietnam ended 20 years ago, the country has struggled to reconcile our feelings of guilt, of anger, of patriotism, of shame, of confusion. My generation came of age during Vietnam. Our classmates were killed there. Our friends faced the draft boards and prayed for a high lottery number when the student deferments ran out. Our music played on the radios over there while it played on the radios here. We danced to it, and they fought

and died to it. Such a jumble of feelings, of images, as the war came into our homes in living color on the evening news. In 1966, we had a bumper sticker that said, "Make love, not war." As if the words could make it so. Now, *Aharei Mot*, we go to the memorial in Washington, and stand before the black stone and read the names of lives snuffed out. Mr. MacNamara spills his guts and tells us now that he knew it was wrong then, but he sent those boys to kill and die anyway. For what purpose does he open these wounds? For his own therapy? Would that he had spoken when it could have made a difference, or taken Aaron's model, and remained silent.

Aharei Mot—after the deaths of six million Jews, after the deaths of one and a half million Jewish children—what can we say? Rabbi Yehiel Poupko has written a meditation for Yom ha-Shoah that captures the impossibility of speaking about the Holocaust, but the necessity of doing so anyway.

The moment one begins to speak of the Holocaust, a betrayal has been committed. If one begins, one must conclude. If one talks of Vilna, one must talk of Lublin. If one talks of Poland, one must talk of France. If one talks of a victim, one must talk of all victims. If one begins, one is doomed to failure. All must be told, and having not been told, a betrayal has been committed, a betrayal of all that is left out; of all those incidents, cities and persons that stand on the threshold of memory and verge of speech crying out, "Do not silence us. Tell our tale." This prayer, too, is one of penance for silencing the forgotten and unspoken voices that we

are doomed as humans to omit—an affirmation of our limitations.

Holy sisters and brothers of Moriah, forgive us for violating your dignity, sanctity and privacy; but all that we do seeing, hearing and thinking—we do only for the sake of the honor of your memories.

Were all the heavens parchment, all the oceans ink, every blade of grass, a quill,   and all the persons scribes, the Holocaust would still remain veiled in terrible mystery.

Aharei Mot—after death comes rebirth. After the pain comes healing. Perhaps that is why we read this passage in the spring, why we observe Yom Ha-Shoah in the spring, when the new leaves on the trees are that tender, beautiful light green, and the daffodils wave in the breeze. After death, life goes on. Babies are born, there is new life—hope rekindled. For after the silence, eventually we are able to speak, and eventually we are even able to sing. Aaron was silent after the deaths of his sons, but he continued, he served God, and was father to his other children.

Aharei Mot—after the death of so many, we still live. We live as a people—a community who cares, an America who will never be embroiled in another Vietnam, and a Jewish people alive and vibrant, here and in Israel. There is still room for our silence, but we can regain the power of speech, when we have something to say. **(Written for the *Chicago Jewish News*)** •

Aharei Mot—223

Kedoshim

Leviticus 19.1–20.27

Rabbi Elliot N. Dorff

RABBI ELLIOT DORFF IS PROVOST AND PROFESSOR OF PHILOSOPHY AT THE UNIVERSITY OF JUDAISM, LOS ANGLES

"**Y**OU SHALL BE HOLY, FOR I, THE LORD, YOUR GOD, AM HOLY"** [Leviticus 19.2]. This verse at the beginning of this section of the Torah is deservedly famous for a variety of reasons. It defines the proper relationship between us and God; it establishes the meaning and the standard for holiness; it describes the way that we should interact with each other in order to reflect holiness in our lives; and it designates our mission in life. Not bad for one verse!**

English is a Christian language: It was created by Christians, and even though it has come to be close to an international language, well over 90% of the people who speak it as their first tongue are still Christian. It should not be a surprise, then, that English terms, especially religious ones, will have Christian connotations. That is certainly true for words like messiah and salvation, but it is also true for words like religion, prayer and holiness. Even though I am a rabbi, and even though I continue to devote significant time to the study of Jewish sources, it still is the case to this day that whenever I hear or use the word "holy," I think first of the "holy ghost," and I picture heavenly entities flying around. The same does not occur when I use Hebrew equivalents of those words, for then Jewish connotations come to mind. Thus when I think of "*kadosh*," the Hebrew word for holy, I think of its

---

דָּבָר אַחֵר **DAVAR AHER. YOU SHALL BE HOLY, BECAUSE I THE ETERNAL, YOUR GOD, AM HOLY... [Lev. 19.2].** MISHNAH AVODAH ZARAH 1.1: ON THE THREE DAYS BEFORE THEIR CELEBRATIONS, ONE IS FORBIDDEN TO DO THE FOLLOWING WITH THE STAR WORSHIPERS/PAGANS: IT IS FORBIDDEN TO TRANSACT BUSINESS WITH THEM, TO LEND THINGS TO THEM, TO BORROW FROM THEM, TO ADVANCE OR RECEIVE ANY MONEY FROM THEM, TO REPAY OR COLLECT A DEBT. BUT, RABBI JUDAH SAYS, "WE CAN COLLECT DEBTS BECAUSE THAT NEVER MAKES THEM FEEL BETTER..." This week the Torah is doing the "*HOLY, HOLY, HOLY...*" thing. I am thinking paganism. Everyone is trotting out their sermons on free loans, stumbling blocks, fearing mom and dad, leaving the corners uncut, etc. Been there.... This week I am doing the pagan shuffle. I talked about a navel piercing with one of my students, Randi, 17, and the bottom line ques-

cognates—*kiddush* (the prayer over wine on Sabbaths and Festivals), *Kedushah* (the high point of the *Amidah*), *Kaddish* (the prayer used in many points of Jewish liturgy, perhaps most famously when we sanctify God despite the death of someone near and dear), *Kiddushin* (the Hebrew term for betrothal)— and I understand that it means set apart, special, distinctive and unique. It denotes that which is not like the rest, which is set apart for special purpose.

Our verse in Leviticus defines exactly what that special purpose is supposed to be. We are to be different from other people in that we are to model ourselves after God. We are to be holy because our God is holy. This is not the calculus of reward and punishment; this is instead the realm of aspiration, of reaching out, of loving God so much that we want to be like the Eternal.

How does one do that? Chapter 19 of Leviticus is careful not to let that be vague and ephemeral. It defines a series of actions that we are either to take or eschew in order to live in a holy way. Some of these are ritual in nature, as, for example, keeping the Sabbath and avoiding Canaanite cultic practices. Some speak to our relationship with the environment: We are to give trees time to grow before using their fruit, and we are not to mix diverse kinds in breeding animals or seeds. Others affect the world of business: theft and fraud are to be shunned, workers are to be paid promptly, and honest weights and measures insured. Other parts of being holy are social: We are to care for the poor, establish an impartial judicial system, and treat aliens like fellow Israelites. Still other components of holiness are interpersonal: We are to respect our parents and rise before the aged; refrain from insulting the deaf, putting obstacles

Synopsis: "YOU SHALL BE HOLY, FOR I, THE ETERNAL YOUR GOD AM HOLY" (Lev. 19:2). These 7 words form the basis for many well-known laws in Chapter 19. Probably the most famous verse, "...LOVE YOUR NEIGHBOR AS YOURSELF; I AM THE ETERNAL" stands boldly in mid-chapter. The second part of the parashah places laws of the family in the context of the religious community, concluding with a challenge to the people of Israel to distinguish themselves from other nations.

tion was "Is a tattoo an act of pagan worship?" Got an e-mail response to the Christmas tree question. It asked, when it comes down to honoring father and step-mom by accepting a livingroom Christmas tree, what should a good Jewish kid do? Two Orthodox friends both quoted the Rambam, that because of thee gods, Catholics are pagans. (I can hear Carol asking, "Is that *right*?" in my ear! Yes, if you read with the Rambam against most other Halakhic authorities.) But the question remains, "What do we consider pagan **today**?" This week, Shmuely Boteach, the Chabad guy at Oxford, wrote that Jews need to boycott Wagner. Pagan! Picasso. Obviously pagan? So here is what I want to know: Is *Metallica* "star worship"? Is Beverly Hills 90210 *Avodah Zarah*? And, "What is rap, anyway?" As Jews, we almost, sort of, kind of, know where we stand maybe. It is even more difficult to know where we do not stand. Without knowing what is pagan, can we know what is *Kadosh*? I fully confess that I no longer know the boundary. I fully admit I am going to work on it. **Joel Lurie Grishaver** <gris@torahaura.com>

Kedoshim

before the blind, or bearing a grudge; we may not stand idly by while our neighbor suffers; and, in general, we must love our neighbor as ourselves. The verse calling us to imitate God's holiness, in other words, is a headline for the entire chapter, and the chapter, in turn, delineates in very concrete terms exactly how we are to achieve holiness. That aim is not left as a pious platitude or an empty hope; holiness is to pervade our lives.

Since God is the standard of holiness, though, all human efforts to be holy will, of necessity, be only partial fulfillment of what holiness can be. This is a crucial lesson to learn: No person has the right to consider him/herself "holier than thou." We must all strive to be like God, but because each of us is human, none of us will totally succeed. That should instill some humility in each of us and should make us hesitant to judge others harshly. Courts there must be, and some of us will achieve a greater approximation of divinity in our lives than will others; the absoluteness of God's holiness and the consequent relativity of ours should not be seen as a reason to undermine standards of behavior or judgments made according to those standards. At the same time, though, we must recognize that only God embodies absolute holiness, that human beings can, at best, only reach a relative degree of that divine quality, and that we, therefore, should think twice or more before judging others.

Still, even with this caution, the summons for holiness remains. The Torah issues a clarion call to us to strive to be like God, and it would have us do so in ways that are concrete and meaningful for us, for our neighbors, for society as a whole, and for the world in which we live. God's absolute holiness is not supposed to be a damper on our spirits, a notice that no matter what we do we cannot be like God. Quite the contrary, the imperative form of the verb in our verse tells us loud and clear that, for Judaism, we can be like God, we can treat each other and the environment in godly ways, we can create a society that reflects God's holiness—and we are duty-bound to try.

This is the ultimate mission that the Torah puts before us, the purpose of our life that can give it meaning: in everything we think and do, we are to strive to be holy like God. Only then can we be, both individually and collectively, what God calls us to be here and at the very foot of Sinai—namely, "A KINGDOM OF PRIESTS AND A HOLY PEOPLE" [Exodus 19.6]. Only then can we be worthy of God's covenant with us. Only then can we fulfill the distinct purpose that God has created us to achieve, the purpose delineated toward the end of this section of the Torah: "YOU SHALL BE HOLY TO ME, FOR I THE LORD AM HOLY, AND I HAVE SET YOU APART FROM OTHER PEOPLES TO BE MINE" [Leviticus 20.26]. What a privilege; what an obligation.•

The Power of Kedushah

Rabbi Samuel G. Broude

SAMUEL G. BROUDE IS RABBI
EMERITUS, TEMPLE SINAI, OAKLAND.
INTERIM RABBI, BETH EL, BERKELEY.

Kedoshim

***Kedushah* as Raw Power:** Our tradition has always seen *kedushah* as a powerful instrumentality. In its earliest manifestation, *kedushah* is experienced as dangerous, even life-threatening. Uzziah seeks to steady the *Aron ha-Kodesh* as the Ark, on its way back from the Philistines, begins to tip. He is "rewarded" for his effort by being struck dead on the spot, in keeping with his earlier understanding of *kedushah* as raw power making no moral distinctions. (At least in *Raiders of the Lost Ark*, it's the bad guys who are punished by the Ark's powerful laser rays while the good guys are spared.)

The Power to Sanctify: In our Torah portion, *kedushah* is held out as a desirable status, a quality of life attainable through our actions and interactions, a way of participating in God's *kedushah*, of fulfilling the goal of becoming a *goy kadosh*—in Heschel's words, "YOU SHALL BE HUMANLY HOLY UNTO ME." The Rabbis went even further. Not only is *ha-Kadosh barukh Hu* approachable in His/Her *kedushah*; not only does God want us to participate in *kedushah*, but in fact is ready to share this gift with us, even to giving us the power to sanctify. The Etz Yosef on *Kedoshim* in *VaYikra Rabbah* tells us that because the imperative הָיוּ *heyu* ("BE") is not used, but rather the future tense (as imperative) תִּהְיוּ *tihyu* ("YOU WILL BE"), we may conclude that God is announcing that He/She is bestowing the gift of *kedushah* upon Israel. Thus, it becomes our task to sanctify situations, people, things, to make them *kadosh* by our attitude toward them. Nothing starts out as *kadosh*. It is only by virtue of our treatment that others become *kadosh*. The power of *kedushah* is in our hands, It is we who sanctify—or fail to do so.

Redemptive-Messianic Power: Hasidism, says Buber, understood this very well. "Everything is waiting to be hallowed by us…The profane is only a designation for the not-yet-sanctified…Any natural act, is hallowed, leads to God…Hasidism teaches that rejoicing in the world, if we hallow it with our whole being, leads to rejoicing in God." [Maurice Friedman, *The Life of Dialogue*, 139f] Thus Hasidism teaches "the hallowing of the everyday" and *kedushah*—the power to sanctify—becomes the power to redeem, and all action for the sake of God is Messianic action. Not only can relationships between individuals be sanctified, but those between peoples and nations as well.

Reb Yisroel of Rizhyn told that all of the disciples of the Great Maggid handed down his sayings except Reb Zussye, who never managed to hear his master's teachings to the end. Whenever the Maggid would begin to expound, "and God said," Zussye would be seized with such ecstasy that he would begin shouting and hitting his head against the wall so that he had to be led from the room and never heard all of the Maggid's words. "But this I can tell you," said R. Yisroel: "if one speaks in the spirit of truth and hears in the spirit of truth, one word is enough, for with one word can the world be uplifted and with one word can the world be redeemed!" [Buber, Tales, *Early Masters*, p. 236, "The Word"].

God's *Kedushah*: Our Torah portion calls on us to become *k'doshim* by being *m'kadshim*—sanctifiers of life in our everyday encounters. Especially in this post-*Shoah* world, in the face of the very antithesis of *kedushah*, are we bidden to use our power-to-sanctify to restore a sense of *kedushah* to human interaction—perhaps even to God!—"to lift up the name of God and set it over an hour of great care" [Buber, *Eclipse of God*, p. 9].•

Kedoshim

ast week, in *Parashat Kedoshim,* we learned what it is to embody the qualities of God's holiness. As God is holy, so should we be. "LOVE YOUR NEIGHBOR AS YOURSELF; I AM THE LORD" [Lev. 19.18] is a teaching with which most of us are familiar. But we are also taught: "YOU SHALL NOT INSULT THE DEAF, OR PUT A STUMBLING BLOCK BEFORE THE BLIND. YOU SHALL FEAR YOUR GOD: I AM THE LORD" [Lev.19.14]. God's holiness is expressed in this world through our acts of emulation. Clearly we should care, as does God, about those whose bodies do not represent physical perfection.

So it is all the more startling to read the beginning of this week's *parashah.* Leviticus 21.16–23: "THE LORD SPOKE FURTHER TO MOSES: SPEAK TO AARON AND SAY: "NO MAN OF YOUR OFFSPRING THROUGHOUT THE AGES WHO HAS A DEFECT SHALL BE QUALIFIED TO OFFER THE FOOD OF HIS GOD; NO ONE AT ALL WHO HAS A DEFECT SHALL BE QUALIFIED; NO MAN WHO IS BLIND, OR LAME, OR HAS A LIMB TOO SHORT OR TOO LONG; NO MAN WHO HAS A BROKEN LEG OR A BROKEN ARM; OR WHO IS A HUNCHBACK OR A DWARF, OR WHO HAS A GROWTH IN HIS EYE, OR WHO HAS A BOIL SCAR, OR SCURVY, OR CRUSHED TESTES. NO MAN AMONG THE OFFSPRING OF AARON THE PRIEST WHO HAS A DEFECT SHALL BE QUALIFIED TO OFFER THE FOOD OF HIS GOD. HE MAY EAT OF THE FOOD OF HIS GOD, OF THE MOST HOLY AS WELL AS THE HOLY; BUT HE SHALL NOT ENTER BEHIND THE CURTAIN OR COME NEAR THE ALTAR, FOR HE HAS A DEFECT. HE SHALL NOT PROFANE THESE PLACES SACRED TO ME, FOR I THE LORD HAVE SANCTIFIED THEM."

What are we to make of these words? They set the criteria which assure the purity of the sacred Temple rituals, particularly the rites of the sacrifices. Physical perfection is the ultimate value

Emor

Leviticus 21.1–24.23

Rabbi Rachel Cowan

RABBI RACHEL COWAN IS THE DIRECTOR OF JEWISH LIFE PROGRAMS AT THE NATHAN CUMMINGS FOUNDATION IN NEW YORK.

דָּבָר אַחֵר **DAVAR AHER.** "GOD SPOKE TO MOSES AND SAID, SPEAK TO THE PRIESTS, THE DESCENDANTS OF AARON, AND SPEAK THESE WORDS TO THEM…."[Exodus 21.1]. A story is told about Rabbi Israel Salanter, the head of the Lithuanian Yeshivot in the nineteenth century. In one town, the community depended on an elderly woman to bake *matzot* each year. As she got on in years, she became less efficient than she had been in the past. Nonetheless, Rabbi Salanter warned the rabbis of the com-

munity to treat her with respect. "The woman is a poor widow," he said. "This is all she has to give her a sense of worth. Don't be impatient with her, and be careful how you speak to her."

Rabbi Salanter's words put into practice a great lesson of Jewish law. The Mishnah tells us that each day we should wake up and say, "THE WORLD WAS CREATED FOR MY SAKE." This advice teaches the importance of self-respect. The corollary to this concept, however, is that we

represented here—the quality which is most pleasing to, and appeasing of, God. Physical flaws, broken perfection, profane the places sacred to the Lord—both in the object of sacrifice as well as in the priest who offers it.

Invoking the modern consciousness, we may distance ourselves from the harshness of these words. We may see in them a reflection of an ancient dread of death, a people's projection of their fear of their own imperfections onto God, and their reliance on flawless sacrificial rituals to please and appease God. But, as usual, themes or practices which at first seem primitive in the Torah speak powerfully of the modern human condition. This text, in fact, invites self-examination, for it reflects attitudes about human flaws and about leadership that many of us hold today. We, too, value physical perfection, and withdraw from those whose bodies are broken in some way. Many of us are disconcerted by physically or mentally disabled people, and prefer to avoid them. Often our

institutions serve to protect us from them, rather than to embrace them.

By sins of commission and omission, we make many Jews feel as if we find them defective when they come into our midst. Many of our Jewish community spaces are designed with barriers that make it difficult or impossible for physically disabled Jews to enter our buildings or to function comfortable in them. (A wonderful exception to his pattern is Manhattan's West Side Mikvah which installed a special mechanical seat that immerses disabled people in the waters.) Six years ago, we renovated Ansche Chesed, the Upper West Side synagogue to which I belong, and made it one of the few wheelchair accessible synagogues in Manhattan. But even within our building, only this year are we making the bathrooms wheelchair accessible. Ramps, for all that they are necessary, do not by themselves meet the challenge of inclusivity. We convey our attitudes in the ways we do or do not reach out to offer ser-

Emor

should treat others with respect, regardless of their station in life, for they are important, too. To this end, the rabbis derived a moral point from the beginning verse of the Torah portion, *Emor*: "GOD SPOKE TO MOSES AND SAID, SPEAK TO THE PRIESTS, THE DESCENDANTS OF AARON, AND SPEAK THESE WORDS TO THEM…." The rabbis taught that the repetition of the word "SPEAK" indicates God's concern

for the manner of speaking. That is, when Moses was addressing the entire group of priests, he should show as much respect for the lower priests as he would for the High Priest. They may have been the "little people" but they deserved as much respect as the "big people" who stood at the top.

The rabbis wanted all who are in positions of authority to remember this

vices. How many of us belong to congregations that have large print prayerbooks, signing for the deaf, or Braille texts? How many of us have tried to understand what it is like to experience the world as a physically-handicapped person? What if we were to try an experiment and confine ourselves to wheelchairs for two days, and understand what barriers serve to keep us out?

As disturbing as the idea that a physically defective man will profane the places sacred to God is the notion that spiritual leadership depends on wholeness. For a long time, we have wanted our leaders to be as male, as handsome, as physically perfect as possible. We wanted ideals, not role models. We exalted the high priest, not the blemished Moses, who at first declined God's call to leadership because of his speech defect. But in recent years our thinking about spiritual leadership has changed. In these post-Holocaust, post-modern times, many of us have relinquished systems

which assert all-embracing truths. We see a world that has been shattered, along with many of our previous assumptions. Those of us whose families suffered in the Holocaust, or whose loved ones have succumbed to illness or died in tragedy, seek leaders who have learned to find meaning in the domain of the broken, who find pieces and fit them together, who understand that the divine can be sensed in many places, and grasped in the wake of devastating experiences. They can help us find the hope and optimism that has sustained our people for centuries, that gives meaning to the moment, and purpose for tomorrow.

We know that Jews need communities of caring and healing as well as of learning and celebrating. To build those communities, we need teachers and leaders whose faith, whose wisdom has been forged in the understanding of brokenness. The spiritual figure whom the *parashah* rejects as the blemished priest we may embrace as the wounded healer.●

Synopsis: Addressed to the priests (kohanim) rather than to the whole people of Israel, the first two chapters of our parashah contain laws about purity, marriage, physical perfection, and the conditions for eating from the sacred donations. The Sabbath and Festivals are next detailed primarily from the perspective of the priests and the sacrifices that were to be offered. Finally, a miscellaneous collection of laws, including the lighting of the menorah, the rows of bread, blasphemy and other serious offenses concludes our parashah.

important rule: Maintain respect for those who are below you. Though you are the *"machers"*—the big shots—and they are the *"shleppers"*—the ordinary people—you should treat them with as much respect as you would want to receive. Nineteen hundred years ago, there were two rabbis who had dramatically different attitudes on this subject. One was Rabban Gamliel, the head of the academy at Yavneh shortly after

the Temple was destroyed. He was an aristocrat, and he ran the academy with an autocratic hand. He often would excuse himself from observing his own enactments, claiming he was exempt because of his high and refined status. Though none of his colleagues would demean his scholarship, they all chafed at his lordly manners.

The other rabbi was known as "Shmuel Hakatan," Samuel the Small.

He didn't get this name because of his size. He may even have been taller than most men. His name came from the fact that he recognized the honor that came just from being a member of the academy. He never forgot to be one of the little people, those whom he represented and on whose behalf he debated and enacted laws. The interplay between these two men is not recorded in the Talmud, but it

Rabbi J.B. Sacks-Rosen

RABBI J.B. SACKS-ROSEN IS RABBI OF CONGREATION B'NAI JACOB IN JERSEY CITY, NJ.

Emor

Towards the end of our reading, we encounter the child of an Israelite woman and an Egyptian father who blasphemes God publicly. Moses has the man remanded to custody while he consults God on how to proceed. The Torah immediately gives us God's answer: The blasphemer should be removed forthwith from the midst of the community; all who actually heard the offensive words hold the guilty party while the community stones him. God further informs that the same response should be meted out to any further instance of blasphemy.

At the very point that the blasphemer is incarcerated, Rashi hastily and with considerable effort, insists that the offender was placed in the very same prison as the one who violated the Shabbat publicly by gathering wood, during whose incarceration Moses also needed to consult God on how to proceed [Numbers 15.32-36].

Both the God-blasphemer and the Shabbat-desecrater committed grave sins, and both were caught. Why does Rashi inform us that these incidents in two separate books happened at about the same time? That is, what is Rashi's point in insisting that they were maintained in discrete cells?

Apparently the fate of the wood-gatherer was certain—death, even if the manner was in doubt. After all, anyone who violates Shabbat, the Torah informs us their punishment: "ITS PROFANER SHALL BE PUT TO DEATH" [Exodus 31.14]. The Shabbat violator was on death row merely awaiting the decision of which

must have been fantastic to observe. We do know that Gamliel came to Shmuel to ask him to write a new prayer for the liturgy, so even Gamliel had to learn to treat the little people properly in order to get a job properly done.

It is fair to say that Shmuel Hakatan's sensitivity came from the fact that he understood that, at one time or another, each of us stands in a position of inferiority to others. When we do, we don't want to be reminded

that we are little people. We want others to respect us as individuals, and for our ability to contribute something of importance. At the end of his life, Rabban Gamliel learned this lesson, too. Despite his wealth, he decreed that he be buried in a simple linen shroud and a plain casket. He did this so the rich would not try to be ostentatious in death, and so the poor would not abandon their dead relatives out of embarrassment. In so doing, he established a

method was to be employed. The fate of the God-blasphemer, on the other hand, was not certain at all. No clear punishment for such a violation had ever been stipulated.

Now, if the two guilty parties had been placed in the same cell, the God-blasphemer would naturally have assumed that his penalty was also death. And this, undoubtedly, would have created tremendous anguish within him. To avoid unnecessary suffering, therefore, even of one who reviles God shamelessly in public, our ancestors, in Rashi's retelling, decided to keep the two guilty parties separated.

What a beautiful tradition that Rashi disseminates, for our ancestors' behavior is so worthy of emulation: We, too, must be sensitive to the greatest degree of everyone's feelings and needs. True, the blasphemer is not the most savory of people. Sure, this God-reviler is not one with whom

we should want to be cozy. In his manner, bearing and self-presentation he surely bears an imperfection of the type about which my colleague, Rabbi Rachel Cowan, speaks so movingly in the adjacent *D'rash*. How much more remarkable, then, that our ancestors insisted on upholding the blasphemer's dignity and avoided causing him any undue suffering.

We often do not give people entry into our lives, even briefly, because we perceive them as distant from our world or without much to offer us because of their language, their verbal presentation: It in some way does not reflect an upwardly mobile, sophisticated, politically correct, post-feminist smoothness and savvy. But no matter how the person's presentation strikes us—grotesque, nerdesque, whatever—the Torah through Rashi insists on our not hurting another's feelings unnecessarily. And the responsibility for the assur-

ance that such person's feelings will not be lowered nor their self-worth demeaned resides squarely with us, who may be the only ones to challenge it. Indeed, we are to be responsive even to the base and the corrupt who come our way, even to a God-blasphemer.

"LOVE YOUR NEIGHBOR AS YOURSELF" may sound as simple as it is lofty. But as Rashi's teaching challenges, and as Rabbi Cowan demonstrates in her juxtaposition of that commandment with this week's portion, done so lovingly, the directive is a difficult challenge for all of us. To mean anything at all, loving our neighbors must begin with upholding the dignity of even the least obviously worthy neighbor, by empathizing with the plight of those we may dislike for a very good reason, by loving the unlovable with endless love. Our own holiness and lovability are at stake.●

---

principle of having simple funerals, which we still follow today. I think he also showed that he had finally become sensitive to the needs and feelings of the little people.

Let us hope that we will each learn this lesson now, and not just at the end of our lives. We should treat the little people we encounter with the respect they deserve. If we do, we will help build a world where all people will feel important, precisely because they are.
Rabbi Jim Michaels <rabi@temple. microserve.com>

דָּבָר אַחֵר **DAVAR AḤER.** EACH OF YOU SHALL NOT CONTAMINATE HIMSELF WITH DEAD PEOPLE, EXCEPT… [Ex. 21.1]. One debate keeps coming up in my life a lot lately. I first really understood it when Beth Huppin said to me at a Rosh ha-Shanah meal, "I don't feel commanded." Her implication, unstated, was, "I do feel connected." My friend, Carol Starin, at whose house the conversation was taking place, echoed the sentiment. Then over the year, as I have listened carefully, many of the high school students to whom I teach Mishnah at Los Angeles Hebrew High Sschool (mainly, but not exclusively,

the girls), and many of the adults to whom I teach Talmud (mainly, but not exclusively, the women) have balked at the sense of "COMMANDED" spiritual activity. They regularly argue: "I want to do my prayers, rituals, blessings out of a feeling, not out of a rule."

The real question is: "Can rules evoke feelings (in traditional-speak: Can *keva* create *kavanah*)? Or, does it work the other way around? Once we know the answer is "Yes," we have to face the fact that up 'til now, the Jewish tradition has rooted itself in the "rules-to-spirit" process, rather than the "rules-out-of-spirit" orientation.

This week's Torah portion starts with a very specific version of this challenge. The opening rule goes against our basic feelings. *Kohanim* are ordered not to go to funerals (except for their closest relatives) in order to keep themselves "PURE." To our sensibilities, this rule feels wrong. We can think through a good rationalization for it, but it feels wrong. It commands a sense of holiness-via-boundary, rather than growing holiness through the spirit. The Torah seems to sense this, and makes it a doubly strong command. Hear the text: "AND GOD SPOKE TO MOSES: SAY TO THE KOHANIM, SONS OF AARON AND SAY TO THEM: 'EACH OF YOU SHALL NOT CONTAMINATE HIMSELF WITH DEAD PEOPLE, EXCEPT…'"

The Rabbis, of course, ask: "Why two sayings?" Then they collect answers. Rashi, glossing *Yevamot 114a*, says: "This is to make sure that the *Kohanim* understood that they had to model and teach holiness as well as obey its rules." Moshe Feinstein expands the ruling, saying: "Adults have to regulate their behavior in order to set a good example for children." I, however, think the answer that speaks to me comes from Ibn Ezra: He asks: "Why does *Emor* follow *Kedoshim*?" and then answers: "We move from national standards of *kedushah* to personal ones. There, the whole people are given holiness standards, now the *kohein* (in each of us) is asked to embody and not just follow those standards."

So here is the Torah you want to ask your *kinder* to teach you this week: "How is Judaism a religion of connection? Commandment? What are holiness standards (and what do they do)? What things can contaminate your sense of holiness? How can you

Emor

embody and model holiness?" When you've got that down, we're really on the way to being a Nation of *Kohanim*. We win when connection and commandment become the same thing. **Joel Lurie Grishaver** <gris@torahaura.com>

דָּבָר אַחֵר **DAVAR AHER.** "FROM THE DAY ON WHICH YOU BRING THE SHEAF OF WAVE OFFERING—THE DAY AFTER THE SABBATH—YOU SHALL COUNT OFF SEVEN WEEKS. THEY MUST BE COMPLETE: YOU MUST COUNT UNTIL THE DAY AFTER THE SEVENTH WEEK—FIFTY DAYS; THEN YOU SHALL BRING AN OFFERING OF NEW GRAIN TO THE LORD." [Lev. 23.15-16]: It is finally spring! Every midwestern winter, with its cold winds and gray days, seems like it will never end. And every spring surprises us with its freshness. The tulips and daffodils push their way up and open into riots of color that instantly banish gray from our memories. We venture out of our interior decoration to savor the spaciousness and freedom we feel without our overcoats. We hear the songs of birds and notice that wonderful, tender green color of the almost-open leaves. It is spring, and everything around us is growing. And it is time for us to grow, too.

This is the season in which we reenact the historical and spiritual growth of our ancestors in their journey from Egypt to Sinai. This is the time of the *omer*, the counting of days and weeks between Pesah and Shavuot. In the portion assigned to this week, *Emor*, the Israelites are instructed to bring the first sheaf, the first *omer*, of the early harvest to the priest who then waves the sheaf before the Lord.

ויאמר יהוה אל משה אמר אל הכהנים בני אהר

"FROM THE DAY ON WHICH YOU BRING THE SHEAF OF WAVE OFFERING—THE DAY AFTER THE SABBATH—YOU SHALL COUNT OFF SEVEN WEEKS. THEY MUST BE COMPLETE: YOU MUST COUNT UNTIL THE DAY AFTER THE SEVENTH WEEK—FIFTY DAYS; THEN YOU SHALL BRING AN OFFERING OF NEW GRAIN TO THE LORD." [Lev. 23.15-16] This counting of the *omer* continues to this day, for the most part by Jews who are not directly involved in the growing of grain in the land of Israel. The priests no longer wave sheaves as part of a Temple ceremony. But the *omer* still serves as the connection between the two major milestones of Pesah and Shavuot in the ancestral journey that we continue to travel.

Many centuries ago the Rabbis transformed the festivals from purely agricultural and sacrificial rites to commemorations of events in our people's history, events with eternal significance. The focal point of Passover shifted from the Pesah sacrifice to the retelling of the Exodus, the reliving of our liberation from slavery. The rabbis called it זְמַן מַתָּן חֵרוּתֵנוּ *z'man mattan Heruteinu*—the season of our freedom. Shavuot, the spring harvest festival with the offering of first fruits, was designated as the date of the giving of the Torah, מַתָּן תּוֹרָתֵנוּ זְמַן *z'man mattan Torateinu*—the season of revelation.

Each year we retrace this journey from liberation to revelation. In the Haggadah we are instructed: "In every generation, each of us must feel as if we, ourselves, went out from Egypt." We are also told that all the generations of Israel, including future generations, were present at Mt. Sinai for the giving of the law. So our responsibility

is to recall those experiences, hidden in the recesses of our collective memory. We've taken this trip before—last year, and the year before that, and on back into antiquity. Every spring, when the world is growing again.

The *omer* period is the journey, the maturing of a reluctant mob of former slaves into a people willing to accept God's law. As Arthur Waskow wrote in *Seasons of Our Joy*, "The (*omer*) period… became the time of ascent from political liberation to spiritual revelation—the period in which a newly free people moved toward a new devotion, a new service and servitude to the God of freedom." (p. 167)

The people grow from liberation to obligation. They are free enough to realize that they can make a commitment. The process is one we recognize, because it parallels our own individual maturation into adulthood. If a child's growing is a series of lessons in letting go, in becoming independent, then an adult's growing is a series of lessons in holding on, in learning to make commitments of enduring value. The latter cannot occur without the former. If we do not let go of our parents and their protection, we cannot become whole, separate individuals. Once we are persons in our own right, we can link ourselves with others in a mature way. We are then capable of the interdependence of marriage and the awesome responsibility of parenthood.

Before the Israelites were ready to stand at Sinai, they had to grow up. They tested authority, like rebellious teenagers, but eventually they were mature enough to enter into a

covenantal relationship—a marriage, if you will—with God. In the Exodus, the relationship was one-sided. God ruptured history to liberate the people. At Sinai, however, the relationship matured. No longer did Israel simply rely upon God to save them in the nick of time. Now God also relied upon Israel—to live up to our side of the covenant, to complete the work of creation, to share the responsibility of perfecting an imperfect world.

The period of the *omer* is for us an opportunity to re-enact that journey of long ago. Rabbi Shimon ha-Tzaddik said that the world depends on Torah, worship, and deeds of kindness. Let this be a time for us to renew our commitment to Jewish learning, to invite the potential for holiness into our lives, to help bind the wounds of those in pain and in need. Let these be the paving stones of the road from Pesah to Shavuot. Soon we will be at the foot of the mountain, with all the generations of our people, ready to bind ourselves to the living God, ready to have God depend upon us as we depend upon God. It is spring and we are growing toward God and Torah. May it always be so. *ANONYMOUS*

דְּבָר אַחֵר **DAVAR AHER.** NO DESCENDANT OF AARON THE KOHEIN WHO HAS A BLEMISH SHALL COME NEAR TO OFFER THE ETERNAL'S OFFERINGS BY FIRE; SINCE HE HAS A BLEMISH, HE SHALL NOT COME NEAR TO OFFER THE BREAD OF GOD… [Lev 21.21]. Rabbi Cowan—thank you for making *Emor* more palatable, but there is still something missing. I find it most difficult to accept the Torah's law against permitting anyone with a "blemish" from serving God. Whether a person has a "blemish" or not, he or she is still a

Emor

human being. According to the previous Torah portion we are to be like God, "HOLY BECAUSE GOD IS HOLY." The comment is even made that being holy is reaching perfection and that is impossible for human beings to attain—we can only strive for that perfection. Even those with "blemishes" strive for that perfection.

I found the following story in *Sefer Ha-Aggadah* about Resh Lakish who was humiliated by a man, R. Kanana, who he thought was laughing at him. Because of Resh Lakesh's humiliation the man's "soul left him." Resh Lakish, the next day, commented to the other sages, "Have you noticed how this man carried on?" The sages responded, "But such is his natural appearance!" It seems that R. Kanana had a cleft—a physical defect following an accident, which left him looking like he was laughing at you all the time. Resh Lakesh was so shaken by his actions that the went to he cave where the body lay and sought God's mercy and brought the man back to life and said to him, "Had I known that such is the master's appearance, I would not have been humiliated." Resh Lakesh then asked him to come back to the academy and lead them in study. R. Kanana agreed as long as Resh Lakesh would beseech God's mercy should he again be humiliated because of his sensitivity. They studied together for many years after this episode. Well, we no longer 98have sacrifices and if we are all striving for perfection, to be God-like, I don't think that leaves anyone out, including those who might

be physically impaired. I think we have much we can learn from them. Their strength can give us hope and their heart can be an inspiration. **Shirley Barish**, Houston, TX

דָּבָר אַחֵר **DAVAR AHER.** NO DESCENDANT OF AARON THE KOHEIN WHO HAS A BLEMISH SHALL COME NEAR... [Lev. 21.21]. The interpretation by Rabbi Cowan of the injunction not to place a stumbling block before the blind strikes me as forced and unduly narrow. She sees it as the basis for caring about people with physical imperfections, but the text tells us not to actively exploit the weaknesses of others, which is rather different. Traditional commentators (*Sifra, Rashi, Rambam*) see the larger ethical principle as the point here; to reduce it to a teaching about the literally handicapped is misleading. Rabbi Cowan goes on to tell us that "in recent years our thinking has changed." In the era after the *Shoah*, some "find meaning in the domain of the broken." Of course, the Psalmist reminded us that God is close to the broken-hearted [34.19], so this notion is hardly a modern one. But it is a point unrelated to the *parashah*. Even metaphorically, a broken spirit is unlike a physical handicap: the *parashah* speaks of physiological shortcomings which are rarely reversible (scars; being a hunchback, lame, or a dwarf; having crushed testes; blindness), but the heart's wounds can potentially be healed. Rabbi Cowan's teaching is a valuable lesson, but it is hard to find it in the text before us. **Bob Goldfarb, New York** <RSGoldfarb@aol.com>

Be-Har

Leviticus 25.1–26.2

Dr. Deborah Weissman

DR. DEBORAH WEISSMAN, FOR-
MERLY WITH THE HEBREW
UNIVERSITY, IS NOW THE DIRECTOR
OF MACHON KEREM, A TEACHER-
TRAINING INSTITUTE FOR "HUMANIS-
TIC JEWISH EDUCATION" IN
JERUSALEM. HER INTERESTS INCLUDE
WOMEN'S STUDIES AND ISRAEL-
DESPORA RELATIONS.

Parashat *Be-Har* embodies the most central theological and social concepts of traditional Judaism, within the institution of the שְׁמִיטָּה *Shmittah*, or Sabbatical year [Lev. 25.2-7, 18-23]. The Rabbis, in *Pirkei Avot*, say that, "Exile came into the world on account of idolaters, incest, bloodshed, and [neglecting] the laws of *Shmittah*." Thus, neglect of *Shmittah* is compared with the three cardinal sins in the rabbinic taxonomy.

In our day, these words seem empty.

How many Jews throughout the world even know when a Sabbatical year (e.g. 1993-1994) arrives? The laws apply only to agricultural produce grown in the Land of Israel. Many religious Jews follow the dispensation of the Chief Rabbinate, based on an earlier decision made by Rav Kook[1]. The reality is that for most Jews in the world today, the Sabbatical year is an outmoded and irrelevant idea.

A leading religious Zionist educator, Pinchas Rosenblitt, in an article published during one of the previous *Shmittah* years (1979-1980) entitled, "The Sabbatical Year—A Social and Spiritual Challenge," wrote: "Even if we cannot observe these commandments fully, given our circumstances, it is just not possible for them to be devoid of all meaning for us... the commandment of *Shmittah* is a serious test of the religiosity of a modern person, who must confront modern life through the application of the eternal halakhah (Jewish law) to changing life conditions."[2]

דָּבָר אַחֵר **DAVAR AHER. AND YOU SHALL HALLOW THE FIFTIETH YEAR, AND PROCLAIM LIBERTY THROUGHOUT THE LAND TO ALL ITS INHABITANTS; IT SHALL BE A JUBILEE FOR YOU, WHEN EACH OF YOU SHALL RETURN TO HIS PROPERTY AND EACH OF YOU SHALL RETURN TO HIS FAMILY. [Lev 25.10].** While helping Leann Rousso prepare her bat mitzvah reading from Lev. 25.8-10 and Jeremiah 32.6-11 in this season between the *herut* of Pesah and *Yom ha-Atzma'ut* and the *harut* of Shavuot (and having just heard a rousing *Yom ha-Atzma'ut* lecture by my *Sifu*, Prof. H. I. Sober), I've been meditating upon the necessity of possessing land in order to preserve our liberty and prevent us from falling back into permanent slavery and subjugation. Holding on to the deed to some small ancestral plot does more for us than ensuring we have a place to practice subsistence farming. Property requirements for voting were officially abolished quite a long time ago, yet it still remains true in many ways that a

It would appear to me that those of us who try to apply halakhah to, for example, changes in the status and role of Jewish women in modern society, might also consider some of the questions raised by the *Shmittah* laws. To finding meaning within the laws of *Shmittah*, I would like to propose a strategy of exploring some of the reasons for these laws which have been suggested by both classical and modern commentators.

The classical term for the reasons for *mitzvot* would be טַעֲמֵי הַמִּצְוֹת *ta'amei ha-mitzvot,* literally, "the tastes of the commandments." In other words, what "tastes" should we be left with from doing them? What is their spiritual and social relevance from a phenomenological perspective? I would divide the main reasons that have been offered for *Shmittah* into five groups. For each, I will mention some of the traditional approaches,

and suggest some modern applications.

The first, and perhaps most widespread, explanation deals with questions of social justice and eliminating the gaps between rich and poor. Maimonides, in *The Guide to the Perplexed*, wrote, "Of all the mitzvot which we have enumerated for you in the laws of the *Shmittah* and the Jubilee, some of them are inspired by compassion for mankind, and they are designed to promote the well-being of all mankind, as the Torah states: 'AND THE NEEDY OF YOUR PEOPLE SHALL EAT, AND WHAT THEY LEAVE THE BEAST OF THE FIELD SHALL EAT.' Furthermore, the earth will increase its yield and improve its fertility through the *Shmittah*. Some are inspired by compassion for the slaves and the poor, that is to say the release of money and the release of slaves. Others are designed to redress the inequalities of income and the economy [*The Guide for the Perplexed*, Vol. 3, chap. 39].[3]

Be-Har

person or a people that does not have a modicum of land (or at least something upon which to base a home equity loan) is not really free.

In verse 11, Jeremiah calls his deed and its terms "mitzvot," symbolizing the Torah, which also serves as our permanent deed (as long as we keep it) to the Land, guaranteeing our autonomy in the lands of our dispersion and ensuring that we as a people would not be enslaved forever.

But such freedom is only possible as long as we hold that deed, and it will only be realized when we actually possess that land and can live safely behind secure borders that we ourselves defend. **Hazan Ira Rohde, Cong. Shearith Israel, NYC** <75610.1722@compuserve.com>

Here is the full text of Leann Rousso's bat mitzvah speech, Parashat Behar, May 20, 1995. It is the result of discussions

In a time when most of the "social-ist" republics have collapsed, it may seem anachronistic to pursue this line of thought. Still, one would hope that the alternative to commu-nism—"the God that failed"—would not be some kind of heartless capi-talist system, in which values of compassion and social justice are ignored. Can we, as religious peo-ple, develop another way? Can we conceive of a year in which some (if not all) debts are cancelled, interest rates are lowered, special attention is devoted to programs for the fur-thering of socio-economic justice? Surely, the *Shmittah* year could at least be devoted to studying and thinking about these issues.

A second approach sees the institu-tion of *Shmittah* as teaching humankind "THAT THE EARTH DOES NOT BELONG TO THEM BUT IT BELONGS TO THE LORD."[4]

Abarbanel develops this idea in his commentary to the *Ethics of the Fathers*: "Just as the Jewish people give expression to the idea of Divine Creation in their resting on the Sabbath, so does the Chosen Land bear witness to that same principle by lying fallow in the seventh year. That is why the reason for the pre-cept of *Shmittah* is given in the Torah as, 'A SOLEMN SABBATH SHALL IT BE TO THE LAND, A SABBATH TO THE LORD'.[5]

Such a consciousness of "creatureli-ness" or "createdness" should, ide-ally, lead to an ecological aware-ness of our responsibilities vis-a-vis what Christians have termed "the integrity of creation."[6]

The *Shmittah* year should become an opportunity to reflect on the con-nections between Judaism and ecology and to engage in practical projects that express those connec-tions. For example, the mitzvah of בַּל תַּשְׁחִית *Bal Tashḥit*—not wasting any part of God's creation—may have as yet unexplored implications for modern people.

Synopsis: The principles and practices that are at the basis of our unique rela-tionship to land constitute the bulk of our parashah. Beginning with laws concern-ing the Sabbatical year and the Jubilee year, chapter 25 concludes with laws of indebtedness and two brief verses about idols and the Sabbath.

---

between Leann and *Ḥazan* Ira Rohde at *Congregation Shearith Israel, NYC:*

דָּבָר אַחֵר **DAVAR AḤER. AND YOU SHALL HALLOW THE FIFTIETH YEAR, AND PROCLAIM LIBERTY THROUGHOUT THE LAND TO ALL ITS INHABITANTS; IT SHALL BE A JUBILEE FOR YOU... [Lev. 25.10].** For my bat mitzvah, I chanted two sections from today's Bible reading. The first reading is about the Jubilee year, which is the fiftieth year. Every seven years, if you owed someone money and you were sold into slavery for it, your debt is canceled, and all Jews are set free. This happens during the forty-ninth year, as well. But if your family had owned land and you were forced to sell it to pay your debts, you still wouldn't get it back. During the fiftieth year, however, the *Yovel* or Jubilee, all family land went back to the original families and their chil-dren. The Torah calls this "PROCLAIMING LIBERTY THROUGHOUT THE LAND, FOR ALL ITS INHABITANTS." In America, they put this quote from the Torah on the Liberty Bell in Philadelphia, and here at this synagogue we have little models of the Liberty Bell which we used on today's Torah. "LIBERTY" means "FREE-DOM." The question is: What does "FREEDOM" for the land mean? How does giving every family its land back help to make us free?

Having mentioned the Sabbath, we have come to the third group of ta'amei ha-mitzvot. Many commentators have indicated that the Shmittah year is called "THE SABBATH OF THE LAND," "A SABBATH OF THE LORD." It would be appropriate, then, to devote the Shmittah year to an intensification of our efforts to promote Sabbath observance among the Jewish people and to combat its desecration. But, by this, we should also mean its desecration by those who purport to observe it, but actually violate its sanctity by throwing stones at others and the like. Perhaps one of the important ways to promote the observance of the Shabbat is by intensifying our efforts at הַכְנָסַת אוֹרְחִים Hakhnasat Orhim—hospitality—on the Sabbath, welcoming into our homes others who might not have a Shabbat experience without our invitations.

The weekly Shabbat is a time for spiritual re-creation and nourishment, for study. The Sabbatical year would provide a significant unit of time for such endeavors. The Torah enjoins the precept of הַקְהֵל Hak-hel, at the end of the Shmittah year, when the entire people—men, women, and children—assembles to listen to a public reading of the Torah "THAT THEY MAY LEARN" [Deut. 31.12]. Ibn Ezra adds to this "all year long," indicating that the public reading is but the culmination of a year-long process of study. Kalischer adds: "Another reason for the Shmittah: they would not be preoccupied with the tilling of the soil to provide their material wants. One year only he would be free. The liberation from the yoke of labour would give him the opportunity of studying Torah and wisdom."

Jewish communities throughout the world could devote the Shmittah year to an intensification of educational programs, perhaps specifically in the area of adult education. And

Be-Har

Cancelling all debts helps to keep us from being slaves. Being free is important, because we can then be what we want to be. We just finished the holiday of Passover, which is about freeing us from being slaves in Egypt, and the Torah wanted to keep us from being slaves again. Freeing the land also keeps us from being slaves because having your own land is part of being free. A slave doesn't own land. They're owned by someone else, so everything they have is owned by someone else (except the small personal things their masters let them keep). During the fiftieth year people are really completely free because their land is not owned by anyone else. Also, you fall into debt by owing money. In those days, most people were farmers. They made their money by growing crops on their land. They normally fed themsleves or paid their debts with the crops they grew. Sometimes their land wouldn't grow enough for a long time, or they needed a lot of money for something, so they borrowed

not only in that particular year, but in general, they should develop the concept of the sabbatical. All Jewish public servants—rabbis, educators, JCC staff, community workers, etc.—should be given a year of study and rejuvenation at regular intervals. Perhaps even people who work in other fields, outside the Jewish community, could be enabled to emulate their example.

Ideally, such sabbaticals would take place in the most exciting and dynamic venue for Jewish study and Jewish living—the State of Israel. This point leads us to the fifth category of ta'amei ha-mitzvot: the laws of Shmittah emphasize the sanctity of the Land of Israel and its centrality in Jewish spiritual life. R. Itzhak Abarbanel indicated, "The Holy One Blessed be He ordained that just as the whole nation recalls His act of creation by resting on the Seventh Day, so the Chosen Land gives evidence about itself through its release in the Seventh year."[8]

Since several of the laws of Shmittah (and certainly, of the Jubilee year) are incumbent only when most of the Jewish people lives in the land of Israel, it would be appropriate to devote the Shmittah year to greater efforts to encourage aliyah, and also to deepen the connections between Israel and Jews throughout the world.

Thus, the Shmittah laws should properly be seen as spiritual resources to be cherished, rather than economic burdens to be circumvented. The Shmittah year should become an opportunity for spiritual enrichment, for deepening and strengthening the ties among the Jewish people, its land and culture.●

Notes:

[1] Given the precarious economic condition of the Yishuv in his day, Rav Kook allowed for the sale of the land to a non-Jew, so that the Jewish farmers in Palestine could continue to work the land. The halakhic status of this dispensation is similar to the sale of hametz to a non-Jew during Pesah. To this day, the religious kibbutz movement* relies upon his heter, although with increasingly limited applications, while the kibbutzim associated with Poalei Agudat Yisrael have developed other ways of dealing with the agricultural restrictions, including hydroponics.

*Hakibbutz ha-Dati—affiliated with the N.R.P.

[2] The article called Shnat Ha-Shmittah—Etgar Hevrati v'Ruhani appeared in the journal Deut, No. 48, 5740, pp. 161-165. The translation is mine.

[3] For this translation, and many other sources in the present article, I am indebted to Aviezer Ravitsky (compiler) and Mordell Klein (translator), the Shmittah Year: Collection of Sources and Articles, Jerusalem: World Zionist Organization, 1972. This particular source is on p. 34.

[4] Ibid., p. 43.

[5] Kalischer, quoted in ibid, p. 37 (emphasis in the original).

[6] Ibid., p. 44.

[7] In March, 1990, I was priviledged to be a Jewish observer at a convocation of the World Council of Churces, held in Seoul, Korea, the theme of which was "Justice, Peace and the Integrity of Creation."

[8] Op. cit., p. 45.

[9] Ibid., p. 35

---

money. As time went on, they couldn't pay it back. So they would have to sell all the things they owned to the one they borrowed the money from—their jewelry, their furniture, and finally their house and their land. Sometimes they would go to work in the fields or the house of the one who lent them the money, to try to work off their debt. But if you had no land, once it was sold or taken away, you could easily get trapped into even worse problems. If you had no land, you couldn't feed yourself. You'd end up owing rent to other

people, and you'd end up depending upon other people to give you food for your family. You could get trapped into a vicious circle of poverty. Finally, you would be forced to sell the only thing you had left—yourself—to be a slave to the person to whom you owed the money. And even though you would get freed every seven years, it would be hard not to fall back into slavery again during the next six years, as long as you had no land. But if you got your land back, you'd be able to start living on your own again. In this way,

having your own land helped keep you free.

Having land also helps keep a whole nation or a people free, too. If they farm the land or build factories on the land, it keeps the nation from going into debt and becoming dependent upon other nations to give them money. There are other ways that a nation's having its own land helps keep it free. If a nation has its own land, it can defend itself from attack. If a nation has no land and is wandering around, it mostly has to depend on other nations to defend it or suffer the

Rabbi Elias J. Lieberman

ELIAS J. LIEBERMAN, FALMOUTH IS
THE RABBI AT JEWISH
CONGREGATION, EAST FALMOUTH,
MA

Be-Har

In 1979, I headed off to Jerusalem to begin my first year of rabbinical studies. I lived in a lovely neighborhood not far from the Supersol, the American-style supermarket where we did much of our food shopping. In most respects it was a typical supermarket—freezer cases of meat and poultry, aisle upon aisle of coffee, jam, crackers and cereals; and a produce section full of the best Israel had to offer.

But in 1979, there was something extraordinary about the fruits and vegetables to be found there, for some of the produce was sealed in plastic bags to which were attached tags which said, in effect, "The contents of this bag have not been produced on land owned by Jews."

This was my first exposure to the reality of the *Shmittah* year, the sabbatical year in which the land of Israel lies fallow…or at least those portions of the land owned and cultivated by Torah-observant Jews. Growing up, as I did, in the diaspora, the concept of a sabbatical year had been merely that—an idea expressed in this week's parashah. Living (and eating) in Israel, however, the biblical concept took on a new meaning in the form of a plastic bag of fruit with a warning label.

Undergirding the concept of both the Sabbatical and Jubilee years is the unsettling notion that what we think is true is really illusory. We do not, in fact, "own" the land on which we live, despite the deeds,

consequences. If no one came to their defense, other nations might come and hurt and kill them, or capture them and make them slaves. If a person has her own land, her own house, her own room, no one else can come in unless she wants them to. She can protect and defend herself from people she doesn't want coming in and taking her stuff. If it's someone else's house, you can't because you don't own it. Having your own space or land is important if a person or a people wants to be independent.

In the Jeremiah story, God tells Jeremiah to buy land. You might have said that was a dumb thing to do. A war was on, and the Jews were losing badly, and everyone knew that if they lost, the Jews would be captured and taken back to Babylonia to be slaves. I don't think most people would have con-

plot plans and surveyors' documents we might amass in the course of our lives. Torah would have us understand that we are merely "sojourners" on land which belongs to God. The legal fictions we call property laws, which every society has created to keep peace between neighbors, all violate the radical premise on which both the *Shmittah* and *Yovel* years exist, namely the assertion that "THE EARTH IS ADONAI'S IN ALL ITS FULLNESS" [Ps. 24].

In their book, *Sparks Beneath the Surface*, Rabbis Lawrence Kushner and Kerry Olitzky make the intriguing point that the Hebrew language itself reinforces the notion that all material possessions—land, money, cars, computers—are but "on loan" to us for the time we "possess" them. Thus, in

Hebrew, we say יֵשׁ לִי "yesh li" ("there is to me"—for a limited time while it is in my possession) rather than "I have" or "I own." Only God "has"! [*Sparks…*,p. 157].

Historically, Judaism had tended to give the ascetic tradition short shrift. We are not encouraged to throw off our worldly belongings to seek God's presence by becoming mendicants or desert-dwelling contemplatives. Judaism is generally comfortable with acquisitiveness and the amassing of "wealth" and "property." But this Torah portion arises each year to remind us of the flip side of the coin: in God's scheme for this material universe we inhabit, amassing has its limitations. We are not what we own, for, in fact, we do not "own" anything. We better define ourselves

by what we accomplish, with what we "own," by how effectively we use the resources that we acquire and with which we are blessed to do God's work in the world.

The Reform siddur, *Gates of Prayer*, reminds us, "There are days when we seek things for ourselves and measure failure by what we do not gain. On the Sabbath we seek not to acquire but to share." As models for living, *Shmittah* and *Yovel* may seem too archaic and remote to apply to our lives in the late twentieth century . But as this prayer fragment suggests, they, like Shabbat, are powerful indicators of what God demands of all of us—greater awareness of the ever-present disparity between those who "have" and those who have not. •

---

sidered buying a house in the middle of Tel Aviv during the last war, when it kept getting attacked by missiles. In the middle of the war, they wouldn't have considered it a wise investment. But God told Jeremiah to buy the land anyway and make sure he gets the deed to it, because he promised Jeremiah that they would only be enslaved for seventy years. After that, they could return and get their land back, if they had proof it was theirs. Of course, six hundred years after they did return, the Jewish people was captured and sold into slavery again, this time for almost two thousand years. But they knew that as long as they kept the mitzvot, the commandments of the Torah, with them as proof that the land belonged to them, they would eventually get

their land back. Jeremiah calls the "terms" of his deed to the land "mitzvot" on purpose, as a symbol for the Torah, which the Jews would keep with them throughout their wanderings as proof that the Land of Israel belonged to them. They knew that just as God fulfilled his promise to Jeremiah, so He would once more. And so He did recently with the State of Israel.

Having a State of Israel makes Jews freer now than during all those years they didn't have their own land. That land helps them to have a freer, more independent, better off, and more secure life. I am glad I live during this time. I am grateful to my parents and family for having brought me up in such a free country. I am grateful to

my parents for having given me my own "space" to grow in and for respecting my independence, even in a Manhattan apartment. I realize that more independence means more responsibility. That is why I am here today, becoming bat mitzvah, a "Daughter of the Commandments"—to show that I take my duties and obligations to God, to my parents, and to other people seriously. Because I know that keeping my responsibilities, my mitzvot, now, will be the deed, the proof, the promise, that I will be worthy of greater freedom and independence as I grow into adulthood. **Leann Rousso, Congregation Shearith Israel, NYC**

תשמרו ועשיתם אתם

Be-Hukkotai

Leviticus 26.3–27.34

Professor David Kraemer

DAVID KRAEMER IS ASSOCIATE PROFESSOR OF TALMUD AND RABBINICS AT THE JEWISH THEOLOGICAL SEMINARY, AND A SENIOR PROGRAM ASSOCIATE AT CLAL. HE IS THE AUTHOR OF *THE MIND OF THE TALMUD: AN INTELLECTUAL HISTORY OF THE BAVLI*, AND OF THE RECENTLY PUBLISHED *RESPONSES TO SUFFERING IN CLASSICAL RABBINIC LITERATURE* (BOTH OXFORD UNIVERSITY PRESS).

The latter part of *Parashat Be-Hukkotai*, the very last section of the book of Leviticus, articulates the laws of חֵרֶם *herem*—variously translated as "that which is cut off, set outside, proscribed, excommunicated, doomed to destruction, or (accounting for the present context) dedicated." Whatever the best translation, modern commentaries have observed that the term חֵרֶם *herem* ordinarily has a negative connotation; it is the term which describes the remains of idolatrous cities vanquished by the Israelites when they conquered the land of Canaan; in later periods, a person expelled from the community for sinful or antisocial acts is spoken of as "being put in *herem*." Undeniably a negative word. If a person familiar with Hebrew was asked to find a functional equivalent for *herem*, there is no doubt that טוּמְאָה "*tum'ah*" (ritual impurity) would be a likely choice. *Tum'ah*, like *herem*, is to be avoided. *Tum'ah*, like *herem*, has negative consequences for one who comes in contact with it. If this equivalency is only partially correct, then the negative characterization of *herem* referred to above would appear unimpeachable.

For this reason, verse 28 of the last chapter of Leviticus has always been the source of some puzzle-

דָּבָר אַחֵר DAVAR AHER. IF YOU WALK IN THE PATH OF MY LAWS AND GUARD MY MITZVOT... [LEV. 26.1]. In reflecting on the portion which Dina and I studied together in preparation for this day, I had two primary thoughts. The first is in reference to the conditional blessings which are discussed at the beginning of the reading. We read אִם בְּחֻקֹּתַי תֵּלֵכוּ וְאֶת-מִצְוֹתַי תִּשְׁמְרוּ *Im behukkotai teileikhu v'et mitzvotai tishmeru*, "IF YOU WALK IN THE PATH OF MY LAWS AND GUARD MY MITZVOT... וְנָתַתִּי גִשְׁמֵיכֶם בְּעִתָּם *v'natati gishmeikhem b'itam*, THEN I WILL BRING THE RAINS IN THEIR SEASON." And as a parent, I look at this text and see it as a prayer for days such as this: if we do what is right, if we love our children and give them the nurturing and the preparation and the teaching, then, in the time appropriate for each of them, they will grow and mature and develop as they should. It's not

אם בחקתי תלכו ואת מצוו

ment. The verse reads as follows: "EVERY *HEREM* WHICH A PERSON MAKES חֵרֶם *HEREM* TO THE LORD FROM ANYTHING THAT HE HAS, WHETHER FROM A MAN OR A BEAST OR FROM A FIELD OF HIS POSSESSION, IT SHOULD NOT BE SOLD OR REDEEMED; EVERY חֵרֶם *HEREM* IS THE HOLIEST OF HOLIES TO THE LORD" (the translation, overly literal by intent, is my own). The question is, how can something that is apparently so negative be described as the "holiest of holies" or, to reverse the question, if something is indeed the "HOLIEST OF HOLIES," then how can it be negative? The present statement so contradicts the commonly understood meaning of *herem* that it has simply been dismissed as anomalous. It is exceptional—so the same commentators claim—and therefore need not be accounted for when defining *herem* in general.

But the dismissal of this verse is unnecessary and unjustified. Indeed, I would argue that this verse, above all others, actually provides the key to understanding the term *herem*. Though this "*herem*" has no obvious parallel in biblical literature, it does have parallels elsewhere in the Semitic world, and these parallels allow us to gain a deeper and more nuanced understanding of the conceptual foundation of *herem* than any of the Biblical equivalents.

I first realized the key to the present apparent anomaly when a student living in Brooklyn, which has a large Muslim population, asked me the meaning of "*halal* meat"—the Islamic equivalent of kosher meat. At the time I had never heard the term *halal* (we have no local butcher shops with such a sign on the window), but it immediately occurred to me that this Arabic term was the same as that used by the Rabbis—they described their appropriately prepared meat as "*hullin*," a slightly different form of the identi-

Synopsis: "If you follow My laws and observe My mitzvot and do them, then I will ..." Thus begins our final chapters in Leviticus with God's blessings if we obey —and what is to happen if we don't. Chapter 27 concludes with a discussion of how the children of Israel are to pay for the upkeep of the sanctuary.

---

a promise, but it is a prayer; all parents pray that what we give to our children will ultimately bear fruit in its time...The second thought on today's portion.

The sidrah begins with this verse:

אִם בְּחֻקֹּתַי תֵּלֵכוּ וְאֶת-מִצְוֹתַי תִּשְׁמְרוּ וַעֲשִׂיתֶם אֹתָם

Im behukkotai teileikhu v'et mitzvotai tishmeru, va'asitem otam. "IF YOU WALK IN THE PATH OF MY LAWS AND GUARD MY MITZVOT, AND IF YOU WILL DO THEM." When you think about it, the last clause is totally unnecessary. We would logically assume that "IF YOU WALK IN THE PATH OF GOD'S LAWS AND GUARD THE MITZVOT," then of course you are in fact DOING them! So what function does this clause serve? In the *Midrash Rabbah*, Rabbi Hanina bar Papa suggests an answer. [He looked at the word אֹתָם *otam*, meaning "them," and noticed that in the way it is written, it has the same letters as another Hebrew word. And he said: Don't read it as וַעֲשִׂיתֶם אֹתָם *va'asitem otam*, read it as וַעֲשִׂיתֶם אַתֶּם *va'asitem atem*. אַתֶּם *Atem* means "you," and אַתֶּם וַעֲשִׂיתֶם *va'asitem atem* would mean, "and you shall make yourselves." And Rabbi Hanina bar Papa interpreted this to mean: "IF YOU OBSERVE THE TORAH, I THE LORD CONSIDER YOU AS IF YOU HAD MADE YOURSELVES."

The Midrash doesn't explain what this means, but the 16th century book

cal Semitic root. The root is the same as that of the word _hol_, meaning "profane" or "non-holy" (not unholy); for both Muslims and Jews, food that is available for human consumption is food that has been properly prepared for "profane," that is, common use.

I knew that, for the Rabbis, the opposite of "חֻלִּין _hullin_" was "קָדָשִׁים _kodashim_"—holy meat which was used for sacrifice and therefore unfit for common consumption. The equivalent of "kodashim" in the Islamic system, I discovered, is termed "_aram_" meat (that is, meat which belongs to God and is therefore unfit for common consumption). "_Alal_" is "_ullin,_" "_aram_" is "_kodashim._" The Arabic designation for what is still holy— set apart, still, as property of God— is none other than our Hebrew _herem_. Clearly, we have here pre- cisely the same conceptual equa- tion suggested in the verse from Leviticus quoted above. _Herem/aram_ and holy are evidently

synonyms of a sort. The question is, in what does their similarity lie?

The answer, I think, has already been suggested. That which is _kadosh_ and that which is _herem_ are both set aside for the Divine. In the case of the holy, humans have access under certain limited condi- tions, according to specified proce- dures. In the case of _herem_, though, humans have no access— ever. _Herem_ is like holy, only more so. It belongs to God absolutely. It is so holy—the "holiest of the holy"—that, unlike other holy things, humans never have access to it under any condition whatso- ever.

Were we wrong, then, in our thought that _herem_ and _tum'ah_ are somehow parallel or conceptually related? I think not. In this case, the key to understanding is found in the Mishnah, tractate _Nedarim_ [4.3]. Responding to the question of his colleagues, "What is the differ- ence between a pure and an impure animal?" R. Eliezer

Be-Hukkotai

Shnei Luhot ha-Brit (The Two Tablets of the Covenant) explains it. _Shnei Luhot ha-Brit_ says: It is through this doing, through the doing of the mitzvot, that you are continually fix- ing yourself, repairing whatever is lacking in yourself. Living by a higher standard is a way to push each of us to reshape our personalities. He says it is through the doing of the mitzvot, אָז הָיִיתֶם עֹשִׂים וּמְתַקְּנִים עַצְמְכֶם _az hayitem osim umetaknim_

atzmekhem, "YOU MAKE AND REPAIR YOURSELVES…." **Rabbi Danny Horwitz, Kansas City**, _in honor of his daughter's Bat Mitzvah._

דָּבָר אַחֵר **DAVAR AHER. IF YOU REJECT MY LAWS AND SPURN MY RULES, SO THAT YOU DO NOT OBSERVE ALL MY COMMANDMENTS AND YOU BREAK MY COVENANT, I IN TURN WILL DO THIS TO YOU: I WILL WREAK MISERY UPON YOU— CONSUMPTION AND FEVER, WHICH CAUSE**

responds: "The pure, its soul belongs to heaven and its body is his [=the owner's], whereas the impure, its soul and its body belong to heaven [!]." The reason an animal is impure (*tamei*, another form of *tum'ah*) is because it belongs in its entirety to God! You may partake of a pure animal because its body, at least, belongs to you. You may not partake of an impure animal because it does not belong to you. To consume it would be stealing from heaven. Heaven has reserved the right of ownership; you must therefore suffice with the pure animal.

Conceptually, the place of the impure here is identical with the holy elsewhere. According to the Talmud's explanation, "the earth is the Lord's" in its entirety until we recite the appropriate blessings (*berakhot*). To partake of the earth's bounty without reciting the blessing is, the Talmud claims, equivalent to stealing from *hekdesh*, stealing from that which is holy (because it belongs to God). The position occupied by the impure in R.

Eliezer's teaching is here occupied by the holy. Both are to be avoided—to be approached only after taking the appropriate steps—because both belong to God.

If we appreciate that the impure belongs to God (and is therefore unavailable for human consumption or use), we will understand why the dead human body is, according to the Torah, the most powerful source of such impurity. The reason for this impurity, I would now contend, is that the dead person belongs to God—so much to God that he/she is impure in the extreme. Now on the way to the next world, the dead should not be approached by the living (again, with carefully prepared and limited exceptions). The dead is impure and she/he is holy. How could it be otherwise?

This same conception will explain the impurity of a woman as a consequence of childbirth. A woman who gives birth is a partner with God. Through her womb, the life of the new child, which originates in the

Divine realm, breaks through into this, the mundane world. Childbirth is a holy partnership, and holy partnership is to be approached only with care. The residue of this partnership, this enhanced proximity to the Divine, is impurity.

But, you may readily object, aren't impurity and holiness diametrically opposed to one another? Indeed, it would appear so. If someone or something is ritually impure, s/he or it may not approach/be brought into the holy precincts (the Temple). Someone who enters the Temple when impure has committed a sin and is required to bring the appropriate sacrifice. Impurity and holiness are opposites, not synonyms—so it would appear.

But I would propose the following alternative understanding, according to which holiness and impurity are opposites in only the most limited sense. Holiness and impurity both describe approach to God, though on parallel and therefore irreconcilable planes. Humans have permission to

---

YOUR EYES TO PINE AND THE BODY TO LANGUISH; YOU SHALL SOW YOUR SEED TO NO PURPOSE, FOR YOUR ENEMIES SHALL EAT IT [Lev. 26.14]. The *tokhekhah* or "terrible punishment" of this Torah portion can give any person cause to ask what he or she has done wrong to cause illness or problems to befall them. This theme of why bad things happen to good people, and why bad people achieve success has been a recurring theme in our weekly

Scarsdale Synagogue Saturday Morning *Minyan* and Study Session.

I attempt to be an observant and practicing Jew, study Torah weekly, attempt to do as many mitzvot as possible while carrying out my roles of son, husband, father and businessman. I attempt to keep the commandments and rules of Judaism; but I do not keep a kosher home, or follow every rule in the Torah. For example, I drive to Shabbat services. I have

asked myself over and over again as the weeks roll by and I run to doctor's appointments, or lie in bed resting: "Am I doing something wrong to cause my illness?" Why would God punish me by being ill for so long, when I try so hard to study His teachings, follow His commandments, and live by His rules, while keeping His covenant?

I do not have an answer, but I have reached some personal insights that

avail themselves of only one of those approaches—and that only with restrictions. We may approach God through the holy, but the greater the holiness, the more restricted our approach. On the other side, the impure represents a breaking-through to God which humans have no permission to access. We will contact impurity, but we must go no further. God controls passage to this world (birth) and God controls passage to the next (death). This is God's territory (and thus impure), not ours. Similarly, God grants us permission to enjoy parts of this earth's bounty; other parts are eternally God's and we, therefore, must avoid them or use them only in the most limited ways (for they are impure). Impure and holy stand as parallel approaches to the divine. We are directed to one of these approaches and God claims the other.

I am reminded of an experience of my childhood. The child of a Jewishly identified but non-observant home, I found myself for the summer at Camp Ramah. Never having kept kosher before, I felt my diet very much restricted—and I protested. "What right does this religion have to restrict my right to eat what I want?" I asked. My junior counselor—I regret that I have forgotten his name—answered by challenging me: "What makes you think it's yours in the first place?" He was right. For the first time in my life, I was completely silenced.

The world belongs to God. We have been granted permission to enjoy only some of it. As for the rest of it, it continues to belong to God and, one way or the other, our access to it is either restricted or prohibited. And so it should be. When we fully realize this wisdom, we will care for God's world—holy, _herem_, impure, and all—with far greater responsibility than at present.•

Be-_Hukkotai_

have brought me comfort. Man has grown spiritually and intellectually since the time of the Torah's writing. Although the Torah accepts slavery; our modern consciousness has evolved to end slavery, give full rights to women, and end the practice of killing sinners. The Torah gives us a glimpse of God's greater plan, but it is not always clear to us. There is a randomness to everyday events that we do not understand.

God's presence is very real and personal to me, and I still have great trouble reconciling my belief that my illness may be a result of God's will with my suspicion that it is simply some random virus that I have caught by chance. It is hard to accept that a God of goodness and salvation can cause illness and pain. I am trying to resolve in my mind whether every act that hap-

Ira J. Wise

IRA J. WISE, R.J.E. IS THE DIRECTOR OF EDUCATION-ELECT OF CONGREGATION B'NAI ISRAEL IN BRIDGEPORT, CT. HE HAS EARNED A MASTER OF ARTS IN JEWISH EDUCATION FROM THE RHEA SCHOOL OF EDUCATION OF THE HUC-JIR. HE IS THE AUTHOR OF SEVERAL TEXTS INCLUDING *I CAN LEARN TORAH* AND *BETMAN'S BOOK OF HEBREW LETTERS*, BOTH PUBLISHED BY TORAH AURA PRODUCTIONS.

Be-Hukkotai

This *parashah* provides me with a wake-up call each year. It's the big foreshadow that reminds me that the summer is not for coasting—the *Yamim Noraim* are on the way! We've spent the last two months wading through the legalese and Temple ritual of *Vayikra*—it is easy to get caught up in minutiae and detail. We have also just finished celebrating a whole spring of holidays—Purim, Pesah, *Yom ha-Shoah, Yom ha'Atzmaut* and *Lag b'Omer*—and Shavuot is just around the corner. With the exception of *Yom ha-Shoah* (and *Yom ha-Zikaron*), we might tend to lose ourselves in the festive rejoicing of the season. Spring after all is a good time for festivity—especially for those of us in more northerly latitudes.

According to the infamous 1990 Jewish population study, Passover is one of the two most widely observed holidays among Jews. Some of us coast into summer with a renewed feeling of connection to our people and our God. This is a good feeling to have. Coasting is less good. I think that Pesah has the potential of leaving us with a smug feeling—for a few hours or even eight days, we have "done Jewish"—*Dayenu*!! It is enough. For some Jews, the Seder is the final Jewish expression until the High Holy Days—barring a wedding or bar/bat mitzvah invitation.

Then we come to *Be-Hukkotai*, the final *sidrah* of *Vayikra* (Leviticus). Typical of final *sidrot*, we see a review of blessings and curses—a final reminder that we must follow God's commands and prosper, not transgress lest we suffer. There are a lot of important things to be said about that, but my wake-up call comes near the end of chapter 26:

---

pens to me, for good or bad, is a result of God's will.

This is the paradox of modern man in reading the Torah. I try to reconcile my belief that the Torah is God's words, whether directly written or inspired; with my modern consciousness and intellectual understanding of God's granting free will to mankind to choose to do good or evil.

I have grown to accept my illness for what it is: an illness. My illness is neither good nor bad, it exists and I must cope with it every day. I do not have the luxury of deciding if my illness is a punishment for my not keeping every commandment of the Torah; because if I did start keeping every commandment of the Torah now, my virus would not leave me. What I can try to do is use my illness as a force for my own personal good and growth. My illness has allowed

Be-Hukkotai

"WHEN I, IN TURN, HAVE BEEN HOSTILE TO THEM (ISRAEL), AND HAVE REMOVED THEM INTO THE LAND OF THEIR ENEMIES, THEN AT LAST SHALL THEIR OBDURATE HEART HUMBLE ITSELF, AND THEY SHALL ATONE FOR THEIR INIQUITY. THEN WILL I REMEMBER MY COVENANT WITH JACOB; I WILL REMEMBER ALSO MY COVENANT WITH ISAAC, AND ALSO MY COVENANT WITH ABRAHAM; AND I WILL REMEMBER THE LAND.

Be-Hukkotai reminds us: (1) Don't be so smug. *Heshbon ha-nefesh*—the accounting of the soul—still must be done, and you will have to see by how far you have missed the mark; and (2) don't worry. *Teshuvah*—repentance—is available. No matter what you have done, it is possible to reconcile yourself with God, to set things right. As it says in verse 44: YET, EVEN THEN, WHEN THEY ARE IN THE LAND OF THEIR ENEMIES, I WILL NOT REJECT OR SPURN THEM SO AS TO DESTROY THEM, ANNULLING MY COVENANT WITH THEM: FOR I AM ADONAI THEIR GOD. I WILL REMEMBER IN THEIR FAVOR THE COVENANT WITH THE ANCIENTS, WHOM I FREED FROM THE LAND OF EGYPT IN THE SIGHT OF THE NATIONS TO BE THEIR GOD: I AM ADONAI.

Ze'ev Chafets, in *Heroes, Hustlers, Hard Hats and Holy Men,* refers to the period following the Six Day War in 1967 as the "era of high certitude." He describes it as a time when Israelis (and Jews the world over) believed that Israel was the little giant who could do no wrong, militarily, politically, or ethically. There was a "can do" feeling in the air—the national morale was flying high. Likewise, after Entebbe, Jews around the world rejoiced, basking in the glory of the heroic efforts of Yonaton Netanyahu and his team. The spring is like that each year, lifting our spirits as we celebrate: delivery from Haman and Egypt, rebirth of the Jewish nation, the receiving of the Torah (at Shavuot, next week). It is easy to coast into summer.

Be-Hukkotai provides us with an annual slap in the face. It reminds us to remember that while we are celebrating we are not free from acting in concert with Jewish ethics. A spiritually fulfilling Seder experience does not give us license to forget who we are—rather it should remind us that our fathers and mothers were fugitive Arameans, strangers in a strange land, and that we know what that feels like. It should be just enough of a slap to cause us to say "Thanks, I needed that." •

---

me to gain a greater understanding of the fragility of life and how one day you can be strong and healthy, and the next you can be ill and tired. I have gained an even greater patience, understanding and compassion for the sick and ill.

Although the Torah teaches that there is a clear and correct pathway for achieving a holy life; God has given me the free will to do good or evil. God is aware of my faults and weakness, and gives me His love as long as I keep His covenant, rules

אם בחקתי תלכו ואת מצותי תשמרו ועשיתם א

and commandments, and offer תְּשׁוּבָה *teshuvah* (repentance) for my wrongs and errors.

I am ultimately left with my faith in God, that although tested by my illness, will sustain me through this period of challenge and travail. Judaism does not provide an easy answer for facing the problems of life. I have learned that man was intended to wrestle with God and search our souls during these times, as did Jacob in the Torah. Judaism and my faith give me the framework to cope and, I hope to survive whatever happens.

I have been reminded every day of an old ḥasidic saying—that God does not give you challenges to face unless you have the inner strength and faith to overcome them. My illness has allowed me to face the future more dedicated to doing mitzvot, continuing my Torah study and having greater faith in God as a loving force for good. **Noah Goldman, Scarsdale, NY**

דָּבָר אַחֵר **DAVAR AḤER.** EVERY חֵרֶם *ḤEREM* WHICH A PERSON MAKES חֵרֶם *ḤEREM* TO THE LORD FROM ANYTHING THAT HE HAS, WHETHER FROM A MAN OR A BEAST OR FROM A FIELD OF HIS POSSESSION, IT SHOULD NOT BE SOLD OR REDEEMED; EVERY חֵרֶם *ḤEREM* IS THE HOLIEST OF HOLIES TO THE LORD [**Lev. 27.28**]. In a class I gave in *Sefer ha-Hinnukh,* I had problems similar to those of David Kraemer in explaining the uses of the term חֵרֶם *ḥerem.* The Syrian and Morrocan Jews recognized the term as a cognate of the Arabic *ḥaram,* a term I hear often enough when I get into halakhic discussions with Syrian Jews, which is often translated as "forbidden." There are, in fact, many additional instances where חֵרֶם *ḥerem* has the positive connotation of

הֶקְדֵּשׁ "hekdesh," (a dedicated or vowed offering), such as Num. 18.14. But what convinced me most then that the usage of the term in 27.28 is not anomalous was the usage וְלֹא יִדְבַּק בְּיָדְךָ מְאוּמָה מִן הַחֵרֶם "ve-lo yidbak be-yadekha m'umah min ha-ḥerem [Deut. 13.16-18]," the prohibitions against enjoying the spoils of victory in the עִיר הַנִּדַּחַת *ir ha-niddahat,* in the war against Amalek, and the prohibitions of using anything which was used for idolatrous purposes [cf. Deut. 12.3]. What was wrong with King Saul's using the spoils of the war against Amalek and taking captives? If idols are merely sticks and stones, why can't I use wood from an אֲשֵׁרָה *asherah* to light my oven? Or, if not the idol itself, at least the אַבְזְרָיוֹת *avzrayot,* the secondary accoutrements, should be permissible. On the contrary, isn't the fact that we don't use these objects an implicit acknowledgment of their power, that there is a "sacredness" to them?

In answering these questions, I came up with my own twist—not that "everything belongs to God and we only get what He gives us special permission to use" but that some of it is

reserved, so to speak, for His "personal use"—it is designated as God's personal property, preserve, or realm; it belongs to Him personally. This includes dedicated "holy" objects as well as the realm of radical evil….I'm reminded of a scene from a John Wayne movie or a war movie, you know, where the rest of the enemy's allies have been effectively neutralized, and now it's time to take on the ringleader himself. Our hero's friends offer to help him give chase, but he waves them away with a gruff "No. This one's mine." It's part of the warrior spirit that you stand in a special relationship with your closest friends as well as with your personal sworn enemy. You must triumph over him personally, and when you do, the spoils—and the glory— are yours, and no one can ever take them away. קְדֻשָּׁה *Kedushah* and טֻמְאָה *tum'ah* are not merely parallel in that both are off-limits to man—radical evil is also literally *kadosh,* holy, at least in potentiality. For when God triumphs over radical idolatry, evil, and death, the captured spoils become, literally, sacred manifestations of His Glory. **Hazan Ira Rohde, Congregation Shearith Israel, NYC**

חֲזַק, חֲזַק, וְנִתְחַזֵּק
Ḥazak Ḥazak v'nit-Ḥazek

במדבר

Be-Midbar

Be-Midbar

Numbers 1.1–4.20

Dr. Jo Milgrom

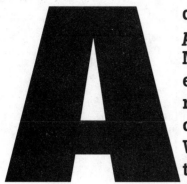

JO MILGROM IS A POET AND ASSEM-
BLAGE ARTIST. DR. MILGROM LIVES
AND TEACHES IN JERUSALEM.
AMONG HER PUBLICATIONS ARE *THE
AKEDAH: THE BINDING OF ISAAC, A
PRIMARY SYMBOL IN JEWISH THOUGHT
AND ART AND HANDMADE MIDRASH.*

A quick perusal of the first *parashah* in the book of Numbers does not exactly fill one with narrative delight. Chapter one opens with a census. Well, they do it here in the USA every ten years, too, for taxes and the draft. Chapter two doesn't hold out that much promise either: the physical design of the Israelite camp as it travels through the desert. It's a square—three tribes on each side, with the portable sanctuary in the center. Pharaoh's camp, in attack formation at Kadesh, was also like Israel's, square in shape, with Pharaoh's tent in the center. After all, Pharaoh was 'god' so his tent was, therefore, a sanctuary.

Doesn't that remind you of the nineteenth century covered wagons in this country on the westward move, arranged to enclose the most precious things in the center, against hostile night marauders? I don't think our cowboy pioneer forebears consulted the second chapter of Numbers, or archaeological reliefs and wall paintings of the ancient Near East. But what is there about this formation that is so instinctive and recurring?

As we work on the solution to this puzzle I invite you to look at the reconstructed drawing from the third-century synagogue of Dura-Europos. The synagoge was located in Syria on the Euphrates River, several hundred miles north of the large Jewish communities of Sura and Pumpeditha where Talmudic academies flourished in late antiquity. Dura was a Roman diaspora town of mixed Hellenistic, Persian and Semitic background. It was located on the silk trading routes leading from the Far East to the Mediterranean. Its arts and culture, therefore, reflected the mix of many contacts and influences.

דָּבָר אַחֵר **DAVAR AHER. AND THEY WHO ENCAMP ON THE EAST, TOWARD THE RISING OF THE SUN, SHALL BE THE STANDARD OF THE CAMP OF JUDAH ACCORDING TO THEIR ARMIES; AND THE PRINCE OF THE CHILDREN OF JUDAH SHALL BE NAHSHON THE SON OF AMMINADAB. [Num. 2.3].**

The east is the holiest direction for it is the entrance to the *Mishkan* (Tabernacle). And there sits *Nahshon*, meaning "THE BIG SERPENT." It is strange, but not uncommon, for a man with an impeccable geneology to be a snake. Here he is descended

Synopsis: A counting of the whole community begins this fourth book in the Torah—primarily for the purpose of determining how many men can bear arms. Surrounding the Tent of Meeting are the military divisions. The number of Levites, both at Sinai and in the wilderness, complete the description of those who are to transport the sanctuary while in the desert.

You are looking with critical disbelief. "You want me to see the arrangement of the tribes during their desert wanderings, three tribes on each side with the sanctuary in the center? Hmmm. Well, I see long spaghettis coming out of the pot in the middle and meandering in various directions to the little guys. Is that what you had in mind? Oh, yes, and the big guy in the middle, I guess he is the chef, stirring the stuff, fixing dinner. Oh yes, there's one little chap down there at about 4 o'clock who's throwing up his hands in disgust because he didn't get anything!"

Well, here's the official version. It is a static composition whose basic elements are organized about a central axis. There are twelve tents or booths, completely filling both sides of this rectangular panel: two pairs of three each radiating out in a diagonal line from the mysterious central structure, and two pairs of

from the tribe of "PRAISE" [Judah], his father is "MY GENEROUS PEOPLE" [Amminadab], his sister is "PROMISE OF MY GOD" [Elisheba], and his brothers-in-law are Moses and Aaron. Perhaps it is his presence which prevents (the spirit of) the common man [Adam] from approaching the *Mishkan* [Num. 3.10]. He has been with us since the garden of Eden [Gen. 3.1-15] biting at our heels. But we can crush his head, for we have the will. [Gen. 3.15].

Michael Kaminski, Price, UT

three each to the right and left in a vertical line along the edge of the panel. Before each entrance stands a diminutive figure, hands upraised, with the exception of the booth at 4 o'clock, whose figure seems to have been squeezed forward by an unequal division of the allotted space.

At center, and high on the panel, is the facade of a different structure, a temple. Two columns are visible, its triangular pediment and a black interior. In front of the temple are ceremonial items: a menorah, two incense altars, and a small, low table for the show bread. Center front and larger than life is a majestic figure in the Greek himation, the garment associated with teacher/leader. The twelve smaller figures wear Persian dress associated with the court, long tunics and full trousers tucked into soft white boots. This central figure stands near a bubbling vessel, holding or placing a staff into it. From the vessel twelve streams lead out to each of the tents.

The clue has been dropped. It's about water. It's about Torah. It's about centering. It's about metaphor. That means, of course, it's also about midrash. To do this right, one has to sleuth in the manner of the scholars. Let's take an educated guess that the big guy is Moses. Then we ask, where in Torah was Moses involved in a water experience, and might there be a visual connection between this painting and the various texts? Water begins the Exodus, through the Red Sea out of Egypt. Water ends the wandering when Israel crosses the Jordan into Israel. Between these two watery brackets there are five water incidents in Exodus and Numbers.

The first is at Marah [Ex. 15.22-25]. *Marah* מָרָה means "bitterness." The waters were bitter, the complaints as well. In verse 25 God shows Moses a piece of wood that he throws into the water, which then becomes sweet. God gives Israel a fixed rule, testing them. In verse 26 God promises health and healing if Israel will keep the Torah. We look at the fresco. Perhaps Moses is, indeed, sweetening the water with that staff. As for giving Israel a fixed rule, or promising rewards for loyalty, that cannot be "seen," nor can we account for the arrangement of the tents, or the ritual objects, or the praying/praising figures, or for the twelve streams.

The second incident is at Elim [Ex. 15.27]. Could the twelve streams be the twelve springs of Elim? Yes, the tents could be the encampment. But what about the sanctuary? What about Moses?

The third is at Rephidim-Massah and Meribah [Ex.17.1-7]. The mood does not accord with the praying/praising figures, but is Moses striking the rock in our panel?

The fourth is at Meribah [Num. 20.2-13]. This episode seems to be a repeat of Exodus 17.1-7 in at least two details: the complaint

Be-Midbar

and the striking of the rock. But for two reasons this seems not to be our panel. Moses does not appear to strike the rock. In fact he is disgraced in this incident. He asks, "SHALL WE BRING FORTH WATER FOR YOU?" We, meaning Aaron and I. Should he not have said, He, meaning God? Moses has become inflated. No wonder he is punished. His leadership is effectively finished.

The fifth at Be'er [Num. 21.16-20] is the remnant of an old poem, mixed in with an itinerary. Verse 16 marks the location, בְּאֵר be'er, meaning "well," and announces the gift of water. In verse 17 Israel then sings the song of the well, "SPRING UP O WELL, SING TO IT, THE WELL WHICH THE CHIEFTAINS DUG, WHICH THE NOBLES OF THE PEOPLE STARTED WITH MACES, WITH THEIR OWN STAFFS." I believe this song accounts for the praying/praising figures whose arms are raised in an orant (praising) posture. Their costumes are associated with nobility, verse 18. Still, it is clear we have another fragment, a composite of water incidents, yet no answer to the arrangement of the tents and the streams, or Moses and the staff.

It has to be midrash! The midrash on Numbers says the well was a rock shaped like a beehive that rolled along with Israel wherever they traveled. If Israel was unfaithful to Torah the well would go underground and Israel would thirst...for both. When the marching camp came to a halt and the Tabernacle was set up, this rock-well would come and settle down in the court of the Tent of Meeting and the princes would come

and say, "Rise up O well," and it would rise.

The New Testament gives evidence of the antiquity of the tradition. Paul speaks of the desert experience of his ancestors: "NOW ALL OUR FATHERS WERE UNDER THE CLOUD AND ALL PASSED THROUGH THE SEA...AND ALL ATE THE SAME SPIRITUAL MEAT; AND ALL DRANK THE SAME SPIRITUAL DRINK; FOR THEY DRANK OF THAT SPIRITUAL ROCK THAT FOLLOWED THEM...." [I Corinthians 10.1-4].

So *Numbers Rabbah* and I Corinthians confirm the potable/portable nature of the well, that its nourishment was also spiritual and that its proper placement was in the courtyard of the sanctuary [the *Tosefta* adds, "opposite the entrance to the Tabernacle."] We begin to get the Dura picture. From the Aramaic paraphrase, *Targum Jonathan*, we learn that the waters were brought directly to each tent (aha! those spaghetti-garden hoses).

And what about Moses and the staff? The first-century work called *Pseudo Philo* says that the tree that God showed Moses at Marah (back there in Ex. 15.25) was no ordinary tree. It would have to be the Tree of Life, i.e., Torah, that made the water sweet as it followed Israel into the mountains and down the plains. So in midrash, water isn't just water; it is heavy water, and trees are not just trees. Narrative always spins into symbol, particularly when word play enters. God *showed* Moses the tree = God *taught* וַיּוֹרֵהוּ *va-Yorehu* Moses the "Tree."

One more point wraps it up. This square configuration that focused on the central circular well is the classic mandala form. The mandala is a structural device for centering and healing, leading to one's inner core. Psychologist C.G. Jung drew mandalas during a period of inner turmoil in his life. The climax for him was the "Liverpool dream" in which the center of a city was marked by a small pool with an island in the middle. The island, despite surrounding darkness, was ablaze with sunlight and at the same time seemed to be the source of the light. On the island stood a single tree, a magnolia with reddish blossoms. The dream gave Jung a sense of his personal myth. It combined the elements of *place, water, light* and *growth* as the desired place to be. And so the Miraculous Well at Dura combines *place*= sanctuary, *water + tree* = Torah, *light*= menorah= tree of light/life. Thus the arrangement of the camp in *Parashat be-Midbar* turns out to be a mandala, centering the Jewish people on the most sacred and most nourishing elements. Finally, it should be noted that the Torah as the Tree of Life is in fact *a portable axis mundi,* a portable God-connection planted, not geographically, but in the heart of the person who is centered. As long as your Tree of Life is rooted in you, the diaspora experience can be validated. It is probably no coincidence that both the parashah and the Dura experience take place outside of Israel. It is also ironic that this is being written two weeks before our departure to Israel, as *olim.*●

Rabbi Ed Feinstein

ED FEINSTEIN IS A RABBI AT CONGREGATION VALLEY BETH SHALOM IN ENCINO, CALIFORNIA, AND TEACHES AT THE UNIVERSITY OF JUDAISM, LOS ANGELES.

Be-Midbar

How do the books of the Torah get their names? It's really rather arbitrary: each name is simply the first significant word found in the first lines of the book. But by some powerful coincidence, these randomly chosen names manage to capture and express the character and content of each book: בְּרֵאשִׁית *Bereshit* (Genesis) is indeed a book of beginnings—recounting the origins of the world, of humanity, and of the Jewish people. More, *Bereshit* sets out the bases of Jewish faith—our fundamental attitudes about God, the world, the nature of human beings, our relationship to nature, the origins of gender and family life and the beginnings of evil.

שְׁמוֹת *Shemot* (Exodus) means "NAMES," because the book opens with names of Jacob's clan who went down into Egypt. But at the center of *Shemot* are those events that give us our identity as a people: the Exodus from Egypt and the Giving (and Receiving) of Torah on Mt. Sinai. *Shemot* is, indeed, the book of our name.

וַיִּקְרָא *Va-Yikra* (Leviticus) translates "AND HE (GOD) CALLED..." which is precisely the book's content: God's call to the people of Israel to attain holiness, and Israel's response through mitzvot and worship.

בְּמִדְבַּר *Be-Midbar* (Numbers) presents the clearest case. *Be-Midbar* means "IN THE WILDERNESS," and the book's story takes us from Mt. Sinai through the wilderness wanderings of the Israelites to the boundaries of the Promised Land. But more than the geographic wilderness, this book takes us through a social wasteland. Every tie that binds Israel falls apart: the driving dream of the Promised Land is violated by the people's fear and doubt. The base physical desires of hunger, thirst, and sexual lust overcome the vision of the people's holiness and duty. It is a book of rebellion, conflict and confrontation, of whining and carping and complaining.

And the tragedy of *Be-Midbar* falls heaviest on Moshe: everyone in his life betrays him in this book. He is betrayed by his people, he is challenged by his tribe, the Levites—his own cousins. He is betrayed by

וידבר יהוה אל משה במדבר סיני באהל מועד

Aaron and Miriam. Finally, and ironically, he is betrayed by God... and for what?... for hitting the rock instead of speaking to it! But what else could be expected? Nowhere in *Be-Midbar* do words function properly! In *Be-Midbar*, there are no shared values, no shared dreams; most of all, *there are no shared words*. Leaders speak, but no one listens. Leaders lead, but no one follows. This is a book filled with screaming and shouting and noise; perhaps the noisiest in the Bible.

Had the Torah ended here, as some scholars suggest it once did, it would be a very different book...and we would be a very different people. Had the Torah ended here, it would take us from the sublime tranquillity of Creation in the first chapter of *Bereshit*, to the noisy chaos of *Be-Midbar*, and leave us exhausted at the boundaries of the Promised Land with a reflection of humanity at its worst. What sort of people would we be? But the Torah doesn't end here.

The Torah's final book is דְּבָרִים *Devarim* (Deuteronomy). *Devarim* means "WORDS," and the book relates all the words shared by the once wordless Moshe with the children of the *Be-Midbar* generation. It's a remarkable revolution: he talks, they listen; he teaches, they learn. Here is dialogue, conversation—shared vision, shared values, shared direction. The most important word in *Devarim* is *Shema*—"LISTEN!" It is a book of listening. It is a book filled with the calm of consensus and confidence. Once again, creation has overcome chaos...and it is good. And at the end, Moshe dies, and he is mourned with heartfelt tears by his people...by the very children of those who would have killed him in *Be-Midbar*.

Why does the Torah juxtapose two such opposite books?...two such contradictory visions of human life and human community? Because all life is an oscillation between them—between periods of *Be-Midbar* and periods of *Devarim*—between chaos and consensus, vision and division. This is the inner life, as we alternatively grasp and then grow out of our conceptions of life's purpose and mission. This is family life—as we learn to hold onto one another, and at the same time, learn to let go. And this is the life of human communities. During the last 50 years, for example, American Jews have enjoyed *Devarim*—a fundamental consensus and shared direction. But now that's changing. We are re-entering *Be-Midbar* to search for a new language, a new vision, a new course. It's not an easy time to be a Jew, and it's especially difficult to be a teacher and leader. But Torah offers this wisdom and comfort: *Be-Midbar* is not the last word. Periods of *Be-Midbar* chaos and wandering will inevitably be followed by the consensus and calm of *Devarim*, just as chaos is overcome by Creation. That's our ultimate faith.●

Naso

**Numbers
4.21–7.89**

Rabbi Bradley Shavit Artson

BRADLEY SHAVIT ARTSON, THE
RABBI OF CONGREGATION EILAT IN
MISSION VIEJO, CALIFORNIA, IS THE
AUTHOR OF *IT'S A MITZVAH! JEWISH
LIVING STEP-BY-STEP* (BEHRMAN
HOUSE & THE RABBINICAL
ASSEMBLY), AND IS CURRENTLY
WRITING A BOOK ON JUDAISM AND
ENVIRONMENTAL ETHICS FOR THE
JEWISH PUBLICATION SOCIETY. HE IS
A SENIOR CONTRIBUTING EDITOR
FOR THE *JEWISH SPECTATOR* AND
WRITES A WEEKLY TORAH COLUMN
FOR THE *SOUTHERN CALIFORNIA
JEWISH HERITAGE*.

To Be A Jew, To Be A Blessing

How do you approach a classic within a classic? The entire Torah represents a pinnacle of literary, moral and spiritual accomplishment. Printed in every language of the globe, the Torah is the all-time bestseller for humanity. Yet, within that great work, there are certain passages which stand out as especially noteworthy, particularly resonant with meaning and with depth.

One such passage is the *Birkat Kohanim*, the Priestly Benediction, found in this week's Torah portion. God instructs Moses to:

דַּבֵּר אֶל-אַהֲרֹן וְאֶל-בָּנָיו לֵאמֹר
כֹּה תְבָרְכוּ אֶת-בְּנֵי יִשְׂרָאֵל אָמוֹר לָהֶם
יְבָרֶכְךָ יהוה וְיִשְׁמְרֶךָ
יָאֵר יהוה פָּנָיו אֵלֶיךָ וִיחֻנֶּךָּ
יִשָּׂא יהוה פָּנָיו אֵלֶיךָ וְיָשֵׂם לְךָ שָׁלוֹם

SPEAK TO AARON AND HIS SONS:
THUS SHALL YOU BLESS THE PEOPLE OF
   ISRAEL. SAY TO THEM:
ADONAI BLESS YOU AND PROTECT YOU!
ADONAI DEAL KINDLY AND GRACIOUSLY WITH
   YOU!
ADONAI BESTOW FAVOR UPON YOU AND
   GRANT YOU PEACE!
THUS SHALL THEY LINK MY NAME WITH THE
   PEOPLE OF ISRAEL AND I WILL BLESS
   THEM.

In part, the prominence of the בִּרְכַּת כֹּהֲנִים *Birkat Kohanim* stems from the rarity of mandated biblical prayers: this is one of only two prescribed blessings within the entire Torah. The other blessing, "MY FATHER WAS A WANDERING ARAMEAN,"

דָּבָר אַחֵר **DAVAR AHER. HE SHALL KEEP HIMSELF FROM WINE AND STRONG DRINK; HE SHALL DRINK NO VINEGAR MADE FROM WINE OR STRONG DRINK, AND SHALL NOT DRINK ANY JUICE OF GRAPES OR EAT GRAPES, FRESH OR DRIED. [NUM. 6.3].** We all know that Samson couldn't cut his hair. A prohibition that is less well-known was the abstinence from any form of alcohol. This, I believe, indicated that for a person to com-

pletely serve G-d, he must use his mind and his body. When a person consumes alcohol, the substance damages both the mind and the body. Therefore, that person cannot fully serve G-d. Alcohol not only distorts the mind but also destroys the important organs of the body. Alcohol is such a killer that 95 percent of all auto accidents are caused by underage drinking and driving.

[Deut. 26.5] forms the core of the Passover *Haggadah*.

The בִּרְכַּת כֹּהֲנִים *Birkat Kohanim's* sense of bounty and of God's sovereignty permeates not only the meaning of the words, but their structure, too. Note how artfully crafted this gem is: in the Hebrew, we see an increasing pattern of words on each line (3, 5, 7), and an increasing pattern of consonants (15, 20, 25), and of syllables (12, 14, 16). The very words, letters, and syllables contribute to a sense of order, climax and completion.

This ancient and inspiring blessing strengthened the institution of the priesthood, by making them the conduit of God's blessing to the people. But the בִּרְכַּת כֹּהֲנִים *Birkat Kohanim's* language also makes it clear that the *Kohein* serves a vital but limited role. Unlike a magician who is the source of the magic, the *Kohen* is only a channel for the blessing to pass through on its way to the Jewish people. The sole source of bounty is God. For that

reason, each line begins by mentioning God as the active agent, and the last line explicitly states "I WILL BLESS THEM." I, God, and not the *kohanim*.

No person in Judaism can approximate or replace God. No human being is holy in a way that is different from the holiness of any other human being. This blessing reminds us of the sanctity of all humanity, and of the awesome otherness of the God of Israel. By promising to bless the people, and by connecting this divine generosity to the rituals of the *kohanim*, the prayer also reminds us of God's love for our people that is at the core of traditional Jewish piety: we are participants in the greatest love story of all time—the perennial passion of God for the Jews, and our reciprocal devotion to the Holy Blessing One.

At the same time that בִּרְכַּת כֹּהֲנִים *Birkat Kohanim* functions as a pronouncement of our mutual love and commitment, this blessing conveys an additional meaning after our

Synopsis: Continuing with a description of the duties of the Levites from last week, our text details the three categories of impure persons who must be removed from the camp. Smaller sections about restitution for breaking faith with God, choice of a Kohein, the suspected adulteress, the Nazirite, and the priestly blessing conclude chapter six. The final chapter of this parashah contains descriptions of the gifts presented by the twelve chieftains to the Tabernacle.

When someone is abusing alcohol, that person is not only hurting himself, but his family, friends and coworkers. Judaism doesn't teach abstinence in drinking. Judaism teaches responsibility. For some people, it is responsible to know when to stop. For others, it is responsible not to start at all. Our tradition should guide us to know our limits, and to be ready to serve G-d with all our capaci-

ties unimpaired. It is important to note that there is a Samson in all of us. Only by being spiritually strong in both mind and body can we succeed in accomplishing our most desired goals in life. **Aaron Luka**, *at his Bar Mitzvah, June 10, 1995, Wilkes-Barre, PA.* As related by **Rabbi Jim Michaels** <rabi@temple.microserve.com>

דְּבָר אַחֵר **DAVAR AHER. AND YOU SHALL PLACE MY NAME BEFORE ALL THE CHILDREN OF ISRAEL SO THAT I WILL BLESS THEM. [Num. 6.27]. God's Bridge:** Undoubtedly, most of the sermons delivered during *Parashat Naso* had to do with what is commonly called the "Priestly Benediction." This makes perfectly good sense since it fits the bill for a d'var Torah to a tee: it is well-known, meaningful and spiritual.

journey through three thousand years: it now provides yet another link to the antiquity of our people and to the vitality of our בְּרִית *brit* (covenant) with God.

When I was last in Israel, I visited the Israel Museum in Jerusalem to see the latest archaeological finds. Among the digs was the excavation of a burial plot, called *Ketef Hinnom*, from the end of the First Temple period (1000-586 B.C.E.)—complete with jewelry, pottery, glass, and other remains. All of those bric-a-brac were impressive, but not particularly gripping. What caught my breath, however, was a small silver plaque, approximately the size of my thumb. On this thin strip of silver, some ancient, anonymous Jew had inscribed the בִּרְכַּת כֹּהֲנִים *Birkat Kohanim* in the ancient Hebrew script of that period. The date of the plaque was estimated at the Seventh Century B.C.E.!

According to the description of the archaeologist, Professor Gabriel Barkay, this metal sheet had been rolled around a cord so it could be worn around the neck of this pious Jew over 2,600 years ago. That same blessing which observant Jews still recite each morning as part of the *Shaḥarit* (Morning) service, which *Kohanim* use to this day to bless the assembled congregation on Yom Kippur, Rosh Ha-Shanah, and the *Shalosh Regalim* (three Festivals of Pesaḥ, Shavuot and Sukkot), that same prayer was a vital part of our ancestors' lives so many centuries ago.

As I stood in the Israel Museum—in a united Jerusalem, capital of the third independent Jewish Commonwealth—I started to cry.

I cried because of the privilege we Jews enjoy in a spiritual continuity which extends back to the very beginnings of our people. Who else can share in the prayers of their most distant ancestors the way we can? The Chinese don't worship the same gods their ancestors did, the modern Greeks don't pray to

Naso

These words are very, very ancient and could very well have been the words spoken by Aaron and the priests in Leviticus 9.22 when they "LIFTED THEIR HANDS TO BLESS THE PEOPLE." The antiquity of these words is also attested to by the fact that a nearly verbatim copy of this blessing was found in *Ketef Hinnom*, near the Valley of Hinnom in Jerusalem, in 1980. In a sense, these words form a living link through the formative years of the monarchies, the divided kingdom, and may well reach back to Aaron and his sons while our people witnessed revelation at the Tent of Meeting. Indeed, these are awesome words.

Though there is much to be gleaned and gained from looking at these words alone, there is also much to be gained by looking at the words of this blessing in the context of the sections before it and

the Olympians, nor do contemporary Egyptians pray to their ancient pantheon or read the *Book of the Dead* for spiritual sustenance. But, every day, I find myself blessed through the same timeless words which moved my unknown ancestor—and all the generations of Jews in between as well. My relationship to the sacred is not solely the result of my own philosophical insight or exclusively through existential openness; my connection to God is primarily nurtured through ancient Jewish words, through specifically Jewish vessels.

The book that contains these ancient words—the Torah—is still a crucial, welcome witness in the lives of many contemporary Jews. Unlike several other ancient works of piety— the *Iliad*, the Egyptian *Book of the Dead*, and so many others—the Torah isn't read simply because of its literary genius or to satisfy historical curiosity. Jews, and millions of Gentiles, too, read the Torah for its spiritual greatness, because it is the

essential starting point for a relationship with God that is firmly rooted. בִּרְכַּת כֹּהֲנִים *Birkat Kohanim* reflects rootedness and depth, the miracle of a continuity borne by the same holy book, read and implemented across the generations.

We pray to the same God as our anonymous ancestors did, implement the same Torah, and celebrate most of the same holy days and festivals, too. And in our age, we have yet another symbol of continuity, the Hebrew language which was the cultural context of the Torah and of our ancestors' spiritual lives. God, Torah, language and land—those threads course through Jewish history from its inception up to the present.

And what of the future?

Here, too, the בִּרְכַּת כֹּהֲנִים *Birkat Kohanim* plays its part: each Friday night, just after lighting our Shabbat candles, my wife and I bless our two-year-old twins, Jacob and Shira. Like other Jewish parents throughout time, we place our hands on our

children's heads and we bless them with the words of the בִּרְכַּת כֹּהֲנִים *Birkat Kohanim*, the same words that God told Aaron to use when blessing the Jewish people. There is a rabbinic teaching that parents stand in the same relation to their children that *kohanim* do to the people at large: representing the values and traditions of Judaism and connecting the past to the future through the way we raise our children. Even when they are not themselves *kohanim*, parents may bless their children with this prayer.

Jacob and Shira are almost two years old, so they have heard this blessing for quite some time now. Recently, for the first time, Jacob responded to my blessing him by putting his hands on my head. Still too young to speak the words himself, his gesture was itself a blessing for me. In his act, I felt the surge of history and the promise of God's ancient covenant fulfilled: assuring me that the continuity I prize will continue, that the Torah will remain a commanding

after it. The section before the Priestly Benediction deals with the elusive and not altogether well-understood rights of the Nazirite; a man or woman whose sense of purpose and dedication to God involved restrictions on behavior such as abstention from wine, certain sacrifices, letting the hair grow and avoiding contact with the dead. When the period of *nazirut* is over, the *nazir* would undergo another series of rituals to

re-enter the community. Most *nazirim* would be *nazir* for a short period of time but, as in the case of Samson, one might be a *nazir* for an entire lifetime. Though the actual meaning of *nazirut* is elusive today, it is obvious that it involved an **individual** who wanted to achieve a greater sense of the holy, if only for a short time. The section immediately followig the Priestly Benediction is the recounting of the completion of the Tabernacle,

the *mishkan*, which was placed at the very center of the camp and which served as the focal point for every Jew. It was here that Moses would ask God for guidance both when God felt like communicating with him and when Moses himself had a question regarding a point of understanding or law brought to him by a concerned Jew. In contradistinction to the vow of the Nazirite which was an individual enterprise, the completion and

presence and a gift of love for yet another generation.

Whether or not each of us are parents, whether or not each of us lives with other people or alone, we are all connected through our membership in the Jewish people, all covenanted to God in the sacred task of linking past to future, of raising up the next generation and of reassuring the generation before us that we will be links in an ancient chain, transmitting God's covenant to yet another seeking age.

Much in human history changes—our customs, fads, styles, and cultures swell and shift throughout the years. But three things remain eternal—the human heart retains the same needs, urges, and concerns across time; the God of Israel has not changed despite our shifting perceptions of who God is; and the bridge between the human heart and the God of Israel—the Torah and the mitzvot—is still the encapsulation of the brit, the covenant, which binds our people to each other throughout time and to our God, who transcends time.

That, indeed, is quite a blessing.●

Naso

use of the Tabernacle was a community-wide event. And in between these events, one personal and one communal, lay the Priestly Benediction.

When we look at the Benediction we see something fascinating. The pronoun at the end of the first sentence "MAY THE LORD BLESS AND KEEP YOU" [Num. 6.24] is in the singular. This corresponds to the singular nature of the Nazirite's vow and responsibilities. The last word of the last sentence, "AND YOU SHALL PLACE MY NAME BEFORE ALL THE CHILDREN OF ISRAEL SO THAT I WILL BLESS THEM," [Num. 6.27] corresponds to the communal event of finishing and dedicating the Tabernacle.

The Priestly Benediction serves as a kind of a bridge between the individual and the community. Like all bridges that span a space, God's blessing is the bridge that spans the space between the individual and the community. As bridges are not wont to judge between the two sides of the river, so too, does this bridge refrain from judgment between the individual and the community. In both cases, God's blessing is ours.

There are times when we want to express our faith individually, perhaps through personal mitzvot or acts of gemilut hasidim. Or, perhaps we, like mystics, find it necessary at times to distance ourselves from the community, find a forest to sit in and meditate. Or, maybe we find ourselves involved in community prayer, but there to pray not as a part of the community but apart from the community. Indeed, the individual's prayer seeks to strengthen, make wise, console and

Approaches to the Numinous

Dr. Steven M. Brown

DR. STEVEN M. BROWN IS
HEADMASTER OF THE SOLOMON
SCHECTER DAY SCHOOL OF GREATER
PHILADELPHIA.

Naso

Rabbi Brad Artson in his beautiful commentary on *Parashat Naso* reminds us of the strikingly different ways that the priestly blessings are evoked in Jewish tradition. On the one hand they are the intimate, loving, and affectionate touch of parents blessing their children, a mitzvah open to all Jews regardless of ancestry, position or socioeconomic status. At the same time they are the grand and awe-inspiring evocation by the priests of the Power of the Universe to bless the people of Israel in a rather regal and extraordinarily impressive ritual. These two approaches to the priestly blessings reflect a dichotomy in Jewish tradition as to how we approach the divine and how we access the numinous in the universe. Ralph Otto, in his book *The Idea of the Holy,* refers to the quality of the numinous or the holy as an awesome, ineffable confrontation with the wholly other that evokes a sense of liminality between the human and the Divine, but which draws us close to the Ultimate Source of all Being.

In Jewish tradition, accessing the awe, wonder, and mystery of the Divine has taken at least two primary forms represented by the schools of *Beit Hillel* and *Beit Shammai*. Whereas many Jews view the differences between *Beit Shammai* and *Beit Hillel* as ones of stringency and leniency on various ritual matters, it is my contention that these two schools often represent different approaches toward the liminality which separates the human from the divine,

inspire the one who utters it and there are times in all our lives when such prayers have to be uttered in the silence of our own minds and hearts. It is reassuring to know that God's blessing reaches into our hearts.

There are times when we want to express our Jewishness collectively. To be sure, the excitement of "SINGING A NEW SONG UNTO THE LORD" is truly appreciated in community worship. Social action programs, synagogue committees, rallies in support of Jewish causes, and the inner strength which is generated from knowing that we are part of a community of Jews no matter how large or small, all lead us to feel our Judaism and to express it among the presence of other Jews. Such a feeling is very comforting. It is reassuring to know that God's blessing, here, too, reaches into the body of Jews no matter how many or few there are. Either as an individual involved in an act of faith, *emunah*, or as part of a

each prescribing different methodologies of bridging the gap.

Beit Hillel seeks to normalize and insert into everyday living our relationship with the numinous, whereas *Beit Shammai* wants to maintain a liminality or separateness which inspires awe, wonder and trembling. The recitation of the *Shema* is a good example. *Beit Hillel* maintains that the *Shema* be recited in whatever position the worshipper finds him or herself. Thus, if you are sitting, you recite it sitting. If you are standing you recite it standing, and if you are traveling you recite it while you are traveling. *Beit Shammai's* position is that the *Shema* needs to be uttered in a very special, separate and unique way, preferably standing with great reverence, awe and majesty. In their dispute over the order of the Friday evening *Kiddush*, *Beit Hillel* (which the tradition follows), states that the *brakhah* over wine precedes the *brakhah* over the holiness of the

day. *Beit Shammai* maintains just the opposite! Some have suggested that *Beit Hillel* was playing to a middle or lower class audience which was not accustomed to drinking wine during the week, and so it wanted to make wine special and preceded the blessing over the Shabbat with that of the specialness of the wine. According to *Beit Shammai* it is the very onset of the Shabbat itself which is unique and awesome, thus its *brakhah* should take preference over the blessing for the wine. In the great debate over the laying of hands on the heads of animal sacrifices *Beit Hillel* contended that anyone is permitted to lay hands, whereas *Beit Shammai* maintained that only the priests could rightfully perform this ritual. One sought to normalize and democratize the ritual, the other sought to maintain the liminality between the numinous and the mundane.

Clearly, Jewish tradition has followed *Beit Hillel*, but something

Naso

community of other Jews, how wonderful it is to hear a blessing which inspires us, individually and collectively, to fulfill. **Rabbi Stephen Robbins, Congregation N'vay Shalom, Los Angeles, CA.**

דָּבָר אַחֵר **DAVAR AHER. THE ONE WHO BROUGHT HIS OFFERING ON THE FIRST DAY WAS NAHSHON SON OF AMMINADAV, OF THE TRIBE OF JUDAH** [Num. 7.12]. The Lessons of Nahshon ben Ammi-

nadav: A nuance in *Parashat Naso* triggers reflection on a fundamental issue confronting the contemporary Jewish community—the *tzedakah* ethic. When the twelve tribal chieftains present their offerings to the Sanctuary at the end of the *parashah*, Nahshon ben Amminadav is the first to present his rich gifts. Whereas all the other gift-givers are referred to as "chieftains," Nahshon alone is not so titled. The rabbis

נשא אֵץ ראש בני גרשון גם הם לבית אבתם

has to be said for the power of Shammai's vision. To the extent that Judaism gave over to the church many of the awe-inspiring and over-powering rituals which marked the sacred space and sounds of the Temple, we have lost something. To the extent that Christianity under-stands the needs of the worshipper to be surrounded by awesomeness in the form of architecture, music and art, and since not everyone is always capable of reaching the level of כַּוָּנָה *kavvanah* or spiritual and intellectual devotion that our rather scholastic

Rabbinic tradition would have us do, the church's adaptation of Shammai's point of view has enriched it and enabled it to inspire masses of peo-ple. Judaism, in almost totally sur-rendering *Beit Shammai*'s point of view in favor of Hillel's, has perhaps lost an opportunity to engage the contemporary worshipper in a more awesome and powerful religious experience than the normalized, democratized synagogue setting and rituals which have come down to us to this day. Though it is fashionable in many Jewish circles today to be

simple and understated in worship when confronting the great and awesome mysteries of the universe, the power of great music, great space, and awesome ritual should not be totally rejected as helpful vehicles enabling today's worship-pers to access the numinous, permit-ting them a glimpse through or over the boundaries separating human beings and God.•

---

commented that this was to lessen any chance of self-importance or self-aggrandizement stemming from his being the first in line. Though first, Nahshon was no more important than anyone else who offered a gift. The deletion of his title was to remind Nahshon and us of the need for humility and graciousness in giving.

We recall that, according to Rabbinic tradition, this same Nahshon ben Amminadav was also the individual responsible for the splitting of the Sea following the Exodus. Although Moses held out his rod at God's com-mand, the sea did not open until Nahshon edged into the water; first with his toe, then to his knee, then to his waist, to his chest, chin; and finally, when the water was just about to overtake his nostrils and drown him, the sea split and dry land appeared. The lesson taught here was that until a person is willing to take a risk, God does not make a mir-acle. There is a partnership between human action and divine providence,

and it's not always easy to see who initiates salvation!

Nahshon's "firsts" have important implications for today's Jewish com-munity. On the one hand, people need to take a risk if the miraculous is going to happen: risks for peace, risks for investment in Jewish educa-tion, risks in how we raise our chil-dren and what values we teach them that may be countercurrent to the in friends' and society's as a whole; risks in the choice of lifestyles and profes-sions that may bring personal fulfill-ment, though not necessarily finan-cial reward. Until and unless we are willing to take those risks, the mira-cles of peace, of Jewish continuity and of truly contented living may not occur.

Similarly, we are seeing new and radi-cally different patterns of giving in today's Jewish community. Donors want more control over where their gifts are directed; they want more input into how their gifts are used.

Few wish to be first, to take leader-ship roles in major fundraising cam-paigns, but many seek the maximum of *kavod.* This creates tension and uncertainty in the ethical implementa-tion of an institution's missions and standards. It's not who gives first, most, or best which counts, but that we give with proper intention, devo-tion, and humility. This is the true ethic of *tzedakah.*

As a Jewish educator, I have an important role to play in the training of children to be risk takers and future gift givers in the American Jewish community. But I plead guilty to the charge that, while we have trained our children to be wonderful fund-raisers, I am not sure we have trained them in a personal ethic of *tzedakah.* Our students are terrific at raising all kinds of monies for all kinds of causes—MS Read-a-thon, the American Heart Jump-rope-a-thon, the Federation Allied Jewish Appeal, JNF. Through white elephant sales, the selling of every kind of foodstuff, walk-a-thons, and even the weekly solicitation of *tzedakah* money from their parents, our children have proven to be terrific fund-raisers. We only need to look at the American Jewish community as a whole to see that as fund-raisers we are unparalleled. The UJA is considered the most efficient charity in the United States. However, the ethic of personal *tzedakah*, of taking a risk with one's own funds, of risking the possibility of not affording something we want for ourselves by giving until it hurts, sacrificing one's personal pleasures to improve the lot of the community, does not seem to have penetrated very deeply into the American Jewish psyche, especially as more and more Jews become professionals and fewer are entrepreneurial business people.

One need only look at the levels of various Federation campaigns throughout the country to see that giving has not dramatically increased, though the quality and efficiency of fund-raising organizations is probably at an all-time high. Our task as Jewish educators must be to train future generations of children to be fine fund-raisers, but more importantly, champion givers, with a desire to innovate and take risks to bring about the miraculous transformation that will be necessary to preserve the American Jewish community and world Jewry as a whole.

This ethic of giving is very much represented by Nahshon's willingness to take a risk and the Torah's demand that Nahshon be humble in his giving. Would that those of us

Naso

who are capable of using our resources to move the American Jewish community forward would be willing to take the risks for greater return on investment, doing so with the humility and graciousness exemplified by Nahshon. **Dr. Steven M. Brown, Philadelphia, PA**

דָּבָר אַחֵר **DAVAR AHER. THE WOMAN BORE A SON, AND SHE NAMED HIM SAMSON. THE BOY GREW UP, AND THE LORD BLESSED HIM. [Judges 13.24].** This Torah and haftarah portion are especially dear to me because they were mine at my own bar mitzvah, twenty-four years ago. I shared my bar mitzvah with another fellow in our suburban Long Island congregation, and I will never forget the sight of all those people in the pews. I knew we were having 150 or so guests; I knew he was having 150 or so guests. But I did not realize until that morning that 150 + 150 = 300! I do not remember what the Rabbi said to me in his blessing; I do not remember what I said to the congregation in my speech. I do remember the suit I was wearing, however—very 70's, beige polyester with a double-vented jacket and a very wide brown tie.

I also remember my haftarah portion, which told the story of the birth of Samson. To a thirteen-year-old, this was the story of grown-ups running around like chickens without heads, all because they were going to have a baby. Now, as a grown-up and a father, I find that the story seems very modern and it makes perfect sense. I think now of the fundamental mystery and holiness of conception. The news of pregnancy comes as no less a wonder today when it is announced by the over-the-counter pharmaceutical kit than it did twenty centuries ago when it was announced by an angel of the Lord. I think of all those books filled with prenatal advice that couples read today, particularly while awaiting a first child. Our favorite was called *What to Expect When You're Expecting*. "Don't drink this; do eat that; exercise; don't exercise; talk to the fetus (like you would to a plant); create a soothing environment"—all to the end that the child be allowed to develop to his or her full potential, just like Samson.

I think also of the excitement of not knowing who your child will be, an excitement that does not end with birth. This could be the messiah, this could be a great genius, an athlete, a musician. This could be the sweetest boy or girl in the whole world. The anticipation and excitement, I am learning, never go away.

THE WOMAN BORE A SON, AND SHE NAMED HIM SAMSON. THE BOY GREW UP, AND THE LORD BLESSED HIM. [Judges 13.24] No less happens for any child, for any child could grow up to do anything. Amen. **Rabbi Michael Joseph, Temple B'nai B'rith, Kingston, PA <michjose@aol.com>**

Be-Ha'alotekha

Numbers 8.1–12.16

Arthur Kurzweil

ARTHUR KURZWEIL IS VICE PRESIDENT OF JASON ARONSON, INC., AND EDITOR-IN-CHIEF OF THE JEWISH BOOK CLUB. HE TEACHES INTRODUCTORY COURSES IN TALMUD AND JEWISH MYSTICISM AT THE MIDRASHA OF THE JEWISH EDUCATION ASSOCIATION IN NEW JERSEY. HIS BOOK FROM GENERATION TO GENERATION: HOW TO TRACE YOUR JEWISH GENEALOGY AND FAMILY HISTORY (HARPERCOLLINS) HAS RECENTLY BEEN COMPLETELY REVISED AND UPDATED.

G OD SPOKE TO MOSES, TELLING HIM TO SPEAK TO AARON AND SAY TO HIM, "WHEN YOU LIGHT THE LAMPS, THE SEVEN LAMPS SHALL ILLUMINATE THE MENORAH." [Num. 8.1-2] A few years ago, Rabbi Adin Steinsaltz accepted an invitation to speak to a gathering of the New York Board of Rabbis. Its membership, spanning all flavors within the Jewish community, filled the space where the extraordinary Rabbi Steinsaltz was scheduled to speak.

דָּבָר אַחֵר **DAVAR AHER. GOD SPOKE WITH MOSES, TELLING HIM TO SPEAK TO AARON AND SAY TO HIM, 'WHEN YOU LIGHT THE LAMPS, THE SEVEN LAMPS SHALL ILLUMINATE THE MENORAH'. [Num. 8.1-2].** In his comments to *Parashat Be-Ha'alotekha*, Arthur Kurzweil cites the "provocative statement" of Rabbi Adin Steinsaltz to the New York Board of Rabbis in which Steinsaltz claimed that "*Kabbalah* is the official theology of the Jewish people."

Though he is perhaps best known for his remarkable translation and commentary on the Talmud, Rabbi Steinsaltz's reputation also includes his highly-regarded writings on science, mysticism and a wide variety of other topics.

Rabbi Steinsaltz reached the podium, looked out at his audience, and said, "*Kabbalah* is the official theology of the Jewish people. As rabbis, if you are not studying *kabbalah*, if you are not teaching it to your students and your congregations, you are not doing your job."

He then repeated, "*Kabbalah* is the official theology of the Jewish people."

When I was a teenager, I went to the local public library and systematically read just about every book in 296 of the Dewey Decimal System. Tht is the place where books on Judaism are catalogued. I never encountered a book that spoke of *kabbalah* as official Jewish

Steinsaltz, as well as other *Kabbalists*, fail to explain how they know that this esoteric "Torah" is indeed Torah, the word of God, and they do not demonstrate on the basis of citation why this "word of God" should be binding or "official." Is he suggesting that the Torah of Moses and the Talmud of Babylon are so deficient that a new revelation must be discovered in order to demonstrate the inner secrets of Torah?

בהעלתך את הנרת אל מול

theology. On the contrary, *kabbalah* was hardly mentioned, and when it was, it was described as a fringe, an esoteric branch, a minority view, and frequently as a desperate invention to ease suffering.

In Hebrew school, I never encountered a single reference to *kabbalah*. In the hundreds of sermons I've heard, I never heard a single reference to *kabbalah*. I've asked scores of rabbis if they studied *kabbalah* in their rabbinical schools and have never received a positive answer. And yet Rabbi Steinsaltz, with absolute confidence, insisted, "*Kabbalah* is the official theology of the Jewish people."

In his lecture to the New York Board of Rabbis, Rabbi Steinsaltz did not just leave his audience with this provocative statement. He went on to explain his statement, pointing out, for example, that one need only look at the *Code of Jewish Law* and see that on each and every page

there are *kabbalistic* references to every halakhah that is presented. He then went on, showing his rabbinic audience that the very heart and soul of Jewish thought is being profoundly neglected. Is it any wonder that we are losing our young people when we see that the part of Jewish tradition that deals with the basic questions of life's meaning, namely kabbalah, is neglected or ignored by the vast majority of American rabbis?

This week's Torah portion begins, "GOD SPOKE WITH MOSES, TELLING HIM TO SPEAK TO AARON AND SAY TO HIM, 'WHEN YOU LIGHT THE LAMPS, THE SEVEN LAMPS SHALL ILLUMINATE THE MENORAH.'" [Num. 8.1–2] Who has not learned about the menorah? We see reproductions of it in local synagogues, it is used frequently in Jewish art, and is surely one of the most familiar of Jewish symbols. Yet, while thousands of Jews look at representations of menorot in their houses of worship every week, surely few

Synopsis: Our parashah continues with details concerning lighting the menorah and the purification of the Levites so they can perform the duties assigned to them as standing in place of the first-born of all the Israelites. The first celebration of Passover in the desert is described and followed by the second Passover for those who were unclean at the time of the first. God's signs, the cloud and the fire, lead the people during the day and at night. Two trumpets (hatzotzrot) are sounded to gather the Israelite camp—for marching and (later) on sacred occasions. The march begins and Moses seeks assistance from his father-in-law, Hovav. The complaints at Taveirah (on the journey), and Kivrot ha-ta'avah (food), Moses' complaint to God and God's response (70 leaders and food) portray an all-too-common pattern. The parashah concludes with the famous incident about healing that concerns Aaron, Miriam and Moses.

Even if it could be demonstrated that R. Shimon is indeed the *tanna* who is also the author of the Zohar, he remains an individual *tanna* whose views, per se, are not binding. Only the recorded decision of the majority of the court which has been handed down and accepted by all Israel continuously from the time of Moses to the Mishnah to the Geonim of Babylon [this is the real meaning of Kabbalah/tradition according to

Maimonides] is normative. When R. Eliezer b. Hyrcanus claimed that God was on his side of the argument, and actually produced an oracle from the Almighty to affirm this contention [*Bava Metzia* 59b], his argument, as well as his very presence, was rejected. It would be sacrilegious to impute a similar sin to R. Shimon. The Mishnah [*Hagiga* 2] teaches that issues of creation, revelation, and sexuality must be taught privately,

appropriately, discreetly and responsibly. **Rabbi Alan J. Yuter, Congregation Israel, Springfield, NJ**

Be-Ha'alotekha

know that for the last several centuries, if not longer, the menorah has been seen as a basic symbol of *kabbalah*.

Recently I ended a ten-year period of living among the ḥasidim of Brooklyn. The prayerbook we used each day begins with a meditation of basic vocabulary of *kabbalah*. I suggest that you take a look at the *Artscroll Siddur*, specifically the edition called "*nusaḥ sefarad*" (which is the style of praying common among ḥasidim and many others). In this meditation, we are asked to contemplate the ten *sefirot*.

I suspect that the local rabbi in most communities in the United States has never studied these ten *sefirot* in depth and probably could not name them all. Yet, in the prayerbook that so many of our ancestors have used for centuries, the very first prayer asks us to meditate on them.

In *The Thirteen Petalled Rose*, his 180-page introduction to essential concepts in Jewish thought, Rabbi Steinsaltz spends the better part of two chapters (out of ten) describing and discussing the ten *sefirot*. How startling it is to realize that while the average American Jew has never even heard of the ten *sefirot*, Rabbi Steinsaltz finds them important enough to include them in his rather brief book containing Judaism's essences!

The ten *sefirot* are considered to be the basic, fundamental elements that make up the world. When our tradition speaks of the ten utter-ances of God resulting in Creation, it is referring to the ten *sefirot*. Our ancestors have meditated on them and written about them, and they are a key to one's understanding of how the world itself functions. Our sages teach that just as the world is continually sustained by the flow of divine plenty as manifested by the ten *sefirot*, so, too, are we as individuals made up of the ten *sefirot*, which, Rabbi Steinsaltz says, "constitute a fundamental and all-inclusive reality."

The term *Habad* has become increasingly known in the Jewish world by its use among the Lubavitcher Ḥasidim. In fact, Lubavitch Ḥasidism is often referred to as *Habad* Ḥasidism. The term *Habad* is actually an acronym for the first three *sefirot*, חָכְמָה *Hokhmah* (wisdom), בִּינָה *Binah* (understanding) and דַּעַת *Da'at* (knowledge). These three *sefirot* are considered to be the basic elements of human consciousness. The remaining seven *sefirot*, known as the *sefirot* that actually impact on the physical world of human experi-ence, correspond symbolically to the seven branches of the menorah. When our learned ancestors looked at the menorah and considered its structure, they kept the seven *sefirot* in mind. This understanding of the menorah has been documented in great works of Jewish thought for several centuries.

Many of us ask the questions: who am I? Where am I going? Where have I come from? What for? Why? Many of us find that these questions challenge us each and every day. We find that the pursuit of these questions is at the heart of our lives. And yet, many of us are troubled by the fact that the Jewish pursuit of these questions has, for too long, been distorted or ignored.

My good friend and noted author and educator, Gary Eisenberg, as a result of the intensive investigations he has done regarding religious cults, quickly verifies that a disproportionate number of young Jews join these groups. These spiritually sensitive Jews, hungry for guidance and learning about the purpose and meaning of life, find little spiritual nourishment in their local synagogues. This it is not surprising, for nobody bothered to tell these young people that the seven-branched candelabrum that is flickering with the fancy electric light bulbs at the front of the sanctuary is actually a *kabbalistic* symbol that represents the Jewish cosmology of the universe.

Another spiritual notion that Rabbi Adin Steinsaltz teaches as a basic and fundamental idea of Jewish theology is reincarnation. Ask the local rabbi if Judaism teaches a belief in reincarnation and you will probably be told that it does not, or at best that some people might have written about it but that it is not "mainstream." Yet it is not only Rabbi Steinsaltz who discusses reincarnation as a part of the core of Jewish theology. Two examples will be sufficient:

When we learn about the *Code of Jewish Law*, the *Shulḥan Arukh*, we are told that this authoritative work was written by Rabbi Joseph Caro.

The impression one gets from the secondary sources is that this code and its author were preoccupied with the do's and don'ts of Jewish tradition. If you say the name "Joseph Caro," the immediate association for so many Jews is that he is the author of the dry, legal *Code of Jewish Law*. How many Hebrew school students who get turned off by this are aware that the same Joseph Caro who compiled the *Code of Jewish Law* was also a mystic who believed in reincarnation, who wrote about it, and who had a fascinating variety of personal mystical experiences?

The second example is this: when American Jews attend their houses of worship on Friday evening they chant the words to *Lekha Dodi*. Yet, how many of us know that its author was a mystic who also believed in reincarnation and who wrote that he witnessed Rabbi Joseph Caro serve as a "channeller," creating manuscripts through "automatic writing"?

For many reasons (which Rabbi Steinsaltz discussed in his talk to the New York Board of Rabbis, and which it would be well worth the effort to more fully understand), the mystical and spiritual aspects of Jewish tradition have been hidden away. Local rabbis are quick to quote the statement that one must not study *Kabbalah* until age forty. As Rabbi Steinsaltz points out, the greatest *Kabbalist*, Rabbi Yitzḥak Luria, died before he even reached forty! In my ten years among the ḥasidim, I saw *kabbalah* taught every day to all ages.

Kabbalah is an essential part of Jewish thought. It is the official theology of the Jewish people.

Rabbi Steinsaltz has a motto: "Let my people know." It is long overdue that those of us who are hungry for spiritual nourishment find out about our tradition for ourselves. No longer will I trust the books that people write "about" Judaism. As Rabbi Steinsaltz teaches, "Don't take someone else's word for it; go to the sources yourself; find out what they say; find out for yourself."

When Jewish families gather together for Shabbat dinner on Friday evening, the Kiddush is recited. Yet so few people who participate, week after week, in the Kiddush ritual know that each detail of it is rich with *kabbalistic* imagery and symbolism.

May the light of the menorah stand as a symbol for all of us to uncover our tradition and revive the very ideas and visions that have sustained our ancestors for centuries.●

Professor Shulamith Reich Elster

SHULAMITH REICH ELSTER IS AN ASSOCIATE PROFESSOR OF JEWISH EDUCATION AT BALTIMORE HEBREW UNIVERSITY.

Be-Ha'alotekha

1.

WHEN THE ARK WAS TO SET OUT, MOSES WOULD SAY:

ADVANCE, O LORD!

MAY YOUR ENEMIES BE SCATTERED,

AND MAY YOUR FOES FLEE BEFORE YOU!

AND WHEN IT HALTED, HE WOULD SAY:

RETURN, O LORD,

UNTO THE TEN THOUSANDS OF THE FAMILIES OF ISRAEL! [Numbers 10.35-36].

In the Torah and in printed texts these familiar verses are set between the נוּנִים חֲפוּכִים *nunim hafukhim*: the two inverted letters נ *nun*. According to the Rabbis—with their eighty-five letters—the group of verses is sufficient in number to be considered sacred text in itself.

Rabbi Judah ha-Nasi referred to them as סֵפֶר בִּפְנֵי עַצְמוֹ *Sefer Bifnei Atzmo*: a book unto itself.

It has been suggested that they (in themselves) are one of the seven books of the Torah!

The Song of the Ark may seem out of place at this point in the text—between the order of march, Moses' conversation with his relative, Hovev, and the people's fond recollections of life in Egypt! Some suggest that this is why the verses are set apart by the inverted *nunim*. Others add that they are placed there to elaborate the marching and resting themes of the two prior verses:

2.

THEY MARCHED FROM THE MOUNTAIN OF THE LORD...

THE ARK TRAVELED IN FRONT OF THEM...

TO SEEK OUT A RESTING PLACING FOR THEM.... [Num. 10.33]

In a traditional view, the verses suggest the special relationship between God and Man. The *nunim* represent נֵר הַשֵּׁם *ner ha-Shem* and נִשְׁמַת אָדָם *nishmat Adam*—the light of God and the soul of Man.

It may well be that the *nunim* are simply a form of punctuation not unlike the small dots that appear over a text. Perhaps they are inverted to avoid confusion with a letter of the *alef-bet* within the text.

2540When the Ark rested the people rested. Israel could not march alone "into battle." This same Ark was to guide Israel through the Wilderness, lead them across the Jordan, encircle Jericho and, as God Himself, frighten the Philistines: their God has come into our camp! The Ark and God were one and the same.

The verses we recite during the Torah service—among them those that rest between the *nunim*—are not about Torah; they are about God and specifically His majesty, power and glory. And they curiously refer to His enemies and foes! *Can God really have enemies? Who/what are the enemies of our God?*

3.

Commenting on the עַם סְגֻלָּה *am segullah*, Israel's special relationship with God, the Rabbis comment: anyone who hates Israel is as though they were enemies of God. [*Sifre 22b*]. "Those who uphold God's world are *ohavei Adonai* and those who seek to destroy it are *sonei Adonai*...."

Perhaps when we model God-like qualities we are אֹהֲבֵי ה' *ohavei Adonai*. When we do not measure up, while we may not 'hate' God or consider ourselves 'enemies,' we may well be שֹׂנְאֵי ה' *sonei Adonai*. We are only human and often ambivalent as we march through our lives and encounter our friends and our loves and our struggles and our foes. God, Himself, exhibited this ambivalence on more than one occasion.

God does have enemies today! And in some ways they may be like those enemies of old...the violent, the false, the hypocrite, the bigoted, the destroyers of His World.

Does the Ark still travel with us today? The route of the Torah is not always the most direct or the most comfortable. But the text suggests that it is Moses who determines the comings and going of God.

4.

"WHEN THE ARK WAS SET OUT, MOSES WOULD SAY...ADVANCE!... REST!...." [Numbers 10.35-36] suggesting, again, a unique relationship between God and man.

Could it be that those who journey with the Ark can call to God:
קוּמָה יהוה *Kuma, Adonai!*...
שׁוּבָה יהוה *Shuvah, Adonai!* and expect that He will march with us on our side? ●

Ira J. Wise

IRA J. WISE, R.J.E. IS THE DIRECTOR OF EDUCATION-ELECT OF CONGREGATION B'NAI ISRAEL IN BRIDGEPORT, CT. HE HAS EARNED A MASTER OF ARTS IN JEWISH EDUCATION FROM THE RHEA SCHOOL OF EDUCATION OF THE HUC-JIR. HE IS THE AUTHOR OF SEVERAL TEXTS INCLUDING *I CAN LEARN TORAH* AND *BETMAN'S BOOK OF HEBREW LETTERS*, BOTH PUBLISHED BY TORAH AURA PRODUCTIONS.

Be-Ha'alotekha

Among other things, the parashah this week tells us about the method by which the people made and broke camp during their forty years of wandering after Sinai. It seems that on the day that the מִשְׁכָּן Mishkan tabernacle was erected a cloud covered it by day, and in the evening the cloud turned to fire. When it was time to break camp and move on, the cloud would lift up from the tent. When it settled back down, it was time to make camp. Numbers 9.23 tells us

עַל-פִּי ה' יַחֲנוּ
וְעַל-פִּי ה' יִסָּעוּ

Al pi Adonai yaḥanu v'al pi Adonai yi'sau, "ACCORDING TO GOD'S WORD THEY RESTED AND ACCORDING TO GOD'S WORD THEY TRAVELED."

It was no doubt both disturbing and comforting for the generation of the Exodus to have this cloud of smoke and fire in their midst. On the one hand, they were cut off from everything they ever knew during their life in Egypt. Some commentators say that the time for the Exodus came when the people no longer complained about their slavery—they had grown used to it. Separated from all that was familiar, it must have given them some sense of security that their God—who, after all, had brought plagues upon Egypt, parted the Sea of Reeds and been revealed at Sinai—was visibly in their midst, dwelling among them. It must have given, on one level, a feeling of security, knowing always that the Shekhinah—the Divine Presence—was always in their camp. Sure, Moses was good, but hey, we're talking about God.

How often has one of our students (or one of us) agonized over a sense of detachment from the Divine? Demanded and not received proof of God's presence among us? Felt a need to know to a certainty that God's end of the covenant was kept? It would be most reassuring to have such a cloud, acting like a parent's steadying hand on our shoulder, just saying "I am here." It would be nice not to always rely on faith. It would also make it much easier to help our students connect with and talk about God.

On the other hand, consider how frightening the cloud and fire must have been for them. They have left Egyptian bondage following ten horrible plagues, witnessed the drowning of the Egyptians in the Sea of Reeds, attended the giving of Torah and the destruction of the Golden Calf. It's possible that not everyone remained comfortable in the presence of The Presence. The Gold Calf episode didn't turn out for the best for those directly involved. Nadav and Avihu didn't do so well with their experiment in personal initiative. At the end of this parashah, Miriam (and some contend Aaron) is punished for criticizing Moses and claiming a stake in leadership. For some, having a flaming reminder of God's presence might bring about the fear of Big Brother, of having someone looking over your shoulder all the time. In spite of this, Korah and his followers rebel two *parashot* later, and come to a sudden and final end, as did Nadav and Avihu.

How often have our students told us that they are tired of being told what to do? How many leave formal Jewish education after their Bar or Bat Mitzvah because they do not feel their needs are being met, but rather, that they are forced to learn based on some narrow "adult" agenda rooted in tradition? How often do we, as teachers and educators, feel that we are being micromanaged by administrators, lay people and parents of our students? Perhaps having the cloud in our midst would be more

unsettling than comforting—a God who is visibly present is much more demanding than the concept rooted in our faith.

What do we, as teachers, take from this parashah? I think at least three things: (1) If we can see the cloud/fire, it is our sacred task to help our students and ourselves perceive God's presence. We may do this best by talking and singing about God, by providing experiences and ways in which to reflect about the Divine. At a Jewish summer camp some of us have attended, there is a climbing tower. A rope attached to a harness at the climber's waist is gradually drawn in, not supporting the climber, but ready to belay her fall—should she slip, it will save her. We must create more experiences like this. (2) The cloud/fire is there if we will but see it. I believe that the clues we need to tell us when to move forward and when to make camp are all around us if we are willing to see them. I mean that, in terms of the classroom—knowing when the students need to review something one more time, and when that review will be counterproductive. If a spark of the Divine is indeed in each of us, then we should be able to take our cues in part from our students. (3) We must remember that the Divine presence can be both comforting and unsettling, and that both of these feelings are important. It is good to be comforted, but we must beware of complacency. Our students won't stand for it, and neither should we. Being agitated can be disturbing and

troubling, but it can also keep us fresh, challenge us to reach new understandings. Change is good, especially if it leads to growth. Change merely for the sake of change is merely unsettling.•

Not "If" but "How"

**Shela<u>h</u>
Lekha**

**Numbers
13.1–15.41**

**Rabbi
Eliezer
Diamond**

ELEIZER DIAMOND IS ASSISTANT
PROFESSOR OF TALMUD AND
RABBINICS AT THE JEWISH
THEOLOGICAL SEMINARY OF
AMERICA. HE IS CURRENTLY
COMPLETING A BOOK ON FASTING
AND ASCETICISM IN THE RABBINIC
PERIOD.

As a child I always felt a great deal of indignant sympathy for the scouts sent by Moses to reconnoiter the land of Canaan. God's anger at them seemed to me to be indefensible. Here were ten who carried out their assigned task (as did the other two spies, Caleb and Joshua, but in a different way). They travelled the length and breadth of the land and gave their honest assessment of the possibilities of conquering it.

דָּבָר אַחֵר **DAVAR A<u>H</u>ER. "SEND FORTH MEN FROM YOURSELF, AND LET THEM SPY (SCOUT) OUT THE LAND OF CANAAN" [Num. 13.2].** Most people think the Torah is just a boring, bland, codex or book of statutes, telling us how to run our lives. But it's more. It's a story. A good one at that, especially my Torah portion *Shelah Lekha*, in the book of Numbers. It has all the makings of a

It so happens that their assessment was pessimistic. So what? If there was a "canned," preordained report with which the spies were supposed to return, why bother sending them in the first place?

In Deuteronomy, Moses justifies the terrible fate suffered by the spies and their generation—forty years of wandering in the desert without ever reaching Canaan—by claiming that his sending of spies was not in fulfillment of a divine imperative but rather a response to the *vox populi*. By their very request for spies, according to this view, the people insured disaster. This account is difficult, if not impossible, to reconcile with the account in Numbers, which begins with God's explicit command to Moses to dispatch scouts.

Our sages, as usual, strive mightily to square the circle. The שְׁלַח-לְךָ *Shela<u>h</u> lekha* of Numbers 13.2, they suggest, is not a command but a Divine concession to the popular

great Hollywood picture. It includes: spies, adventure, deceit, death, threats, blackmail and repentance.... As the camera pans the vast desert that the Israelites have covered in the two years since fleeing Egypt, it focuses on the Israelites as they are preparing to enter the Promised Land. It zooms in on Moses sending out twelve spies, one from each tribe, to scout out the inhabited land

demand for spies conveyed to God by Moses. The word לְךָ, lekha, rather than simply being a stylistic reflexive (see Nahmanides on Genesis 12.1), is understood as disassociating God from the mission of the spies. שְׁלַח-לְךָ Shelah lekha, they argue, is to be translated: "SEND THEM FOR YOURSELF" or "SEND THEM IF YOU WISH" or, in idiomatic English, "Suit yourself." "It's up to you," says God to Moses, "whether or not to send spies; as for me," says God, "I wash my hands of the whole business."

This rabbinic solution is ingenious but hardly convincing. Are we to understand, for example, when God says to Abraham לֶךְ-לְךָ Lekh lekha mei'artz'kha, "GO FORTH FROM YOUR LAND" [Gen. 12.1], that God is not commanding but merely suggesting? Hardly likely—though we American Jews seem to read the verse that way. Moreover, even if we were to accept the Rabbinic interpretation, we are left with a

second problem. In this retelling of the episode of the spies, Moses recalls that he considered it a good idea to send scouts [Deut. 1.23]. If this plan of action was so reprehensible that those who executed it brought down God's wrath upon themselves and their entire generation, is not Moses' acquiescence blameworthy as well?

A compelling solution to our difficulties is proposed by Nahmanides, a thirteenth-century Spanish exegete. He dismisses the notion that sending spies at this stage of the Israelite journey was an inherently evil or faithless act. Moses subsequently sends spies [Num. 21.32] as does Joshua [Joshua 2.1]. Even when in the presence of God it is wrong to depend upon miracles; the Israelites had to plan military strategy like any other nation. The request for scouts, then, was reasonable, even appropriate. Wherein lay the sin?

The spies did not carry out the mission they were assigned. For Moses,

Synopsis: Under the leadership of Joshua and Caleb, the expedition into Canaan opens our parashah. The scouts return with a detailed, accurate description, but give a negative recommendation. Only Joshua and Caleb dissent. The people cry out against Moses—God responds. Moses argues for the lives of the people, and God relents but will not permit this generation to enter the land. A final chapter of miscellaneous laws ending with tzitzit concludes this week's reading.

in order to conquer it. Upon the return of the twelve spies, ten are cowards and speak ill of the land out of fear of not being able to conquer it. Only two spies, Joshua and Caleb, who trust in God, tell the truth, trying to convince the Israelites to conquer it. Outnumbered, Joshua and Caleb are not able to persuade them to have faith in God's promise and to take the land. The people are con-

vinced that they would have been better off staying in Egypt as slaves.

Cut to God, who is infuriated by their unfaithfulness, and would have killed the Israelites immediately if Moses had not then interceded and informed God that He would get a lot of bad press by doing so. God is apparently swayed by this argument and decides not to destroy them all,

but to keep them in the desert another thirty-eight years, making it a total of forty years, one for each day the spies were in Israel. By doing this, no one over the age of twenty years at that time would enter Israel...guaranteeing a sequel with the next generation called, *Shelah Lekha Two—The Next Generation.*

The foolish Israelites, seeing their imminent doom in the desert, rise up

it was a foregone conclusion that Israel would conquer the Canaanites. Had not God promised that they would? The role of the spies was merely to determine how that might best be done. The spies, however, did not understand their role in that fashion. They viewed the ability of the Israelite armies to prevail as an open question. They saw themselves engaged in a feasibility study: would it be possible to defeat the Canaanites or not? In short, the mandate the spies received from Moses was to determine *how* to conquer the land; the mandate as they willfully misunderstood it became seeing *if* the land could be conquered.

We should realize that the sin of the spies goes far beyond the distortion of Moses' directive. There is all the difference in the world between believing that something can be done and then seeking ways to do it, and, on the other hand, having grave doubts as to whether an objective can be achieved and,

therefore, feeling the need to allay one's uncertainty. The truth is, as our sages taught, "Everything is in the hand of heaven other than the fear of heaven." No project can be successful unless God wills it so; on the other hand, even the most unlikely endeavor can prosper with divine assistance. What Moses asked of the scouts and of the people was to trust in the divine promise of success, and to be partners in that promise by doing whatever was humanly possible to bring it to fruition. The spies, however, were determined to take destiny into their own hands. They, not God, would determine if this enterprise were possible. Of course, once God was left out of the equation, conquering the powerful Canaanite nations seemed—and was—an insurmountable challenge.

The distinction between "how" and "if,' between the engaged behavior of belief and the static questioning of the agnostic is crucial to how we live our daily lives. When we see our-

Shelah Lekha

and wish to go into Israel, but they had already insulted God and were prohibited. However, the people are reassured that their descendants will eventually enter the Promised Land. God tells the Israelites to wear fringes in the corners of their garments to remind them to lead holy lives and abide by the commandments. Of course, just as every Hollywood film must have its gratuitous violence, my portion tells of the gruesome fate of a man who

decided to flagrantly violate the laws of God by collecting sticks and working on the Sabbath...he was stoned to death. The Torah doesn't report any further violations of *that* commandment!

In every good film, there is meaning beneath the surface of the story. If we go back and relook at the story closely, we begin to see that it's a little more complex than we first imagined. Take, for example, in scene one with the spies, it is writ-

selves as God's earthly messengers, entrusted with the mission of leading a life of Torah, we need not ask ourselves constantly whether our goals are feasible. They are God's will, and we carry them out to the best of our ability. The ultimate degree of our success is not in our hands but in God's. If we demand assurances of success before we commit ourselves to a project, we have doomed ourselves to failure. When we risk nothing, when we have no faith, we achieve nothing.

This notion is powerfully reinforced at the end of our *parashah*, which commands us to wear *tzitzit*. In Numbers 15.39 we read: "LOOK AT [the *tzitzit*] AND RECALL ALL THE COMMANDMENTS OF THE LORD AND OBSERVE THEM, SO THAT YOU DO NOT FOLLOW YOUR HEART AND YOUR EYES IN LUSTFUL URGE." The Torah's word for "FOLLOW" is תָּתֻרוּ *ta'turu*, derived from the same root, [תוּר] *tur* as the word וְיָתֻרוּ *v'ya'turu*, which is used in Numbers 13.2 to delineate the mission of the spies. Rashi strengthens this connection when he comments: "The heart and the eyes are the body's spies." In short, we,

like the spies, are engaged constantly in scouting out the terrain around us, be it physical, emotional, psychological or spiritual. Like the spies of the desert we, too, run the risk of misunderstanding our mission. It is all too easy for us to use our eyes and hearts to find seemingly insurmountable barriers to the fulfillment of the divine will. The צִיצָת *tzitzit* is a reminder of God's eternal presence through God's Torah. Our mission's directives are to be found there; we need never fear failure so long as we are engaged in their fulfillment.●

---

ten: "And the Lord spoke unto Moses, saying: 'Send thy men, that they spy out the land of Canaan, which I give unto the children of Israel....'" Now one may ask, why would God tell Moses to send spies? He knows what's to be found there!

What's He up to? Perhaps He was fed up with the people's murmurings. God knows it is time for the people to start to take responsibility for their own lives. They have to feel that they are part of the decision. If the spies came back with reports of a "LAND OF MILK AND HONEY," the people will be anxious to get there and finally stop their annoying complaining. Perhaps God knew that their lack of faith in Him was a sign of their own spiritual immaturity. By forcing them to take some responsibility, some of their skepticism of Him would be washed away and they would finally have more trust in Him.

The movie doesn't make clear whether or not God did know that the spies would return and spread evil

reports, or if He did, at which point God knew it. In any case, it seems that God gave the spies and people free will. He could have struck them with lightning or closed their mouths, but He didn't. Having given them free will, God has to let them do as they would, and suffer the consequences.

But maybe there is another explanation. This movie, not unexpectedly, has something of a surreal twist. The same story is told again later in the Torah, but with just enough of a difference to suggest a completely different meaning. Perhaps God didn't actually tell Moses to send the spies. Rather, Moses sent them in response to the people's pleas. In Deuteronomy I, verse 22, when Moses retells the story to the new generation, which is on the verge of entering Canaan, he says, "AND YE CAME NEAR UNTO ME EVERY ONE OF YOU AND SAID: 'LET US SEND MEN BEFORE US THAT THEY MAY SEARCH THE LAND FOR US AND BRING US BACK WORD OF THE WAY BY WHICH WE MUST GO UP AND THE CITIES UNTO WHICH

WE SHALL COME.'" According to the version in Deuteronomy, you can see that it was not God, but the people themselves who requested the spies or scouts.

Spies or Scouts—that seems to be an essential question. Which was it? What does the word מְרַגֵּל *meragel* actually mean? Spy or scout? And what does the word לָתוּר *latur* mean, "to scout around" or to "spy" in our modern sense of the word? In other words, had they the bellicose intentions implied by the use of the word spies, or were they merely curious about what the land held for them?

The answer to this question would reveal their attitude toward God. If they sent spies, it would indicate their intentions of accepting God's word and taking the land promised to them. However, if they sent scouts, it would show mistrust of God's promise by doubting the worth of the land, and thereby insulting Him. In other words, in the Deuteronomic version, did they send

Rabbi Laura Geller

RABBI LAURA GELLER SERVES AS THE SENIOR RABBI OF TEMPLE EMANUEL IN BEVERLY HILLS, CALIFORNIA. BEFORE TEMPLE EMANUEL, SHE SERVED AS THE EXECUTIVE DIRECTOR OF AMERICAN JEWISH CONGRESS, PACIFIC SOUTHWEST REGION, AND AS HILLEL DIRECTOR AT THE UNIVERSITY OF SOUTHERN CALIFORNIA.

Shela<u>h</u> Lekha

This parashah has particular significance for me—it is the one my firstborn will read when he is called for his bar mitzvah. I've heard many parents speak to their children on the occasion of their becoming *b'nai mitzvah*. Some parents review the child's entire history, all of his or her accomplishments, sports triumphs, scholastic achievements. Other parents talk about themselves, how much they sacrificed to bring this child to this moment.

Sometimes parents manage to find the right balance between words of love and words of guidance. Some of the words are moving; some are not. So what should a parent say to her child at the moment when the tradition has us say: בָּרוּךְ שֶׁפְּטָרַנִי מֵעָנְשׁוֹ שֶׁלָּזֶה *Barukh Sh'petarani me-onsho shelazeh*: "Blessed is the One Who has freed me from the responsibility for this one."

Rabbi Diamond's insight into the *parashah* is the beginning of a message to the bar mitzvah. As my son stands at this important juncture in his life, he needs to ask himself not only what he can spy out in the landscape ahead, but more importantly, how he sees his mission in life.

The *Hatam Sofer* amplifies Rabbi Diamond's theme that the spies misunderstood their mission. Instead of scouting the land to breathe in its holiness, they responded to the clamor of the Israelites to find out whether the

out spies to be part of God's plan, or did they send out scouts in order to decide whether it was worth their while to be part of God's plan?

Several sages, Rashi among them, seem to believe that it was a military reconnaissance mission. I beg to differ. These people, who were so quick to believe they would have been defeated by the local inhabitants, did not seem so self-assured as ones who would have waged war on several powerful communities. They were full of fear.

You would think that God would be pretty tired of them by now. In fact, God does, indeed, continually threaten to destory them. On the surface, God comes off looking a bit like a whiner, always moaning, "How long must I suffer this evil nation?" I have learned that some commentators see this as a sophisticated psychological ploy on God's

land was fat or lean and whether one could earn a living in it. While these are not insignificant questions, if they are the only questions one asks, the life that unfolds is a life bereft of meaning.

Another teacher, Noam Elimelech, has a similar insight on verses 17 and 18: "AND MOSES SENT THEM TO SPY OUT THE LAND OF CANAAN AND SAID UNTO THEM, 'GET YOU UP THIS WAY IN THE SOUTH AND GO UP INTO THE MOUNTAIN AND SEE THE LAND, WHAT IT IS....'" For him, "AND GO UP INTO THE MOUNTAIN" means: when you reach the highest levels of wisdom, "YOU WILL SEE THE LAND WHAT IT IS" you will see that earthliness and materialism are not the most important goals.

Now, perhaps these ideas are a little heavy for a thirteen-year-old young man to understand, but in this world of theme bar mitzvah celebrations,

fancy parties and deejay's, they certainly speak to the reality of our lives.

"AND MOSES CALLED HOSHEA, THE SON OF NUN, YEHOSHUA JOSHUA." [Num.13.16] HOSHEA signifies "*He has saved*"; by adding the *yod*, a letter of the Divine Name, the name means "*God will save.*" My son is also called Joshua, so Rashi's understanding of why Moses changed the name of this biblical namesake seems relevant: "*May God save you from the plot of the spies,*" may God save you from misunderstanding your mission as the spies will misunderstand theirs.

So, to my son, Joshua, I want to say: may God save you from believing that the only important questions are about the value of things, about what you will do when you grow up, about whether you are stronger than the next guy. May God help you discover

a mission for your life, a mission that will help you breathe in the holiness that is all around you, the holiness present in the faces of other human beings and the holiness present in working to repair what is broken in the world. And may God help you go up into the mountain and reach the highest levels of wisdom, wisdom that comes from wrestling with Torah, your Torah, your inheritance.

As Joshua wraps himself for the first time in his own *tallit*, and looks for the first time at his own *tzitzit*, I hope he will be ready to trust his heart and his mind to be his faithful spies, to help him discover a holy mission. And I hope that each time he puts on his *tallit*, he will feel sheltered by the love and the pride that will envelope him as he becomes a bar mitzvah.•

---

part. God knows that His covenant with us is eternal, but He knows that Moses' patience is not. When God acts fed up, it forces Moses to come to our defense. Moses then listens to his own words, and is recommitted to leading us.

Like all great works of art, you don't expect the end. What you would expect from the beginning of the Torah portion is Moses and Joshua leading the Israelites to a great battle and overcoming their enemies. What you don't expect is bittersweet tragedy. They never get to fight. They miss their chance at retaking their ancient homeland. But God does not

cast them away. God gives that generation and all generations to come, the commandments of the tallit, to remember that it is not upon us to finish the task. The movie ends with God giving the commandment of the tallit. I imagine a great last scene, a shot panning hundreds of thousands of Israelites, all putting on their tallitot for the first time as the crimson sun sinks below the horizon and the music reaches its poignant climax.

They are sad that their lives did not turn out the way that they had thought they would. But now they have the holy task of raising a new generation which will complete their

unfinished work. Perhaps they realize that they can create the potential for a holiness greater than they had ever imagined. **Yoni Pressman, Ohr ha-Torah, Los Angeles, CA– His Bar Mitzvah Drash, June 24, 1995**

דָּבָר אַחֵר **DAVAR AHER. MOSES SENT THEM FORTH FROM THE WILDERNESS OF PARAN AT GOD'S COMMAND; THEY WERE ALL DISTINGUISHED MEN; HEADS OF THE CHILDREN OF ISRAEL [Num. 13.3].** What God says to Moses is crucial to our understanding of the sequence of events that are about to unfold through the language of the narrative text. God instructed Moses to send the נְשִׂיאִים *nesi'im* (the princes) of each tribe that

Shelah
Lekha

are named specifically in the opening verses to *Bemidbar*, the Book of Numbers. If we look at the actions of Moses immediately following God's instructions to him, we discover that Moses sent רָאשֵׁי בְּנֵי-יִשְׂרָאֵל *"rashei B'nei-Yisrael"* (the leaders of children of Israel). This list of names, which can be found in this week's *parashah,* is indeed a different list of characters. (Compare the differences between Numbers 13.2 and 13.3.)

The major differences between these two parties of men are their distinct roles in the communal life of the twelve tribes as they wandered in the *midbar.* The title *Nesi'im* appears in the *Tanakh* many times, and refers to those leaders from the children of Israel who were given administrative functions within the inner circle of the Tabernacle. They were concerned with priestly functions and their authority was not to be undermined as we are told in Exodus 22.27: "Do not revile Elohim, nor should you curse the נָשִׂיא *NASI* (prince) of the nation." Each was endowed with the greater responsibility of providing leadership and direction for the entire community of Israel. Like the senators of the American judicial system, Moses called upon this group of individuals to look beyond their individual constituant tribes to resolve the problems of the Israelites in their present journey.

In contrast, the רָאשֵׁי בְּנֵי-יִשְׂרָאֵל *rashei B'nei-Yisrael* (heads of the individual tribes) were more concerned with lobbying explicitly for the individual needs of their own tribes. They were charged with the role of military advisors, to help Moses with the vital need to provide protection from Israel's enemies as they moved from one location to another. Moses was well aware of their physical strengths and their mental weaknesses in governing the people of the fledgling nation.

These military leaders are not the ones that God instructed Moses to send into the land of Israel to spy out the territory. God asked that Moses send men of broad vision and intelligence. God needed leaders who would be able to "lift up," *Nesi'im\Nasa,* the spirits of the people with a positive scouting report. Because of their intimacy with God, these men would be in a position to report to the Israelite leadership and the people a vision that would take into consideration God's promise to help the Israelites in their attempt to conquer the land.

When Moses selected the military chiefs to assess the territory, he chose to send men with a completely different agenda. He sent men whose eyes were blind to everything except the military strength of the present occupants of the land. That is why they reported to the people that they were like grasshoppers in comparison to them. They lacked the faith and understanding that was required by God to continue into the promised land.

As Commander-in-Chief, did Moses make a tactical error by deliberately sending the "military" leaders in place of the "priestly" leaders? Or, did Moses truly misunderstand God's directions? Perhaps Moses doubted God's words and he sent what he thought God meant to send, without realizing the greater implications of this "mistake" in judgement. Moses may have meant well. However, he, too, was subject to the same fate as the rest of the Israelite nation which was doomed to wander in the "*Midbar*" until they died. One of the lessons that I have drawn from this series of events is that God remains a mystery to humanity. We have not been placed on this earth to question God's motivation, but to understand the depth of God's wisdom by observing God's word—without embellishment. **Steven J. Rubenstein <RABBIOLI@aol.com>**

דָּבָר אַחֵר **DAVAR AHER. MOSES SENT THEM TO SPY OUT THE LAND OF CANAAN [Num. 13. 17].** There are some commentators who explain that the purpose of Moses sending the twelve spies to Canaan was not to assess the military might of the Canaanites nor to lay the foundations for a military campaign against them, because God promised that Israel was the land that He was giving to them.

Then what was the reason for their exploring the land? Could the meaning of the English word "*tour*" be related to the Hebrew word [תור] "*tur*" as in לָתוּר אֶת הָאָרֶץ "*la-tur et ha-aretz*"? The word "*tour*" in English denotes traveling around the country to become familiar with the people, the land and the various sites. Is that not what God commanded Moses to do? He sent forth twelve men "*latur et ha-aretz*" to become familiar with the conditions of the land, with the customs of the people, with the cities and towns. Moses wanted to know whether the land was fertile and productive; whether the people were friendly or hostile; whether the cities and towns were well-built and had the proper water supplies.

Did the English word "*tour*" have its origin in the Hebrew word "*la-tur*?" **Rabbi Jacob Friedman, Temple Beth Torah, Ocean, NJ**

דָּבָר אַחֵר **DAVAR AHER. ADONAI SAID TO MOSES: "HOW MUCH LONGER IS THIS PEOPLE GOING TO GET ME P.O.ed?" [Num. 14.11].** This weekend I will speak at the Confirmation of Kent, Danny, Ben, Davida, Erika, David, Andy, B.J., and Brett. These are my "faux children," the former twelve-year-olds who terrorized me four years ago when I returned to the classroom to be the Jewish Tracy Kidder—their seventh grade Hebrew School teacher. Then they wouldn't go away. This is the message I will share with them, and this is the message of this week's *sidrah*. God gets angry. God hides. God cries. God remembers. God comes back. And God starts again. Not only are we supposed to be a lot like God, but, surprisingly, God is a lot like us.

This week, God has Moses send the spies into *Eretz Yisrael* to scout out the farm teams. They come back in need of the Torah of *The Little Engine That Could*. At that, God gets mad. ADONAI SAID TO MOSES: "HOW MUCH LONGER IS THIS PEOPLE GOING TO GET ME P.O.ed?" [Num. 14.11] When my kids graduated from their last year of Hebrew school, there was a service and a party. I was all set to be thanked. I—after all the games and crap, after all the patience I had shown—expected kind words. Instead, when Kent and Ben came up to make a presentation from the class, they smashed a piece of chocolate cake in my face. "HOW MUCH LONGER WON'T THEY TRUST ME DESPITE ALL THE SIGNS THAT I HAVE PERFORMED IN THEIR MIDST?" [Num. 14.11] I went home crying. While I knew it was some kind of adolescent "bonding" thing, I needed more. My heart was broken. I understood. Understanding didn't help. I felt like God. I needed the kind word. I needed to know that some of my suffering and effort had accomplished something. The families vanished immediately. They were too embarrassed to talk to me. The rabbi and the educator went into action, punishing the offenders, defending my honor, not ministering to my feelings. They were ready to kill; I was left alone. I had cake on my face. Everyone was saying: "I WILL KILL THEM WITH A PLAGUE, WIPE THEM OUT AND YOU…." [Num. 14.12] Moses says: "Cool it God. Deja vu. We did this number at the Golden Calf. Same anger. Same threat. I know: 'I WILL MAKE YOU INTO A GREATER AND MORE POWERFUL NATION.' [Num. 14.12] But that is not what I want. That is not what You want. Let's do Your names by the numbers: (1) Adonai, (2) Slow-Anger, (3) Lotta Hesed, (4) The Sin-Forgiver, (5) The Cleaner of Souls, (6) The Not Complete Soul Cleaner, (7) The One Who Teaches Kids about their ParentsÑfor bad (and for good). PLEASE FORGIVE THIS PEOPLE'S SIN—BECAUSE YOU ARE BIG INTO HESED!" Then God says, "KEWL." Then God says, "But you've got 40 years detention." I know just how God felt. That is what I am going to say to Ben and Kent and the rest this Sunday. (That is the Torah of the Neil whose name used to be *Tzedakah*.) **Joel Lurie Grishaver <Gris@Torahaura.Com>**

Korah

**Numbers
16.1–18.32**

Professor
Everett Fox

EVERETT FOX IS ASSOCIATE
PROFESSOR OF JUDAICA AND
DIRECTOR OF THE PROGRAM IN
JEWISH STUDIES AT CLARK
UNIVERSITY. HE IS THE AUTHOR OF
*THE SCHOCKEN BIBLE: VOLUME 1:
THE FIVE BOOKS OF MOSES,* A NEW
TRANSLATION/COMMENTARY ON THE
TORAH PUBLISHED BY SCHOCKEN
BOOKS.

n the climactic banquet scene of Mozart's *Don Giovanni*, the audience is, so to speak, served the just desserts of a scoundrel. The title character, unrepentant to the last, is dragged down to Hell by the stone statue of the old commandant he had killed in the opera's opening moments. The Don's precipitous descent into the netherworld is accompanied by smoke, orchestral thunder, and a spectral choir, and is followed immediately by the finale, where the surviving characters sing a stern warning to the audience to watch their behavior, lest they suffer the same fate.

How different from this scene, which came down to Mozart's librettist filtered through medieval Christian eyes, is its remote precursor, which occurs in the climactic moment of this week's parashah. Here it is not, of course, the punishment meted out to a master seducer of women, but rather the fate of the Torah's great rebel, Korah, and his associates Datan and Aviram, that is so graphically described:

"THE GROUND THAT WAS BENEATH THEM SPLIT, THE EARTH OPENED ITS MOUTH AND SWALLOWED UP THEM AND THEIR HOUSEHOLDS, ALL THE HUMAN BEINGS THAT BELONGED TO KORAH AND ALL THE PROPERTY. SO THEY WENT DOWN, THEY AND ALL THAT BELONGED TO THEM, ALIVE, INTO SHEOL; THE EARTH COVERED THEM, AND THEY PERISHED FROM THE MIDST OF THE ASSEMBLY. NOW ALL ISRAEL THAT WERE

דָּבָר אַחֵר **DAVAR AHER.** "WHY DO YOU RAISE YOURSELF ABOVE THE CONGREGATION OF THE ETERNAL ONE?" [Num. 16.3]. The villain of this week's Torah portion, Korah, appears mean, vindictive, angry and jealous. He is peeved at Moses, and rather than discussing the problem directly with him, lashes out at him. He seems to want Moses' power. He wants a piece of the action.

He takes himself out of the community and sets himself aside the group (Rashi). He desires the prestige and authority that come with Moses' position. Unfortunately, only Moses has been appointed to lead the Jewish people by God. Korah, who had a unique role as a Levite, yelled at Moses [Num. 16.3], "WHY DO YOU RAISE YOURSELF ABOVE THE CONGREGATION OF THE ETERNAL ONE?"

AROUND THEM FLED AT THE SOUND OF THEIR VOICE, FOR THEY SAID: LEST THE EARTH SWALLOW US UP!" [NUM. 16.31-34]

In the Bible's typically brief style, the whole thing is over in four verses. Yet everything that needed to be said has been said. The men who had accused Moses of seizing political and religious power for himself have been quickly and dramatically disposed of (*Sheol* is the biblical netherworld), and the onlookers are properly unnerved.

Martin Buber once characterized the death of Korah as "sinister," and there is certainly something disturbing about this story that goes beyond the usual bounds of divine punishment. Perhaps, it is the natural human revulsion at the possibility of being buried alive (familiar in folklore and in literature such as Poe's classic tale "The Cask of Amontillado"), or the summary judgment of God, who obliterates Korah without so much as a trial, that

makes this scene so terrifying. As the fate of a biblical rebel it is quite unique, as becomes clear from looking at the deaths of other "villains" in biblical narratives.

For an anthology that is concerned with human behavior, the Bible has surprisingly few real villains in the sense that we like to think of them (e.g., Snow White's stepmother). While there is a good deal of bad behavior and punishment in the Bible, the text generally seems more concerned with gifted people and their strengths and weaknesses than with the satisfaction to be gained from seeing a true villain die.

In the Torah, Korah has only one rival for evil—the Pharaoh of the Exodus story. Interestingly, this key personality is neither named nor his death mentioned (unless one takes the drowning of the Egyptians at the Red Sea to include him, which is not clear from the text). In the

Synopsis: Rebellion led by Korah against the Tabernacle is the theme of our parashah. Together with 250 chieftains, Korah instigates a rebellion against Moses and Aaron. God threatens to destroy everyone; Moses and Aaron intercede; the rebels are punished; and the fire pans are made into a reminder. A plague breaks out and Aaron and Moses intercede successfully again. Twelve staffs are gathered and Aaron and the Levites are assigned, once again, the responsibilities of the Tabernacle. The parashah concludes with a list of all the gifts that the Levites get in return.

Korah's angry rebuke was both unfounded and ill-mannered. After all, God is the One who chose the leaders in the wilderness, and Korah, as a Levite, already had a hereditary position. God set the Levites apart from other Israelites, as Moses says, "GIVING YOU ACCESS TO GOD, TO PERFORM THE DUTIES OF THE TABERNACLE OF THE ETERNAL ONE, AND TO MINISTER TO THE COMMUNITY AND SERVE THEM."[Num. 16.9]. This is certainly a role of prestige, sacred

authority, and great standing within the community. Korah is a chieftain, a man of renown. But this was not enough for him. His jealousy overtook his rational thinking.

Sefer ha-Aggadah, quoting *Numbers Rabbah* 18.3, suggests that Korah was a man of great cunning and one of the bearers of the Ark. When Moses commanded, in the previous portion, "THAT THEY PUT WITH THE FRINGE AT EACH CORNER A THREAD OF BLUE" [Num. 15.38],

Korah ordered that 250 cloaks of blue be made, in which the 250 heads of the Sanhedrin who rose against Moses were to wrap themselves. Then Korah made a feast for them, before which they wrapped themselves in their blue cloaks. When Aaron's sons came to receive their dues of the animals slaughtered for the feast, the 250 rose against them, saying "Who told you that you are entitled to take these? Was it not

Exodus material, what seems to be more important than Pharaoh's precise fate is the judgment wrought on the gods of Egypt (himself included) via the plagues, and the liberation of the people of Israel from Egyptian servitude.

Another high-class biblical villain, this time from the former Prophets, is Jezebel, a Phoenician princess and Ahab's queen in Samaria. Since her crime, the introduction of full-scale Baal worship into Israel, is considered unspeakably monstrous by the biblical historians, her death is also appropriately so—she is thrown out of a palace window, and the dogs eat her so thoroughly that when servants are sent to bury her body, all that remains are the skull, the hands, and the feet [II Kings 9.33-35].

From the same part of the Bible, one could also mention two slightly lesser villains, the throne-grabber Avimelekh [Judges 6-9] and the rebellious prince Avshalom [II Samuel 13-19]. They each meet a somewhat unorthodox death—Avimelekh is mortally wounded by a woman who throws a heavy millstone on him from a roof, and Avshalom is caught in a tree by his luxurious hair, to be killed by his father David's servants (despite the king's express order to the contrary).

Lastly, one thinks of Haman, the archetypal Jew-hater and a stage character with no redeeming social values. Yet his death has more of a poetic justice than the gruesome detail we all crave; what is important for the writer of the book of Esther is that Haman is hanged on the same gallows (or, as some scholars would have it, impaled on the same stake) as he had planned for Mordechai.

Korah's death, then, is unique in its unearthly character. It occurs solely by divine agency, in contrast to the fate of Jezebel, Avimelech, Avshalom and Haman, who are executed by kings' servants. In addition to this, it uses a com-

Korah

Moses? We will give you nothing. *Ha-Makom*—the Holy Place said no such thing." When the priests who were thus repulsed went back and told Moses, he tried to pacify the people, but they rose against him, also.

Korah's not-so-subtle move to unite with 250 Israelites was totally inappropriate! How could Moses deal with the problem in such a large gathering? Wouldn't it have been better for Korah to pull Moses aside, talk with him about the problem, his concerns, and work it out, face-to-face, man-to-man? But this was too proper for a man with such a hot-headed temper. It was easier to discuss it apart from Moses; to gossip and slander him among the other leaders, and then confront him in a surprising way. Moses, dumbfounded, fell on his face to

pletely different means from God's usual methods of punishment, plague or fire. The image of the earth swallowing up humans alive must have been particularly ominous to the ancients. After all, the earth, even in partially demythologized Israel, still bore the connotation of a mother, or at least that of a nurturing environment, blessed with abundance by God. The long-standing Jewish practice of gently interring the dead in the grave bears testimony to the normally close bond between humans אָדָם-*adam* and the soil אֲדָמָה *adamah*. Yet in the Korah story, the earth turns into a kind of monster, opening its mouth and literally swallowing up the rebels. Indeed, a common way of depicting this moment in the story in medieval Jewish art was to portray Korah's band disappearing into the mouth of a gigantic serpent-type creature.

The wording of the biblical text gives us yet another clue to the significance of Korah's fate. תִּבְלַע *Tivla* ("swallowing") (verses 32 and 34) is

sometimes used biblically to indicate cosmic destruction. Thus, it appears in the Song at the Sea in Exodus 15.12, in conjunction with תִּבְלָעֵמוֹ אָרֶץ "underworld," just as it is used in conjunction with *Sheol* in our text. Therefore, one can say that the Korah story portrays a rebellion on an epic, not just a local, scale. Given that the story may well reflect either a political struggle as to status among priests and Levites (in one standard interpretation), and/or a family squabble (in another one, Korah was Moses' and Aaron's cousin), why has the text transformed these differences of opinion into a matter of cosmic import?

There are a number of unforgivable sins in the Torah, among them, say the Rabbis, idolatry, incest and murder. In addition, particularly in the book of Numbers, there are the unforgivable rebellions against God and against the Divine representative, Moses, which lead to the death of an entire generation. Yet nowhere more than in the Korah narrative do we

find such a frontal attack on Moses' right, not only to be leader, but also to designate (in God's name) who is "holy"—first priests, and then on a lower level, Levites. Korah's accusation against Moses, "Too much for you! Indeed, all the community, all of them, are holy, and in their midst is the Lord! Why do you exalt yourselves over the assembly of the Lord?" [Num.16.3] calls for not only a radical restructuring of leadership but also for a fundamental change in the Sinaitic concept of Israel. At the flaming mountain [Ex. 19ff.], God had told the people that they would be "a kingdom of priests and a holy nation" [19.6], but that characterization is conditional on the concept expressed in the previous verse: "If you will hearken, yes, hearken to my voice and keep my covenant…."[19.5] Everything here is predicated on the "if." In the Bible, holiness is seldom a given; things (places and objects) become holy and people become holy, the former by ceremonies and usage, and the latter by ceremonies, but also by behavior. Korah's statement, while

---

pray: for guidance, for wisdom, for understanding, and for forgiveness.

Often in our synagogue communities, people act like Korah as well. They surprise the leadership of a congregation or community with irrational arguments; they are jealous of the president or rabbi's perceived power or authority; they are jealous that others are accorded honors when they feel they are more deserving; they may feel slighted or passed over.

Rather than dealing with the problem in a calm, cool and rational way, they lash out with words and gossip, frustrating everyone and not dealing with the problem.

Numbers Rabbah 18 suggests that Moses tried to win Korah over by exposing his argument as blind arrogance and a power grab: "it is against the Eternal that you and all your company have banded together."[Num. 16.11] But Korah did not respond.

Korah thought to himself "If I answer Moses, I know that, being resourceful, he will certainly overwhelm me with these arguments, so that I might find myself reconciled with him against my will. It is better for me not to respond." There was no further communication with Korah, and so Moses parted from him. Sometimes it is wisdom to walk away from someone unable to heed a message.

it may well have been driven by personal ambition, puts forward a view of the people that by and large is rejected by the Bible itself, and especially by the prophets. For them, holiness is intrinsic solely to God and not to any human value—not land, not Temple, not kingship, not even sacred time. The land must be "hallowed" by proper human behavior; the Temple sacrifices may be rejected if not accompanied by genuine repentance and social action; the king is not above the law and does not serve as the representative of the holy; and the Sabbath, as an example of sacred time, must be "hallowed" by the people of Israel, just as God did at Creation. In this context, the holiness of the people is basically a potential, which needs to be realized and not merely stated as a fact.

The text suggests that the survivors of Korah's rebellion and its aftermath, in which more rebels were killed by divine fire, did not fully understand what was at stake. Further on in the parashah they rise up against Moses again, because "YOU HAVE KILLED THE LORD'S PEOPLE!" [Num. 17.6]. Thus, the parashah must end on a prosaic note, with chapter 18 spelling out in precise detail—the duties of the Levites, so that there will be no further mistaking the proper boundaries. As so often happens in the Torah, out of the disorder of narrative events comes the order established by law. The last line of the parashah, after the giving of certain injunctions, reads, "so that you do not die." It is a fitting ending to a reading that began with an unprecedented form of death.●

Korah

What do we learn from Korah? Not to act like him! Better we should deal with the problem as Moses does with God: personally, passionately, with great intuition and insight, with good elocution and a proper choice of words. And most importantly, we should think rationally at moments of crisis, rather than let our emotions sway us. **Rabbi Morley T. Feinstein, Temple Beth-El, South Bend, IN**

דָּבָר אַחֵר **DAVAR AHER.** MOSES SAID TO KORAH, 'YOU AND YOUR ENTIRE ASSEMBLY, BE BEFORE GOD... LET EACH MAN TAKE HIS FIREPAN AND YOU SHALL PLACE INCENSE ON THEM AND YOU SHALL BRING BEFORE GOD EACH MAN WITH HIS

FIREPAN, [Num. 16.16-17]. As I peruse the story of Korah and his "Great Rebellion," I am transported back to a story of another Great Rebellion; the episode of the Golden Calf. I see a situation in both stories that reminds us of the immanence of God's presence and the importance of arguing for the sake of Heaven alone.

In the story of the Golden Calf, I am of one opinion with some of the sages who suggest that Aaron was, indeed, trying to bide his time until Moses came down from the mountain. Yet, I would like to go a little bit beyond the Rabbis' suggestion

Rabbi Melanie Aron

MELANIE ARON IS THE RABBI AT CONGREGATION SHIR HADASH IN LOS GATOS, CA.

Parashat Korah is usually read at about the same time of year that congregations hold their end-of-year annual meetings, bringing to mind the well-known passage from the fifth chapter of *Pirke Avot:* "Any controversy which is for the sake of heaven, is destined to result in something permanent; any controversy which is not for the sake of heaven, will never result in something permanent. Which controversy was for the sake of heaven? The controversy between Hillel and Shammai. And which was not for the sake of heaven? The controversy of Korah and his company."

Musarists writing about *Parashat Korah*, remind us that one of the *taryag* (613) *mitzvot*, based on Numbers 17.5 is: "YOU SHALL NOT ACT SIMILAR TO KORAH AND HIS COMPANY." Unfortunately, sorting out different types of controversy is not always so simple. The Talmud provides us with some guidance. An argument over a *halakhic* matter or interpretation of Torah is proper, if the participants, while adversaries for the moment, ultimately feel love for one another [*Kiddushin* 30b]. This is the image we have of Hillel and Shammai, who, though involved in *halakhic* disputes, were close friends, and this is the picture the Talmud paints of the continued interaction between their schools of followers [*Yevamot* 13b]. However, many of us have witnessed discussions, which start out *l'shem shamayim* and then disintegrate into *ad hominem* attacks. At the receiving end of "constructive criticism," we sometimes react defensively as Moses did to Korah and his company, "I HAVE NOT TAKEN THE ASS OF ANY OF THEM, NOR HAVE I WRONGED ANY ONE OF THEM." In addition, disputes are danger-

Korah

which seeks, for the most part, merely to exonerate Aaron.

The making of the Calf is very mysterious. In the words of my mentor, Rabbi Chanan Brichto, the verse in which the Calf is made is awkward, at best. Rabbi Brichto teaches us that the verse literally says, "HE TOOK FROM THEIR HAND, ENGRAVED IT WITH A STYLUS AND MADE IT A CAST BULL"[EX. 32.4]. What is "IT?" The verb "took" has no object and the object of engraved is clearly the gold in some form but not in

the original form of the earrings. We do not know what he engraved (a word, a phrase, an image). We do not know why the people would believe that what is clearly man-made would be hailed as their liberator. We do not know had Aaron produced an ass or an ape, the reaction of the people would have been the same.

The answer to these questions comes from the people's reaction itself. Something miraculous must have happened

ous, the Musarists remind us, because they can lead to other sins, including, but not limited to, unwarranted hatred, *lashon ha-ra*, *rikhilut*, anger, insults, humiliating words, revenge, grudges, curses, and *hillul ha-Shem*. Arguing can become such a passion, Rabbi Samson Raphael Hirsch warns, that we quarrel for the sake of quarreling and need always to be right and have the last word.

Recognizing our own motivation for entering a dispute is the key to directing our disputational energies appropriately. In the Talmud, Korah is grouped in ways which give us indications of the rabbis' understanding of his character. In one passage [*Sotah* 9b], there is a list of those who "set eyes upon that which was not proper for them: what they sought was not granted and what they possessed was taken from them." These were Cain, Korah, Balaam, Doeg, Ahitofel, Gehazi, Avshalom, Adonijah, Uzziah and Haman.

Another passage, *Sanhedrin* 37b, relates Cain and Korah, because the earth opened its mouth in both passages.

Korah presented his attack on Moses as motivated by communal concerns. He raged and ranted about increasing democracy and discouraging nepotism. Yet, the midrash reads Korah's motivation as entirely personal and emotional—jealousy over the appointment of his cousin, Elizafan, as head of the clan. One wonders whether Korah was aware of his own motivations. Did he consciously devise a cover story, like Haman, or was he like Cain, who I believe never gained the self-awareness necessary to realize that his anger at Abel was the displaced rage that resulted from God's rejection of his sacrifice and his own unwillingness to accept God's forceful statement of personal responsibility ("SURELY, IF YOU DO RIGHT, THERE IS UPLIFT"—[Gen. 4.7])?

Korah

for the people to think that this was some kind of representation of Deity. This is further reinforced when the Torah tells us that "AARON SAW" [Ex. 32.5] and then declared a festival to the Lord. According to Brichto, "he flung an ingot into the fire, waited confi-dently for its reduction into a blob, ready to turn on the image-demanding instigators with this proof of their folly. Instead, a miracle occurred. A miracle which

could have been worked only by the will of YHVH."

Clearly the people who demanded the making of the Calf have already failed the test of faith—which is but a manifestation of their rejection of the theophany at Sinai. God only completed the miracle to underscore their folly. God, suspended natural law and performed a miracle to demonstrate the conse-

ויקח קרח בן יצהר בן קהת בן לוי

In *Parashat Kedoshim*, we are told to "REBUKE OUR NEIGHBOR, BUT INCUR NO GUILT BECAUSE OF HIM" [Lev. 19.17]. Coming as this does as the second half of a verse that begins, "YOU SHALL NOT HATE YOUR NEIGHBOR IN YOUR HEART," we are reminded that a proper rebuke must be based only on love, not on animosity, jealousy, or a desire for power. However, this is very difficult—so difficult that the commentaries wonder whether any human being can give a proper rebuke.

I wonder if we aren't in a similar situation with regard to *mahloket* (argument). A healthy dispute is a positive thing; without it we are in danger of stagnating. Yet disputes are also dangerous things because of their potential to hurt. Our sages warn us against maintaining and participating in disputes, yet continue to further the study of Torah through adversarial discussion. It is only in the careful and honest probing of our motivations that we move ourselves and our communities toward a style of disagreement and discussion which is healthy, productive and has enduring results.•

quences of rejecting the Sinaitic convenant.

How similar this is to the episode of Korah! Korah and his band annoy Moses to such a degree that Moses himself utters their punishment and when it does happen, Moses orders their firepans to be used at the Tabernacle. Why would he do that?

I suggest that Moses, like Aaron before him, was totally surprised when the miraculous event he uttered was actually executed by God! Moses is depicted on many occasions begging for mercy for the Children of Israel. But on this occasion, he was simply fed up with their contentiousness, lost his temper, and put God in the position of fulfilling his words, thus proving to all Israel that God was, indeed, among them, watching their actions and listening to their every word. After the earth swallowed Korah and his followers, Moses realized that it was God, not he, who was ultimately the Holy One. Thus, in a sort of penance, Moses required that Korah's firepans be used in holy service.

The use of Korah's firepans as altar plating was not exclusively, as some rabbis have suggested, to keep alive the notion that Korah's complaint was somehow valid. It was also a perpetual symbol and reminder of the consequences of Moses' temper. The people would look at that metal on the altar and recall how it was Moses' utterance that caused the death of so many. One can only wonder how the story would have unfolded if the test of the incense had been proven without Moses' losing his temper and specifying the punishment.

To be sure, Moses was at fault to some degree and, as a consequence, his repentance was visible and constant. But more important than that was that God, Himself, demands faithfulness to the Covenant and that, in some fashion or another, there is an accounting. To paraphrase the Talmud, "Let every argument be for the sake of Heaven, for if it is not it is surely doomed to failure." **Rabbi Cy Stanway, Temple Beth El, Las Cruces, NM**

דָּבָר אַחֵר **DAVAR AHER. BUT IF THE LORD CREATED AN [UNUSUAL] CREATION [Num. 16.30].** The Torah uses the term בְּרִיאָה *"beri'ah," "creation"* to mean "miracle." Rebelliousness stems from taking things for granted. Thus, Moses reminds the people that their very existence depends upon the constant miracles of God in the renewal of Creation. **Hazan Ira Rohde, Cong. Shearith Israel, NYC**

Hukkat

**Numbers
19.1–22.1**

Rabbi Mordecai Finley, Ph.D.

MORDECAI FINLEY IS THE RABBI OF OHR HA TORAH, CO-RABBI OF MAKOM OHR SHALOM AND IS AN ADJUNCT FACULTY MEMBER AT HEBREW UNION COLLEGE IN LOS ANGELES, CALIFORNIA. HE IS ALSO PART OF THE FACULTY OF THE DEPARTMENT OF CONTINUING EDUCATION AT THE UNIVERSITY OF JUDAISM IN LOS ANGELES, CALIFORNIA.

The Torah is a tapestry of archetypes, woven together in a narrative landscape, revealing the contours of our own souls. Our souls and the Torah emanate from the same place, *Ha-Makom,* the soul of the universe. We study Torah to know truth, ourselves, our duty and our place in the world.

THE PARADIGMATIC CONUNDRUM

The truth we encounter in this Torah portion begins a puzzle, in fact the archetypal puzzle of the Torah. Here is the law we find in the narrative: A red cow, פָּרָה אֲדֻמָּה *parah adumah,* unblemished and unworked, shall be slaughtered. Some of the blood is sprinkled toward the Tent of Meeting, and the cow is burnt entirely.

The kohein throws into the burning cow cedarwood, hyssop and crimson thread. The kohein then is טָמֵא *tameh*, impure, unclean until evening, at which time he immerses himself. The one who burns the cow is similarly *tameh*, impure. The one gathering the ash and storing them is also *tameh*.

And the purpose of this gory ritual in which everyone who prepares it becomes impure? The ashes are mixed with water to create a "water for the removal" of impurity. Which impurity? The archetype of all impurities, the contamination of death. Everyone involved in the process of creating the mixture for the removal of impurity becomes impure, while the one upon whom the mixture is sprinkled becomes pure. Go figure.

For the sages, this was a paradigmatic example of *hukkah*, a statute commanded by God which has no reason, no logical explanation. The term "red cow," פָּרָה אֲדֻמָּה *parah adumah*, has come into modern Hebrew meaning an insoluble conundrum. A person observing another's inexplicable behavior might comment, "*Mamash parah adumah*," a real red heifer.

THE REVENGE OF THE IRRATIONAL

What do we do about this conundrum? Does not everything have a reason? Traditional Judaism is of

זאת חקת התורה אשר צוה

two minds concerning finding reasons behind the commandments. Commandments which seem to have some rational bases are called מִצְוֹת שִׂכְלִיּוֹת mitzvot sikhliyyot, roughly, "sensible commandments." Commandments that seem to have no rational bases are called מִצְוֹת שְׁמָעוֹת "mitzvot shema-ot," the later word from the same root as the Shema, "Hear O Israel." We do them because we have heard them and we must hearken—in other words, commandments of obedience. Some voices in our tradition lean toward saying that all the commandments make sense somehow. Either we have not figured them out, or God has not yet revealed their meaning to us. Other voices in our tradition say that the reward for the commandments is doing them, obeying the law, not because we understand, but because we obey the word of God.

One voice says, "It all makes sense, there is a reason for it all." The other voice says, "Sometimes God gives us commandments that do not make sense, just so that we will obey." The commentaries and discussions around this Torah portion are evidence of the gravitational pull this Torah portion has on Rabbinic literature as a place to knead this issue of the nature of the commandments and whether they all have a rational foundation or not. The basic dichotomies, rational/irrational, sensible/nonsensical, reason/obedience are examined and worked out in the commentaries on this Torah portion. In this particular slice of Rabbinic literature, the cognitive conquers the intellectual, even if only on points. At times, God just wills and we obey. But not without an argument. The basic question seems to be: "Do the commandments always have to make sense?" The anwer is simply, "No!"

A DEEPER CONUNDRUM

But have we even arrived at the real question? Is the root conundrum really about how it could be that those who prepare the mixture for the removal of the taint of death become tainted themselves? The Torah reveals its secrets in many ways. One of the ways we find out what is going on in the subterranean levels of the Torah is to ask what happened just before and what happens after. So we ought to ask, "Why is the chapter on the red cow at this place in the Torah?"

Some commentators say that it's just part of the great, instructive disorder. There is no chronological order in the Torah, or at least none that you can count on. Others see that these laws are a fitting conclusion to the laws of the tabernacle and priests begun in the book of Leviticus.

Neither view—that there is no order, or that this is a conclusion to Levitical law—seems convincing to me. Is it an accident that further on

Synopsis: Contamination by a corpse and subsequent purification (red heifer) begins this week's parashah, and the journey continues. After Miriam dies, Moses and Aaron commit a sin akin to heresy when they are instructed by God to bring forth water from the rock. Israel then encounters Edom and the death of Aaron is reported. The Canaanites are then engaged in battle, the incident of the copper snake is described, and the victories over Sihon and Og conclude the reading.

Hukkat

in our Torah portion, in the next chapter, Miriam dies, Aaron dies and Moses is told that he will die before he enters the promised land? Whether or not these laws concerning the contagious impurity of death were given at this point in the actual history of the Israelites in the desert, in the fortieth and last year in the desert, it seems clear that God wanted these laws concerning the taint of death placed next to the stories of death and punishment that follow. The Torah portion begins with the contagion of death, and then the greatest Jews in history start dying. This portion is about death, and the response to death.

BREAKDOWN AND BEREAVEMENT

Miriam dies in the first verse of the next chapter—chapter 20. The people immediately cry that they have no water. The Midrash tells us that as long as Miriam was alive, there was a well that provided a constant stream of water. She dies, and it seems that the grief-stricken well pauses, allowing us to shed water for a change. We read that the people displaced their grief for her onto the ramification of her presence, Miriam's Well of Living Waters. Our grief, however, becomes anxiety; we do not cry for Miriam, instead, we cry for water. The well closes up, shocked at our lack of tears. We go after Miriam's surviving brothers: Numbers 20.2: "The community was without water, and they joined together against

Moses and Aaron." We say to them, "if only we had died like the others died. You've brought us here to die."

But God gives us a way back. He tells Moses and Aaron to attend the people's crying for water, and speak to the rock, which according to the Midrash, was the source of Miriam's well. Perhaps we will see that water and learn to properly grieve for Miriam. Perhaps the well can be consoled of its grief, and coaxed back to life. As we know, Moses strikes the rock, instead of speaking to it. He says to the people, "Listen, rebels, shall we get water for you out of this rock?"[Num. 20.10].

What was Moses doing? Was he striking out at God for taking his beloved sister? Was he striking out at the people who could not stop complaining long enough for him to grieve for his sister and/or work at his anger at God or both? This seems obvious: when God told Moses to speak to the rock, Moses didn't know what to say. So he spoke to the people instead, full of wrath. And he whacked the rock, as he did back in Exodus 17. That felt familiar. But that time it was God who told him to do it, Who knew what the people needed to see. This time Moses hit not for God, but for himself.

Anyway, he struck the rock. It gushed one last time, the heart of stone broken. God said to Moses and Aaron (the latter of whom, as at the Golden Calf incident, was a willing, if passive, accomplice. That time he collaborated with the riotous Israelites, this time he acquiesces to Moses' expression of contempt), "YOU WILL NOT BRING THIS CONGREGATION TO THE LAND THAT I HAVE GIVEN THEM" [Num. 20.12]. Aaron dies in the next chapter, and the cloud of glory that protected us from our enemies that the Midrash associated with Aaron went the way of Miriam's well. The Torah portion ends with us fighting and dying on our way to Canaan. Moses is given the opportunity to write a eulogy before he is to die (the book of Deuteronomy). The Torah portion smells of breakdown and bereavement. We have left the womb and entered history. We have to face death.

THE REAL MYSTERY

The real mystery is not how that which makes pure impurifies those that prepare it. The mixture is a toggle switch, it reverses the status of those who touch it. If you are in a pure state, it makes you impure for a little while. But if you are in an impure state, it removes that impurity. Toggle switch theory is not rocket science. Maybe all the Rabbinic discussion about the whys and wherefores of this law reflect the displaced anxiety of the ancient sages about statutes that surpass their understanding, because the real mystery is not the statute of how burnt cow mixture removes the taint of death. The real mystery is why we die at all.

Why we die is the subject of a different Torah portion, the first one. This

Torah portion addresses another issue: what we do under the specter of death. Hasidic commentators take the phrase from our Torah portion, "*Zot* זֹאת הַתּוֹרָה אָדָם כִּי-יָמוּת בְּאֹהֶל *hatorah, adam ki yamut ba-ohel*—THIS IS THE TEACHING [CONCERNING] THE ONE WHO DIES IN A TENT" [Num. 19.14], and cut it down to: "*Zot hatorah: adam ki yamut*—THIS IS THE TORAH, BECAUSE HUMAN BEINGS DIE."

We are taught that the Torah is given in response to that ultimate conundrum, that ultimate *hukkah*, unreasonable statute, that ultimate disorder, death. Our response to death is the entire system of pure and impure, right and wrong, the spiritually true and false. If we are to die, then we cleave to what is eternal. If others, whose presence is the very living waters of our lives, a shelter from life's storms, are to die, then we must learn to grieve and find water and shelter. And if we are to die short of our promise, then we should leave a good word behind us, a map for others to carry on the task.

Death is the ultimate *hukkah* which we will all obey. This is our truth, even if we can't fully understand it. We certainly don't have to like it. Facing it, we come to know our duty of containing and channeling its energy into the service of the holy.

And why the red cow? Perhaps because of the Golden Calf—we had once given ourselves over to the spiritual death/idolatry of that beast, and called it a god. In this ritual, perhaps, we recognize that "god" had a mother, a source. We move from the

potency of animal worship to the nurturing of a God who gives us life. The Red Cow for purity is the ritual *teshuvah* for the Molten Calf of death. The Red Cow symbolizes, perhaps, our return to the living God who implants eternal life within us, who removes from us all impurity when we are gathered in death to the living waters of eternal life.●

Rabbi Daniel Isaak

DANIEL J. ISAAK IS RABBI OF CONGREGATION NEVEH SHALOM IN PORTLAND, OREGON.

Hukkat

Before and After is the title of a novel by Rosellen Brown. In it she traces the transformation of each member in a family as the result of an act, a criminal act committed by one of them. This otherwise ordinary family is not only marked, but husband and wife respond independently in unexpected ways as a result of the trauma that has befallen their family. We might wonder, confronted by similar stimuli, God forbid, with the same equally unenviable alternatives, how would we respond? What would any of us do? How might we be altered by a similarly shocking event? How might we survive such a "before and after" experience?

While the Torah records numerous such "before and after" experiences, *Parashat Hukkat* draws our attention to Moses' own personal trial.

We are curious as to whether Moses had any idea of the severe consequences that would ensue upon his intemperate "striking" of the rock rather than "ordering" the rock to yield its water. "BECAUSE YOU DID NOT TRUST ME ENOUGH TO AFFIRM MY SANCTITY IN THE SIGHT OF THE ISRAELITE PEOPLE THEREFORE YOU SHALL NOT LEAD THIS CONGREGATION INTO THE LAND THAT I HAVE GIVEN THEM" [Num. 20.12]. Moses' ultimate goal, to lead the people to the final destination of *Eretz Yisrael,* is dashed for a seemingly insignificant indiscretion. Moses' response is not recorded. Was he shocked? Did he remonstrate with God, plead his innocence, ask God for another chance? We can only imagine, as did the Rabbis of the Midrash who projected a whole series of protests and pleadings onto Moses.

However, the more important question, it seems to me, is how did this "before and after" experience transform Moses? In order to fully comprehend this phenomenon, perhaps it would be helpful to examine how "before and after" experiences affected other biblical characters. Saul is a good example. Having disappointed God in not wiping out King Agag as he had been ordered, and preserving Amalekite sheep and oxen alive, Saul begs for forgiveness, but to no avail. It is a tragic moment and one from which Saul never recovers. The once proud king becomes a prisoner of his punishment. Convinced that David, rather than his own son, will succeed him,

298—חקת

זאת חקת התורה אשר צוה יהיה לאמר

Saul can apparently think of nothing else but David's destruction.

David's fate is not much better. His adultery with Batsheva and killing her husband, Uriah the Hittite, prompt the prophet Nathan's scathing pronouncement. David's fate is sealed. All that has been foretold comes to pass and David never recaptures his former glory. He continues to rule and survives Avshalom's challenge, but in a much weakened state.

Not so with Moses. Though already quite an elderly man, Moses persists and perseveres. He provides for his people as he did previously. He continues to intercede with God on their behalf. He defeats the Amorite King, Sihon, the Bashan King, Og, and the Midianites, determining an equitable means of distributing the spoil. He rewards Pinhas for his zeal. He apportions the land, assigns cities of refuge, and negotiates with the Reubenites and Gadites over Trans-Jordan. After inquiring of God, he pronounces judgment for the daughters of Zelophehad. And, he asks God to appoint a successor when told that it is time to give up leadership. Moses is not side-tracked. Despite God's harsh verdict, Moses remains focused, vital and determined. He will complete his mission to the best of his ability. He refuses to be shaken.

One might find in this reason to criticize. Has Moses no feelings? If someone had a heart attack during one of his lectures, would he have just kept on speaking? Would he even have noticed? But there is also something

very special about someone whose mission is so clear, whose purpose on earth is so absolute, that he will devote his full energy, despite setbacks and reverses, to bringing it about. There is something very refreshing, healthy and wonderful in Moses' example. Few of us are as undistractable. We look for excuses. We give up too easily. We experience multiple "before and after" events, a troubled marriage, an unfulfilling job, disappointments of various sorts, and we are all too ready to give up. While perseverance ought not become anyone's religion, pursued for its own sake without continual re-examination, it is nevertheless a valuable attribute which we should seek to emulate. A righteous cause is always worth pursuing.•

THE ASHES OF THE RED HEIFER

Howard Schwartz

HOWARD SCHWARTZ TEACHES AT THE UNIVERSITY OF MISSOURI–ST. LOUIS. HE HAS EDITED A FOUR-VOLUME SET OF JEWISH FOLK TALES, CONSISTING OF *ELIJAH'S VIOLIN*, *MIRIAM'S TAMBOURINE*, *LILITH'S CAVE* AND *GABRIEL'S PALACE*, WHICH IS AVAILABLE FROM OXFORD UNIVERSITY PRESS.

Ḥukkat

In addition to describing the deaths of Aaron and Miriam, *Sidrat Ḥukkat* [Num. 19–22.1] includes two enigmatic episodes, one concerning the ritual of using the ashes of a red heifer to purify a person who has become ritually unclean, and the incident in which Moses strikes the rock in the desert with his rod rather than speaking to it, as the Lord had commanded. Both episodes are worthy of extensive commentary and have received it, but since there is only space to consider one of them, let us consider the most obscure of the two, that concerning the red heifer.

The *sidrah* opens by describing in great detail how the red heifer was to be selected and burned.

The preparation was to be done by the assistant to the High Priest and the ashes were to be mixed with water taken directly from a well of מַיִם חַיִּים *mayim ḥayim* and sprinkled on the third and seventh day on anyone who had come into contact with a dead person, for in doing so that person had become ritually unclean טָמֵא *tamei* and could not enter the Temple until the ritual of sprinkling the mixture of the ashes and water had been performed. Only this ritual could make them טָהוֹר *tahor*, ritually pure.

There is an interesting paradox associated with the potent ability of this ritual to turn the unclean clean. For if a ritually pure person should accidentally come in contact with the ashes of a red heifer, he would be rendered impure. It is this paradox that has remained a mystery over the centuries, causing the ritual of the ashes of the red heifer to be considered so enigmatic that only Moses was said to understand its true meaning. King Solomon said that this was the only mystery he could not penetrate. Therefore assumptions about the meaning of this paradox must remain speculative, but it was on such unresolved problems that Rabbinic commentary thrived. Such commentaries are found in the Talmud, the *Tosefta,* and midrashic collections such as *Pesikta de–Rav Kahana,* which devotes an entire chapter (4) to this question.

זאת חקת התורה אשר צוה יהיה לאמר

The dual ability of the ashes of the red heifer to render the impure pure and the pure impure may be seen to suggest the essential nature of a polar structure, such as the soul, which is subject to the influence of both the יֵצֶר הָרַע *yetzer ha-Ra*, the Evil Inclination, and the יֵצֶר הַטּוֹב *yetzer ha-Tov*, the Good Inclination. This notion suggests that a soul under the sway of the *yetzer hara* may restore itself to purity by some kind of תִּקּוּן *tikkun*, restoration, in order to re-achieve the state of purity. In any case, this ritual has meaning only in this world, while in the World to Come it is God who will purify Israel: "AND I WILL SPRINKLE CLEAN WATER UPON YOU, AND YE SHALL BE CLEAN; FROM ALL YOUR UNCLEANNESSES, AND FROM ALL YOUR IDOLS, WILL I CLEANSE YOU" [Ezek. 36.25].

Judaism has always recognized the need for and importance of rituals of purification. The מִקְוֶה *mikveh* is one primary means and fasting is another, as is reciting the Psalms. Rabbinic and Hasidic tales are filled with inventive methods proposed by the sages to attain purification from a variety of particular sins. Using the ashes of the red heifer was the most powerful of these methods because of the almost magic powers associated with them. But the mitzvah of using this ritual, which is one of the 613 commandments, is no longer observed, for a cow perfect enough to serve for it—which may not have as many as three hairs that are not red—has not been found for many centuries. Therefore we are all ritually impure, since virtually everyone has come into contact with a dead person at one time or another—even to be in the same house is to render one impure in this sense—and that is why Jews are not permitted to go to the Temple Mount at the site of the Temple in Jerusalem.

Thus, this mitzvah is in the category of those commandments. It is impossible to fulfill, such as those which had to be performed in the Temple, or the one concerning the use of תְּכֵלֶת *tekhelet*, the special blue dye that is required to dye the middle thread of the fringes of the tallit. The secret of how to make this dye was lost even in the time of the Talmudic sages, and thus the rabbis chose to leave the thread white rather than dye it incorrectly. (However, the Radzinim Hasidim believe that their Rebbe, known as the Baal Tekhelet, rediscovered the secret of how to make the dye, and observe the mitzvah.) Yet even though the ritual of using the ashes of the red heifer cannot be performed, it offers an intriguing mystery to ponder: one whose meaning is relevant even if the act, itself, is not.

And when will the practice of using the ashes of the red heifer be taken up again? The midrash tells us that nine red heifers were furnished by the Holy One, blessed be He, beginning with that of Moses, and that the tenth will be furnished by the Messiah.•

Balak

Numbers 22.2–25.9

Rabbi Neil Gillman

NEIL GILLMAN IS THE AARON RABINOWITZ AND SIMON H. RIFKIND ASSOCIATE PROFESSOR AND DEPARTMENT CHAIR IN JEWISH PHILOSOPHY AT THE JEWISH THEOLOGICAL SEMINARY OF AMERICA. HE IS THE AUTHOR OF *SACRED FRAGMENTS: RECOVERING THEOLOGY FOR THE MODERN JEW* (JPS), AND OF *CONSERVATIVE JUDAISM: THE NEW CENTURY* (BEHRMAN). HIS NEW BOOK ON *RESURRECTION AND IMMORTALITY IN JEWISH THOUGHT* WILL BE PUBLISHED BY JEWISH LIGHTS, WINTER, 1996-1997.

Some years ago, the British dramatist, Tom Stoppard, wrote a play entitled *Rosencrantz and Guildenstern are Dead* retelling the Hamlet story from the perspective of these two totally peripheral participants in the drama. I had reason to recall that play recently when I was searching for an imaginative final assignment in a course I was teaching on the *Akedah*, the story of the binding of Isaac in Genesis 22.

What would emerge if we retold that terrifying story from the perspective of the two servants who accompanied the central characters on their journey to God's sacred mountain? Or from the perspective of characters who are not explicitly in the story at all but were surely affected by the events, such as Sarah, Hagar, or Ishmael? Or by biblical personalities who underwent similar trials such as Job? Or stretching it even further, what if the ram who was substituted for Isaac could speak? Or, finally, Abraham's ass?

This week's Torah portion also features an ass—this time, one who does speak. How would this ass tell his story? What if these two asses met and shared their different experiences? That possibility—not at all outrageous from the perspective of midrash—was enough to set me off on an inquiry regarding the common themes in these two stories.

Coincidentally, the stories occupy the same chapter (Chapter 22) in their

---

דָּבָר אַחֵר DAVAR AHER. "PLEASE COME AND CURSE THIS PEOPLE FOR ME, FOR IT IS TOO POWERFUL FOR ME; PERHAPS I WILL BE ABLE TO STRIKE IT AND DRIVE IT AWAY FROM THE LAND. FOR I KNOW THAT WHOMEVER YOU BLESS IS BLESSED AND WHOMEVER YOU CURSE IS ACCURSED." [Num. 22.6]. Balak, son of Zippor, King of Moab, is frightened by the large number of Israelites who have come from Egypt. He seeks out Balaam, a well-known prophet, to

come and curse the Israelites. He is perfectly willing to minister to all of Balaam's requests: build me altars and have a bull and a ram on each. An expensive demand, yet to be repeated twice more. Balak must have been quite frustrated with Balaam since at one point he says "DON'T CURSE THEM AND DON'T BLESS THEM". [Num. 23.25]. Question: why didn't Balak simply have Balaam

וירא בלק בן צפור את כל

respective books, Genesis and Numbers. But there are numerous textual parallels as well. Both Abraham and Balaam saddle their asses themselves, and the midrash comments that both love (Abraham's love of God) and hatred (Balaam's hatred of Israel) upset the natural order, for surely both could have had their servants do this menial task. In fact, both take two servants with them on their respective voyages, and the midrash notes that this is the proper conduct for a noble man, for both Abraham and Saul (in 1 Samuel 28.8) did the same thing. In each case, the servants are completely passive; neither set utters a word.

In each case, Abraham's in the midrash and Balaam's in the biblical text itself, an angel is introduced to impede their way. (Note that the Hebrew in the midrash on Genesis identifies this impeding angel with the Satan, and Numbers 22.32 uses the same root to describe the func-

tion of this angel.) In each case, the story concludes with the main characters returning home, Abraham to Be'er Sheba and Balaam to an unspecified place.

And then there are the two asses. The midrash is singularly unconcerned with the fact that the Bible uses two different words to characterize this animal. In Genesis, the word is חֲמוֹר *hamor* and in Numbers, אָתוֹן *aton*. Not unexpectedly, the midrash conflates Abraham's *hamor* with the *hamor* Moses rode on his journey back to Egypt [Ex. 4.20] and with the *hamor* that, according to the prophet Zechariah [9.9], the messianic king will ride on his triumphant journey into Jerusalem. There is ultimately only one mythical *hamor*.

But the midrash also conflates Abraham's and Balaam's asses. Of the second, we are told that its mouth was one of ten things that were created at twilight between the sixth

Synopsis: On the journey, Israel encounters the nation of Moav. Balak, the king, hires Balaam, the seer, to curse Israel. Instead of the curse, Balaam blesses the people in the famous story of Balaam and his ass. Four oracles follow, and the parashah concludes with the story of idolatry at Baal Peor.

hung, beheaded or whatever the punishment of the day was?

The Midrash says: Balaam was a true prophet, although a pagan. God gave the gift of prophecy to men like Balaam so that other nations could not say that God loved only the Israelites. *The Talmud says:* first, Balaam was a true prophet and spoke God's words. Then he deserted God and became a magician. Most prophets of Israel did not seek the

job. In fact, most objected and tried to escape the possibility (like Moses: "I'm not worthy—I can't speak well"). Not so with Balaam. Most prophets would add to their prophecy "said God" or "The Lord has spoken;" not so Balaam (he often added "said Balaam, son of Beor."

In spite of all the problems with Balaam, his blessings (*Ma Tovu*) appear at the beginning of our siddurim, distinguished for the poetic beauty of

the sentiments expressed. Balaam emerges as a neutral figure, Balak as the villain.

A word or two about the talking ass. The incident might have been a dream or a reversal of characters—Balaam becomes the ass: the ass becomes Balaam. Another note about the ass (The only other instance of an animal's speaking is the serpent to Eve. The serpent speaks in a sly, cunning Biblical voice enticing Eve to eat the fruit and

and seventh day of creation [*Mishnah Avot* 5.6]. Of Abraham's ass, we are told that it was the foal of that very same ass. And then to compound the commonalities between the two stories, the midrash also notes that Abraham's ram was created at that very same time.

The list of other things created at twilight between the sixth and seventh day of creation is instructive. It includes, among other creations, Moses' staff, the rainbow, *mannah*, the twin tablets and Moses' tomb. What all of these have in common is their somewhat mysterious state of being "neither here nor there," of occupying some "in between" status. Moses' staff is both an ordinary staff and a staff that can be transformed into a serpent. The rainbow is both palpably "there" and yet evanescent. We are told precisely where Moses is buried [Deut. 34.6] but the text adds "AND NO ONE KNOWS HIS BURIAL PLACE TO THIS DAY." And Balaam's ass is both an ordinary ass and a miraculous one that has the power of speech.

It is this somewhat mysterious "neither here nor there" quality that has all of these created precisely at a time which is also "neither here nor there," neither on the sixth day nor on the seventh. Today, in the language of the phenomenological study of religion, that moment would be identified as a "liminal" or "boundary" moment and all of these creations as occupying a liminal status.

Abraham's ass does not speak, neither in the Bible nor in the midrash, and Balaam's ass does. The midrash comments that this ass had the power of speech from its very creation, but had not used it until this very moment. The midrash also notes that this phenomenon of a talking ass underlines the basic thrust of this story which deals precisely with the power of speech to curse or to bless. Balaam's ass speaks in order to remind his owner that, ultimately, the power of speech belongs to God alone.

It also points out the contrast between the nobility of the animal

Balak

pointing out that "YOU WILL NOT DIE— YOU WILL JUST KNOW WHAT GOD KNOWS, SO GO AHEAD EAT!" [Gen. 3.4-5].

The lowly ass, on the other hand, seems to see things more clearly than Balaam, and her wise speaking eventually causes Balaam to see the light. **Unknown.**

דָּבָר אַחֵר **DAVAR AHER. THE SHE-DONKEY SAW ME AND TURNED AWAY FROM ME THESE THREE TIMES [Num. 22.33].**

Many ask "Why did the ass speak?" and forget to ask "Why did the ass see angels?" Seeing angels + speech = prophecy, for which speech is a metaphor. The ass bests Balaam in more than her ability to talk back; in seeing angels which Balaam can't, she is actually a better prophet than Balaam, the "professional." The spiritual vision and power of prophecy does not belong, by right, to humans, but is a gift from God, who

and the folly of its human owner. That's why the midrash tells us that God killed Balaam's ass immediately after it had spoken in order to preserve Balaam from further embarrassment, so that people should not see this ass and comment, "This is the ass that bested Balaam."

But to return to the parallels with the story of the *Akedah*, the most striking commonality is that both stories deal with a transformation. In the story of Abraham, what began as the worst possible trauma that could ultimately affect a man became a source of blessing and redemption. For in Israel's historical memory, Abraham's readiness to sacrifice his son is recalled by all future generations as the very paradigm of Jewish loyalty to God, and as the basis for God's promise to forgive and to redeem Abraham's posterity evermore.

Liturgically, that promise is recalled annually at the very heart of the Rosh ha-Shanah Musaf liturgy in the conclusion to the *Zikhronot* (or "Remembering") benediction when

we ask God to remember how "Abraham subdued his compassion to do Your will whole-heartedly, binding his son Isaac on the altar. Subdue your wrath with Your compassion. In your great goodness favor Your people, Your city and Your inheritance."

In the Balaam story, again what began as a plan to curse Israel is transformed into a blessing. And startlingly, again, it is precisely Balaam's blessing that is recalled liturgically, this time daily, when Balaam's words, "HOW FAIR ARE YOUR TENTS, O JACOB, YOUR DWELLINGS, O ISRAEL" [Num. 24.5] are recited every morning as the very opening words of the *Shakharit* liturgy. Both of these stories, then, have lived on in our historical consciousness.

This double transformation is surely the source of the liminal quality that is discovered in both of these extraordinary narratives. Both deal with dramatic turnabouts, both begin as potential tragedies and conclude as triumphs and in both instances, the transformation is wrought by God,

whose power is not simply in the creation of speech but also and mainly in the transformation of history.

If in some mythical space and time, these two asses might meet and share their experiences, they would have much to talk about: the striking difference in the personalities of their two masters, their encounters with impeding angels, their feelings as they proceeded on their respective journeys. But above all, they would surely testify to God's ultimate power to shape and transform historical events to God's purposes.

In fact, they might even quote Joseph, the hero of one of the great turnabout stories in the Bible, who reassures his brothers: "THOUGH YOU INTENDED ME HARM, GOD INTENDED IT FOR GOOD, SO AS TO BRING ABOUT THE PRESENT RESULT—THE SURVIVAL OF MANY PEOPLE." [Gen. 50.20]

(For further study and for bibliographical references to the material used above, consult Volume III of Louis Ginzberg's *The Legends of the Jews* (Philadelphia: The Jewish Publication Society of America, 1954) pp.363-366, and the corresponding footnotes in Volume VI.) ●

---

has the power to bestow it upon whomsoever He wills, human or even beast, if so He desires, and to direct it for good or for bad: this is the lesson of Parashat Balak. **Unknown**

דָּבָר אַחֵר **DAVAR AHER.** How GOODLY ARE THY TENTS, O JACOB, THY TABERNACLES, O ISRAEL [Num. 24.5]. In Numbers 22.2-25.9, Balaam personifies, for me all who would listen to G-d, proclaim His name and carry out

His word, but who have a blind prejudice, a blind spot, the ability to put their conscience on freeze, to hate without reason. And Balaam's words echo over the generations, for we are told that it was he who counselled the Malakites and Medianites that, though he could not himself curse the Israelites, he knew a way whereby the Israelites would curse themselves and be ruined by their own sins.

Here in America, assimilation is our own greatest danger to ourselves. To be Jewish is to know hope. The honor and faith of all Jews is in each of our hands, as Jews. Times have changed, but Jewish values have not. From the *Gates of Prayer*: "We are Jews. Each of us is unique, yet we are one in search of life's meanings." Let us not be fooled, for Balaam's mentality has survived the ages. May we cling always to the words that G-d put

Rob Fire

Rob Fire is a 9th grade teacher at Congregation B'nai Israel Hebrew High School.

Balak

What does it mean to have choice? What does it mean to be good? Is the person who never notices temptation a better person than someone who overcomes temptation? Should we never question authority? How often do we confuse permission with approval?

I am struck by how much Balaam's relationship with G-d is like that of a child with a parent. Balaam doesn't question G-d's authority any more than a child would question his parent's authority.

Yet accepting authority is not the same as being content with all of that authority's decisions. If a child is unhappy with a parent's decision, the child may not disobey, but the child will probably try to get the decision changed, often by simply repeating the request, just as Balaam does. Sometimes the parent will relent and sometimes not. So why would the simple repetition of a request cause a parent, or in Balaam's case, G-d, to have a change of heart when a simple "because I said so," is, after all, so much faster?

I suspect that the answer may be found in the similar nature of these two sets of relationships. Parents typically take little pleasure in saying "because I said so," because as parents the most important facet of our relationship with our children is that of teacher, not judge or law enforcement official. A child who never learns to obey may not live to see adulthood. But a child who

---

into Balaam's mouth, "How goodly are thy tents, O Jacob, Thy Tabernacles, O Israel" [Num. 24.5]. **Kathleen Parker, Homer, AK**

דָּבָר אַחֵר **DAVAR AHER.** Pinhas, son of Elazar, son of Aaron the Kohen saw, and he stood up from amid the assembly and took a spear in his hand [Num. 25.7]. A closer look at the literal text at the end of *Parashat Balak* made me wonder if

Pinhas' "zealotry" was anywhere near what it's been cracked up to be. It can hardly be called a case of taking the law into your own hands; on the contrary, Numbers 25.6 and 7 make it clear that there were standing orders to string up or otherwise kill, in the most public manner, all those involved (with special emphasis, at least in God's command to Moses, upon the "heads of the people"). Only in this

never learns to choose won't ever be much of an adult no matter how long he lives.

So, sometimes parents will give permission to their children, just as G-d does with Balaam, to make the wrong choice because, in the end, there is no other way to learn how to choose. Our children will often protest that they are not really free to choose in these circumstances because our wishes are so obviously contrary to their desires. But there is no lesson to be learned when our children agree with us. It is only when they do not see what we see that we want to open their eyes, just as G-d does with Balaam.

In a world driven by commerce, where we are relentlessly encouraged to make decisions that are, at the very best, shortsighted, we may have no greater gift to give our children than the lesson of how to see.●

way will the "WRATH OF GOD" (which, we infer from context later, manifested itself in the form of a "plague") be turned back. These orders do not seem to have been implemented; Pinhas seems to have been the first to do so. In addition, the description emphasizes the public and flagrant nature of the act, as if to say that all of Israel were Zimri's witnesses, jury, and judges. But if Pinhas is simply the first one to execute orders, it is ordi-

nary bravery, not zealotry, it would seem.

However, one could answer that "ZEAL" or "JEALOUSLY GUARDING" (thanks to Sylvia Gamal for this translation of קִנְאָה "qin'ah") is inherent in a situation when one is willing to hurt one's own people in the fight. To fight an outside enemy requires courage; to fight an internal one requires such faith that one is willing to go out against one's own people. To single-

mindedly pursue justice (not to be lead astray through sexual enticements, nor to be fearful of the repercussions of killing a major tribal leader, nor be swayed by the bonds of loyalty to one's people, but rather to single-handedly and directly score a blow for the right—these are what make Pinhas one of the paradigms of the kabbalistic *sephirat yesod*, the paradigm of the tzaddik. **Hazan Ira Rohde, Cong. Shearith Israel, NYC**

When we look at a particular biblical story from the perspective of the Wisdom tradition, from the esoteric line that is foremost in the Kabbalah, we often discover that what we see is not the whole truth, or even necessarily the main truth. Very often there is a deeper, hidden teaching that we can perceive only by looking at signs pointed out by our teachers. These are so rare, so precious, so mysterious, that alone we would never have deduced them.

One of the most marvelous of these teachings regards the events described in this and last week's Torah portions, the story of Pinhas and of Zimri and Cozbi.

On the external level, this is a story that is not only deeply disturbing, but is even repugnant to the modern sensibility. It is the kind of story that, on the level of *p'shat*, we would prefer weren't in the Torah at all. Toward the end of their journey through the desert, while encamped at Baal Peor in the Midianite territory, the Israelites are drawn into a cult of worship that apparently involves orgiastic rites. Israelite men are seduced by Midianite women (guess who's to blame). This licentious behavior evokes God's wrath, and the people begin to repent. Just at this point, in an episode connected more by counterpoint than by thematic continuity, two people, a Jewish aristocrat named Zimri, and a Midianite

Pinhas

Numbers 25.10-30.1

Rabbi Jonathan Omer-Man

JONATHAN OMER-MAN IS THE DIRECTOR OF METIVTA, CENTER FOR JEWISH WISDOM, IN LOS ANGELES, CALIFORNIA.

דָּבָר אַחֵר **DAVAR AHER.** "PINHAS, SON OF ELAZAR, SON OF AARON THE KOHEN SAW, AND HE STOOD UP FROM AMID THE ASSEMBLY AND TOOK A SPEAR IN HIS HAND" [Num. 25.7]. The Biblical story of Pinhas, begun in last week's *parashah* and continued this week, raises anew each year questions about the danger of fanaticism. The story itself is rather simple. The Israelites, during their wilderness sojourn, are encamped at a place

called Shittim, where they are tempted away from the Covenant by the Moabites. They take to sacrificing to the Moabite god Baal-peor, and, in the words of the text, whoring with the Moabite women. God, understandably, is upset. He orders Moses to take all the ringleaders of the insurrection and have them impaled, so that the Lord's wrath may turn away from Israel. Just as Moses transmits this directive to his

princess called Cozbi, become sexually involved. They behave flagrantly, and sport together in a tent in the middle of the camp. Pinhas, Moses' grand-nephew, is incensed by anger and consumed by zeal for God, and he bursts into their chamber and skewers them both through the belly with a single thrust of his spear. The plague that is decimating the people of Israel is brought to an end (though only after 24,000 have died); Pinhas is rewarded by God for his zeal, and is given a covenant of peace (!), the high priesthood for himself and his descendants for all time.

In most Rabbinic interpretations of this story, condemnation of the lovers is outright and absolute: they are irredeemable sinners. Predictably, Hertz calls their act "heinous." In Jewish folklore, Zimri is the worst of the worst. (In the 1960's, when David Ben Gurion was being challenged by a poten-

tial rival named Pinhas Lavon, he attempted to discredit the latter with the phrase

עֹשֶׂה מַעֲשֶׂה זִמְרִי וּמְבַקֵּשׁ שְׂכַר פִּינְחָס

"Oseh ma'aseh Zimri um'vakesh s'khar Pinhas"—"He does an act of a Zimri and claims the reward of a Pinhas.") Nevertheless, some commentators did feel uncomfortable with Pinhas: he had ignored all appropriate legal process and had acted out of passion. He hadn't warned the couple, or tried to separate them. He had in no way been threatened by them. He was a witness, and had appointed himself judge and executioner as well. Ultimately, however, Pinhas is justified, with the clear caveat that this is not a precedent. Pinhas is coupled in the haftarah with Elijah, another man whose zeal for God was excessive.

The p'shat narrative doesn't seem to give much leeway for radical reinterpretation of the text, but

Synopsis: Pinhas, the son of Elazar son of Aaron the Kohen is rewarded for his zeal by God's giving his offspring, the Zadokites, the priesthood. The second census is taken to prepare for war with the Midianites and to apportion the land, after which the case of the daughters of Zelophehad is pleaded and judgment rendered. Moses goes up the mountain of Avarim to view the land and Joshua is appointed to succeed him. The parashah concludes with the listing of all the public sacrifices offered on the holy days.

loyal leaders among the people, an Israelite named Zimri ben Salu openly defies Moses and the loyal elders by engaging in lewd behavior with a Moabite woman. The first to respond is Pinhas, who is one of Aaron's grandsons. He grabs a spear, follows Zimri and the woman into their tent, and stabs them together through their bellies. For this rash, though perhaps heroic, act, Pinhas is rewarded by God' s eternal friendship: "I GRANT

HIM MY PACT OF FRIENDSHIP. IT SHALL BE FOR HIM AND HIS DESCENDANTS AFTER HIM A PACT OF PRIESTHOOD FOR ALL TIME, BECAUSE HE TOOK IMPASSIONED ACTION FOR HIS GOD" [Num. 25.12-13]. Yet I feel that we, as modern Jews, must be deeply suspicious of this kind of sudden, impulsive, violent action that completely suspends any notion of due process and legal procedure.

We have been victimized too many times by fanaticism to be easily con-

vinced, even by a biblical imprimatur. The type of fanaticism practiced by Pinhas seems to me a particularly dangerous one today. It is a fanaticism that seeks to "divide and destroy," that says not only, "Your action is sinful," but also, "You, yourself, are irredeemable." This kind of thinking, when brought to a violent extreme, creates terrorists and assassins. But even without violence, "divide and destroy" fanaticism is a

there must be a clue somewhere. It is, in fact, found in a scribal quirk in the way the Torah is written. The letter ו *vav* in the word שָׁלוֹם *shalom* (*peace*) in Pinḥas' reward is broken. The covenant of peace is not perfect, or at least it is not unequivocal. Proceeding from this minuscule sign, certain mystical teachers, starting with Isaac Luria, and including Chaim Vital, Abraham Azulai and the Izbeca Rabbi, offer the following:

"There are ten degrees of fornication in the world. At the lowest level, the worst, the will to sin is even greater than the desire to perform the act, and the person has to urge himself on to sally out into the world and sully it. At each ascending level, however, the protagonist's will becomes weaker relative to the desire, which becomes progressively more powerful. At the tenth and final level, which is extremely rare, the desire is so powerful that no human will in the world would be strong enough to

vanquish it. We must conclude that it was not a sin at all, but God's will. Zimri and Cozbi, then, far from being wicked sinners, were a couple ordained from the beginning of creation."

If this is the case, their fate is outrageous. If, in fact, they were two souls destined for one another at such a high spiritual level, why were they slain so brutally at the moment in which they consummated their love on the physical plane? How could God let this happen? The esoteric answer is one that today we do not find to our liking: what exists on higher planes may not be possible in "real" life. True love is not always vouchsafed a happy ending. At least not immediately. There is a Kabbalistic resolution, according to which the souls of Zimri and Cozbi, the couple who were one on high but whose physical union was not possible here on earth, were reincarnated again and again, variations on a tragic theme. And then they were manifest in

Pinḥas

grave danger. This kind of thinking also threatens to "divide and destroy" the Jewish people. The most recent issue of *Reform Judaism Magazine* includes a forum on Jewish peoplehood where a leading moderate Orthodox rabbi states that Jewish religious pluralism needs to be abandoned in favor of strict Orthodox hegemony. In response, Reform Jewish leader Albert Vorspan asks rhetorically,

"Am I more connected to a Lubavitch Ḥasid, a racist JDL hoodlum, and a rabbi who panders to Pat Robertson than I am to a Christian who takes the social gospel seriously, respects my interpretation of Judaism, and appreciates my Jewish identity in the spirit of genuine pluralism?"

Commenting in his weekly column in the *Forward*, Leonard Fein responds that the correct answer [to

פנחס בן אלעזר בן אהרן הכהן השיב את חמתי

Rabbi Akiva and the gentile philanthropist who assisted him in building his academy.

Who then was Pinhas, according to this reading, and why did he do what he did? The answer is that he was a true seeker after truth, but that he was mistaken. He thought that Zimri and Cozbi were deceiving themselves, that they were, in fact, only at the ninth level, and that with enough willpower they could have overcome their desire. Ultimately, Pinhas was immature: he was a young soul that still had a lot of work

to do in clarifying his own sexuality. Why then was he rewarded, made high priest? No answer, except perhaps to note that the best thing to do with a fanatic is to make him a bureaucrat.

Is there a teaching for us in this arcane understanding of a brutal episode? Clearly it is not a justification for promiscuity, or the glorification of one's desire. It is, rather, at one level, a call upon us to be less judgmental in *interpreting* the behavior of others. Apparent sinners may, in fact, be acting out their part

of a Divine plan that is unknown and unknowable to us. This does not mean that their behavior will not draw unpleasant consequences in this world, that there will be no punishment, but that we are not equipped to understand. Ultimately, the esoteric meaning of the story of Zimri and Cozbi is that there is light when we can only see darkness.●

Vorspan's questions] is—yes—for most purposes, the Jewish connection overrides most, if not all, ideological differences. Those purposes cluster around crisis. When Jews are in trouble, virtually all of us say, "Damn our differences, full speed ahead." Yet Fein goes on to assert that most of the time, on a non-crisis basis, the rifts are more relevant than the family connection. But Leonard Fein does not live in northeastern Pennsylvania. In most of our communities here, we are in the midst of a crisis, albeit a long drawn-out crisis of aging and declining population. It is not just our family feeling that is threatened by "divide and destroy" thinking; it is the very survival of our Jewish communities. The obligations for compromise go both ways on the ideological spectrum. Liberal and Reform Jews usually bear the onus of compromise, and even if that remains true we must not lose patience or interest in the vital project of nurturing community.

Sometimes we must uphold standards to which we do not, strictly speaking, subscribe, and always we must respect the sensibilities of our more Orthodox neighbors. We do not all have to become *shomrei Shabbat*, but neither can we afford to revel in non-observance. By the same token, the Orthodox leaders and laity need to respect and understand their more liberal neighbors. Our Reform congregations are not churches—we practice Judaism pure and simple, and we excel in efforts to rescue marginal Jews and to improve the lives of our communities through outreach and social action. If maintaining community in the face of our long-term crisis means anything, then Orthodox Jews have to know that certain questions of personal status should not be asked, certain feelings about the level of ritual observance should not be expressed.

"Divide and destroy" thinking is not a luxury we can afford in northeastern

Pennsylvania. What is at stake in our efforts to respect each other is nothing less than the survival of Jewish communities that have existed for as many as 150 years. As uncomfortable as it may sometimes be, we must, indeed, all hang together, or, most assuredly, we shall all hang separately. **Rabbi Michael Joseph, Temple B'nai B'rith, Kingston, PA <michjose@aol.com>**

דָּבָר אַחֵר **DAVAR AHER. AFTER THE PLAGUE, THE ETERNAL SPOKE TO MOSES AND ELEAZAR, THE SON OF AARON THE PRIEST, SAYING: "TAKE A CENSUS OF THE WHOLE COMMUNITY OF THE FAMILIES-OF-ISRAEL, COUNT EVERY MAN OVER TWENTY WHO CAN GO TO THE ARMY"** [Num. 26.1]. In this week's *sidrah*, God celebrates Pinhas' fanaticism in the last *sidrah*, and curses Midian. (In case you need a review, Pinhas, a grandson of Aaron, makes shishkebab out of Zimri, a prince of Simeon, and Cozbi, his Midianite squeeze.) **"AFTER THE PLAGUE, THE ETERNAL SPOKE TO MOSES AND**

Rabbi Yosi Gordon

RABBI YOSI GORDON IS A RABBI IN EAU CLAIRE, WISCONSIN, AND IS A WELL-PUBLISHED AUTHOR IN THE AREA OF HEBREW LANGUAGE ACQUISITION.

Pinhas

"JUST THEN ONE OF THE ISRAELITES CAME AND BROUGHT A MIDIANITE WOMAN OVER TO HIS COMPANIONS, IN THE SIGHT OF MOSHE AND OF THE WHOLE ISRAELITE COMMUNITY WHO WERE WEEPING AT THE ENTRANCE OF THE TENT OF MEETING. WHEN PINHAS BEN ELAZAR BEN AHARON THE KOHEN SAW THIS, HE LEFT THE ASSEMBLY AND, TAKING A SPEAR IN HIS HAND, HE FOLLOWED THE ISRAELITE INTO THE CHAMBER AND STABBED BOTH OF THEM, THE ISRAELITE AND THE WOMEN, THROUGH HER GENITALS. THEN THE PLAGUE AGAINST THE ISRAELITES WAS CHECKED."

[Num. 25.6-8]

"The violins are proud people. During breaks in rehearsal they sit and go over the hard parts, so everyone knows it wasn't them who screwed up. The violins hardly ever look at the conductor. They know that he's taking his tempo from them anyway, so what's to look at? It's the winds he's conducting. It's not them. The violins believe that the conductor waves his baton in time to their bows going up and down, and that if he left, nobody in the audience would notice any difference except that they now have an unobstructed view of the orchestra. The violin is an instrument for neurotic geniuses; it's not for Lutherans. It has soul. It weeps. It cries out. It argues. Honey, this is a Jewish instrument. There's no Itzhak Peterson. There's no Pinhas Soderberg or Jascha Hanson. If you're Jewish, go, play already; Lutheran—uh-uh." *The Young Lutheran's Guide to the Orchestra.*

ELEAZAR, THE SON OF AARON THE PRIEST, SAYING: TAKE A CENSUS OF THE WHOLE COMMUNITY OF THE FAMILIES-OF-ISRAEL, COUNT EVERY MAN OVER TWENTY WHO CAN GO TO THE ARMY [Num. 26.1]. Rashi asks one question. Jacob Milgrom asks another. Rashi asks: "Why the census?" Milgrom asks: "Why tell Eleazar?"

Rashi answers, "Because they wanted to see how many people were left. And, because Moses was going off watch. He was like a shepherd—when they left Egypt, God trusted Moses with the flock. Now, he has them counted, to show that he has been responsible." Milgrom answers: "Because Aaron was dead." And then points out that this is the only time that God actually "spoke" to Eleazar.

Plague is an easy metaphor for era. We often feel like doing the Pinhas thing and finding a heroic solution

Garrison Keillor advised Lutherans to take up the flute or the harp. Not the violin. Pinhas played the violin. He was not Lutheran (Aharon played the viola).

Let's begin by not underestimating the desecration that was taking place. First, it was unseemly; that is, it was bad-for-the-Jews. Those of us who have dabbled in Jewish community relations know how bad bad-for-the-Jews can be. This was bad-for-the-Jews in a very big way. It is bad-for-the-Jews when lots of Jews, including lots of important Jews, engage in cultic orgies under the *hupah* in front of the Tent of the Meeting with ritual prostitutes of pagan gods and goddesses. It upsets things and does not look good in the press or in the Torah.

But this was desecration in a second sense. It violated holiness; or, we might say, it undid holiness. All the holiness that God and Moshe and Miriam and Aharon and others had carefully layered in the Wilderness journey, patiently stitched into the communal lives of the wandering riffraff, solidly nailed into the edifice of law and worship in preparation for the utopian assault—all that was about to be undone at the border. It was time for the violins.

("Why is everybody against violins
  What's wrong with violins?"
"That's violence."
"Not violins?"
"No, Miss Pattella. Violence."
"Never mind." *Emily Pattella*)

What Pinhas did was right. The rabbis were as shocked as we, and they found midrashic ways to cast a pall on Pinhas' impetuousness. But God didn't print a disclaimer: killing idolatrous princes and evangelizing harlots by stabbing them in their offending parts was the correct and only antidote for desecration on this scale. God saw, cheered and rewarded Pinhas with a special covenant: appropriately, a *b'rit* of *shalom*, of peace, of wholeness.

There are those who ask whether the Torah still speaks to us. Sometimes it speaks too loudly.

Pinhas, in midrashim, came back as Eliyahu, proving the reality of YHWH against Baal, then executing Baal's missionizing emissaries. He was Y'huda ha-Maccabee, attacking Jew and Greek for the purity of our practice and our belief. But was he Bar Kokhba, whose misbegotten revolution ended in 2000 years of exile from the Land of Israel? Was he that man who slaughtered almost 30 innocent Muslims in Machpelah in Hevron last year?

It's probably a matter of knowing. How did Pinhas know that turning Zimri and Cozbi into shishkabob was a mitzvah? Rambam says Pinhas got the Torah directly from Moshe. (Knowing is having well-educated teachers.) Rashi and the Vilna Gaon list Pinhas among the Prophets. Good students and good prophets know their mitzvot. And if it's a mitzvah, then it's a mitzvah. Knowing is not the same as zeal or a sense of purpose or self-confidence. Those can be very dangerous attributes.

---

to all our problems. But, reality is, we too, are usually left to the priesthood of demography—taking count of who is left after the plague. This, too, is holy work. When the census is done, God says to Moses: "FOR THESE YOU SHALL DIVIDE UP THE PROMISED LAND FOR AN INHERITANCE" [Num. 26.53]. I have my calipers ready. **Joel Lurie Grishaver** <Gris@TorahAura.Com>

דָּבָר אַחֵר **DAVAR AHER. THE DAUGHTERS OF TZELOFHAD...** [Num. 27.1]. Torah from *Written Out of History, Our Jewish Foremothers*, by Sondra Henry and Emily Taitz: "In 1901, a series of scrolls from the ancient Elephantine colony were discovered by diggers near Aswan, Egypt, and through them, Mivtahiah was reborn. She may be the earliest Jewish woman to become known through original documents...Mivtahiah may have been

an only daughter, with no brothers to inherit. But whatever her status within her family, she received property from her father, Mahseiah, who put no limit on whom she might marry.... Mivtahiah married three times, twice to non-Jews. The practice of intermarriage, although officially forbidden to Jews, was very common in Diaspora communities as well as in the Jewish nation itself. Mivtahiah's first husband was a Jew, her second a gentile, and

Rambam looks at prophetic knowing and finds seven pre-reqs:

(1) Complete physical and mental health,
(2) Perfect learning and rational intellect,
(3) A wholly-balanced character,
(4) Total commitment to understanding the laws of the universe,
(5) Unconditional and boundless *kavvanah* (devotion) to know God, God's laws and God's purposes,
(6) Full control of all lower appetites, and,
(7) Radical selflessness.

Then comes the word of God.

This is how I can understand Pinhas (and the only way I can understand Pinhas). He is not like you and me, not like Bar Kokhba and that man, because he possessed all the prerequisites, and then came the word of God. Thus, he was able to slaughter without

benefit of Rabbinic Court or state authority or even Torah (which includes no "*Thou-shalt-skewer*" commandments). Otherwise, God could not have honored Pinhas. Otherwise, Pinhas would have died in the ignominy I so wish upon that man.

The moral of this story is that we, too, have the right and the *obligation* promptly to annihilate all evil-doers and all who cause others to do evil, i.e., to be just like Pinhas…provided that we, too, truly possess all the prophetic qualifications and *know* that we have heard the word of God. Lacking that, we shall have to be like Moshe in the ways of law and Aharon in the paths of peace, with the hope that this, too, will bring *Mashiah*. Slowly.●

Pinhas

her third, a gentile who converted. Mivtahiah's first two marriages ended, either by death or divorce. Her third marriage, to As-Hor who became Nathan, produced two sons who ultimately inherited all her property…. Mivtahiah is important for the information she gave us about the life of a Jewish woman in that period, the decree of power she could attain, her freedom, and her recognition as an independent person in her world." **Joel's Comments:** (1) In checking out my "Women's Shelf" the Daughters of Tzelofhad are all but missing. Why haven't Jewish feminists rooted themselves more in an economic text? (2) If you don't understand the connection between Mivtahiah and the *sidrah*, look up Numbers 36.1-12. **Joel Lurie Grishaver** <Gris@TorahAura.Com>

nique among mitzvot in the Ḥumash is the one dealing with vows.

AND MOSHE WAS SPEAKING TO THE HEADS OF THE TRIBES OF THE CHILDREN OF ISRAEL. "THIS IS THE CONVERSATION WHICH YH HAS CONVEYED. A PERSON WHO WILL AGAIN AND AGAIN MAKE VOWS AND PLEDGE OATHS THUS BINDING AND TYING THEIR BREATH-SOUL TO A PROHIBI-TION—LET THEM NOT INJURE THEIR WORD—FOR ALL THAT COMES FORTH FROM THEIR MOUTH MAKES FOR ACTION.

A WOMAN, HOWEVER, WHO WILL AGAIN AND AGAIN MAKE VOWS AND PLEDGE OATHS THUS BINDING AND TYING HER BREATH-SOUL TO A PROHIBITION ALL THE WHILE SHE IS IN THE HOUSE OF HER FATHER AND IN HER STILL TOO YOUNGNESS. AS HER FATHER HEARD HER VOW-ING AND FORBIDDING TO-SELF-BY WHICH SHE HAS BOUND HER BREATH-SOUL AND HER FATHER WAS QUIET TO HER ABOUT THIS THEN ALL THE VOWINGS AND ALL THE BINDINGS ONE'S BREATH-SOUL TO REFUSE THEY SHALL BE MADE REAL. BUT—IF HER FATHER SAYS 'NO! NO!' THAT VERY DAY HE FIRST HEARS OF IT, THEN HER VOWING AND FORBIDDING TO-SELF-BY WHICH SHE HAS BOUND HER BREATH-SOUL THEN ALL THE VOWINGS AND ALL THE BINDING OF ONE'S BREATH-SOUL TO REFUSE HAVE NO LEG TO STAND ON. AND YH WILL RELEASE HER FOR HE, HER FATHER, WAS THE ONE WHO NO-NO'ED HER. [NUMBERS 20.2-6]

Then the same is repeated in the situa-tion of an espoused lass, for whom both father and bridegroom share responsi-bility, and in the case of a married woman and her husband. This is the only time when the Torah Giver insists that a mitzvah is first addressed to the heads of tribes.

Mattot

Numbers 30.2–32.42

Rabbi Zalman Schachter-Shalomi

RABBI SCHACHTER-SHALOMI IS THE RABBINIC CHAIR OF ALEPH ALLIANCE FOR JEWISH RENEWAL.

דְּבָר אַחֵר **DAVAR AḤER.** "TAKE VENGEANCE FOR THE CHILDREN OF ISRAEL AGAINST THE MIDIANITES" [Num. 31.2]. Deb-orah Enelow writes that "the Torah is our teaching, the central text of Jewish reve-lation," but apparently she looks to other authorities for her standards of morality. She flatly declares that parts of *parashat Mattot* are "morally wrong" and "unac-ceptable," and what's more, she writes as though her position is so self-evident that it needs no justification. In the spe-cific case, she objects to the waging of all-out war with Midian, and measures all the commentators according to how much they agree with her. That view seems shortsighted as well as in the minority: it is only very recently that war involving civilian slaughter has been seen as problematic, and even now, few people are so troubled by it that they would intervene to stop it in Bosnia, or would object in hindsight to the fire-bombing of Dresden. We may be

First, I want to talk about the concern over both authority and responsibility that the heads of the tribes were to have had. Second, about making promises to oneself before G-d. If I want someone else to shoulder some of my responsibility, I must also empower them to fulfill it and, therefore, limit my freedom. In the world of free choice, I abdicate some of my freedom to one whom I trust to do it well for me and my relations. In this act, I testify to my belief that they can indeed be relied on to do it well.

To be one of the heads of the tribes is a heavy responsibility. No one could share with them the secret of leadership better than Moshe! So he began by giving an example from their own lives as heads and members of families and taught that law (that people these days see in need of being gender equalized), which in their day was their life situation. Imagine you really mean what you say in the Shema: "Train your children to good habits and talk with them when you are at home in your house, etc."

Being a spouse to a spouse, a parent to a child always poses dilemmas in relation to authority and responsibility. "As long as you are in my house and eat from my table you will have to..." is one horn of the dilemma, and "I am my own person and I know best what I want and what is right for me" is the other.

When Moshe taught them this, they must have felt what it would be like in their own families. They realized the web of relationships and how one person affects the others they relate to. I have no right to determine something for someone else without their consent and even less so when that other has taken on responsibility for me.

In this way, Moshe prepared the heads of the tribes, the people in

Mattot

appalled by the violence of this episode, but it is the way human beings behave even now; God's command was certainly not anomalous or extraordinary by the standards of that time and place. More importantly, there are surely lessons we can learn from this passage—but we won't have the chance if we simply "condemn" it, as Ms. Enelow has done.

She evidently believes that her personal views represent a higher morality than the Torah, and that the Torah should be called to account for its deviations from her views. We live in solipsistic times, when individuals' feelings, perceptions, and pronouncements are treated as sacred. As Jews, we are fortunate to have the Torah to combat that impulse. We just have to take it seriously enough to listen to

וידבר משה אל ראשי המטות לבני ישראל לא

positions of responsibility and authority, to see the whole tribe as their extended family and in this way taught them how to discharge their responsibility.

Now what is a VOW? A part of me—here and now—wants to take away the freedom of my decision from me at a later time and different place and situation when I will be there and then. It feels imperative that I do so now. I have battled with the same urges in me for a long time. I will not again do that battle. I decide now and for such and such a time that in case of an oath that binds me, I will not act on that urge or, in case of a vow, I promise not to open inner debate again, but I decide now that I will fulfill my word without delay.

At issue is the power of my word. If I am fickle and I say one thing today and don't keep it tomorrow then my word loses power—it has a puncture—one of the meanings of

יָחֵל yahel—to make a חָלָל hallal, a hole, a puncture—and it is weakened, made powerless. My extended family cannot rely on it and it has no power in Torah or in prayer. Without the power of the Word all leadership ceases to function. The word has become empty of power and Moshe wants us to have a strong Word. Look what we call the Ten Commandments which obligate us and the Ten "Let there be's!" that have the power to create: עֲשֶׂרֶת הַדִּבְּרוֹת Asseret ha-Dibrot and עֲשָׂרָה מַאֲמָרוֹת Assrah Ma'amarot. They are power words.

The Ishbitzer Rebbe, Rabbi Mordechai Yossef, points out that there are some people who wonder why the Torah did not forbid such an act that they found to be destructive to the life—imagine how an alcoholic would feel about alcohol. Why is it not totally forbidden? So the Torah gives each person the power to make an oath-vow and to

Synopsis: Moses speaks to the heads of the Israelite tribes about oaths—those made by themselves, women, wives and widows. The war against the Midianites occupies all of chapter 31, while in chapter 32, the tribes of Gad and Reuven negotiate to settle the east side of the Jordan in return for their acting as shock-troops in the conquest of the land.

---

what it says, instead of using it as a palimpsest on which to project our own issues. **Bob Goldfarb, New York, NY** <RSGoldfarb@aol.com>.

דָּבָר אַחֵר **DAVAR AHER.** "TAKE VENGEANCE FOR THE CHILDREN OF ISRAEL AGAINST THE MIDIANITES" [Num. 31.2]. *To Deborah Enelow:* Hallelujah for daring to question, for the expanded understanding of "Turn it over, turn it over." You might find it wormy under the

rock. Love, **Jo Milgrom** <milgrom@hum.huji.ac.il>

Mattot

treat it in their own life as if it were a Torah prohibition. So making a vow-oath can be very helpful. It becomes for me an individual mitzvah and it does not obligate everyone else.

What happens if at some later day I really regret that I made a hasty vow or oath? When I made it, I had no idea how it would impact my life and I experienced regret. I cannot ignore it without damaging the Word and I cannot keep it without damaging some of my relations or myself. Then I come to the head of the tribe—a Rav, a Rebbe—someone who has authority over the extended family, a respected counselor, to help me to find a פֶּתַח חֲרָתָה *petah haratah*, a door for regret, and thus to arrange for me to have הַתָּרַת נְדָרִים *hattarat n'darim*, the unbinding of the vow. In this way, I will give the Word all the respect it deserves and, in the right context, discover a way to annul the vow without weakening the Word.

This is why Moshe had to charge the heads of the tribes with this law. They have the responsibility of being friends and counselors to the people as well as keepers of the Word. So they need to create a safe and sacred space of spiritual intimacy to explore one's feelings and motives and, in this way, rethink and re-feel the whole thing and, if it is right, open a Gate for Regret to annul the vow.

A man confided to me that he had once—when as a young man he was sick—prayed to be allowed to live to be sixty years old. He was now going to be that age and he was showing symptoms of disease. We called a group together to perform הַתָּרַת נְדָרִים *Hattarat N'darim*. AND WHEN THERE ARE PEOPLE WHO WANT TO MAKE POLICY FOR OTHERS THAT IS NOT GOOD—THEN ON THE DAY THEY HEAR OF IT THEY NEED TO OFFER THEIR PROTEST.

They were once going to make a new law in Berditchev, that beggars not go from house to house to beg, but that there should be a fund that the poor be given a stipend. Since Rabbi Levi Yitzchak had requested to be present when a new law was about to be enacted, they invited him to come to the meeting of the town council. When he heard what it was all about he rose to leave. They asked him, "Rabbi, why are you leaving? This is a new law and you asked us to call you." And he said "No! It is an old ordinance that was long ago enacted in Sodom and Gomorra, not to have to see the poor face-to-face." This is how he NO-NO'ed that new law. That is leadership and responsible authority.•

וידבר משה אל ראשי המטות לבני ישראל לאמר

Deborah Enelow

DEBORAH ENELOW IS THE EDUCATOR AT CONGREGATION BETH EL RELIGIOUS SCHOOL IN BERKELEY, CA.

As I reread these chapters at the end of *Be-Midbar*, I found myself increasingly disturbed by them. I might be tempted to explore the personal meaning of vows [Num. 30.2-19] or to comment on the midrash [*Tanhuma* B on Num. 33.1-48] which spiritualizes the stages of the journey through the wilderness; I would surely find discussing the first two sections of the *parashah*: the first recounts the laws involving the vows of women living in their father's or husband's houses (Num. 30), the second, the war against the Midianites (Num. 31)? Thinking about these passages has led me to a broader question: How should we talk about sections of the Torah that are morally wrong?

Needless to say, many others before me have seen the ethical problems in these sections, but when I examine the commentaries—both ancient and modern—I am not pleased with what I see. All of them refuse to confront squarely what is unacceptable in the text.

To begin with, let us look at the section on vows [Num. 30.2-19]. Here's a summary: If a man makes a vow, he must carry out what he has said. If a woman makes a vow while in her father's house, he is able to negate her vow if he does so when he hears of it. The same provision is true if the woman is married: Her husband can negate her vow when he hears of it. In short, women are treated as children while the men in their lives act as their parents.

Ancient and medieval commentators hardly objected to this disparagement of women; it reflected their own bias. To cite one related example, Rashi comments on *Kiddushin* 23b: "For a wife is like a slave in that her husband is entitled to the work of her hands and whatever he may find." Modern commentators like Gunther Plaut (*The Torah: A Modern Commentary*) and Jacob Milgrom (*JPS Torah Commentary*), are less at ease with such assumptions of inequality, and have, therefore, approached the passage containing this series of laws by treating it as an historical document, then arguing that in its view of women the Torah as a whole was progressive for its time. Though women, it is argued, are treated here as children, in many cases in Biblical law women are given more respect and autonomy than in other legal codes of

Mattot

that era. This approach, however, conveniently forgets the authority of the Torah as sacred scripture today. The Torah is our teaching, the central text of Jewish revelation. We cannot just look the other way when the text says that women's words have no authority without the approval of men! Lack of space here precludes my going any further than noting the omission in the modern commentaries of an honest recognition of the depth of the problem.

Let me turn to an even more difficult section—what Rabbi Plaut euphemistically calls "the campaign against the Midianites" [Num. 31]. What is described is, in fact, a genocidal war against the people of Midian. Plaut and Milgrom treat this section as historical fiction possibly surrounding a core of historical fact. The Israelites, they argue, never got close to exterminating the Midianites who appeared later on as a dominating power. In discussing the historical issues surrounding the war, Rabbis Plaut and Milgrom both talk about the exaggeration of the numbers of people slain and the booty captured. Though Milgrom discusses the historical problems and the literary structure of the text, he never goes into the moral problems that it raises. Plaut, in contrast, recognizes the moral issues of this passage. The historical analysis, for Plaut, only makes the moral issues more glaring. How could the slaughter of so many, he asks, stand side-by-side with "the humanitarian ideals and deep sense of compassion that are the very heart of the Torah?" We might, indeed, remember the injunction "Do not stand by while your neighbor's blood is shed" [Lev. 19.16]. At this point, however, Plaut refuses to take the next step and denounce this section of the Torah as immoral, instead softening the sting of his own question by looking to the midrash and claiming that the ancients were also disturbed by this passage. He specifically mentions a midrash implying that it was Moses' anger that led to the slaughter and that God was not responsible. One commentary he refers to, however, makes the opposite point. In *Numbers. Rabbah* 22.4, God tells Moses to avenge the Midianites himself, yet Moses goes against God's words and calls upon the tribes to contribute soldiers. Why does Moses go against God's words? Moses has a moment of conjunction: He remembers that he grew up in Midian and that one should not hurt that which has nourished one. A moment of moral conjunction—and then the midrash goes on to say this was really not the same Midian where Moses grew up, so Moses' squeamishness was unnecessary.

The rest of the midrashim that I found only makes matter worse! While I searched to find a text equal or even close to the wonderful midrash about God stopping the angels from cheering as the Egyptians drowned in the Sea of Reeds, I found only texts that seem to glorify the whole affair. For example, in *Numbers Rabbah* 22.5, it says that Moses longed to see the vengeance upon the Midianites before he died and begged God for the chance to see it with his own eyes. Worse than the picture of Moses in this midrash is the picture of God in the original text. *Be-Midbar* justifies genocide because the Midianites seduced the Israelites into idolatry and harlotry. God first punishes the Israelites involved in the apostasy. But for God, punishing the guilty parties was not enough. For not only the Midianite women, who were presumably the seducers, but the whole tribe of people must be collectively responsible for the sin of the Israelites and so must be avenged. Not just the adult women and men, but all the male children and all women who were not virgins. None of the commentators are willing to discuss the character of God implicit in this text, which attributes to Him the indiscriminate hatred and fury of an insanely jealous husband who has witnessed his wife's adultery.

What are we to say? "*Turn it, turn it, because all is in it*" must mean that the worst aspects of human nature are projected onto God as well as the best. And what does it mean to treat the Torah as sacred? It is to find within the text the standard by which to condemn its worst parts. It is to question the Torah as Abraham questioned God: "SHALL NOT THE JUDGE OF ALL THE EARTH DO WHAT IS JUST?" [Gen. 18.25].•

צֵאוּ מֵאֶרֶץ מִצְרַיִם

Masei

**Numbers
33.1–36.13**

Howard
Schwartz

HOWARD SCHWARTZ TEACHES AT
THE UNIVERSITY OF MISSOURI–ST.
LOUIS. HE HAS EDITED A FOUR-VOL-
UME SET OF JEWISH FOLK TALES,
CONSISTING OF *ELIJAH'S VIOLIN*,
MIRIAM'S TAMBOURINE, *LILITH'S CAVE*
AND *GABRIEL'S PALACE*, WHICH IS
AVAILABLE FROM OXFORD
UNIVERSITY PRESS.

Cities of
Refuge

"T HEN YE SHALL APPOINT YOUR
CITIES TO BE CITIES OF
REFUGE FOR YOU; THAT THE
SLAYER MAY FLEE THERE,
WHO KILLS ANY PERSON
UNAWARES" [Num. 35.11].
Among the legendary
traditions of the world,
that of the Jews is
unique, in that it is possible to trace its evolu-
tion. In most cultures,
myths and legends gen-
erally exist orally until
they are written down,
then they tend to
remain fixed.

דְּבָר אַחֵר **DAVAR AHER.** Dear
Judy: Although I have never
responded to a contribution of the
"**Learn Torah With…**" publication, I
had a thought that might interest
you. You have written (of the daughters of Tzelofhad) that "some
midrashim even say that their intelligence diminished when they
become mothers." What word in
Hebrew is used for diminished? Is it
related to "that which gets smaller as

But in Judaism the stories of the
Torah and the rest of the Bible
were constantly retold and re-
imagined, giving birth to a host of
new legends. These legends
gained acceptance because they
were said to be part of the Oral
Law that Moses was said to have
received at Mount Sinai, along
with the Written Law. As one
midrash puts it, Moses received
the Torah during the day, and at
night God explained it to him
[*Pirke De Rabbi Eliezer* 46].

One of the great wonders of the
Jewish tradition is in the way in
which these new legends came into
being. In seeking to investigate
(*darash*, the root of midrash) the
true meaning of the text, the rabbis
of the talmudic and midrashic eras
would look for clues in other portions of the Torah. In the process
they would combine separate myths
and legends in a way that produced
new legends, which would them-

it moves into the distance?" This is
what I'm thinking: Marguerite
Porete, a Christian mystic, burned at
the state in 1310 and possibly a
"teacher" of Meister Eckhart, probably the greatest Christian mystic,
wrote a play called *A Mirror for Sample Souls*. The play is an incredible
description of higher states of consciousness involving a dialogue
between love and reason and the
soul. In chapter 7, Porete writes:

אלה מסעי בני ישראל אשר

selves later undergo this same process of embellishment. In this way the rabbis re-imagined the Bible, remaking it in the image of each generation.

One good example concerns the Cities of Refuge, as defined in Numbers 35.11 and related passages. These cities were created as a safe haven for those who had accidentally slain another, to protect them from revenge. Some of those living in these cities of refuge were awaiting trial, to determine if the death they caused was accidental or not. After the trial, a person judged innocent was sent to live in the city of refuge to which he or she had fled. They were required to remain there until the death of the high priest. Thus, the cities of refuge functioned both as a place of refuge and as an enforced exile. But the primary purpose of this exile was to protect an innocent person from revenge by the family of the

victim, for in the culture of that time, the family of the victim would likely seek revenge. Those who had not killed on purpose had to be protected, and, thus, the concept of the Cities of Refuge came into being.

The biblical text is very specific about the locations of these cities, and equally clear about their purpose. In later verses, the identity of those who sought refuge in these cities is refined: "THESE SIX CITIES SHALL BE A REFUGE, BOTH FOR THE CHILDREN OF ISRAEL, AND FOR THE STRANGER, AND FOR THE SOJOURNER AMONG THEM; THAT EVERY ONE THAT KILLS ANY PERSON UNAWARES MAY FLEE THITHER." [Num. 35.14]

The establishment of the Cities of Refuge was a sign of great moral responsibility. We cannot but be struck by the powerful sense of justice they demonstrate; they embody the biblical injunction "JUSTICE, JUSTICE, SHALT THOU PURSUE" [Deut. 16.20]. This concept of justice is the under-

Synopsis: The trek comprising 42 stops through out the wilderness is recounted and the boundaries and apportionment of the land of Canaan are detailed, complete with the Cities of Refuge. The final chapter in the Book of Numbers concludes with laws of inheritance and the case of the daughters of Tzelofhad.

"The soul: Within him she is queen of virtues, daughter of the godhead, sister of wisdom and bride of love. Reason will wonder at such language, but he has reached his limits whereas I was, am and shall be for evermore: love has no beginnng or end, and is beyond understanding and I am pure love. How then can I ever end? Reason: This is too much for me! I cannot bear it! My heart fails me and I am slain! (dies) The soul: He should have

died before. Now I can come freely into my own. The wound of love is the death of reason." Regarding Porete's phrase "Sister of Wisdom" See Daniel Matt's *The Essential Kabbalah* (p. 112): Say to wisdom, "you are my sister." Join thought to divine wisdom, so she and he become one. New drash on old drash. When we love, our world changes, the world of boundaries is diminished and the world of unity becomes our lived real-

ity. See Matt p.113 (beyond knowing) and p. 117 (gathering multiplicity) and all the many, many references among the writings of Jewish mystics. **Nancy Freund**

Masei

lying principle behind democracy, and is at the core of the Jewish passion for justice.

At the same time, it seems likely that the biblical concept of the Cities of Refuge inspired the Jewish legend of the ultimate city of refuge—one that offered escape from the Angel of Death. This is the legend of the city of Luz, which first takes form in the Talmud and Midrash and continues to evolve in medieval Jewish folklore.

Just how the legend of the City of Luz emerged is a case study in the evolution of Jewish folklore. There are four passing references to Luz in the Bible, but it is the first reference that supplies its attributes as a place unique in the world, for it was there that Jacob had the dream of the ladder that reached into heaven, with angels ascending and descending on it [Gen. 28.121]: "AND JACOB ROSE UP EARLY IN THE MORNING, AND TOOK THE STONE THAT HE HAD PUT UNDER HIS HEAD, AND SET IT UP FOR A PILLAR, AND POURED OIL UPON THE TOP OF IT. AND HE CALLED THE NAME OF THE PLACE BETHEL {HOUSE OF GOD}, BUT THE NAME OF THE CITY WAS LUZ AT THE SAME TIME" [Gen. 28.18-19].

The rabbis were curious to know what there was about this city that made it so special that Jacob had this holiest of dreams there. A talmudic legend embellishes its history and purpose: "That is the Luz against which Sennacherib marched without disturbing it, and even the Angel of Death had no permission to pass through it. But when the old there become tired of life they go outside the wall, then die." [B. Sot. 46b]

In this legend, we see that the City of Luz has been identified as a city of refuge—from conquerors such as Sennacherib and Nebuchadnezzar, and, above all, from the ultimate conqueror, the Angel of Death. Where did the rabbis of the Talmud find their inspiration? Surely in the Cities of Refuge. After all, it is not a great imaginative leap from a city of refuge for those whose lives were in danger to a city of safety from the Angel of Death.

From this time on, the City of Luz is described as a city of immortals. Another talmudic legend links King Solomon to this city:

"One morning, as King Solomon awoke, he heard a chirping outside his window. He sat up in bed and listened carefully, for he knew the language of the birds, and he overheard them say that the Angel of Death had been sent to take the lives of two of his closest advisors. King Solomon was startled by this unexpected news, and he summoned the two doomed men. And when they stood before him, he revealed what he had learned of their fate. The two were terrified, and they begged King Solomon to help them. Solomon told them that their only hope was to find their way to the city of Luz. For it was well known that the Angel of Death was forbidden to enter there. Therefore, the inhabitants of Luz were immortal—as long as they

אלה מסעי בני ישראל אשר יצאו מארץ מצרים

remained within the walls of the charmed city. Very few knew the secret of how to reach that city, but King Solomon was one of those few. So it was that King Solomon revealed the secret to the two frightened men, and they departed at once. They whipped their camels across the hot desert all day, and at nightfall they saw finally the walls of that fabled city. Immortality was almost within reach and they rode as fast as they could to the city gates. But when they arrived they saw, to their horror, the Angel of Death waiting for them. "How did you know to look for us here?" they asked. The angel replied, "This is where I was told to meet you." [*B. Sukkah* 53a.]

In later midrashic commentary, additional details about the city of Luz emerge. It turns out that the city does not have an entrance, or else everyone in the world would seek refuge there. Further, it has an almond tree (one meaning of "Luz") in front of it. Then, in a flash of inspiration, one rabbi links the almond tree and the missing gate, and we can virtually see a legend evolving before our eyes. Rabbi Abba ben Kahana said, "Why was it called Luz?—Because whoever entered it blossomed forth into meritorious acts and good deeds like a *luz*" The Rabbis said, "As the nut has no mouth (opening), so no man could discover the entrance to the town." Rabbi Simon said, "A nut tree stood at the entrance of the city." Rabbi Leazar ben Merom said in the name of Rabbi Phinehas ben Hama, "A nut tree stood at the entrance of a cave; this tree was hol-

low, and through it one entered the cave and through the cave the city." [*Genesis Rabbah* 69.8]

In later Jewish folklore, all of these elements come into play in several folktales about quests to the city of Luz. In one of these tales,"The City of Luz,"* two Jews travel through enchanted caves to the Holy Land, and then find their way to the ancient city. Once they discover the entrance hidden in the hollow trunk of the almond tree—as described in the midrash from *Genesis Rabbah*—they enter the city and meet an old man three hundred years old, who confesses that living so long is not necessarily a blessing. That is why the old inevitably go outside the city, where the Angel of Death awaits them.

Thus does the midrash give birth to a quest to this city of immortals, the only refuge on earth from the Angel of Death. At this point the legend of the city of Luz has come to exist independently of the concept of the Cities of Refuge that almost certainly inspired it, along with Jacob's dream. It is this kind of ingenious embellishment that lies at the heart of the oral tradition reflected in the *aggadah*, where the rabbis found a way to resolve the mysteries and contradictions of the Torah by re-imagining the Bible. In the process, they created a book of the Book, in which these kinds of gems lie scattered everywhere in the rich midrashic texts.

*A version of this story can be found in *Elijah's Violin & Other Jewish*

Fairy Tales, pp. 279-293. For another story about the city of Luz, see "The Cave of King David" in *Gabriel's Palace: Jewish Mystical Tales*, pp. 139-141.•

Judy Aronson

JUDY ARONSON IS THE DIRECTOR OF EDUCATION AT LEO BAECK TEMPLE, LOS ANGELES, CALFORNIA, AND A MEMBER OF THE CLINICAL FACULTY AT THE RHEA HIRSCH SCHOOL OF EDUCATION AT HEBREW UNION COLLEGE.

Masei

In his essay, Howard Schwartz speaks of the process of *aggadah*, where the rabbis found a way to resolve the mysteries and contradictions of the Torah by re-imagining the Bible. He has demonstrated how stories grow from generation to generation, deepening our understanding of the text through ingenious invention. In our own generation, interpreters searching for women mentioned in the Bible as well as women not mentioned (but clearly somewhere in the background) have turned to classical Rabbinic literature for fresh interpretation. A welcomed addition to the field is a new book by Leila Leah Bronner called *From Eve to Esther: Rabbinic Reconstructions of Biblical Women*, part of the Gender and the Biblical Tradition series of Westminster John Knox Press published in 1994. This book was recommended by a friend who knew I was studying *Masei*. In the chapter called "The Estate of Daughterhood," Bronner uses Rabbinic sources to write a success story about the five sisters. Our story began in *Pinhas* [Num. 26.33] when we heard of Tzelofhad who died in the wilderness leaving no male heirs. His five daughters, Mahlah, Noah, Hoglah, Milcah and Tirzah, appear in a census taken by Moses and Eleazar, the son of Aaron. The purpose of the census was to divide the land of Israel among the tribes when they cross the Jordan. It is rare that women are mentioned by name in Biblical lists. (See Bronner on Serah Bat Asher). Even if the purpose is only etymological, it is still important. Subsequently, in Numbers 27.1-11, the daughters of Tzelofhad present such a good case for themselves concerning the disposition of their father's promised land, that Rashi says of them, "Happy is that mortal, whose words are acknowledged to be true by God." God decrees that the daughters can inherit.

In *Parashat Masei*, what Hertz calls the "Law of Heiresses" gives the decision a broader definition and application. (Just an aside: One of my friends was an heiress. I asked if her father treated sons and daughters equally. She said her father had not discriminated by gender in the amount of his bequests. However, only sons could be executors. As a result, since her father's death years ago, the opinion of the sisters has been ignored and the estate has dwindled considerably through mismanagement. Keep this story in mind as we return to the text.)

There is a verse in this parashah that is causing me no end of consternation. Periodically, when I study Torah, a verse jumps off the page and into my mind. I begin to obsess about it wondering why I never paid attention to it before. Leila Bronner says that the Bible is a laconic, elliptical, and at times ambiguous text. Yet the verse is reasonably straightforward at first reading. I think I missed its significance before because most commentaries pay attention to the second half of the verse and rush past the first. Chapter 36.6 begins, "THIS IS THE THING (HA-DAVAR) THAT GOD COMMANDED ABOUT THE DAUGHTERS OF TZELOFHAD, SAYING: 'LA-TOV B'EINEIHEM TIH'YENAH L'NASHIM' 'LET THEM MARRY TO WHOM THEY THINK BEST.'" How had I missed this show of confidence in the ability of these fatherless and perhaps even orphaned women to choose their own husbands? (Don't bother to look for their mother's guidance in Torah; she doesn't even get a mention. Perhaps she will resurface in a yet-to-be-written midrash.) Because it is in the interest of the tribe to preserve the integrity of their land grant, the daughters can choose that which is pleasing in their eyes, as long as they marry into their own tribe. That is the biblical ruling.

One of my cousins considers this verse a cynical joke against the daughters. They would not have had any choice at all in his opinion. This was such an outlandish notion that no one would take it seriously. However, Leila Bronner says that Rabbinic praise of the daughters knows no bounds. They were wise, exegetes, and they were virtuous. So why not trust them to pick appropriate mates? My cousin's wife and I are not so sure. The words are there on the page, clearly written. Without taking anything out of context and simply looking at the *p'shat* level, I, as a feminist, accept this as validation of a woman's right to make important choices that affect her life and body. To support my argument, I turn again to Bronner's research that the daughters were called virtuous by the rabbis, for they were willing to marry only such men as were worthy of them, to wait a long time to marry, and marry only when they found the proper spouses. These women, according to the rabbis, sound like they would be good managers of their own property and destiny. However, their husbands

became the holders of the land for the tribe. Who knows whether their wives were valued after marriage as they were before? Some midrashim even say that their intelligence diminished when they became mothers. What do you think about this rather peculiar idea? I welcome your opinion. I am deeply grateful to Leila Leah Bronner who through her work helps me to re-imagine and become more inventive in looking at text. We need more of this thoughtful scholarship to help us establish a balanced role for women in Judaism. We are all heirs and heiresses of a great tradition. Our devotion to its study will water the roots of the Tree of Life and give it continued growth and vigor.

חֲזַק, חֲזַק, וְנִתְחַזֵּק

Hazak Hazak v'nit-Hazek

דברים

Devarim

Devarim

**Deuteronomy
1.1-3.22**

Professor Sherry Israel

SHERRY ISRAEL IS AN ASSOCIATE PRO-
FESSOR, HORNSTEIN PROGRAM IN
JEWISH COMMUNAL SERVICE, BRANDEIS
UNIVERSITY, WALTHAM, MA.

This week, we begin reading the last book of the Torah, דְּבָרִים, Devarim. The first parashah of the book, as is always the case, has the same name as the book it begins. Parashat Devarim has another distinction: it is always read on the Shabbat before Tisha B'Av. There is something to be learned from this, or, rather, a couple of things, intricately intertwined.

We can start with history. *Melakhim Bet* [II Kings], chapters 22-27, reports a story. It was the eighteenth year of the reign of King Josiah in Judah (621 B.C.E., by our count). The high priest, Ḥilkiahu, reported to the king's scribe that he had found *Sefer haTorah,* the Book of the Law, in the Temple.

The scribe took the book back to the king and read it to him. Josiah may have been unable to read, but apparently he knew how to listen. Struck by his kingdom's departure from the Word of God, he initiated a campaign of moral and theological reform.

It didn't last long. Josiah's son and grandson "DID ALL THAT WAS EVIL IN THE SIGHT OF THE LORD." The Great Reform was over, a divided populace and court challenged their Babylonian overlord, and in 586 B.C.E., Nebuchadnezzar's soldiers laid siege to Jerusalem. They starved its people, conquered it, and burned the Temple. And the Ninth of Av became the anchor date for Jewish national calamities.

Contemporary Biblical scholarship describes the book of *Devarim* as being built around a central core, which runs from about the middle of *Parashat va-Etḥanan* to almost the end of *Parashat Ki Tavo*. This core is believed to be in its essence that same "Book of the Law" that Ḥilkiahu found and turned over to King Josiah. (The first chapters and the last, which provide a setting for the core, are believed, on testimony of language and other internal evidence, to have been attached to it much later.) Knowing all this, we can see that reading *Devarim* as we approach *Tisha B'Av* is good historic pedagogy. The reading today is preparatory, reminding us of the Jewish people's ever-recurring

אלה הדברים אשר דבר מ

need for reform, of the fragility of social and moral change, of the tradition's view of the results of national indifference to God's law.

The rabbis, who were the successors not to kings or priests, but to the prophets and scribes, had a different understanding of this fifth book of the Torah. By rabbinic tradition, *Devarim* is our record of the final teaching of Moses, the Great Lawgiver, to the children of Israel before his death. It is the recapitulation of the Sinaitic Covenant to the new generation, to inscribe the Covenant in their hearts as they were about to cross over to inherit and settle the Land.

Yet these same rabbis set up our calendar to make a connection between this parashah and the fast of the Ninth of Av. Their connection is not historic, but poetic and homiletic, which is to say, midrashic. The link is through the word אֵיכָה, *eikhah*, which resonates through all the public readings of both Shabbat *Devarim* and *Tisha B'Av*.

In chapter 1, verse 12 of this parashah, Moses despairs that the tasks of governing the people have grown beyond his capacity. He exclaims

אֵיכָה אֶשָּׂא לְבַדִּי טָרְחֲכֶם וּמַשַּׂאֲכֶם,
"*eikhah esah l'vadi, torhakhem u'massa'akhem?*" "HOW CAN I BEAR UNAIDED THIS BURDEN OF YOU?" Lest we miss the point, this sentence is traditionally read not in normal Torah

trope, but in the trope of the Book of Lamentations.

The haftarah for the day, from the book of Isaiah [1.21], uses that same word:

אֵיכָה הָיְתָה לְזוֹנָה קִרְיָה נֶאֱמָנָה
"*Eikhah haytah l'zonah kiryah ne-emanah!*" "HOW IS THE FAITHFUL CITY BECOME A HARLOT!" The haftarah, too, is traditionally read in the trope of Lamentations (beginning after the first verse). On *Tisha B'Av* itself (this year, observed starting in the evening as we take leave of Shabbat), we will read from Lamentations, the book named in Hebrew for that same word, its first word,

אֵיכָה יָשְׁבָה בָדָד הָעִיר רַבָּתִי עָם
"*Eikhah yashvah vadad, ha'ir rabbati am.*" "ALAS, HOW SOLITARY THE CITY SITS, THAT WAS FULL OF PEOPLE."

This word אֵיכָה *eikhah* appears in the Tanakh sixteen times—five times in Deuteronomy, twice in the Early Prophets, three times in the Latter Prophets, and six times in the Writings—four of those in the Book of Lamentations itself. It has different meanings in different places. Most of the time, it means "how" in a pragmatic sense, expressing puzzlement at some situation. It is a "how" to which an answer can be given. So, for example, the answer to Moses' "how," is to delegate some of his judicial authority to others, who will hear and resolve the common issues.

In the Prophets and Lamentations, אֵיכָה *eikhah* is used rhetorically. In

Synopsis: The first verse of this fifth book of the Torah sets the stage for what is to follow: "THESE ARE THE WORDS THAT MOSES ADDRESSED TO ALL OF ISRAEL ON THE OTHER SIDE OF THE JORDAN...". (Deut. 1.1). Three discourses are to follow. But at the beginning, Moses recounts the start of the journey from Horev and the establishment of the judicial system. At the second stop in the journey, at Kadesh Barnea, the scouts are sent, report back, the people are disaffected, as a result of which God decrees the fate of the desert generation and we learn about the battles against other nations. Now, close to forty years have passed and the new generation is ready to enter the land. The battles against Sihon and Bashan are clear indications that God is the One who is running the show—there is no need for fear.

Devarim—331

Devarim

our haftarah, Isaiah's אֵיכָה *eikhah* is such a rhetorical "how." It expresses indignant rebuke, that the people are straying away from God: "HOW COULD YOU LET YOURSELF, ZION, TURN TO OTHER GODS, TO IMMORALITY?" [Isaiah 1.21]. The situation, in the prophet's eyes, isn't yet entirely hopeless. Rebuke is the appropriate stance when there is still the possibility of change, when disaster can still be avoided. This אֵיכָה *eikhah* has the aspect of a call, the aim of which is to evoke in the other an *awareness* of distance from God and God's ways. Sometimes, the prophet knows, we are not so far gone, and the אֵיכָה "*eikhah*" of rebuke will bring us to our senses.

Finally, there is the wailing אֵיכָה *eikhah* of Lamentations. "אֵיכָה *Eikhah*, alas, how awful everything is, how hopeless." Contact has been *lost*. All one can do is grieve. But are we to be left only with hopeless grief?

No. There is one more time when the word אֵיכָה (*alef-yud-khaf-hay*)—which is how אֵיכָה *eikhah* is spelled—appears in the Tanakh. It, too, is related to the notion of contact. In the Garden of Eden, after Adam and Eve have eaten the fruit and clothed themselves, they hide when they sense God's approach. God says to Adam, אַיֶּכָּה "*AYYEKKAH*," "WHERE ARE YOU?" [Gen. 3.9]. Usually, this word is spelled [אַיְ] *alef-yud-khaf*. But there it is spelled out in full, with a ה (*hay*) added to the end. In the midrashic framework, changes like these in the text are

never taken for granted. So the question is asked, what can we learn from this extra ה (*hay*)? Lamentations Rabbah tells us:

"R. Abbahu opened his discourse… [GOD SAID], I BROUGHT HIM [THE FIRST HUMAN] INTO THE GARDEN OF EDEN…BUT HE TRANSGRESSED…SO I PUNISHED HIM BY DRIVING HIM OUT… AND [I] LAMENTED OVER HIM, אֵיכָה *EIKHAH*, AS IT IS SAID, 'WHERE ART THOU?—אַיֶּכָּה, *AYYEKKAH*,' THIS BEING WRITTEN אֵיכָה, *EIKHAH*.

"Similarly with his descendants, I brought them into the land of Israel…I gave them commandments…They transgressed my commandments…So I punished them by driving them out…and I lamented over them, 'How אֵיכָה (*EIKHAH*) SITTETH SOLITARY.'" [*Lamentations Rabbah, The Proems of the Sages, IV*, Soncino edition, *The Midrash Rabbah*, Volume IV, 1977, pp 6–7.]

The Midrash asks us to imagine God saying two things at the same time to Adam: the "WHERE ARE YOU?" of our usual translation, but also, at the same time, "ALAS." God must banish Adam and Eve from the Garden, but at the same time compassionately grieves the separation; and by analogy, the Temple has been destroyed, God has driven the Jewish people into exile, but the rabbis still experience God's caring concern for the Jewish people.

Even at the times of deepest tragedy, when all we are able to do is wail "*Eikhah*, alas," the Tradition teaches that Another is looking for

אלה הדברים אשר דבר משה אל כל ישראל

us, that the אֵיכָה "*eikhah*" is also אַיֶּכָּה-"*ayyekkah*." It says that at these times, if our "alas," our grief, is deep enough, it can awaken a yearning to have contact re-established. Then we may be able to hear, through our tears and our mourning, the call of אַיֶּכָּה "*ayyekkah*."

So we get our choice of approaches to the timing of this parashah—scholarly and historic or traditional and midrashic. Either way, we come back to those events of 586 B.C.E. Reading *Parashat Devarim* and its haftarah, we are offered a way to begin thinking about our people's paradigmatic national tragedy, about the grief we will keen out, for that loss and so many others. We must remember, the readings tell us, that grief is real, but so are compassion and hope. •

Dr. Peter Pitzele

PETER PITZELE IS A PSYCHOTHERA-
PIST AND AN ADJUNCT FACULTY
MEMBER AT THE HEBREW UNION
COLLEGE-JEWISH INSTITUTE OF
RELIGION, THE JEWISH THEOLOGICAL
SEMINARY, AND UNION
THEOLOGICAL SEMINARY. HE IS THE
AUTHOR OF *OUR FATHERS' WELLS*.

Devarim

Joshua's Moses

At night, when the last of the tribes and their elders had dispersed, we would sit together in his tent. He had spoken all day before the Tent of Meeting, speaking to each tribe in turn, saying the words the Lord had given to him. "Words," he would often say to me as we sat by a small fire, "our God is a God of words, and we will be a people of words." And indeed, because I stood by him all these days, hearing the variations and the repetitions of words, I, as much as anyone who heard him, felt how the words were founding our wilderness travail into a story and building the bulwarks of our law.

And he was old in those days, very old. There were few beside him who had survived since the holocaust of Passover night.

Aaron was gone. Miriam was gone. He was alone now, this small man. I was always surprised standing next to him at his slightness, but now in his great age he seemed to grow frail. He had been a father to me, and increasingly now in his exhaustion I felt I was the son upon whom he leaned. With a touch of mirth he would call me his staff, sometimes his right hand, his Benjamin. Yet in spite of this intimacy he was always Moses, the mysterious man whom we knew and never knew, and whom we obeyed in the belief that in obeying him we obeyed his God that was still becoming our God. We were still in many ways a servile people, though war had bloodied us and plague had hardened us. Sometimes I thought our victories and our losses, the terrible legions of losses, had made the wilderness this side of the Jordan an immense burial ground for the dead.

When he began to speak on that day—and I listened to him, handing him the skin of sweet water through the long hours—I felt that I was hearing a great and final summing up. Others hearing felt it, too; this sense of a familiar story now being told as a summation, as a version to be remembered, as his last words. God's last words through him to us. I thought of him as a weaver. I knew the incidents, dark and light, red and blue, purple and gold, that he was weaving together into a story. I marveled at

אלה הדברים אשר דבר משה אל כל ישראל

his skill and memory. And though he was old now—his sentences full of pauses and waverings—he spoke in a voice that seemed to come from a place of depth and darkness, as from the depths of a well or from the darkness of a cave. The well of his heart, I would think, listening to the words spill out full of memory and prophecy; from the cave of his mind, I thought, as the words in their astonishing sequences seemed to resound with meaning and allusion. He was performing. His power was drawn from the years of having lived at our center and been the center of our attention, and he had the bearing that comes from having stood for half a century in the role of God.

On this particular night, this first night, this beginning of the end, I remember he was not only tired but seemed, in fact, troubled. Usually, he wished simply to rest, to refresh himself modestly with food and to sleep. But this night sleep would not come, and he rose in the middle watch and left his tent to stand under the stars. I was there on guard. I woke and rose to stand beside him. For a time he was quiet, gazing up into the heavens, then he drew his breath and seemed to notice me. Making small talk, he spoke of how long the day had been; he made a little joke about getting too old to stand all day under the sun. It was a little play on words: he was saying both that the heat had wearied him, and that he was becoming too old to understand the sun. That glint of mirth again, but then he grew grave.

"I killed a priest today," he said. He was silent for a while, and I did not speak. He had killed no man today, not that I saw, and I was with him. "A priest of Midian."

"Sir?" I said, for now my confusion was complete, and I thought him confused also, for the campaign against the Midianites, though recent and one of the most savage of our terrible wars, was over.

"Joshua," he said to me, "Today God had me recall the time after our first warring with Amalek when I created new leaders among the tribes, new judges, new lines of authority, new delegations of power. I heard myself say these words: I CANNOT BEAR THE BURDEN OF YOU MYSELF. THE LORD GOD HAS MULTIPLIED YOU UNTIL YOU ARE AS NUMEROUS AS THE STARS…HOW CAN I BEAR THE BURDEN AND THE BICKERING [Deut. 1.9-12]? You were there today, Joshua; you heard. You were there then, Joshua; you fought."

Yes, I thought to myself, I remember that time; we fought Amalek, but in my mind's eye, I did not see the battle but rather the figure of Moses standing on the hilltop with Aaron and Hur beside him propping up his hands so that he might hold his staff above his head, fierce and still as a statue, unmoving until the sun went down and the field was red with the blood.

"And, Joshua," pulling me back to the present, "I said today further: PICK FROM EACH OF YOUR TRIBES MEN WHO ARE WISE, DISCERNING AND EXPERIENCED, AND I WILL APPOINT THEM AS YOUR HEADS. YOU ANSWERED ME AND SAID, 'WHAT YOU PROPOSE TO DO IS GOOD'" [Deut. 1.13-14].

I remembered that, too, the great reorganization of our clans, the establishment of a new clan among the clans, elders and judges, who reported to Moses.

"But," he then went on, "I made no mention today of Jethro."

Ahh, yes, I thought; it was about this time that Jethro came, his father-in-law, with his daughter—Moses' wife and two sons. And I remembered the quarrels with Miriam and Aaron that blackened the camp back then. "In telling our people the story of that time I have left out—God has had me leave out—Jethro, yet it was through Jethro that God spoke to me then, and it was from Jethro's lips that I learned to change our ways of judging and settling disputes. It was Jethro who guided me then. God through Jethro. And now God omits the guide. Have I not conspired, Joshua, to wipe out this Midianite priest from the sacred history of our people? It seems as if this last—for I feel this is the last time I shall speak before all the people—this last story God is telling through me will not have this good man in it, this man who was a father to me. I have been wondering in my heart all night—why."

"Why here at the end am I kept from speaking of Jethro? Is not history to be remembered? Is that not what I am doing now with these people, passing on a history only I fully know? If I, who have such reason to revere him, do not remember Jethro, who will? Is not history, Joshua, to be recorded accurately? Surely, we

are to keep faith with God? Or is God who makes history able to remake history? Can the past be changed as one changes a story in retelling it? Is there something deeper or more important than the record of the actors and their acts, something separable from them, beyond them, invisible at the time, visible only in remembering? Is the hidden pattern in the past more important than its evident chaos?"

"I wonder these things, Joshua, remembering Jethro. He welcomed me among his people, the very Midianites we so recently slaughtered. He gave me his daughter and a place in his home. Later he brought my family to me here in the wilderness when my heart was too full of God and these people, and he gave me back my sons. He watched me administer, and he counseled me with wisdom. This was Jethro, the priest of Midian. He was also the father to me, wise and kind. He was the only father I ever had. Am I never to have my father, Joshua?"

"And, Joshua"—here he turned to look up at me, for I was taller than him by almost a head, and as he looked up I could see that his eyes glimmered in the darkness with something between mirth and resignation—"How much of Moses will be lost? How much of Moses—his life, his kin, his thoughts, his deeds—really matters?"

Then he wished me a good night and retired back into his tent to sleep.•

Devarim

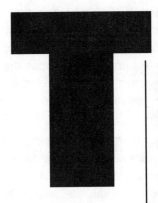

The preeminent and overarching theme of this parashah—and of Deuteronomy as a whole—is the act of covenanting between God and the Jewish people. None of the distinct pericopes in this parashah—and there are many—can be understood outside a frame of reference of covenant. The covenant idea creates one unitary whole, connecting all of the strands, even ideas that seem unrelated to each other or lofty speeches that seem to wander.

So, we should first ask—what is a covenant? In ancient literature, the word בְּרִית *brit* (covenant) generally meant a pact or treaty of faithfulness and friendship between human beings. But for most of its 283 references in the Tanakh, בְּרִית *brit* refers to the bond that exists between the Jewish people and God, beginning with Abraham and lasting until the end of time.[1]

At first blush, it seems like a preposterous idea. Human beings on a par with God, equals in the sense that some sort of deal can be struck? Hardly. "Servants of the Lord" more aptly describes the relationship and suggests no manner of equivalence. But it need not, for the very essence of a covenant is a contractual relationship between unequals. Moreover, a covenant of mutual obligation is less an attempt to bridge the gap in parity than to recognize a basic interdependence between the two partners.[2]

Contemporary scholarship confirms this theological insight of the Torah. We now know that covenants were used

Va-Ethanan

Deuteronomy 3.23-7.11

Blu Greenberg

BLU GREENBERG IS THE AUTHOR OF *HOW TO RUN A TRADITIONAL JEWISH HOUSEHOLD* AND *ON WOMEN AND JUDAISM*.

דָּבָר אַחֵר **DAVAR AHER.** MOSES SAID, 'O GOD, LET ME, I PRAY, CROSS OVER AND SEE THE GOOD LAND ON THE OTHER SIDE OF THE JORDAN, THAT GOOD HILL COUNTRY, AND THE LEBANON [DEUT. 3.25]. Torah tells us that God withheld this wish from Moses "BECAUSE YOU BELIEVED NOT IN ME…" [Num. 20.12], at the waters of Meribah. What the Torah does not tell is that Moses was scheduled to die ten times in the Wilderness already, and at the end of forty years, as Moses stood on Mt. Nebo

and gazed at the Promised Land in the distance, he argued his case with God. Moses said, "You called me as your servant and I served." God said, "No." Moses said, "Let me sneak into the Land alone, by the back door. No one has to know." God said, "No." Moses said, "Let someone carry my bones after my death into the Land, like Joseph." God said, "No." Moses said, "Adam disobeyed and you forgave him…" God said, "No." "Let me enter for two or three years, then I'll

widely in the ancient Near East. The covenant idea was not unique to the Jewish people. Its most frequent use was as an instrument between two very unequal entities, vassals and serfs. Though it may initially startle the faithful reader of a canonical text, critical analysis shows that the organization of Deuteronomy (also called *Sefer ha-Brit*) follows the standard covenant form of Near East suzerainty treaties: (1) a preamble in which the suzerain, or lord, identifies himself; (2) an antecedent—and motivating—history of gracious deeds (i.e., look what I did for you); (3) stipulations of the covenant, e.g., exclusive loyalty on the one side and the promise of protection on the other; (4) deposition of a text; (5) a list of witnesses—often natural phenomena such as heaven and earth; (6) and curses and blessings, for breach or performance, respectively.[3] The genius of Moses, and of

God, *kevyakhol,* is that they appropriated a form that was in wide use in those times and fashioned it into a testament that became the essence of a sacred relationship between God and the Jewish people.

But there, with inherent inequity of partners and with commonality of form, the resemblance ends. From our parashah, and largely from the *p'shat,* we can extrapolate the extraordinary and unique characteristics of the Jewish covenant:

(1) It is a covenant of love and of law. More importantly, a unique relationship exists between love and law.

(2) The sacred covenant between human and God incorporates within it both civil laws and societal ethics. This carries important implications for the examined life.

(3) The covenant is irrevocable, eternal, automatically renewed

Va-Et<u>h</u>anan

die…" God said, "No. I have resolved that you should not go there." So Moses went to the Earth. "O Earth, speak to God for me. Perhaps then God will have pity on me and allow me to enter the Land." The Earth said, "I have my own troubles, 'dust you are and to dust shall you return', we're all in the same boat. I, too, grow old and pass away." He went to the Heavens. He went to the Sun and Moon. He went to the Stars

and Planets. He went to the Hills and Mountains. He went to Mt. Sinai who told him she was still sore from the fire and smoke during his last visit. He went to the Rivers. He went to the Deserts. He went to the Great Sea who told him that she had been beaten up enough by Moses, when he parted her waters. Moses recalled all the wonderful things he had done in his youth. "In those days I was King of the World, now I'm a

ואתחנן אל יהוה בעת ההוא לאמר

and renewable in each generation. This, no matter who says otherwise.

(4) The covenant is independent of the land, yet also inextricably linked to it.

(1) A covenant of love and of law

Love: What is the basis of the covenantal relationship, its underpinning? It is love, mutual love. The covenant is both fruit of love and expression of love. This is truly quite an incredible thought. It may well be that, in addition to the concept of monotheism, love between God and human is an idea that Judaism has contributed to the entire world.

"FOR YOU ARE A HOLY PEOPLE UNTO GOD... [WHO HAS] CHOSEN YOU TO BE A SPECIAL NATION FROM AMONG ALL THE NATIONS OF THE EARTH. NOT BECAUSE OF YOUR NUMBERS DID GOD DESIRE YOU AND CHOOSE YOU FROM AMONG ALL THE NATIONS—FOR YOU ARE THE SMALLEST OF THEM—BUT BECAUSE GOD LOVED YOU AND...WOULD KEEP THE OATH [GOD] SWORE TO YOUR ANCESTORS...KNOW, THEREFORE, THAT GOD IS THE FAITHFUL GOD WHO KEEPS THE COVENANT AND THE LOVINGKINDNESS WITH THOSE WHO LOVE [GOD] AND WHO KEEP [GOD'S] COMMANDMENTS, UNTO A THOUSAND GENERATIONS... AND WILL LOVE YOU AND BLESS YOU AND MULTIPLY YOU AND BLESS THE FRUIT OF YOUR BODY AND BLESS THE FRUIT OF YOUR LAND...AND PROMISED TO YOUR ANCESTORS TO GIVE YOU.... [Deut. 7.6-13]

"AND BECAUSE [GOD] LOVED YOUR ANCESTORS AND CHOSE THEIR SEED AFTER THEM AND BROUGHT YOU OUT PERSONALLY...." [Deut. 4.37]

And what is the human partners' appropriate response to this love?

"AND YOU SHALL LOVE YOUR GOD WITH ALL YOUR HEART, AND WITH ALL YOUR SOUL, AND WITH ALL YOUR MIGHT...." [Deut. 6.5][4]

Because the covenant, love was in their bones, not just in their minds, because of an inherent—or perhaps

Synopsis: Our parashah begins with one of the most famous scenes in the Torah: Moses is standing on the top of a mountain called Pisgah on the eastern side of the Jordan and is told to look west, north, south and east— to view the land that he is not to enter. That privilege is left to Joshua. The discourse to the people continues with Moses' appeal not to forget what they have experienced. Brief mention is made of the cities of refuge and the parashah continues with Moses' second discourse, which, appropriately enough, begins with the Ten Commandments followed closely by the Shema. Again, the people are warned not to forget and to use the lesson of the Exodus as a way of remembering.

---

beggar for my life." He began to cry. The angels came and snatched Moses' tears and words away so that God wouldn't hear them, but God loved Moses like a mother and always knew when something was troubling him. God came to Moses and said, "Don't be afraid. It isn't written that you should enter the Land" (Moses, of course, knew this since he was the one who had done the writing). "It was decreed before I created the World, and yours is not to ask why. It just is." Moses said, "I am their leader. I earned it." God said, "It is time for Joshua to take over." So Moses spent his last days on a mountain top, gazing into the Promised Land in the distance, only partly resigned to the fate that had been apportioned him, thinking, "It should have been me." **James Stone Goodman, <Stavisker@aol.com>**

Va-Ethanan

inherited—ability to stand inside of this love relationship, the Jewish partners throughout the generations were able to hear the admonitions and even the curses in a different way. Not as texts of terror, nor as emanations from a God of Wrath (as some have described the God of Deuteronomy) but as the voice of a momentarily disappointed lover or distressed parent, sometimes stern but always loving.

Law: To reduce it to a simple equation: the children of Israel must be faithful to God alone and follow God's laws; in return, God will give them the land of Israel and a life of blessing and of extended years.

But it is not so simple, this connection of law to covenant. That the law was subsumed under the covenant altogether is in sharp contrast to other ancient covenants which were almost exclusively assertions of fealty or political allegiance. Acceptance of this covenant, then, is no mere declaration of infatuation or allegiance. It embodies a most serious commitment, that of wholehearted observance of the law.[5] Thus, observance of the law becomes the measure of integrity in the covenantal relationship.

Law and Love: But even more remarkable than law or love as parameters of the covenant is the continuous coupling of the two, e.g., "TO LOVE [God] AND KEEP [God's] COMMANDMENTS...." [Deut. 7.9]. Compliance with the law, then, is felt not as onerous duty, but as an

expression of love. This explains another mystery in Jewish consciousness: the phrase, עֹל הַמִּצְוֹת ol ha-mitzvot, the "yoke" of the law, would ordinarily be perceived as something burdensome, a heavy load to bear. Yet for Jews, this yoke has always been understood as a beloved mantle, something to wear with self-esteem and a sense of privilege.

Christianity parted ways with Judaism on this very notion of law and love. It held that love and law are dichotomous; love is the fulfillment of law and can therefore replace it. But our parashah teaches otherwise: law and love are inextricably linked. Thus, for a Jew to say, "I will" or "I do" is as powerful a statement of love as is to say the words, "I love" or "I believe."[6]

(2) Sacred covenant and civil law

One should rightly ask—what place does civil law have in a covenant? Ritual law, yes, but civil laws are adjudicated in the courts of human enterprise. What has this to do with God?

Moreover, in the Torah, every type of law is mixed in with every other—בֵּין אָדָם לַחֲבֵרוֹ *bein adam la-haveiro* and בֵּין אָדָם לַמָּקוֹם *bein adam la-Makom* (between human beings and each other and between human and God), מִצְוֹת קַלּוֹת *mitzvot kallot* and מִצְוֹת חֲמוּרוֹת *mitzvot hamurot* (easy laws and heavy-duty ones), apodictic and casuistic law.[7] Absolutely no distinctions are made

ואתחנן אל יהוה בעת ההוא לאמר

in the text; laws of differing types and valences appear virtually side by side, unlike in any other system.

No proof texts are offered to interpret the strange juxtaposition of covenantal law. Consequently, Biblical critical scholars explained away this asymmetrical melange by constructing supplementary and fragmentary hypotheses.[8,9] But scholars of the Torah looked at the same issue and came up with a different insight, one fraught with real meaning for our lives.

For example, they asked, "What is so unique about the Decalogue and why should it be repeated here in *Va-Ethanan*?" After all, each commandment appears elsewhere in the Pentateuch, sometimes more than once.

One answer is, of course, that these ten were the core experience of revelation and reconstitute a basic creed—what one must do or refrain from doing in order to be counted as a member of this special community.

But another answer lies in the distinctive arrangement of the Decalogue. In addition to the novel structure of two tablets, the content itself suggests two distinctive pentads.[10] The first five commandments—all containing the phrase, "THE LORD YOUR GOD"—reflect the divine/human sphere;[11] the latter five, the ethical and moral fabric of society. What it teaches us is that the different kinds of law are of equivalent value. Thus, it is appropriate to repeat it here, in the Book of the Covenant, because it

is paradigmatic of all the laws under the covenant.

One point, therefore, is that no act is trivial. Just as love expresses itself in a thousand details, significant and trivial alike, so, too, the great manifestation of covenant love/obligation is concretized in commandments of differing degrees of gravity. But all of it carries the same covenantal weight.

Another point: that ethical laws are to be considered as laws between human beings and God. If one violates social ethics, it not only offends humanity and upsets the social order but is also a sin against God. No matter that these cases are judged by human peers; hurt your neighbor, and you violate the covenant with Me, says God. The way you act with your fellow human being is determined by your relationship with Me.[12] The line between sacred and secular is overcome. Life is holistically holy.

(3) Irrevocable, eternal, renewed, and renewable

The covenantal trust passes from generation to generation, is renewed in each generation, and will never end.

"THE LORD OUR GOD MADE A COVENANT WITH US AT HOREB. GOD MADE THIS COVENANT NOT WITH YOUR PARENTS BUT WITH US, THE LIVING, WHO ARE ALL OF US HERE TODAY. FACE TO FACE, GOD SPOKE WITH US IN THE MOUNTAIN, IN THE MIDST OF THE FIRE…." [Deut. 5.1–4][13]

These opening words of Moses' second sermon in Deuteronomy are literally an oxymoron. The generation

that stood at Sinai is dead, their children are about to enter the land. These are the plains of Moab; there's no fire here. Yet, the text insists that God made the covenant with those present at the plains of Moab. The point is this: don't think to yourselves that God made a covenant with our ancestors, and, therefore, what is it to us, a generation removed. No, it is here and now that the covenant is being made, again. This also explains why the Decalogue, pure essence and central creed of that covenant, is repeated here in the plains of Moab, repeated but with slight variation as if to remind the later reader of the two distinct covenant experiences.

And just as it is true for the generation in the plains of Moab, so it is true for all succeeding generations.[14,15] Tradition teaches us that each Jew is to feel as if he/she was taken personally out of Egypt and his/her soul was present at Sinai and received the Torah there.

Because it is renewed generation to generation, it becomes irrevocable, able to override conditions of failure and betrayal, never to be forfeited or rescinded or superseded. Even when the people sin, the covenant is not over. Repentance will restore the relationship.

(4) Independent of the land of Israel, yet inextricably linked to it

Receiving the covenant in the desert and renewing it on the plains symbolize the covenant's broad accessibility, open to anyone, in any place.

Va-Et<u>h</u>anan

Among other things, this means that Judaism is not racist.

But independence from turf does not mean that the covenant is not uniquely tied to life on a particular land. "AND NOW ISRAEL, LISTEN TO THE LAWS AND STATUTES THAT I TEACH YOU THIS DAY TO DO IN ORDER THAT YOU MAY LIVE AND...INHERIT THE LAND GOD...GIVES TO YOU." [Deut. 4.1] Throughout *Va-Et<u>h</u>anan*, throughout all of Deuteronomy, faithfulness to God, observance of the laws, inheritance of the land, and life on the land are woven together in a kind of covenantal dance, first one partner's claims, responsibilities, and rewards, then the other's.

To a certain extent, the land factor allows the covenant to remain unbroken. Without exile as punishment for infidelity and breach of the law, the covenant would have to be abrogated when either side fails. Moreover, this fall-back position of land as punishment puts teeth into covenantal expectations. Conversely, the greatest reward for fulfilling the obligations of the covenant is a long life of blessing on the land.

The covenant is the most extraordinary vehicle for defining a human relationship with God, which is why other religions adopted the same pattern. In this generation, perhaps more than in any other since the first covenant was drawn, we are forced to ask the question even as we read the chapter of Deuteronomy: what are the implications of the Holocaust for the covenantal relationship? Or to quote the famous phrase, "No statement, theological or otherwise, should be made that could not be made in the presence of burning children."[16]

What does the human partner do when it seems as if God has failed us? Send God into exile? For how long? There are no easy answers, nor even complex and hard ones. But some of them lie in *Va-Et<u>h</u>anan*. Just as the covenant was not over when the human partner failed in history, so it is not over in this generation. And love can continue for the partners even through incredible pain. And observance of the law binds us up together in a powerful emotional bond. And the promise of the land has been realized in our time and we should maximize that blessing.

Yes, we should ask the questions. But not at every given moment.•

Footnotes

[1] See Abraham Even Shoshan, *The New Concordance to Torah, Prophets, and Writings*, Kiryat-Sefer, Jerusalem, 1993.

[2] A parallel might be drawn to prefeminist construction of marriage, where the inherent inequity of partners was simply not a factor to consider or critique.

[3] It is easy to find these six parameters in a cursory reading of Deuteronomy, item (3) being exclusive faithfulness to God and a host of applications of the loyalty principle in the forms of daily living; item (4), the recitation and then deposition of the tablets in the Holy Ark.

[4] The mutuality of love explains why the rabbis established the *ahavah rabbah* and *ahavat olam* prayers, which speak of God's great love for the Jewish people, as prelude to the Shema.

[5] So central was the observance of the whole law that the cherished Ten Commandments, originally part of the liturgy, was excised from it sometime during the third or fourth century. The rabbis felt that the heavy Christian emphasis on the Decalogue was excessive and constituted an attempt to diminish the significance of the other laws—a wedge toward Christian repudiation of the law. Since the daily recitation of the Shema by Jews seemed to strengthen the Christian claim that the other laws not recited daily were unimportant (superseded), the rabbis removed the Ten Commandments from the daily liturgy.

[6] The classic communal expression of this principle is "na'aseh v'nishma." [Ex. 24.7]

[7] There are different ways of categorizing Scriptural law. One Rabbinic arrangement was to divide the law into mitzvot bein adam le-havero (laws between human beings and each other) and mitzvot bein adam la-makom (between human and God). Another division was by weight or significance, the so called trivial laws and the heavy-duty ones. Contemporary critical Bible scholars distinguish between casuistic and apodictic law in Deuteronomy. While not exactly falling into neat divisions of sacred and evil, they closely approximate them. Oftentimes in the Torah, laws with these very different valences appear side by side, sometimes in the same unit.

[8] The fragmentary hypothesis posits that Deuteronomy is composed of many independent fragments, of varying sizes, entered into the text at different times. This is in contrast to the supplementary hypothesis—that the Book is one basic document with numerous accretions.

[9] Though the Rabbis would have no part of an interpretation that questioned the unitary word of God at Sinai, they were not unmindful of the strange contiguity. Long ago and in many places they raised the code question: mah inyan shmittah etzel har Sinai? "What does the issue of Sabbatical year have to do with Sinai? What does this law or issue have to do with the adjacent one? This was, in a sense, a rabbinic form of critical scholarship.

[10] Remember, the text only suggests tablets [Deut. 4.13; 10.4], not five and five, which are a product of later division. By sheer volume, the division would have been quite different.

[11] This is not perfectly consistent: at surface reading, the fifth commandment doesn't fit neatly into this category. More accurately, it's a bridge between the two categories, linking the divine and socio-moral spheres. The relationship to parents is different from other human relationships because a mother and father belong to a higher authority than one's fellow human beings, with whom there is a basic equality. Giving parents honor is not a matter of reciprocity, as are the laws of the second pentad. It is continuously uni-directional, generation after generation. Parents should honor children, for it shows love and engenders a child's self-esteem. But it is not a relationship of equals, as I have often tried to tell my teenage children.

[12] In many a law, the connection is made explicit: "IF THERE BE AMONG YOU A NEEDY MAN... IN THE LAND WHICH GOD HAS GIVEN YOU,... OPEN YOUR HAND AND LEND HIM WHAT HE NEEDS [DO NOT HOLD BACK] SAYING THE SEVENTH YEAR OF RELEASE OF DEBTS IS AT HAND... AND HE CRIES UNTO GOD AGAINST YOU AND YOU WILL BEAR SIN... GIVE TO HIM AND YOUR HEART SHALL NOT BE GRIEVED WHEN YOU DO BECAUSE FOR THAT GOD WILL BLESS YOU IN ALL YOUR WORK.... [Deut. 15.7-10] See also 24.17-18; 25.13-16; also 27.15-26 regarding sins that one commits in secret and assumes will not be discovered. No, they, too, will draw a curse.

[13] In some ways, this had a powerful impact on feelings for others in the covenantal family. I think that the tight bonds Jews feel for each other have something to do with the covenant running from generation to generation—each Jew connected with every other Jew in the covenant.

[14] Perhaps the most powerful articulation of this theme appears in Nitzvaim. "NOT ONLY WITH YOU DO I MAKE THIS COVENANT... BUT WITH HIM WHO STANDS HERE THIS DAY BEFORE GOD AND ALSO WITH HIM WHO IS NOT HERE TODAY.." [Deut. 29.13-14]

[15] What happened to the covenant renewal ceremonies of ancient times? The best answer is to be found in an extraordinary, must-read book by Jon Levenson, Sinai and Zion. Levenson suggests that the Shema prayer [Deut. 6.4-9; 11.13-21; also Num. 15.37-41] was established as a central text of Rabbinic liturgy because it is, in essence, a covenantal renewal ceremony. a constant declaration of covenantal faith. The rabbis organized it to be so, selecting and arranging the different segments of Shema in a manner that was consistent with covenantal affirmation. Levenson even identifies all the elements of the covenant formulary in the Shema. So why is the word covenant or renewal ceremony not mentioned? This is wholly consistent, says Levenson, with the Rabbinic pattern of making the everyday holy, and the sacred, routine.

Just as they moved the sacrificial cult from an occasional dramatic offering into the home with continuous blessings, worship and service of the heart, so they moved what was an extraordinary covenantal ceremony into daily life where consciousness of the covenantal relationship could become deeply and permanently embedded in the soul and psyche of every Jew. And it worked!

[16] Irving Greenberg, "Cloud of Smoke, Pillar of Fire" in Auschwitz: Beginning of a New Era, Eva Fleischner, ed.

I wish to acknowledge the influence of my husband, Irving Greenberg, on this Learn Torah With... text. Most of my understanding of and thinking about covenant comes from him. It is a theme that he has dealt with in a variety of ways, and it is the underpinning of much of his work in contemporary Jewish theology.

Shoshana Silberman

SHOSHANA SILBERMAN IS AN EDUCATOR AT THE JEWISH CENTER IN PRINCETON, NEW JERSEY.

Va-Ethanan

Parashat *Va-Ethanan* opens with Moses' "laying a guilt trip" on the Israelites. He reminds them that it was because of their constant complaints and demands that his anger was provoked and God then denied him entrance to the Promised Land. Moses proceeds to warn the Israelites to give heed to the commandments so that they may enter the Promised Land with Joshua, their new leader. Their good behavior will not only give them entry to the land, but also will gain them (and God) the respect of other nations.

Invoking the memory of both the Exodus and of Sinai (and all that the Lord did for the Israelites), Moses reviews the key teachings that are to be followed and passed down to their descendants.

They include the Ten Commandments and the *Shema/V'ahavta*. He concludes with the message that God will uphold the covenant if the Israelites are faithful. However, destruction awaits them if they reject God's ways.

This parashah is so intense that it is almost overwhelming. The warnings are so frequent and so ominous that it is frightening. Yet, a part of us holds back. We want to be spoken to as responsible adults. We don't like to be threatened. We want to do deeds because of their intrinsic merit. Moses is beginning to rattle us, to get on our nerves.

Just when I am beginning to be increasingly put off by Moses, my mind wanders back to a clear cold night in January; the year is 1960. I am a teenager with an independent streak, who likes to be responsible for her own affairs. One of my favorite activities is talking on the phone to my boyfriend, Mel. This is a nightly ritual.

On this particular night, my father, who has stayed home from work that day because he doesn't feel well, calls up to me. With an "I'll call you right back," I go to his room. My father's face is pale with a serious expression. He begins with these words: "Have you finished all your homework?" "Sure," I say in a puzzled voice, "I did some at school and some when I got home."

ואתחנן אל יהוה בעת ההוא לאמר

I'm startled by how strange this is. My father never questions me about school-work. Why is he so concerned? I haven't been avoiding my responsibilities. Then he interrupts my thoughts with another query. "Have you taken care of everything you should?" I reassure him that everything is in order. Yet, I sense everything is out of order. He seems tired, so I kiss him and leave.

On the phone again, I say in a trembling voice, "Something is wrong; something terrible is going to happen. I can feel it." It did. My father died that night of a heart attack at age 49. Unlike Moses, he did not live to a ripe old age. Ironically, he had just learned he was to direct a convention in Israel. Like Moses, his dream of going to the Promised Land was also not fulfilled.

I think the experience with my father has helped me to empathize with Moses. Each year as I read this parashah, I find that my heart goes out to this stern old man who is about to die. I understand why he wants to give every last warning to the people. His concern is for their survival and spiritual well-being after he is gone. I understand why he feels the need to pound the message into them: follow the path; don't go astray. Conversely, this parashah has helped me to better understand the encounter with my father before his death. I've come to see that like Moses, his words of warning were an expression of his love.

The tone of *Va-Ethanan* may be harsh but the message behind the tone is one of care and concern. How can we not feel for Moses? How can we respond except by assuring him that we'll try to put everything in order?•

The Test of the Good Life

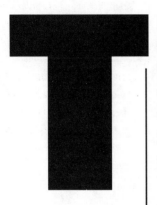

This is one of these rich multifaceted *parashot* that is a *drash*-giver's dream. It begins by enumerating the blessings God will provide the Israelites *if* they "OBEY THESE RULES AND OBSERVE THEM CAREFULLY" [Deut. 7.12]. Their families, produce, and livestock will multiply. They will be protected from sickness and none of the men and women in their midst will be barren.

Ekev

Deuteronomy 7.12-11.25

Dr. Deborah E. Lipstadt

DEBORAH E. LIPSTADT IS DOROT PROFESSOR OF MODERN JEWISH AND HOLOCAUST STUDIES AT EMORY UNIVERSITY IN ATLANTA, GEORGIA

Moses continues his farewell speech by asking the people to "REMEMBER THE LONG WAY" [Deut. 8.2] God made them travel in the preceding forty years. He recalls for them the many tests they had to face in the desert, among them the hunger they felt and the manna they were given to sustain themselves. He warns them against assuming that their own prowess is solely responsible for their success. He admonishes the Israelites for past wrongs and describes them as a stiff-necked people—a phrase that has become a staple of the Yom Kippur confessional. *Ekev* also contains the second paragraph of the Shema and the commandment that we thank God after we have eaten our fill. Finally, in one of those all-powerful, oft-quoted verses of Bible, Moses tells the Israelites [and us] just what it is God wants of them [us].

דָּבָר אַחֵר **DAVAR AHER.** THIS SHALL BE THE REWARD WHEN YOU HEARKEN TO THESE ORDINANCES, AND YOU OBSERVE AND PERFORM THEM; HA-SHEM, YOUR GOD, WILL SAFEGUARD FOR YOU THE COVENANT AND THE KINDNESS THAT HE SWORE TO YOUR FOREFATHERS [Deut. 7.12-13]. Rabbi Plaut, since I heard your sermon at the Canadian Kallah last summer on עֵקֶב *ekev* (obey/heel), also a derivative of יַעֲקֹב Ya'akov (supplanter), I was challenged to address the question of where עָקוּב *ikkuv*, which means "raised to the third power," fits in. When we say God of Abraham, God of Isaac, God of Jacob (1x1x1 or 1 cubed), we may be talking about a God who represented different aspects or qualities to these three individuals. God, however, is still unified (the unified field theory to physicists and TM people alike), represented by the fact that one raised

והיה עקב תשמעון את המ

Let us begin our short excursion through this parashah by looking at the tests Moses recounts. He recognizes that the hardships the Israelites faced during their long trek through the wilderness were difficult experiences that tried their faith. Despite his, at times, total exasperation with their antics and unceasing complaints, Moses seems to comprehend the trying quality of those crucial moments in the desert. But he warns them that now, as they are poised to reach their ultimate destination, a land of milk and honey, they are destined to face yet another test, a test that will be equally as trying but dramatically different from the tests they faced in the wilderness. They will come into a uniquely good land, a land flowing with streams, springs and fountains; a land of wheat, barley, vines, figs, pomegranates, olives and honey; a land rich in mineral resources, including iron, gold, cop-

per and silver. In short, a land where they will lack nothing. They will be able to eat their fill easily, build fine houses in which to live, accumulate gold and silver, and watch their flocks grow and multiply. Everything their hands touch will prosper. But Moses recognizes that there is danger in this bounty: intoxication by plenty. It is the kind of intoxication that will lead them to forget the source of their blessing, so that having eaten from their manifold resources, instead of "GIVING THANKS TO THE LORD YOUR GOD FOR THE GOOD LAND" [Deut. 8.10] (a verse which is, by the way, the source of the *birkat ha-mazon*), they will say "MY OWN POWER AND THE MIGHT OF MY OWN HANDS HAS WON THIS WEALTH FOR ME" [Deut. 8.17]. Moses is cognizant of the danger of plenty. Manifold blessing is just as much of a test as a long trek through the wilderness with its serpents and scorpions. It is no less a test than the hunger they

Synopsis: Ekev begins with the blessings that come from attending to the Law and the consequences of noncompliance. Remember, God was the One who gave Israel victory as is evident from the many rebellions by the people. The second set of commandments is a sign of God's continuing love. Let the memory of those experiences lead to obedience to the Law and love of God. The parashah concludes with what is now the second paragraph of the Shema— the consequences of one's actions and the difficult twin concepts of reward and punishment.

to any power still is one. But when others are added to the drama and two individuals interact with each other, as in the confrontations between players in Genesis, the repercussions ripple through the family, the community, and the world. Thus, two raised to the third power (2x2x2) has exponential (literally and figuratively) results. Actions taken in the material world reach into the three dimensions and the four cor-

ners of the universe. Because the repercussions no longer center around the individual, it is imperative that we *ekev*, obey laws of Torah decency, in order to live in a civilized world.

This is Jewish Mathematics (thank you Rabbi Nancy Wechsler). That looking out for "Number One" is of great and grave importance in our relationship with God but that when another "number one" enters the pic-

ture the consequences for self, God, and community become astonomical very quickly. And this is Ya'akov's and our story. His misjudgments, mistakes, and miscalculations are the human condition and our own drama. **Diana Lynn, Bermuda Biological Station, <dlynn@sargasso.bbsr.edu>**

experienced and the strange thing called manna they had to eat in order to satisfy themselves.

Both deprivation and bounty constitute tests of our faith. Deprivation tests our ability to maintain belief in the face of hardship, suffering, fear and travail. It is a challenge to sustain a belief in God's promise when one feels vulnerable. This is the test endured by those who have faced severe illness or have watched family members or loved ones suffering. Recognizing how fragile they are, they wonder—will they be helped? From whence will that help come? Will it come in time? And why are *they* or *their* loved ones in such pain?

But there is another kind of test facing the Israelites who are about to enter the land. And it is this latter trial which is as applicable, if not more so, to our lives today as the test of deprivation. Moses fears that the Israelites will become so engrossed by their physical and material success that they will forget the source of that blessing. They will assume their success is all of their own making. So, too, we face the danger of coming to believe that the professional and personal success we have achieved is the result solely of our talents and abilities. The greater our achievements, the less inclined we are to believe in anyone or anything other than ourselves. We do not say so aloud but we are convinced that our own power and the strength of our hands has won this wealth for us. (In American society it is, in fact, quite acceptable to make such a declaration. It constitutes the realization of a starkly American image: the self-made person.) Intoxication by plenty can leave us beset by the most dangerous of vanities: hubris. And even if not beset by hubris, then at the very least we take what we have for granted and forget to "give thanks."

As a means of preventing the Israelites from becoming wrapped up in their own success, Moses

Ekev

דָּבָר אַחֵר **DAVAR AHER.** YOU WILL DEVOUR ALL THE PEOPLES THAT **HA-SHEM**, YOUR GOD, WILL DELIVER TO YOU; YOUR EYE SHALL NOT PITY THEM; YOU SHALL NOT WORSHIP THEIR GODS, FOR IT IS A SNARE FOR YOU [DEUT. 7.16]. Today's Torah portion, *Ekev*, is very interesting, but raises a very difficult question. If everyone is Ha-Shem's child, why did God order our ancestors to kill the Canaanites and take all of their possessions? Why would God want to kill his children? Could it just be that Ha-Shem wanted the land to be available for our people to inherit? Or was there something more? There is a better reason. The Canaanites worshipped idols, and they did not believe in God. God was afraid that the Canaanites might infect our people with their beliefs. Even more important was the fact that the pagans sacrificed their children as part of their wor-

recalls the sins they committed—the Golden Calf, their murmurings, the evil reports on the Promised Land brought back by the spies—and reminds them that God forgave them each time. And then, in what Nechama Leibowitz describes as the rhetorical equivalent of starting a new page in history and leaving behind the wrong doings of the past, Moses moves beyond their shortcomings. He turns his back on their failings and asks with a dramatic flourish:

"WHAT THEN DOES GOD DEMAND OF US? ONLY THIS: TO REVERE THE LORD YOUR GOD, TO WALK ONLY IN HIS PATHS, TO LOVE HIM AND TO SERVE THE LORD OUR GOD WITH ALL YOUR HEART AND SOUL; TO KEEP THE COMMANDMENTS OF THE LORD AND HIS STATUTES WHICH I COMMAND THEE THIS DAY FOR THY GOOD." [Deut. 10.12-13].

Nachmanides points out that the question "WHAT DOES GOD DEMAND OF YOU?" must be understood in terms of the final phrase: "FOR THY GOOD." A basic premise of Judaism is that nothing God asks of us is for God's personal benefit, but for our own.

Immediately after telling them what it is God wants of them, Moses proceeds to describe this God, who only demands of all people that they revere him and walk in his paths and love him, as a God who plays no favorites and who does not render judgments based on an individual's wealth, social status, or family lineage. This is a God interested only in people's true human values. As a demonstration of that quality, Moses reminds the Israelites that his God guards the rights of the orphan and the widow and loves the stranger. The Israelites must, therefore, do the same. They must particularly love the stranger because they, too, were strangers in Egypt.

This juxtaposition of the commandment to help the widow, orphan and stranger with keeping the commandments for your own good is worth noting. How does helping the stranger, the widow and the orphan—laws commanded to the Israelites no less than 36 times in the Torah [neither Shabbat, circumcision, kashrut

nor stealing is mentioned so often]—serve our own personal benefit? And why is that injunction always accompanied by the command to remember that you, too, were strangers in the land of Egypt? Why not simply say: Do not oppress the stranger because that is the moral way to behave? Wouldn't that be enough? For some people past memories, particularly memories of bondage and suffering, serve to prevent them from succumbing to the evil impulse or lording it over the stranger. Memories of the past suffering will evoke feelings of empathy and compassion. But past memories do not always make former sufferers more tolerant. In fact, sometimes the opposite will happen. *"I suffered. I came here with nothing. We became successful. We sent our children to college. Why can't they do the same?"* Lest that happen the Torah warns: Do not think that your bounty comes from your own powers. Remember the source of that blessing and share it with the least fortunate and most vulnerable in your society.

---

ship. Ha-shem despised that. Therefore, he gave the worst punishment possible…death.

This raises a very confusing issue for me. When God killed the Egyptians at the Red Sea, our tradition tells us that Ha-Shem cried. How could Ha-Shem cry over the Egyptians and then tell Moses to kill all the Canaanites?

When our ancestors killed the Canaanites they were ordered to do it

for two reasons. For punishment and to protect themselves from the infection of human sacrifice. Killing people in the name of worshipping God is an abomination, deserving the most serious of punishments. Is there another reason Ha-Shem wanted to punish them? Yes, there is. The pagan religion that was the religion of the Canaanites included human sacrifice. They didn't believe in Ha-Shem, and they prayed to idols.

The Egyptians, however, were trying to maintain a nation that, although it enslaved our ancestors, was basically a moral government. God, therefore, cared when he had to take the lives of the Egyptians to save our ancestors. The death penalty that God decreed for the Canaanites, by contrast, was deserved by their immorality. **Joel Frank, Charlotte, NC**

And how does it rebound to your own personal benefit to help others? There is, of course, the change that occurs in virtually every person who helps those who are more needy than they. That is why even the poor are commanded to give *tzedakah*. They cannot help but subsequently look upon what they have—and what the person they are helping does not have—differently. They are less likely to take their material and emotional comforts for granted. For Jews looking out for the stranger, recognizing strangers' vulnerability in society contains a historical message as well. By helping the vulnerable and by remembering our own experiences with suffering—whether in Egypt or Auschwitz—it becomes harder to believe that we are in total command of what will happen to us. Many of those who ended their lives in Auschwitz lived most of their years in a secure, materially comfortable, privileged, acculturated climate, as does much of American Jewry today. Physical security and good health can be temporary. For the vast majority of the Jews who ended up in concentration death camps, that end was as great a shock as it would be to us. I recently read a memoir by a Hungarian Jewish woman who recalled that one week before the Nazis took over Hungary, and a few months before her family was deported, she received a red Schwinn bike from her parents for her birthday. Her only concern—until the heavens darkened—was riding that bike through the streets of her neighborhood, glorying in its bright color, sleek lines and thick tires.

Even as we bask in the blessings of this life, we must remember that each element of that life is a blessing and comes with no guarantees. So let us thank God daily [*yom yom*] for the good and the abundance of blessings in all our lives. Let us revel in its bounty, let us share it with others. And let us never fail to remember that it is when we are full and satisfied that we are to thank God, for that is the real challenge.•

Ekev

דָּבָר אַחֵר **DAVAR AHER.** "YOU WILL DEVOUR ALL THE PEOPLES THAT HA-SHEM, YOUR GOD, WILL DELIVER TO YOU" [DEUT. 7.16]. Nechama Edinger, of Beit Rabban Day School upstairs, was teaching her class about the afternoon prayer service and inquired about the meaning of the term מִנְחָה *minḥah*. We talked about the derivation of the "afternoon" offering from the biblical בֵּין הָעַרְבַּיִם *bein ha-arbayim* daily sacrifice, which was interpreted to mean not "evening" but rather "as the shadows lengthen [in the afternoon] toward evening," and how the preferred time was later in the afternoon, but on a busy day in the Temple, such as the day before Pesaḥ, it could be made as early as half-past noon. We discussed the different meanings used here: gift,

וְהָיָה עֵקֶב תִּשְׁמְעוּן אֵת הַמִּשְׁפָּטִים הָאֵלֶּה

Diane Bernbaum

DIANE BERNBAUM IS THE DIRECTOR OF MIDRASHA, AN INTERCONGREGATIONAL HIGH SCHOOL IN BERKELEY, CALIFORNIA.

Ekev

As an educator, one of my summer projects is to help colleagues rework an ethics curriculum. People are always asking us, "What is the Jewish view about...." If only it were so simple. For every text quoting the "Jewish" view on one side of an issue, another one pops up on the opposite side.

The beginning verses of *Ekev* are a case in point. Just a few weeks ago, my younger son wrote a beautiful Bar Mitzvah *drash* on a verse in Numbers [15.15], stating that strangers should be treated under the same laws as the Israelites.

I sat there, beaming, filled with maternal pride as he expounded how the Torah says "no racism allowed." I marveled at his insight into this moral document that has been with the Jewish people for millennia.

I quickly came down from my euphoric moral mountain, however, when I began to read the first verses of *Ekev*. The Israelites are commanded to destroy (literally, "eat up") all the Canaanites, showing them no pity. [Deut. 7.16] Are these the same people who only a few chapters before were commanded to treat strangers the same way they treated themselves? And if they can't do the job alone, God tells us, He will send a plague against the Canaanites to ferret out those who are in hiding. He will "OBLITERATE THEIR NAME FROM UNDER THE HEAVENS." [Deut. 7.20, 24] Do we want to even be related to these folks?

The classic response, of course, is that we must see the Tanakh in its own time, and not ours. This bloodthirstiness was the modus operandi at the time in the Middle East. The first listeners

offering, [animal] sacrifice, meal-offering, as well as the usage in the story of Elijah at Mt. Carmel: וַיְהִי בַּעֲלוֹת הַמִּנְחָה *vayehi ba`alot ha-minhah* [MELAKHIM ALEF 18.36], which is interpreted as afternoon, in consonance with our usage. I looked up various other derivations, from "rest" time, Abudraham's "from the wind of the day" during which God took His stroll in the Garden (which the Targum translates לְמָנָה יוֹמָה *le-manah yoma*). I've suggest-

ed that because the afternoon prayer varies and is less tied to a specific astronomical cue such as dawn, sunrise, sunset, or dark, it was simply known as "offering time." Other suggestions?
Kaplan Kleinberg

Ekev

would not have been shocked by admonitions to commit genocide. Others say that this was written in a time when morals were immature. But don't we want our Torah to rise above the morals of its neighbors and its times? Should it have remained our moral guide for so many generations if it only caused us to act like everybody else?

It helps calm down my moral indignation to look at this as just rhetoric. It's a prebattle pep talk. It's the coach talking to his team in the locker room before the game. First he tells them that if they follow the rules, God will love and bless them and multiply them and their crops and flocks. [Deut. 7.12-15] (Coach: "Exercise, eat right, get lots of sleep and you'll be able to play a lot better.") He warns them not to get nervous about the fact that the Canaanites are more numerous, because God will deliver them [Deut. 17.17-24]. He needs to boost their very low self-esteem. (Coach: "I know you're afraid to play our opponents because they haven't been losing much lately, but our starting pitcher has a great fast ball, and besides, their .400 hitter is out sick today. You can do it. You're great.") And then, lest they get too cocky that it will be a snap to overtake the Canaanites, Moses reminds them of the despicable way they acted with the golden calf, but tells them he's going to make a new set of tablets. [Deut. 9.6-10.11] (Coach: "You took your eye off the ball and swung at

a pitch that was over your head. I'm giving you a second chance, but you do that one more time and you're off the team.") The problem about rhetoric, however, is that most people, even when they know it's "just rhetoric," still take words seriously. If the Israelis hadn't given appropriate respect to the famous "we will drive you into the sea" comment, would the IDF be as prepared as it is today?

Moses' flock are a group of people who are frightened. Remember, according to their most recent scouting report, albeit one that is nearly 40 years old, Canaan is an unconquerable land. God and Moses have to use a little psychology to get them to fight: tell them that if they follow the rules, God will be on their side and they will win. Tell them that last time they really goofed and that this is their second chance.

We can try to calm down our 20th century outrage—probably unsuccessfully—at the command to wipe out an entire people, by remembering that this total obliteration of the Canaanites never happened. Assuming that this was actually written after the Israelites were already in the land, it was a warning against religious assimilation that was probably taking place at the time of the writing. This was a way to remind readers—sort of written in code—not to pray to their neighbors' gods. [Deut. 7.25-26]. A college history professor of mine taught that societies only legislated against things that were already

והיה עקב תשמעון את המשפטים האלה

occurring. But even if this genocide never happened, isn't it problematic that an admonition to commit it remains in our sacred text?

As a parent of the 80s and 90s (and a child of the 60s), it has always been very hard for me to counsel my children to fight, and I usually suggest another way out of a situation. Surely there are good causes worth fighting for. Voltaire writes "I know I am among civilized men because they are fighting so savagely." But should fighting for a cause be extended to include genocide?

Ekev may have told us to fight, but it also tells us [Deut. 10.19] "You, too, must befriend the stranger, for you were strangers in the land of Egypt." The trouble with trying to follow the biblical moral compass is that it points in too many directions at once. Our task is to choose which needle to follow.•

What Seems Like a Curse May be a Blessing

RE'EH: Anokhi notein lifneikhem ha-yom berakhah u-kelala,

רְאֵה אָנֹכִי נֹתֵן לִפְנֵיכֶם
הַיּוֹם בְּרָכָה וּקְלָלָה,

"SEE: THIS DAY I SET BEFORE YOU BLESSING AND CURSE." [Deut. 11.26]

With these stunning words the Torah begins *Parashat Re'eh*, a portion that surveys many of the mitzvot incumbent upon the Israelites as they entered the land of Israel and upon all Jews to this day.

Re'eh

Deuteronomy 11.26-16.17

Rabbi Amy Eilberg

RABBI AMY EILBERG WORKS WITH THE NATIONAL CENTER FOR JEWISH HEALING IN NEW YORK, AND IS MARRIED TO DR. LOUIS NEWMAN. SHE IS THE MOTHER TO PENINA, AND STEP-MOM TO ETAN AND JONAH.

The opening words of the parashah cry out with bold clarity. Their clarion call shakes us to the core, calling for our attention like the stark sound of the shofar blast. The words are intended to stop us in our path, insisting that we take notice: THIS DAY I SET BEFORE YOU BLESSING AND CURSE.

What am I supposed to see, to take note of, in this call? I always understood the words of the text to mean that blessing and curse were distinct realms, and that I/we, the Jewish people, were to choose between them. Yet somewhere along the way the worlds of blessing and curse came to seem less distinct in real life than the Torah describes them here. The more I age and the more I see suffering in the world, the less I feel we really have a choice about the blessings and curses in life. So what, indeed, am I to notice?

I recently heard a folk tale, retold by storyteller Joel ben Izzy on his tape *Stories From Far Away*, where a man in a small village in China acquired a beautiful horse. "How

דָּבָר אַחֵר **DAVAR AHER.** For the benefit of readers, let me help identify the source of Va-Yedaber Moses. It is a collection of comments on the Torah made by Rabbi Moses Pollak (1846-1889) who lived in Bonyhad (South Hungary) and whose yeshivah developed a rather significant reputation in that part of

Europe. **Dr. Kerry M. Olitzky, Hebrew Union College, New York, NY <olitzky@huc.edu>**

דָּבָר אַחֵר **DAVAR AHER.** "SEE, I PRESENT BEFORE YOU TODAY A BLESSING AND A CURSE" [DEUT. 11.26]. As I read the opening lines, I wondered, as do many others, about the exact nature

wonderful!" exclaimed the villagers, "What a blessing has come to you!" He said, "What seems like a blessing may be a curse." The villagers, puzzled by his reaction, went on their way. Sometime later, the man awoke one morning to find that his beautiful horse had run away. The villagers rushed to his side to comfort him on the loss of his prized possession. Again, he puzzled them by saying, "What seems like a curse may be a blessing."

Sure enough, sometime later, his horse returned, surrounded by a whole herd of beautiful stallions, worth a veritable fortune. The villagers, struck by the man's extraordinary good fortune, congratulated him with great zest. The person replied, "What seems like a blessing may be a curse." Sometime later, the man's son, riding on one of the stallions, was thrown from his mount and broke his leg. The villagers rallied to offer support to the man on his son's injury. The man was sanguine, saying, "What seems like a curse may be a blessing." Not long afterwards all the young men

of the village were conscripted into a terrible war far away, in which all were killed, except for this man's son, who could not go, because of his broken leg. What seems like a curse may be a blessing.

No, it is not always so clear in my life, and in the lives of people I work with, which events are blessing and which are curse. Some events that seem graced with light and joy suddenly turn dark and agonizingly painful. From some losses, a thousand blessings flow. What is more, one almost never knows at the time of the event which this one will be. Will this be one of those tragedies that will scar me forever? Could this be one of those times that will lead to new births, new ways of being, a new world of blessings?

The anthology *Itturei Torah* explains this mystery, in the name of the vayedaber Mosheh [and let me confess that I have no idea about his identity]: BEHOLD I PLACE BEFORE YOU TODAY BLESSING AND CURSE...THE BLESSING IF YOU ATTEND...AND THE CURSE IF YOU DO NOT ATTEND...." [Deut. 11.26-28].

Synopsis: "SEE, THIS DAY I SET BEFORE YOU BLESSING AND CURSE: BLESSING IF YOU OBEY THE COMMANDMENTS OF THE ETERNAL, YOUR GOD, THAT I ENJOIN YOU THIS DAY; AND CURSE, IF YOU DO NOT OBEY THE COMMANDMENTS OF THE ETERNAL, YOUR GOD, BUT TURN AWAY FROM THE PATH THAT I ENJOIN UPON YOU THIS DAY AND FOLLOW OTHER GODS, WHOM YOU HAVE NOT EXPERIENCED." [Deut. 10.26-38] Here, in the opening verses of our parashah, we are presented with THE classic choice. Although it is the end of the previous chapter in Deuteronomy, nevertheless, it is an appropriate introduction to Moses' second discourse (which ends in Chapter 26). Starting with the laws regarding the destruction of foreign religions and the construction of a central place of worship (rather than private altars), we are warned about the blood in animals that we slaughter—for that is the sign of life. In this and in our worship, we ARE to be different from the other nations. Be wary of false prophets and of those who would wish to add or diminish the mitzvot. Cities that are completely corrupted with idolatry are to be destroyed. You (we) are to be a holy (kadosh) nation—in our eating practices, in how we treat our bodies, in how we distribute wealth, in how we preserve our natural resources, in how we treat the poor, the slaves, the foreigners, and in the uniqueness of our firstborn. This very rich parashah concludes with passages about the three pilgrimage festivals, Pesah, Shavuot and Sukkot—describing, in particular, the mitzvah to journey to the "central place of worship" (not yet identified as Jerusalem).

---

of the blessing and the curse. Perhaps the text tells us that the Children of Israel had the opportunity placed before them to "perform" a blessing or a curse. The blessing: if they (we) observe God's mitzvot, then our actions will, in effect, serve as a blessing for God. The curse: if they (we) disobey God and pursue

false gods, that will be quite a slap in the face for God, and hence, a curse. In any case, whether or not we are granting or receiving, our actions will determine whether it is a blessing or a curse. **Elon Sunshine, rabbinic student, University of Judaism <al280@lafn.org>**

"Goodness and abundance are not always a blessing, for sometimes wealth turns bad for its owner. 'THE BLESSING...IF YOU OBEY...' if you do mitzvot and good deeds with your wealth, then will it be a true blessing? However, if wealth brings forth pride, envy and competition, and you become obsessed to acquire even more money, then the blessing itself will become a curse. The same is true for the giving of Eretz Yisrael, which will be for blessing if they observe the Torah and mitzvot, but danger if they diverge from the way of God. This is the meaning of the teaching, 'Any *brakhah* that does not include mention of *Ha-Shem*—God's name—is no *brakhah* [*Brakhot* 40b].' Any good thing that is not based in the recognition that God gave the means to achieve it, rather than in the spirit of 'My strength and the power of my own hand gave me this success' will end up in curse." [*Itturei Torah*, vol. 6, p. 82]

The author, conveniently, uses moral categories of blessing and curse. If you amass wealth and use it for the sake of God and humankind, to deepen your spiritual life and your capacity to contribute to the world, it is for blessing; if you forget God and allow wealth only to make you hunger for more, it is a curse. If the Jews entered Israel with God's presence in mind, they would be blessed; but curses would abound if they were to fail to be mindful of God.

So, too, I dare say, for other points of crisis in our lives. Sometimes, when we stand at a crossroads—even one shaped by loss and pain that was beyond our control—we still have many choices about how we respond. For one person, a time of multiple or traumatic losses gradually unfolds into a time of profound renewal, giving birth to new gifts, relationships and opportunities. For another, a time of loss brings darkness so thick that no one can penetrate it, even to help.

By no means do I want to advocate a simple-minded "right way" to

Re'eh

דָּבָר אַחֵר **DAVAR AHER.** "See, I PRESENT BEFORE YOU TODAY A BLESSING AND A CURSE" [Deut. 11.26]. The text could have begun: *Anokhi notein lifneikhem berakhah u-kelalah*, "I PUT BEFORE YOU THE BLESSING AND THE CURSE..." but we need the *Re'eh* (see) to indicate "sight." There is an *inyan* in Gemara stating that *Ayin od na'aseh din*, "We still make law by eye" because once a person sees a crime or an incident, that sighting becomes part of the person's experience. *Hazal* teaches us that everything involved in *Torah u'mada* must be related internally by Ha-Shem. *Re'eh* = "Open up your eyes and see that through free choice, we have a choice between receiving *brakhot*/blessings or *k'lallot*/curses. Ha-Shem desires a dwelling place in this world. We hope that when one looks at evil it will penetrate him in order to per-

ראה אנכי נתן לפניכם היום ברכה וקללה

respond to personal loss or tragedy. Yet the teaching of the Vayedaber Moses on *Re'eh* suggests an aspect of choice that is always available to us, no matter what experiences life sends our way. The most important events of our lives are often the ones over which we have little control. Yet we usually exercise significant choice over our response. Most of the time, we have the opportunity to choose blessing. This is the path that our tradition offers us, in a thousand ways each day.

Our tradition does not, after all, promise that our days or our lives will be free from suffering. What we are assured of is the constant opportunity to perceive the blessings that are available on any day, in any situation. It is one of Judaism's most ever-present teachings—what my friend, Barry Barkan, calls "the way of blessing." To notice what is beautiful, what is blessed around us and within us, is a choice that is always open to us, if we choose to walk that path.

We can choose to begin any day with the prayer,

מוֹדֶה\מוֹדָה אֲנִי לְפָנֶיךָ

"*Modeh/modah ani lefanecha…*" thanking God for the gift of returning us to life after a night of unconsciousness. Every morning, we can thank God for the gift of life, the gift of breath and spirit that is with us at every moment. We can thank God that our eyes can see again, our limbs can move again, that the earth is still steady beneath our feet. We can give thanks that we can use the bathroom. We can notice Gods presence in a sip of water, a slice of bread, a piece of fruit. In the way of blessing, Judaism's way of mindfulness, we stop and notice—a hundred times a day and more—that we are awake, that we are alive, that there are wonders everywhere around us, and that God reveals Godself to us through these everyday wonders, whenever we choose to take notice. This is a choice we are given: the choice to notice the blessings.

No, the course of our lives is not shaped only by our own moral choices. Pain and loss show up, others fail us, we are hurt in many ways despite the right choices we try to make. But this day, every day, we are offered the choice to pay attention to the beauty and wonder that surrounds us and pervades our lives, morning, noon and night.

May the call of *Parashat Re'eh* inspire us to see, to notice, and to respond to the many blessings that we receive this day. May we see the blessings, and give thanks. ●

---

mit him to use free choice and choose life. For this reason *Parashat Re'eh* is always read at the onset of the month of *Elul*. "I AM FOR MY BELOVED AND MY BELOVED IS FOR ME." G-d is waiting for us to "open our eyes" and choose good things—understanding that every moment is precious. With our choice of *brakhah* and the spirit of *teshuvah* of *Elul* we should usher in a period of happiness. **Dr. Jeffrey C. Ratz, Brooklyn, NY**

דָּבָר אַחֵר **DAVAR AHER.** "NO PART OF THE BANNED PROPERTY MAY ADHERE TO YOUR HAND, SO THAT HA-SHEM WILL TURN BACK FROM HIS BURNING WRATH" [DEUT. 13.18]. IN a class I gave in *Sefer ha-Hinnukh* on *Parashat Re'eh*, I had problems similar to those of David Kraemer in explaining the uses of the term *herem*. The Syrian and Morrocan Jews recognized the term as a cognate of the Arabic *haram*, a term I hear often enough when I get into

halakhic discussions with Syrian Jews, and which is often translated as "forbidden." There are, in fact, many additional instances where *herem* has the positive connotation of *hekdesh*, a dedicated or vowed offering, such as Numbers 18.14. But what convinced me most then, that the usage of the term in Deuteronomy 27.28 is not anomalous was the usage מִן-הַחֵרֶם וְלֹא-יִדְבַּק בְּיָדְךָ מְאוּמָה *Velo yidbaq beyadekha me'umah min ha-herem*

Rabbi Ronald Shulman

RONALD SHULMAN IS THE RABBI OF
CONGREGATION NER TAMID OF
SOUTH BAY IN RANCHO PALOS
VERDES, CALIFORNIA. HE IS ALSO A
LECTURER IN BIBLE AT THE
UNIVERSITY OF JUDAISM IN LOS
ANGELES.

Re'eh

Here are four words I use to describe the religious imperative I derive from Judaism. Faith Is Not Fact. Faith is the measure of my ideals. It is the way I believe things ought to be. Quite often the facts with which I live demonstrate a different reality. The essential purpose of my faith is to bring its truths to bear on the facts I know. The goal of my faith is to draw those facts I know closer to the ideal vision of God's presence in which I believe.

Children have a much greater capacity to do this than adults. My ten-year-old daughter is filled with questions and wonder about the world's order. She often comments about the unfairness she sees around her every day. She is concerned about people who are disabled, reflecting an aspect of her own identity. Behaviors that cause hurt to others also get her attention. Some are things I know she has done herself, though she has trouble acknowledging them. These are realities that she believes should not be. My heart knows that she is right. My head struggles to explain why these things are so.

For me, faith is about such contrasts. The eternity of God's essence teaches the sanctity and importance of my time. God's boundless spiritual nature underscores the limits of my physical strength. This contrast also attaches moral consequence and importance to my actions in life and human society.

The very last words of *Parashat Re'eh* teach me this awareness. Three times each year festival gifts were to be brought to Jerusalem.

[Deut. 13.16-18], the prohibitions against enjoying the spoils of victory in the `ir ha-niddahat, in the war against Amalek, and the prohibitions of using anything which was used for idolatrous purposes (cf. Deut. 12.3). What was wrong with King Saul's using the spoils of the war against Amalek and taking captives? If idols are merely sticks and stones, why can't I use wood from an אֲשֵׁרָה *asherah* (ritual tree) to light my oven?

Or, if not the idol itself, at least the אֲבִזְרַיּוֹת *abizrayot*, the secondary accoutrements, should be permissible. On the contrary, isn't the fact that we don't use these objects an implicit acknowledgment of their power, that there is a "sacredness" to them? In answering these questions, I came up with my own twist on David Kraemer's approach. Not "everything belongs to God and we only get what He gives us special

"THEY SHALL NOT APPEAR BEFORE THE LORD EMPTY-HANDED, BUT EACH WITH HIS OWN GIFT, ACCORDING TO THE BLESSING THAT THE LORD YOUR GOD HAS BESTOWED UPON YOU" [Deut. 16.16-17]. We are each endowed with Divine gifts in consonance with our individual nature and condition. It is from that which is my blessing, my power to act in response to God, that I am asked to give to others of what I have received.

A text in the Mishnah which grows out of a different section of this parashah complements this recognition. In Deuteronomy 14.22-29, we read the command of God through Moses to Israel of *Ma'aser Sheni*, a second tithe of produce required to be eaten at the Temple itself, an act that brings sacred purpose to the fulfillment of our physical needs.

The Mishnah describes a vow to have been spoken when the *Ma'aser Sheni* was brought to the Temple. It concludes with the declaration, "I have done according to all that You have commanded me. I have rejoiced and caused others to rejoice." In this Torah commentary, Rabbi Shimshon Raphael Hirsch points out, "observance of these procedures has been entrusted entirely to the conscience of the individual."

I hope my conscience is a reflection of my faith. I hope my conscience challenges the ideals of my faith to respond to the facts in life I cannot accept. I hope my conscience keeps me aware of others so that I may give something of myself to them.

Following the tithe comes the law of *Shemitah*, a release of debts and servitude to others every seven years. As a result of this release we are taught that God's blessing will remove the needy from Israel's midst ("THERE SHALL BE NO NEEDY AMONG YOU...") [Deut. 15.4], but only if we act on the imperatives of our faith ("IF ONLY YOU LISTEN TO THE LORD YOUR GOD AND TAKE CARE TO PRESERVE AND DO ALL OF THIS MITZVAH...") [Deut.15.5]. This is the ideal, the faith in which I seek to believe.

The text also reminds us that it is each of us who is called upon to lend help to the needy among us. We are to act willingly and out of conscience. Rashi reminds us in his comments (on verse 7) that if we do not give to one in need we are destined to become his brother, another who needs the help of others.

But soon after, verse 11 in chapter 15 is read. Human reality will not be changed without a call to my conscience. "FOR THERE WILL NEVER CEASE TO BE NEEDY ONES IN YOUR LAND, WHICH IS WHY I COMMAND YOU: OPEN YOUR HAND TO THE POOR AND NEEDY KINSMAN IN YOUR LAND." Still others who need will always be there. A lesson I learn from *Parashat Re'eh* is that I must always be there, too. Motivated by my faith and inspired by my ideals, it is here in the real world that I am asked to live and to give.•

---

permission to use"—that's fine for the "I am but dust and ashes" pocket. But what about "the world was created for my sake" side? I'd rather say that God gives us the earth outright, placing it at our pleasure (the ecological crowd will lynch me if I say "at our disposal"). Some of it, however, is reserved, so to speak, for His "personal use"—it is designated as God's personal property, preserve, or realm; it belongs to Him personally. This includes dedicated "holy" objects as well as the realm of radical evil. Amalek represents radical evil, as do idols. They are the "sworn enemies" of God and of everything our people holds sacred. When we triumph over them, the victory and the spoils belong to God, not to man. You can't gain benefit from radical evil; the only way is eradication. The idols do, in a sense, become holy. I'm reminded of the story in I Samuel 5.3, where the Philistines capture the Ark and place it next to the idol of Dagon, and the next morning they find Dagon face down biting the dust before the Ark. There are similar Midrashim about how the idols of Egypt were also wiped out during the plagues, as it says: *"uveloheihem e`eseh shefatim."* If the idols meant nothing, why bother? "To the victor go the spoils"—the custom was that the head general got first pick of the spoils. This is why

Melchizedek offers first dibs on the loot to Abram. All wars of the Jewish people are in a sense holy wars, for we represent God. In the war against Midian in Numbers 31, a certain part of the spoils are given to the Levites. But some are holier than others: the real *jihads*, the ones against radical evil incarnate, the head honcho, the personal enemy of God. When the offense committed is so heinous that it involves an "in your face" affront to the power of God, He "takes it personally," and the revenge—and the spoils—are His alone. The enemy forfeits his rights as the Avenger confiscates and appropriates all. I'm reminded of a scene from a John Wayne movie or a war movie, you know, where the rest of the enemy's allies have been effectively neutralized, and now it's

time to take on the ringleader himself. Our hero's friends offer to help him give chase, but he waves them away with a gruff "No. This one's mine." It's part of the warrior spirit that you stand in a special relationship with your closest friends as well as with your personal sworn enemy. You must triumph over him personally, and when you do, the spoils—and the glory—are yours, and no one can ever take them away. Kedusha and *tum'ah* are not merely parallel in that both are off-limits to man—radical evil is also literally *kadosh*, holy, at least in potentiality. For when God triumphs over radical idolatry, evil, and death, the captured spoils become literally sacred manifestations of His Glory. **Hazan Ira Rohde, Cong. Shearith Israel, NYC**

Re'eh

Deuteronomy 18.13:

תָּמִים תִּהְיֶה עִם ה׳ אֱלֹהֶיךָ

"YOU MUST BE WHOLEHEARTED WITH THE ETERNAL YOUR GOD."

When we enter the month of Elul, we begin that thoughtful preparation to move us toward the High Holy Days, the Days of Awe. I love this time of year, as summer draws to a lingering close and the New Year is still in the distance. It is now that I try and focus on the coming period of introspection and self-evaluation known in Hebrew as חֶשְׁבּוֹן הַנֶּפֶשׁ

heshbon hanefesh,"taking stock of your soul."

Shoftim

Deuteronomy 16.18-21.9

Rabbi Elyse Goldstein

RABBI ELYSE GOLDSTEIN IS THE DIRECTOR OF KOLEL: A CENTRE FOR LIBERAL JEWISH LEARNING, ONE OF NORTH AMERICA'S ONLY LIBERAL ADULT YESHIVOT, IN ONTARIO, CANADA.

This week's Torah portion, _Parashat Shoftim_, is a good place to start.

It seems, on first glance, to be an administrative section, dealing with the assignment of judges and magistrates, potential kingship, levitical rights. Laws of warfare are juxtaposed with laws of testimony. The Hebrews are preparing to enter the land and must also be prepared, like any modern nation, to govern themselves in that land. The _parashah_ also speaks of the nation's responsibility to—dare we say it—a higher standard of governance. "JUSTICE, JUSTICE SHALL YOU PURSUE, THAT YOU MAY THRIVE AND INHERIT THE LAND THAT THE ETERNAL YOUR GOD IS GIVING YOU." [Deuteronomy 16.20] The right to finally occupy the land is tied inexorably to being a government of justice. Rashi suggests, quoting _Sifre_:

כְּדַאי הוּא מִנּוּי הַדַּיָּנִין הַכְּשֵׁרִים לְהַחֲיוֹת אֶת יִשְׂרָאֵל וּלְהוֹשִׁיבָן עַל אַדְמָתָן

"The appointment of honest judges is sufficient merit to keep Israel alive and to settle them in their land." But Ramban, quoting Rashi, says it is not

דָּבָר אַחֵר **DAVAR AHER.** "JUSTICE, JUSTICE SHALL YOU PURSUE" [Deut. 16.20]. Nathaniel, you know I've struggled with this talk to you today. For weeks I've been thinking about what I wanted to say, about who you are, and the significance of this special day. I think I've had such a hard time writing this because of the attachment we've had. You, yourself, said it most succinctly…"We're close because we like all the same things, and we think the same way." Maybe that's

why this has been so difficult…there are so many things I want to say, but then you should already know what they are.

I have thought about your Torah portion and what _Shoftim_ offers us. I've thought about your becoming a bar mitzvah and how significant this day is not only for you, but for your family as well. And when I think about how all this ties together, the same theme keeps coming back to me…family.

enough to be a government of justice. The doubling of the word "JUSTICE" suggests that *each individual must also actively pursue justice* as well:

וְטַעַם הַכֵּפֶל לוֹמָר הַדַּיָּנִים
צְרִיכִין שֶׁיִּשְׁפְּטוּ אֶת הָעָם
מִשְׁפַּט צֶדֶק וְגַם אַתָּה
צָרִיךְ לִרְדֹּף הַצֶּדֶק תָּמִיד

"The reason for the doubling is to say that while the judges must exercise judgment of the people righteously you also need to always pursue justice." One person *can* make a difference. Thus our *parashah* is not only for the people, but for each person.

If one person makes a difference, then it makes a difference what kind of people we are. Let us focus in on one word in the parashah: Deuteronomy 18.13: תָּמִים—*tamim.* Noah and Abraham were both called תָּמִים "*tamim.*" In Noah's case, his behavior is contrasted with that of others. He is "RIGHTEOUS IN HIS GENERATION" [Gen. 6.9]. His wholeness is in relation to the wickedness of

the generation of the flood. Remember that the Torah judges Noah's generation as utterly corrupt, and so his being *tamim* really stands out. Here, wholeness is understood as bravery: stand out and speak up even when the rest of the world around us is silent; be innocent when others are guilty. Noah was whole—*tamim*—in a broken world.

In Abraham's case, the word תָּמִים *tamim* appears in the command "WALK BEFORE ME AND BE WHOLE" [Gen. 17.1]; a command he receives while he is still named Abram. Immediately after this command, he receives the additional "ה" in his name, becoming Abraham. The tradition teaches that this extra letter is no ordinary letter, but one signifying his new spiritual being: with God "הי." Thus, being *tamim* means being in relation to God, a spiritual wholeness that may radically change us, cause us to be "with God." Abraham was whole—*tamim*—because he was willing to be less, to make room, to let God in.

Shoftim

You have shown incredible devotion, loyalty, and unconditional love to family. Whenever I've been sad, or as your Aunt Hannah would say, "feeling a little blue" you would be there to comfort me. When Daddy goes to a swim meet, it's always you who goes along to root and cheer him on. And when Bubby's friend Julius died, you immediately went to Bubby's to stay with her so that she wouldn't have to be alone,

and to give her your love, support and comfort. When your sister Nira was ill, or had recently returned from one of many hospital stays, you were always there for her. You passed up many invitations to be with friends when you thought your sister needed you…truly amazing for a seven-year-old.

Your great grandmother, Bubby Riva, took one look at you when you were born, beamed and pro-

שופטים ושטרים תתן לך בכל שעריך

Furthermore, Rashi adds that this extra letter will make Abram's new name, Abraham, add up in gematria to 248, the number of bones in the body and the number of positive mitzvot in the Torah. Being in relation to God through the mitzvot is a full body affair, a partnership of brain and heart and anatomy, causing one to be whole in body, not only whole in spirit. Being *tamim* means taking care of yourself physically so that you can be spiritually alive.

Tamim can also be translated as "simple." In the Haggadah, the "simple" (תָּם *tam*) child merely asks, "*Mah zot,* מַה זֹּאת" "What is all this?" She is interested, open-minded, non-judgmental. He is not simple in a pejorative way, rather, in a pleasing way. As with all children, she is a blank slate. Being whole means seeing yourself as an open book, full of possibility; seeing this coming New Year as a clean page. "YOU MUST BE SIMPLE WITH THE ETERNAL YOUR GOD" means no preconceived notions about old men with white beards on

thrones. It means asking, "מַה זֹּאת" "What is all this?" and being ready to hear all possible answers.

And so we are told in our parashah, "YOU MUST BE WHOLEHEARTED WITH THE ETERNAL YOUR GOD" [Deut. 18.13]. Dear friends reading this: Our world is a mess of broken pieces, hearts that are worn and torn, dreams dispossessed. A recent survey said that a startling number of North American children fear they will not grow old because there will be a nuclear destruction. Yet we Jews live in two realities, because Judaism is a religion of hope, wholeness and grounding. I am not the only one who knows this. You know it, too. Thus not only must we be wholehearted *with* God, we must be wholehearted *for* God.

Rabbi Shalom ben Joseph Alsheich, comments on our verse: "Even in the most private of rooms, when no one sees you and you are only with The Eternal your God alone and there is no stranger there, then too, 'be whole with The Eternal your God.' Outward religiosity should match

Synopsis: Civil government along with the pursuit of justice is the subject of this week's parashah. Specific laws concerning idolatrous worship, the supreme court, and the king follow. The Kohanim and Leviim are not given land and the role of true prophets is defined. A miscellany of laws dealing with crime, landmarks, plotting witnesses, laws of warfare (exemptions from service, capture of heathen cities, destruction of trees, banning of the Canaanites), and expiation of untraced murder concludes this week's reading.

---

nounced "He's a good one … look in those eyes…a *gute nashuma.*" She was right.

Your devotion to family is not just limited to your immediate family, but to your extended family as well. You were allowed to invite a friend to vacation with us, but you immediately asked if your cousin Eric, from Connecticut, could come. I think of the spark created when you and your Uncle Jerry were trading baseball

cards. And I've rarely seen you happier than when your Uncle Johnny comes to stay with us. Putting up with you when he leaves, however, is another story.

Today when you and the others read from the Torah, the pointer you used, the yad, belonged to your great-uncle Benny. How proud he would have been to hear you today. And later, at kiddush, when we say the blessing over the wine, you will drink from the

kiddush cup that was given to your great-grandmother in Russia upon her engagement. Your sister did this as well at her bat mitzvah, yet another family tie.

Your love of family must be truly obvious to all. It is a testament to you that so many family members are here today to celebrate with you on this special occasion. Your cousins Zhenia and Tanya from Moscow came an incredible distance to be

inner spirituality. Don't do it for show. Don't do it just when you are in shul."

Be brave. Be sound of mind and sound of body. Be simple. But most of all, be whole with God, even when you are alone, even when everyone else around you is broken and trying to break you, too. The Seer of Lublin asks, "Which is the higher attainment: greatness or wholeness? Wholeness! Here is the proof: if you have two *Hallot*, one large and sliced and one small but whole, you bless the whole one. Thus wholeness has more value

than greatness." In the Torah scroll, the ת of *tamim* is enlarged. Maybe the first letter of the word for wholeness is made bigger to show that all we need to do is merely begin the process of striving to be "*tamim*" and we are already a little taller, a little prouder. "HAPPY ARE THEY THAT ARE '*TAMIM*' IN THE WAY, WHO WALK IN THE LAW OF THE ETERNAL." [Psalm 119] *Hag Sameah,* חַג שָׂמֵחַ Happy New Year!•

Shoftim

here, to meet you for the first time and to witness their first bar mitzvah. Also here today is your great-great aunt from South Africa, and your cousins from England, one of whom read Torah today. And the numerous aunts, uncles, cousins from all over the U.S., from the East Coast, from Texas, and from Northern and Southern California.

Today is such a sweet day for me, yet is also difficult. By Jewish tradition, you have become a man. It's a time of transition. You're grown up! I know I have to, but it's hard to begin letting go. But you are doing that yourself. You are starting a new school, will make new friends, yet I know your ties with your old friends will remain strong. I know your loyalty. I know who you are. In this respect you remind me so much of your grandfather, your namesake. You carry more similarities with him than just his name.

In *Shoftim*, the Torah portion you read today, a central theme is justice. Moses said to the Israelites "Justice, justice shall you pursue." And in your *drash*, you stated, and I quote: "I must strive not only to live a just life, but also to exercise justice to all those around me." You have already achieved this goal. You ARE a just person, and I know you will continue to exercise justice to all those around you. I am so proud of the person you have become. I love you very, very much. **Lisa Schwartz's talk to Nathaniel Feeley on his Bar Mitzvah–September 2, 1995**

דָּבָר אַחֵר **DAVAR AHER.** "WHEN YOU COME TO THE LAND THAT HA-SHEM, YOUR GOD, GIVES YOU, AND POSSESS IT, AND SETTLE IN IT…" [Deut. 17.14]. Nathaniel, I think you know how difficult it has been for me to prepare for this day. You know the struggle I have gone through in finding a meaning for today for both you and

Rabbi Chaim Seidler-Feller

RABBI CHAIM SEIDLER-FELLER IS THE EXECUTIVE DIRECTOR OF UCLA HILLEL, LOS ANGELES, CALIFORNIA.

Shoftim

Shoftim—the structures and operations of Jewish government, of the Judaic system of justice. For such a legal system to function it must establish a mechanism for continuous legislation and judicial review as well as the ground of its authority. Indeed, our parashah contains a passage that serves as the source of Rabbinic authority throughout the generations. As we read: "IF A CASE IS TOO BAFFLING FOR YOU TO DECIDE...YOU SHALL PROMPTLY...APPEAR BEFORE...THE MAGISTRATE IN CHARGE AT THAT TIME...YOU SHALL ACT IN ACCORDANCE WITH THE INSTRUCTIONS GIVEN YOU AND THE RULING HANDED DOWN TO YOU; YOU MUST NOT DEVIATE FROM THE VERDICT THAT THEY ANNOUNCE TO YOU EITHER TO THE RIGHT OR TO THE LEFT" [Deut. 17.8-1].

What is fascinating about the last phrase is that it can be construed as both a limiting principle that enjoins even the slightest departure from the determined law and, at the same time, as a pronouncement that provides the license for a perpetually evolving interpretative tradition.

The expansive reading is offered in Tractate *Shabbat 23a* where the Talmud puzzles over the fact that although Hanukkah is a post-Biblical festival that is not ordained by the Torah, the blessing chanted upon kindling the Hanukkah lamp refers to the act as God's commandment. "Where have we been commanded?" asks the Gemara. And it answers: "In the words, YOU MUST NOT DEVIATE...לֹא תָסוּר *Lo tasur*." The rabbis argue that the authority for all Rabbinic legislation derives from the Torah. But they are actually saying much more, since the *brakhah* asserts

me. For Jewish parents, grandparents, family and friends the meaning of this day comes quite naturally, it's part of a tradition that dates back thousands of years. Jewish parents may have celebrated their own bar and bat mitzvahs. They probably grew up witnessing and celebrating with cousins, brothers, sisters, and friends. Days like this are part of the normal ebb and flow of life for Jews.

But I think you know, I don't have a connection to this day by birthright. In anticipation of this day, I got a little anxious as it approached. I got a little cranky, I lost some sleep, I did a lot of reading, pulled weeds, swam a little farther and harder, went to Peet's more often (although I'm not sure why I thought that would calm me down). You know, I did just about anything that would burn a little more energy as I struggled to find the right context in our lives as father

that we were commanded by God to light, when, as a matter of fact, we're not. The proof text is really taken to mean that the authoritative teachers of each generation mediate God's word and, in legal terms at least, determine the nature of God's will. God's mitzvah is such because the rabbis have established it as such. In other words, according to this teaching, the concept of "God's word" is only a legal category and not a substantive description. The implication for the doctrine of revelation is, of course, far-reaching. In one bold move the rabbis suggest that what is denoted as God's word is not intended as a statement of fact but as a legal construct. Is it possible that herein is a seed for developing a new understanding of mitzvah and of revelation, in general?

The narrow reading of "*LO TASUR—YOU SHALL NOT DEVIATE*" is presented by Rashi who rephrases the *Sifre* [194]. Troubled by the seemingly superfluous addition of "EITHER TO THE RIGHT OR TO THE LEFT" (it would have been enough to say, "You must not deviate from the verdict that they announce to you") Rashi comments, "Even if he says to you that right is left and left is right (you must not turn away), and certainly if he says right is right and left is left." Rashi appears to be laying the groundwork for an authoritarian system of total control whose legal decisions are independent of reason. After all, the plain meaning of the Rashi text is that you must follow the decision rendered by the judge even if he teaches that what is right is wrong and what is wrong is right. Even though you recognize the error, nevertheless you must do what you know to be wrong. One hears in this formulation an echo of Tertullian's, "I believe, because it is absurd." And one senses that it is this Rashi that energizes contemporary fundamentalist forces that seem to hold that the more a particular belief or prac-

Shoftim

and son that would define where this event belongs. The irony and difficulty about this day, is that I'm one of the two people who know you best, and yet this day is one that I feel both intimately included and excluded at the same time. It is a day on which I feel immense pride because I know that you, your mom and I have made the right decisions and choices. Decisions and choices that have brought you here today.

And yet I struggle with the questions: "What is our connection to this celebration?"

There are two very strong connections to you that I feel on this day. The first connection is family traditions. I think most people who see you today see a strong Jewish identity based on thousands of years of Jewish tradition and family ties. But

tice defies reason, the more religiously significant it is.

In contrast to Rashi, the Jerusalem Talmud in Tractate *Horayot* [1.1] writes that we are required to listen to authority only if "they will say to you about the right that it is right and about the left that it is left." If, however, we know the sages to be in error, we're obligated not to listen to them. Thank God for reason! At least the *Yerushalmi* seems to be supportive of a Maimonidean ethic that appreciates the religious value of intellectual integrity. As Maimonides avers: "for the intellect is the glory of God" [*Commentary to the Mishnah*].

Yet, one senses that the religious impulse favors Rashi's position since there is always the concern that the opinion that places a premium on individual reason might lead to a breakdown of the authority structure in the community. That precise concern is articulated by Nachmanides, who writes "controversies would multiply and thus the Torah would

become (as though it were) many Torahs" (commentary to Deuteronomy 17.11). The 13-14th century author of the *Sefer Hinukh* elaborates further when he warns: "Even if the sages should be in error about one particular thing, it is not right for us to oppose them, *but we are rather to act according to their error*. It is better to suffer one error, all being thus subject to their good thought, and not that everyone should act according to his thinking. For this would lead to the ruin of the religion, dissension in the heart of the people, and the total loss of the nation."

I am emphasizing this mode of argumentation because it has found new currency in contemporary Jewish life. Indeed, the conflict over the interpretation of "*LO TASUR*—YOU SHALL NOT DEVIATE" that raged in the Middle Ages is very much alive today. Reason is not a valued commodity in the halakhic community and one fears that were Maimonides to make an appearance, he would not be welcomed by the contemporary "cus-

todians of the law." As a response to this fundamentalist tendency I want to propose that we give *Rashi* and the *Sifre* a new spin. Rather than providing a justification for "know-nothing obedience," Rashi might actually be arguing for openness, encouraging his readers to be accepting of change. For "even if he says to you that the right is left..." that is, even if a later judge (or court) teaches the opposite of what an earlier judge taught so that he transforms the 'right' into the 'left,' even so, you should not deviate from the latter's instructions, so long as the teaching of the second judge (or court) is reasonable and verifiable (a variation on the well-known *mishnah* in *Eduyot 1.5*).

Although this rendition of Rashi may be farfetched, my goal is to overcome a particularly damaging and humiliating interpretative stance (without resorting to textual emendation) and return the crown of reason to its rightful place in the *halakhic* process.●

I know how much you are the product of two very rich traditions. Traditions that are at times as similar as they are dissimilar.

You remember a few years back when we were in Ireland and somewhere between Cork and Kilkenny we left the main road in search of a small town called Glenville. Based on the research your Aunt Ann had done, we knew that our ancestors were forced to leave this town at the time of the

Irish potato famine. You exist because two very distant groups of people came to this country to make a better life.

I know that I have enriched your Jewish traditions with many of my and my ancestors' traditions. Even though at times it may only seem that I have given you a rather neurotic obsession with English grammar, you are the product of two very rich cultures that

value family, justice, education, storytelling, and humor.

Here is the second more important connection I feel with you today. What's really special about today, is that today our lives begin to part. Think about it. You now have a separate status and position in life. This event truly is the first event in your life that begins to blur the distinction between parent and child. You are doing something that is your own,

Shoftim

that will forever distinguish you as a unique individual, different from me.

In thinking about the uniqueness of this event in our relationship, I can't help but reflect on your Torah portion *Shoftim* and all of the book of Deuteronomy and the situation that Moses was in as he spoke to the Israelites.

I think I know exactly how Moses must have felt. He and I, although a few thousand years apart, have now shared, I believe, some very similar emotions. With the Israelites on the verge of entering the promised land, Moses must have felt a little like the guy on the outside looking in. He was not going to be able to enter the land of Israel. As his people prepared to enter the land of Israel, he must have felt a bit confused, maybe hurt, maybe angry. He must have felt that he had done a considerable amount of work, and couldn't reap the ultimate reward for his work. Yes, I'm pretty sure he was probably feeling a little sorry for himself (but of course didn't have Peet's coffee for that special little pick-me-up). And yet, despite these emotions, he must have also felt immense pride, joy and happiness, for he had accomplished his goal. For his goal was not to enter the land of Israel himself, but for his people to enter the land of Israel and to establish a nation.

So, too, for me today. Just seeing you here today celebrating your Bar Mitzvah, I feel enormous pride at your accomplishments and pride in the knowledge that I have played a part in bringing you to this point. I know that I have played a significant role in your development including your Jewish development. For this alone, I really am a full participant today, sharing the joy and happiness that you must feel.

You know Nathaniel, life takes many interesting twists and turns. If I think back twenty years, it would have been impossible for me to imagine that I would be standing here today. If someone twenty years ago predicted that I would marry a Jew; that I would have two kids both of whom would go to Jewish school and celebrate their bar and bat mitzvahs; that your Jewish relatives from Russia could freely leave Russia to attend your bar mitzvah; that I and my three siblings would only rarely all get together and then only at special occasions like weddings and bat mitzvahs; it would have been hard to believe. But I guess not impossibly so, because life is unpredictable. For all the unpredictability you face in your life, may you have many moments in your life that you feel the joy, happiness and pride that I feel today. I love you very much. Mazel Tov. **Michael Feeley's talk to Nathaniel Feeley at his Bar Mitzvah—September 2, 1995**

דָּבָר אַחֵר **DAVAR AHER. "AND WHEN HE SITS ON THE THRONE OF HIS KINGDOM, HE SHALL WRITE FOR HIMSELF IN A BOOK A COPY OF THIS LAW, FROM THAT WHICH IS IN THE CHARGE OF THE LEVITICAL PRIESTS; AND IT SHALL BE WITH HIM, AND HE SHALL READ IN IT ALL THE DAYS OF HIS LIFE, THAT HE MAY LEARN TO FEAR THE LORD HIS GOD, BY KEEPING ALL THE**

שופטים ושטרים תתן לך בכל שעריך

WORDS OF THIS LAW AND THESE STATUTES, AND DOING THEM [DEUT. 17.18-19]. *My question is: Why does the king have to keep the Sefer Torah with him?* **Shaye Horwitz.**

This one is easy. Open up First Kings and read the famous story which starts at 3.10. Here, Solomon acts as a judge. Normally, according to the "oral" Torah, you need three judges to do a trial. According to the Torah you need witnesses to have a verdict. Jewish courts do not allow "circumstantial evidence." According to the "oral" Torah, it would be wrong to cut a baby in half. Solomon does things which are not allowed—and they turn out good. Because he is a king, he can play faster and looser with the law, and solve some problems that ordinary judges can't. But that could be a problem.

Now, turn back to II Samuel and read the story of Bat-Sheva in 11 and 12. Here King David goes crazy with power. He begins to believe that whatever he does is right, just because he is the king. It takes Nathan, a prophet, to set him straight. Kings tend to go crazy with King power. They need King power in order to solve problems for their countries that no one else can solve. But, they are still at risk from going King power crazy. That is why they must write and keep a Torah. It is like their Nathan. It reminds them that someOne is always watching and judging their actions. That is what I think I know. What do you think? **Joel Lurie Grishaver** <gris@torahaura.com>

A
Ki Tetze

**Deuteronomy
21.10-25.19**

Arthur Waskow

ARTHUR WASKOW IS A FELLOW OF
ALEPH: ALLIANCE FOR JEWISH
RENEWAL, AND DIRECTOR OF THE
SHALOM CENTER (A DIVISION OF
ALEPH) FOR JEWISH THOUGHT AND
ACTION TO PREVENT GLOBAL ENVI-
RONMENTAL DISASTER. SINCE 1969,
WASKOW HAS BEEN ONE OF THE
LEADING CREATORS OF THEORY,
PRACTICE, AND INSTITUTIONS FOR
THE MOVEMENT FOR JEWISH
RENEWAL. HE IS THE AUTHOR OF
THE FREEDOM SEDER (1969);
GODWRESTLING (SCHOCKEN, 1978;
2D ED., JEWISH LIGHTS 1995);
SEASONS OF OUR JOY (BANTAM,
1982; REVISED ED., BEACON,
1991); *AND DOWN-TO-EARTH
JUDAISM: FOOD, MONEY, SEX, AND
THE REST OF LIFE* (WILLIAM
MORROW, 1995).

TO REMEMBER, TO BLOT OUT

t the end of *Ki Tetze*, a parashah of great compassion for the poor man who cannot redeem his debt pledge; for your neighbor who might fall from the unprotected roof of your house; for your enemy whose sheep has wandered away; for a mother bird who is sitting on her eggs—suddenly there is this puzzling, paradoxical command: "REMEMBER WHAT AMALEK DID TO YOU ON THE ROAD AS YOU CAME FORTH FROM MITZRAIM, THE NARROWS:

HOW HE MET YOU ON THE ROAD AND SMASHED THE STRAGGLERS AMONG YOU, ALL WHO WERE ENFEEBLED IN YOUR REAR, WHEN YOU WERE FAINT AND WEARY. FOR HE DID NOT REVERE THE DIVINE CREATIVE POWER. WHEN YHWH YOUR GOD HAS GIVEN YOU SAFETY FROM ALL YOUR ENE-MIES THAT SURROUND YOU, IN THE LAND THAT YHWH GIVES YOU FOR AN INHERI-TANCE TO POSSESS IT, YOU SHALL BLOT OUT THE MEMORY OF AMALEK FROM UNDER HEAVEN. DO NOT FORGET!" [DEUT. 25.17-19]

Until Purim morning of the year 5754 (our count since the Creation), this passage was only paradoxical and puzzling. "REMEMBER...BLOT OUT THE MEMORY...DO NOT FORGET...." Are these a contradiction? Or a—what?

Until Purim 5754, Jews resolved the paradox with a joke—a Purim joke. Jewish tradition linked the command about Amalek to Purim, on the ground that Haman—the villain of the Scroll of Esther, who in the story would have destroyed the

---

דָּבָר אַחֵר **DAVAR A<u>H</u>ER.** WHEN YOU GO FORTH TO WAR AGAINST YOUR ENEMIES, THE ETERNAL YOUR GOD WILL DELIVER THEM INTO YOUR HANDS, AND YOU WILL TAKE THEM CAPTIVE [Deut. 21.10]. We are all living contradictions. I like Jewish values. I like Clint Eastwood movies. I like quoting:"YOU ARE STANDING HERE, THIS DAY, ALL OF YOU..." [Deut. 29.9]. I like saying "Go ahead, make my day!" (Dirty Harry) Some of my best and my worst

teaching moments are "Clint does Moses."

It was Sunday morning, post-senior prom. Adam and David had "doubled" with two "female-friends" (not dates) and all four of them showed up to my Hebrew High Class. (A Real Compliment—more so, because they were in street clothes and didn't do "the walk into McDonalds in tuxedo things"). They had been up all night. Adam was making a lot of noise and

Jews—was both a biological and an ideological descendant of Amalek. So what Jews did to "BLOT OUT THE MEMORY" of Amalek was to shake noisemakers at the mention of Haman's name, write his name on the soles of shoes to be rubbed out in dancing…. How do we know this was a joke? Because we are, at the same time, commanded to hear every word of the very Scroll that we drown out with our noise. Laughter and derision. To kill a tyrant, laugh at him.

But on Purim morning of 5754, the paradox became a terror, the puzzle a *shandeh*.

Purim morning—I have been up half the night, celebrating the hilarious festival of spring fever: reading Esther's tale of masks and ridicule; wearing my Hasid-diamond-merchant costume and drinking enough, as the Talmud commands, to forget the difference between the blessed liberator and the cursed murderer, swinging a noisemaker, dancing and telling bawdy jokes, and acting out a Purim spiel that pokes fun at rabbis, at Jewish life and at the Torah itself.

But now on Purim morning, the radio is muttering at me. It will not stop.

What is it saying? No. Some Jew has entered the mosque in Hebron with a machine gun—no, no—and has fired at Moslems kneeling in prayer—no, no, no, no—and killed maybe forty, maybe fifty or more—no, no, no, no, no—It is the mosque at the Tomb of Abraham, Abraham our Father, father of Jews and Arabs, blessing to the world—oh no, oh no, oh no.

No, no, no, no, no, no, no, no, no, no.

I lie in the bed sheets, dazed into silence, into a trance, but I know, know, know, know, no, no, no, no, no, no, no.

Synopsis: Laws dealing with family comprise the beginning of our parasha. Marriage with a female war-captive, punishment for a disobedient son, and the rights of the firstborn lead to a second group of laws about the exposed corpse of a criminal, restoring lost property, parapets on house roofs, mixing of seeds and helping to raise fallen animals. From here until the end of the parashah, there is a miscellaneous collection of laws among which are: sparing the mother bird, shaatnez, tzitzit, charges against a bride, adultery, marriage prohibitions, fugitive slaves, immorality, interest, vows, divorce, kidnapping, injustice to the stranger, orphan and widow, against excessive punishment, generosity to the landless, kindness to animals, levirate marriage, immodesty, and a final command to remember Amalek.

---

just goofing. It was hard to start teaching. In my best inner-Clint Eastwood, trying to get to my inner-Moses, I said, calmly, "Just because you had a bad prom night, doesn't mean you have to take it out on me." The whole class laughed. Everyone knew the story. It was a close class. Then I said, "Adam, just put your little head down on the desk and go to sleep." He did. I was proud of the moment. It was deep into the world of loving "put downs." It proved that I knew my students well enough to know them.

Then I started to read all the *musar* stuff about "*Busha*"—the mitzvah of not embarassing anyone. Rabbinically, my loving put-down is not justifiable. This week's sidrah begins, WHEN YOU GO FORTH TO WAR AGAINST YOUR ENEMIES, THE ETERNAL YOUR GOD WILL DELIVER THEM INTO YOUR HANDS, AND YOU WILL TAKE THEM CAPTIVE. *Itturei-Torah*

quotes the *Besht* (Baal Shem Tov) in saying, "Jews have no greater enemy than their own individual *Yetzer ha-Ra* (Evil Inclination). With God's help, we can each take and hold it captive."

Once, Armando, an Hispanic receptionist, spell-checked a monograph of mine about gender and the evil inclination. When he was done, the paper talked about the *Jester ha-Tov* and the *Jester ha-Ra*. ("Killer Clowns" took on a new meaning.) Now, thinking about

I know at once this is no isolated crazy, this "Baruch Goldstein" who has murdered forty of my cousins. I know at once: he has decided on this Purim to "BLOT OUT THE MEMORY OF AMALEK" not with a noisemaker but a machine gun, not with rivers of Schnapps and a *l'ḥayyim* but with rivers of blood and *l'Mavet* "To Death."

Most scholars and most celebrants take Purim as a day of hilarity and joking. The seemingly nightmarish story of the Scroll of Esther is a fantasy, a joke. On the very day Haman/Amalek intended to destroy us, we, instead, killed 75,000 of our enemies—the fantasy of the powerless that once, just once, they could fight back and destroy everyone who ever sneered at them.

But Goldstein took the story at face value. Why?

In the generation after the Nazi Holocaust—the Holocaust that actually did happen, the one from which no Esther saved the Jews—this archetypal myth of disaster bites home with intense cruelty and fear. Suddenly, Jews for whom the Amalek mythos had become somewhat quiescent, become attuned to it.

In our generation and for some Jews, the Palestinians become Amalek. Some Palestinians are terrorists? Some Palestinians call publicly for the State of Israel to be shattered? The archetypes of fear slide into place: all Palestinians are Amalek.

And the fantasies of the powerless become the actions of the powerful. For in our generation, Jews have power.

If the Scroll of Esther is a fantasy of the powerless about revenge upon the powerful, a dark, hilarious tale of masks and reversals, then in a generation when Jews are not, in fact, powerless we have to reimagine Purim.

And we have to reimagine Amalek. What does it mean to blot out the

Ki Tetze

the coming year of teaching, I'm wondering when to hold my *Jester ha-Ra* captive. **Joel Lurie Grishaver <Gris@TorahAura.Com>**

דְּבָר אַחֵר **DAVAR AḤER. REMEMBER WHAT AMALEK DID TO YOU, ON THE WAY WHEN YOU WERE LEAVING EGYPT, THAT HE HAPPENED UPON YOU ON THE WAY, AND HE STRUCK THOSE OF YOU WHO WERE HINDMOST, ALL THE WEAKLINGS AT YOUR REAR, WHEN YOU WERE FAINT AND EXHAUSTED, AND HE DID NOT FEAR GOD. IT SHALL BE THAT WHEN HA-SHEM, YOUR GOD, GIVES YOU REST FROM ALL YOUR ENEMIES AROUND, IN THE LAND THAT HA-SHEM, YOUR GOD, GIVES YOU AS AN INHERITANCE TO POSSESS IT, YOU SHALL WIPE OUT THE MEMORY OF AMALEK FROM UNDER THE HEAVEN—YOU SHALL NOT FORGET! [Deut. 25. 17-19].** In his article on *Ki Tetze*, Arthur Waskow touches on the apparent paradox in the passage on Amalek [Deut. 25.17-19]:

כי תצא למלחמה על איביך

memory of Amalek? The key command has two parts: first, "REMEMBER WHAT AMALEK DID TO YOU." Then, "WHEN YOUR GOD BRINGS YOU SAFELY INTO THE LAND, YOU SHALL BLOT OUT THE MEMORY OF AMALEK."

The chair of the board of the ALEPH Alliance for Jewish Renewal, Barbara Breitman, drawing on her own experience as a psychotherapist, teaches that this means:

First, the victim must clearly and fully recover the memories of victimization and abuse.

Then, when the victim is no longer weak and powerless, but safe in a good land, we must no longer be obsessed with Amalek; for it is exactly an unrealistic and obsessive fear that will drive us to repeat the abusive acts of Amalek.

Rabbi Tirzah Firestone points out that Amalek was a descendant of Esau, grandson of Abraham, who was cheated out of the birthright and the blessing that would have let him follow in Abraham's footsteps. So

Amalek is part of our own family—the residue of rage that sprang from the grief and anger Esau felt. Amalek is always a possibility within us, as well as in others. The Torah is teaching that we must blot out every urge to become Amalek, our own as well as others, by turning that urge toward compassion.

On Purim morning in the Tomb of Abraham, Goldstein, himself, was Amalek, attacking people from the rear, attacking those who had humbled themselves in prayer.

Purim 5754 taught us that Amalek is a way of living, not a specific ethnic community. Persians, Germans, Arabs and Jews can choose to behave like Amalek or like Queen Esther—who risked her life to challenge a king to do justice.

Purim 5754 also taught us that we have to change what we teach. Under new conditions, the old ways of interpreting Torah can lead straight to murder. Jews have long demanded that Christians and Muslims face the ways in which their

traditions have been used to justify the murder of Jews. Now Jews as well—Jews alongside Muslims and Christians—must look inward. We must all repudiate the elements of our different religious traditions that lead to the dehumanization and murder of Palestinians and Israelis.

Both peoples must affirm that they are hooked to each other like Siamese twins. So each has a positive need and goal not only to keep itself healthy, but also its twin. Both peoples must face the always-recurring "Amalek-urge" within themselves, and act to prevent the urge from turning into action.

How do we translate such a new vision into public policy? By demanding that each side seek to create the maximum degree of self-government and security for the other side that is consonant with its own basic security, not the minimum it can get away with. By that test, for example, most Jews would probably conclude that many West Bank settlements are a disadvantage to Israel.

---

how can one both remember Amalek and blot out the memory of Amalek? The answer, I believe, lies in the text. We are not commanded to remember Amalek but rather אֲשֶׁר עָשָׂה לְךָ עֲמָלֵק אֵת et asher asah l'kha Amalek— what Amalek did to you. That is, we are commanded to remember Amalek's evil deeds, not to become obsessed with the tribe which perpetrated them. "Forget about Amalek," the text appears to be saying, "once you have

been settled in the Land you no longer need fear him." Rather, remember how it felt to be attacked when you were down, and don't treat others in this way." Such an interpretation would certainly be in keeping with the enlightened tone of the rest of the parashah. **Stuart Lewis, Prarie Villiage, KS**

Most Palestinians would probably conclude that the Arab boycott of Israel is a disadvantage to the Palestinians.

For Jews, Muslims and Christians, these new understandings of their religious traditions must become not only the test of public policy but the fabric of prayers and celebrations, so that they become profoundly part of everyday life and sacred truth.

So, every year on the day before Purim (traditionally a Jewish fast day, the Fast of Esther), Jews could fast and invite Muslims, and others to join with them in holding public meetings of grief and rededication in memory of all the Arab and Jewish victims of terrorism, with a commitment to make a "Peace of the Children of Abraham."

On Purim, when Jews read the Scroll of Esther, we could chant in the wailing melody of the Book of Lamentations the troubling verses that express the fantasies of the powerless for revenge. We could pause to explain that we do this in sorrow over the deaths on Purim 5754 of our cousins, the children of Ishmael, in the Tomb of Abraham, lest anyone think that these verses are a call to wanton murder. (It is already traditional to read some earlier verses of Esther in this Lamentations wail: the verses in which Mordechai reports that we Jews are in danger. How powerful to make the parallel!)

And in the same way, we could read with wailing trope the passage in *Ki Tetze* about remembering/blotting out the memory of Amalek: remembering to confront Amalek within our own individual selves, within the Jewish people, and within all peoples.•

Ki Tetze

Allan Gould

ALLAN GOULD IS A TORONTO-BASED AUTHOR, JOURNALIST AND LECTURER, WHOSE BOOKS INCLUDE THE ANTHOLOGY *WHAT DID THEY THINK OF THE JEWS?*

Ki Tetze

Imagine, for a moment, that nearly the entire Torah was lost in our wanderings in the desert! The beautiful account of the Creation; the powerful stories of our Patriarchs and Matriarchs; the Burning Bush; the Exodus from Egypt; the astounding Revelation at Mt. Sinai; our wanderings in the desert; even the death of Moses! But, thank the good Lord, one, tiny fragment was somehow saved—the one that will be read this coming Shabbat in synagogues and homes around the world: *Ki Tetze*, that single *she'erit*, which had been preserved from the final book of the five, *Devarim*, covering the chapters 21, verse 10, through chapter 25.

Now, why should I ask you to imagine this horrible possibility? To suggest that Judaism could well have survived on this single parashah alone, because, like the glorious Torah itself, you can turn this portion, and turn it, and there is always more! Indeed, an entire religion could be built upon *Ki Tetze* alone! And a religion that, if it had become the cornerstone of both Christianity and

Islam (as Judaism is claimed to be, but rarely is), our world would be so much different—and so much more spiritually and physically healthy, than it is today.

True, this religion of *Ki Tetze* would have its obscurities, or *hukkim* (for this is the parashah that contains both the prohibition against wearing *Sha'atnez* [Deut. 12.11] and even the strange, mysterious *halitzah* ceremony [Deut. 15. 5-10]. And, yes, it cannot be denied, this religion of *Ki Tetze* would also have its harsh, "primitive" aspects as well, ranging from the suggested stoning of a disobedient son [Deut. 10.18-21] to the stoning of an adulterous couple [Deut. 12.22]. But even in the latter case, our tiny Torah fragment is light years ahead of many cultures and faiths today; as Dr. Hertz noted, "the man as well as the woman [die]; there is to be no double standard of conjugal morality in Israel."

The great Maimonides wrote that *Ki Tetze* may be the single most "halakhic" sidrah, containing over 70 of the *Taryag* (613) mitzvot—and who could disagree? Indeed, more than any other parashah (yes, a good case could be made for the centrality of *Shoftim*, last week's portion), this one can nearly stand alone as the moral and ethical basis of a better world than we see among us in the 1990s.

The very opening lines of *Ki Tetze* order us to not molest, or sell into slavery, a captive woman in wartime. (Would that the combatants in the former Yugoslavia had been observing this commandment over the past few years.) At the start of the very next chapter [XXII, 1-4], we are commanded to return lost objects to our

Ki Tetze

"BROTHERS"—an act of generosity and respect for property that was quickly expanded in the Talmud to include "heathens" as well, so that they might "bless the God of the Jews" [Jerusalem Talmud, Bava Metzia, Ch. 2.5].

Ki Tetze tells us to sweep away a mother bird from its eggs before we take the latter for ourselves [Deut. 12.6-7], displaying a respect for an animal's feelings that millions do not even show to their human neighbors. (An even more powerful and related commandment comes soon after. In 15. 4, we are told not to muzzle an ox while it treads grain; like the mother bird, why should it suffer such indignities?)

We are ordered to build safe guardrails for our homes [Deut. 12.8], a mitzvah that could be interpreted, if observed, as preventing the manufacture and sale of cigarettes and maybe even junk food.

And would not U.S. history be different and the tragic state of Afro-Americans be so much healthier, if the good Christians who supported traffic in slaves had accepted, as the word of G-d, 13.16-17, that runaway slaves must not be returned to their masters? (Precisely the opposite of accepted 19th century practice.)

Yes, it can be argued that *Ki Tetze* has enough laws of family life, human kindness, respect for property, animals and more, to create an entire religion. But it is the second half of Chapter 14 which most moves this Torah-loving Jew, for it is there that Judaism's genius for *tzedakah* fully blossoms. Don't enter a home to get back your "pledge!" Pay your worker on the same day! (So much for the long-established tradition of "the check is in the mail!") Don't go back and pick up dropped sheaves of grain, and don't shake your olive tree too much as you harvest for "IT SHALL BE FOR THE STRANGER, THE ORPHAN, THE WIDOW"[Deut. 24.19].

The rabbis later rhapsodize on the magnificent humanity of these mitzvot in the Midrash [Numbers Rabbah 5.2], by quoting the Proverbs' seemingly obscure "DO NOT ROB THE POOR BECAUSE HE IS POOR [Deut. 22.22]. "If a person is poor, what could he possibly be robbing him of? This verse must refer to the gifts to the poor that the Torah requires the person to give.... The Holy One issued a warning that a person should not rob him of these gifts that are rightfully his because he is poor. His poverty is as much as he can handle." (Ahhh, these bleeding-heart Jews!!)

There you have it—my new religion of *Ki Tetze*, based entirely upon this one, brief parashah. I urge all rapists of women in wartime, teasers of animals, former and neo-Nazis, keepers of lost property, manufacturers of unsafe cars and products, and people who turn their backs on the poor to join up. This planet would be in much better shape if they did.•

GOD'S MAILBOX:
A Modern Midrash for Children

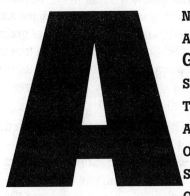

AND YOU SHALL BUILD THERE AN ALTAR TO THE ETERNAL, YOUR GOD, AN ALTAR OF STONES; YOU SHALL USE NO IRON TOOLS ON THEM. YOU SHALL BUILD AN ALTAR TO THE LORD YOUR GOD OF UNHEWN STONES; AND YOU SHALL OFFER BURNT OFFERINGS ON IT TO THE ETERNAL, YOUR GOD. [Deut. 27.5-6]

The best builder of anything in the Bible was a guy named Bezalel. Whenever something had to be built, the people ALWAYS called on Bezalel to build it.

Even God chose Bezalel to build all the important things God wanted built. Bezalel built a terrific seven branched candle stick make of gold for the Temple in Jerusalem. Each one of the seven cups for the oil and the wick light looked like the flowers of an almond tree, and when the wicks were lit they looked like little fireflies glowing inside seven golden flowers.

Bezalel's best work was the box to hold the Ten Commandments. The box was acacia wood covered in gold with two golden angels on top whose big wings covered the box. There were rings and poles on the side of the box to carry it around. The problem with the box holding the Ten Commandments was that God told the people not to look at the box because it was so special. A few people who did look at it had their faces melt off, and after that NOBODY wanted to look at the box that held the Ten Commandments. Bezalel was somewhat sad about this because the

Ki Tavo

Deuteronomy 26.1-29.8

Rabbi Marc Gellman

MARC GELLMAN IS THE RABBI OF TEMPLE BETH TORAH, MELVILLE, NEW YORK. HE IS THE AUTHOR OF *DOES GOD HAVE A BIG TOE?*, *WHERE DOES GOD LIVE?* AND MOST RECENTLY, *HOW DO YOU SPELL GOD? ANSWERS TO THE BIG QUESTIONS FROM AROUND THE WORLD* WITH MONSIGNOR THOMAS HARTMAN. THIS MIDRASH IS FROM *GOD'S MAILBOX: MORE STORIES ABOUT STORIES IN THE BIBLE*, PUBLISHED BY MORROW JUNIOR BOOKS.

דָּבָר אַחֵר **DAVAR AHER.** "MOSES SUMMONED ALL OF ISRAEL AND SAID TO THEM, 'YOU HAVE SEEN EVERYTHING THAT HA-SHEM DID BEFORE YOUR EYES IN THE LAND OF EGYPT, TO PHARAOH AND TO ALL HIS SERVANTS AND TO ALL HIS LAND—THE GREAT TRIALS THAT YOUR EYES BEHELD, THOSE GREAT SIGNS AND WONDERS" [DEUT. 29.1-2]. As one who deplores model *Sedarim*, I welcome a different understanding of the Seder. But, I believe in the metaphysical. The Seder is all about teaching the participant this

metaphysical principle: It's 1250 BCE and you were there. We were slaves in Egypt and with a mighty outstretched arm, God delivered us unto freedom. And if you don't believe that you were there, then the Seder recreates the experience for you, persuading you by use of the senses and the heart. One final thought: a story told in shorthand in order to preserve space. A boy comes home from religious school and gets the typical parental question: "So what did

box was his best work, but he did understand that nobody wanted to get a face melt.

Because Bezalel was so good, the other artists and builders were jealous of him. Some would say behind his back, "Sure, Bezalel makes great things, but God gives him all the great designs. All Bezalel has to do is put them together." Bezalel didn't care what people said. Bezalel was happy to give all the credit to God. "I am just God's hands," Bezalel would always say. God was not happy that Bezalel was not getting enough credit for what he did and so one day God did a very strange thing, even for God. God announced a contest. One day everybody saw pieces of paper floating down from the sky, and on each piece of paper there was this very strange announcement:

Build me a mailbox!
Take a week to do it.

Signed, God

Everybody was excited to build God a mailbox and they scurried off to draw, hammer, nail and paint. All the big designers were working in secret, but even the children were building mailboxes for God. Everybody thought they had a chance to build the best mailbox for God because God had not GIVEN OUT the design.

The next week came so fast that not everybody had finished their mailboxes at dawn when the contest began. All the people who had finished their mailboxes had them covered up so that nobody else could see them. Then God said, "Show me your mailboxes."

The first one to show his design for God's mailbox was Ziptor the grape grower. Ziptor made his mailbox with many grape-colored balloons all tied on with strings to a mailbox that had the name GOD painted on both sides. Hanging from the strings was also a card that read, "Dear God, the prayers and letters in this mailbox have been lifted up

Ki Tavo

you learn today?" (He learned about the Exodus.) He proceeds to tell the story of the 1973 War (you know, the Israel army surrounds the Egyptian army in the Sinai and puts pontoon bridges across Suez—read: Red Sea) all couched in terms of the Exodus from Egypt. Flabbergasted, the father responds, "Is this what you really learned today?" "No," came the reply, "But if I told you what they told me"—referring to the

traditional story of the Exodus—"you wouldn't believe it." Well, some of us believe it and variant understandings of the Seder threaten to rob us of what Heschel called "radical amazement." **Rabbi Kerry M. Olitzky, <Olitzky@huc.edu>**

דָּבָר אַחֵר **DAVAR AHER. These shall stand to bless the people... [Deut. 27.11]** Dear Joel, Shaye and I went through the segments in Ki

to you by Ziptor the grape grower. Any sunshine and good rain on our vineyards would be greatly appreciated! Yours truly, Ziptor."

Ziptor was quite proud of his design and said, "My grape balloon God mailbox will deliver prayers and packages to God faster than any other way. I am sure to win." Then Ziptor let go of the balloons and they flew up into the sky, but birds pecked at the balloons and popped them thinking that they were humongous grapes. Ziptor's mailbox crashed to the ground.

Then Barukh, the sign painter, uncovered his design for God's mailbox. It was a four-sided box with a red flag on top and huge signs painted on every side. One of the signs read, "Eat Ziptor's grapes, and get a free balloon." Another sign said, "Coming to Jerusalem for the holidays? Why not stay at the Jerusalem Grand Hotel? We put a camel in every room." Barukh explained that the signs were a new idea he had been working on called

advertising. He said, "I figure there will be lots of people coming to God's mailbox, and everybody will see the signs. I sold space on the mailbox for people who want to sell stuff to the folks bringing letters to God's mailbox. Nobody believed Barukh that folks would buy something just because they saw it on a sign.

Then came Oholiab's turn. When he took the cover off the mailbox he designed for God, people gasped. Some could not say a single word. Some just muttered, "Wow! Golly! Gee Whiz!" Oholiab had built a golden tower. The tower had flags and bells and little carved animals and flowers decorating every part. The tower had little shelves and drawers and slots for letters and packages and the whole thing shimmered and tinkled in the wind like a great big chime. Nobody had ever seen anything more beautiful. Some people said, "It's more beautiful than the golden box Bezalel made to hold the Ten Commandments," but since

Synopsis: "When you come into the land," is an appropriate beginning to this week's parashah which opens with the acknowledgement of God as giver of all (to whom we pay tribute to by offering our first fruits and other tithes). Procedures for crossing the Jordan are next, the building of an altar, the alternating recitation of blessings and warnings, are all part of the renewal of the covenant played out now upon acquiring the land.

Tavo, chapter 28. From verses 1-14 we counted about 16 blessings, then in verses 15-68 we counted over 50 curses (we lost count, and some interest, by that point). **Danny Horwitz**

Dear Shaye, Here are three answers to your question. (1) I think the blessing is mightier than the curse (so it takes fewer).

(2) If you go into chapter 28 of Deuteronomy (and I don't know

which of the lists of blessings and curses you were counting), you can find this secret message. Count the number of times the root for blessings and the root for curses are used. You come up with 10 on the bless side, only 9 on the curse side. 10 is a perfect number in the Bible. God created the world with ten speakings. The essence of Torah came in ten utterances. Ten Plagues. All kinds of tens. The message is simple: When

we fill the things created (ten speakings) with Ten commandments (teachings) we wind up with a perfect 10 blessings. Otherwise, it may look like there are a lot of curses in life, but they don't add up.

(3) If you read carefully, the basic blessing is rain. It only takes one: give us rain, and all the other blessings come from that one. If you read the passage below, which comes from next week's Torah portion, it says

nobody had ever looked at that box it was hard to know for sure. Everybody agreed that this was going to be the winner of the God's mailbox contest for sure and that not even the great Bezalel could top the wonderful golden mailbox tower of Oholiab.

Then Bezalel removed the covering from his design. People started to laugh right away. Bezalel had made a pile of stones, just plain stones! "Nice rocks!" someone called out to Bezalel. "Real nice rocks. You didn't even take the time to cut them so that they fit together right. What do you think you're doing? Where do you put the prayers and letters to God? Your mailbox is a joke!"

Bezalel waited for all the laughing to stop and then he said in a quiet voice, "I made God's mailbox out of uncut stones for a whole bunch of reasons.

"I don't think God needs a mailbox that floats, so I made it out of things that are part of the earth.

This way people will learn that God is not just high up in the sky but down here were we live.

"I did not make God's mailbox out of gold because the only words that should be in a golden box are God's words to us, not our words to God. We already have a golden box for God's words and that's enough.

"I did not make God's mailbox to be a place for selling things. God's mailbox is a place where we should remember to be happy with what we have, not a place where we should be tricked into wanting more and more junk.

"Most of all, I decided to make God's mailbox out of uncut stones to teach people that what is true about stones is also true about people. Building with uncut stones is harder than building with stones you cut to fit, but it is better because you let each rock keep its own shape and you don't cut off its edges just to make it fit. It's the same with people. It's harder and it takes more time to teach people

Ki Tavo

that Torah/teaching is like rain, too. It, too, grows blessings. We don't need so many, because they multiply. Curses, on the other hand, come one by one. We cause each new curse by ignoring the Torah.

Dear Joel, I am having trouble with finding out what the blessing and the curse are. **Shaye Horwitz**

Dear Shaye, To understand Blessings and Curses, let's talk about two old horror movies.

But first, one idea. A blessing is a gift from God. God gives us blessings like life, intelligence, rain so we can grow crops, etc. Blessings are all the good things we get in life. When we "say" blessings, we are saying words which are a thank you for the gift. When the Torah says that "ABRAHAM WILL BE A BLESSING" we learn that the highest way to say thank you to God for our blessings is to be a source of blessings

how to work together than to just order them around and make them do things they do not understand. People who fit together to do a big job are even harder to find than stones that fit together to make a mailbox for God. But it's better to wait for the fit. These uncut stones remind us that the best things we build in this world are the things that leave everything whole. God gives

each of us special edges and special gifts that are given to no other person in the whole wide world. Stones are different, too, until they are cut. If we keep our edges, and do the most with our gifts, then each of us will be God's mailbox."

The people were quiet for a long time after Bezalel spoke these words. Some of them were crying and some of them were nodding and some just

said, "Wow! Golly! Gee Whiz!" Then Oholiab said, "Bezalel, we were wrong about you. We thought you just had good hands. You also have a good heart. You can build stuff for us anytime." Then the people put their letters and prayers on God's mailbox and every prayer and every letter was answered.●

---

for other people. So what is a curse? Let's go ahead and take a look at the two horror movies.

One is *The Pit and the Pendulum* starring Boris Karloff and Vincent Price. It shows the wrong idea. It is not at all like the very famous Edgar Alan Poe story. Anyway, in the end, these two wizards have a fight by hurling magic spells at each other. You see them wave their arms and (thanks to animation) these glowing balls or rays of light shoot out at each other. The idea is that you get hit by a "spell" and can't block it; you can get hurt by the black magic. This is the wrong idea about blessings and curses. But, I used to believe it and it confused me for a while. I thought that God was like a more powerful version of one of these wizards, and would hurl good and bad spells at you. If you got hit with a blessing, it was good luck. If you got hit with a curse, it was bad luck. Blessings made you smart, or caused you to always win in Las Vegas. Curses meant that you became ugly and always stepped into the wrong stuff on the sidewalk (and worse).

A better horror movie to understand Blessings and Curses is *Doctor Jekyll and Mr. Hyde*. This is an old black-and-white movie with Spencer Tracy from a book by Robert Louis Stevenson (the same guy who wrote *Treasure Island*). Anway, there is this good doctor who helps everyone and invents this potion which he thinks will be a miracle drug. But, what he doesn't know is that it splits him into two parts. The Doctor Jekyll part, who is basically happy and kind, is split off from the Mr. Hyde part which is dark, angry and dangerous. All the parts of him which are out of control and can hurt other people are gathered together. I think that blessings and curses are like Dr. Jekyll and Mr. Hyde. When we get blessings, we tend to move toward the part of ourselves which is like Dr. Jekyll, one who says thank you, and one who passes blessings on to others. When we are "cursed" we tend to move away from the light. We tend to become Mr. Hyde and to react to the hurt by hurting others. In other words, God is saying what God said to Cain: "WHEN YOU DO GOOD, AREN'T

YOU LIFTED UP? BUT WHEN YOU DO EVIL, SIN HIDES BY YOUR DOOR, READY TO HAUNT YOU." Blessings lead to more blessings. Curses lead to more curses. That is human nature, not luck. **Joel Lurie Grishaver <Gris@TorahAura.Com>**

Shaye liked your explanation about blessings and curses. I also showed him something I learned from Rabbi Saul Teplitz: חַיִּים *Hayyim* (life) and מָוֶת *Mavet* (death) are both irregular nouns. מָוֶת *Mavet*, death is only one: always singular. חַיִּים *Hayyim* is always plural, of infinite variety. **Danny Horwitz <RABBIDANNY@aol.com>**

Rabbi Daniel I. Leifer

RABBI DANIEL I. LIEFER, לז, WAS THE DIRECTOR OF THE NEWBERGER HILLEL CENTER AT THE UNIVERSITY OF CHICAGO, ILLINOIS.

Ki Tavo

A WANDERING ARAMEAN WAS MY FATHER; AND HE WENT DOWN INTO EGYPT AND LIVED THERE, FEW IN NUMBER; AND THERE HE BECAME A NATION, GREAT, MIGHTY, AND POPULOUS. AND THE EGYPTIANS TREATED US HARSHLY, AND AFFLICTED US, AND LAID UPON US HARD BONDAGE. THEN WE CRIED TO THE ETERNAL, THE GOD OF OUR FATHERS, AND THE ETERNAL HEARD OUR VOICE, AND SAW OUR AFFLICTION, OUR TOIL, AND OUR OPPRESSION; AND THE ETERNAL BROUGHT US OUT OF EGYPT WITH A MIGHTY HAND AND AN OUTSTRETCHED ARM, WITH GREAT TERROR, WITH SIGNS AND WONDERS....
[Deut. 26.5-8]

When I was growing up, I was taught by all my Jewish teachers from day school to seminary that at the Pesah Seder we relive the Exodus: We are there at the crossing of the Red (Reed) Sea.

I was also an avid listener of a radio program entitled *You Are There*. I heard Caesar crossing the Rubicon and King John and the English nobles signing the Magna Carta. Sitting at the Seder table, I was puzzled. Why didn't the Seder sound like those programs? I never felt as though I was "at the crossing of the Red Sea with Moses." I knew I was reading a text studded with Biblical quotations and interpretations of the Rabbis.

Years later I learned that Deuteronomy 26.5-8 was the central Biblical passage of the Haggadah. Everybody said so, even Maimonides. Nobody gave a good reason except to say that the passage told the story of the Exodus. I asked myself: I wanted to find a script for reliving the Exodus, I could find much more dramatic passages in Exodus. As a teenager, I had come across the Reconstructionist Haggadah and saw that they had attempted to do this. But their passages were too short and it didn't work.

Many years later, I realized that the purpose of the Seder is not to relive the Exodus. The rabbis who put together our Haggadah were not interested in that. They had a very different goal in mind. I realized that when I studied Deuteronomy 26.5-8 in context. Deuteronomy 26 contains the texts of two declarations [vv. 5-10 and 13-15] to be made by the Israelite head (male) of the household when bringing first fruits [vv. 5-10] and when setting aside the triennial tithe [vv. 13-15]. Remarkable passages! Nowhere else in Tanakh do we have texts to ritual prayer declarations to be enunciated by an "everyman." And note, our Pesaḥ passage is set in a context that has nothing to do with Passover, but rather with a holiday we later came to call Shavuot.

I call Deuteronomy 26.5-8 (10) a narrative historical creed, comparable to the Christian Nicene Creed. What makes it uniquely "Israelite" or "Jewish" is that it is a first person story. "Everyman" Israelite tells who he is when he appears before a priest and God in a sanctuary by recounting the *Heilsgeschichte* of Israel—his personal biography.

The brilliant composers of the Haggadah chose not a "you are there" text but a "this is who I am" text. The rabbis did not want us to attempt to relive the Exodus event but rather to declare who we are at a time when Jewish identity was under attack physically and spiritually. In my view, the Seder is a rabbinic sacred liturgical meal that reconstitutes the Jewish People metaphysically, every year, by the recitation of the first and most ancient Biblical narrative creed. The Seder is our annual Constitutional Congress. Every year at the Seder we are reborn as the Jewish People. Pesaḥ is truly a festival of rebirth and resurrection. Who challenged our self-understanding as God's Covenanted People of Israel? The Romans who conquered and destroyed Jewish political autonomy; the Christians who claimed that they

were now the true People of Israel, the inheritors of the promises.

But our Haggadah was composed after the destruction of the Temple. That is why the authors of this document dropped verses 9 and 10. They were no longer true. They would stick in one's craw, if one said them. Rather, they linked these two verses that contain the predicates יְבָאֵנוּ/הֲבֵאתִי *heveti/v'yevi'enu* with the fifth language of redemption *v'heiveiti* וְהֵבֵאתִי in Exodus 6.8 (the other four languages, verbs, of redemption are in Exodus 6.6-7). And they pinned this verb and its promise of future restoration on Elijah, the harbinger of the Messiah, and his cup.

NOTE: Our Deuteronomy historical narrative creed does not mention the Exodus tradition of Sinai and its covenant and theophany. Yet our chapter 26 contains language similar to that of Exodus 19: "TO BE A TREASURED PEOPLE" (*am segula* עַם סְגֻלָּה) [26.18] and "YOU SHALL BE A HOLY PEOPLE"(*am kadosh* עַם קָדוֹשׁ) [26.19] set within an envelope of language that is characteristically Deuteronomic [26.16-19].

NOTE: Chapter 27 contains what many scholars call the Dodecalogue of the plastered stones set up upon Mt. Ebal and proclaimed by the Levites as "THE WORDS OF THIS TORAH." And it is followed in chapter 28 by the blessings and the curses. Together, all the elements of chapters 26-28 make up the full package of the mid-second millennium sovereign-subject treaty we now recog-

nize as structural precedent of our Covenant with God.

At the Seder table, "we are here" renewing our Covenant as the ever-living Jewish People with their ever-present living God.●

Nitzavim

Deuteronomy 29.9-30.20

Rabbi Harold M. Schulweis

HAROLD M. SCHULWEIS IS THE AUTHOR OF *FOR THOSE WHO CAN'T BELIEVE* (HARPERCOLLINS) AND THE SPIRITUAL LEADER OF CONGREGATION VALLEY BETH SHALOM IN ENCINO, CALIFORNIA.

FOR THIS COMMANDMENT WHICH I COMMAND YOU THIS DAY, IT IS NOT TOO HARD FOR YOU NEITHER IS IT FAR OFF. [Deut. 30.11] Which commandment is not too hard for you? For most commentators the commandment refers to *teshuvah*, repentance. But if *teshuvah* is the mitzvah referred to, it is, indeed, quite hard and not easy to reach. It is hard to admit failures and to acknowledge sins and injuries done to others and to oneself.

Were repentance for such transgressions easy and near at hand one would not have to recite the "*Al-Het*" and "*Ashamnu*" litany of confessions ten times during the Day of Atonement, both in public and in private prayer. The repetition of the confessions indicates that repentance is not quite so facile to achieve. The ten-fold repetitions are necessary because there are layers of sins and levels of repentance that must be excavated in the search for forgiveness.

The rabbinic tradition itself refers to two major modes of repentance. One is called repentance out of fear—*Teshuvah mi-Yirah*. The other speaks of repentance out of love—*Teshuvah mei-Ahavah*. Each of these approaches sin differently. Each understands the intention of repentance differently.

Fear repentance seeks to avoid punishment. Penitence is akin to the Latin "*poena*" or pain. Confession out of fear seeks to minimize the punishment, pleads to erase the transgression from the record, to wipe out the sin and to bury it. Love repentance has a loftier ambition. Here the sin is not to be cast aside but to be retrieved, to be confronted, resurrected and raised up.

דָּבָר אַחֵר **DAVAR AHER.** YOU ARE STANDING TODAY, ALL OF YOU, BEFORE HA-SHEM, YOUR GOD: THE HEADS OF YOUR TRIBES, YOUR ELDERS, AND YOUR OFFICERS—THE MEN OF ISRAEL; YOUR SMALL CHILDREN, YOUR WOMEN, AND YOUR PROSELYTE WHO IS IN THE MIDST OF YOUR CAMP, FROM THE HEWER OF THE WOOD TO THE DRAWER OF YOUR WATER, FOR YOU TO PASS INTO THE COVENANT OF HA-SHEM, YOUR GOD, AND INTO HIS IMPRECATION THAT HA-SHEM, YOUR GOD, SEALS WITH YOU TODAY, IN ORDER TO ESTABLISH YOU TODAY AS A PEOPLE... [DEUT. 29. 9-12].The Torah

This distinction is drawn from a discussion in the Talmud [*Yoma* 86] in which the sages themselves distinguish between fear and love repentance. In the former instance premeditated sins may be turned into "errors," an opinion that draws its proof text from Hosea 14.2 "FOR THOU HAST STUMBLED IN THY INIQUITY." The sin is an accident, a misstep. Out of fear the penitent would turn the sin into error. Fear repentance is the conventional approach to sin. Most of us are raised with fear of discovery and of punishment.

But love repentance seeks to transform the premeditated sin into "merits." The proof text is taken from Ezekiel 33.19 "AND WHEN THE WICKED TURNS FROM HIS WICKEDNESS AND DOES WHAT IS LAWFUL AND RIGHT, HE SHALL LIVE THEREBY."

The difference between these two forms of *t'shuvah* is illustrated by Levi Yitzchak's use of the metaphor of water. On Rosh ha-Shanah, during the ceremony of *Tashlih*, the penitent gathers crumbs symbolizing sins and casts them into the water. Throwing the crumbs away, the penitent recites the verse from

the prophet Micah "THOU WILT CAST ALL THEIR SINS INTO THE DEPTHS OF THE SEAS."[Micah 7.19]

On Sukkot, however, we recall the celebration of the drawing of the waters (*Simhat Bet ha-Sho-eivah*) and recite the verse from Isaiah 12.3 "WITH JOY SHALL YE DRAW WATERS OUT OF THE WELLS OF SALVATION." Levi Yitzchak explained that on Rosh ha-Shanah when we repent out of fear we distance ourselves from the memory of the sins, but on Sukkot it is with love that the very sins cast into the rivers are retrieved and raised into positive merits.

Repentance out of love does not stand in fear and trembling before the sins but heroically recalls the transgressions, and searches out the concealed virtues hidden in our angers, resentments and vindictiveness. Through the eyes of love repentance, something edifying can be done with the transgressions. Sins, rather than be forgotten and uprooted, are to be remembered and traced lovingly to their benevolent roots.

Love repentance looks differently at sin and the *yetzer ha-ra* than does

Synopsis: All of you are standing here today, says Moses, but the covenant God creates with you is for everyone of future generations. Repentance is the key to a true relationship with God. The mitzvah that God commands is close not distant. Therefore, choose life.

stresses it over and over. Today, today, today. Our voices inside of us keep saying "Who are you kidding? Look how you have lived over the last twenty years. You think you are going to change now? What is the key to self-improvement? Forget about yesterday and do not think about tomorrow. JUST DEAL WITH TODAY." Before you know it the days add up and you are a different person. **Jeffrey C. Ratz, Brooklyn, NY**

Nitzavim

fear repentance. Love repentance does not counsel extirpation of the *yetzer ha-ra*, the evil inclination. It seeks to sublimate impulse, to convert its negativism into affirmations of life. Evil remains our foe but "Who is strong? He who makes of his adversary a friend" [*Ethics of Rabbi Nathan*].

The wisdom of love repentance battles the evil impulse with an eye toward redeeming the good ensnared within it. Love repentance takes its clue from the law of Deuteronomy 20.19: "IF YOU BESIEGE A CITY AND MAKE WAR ON IT YOU SHALL NOT DESTROY THE TREES THEREOF BY WIELDING AN AXE AGAINST THEM." Do not destroy the fruitful good in the course of fighting the thickets of evil.

Love repentance recognizes the ambiguity of sin and draws upon the cabalistic metaphysics of the book of *Zohar* [III, 80b]: "When God came to create the world and revealed what was hidden in the depths and disclosed light out of darkness, they were all wrapped on one another. Therefore, light emerged from darkness and from the impenetrable came forth the profound. So too, from good issues evil and from mercy issues judgment and all are intertwined, the good impulse and the evil impulse." The genius of love repentance is to appreciate sin as a generating force that has the power to transform evil into good, sin into sanctity and hatred into love. This is the insight of the philosopher, Rabbi J.B. Soloveitchik, who insists that the human being is his own redeemer. He exalts the human being as his own creator, his own innovator and his own messiah.

Repentance out of fear may lead God to overlook the sin (*oveir al pesha*). But with repentance out of love, God bears the sin and elevates the evil to the point that it is no longer evil (*nosei avon va-fesha*).

There is a subtle art in formulating prayers of repentance. Because good and evil, sin and mitzvah are intermingled, one cannot pray for good as if goodness could be granted whole, a separate, distinct package. When the sages sought to pray that the powers of the *yetzer ha-ra*, such as ambition, drive and creativity be granted, stripped of their darker side, a voice from heaven informed them, "They do not grant halves in heaven, (*palga ba-rakia lo yahavei*)." This counsel flows from Judaism's reality principle. The wisdom of prayer and of penitence accepts the complexity and ambiguity of all power and urges the penitent out of love to squeeze the sparks of goodness out of the husks of evil.

Consider the two tablets of the law. The first revelation was announced publicly accompanied by storm and lightning. Though broken out of resentment and disillusionment, the shattered tablets were not cast aside, discarded or forgotten. They were placed into the Ark of Holiness alongside the whole tablets "*Shivrei luhot v'luhot munahim ba-aron*." The second tablets of the law were hewn out of love and with full remembrance of the transgressions of the first. So we do out of love with the sins we confess.

The evil that I acknowledge must be well understood. My jealousy, my humiliation of another, my arrogance, what drives them but my longing to be loved, a yearning for approval? What is my folly but a perversion of the need to be needed, to be accepted, to be known? The fear of being ignored, of being abandoned turned me into a creature of envy and sarcasm whom I do not respect. Fear distorted my love. Now, out of love, I confront my fear with the love of God: "WHOM SHALL I FEAR...EVEN IF MY FATHER AND MOTHER FORSAKE ME, THE LORD WILL TAKE ME UNDER HIS CARE" [Psalm 27]. I understand my outbursts as cries of the inner soul for the recognition of goodness. I repent of my transgressions, which have tarnished the image of God within me. Out of love I cleanse the stain. Out of love I beat my chest softly, for repentance is meant to purify my ways but not out of fright or fear of punishment. No punitive deity from without threatens me, but a loving God within draws me closer to the image of Godliness. I come to repentance out of respect for myself and that respect includes the negative aspects of my drives. Out of love the whole personality of the penitent may be remolded. The traits of jealousy, anger and hatred can be turned to appreciation, patience and love. Nothing is without its potential for good.

Teshuvah out of love is hard and distant though it is "VERY NIGH UNTO THEE, IN THY MOUTH AND IN THY HEART AND IN THY HEART THAT THOU MAYEST DO IT" [Deut. 30.14]. The hardest things are as close as the soul that breathes and the heart that beats in us. Repentance out of love explores the depth of the soul deeper than the surface repentance out of fear. The litany of repentance is repeated to enable us to explore the strata of transgressions and to cleanse the outer shell of the dirt that disguises the yearnings for goodness.•

Dr. Lois J. Zachary

LOIS J. ZACHARY IS THE
PRINCIPAL/OWNER OF LEADERSHIP
DEVELOPMENT SERVICES IN
FAYETTEVILLE, NEW YORK. DR.
ZACHARY IS A SPECIALIST IN ADULT
DEVELOPMENT AND LEARNING AND
LEADERSHIP DEVELOPMENT.

Nitzavim

Of the many themes in this week's *parashah,* the one that is the most compelling to me is the theme of collective responsibility that emerged as the people stood together to hear Moses' last oration. That theme summons up a profound sense of awe. Perhaps it is because of the moral imperative it places squarely on our shoulders. Perhaps it is because "standing together" is reenacted every day: as parents teaching children the value of mitzvot; as lay leaders sitting together perplexing and planning for a Jewish future; as Jews interacting within and in the name of community; and as individual citizens living on the planet earth together.

Though each circumstance may be different, the age-old question remains the same: how do we ensure that future generations will also stand together?

It was in Moses' last oration that the continuity agenda was first formulated several thousands of years ago, and with it the covenantal obligation of communal responsibility for generations yet to come. In essence, when we stood together, our generative destiny was linked. Community became the vehicle for fostering continuous commitment, expression, fulfillment and peoplehood.

If Torah, then, lives in the collective, it is everyone's responsibility. The first critical step in accepting responsibility for others "not present," is acceptance of responsibility for ourselves. We are told in Nitzavim that a person who is placed in a position of communal responsibility must continuously try to improve the moral stature of the people, even if his/her words appear to be ignored. In fact, even if one does not engage in Jewish learning oneself, one still bears the responsibility, as a member of the community, to provide it for others and to insure its accessibility.

If we believe that we create the future through present actions, then we are obligated to continuously choose Torah. Choosing Torah is a conscious decision of affirmation, study and action. Choosing Torah is an act of holiness. In choosing Torah, we honor our relationship with God. In that code of ethics and relationship lies the most profound sense of awe.

God gave us a mandate and then left it up to us. Just as it is a parent's job to provide a child with a Jewish education that will enable the child to accept increasing responsibility for ethical conduct with maturity, so, too, it is each community's responsibility to make sure that its educational institutions are viable, that its Jewish education is a community priority and that its leaders make decisions informed by Jewish values. Communal responsibility is an expression of individual responsibility and sacred trust.

Without knowledge there can be no commitment. Without commitment there is no future. We cannot wait for others to do it for us nor should we. We are each a link in the chain of generations. Thus, our fate is bound up together as a people. The responsibility for Jewish continuity is fulfilled in standing together, creating Jewish communities that learn and that choose Torah together, from one generation to another.•

אֵלֶּה אֶל כָּל יִשְׂרָאֵל

Va-Yelekh

Deuteronomy 31.1-31.30

Dr. Tamar Frankiel, Ph.D.

TAMAR FRANKIEL IS THE AUTHOR OF *THE VOICE OF SARAH: FEMININE SPIRITUALITY AND TRADITIONAL JUDAISM*. SHE CURRENTLY TEACHES AT THE CLAREMONT SCHOOL OF THEOLOGY IN CLAREMONT, CALIFORNIA.

This very brief parashah—only thirty verses—nevertheless occupies a significant place in our round of Torah readings; it is read either on *Shabbos Shuva*, the Shabbat between Rosh Ha-Shanah and Yom Kippur, or else by itself or with *Parashat Nitzavim* on the Shabbat before Rosh Ha-Shanah. It contains the last two of the 613 mitzvot of the Torah—the mitzvah of הַקְהֵל *Hak-hel*, to gather the nation for a special reading of the Torah, and the mitzvah of writing a *Sefer Torah*.

Moreover, these few verses are witness to the transfer of leadership from Moses to Joshua.

"BRING HIM INTO THE TENT OF MEETING," says God, "AND I WILL GIVE OVER TO BOTH OF YOU THE SONG (*Ha'azinu*, the next parashah), WHICH YOU ARE TO TEACH TO THE ISRAELITES." [Deut. 31.14] Our parashah also continues the warnings and prophecies, some of them quite dire, which occupied previous parashiot and which will follow in *Ha'azinu*. All this in a mere thirty verses!

Let us begin with the warnings that hint to us about the season of the Days of Awe. Specifically, we are told that the Jewish people will stray after other gods and will be punished: "THEN SHALL MY ANGER BURN AGAINST THEM ON THAT DAY, AND I WILL FORSAKE THEM AND HIDE MY FACE FROM THEM, TO BE CONSUMED, AND MANY EVILS AND TRIBULATIONS WILL FIND THEM. AND THEY WILL SAY ON THAT DAY, 'SURELY IT IS BECAUSE GOD IS NOT IN OUR MIDST THAT THESE EVILS HAVE FOUND ME.' AND I WILL INDEED HIDE MY FACE ON THAT DAY, BECAUSE OF THE EVIL THEY HAVE DONE, FOR THEY TURNED TO OTHER GODS." [Deut. 31.17–18]

This unusual sequence has been noted by many commentators. It seems that Israel is repenting,

דָּבָר אַחֵר **DAVAR AHER. HA-SHEM SPOKE TO MOSES, 'BEHOLD, YOUR DAYS ARE DRAWING NEAR TO DIE...' [DEUT. 31.14].** *What do you think Moses was dreaming about near the end of Deuteronomy? Knowing that he was going to die soon, what was in his dreams? Dreams come from the thoughts you had* during the day. Maybe Moses dreamed of not winning a battle, of losing and being killed in a battle. Dad told me that some people say Moses died with God's kiss. So the softest of blows from God can bring you death. **Shaye Horwitz**

390—וַיֵּלֶךְ

recognizing the reason why evil has come upon the people. If so, why should God conceal himself after Israel recognizes the error of their ways? The *Sefat Emet* explains persuasively that their statement did not demonstrate repentance but, in fact, was a counsel of despair. They were not really taking responsibility for their sins, but instead were blaming God for abandoning them. By saying God was not "IN THEIR MIDST," they were denying the existence of God within every human being. The result was that they lost hope and, by a compelling inner logic, God concealed himself even more.[1]

This allows us to reflect on what is expected of us during the Days of Awe. As God renews the world, we are offered an opportunity to reflect on our past year and our lives, to correct our ways through *tefillah, tzedakah, teshuvah* (prayer, charity, and return). This is, above all, a hopeful time. If we see only the fearsome and intimidating aspect of the holidays—that we have to confess our sins, humble and "afflict" ourselves—we are missing the main point. We actually now have the opportunity to bring God "into our midst" again; we can experience and know complete renewal. Without this realization, we will only be drawing a darker curtain around ourselves.

How can we think positively as we are reviewing our sins? The

parashah offers a clue in one of the special mitvot it brings us: הַקְהֵל *Hak-hel* or gathering. The word has the same root as קְהִילָּה *kehillah*, community. The mitzvah in its original form is for the entire Jewish people—men, women and children—to gather in Jerusalem every seven years and hear passages of the Torah read aloud by the king (or, as it was practiced in the time of Josephus, by the high priest).[2] The passages read were a summary of the final covenant of the Jewish people with God, before Moses's departure as their leader—the covenant, as it says earlier, that was given in the land of Moab in addition to the one given at Horeb [Deut. 28.69].

The centrality of *Hakhel* in the parashah is indicated by an esoteric hint. The Masoretic editors' note to the parashah observes that this parashah and *Nitzavim* together contain 70 verses, which is the number, by *gematria*, of the mnemonic which signifies: My Lord is Ha-Shem (God), reminding us to worship only God. The number 70 is also significant in that 70 elders made up the Sanhedrin or supreme Jewish court, reminding us to honor the transmission of authority, as from Moses to Joshua. The two "70s" together, Ha-Shem who rules in the heavens and his "children" who rule on earth, add up to 140, which is itself the *gematria* of הַקְהֵל *hak-hel*.

Synopsis: Moses is 120 years old when he appoints Joshua as his successor. Moses writes the words of the Torah and commands that it be read on the Sabbatical Year. The end of the parashah is the introduction to next week's reading: the Song of Moses.

Va-Yelekh

Surprisingly, the mitzvah of הַקְהֵל *hak-hel* was not to be done at Shavuot; thus it was not intended merely to commemorate the first giving of the Torah.[3] Rather, it was to be performed during Sukkot, on the first day of *hol ha-moed* (the third day of the holiday), following the *Shemitta* (sabbatical) year. Its placement in the joyous harvest season resonates with our celebration, established by the Sages, of *Simhat Torah* and the completion of the yearly reading of the Torah on *Shemini Atzeret*. Its occurrence after the *Shemitta* year suggests also the theme of thanksgiving for a successful year of abstinence from agricultural work (rather than having the impact of warning, which might be an appropriate interpretation if the reading occurred at the beginning of the sabbatical year).

Moreover, the Torah explicitly states the purpose of the gathering—to hear and to learn.[4] Ibn Ezra gives an interpretation here that is somewhat puzzling. He indicates that the mitzvah of הַקְהֵל *hak-hel* is to remind us to learn "the whole year, even on the Sabbath." A subcommentator explains that this means that *Shemitta* is to be a year devoted to learning, just as Shabbat is set aside in that way every week.[5] It seems, however, that if this were the purpose, הַקְהֵל *hak-hel* would have been set for the beginning of the *Shemitta* year, not afterwards. Rather, הַקְהֵל *hak-hel* is to remind us that not only in the *Shemitta* year should

we learn, but we should continue even when we are busy with our ordinary affairs.

The Jewish people were thus to be assembled as one unit, hopefully of one heart and one mind, as at Sinai; but the emphasis on learning reminds us that this was not the first covenant, not the conversion of newly freed slaves to a new awareness of God. הַקְהֵל *Hak-hel* was the reenactment of the ultimate covenant, the covenant of a people who had matured through forty years in the wilderness, having battled within themselves against idolatry, jealousy, and lack of faith, having watched the older generation die, leaving the future in a new land in their hands, and having fought with other peoples for access to that land. It was a covenant for the tough-minded realist, not the tender-minded newcomer.

But this also means it was a covenant of confidence. Such confidence is expressed also in the part of the commandment of הַקְהֵל *hak-hel* that says "*your stranger*" will also come to the gathering. Usually, *ger* is translated as "proselyte," but here it actually means the non-Jew living in *Eretz Yisrael*.[6] The general rule is that we do not seek converts, but for *Hakhel*, we should encourage those non-Jews nearby to come and hear the Torah reading. Our faith, joy, and unity are at such a high level that we can approach the non-Jew out of pure motives, out of a desire to share our gift. It is all the more significant that we read this parashah near the time of Rosh ha-Shanah, when we celebrate the birthday of all humankind, and before Sukkot, when the nations of the world are to bring their offerings to Jerusalem.

The commentators also emphasize that we are to bring our children along. This is the only time besides the holiday of *Pesaḥ,* that the teaching of the children is so emphasized. They will wonder, say the sages, at this great gathering and will begin to ask questions. Just as Moses passed his knowledge and transferred his authority to Joshua, so we must always be passing ours to our children. In order to do this, we must personally make the Torah our own. So the parashah teaches the last of the 613 mitzvot. To write a *Sefer Torah* or, as the sages interpreted it, to contribute to or participate in the writing of one, or to buy books to learn Torah. This mitzvah, interestingly, is derived from God's commandment, "Now WRITE THIS SONG," referring to the song of *Ha'azinu* in the next parashah. But this means, say the sages, the whole Torah—for what would be the point of having just the song? It could not be understood without the background of the Torah itself.

The parashah thus offers a multi-layered message. During these Days of Awe, we must take heed to the warnings—confess our sins, focus on *teshuvah*—but we must at all costs avoid despair. We are urged three times in this parashah, in the words of Moses Rabbenu as he was about to leave his beloved people, "BE

STRONG AND COURAGEOUS!" We have the means of overcoming all difficulties in the two mitzvot of this parashah: to make the Torah our own, and to unite ourselves with the whole people in one great קְהִילָה *kehillah.* Since this year 5755 was a הַקְהֵל *hak-hel* year, we should take every opportunity to focus on אַחְדוּת *aḥdut,* unity, during the Ten Days of *Teshuvah* and in the joyous festival days to come.•

Notes:

[1] Most commentators take a similar view; an exception is the Ramban, who interprets, *haster astir,* "I shall indeed hide my face," as implying a diminishing of God's anger. For a good discussion, see Rabbi M. Miller, *Sabbath Shiurim,* Second Series [Gateshead, England: Gateshead Foundation for Torah, 1979, pp. 328-332).

[2] See the Rambam's description in *Sefer HaMitzvot,* and also *Sefer HaḤinuch,* Vol.5, Mitzvah 612. It appears that this mitzvah is not dependent on the existence of a king in Israel.

[3] I depart somewhat from the Rambam's interpretation, which focuses on the connection to the events of Sinai. I think its placement in the harvest season, after the New Year festival, is extremely important.

[4] This verse is the basis for many judges to affirm that women are obligated to learn Torah, at least the Written Torah. For a superb discussion of this and of related arguments concerning women being permitted to learn the Oral Torah, see Shoshana Zolty, *And All Your Children Shall Be Learned* [Jason Aronson, 1993).

[5] Rabbi S.Z. Netter, as quoted by Rabbi B.S. Jacobson in *Meditations on the Torah* [Tel-Aviv: Sinai Publishing , 1956], p. 310.

[6] Rabbi Yaakov Kamenetsky, in *Emes L'Yaakov,* understands the Rambam and probably the Ramban to interpret the word גֵּר, *ger,* in this way. See *The Stone Chumash,* ed. R. Nosson Scherman [Artscroll Series; Brooklyn: Mesorah Publications, 1993], p. 1097.

Rabbi Janet Marder

RABBI JANET MARDER IS THE
DIRECTOR OF PACIFIC SOUTHWEST
COUNCIL OF THE UAHC.

Va-Yelekh

Parashat Va-Yelekh, which reaches us a few days after the September equinox, is autumnal in mood: short as a fall afternoon, somber, tinged with the chill of imminent winter. The impending death of Moses shades the portion from beginning to end; its beauty, like that of autumn, is pervaded by melancholy. Words of comfort and reassurance are offered repeatedly throughout *Va-Yelekh,* but their very repetition heightens the sense of foreboding. The many exhortations to "BE STRONG AND RESOLUTE," warnings to "FEAR NOT AND BE NOT DISMAYED," promises that "GOD WILL NOT FAIL YOU OR FORSAKE YOU" hint at the crippling anxiety they're meant to dispel.

It is easy to picture a people terrified of losing the leader and patriarch they have trusted all their lives; a young man dreading the new responsibilities he faces and haunted by the stature of his predecessor; an old man fearfully contemplating his last days and the futility of his life's work.

The juxtaposition of this brief, uneasy narrative with *Shabbat Shuvah* may be only a calendrical coincidence created by the fact that the Torah comes to an end as the new year begins. Yet on this Shabbat when the hopeful, joyous mood of Rosh ha-Shanah begins to give way to the solemn intensity of Yom Kippur, it is instructive to immerse ourselves in *Parashat Va-Yelekh.*

What does the drama of Moses' farewell and Joshua's succession suggest about the drama that occurs within each of us as we journey through the Days of Awe? On the simplest level, perhaps, we respond to this portion's theme of change and transition. Each of us engages in the work of *teshuvah* hoping that we can free ourselves of the past's hold and chart a new path. Moral growth is only possible if old instincts and habits pass away and new ones emerge. Knowing this, we face the difficult task of identifying parts of ourselves that ought not to be carried into the new year.

It is necessary, though often painful, to bury Moses—to turn away from impulses that dominated us in years past but that are no longer helpful—in order to make room for Joshua—new ways of thinking and being. Lest we reduce the story of Moses and Joshua to a transparent allegory of *teshuvah*, let us dig a little deeper. The essential theme that dominates their story, it seems to me, is power. Moses must learn to renounce power—to relinquish his leadership, to let go of the people he has guided for so long, to surrender to the inevitable. Joshua, on the other hand, must learn to accept power—to believe in himself, to step forward and take command.

In graphic terms, Moses' task is to open his hands, to loosen his grip on all that ties him to earthly life; Joshua's task is to close his hands—to grasp the reins of power and take hold of his life's work. Both are important lessons for us on the Holy Days.

We, too, are compelled to renounce our illusions of power—to acknowledge that we are frail creatures subject to forces beyond our control, clay in the hand of the Potter. We get old, our strength wanes, everything precious to us leaves us sooner or later.

Yet, even as we learn this lesson—from *Unetaneh Tokef*, from *Yizkor*, from *Avinu Malkeinu* and other prayers of this season—we learn the opposite one, as well. Limited as our power is, few as our days of life may be, they are all we have, and ours to shape as best we can. The Holy Days are about seizing power—believing in our ability to change, taking control

of our actions, turning our life in a new direction.

It is our task, then, to become Joshua as well as Moses—to leave aside hopes of living forever and achieving all our goals, while mustering energy and enthusiasm for the work that is ours to do.

Shabbat Shuvah, which mingles the joy of Rosh ha-Shanah with the solemnity of Yom Kippur, is an appropriate time to contemplate our double task. And *Parashat Va-Yelekh*, a narrative in which hope and comfort struggle with fear and despair, is an appropriate vessel for the message.●

W e wander through life searching for bridges to move us closer to each other and nearer to God. *Parashat Ha'azinu* shows us how to build bridges between heaven and earth while being, as the next-to-last portion of the year, a bridge itself between the end and the beginning. Its very form, a song, opens the heart to receive its urgent message of hope and direction; as we reach the inevitable end of the book, its passion inspires and propels us to begin the study again.

Ha'azinu

Deuteronomy 32.1-52

Malka Drucker

MALKA DRUCKER IS THE AUTHOR OF MANY FINE JEWISH BOOKS INCLUDING *JACOB'S RESCUE, THE FAMILY TREASURY OF JEWISH HOLIDAYS* AND *GRANDMA'S LATKES.* MALKA IS A RABBINICAL STUDENT AT THE ACADEMY FOR JEWISH RELIGION IN NEW YORK.

The portion opens with Moses declaring, "LISTEN HEAVEN! I WILL SPEAK! EARTH! HEAR THE WORDS OF MY MOUTH!"[Deut. 32.1]. Like a dying father who warns his children that he no longer will guide, scold, or defend them, Moses calls upon heaven and earth to be witnesses: human beings are inclined to do better when they know they're being watched. If Israel does right, earth will open with fecundity, and likewise, if we sin, earth will close itself to us. Like parents, heaven and earth will watch and keep us on the path by their example. Heaven and earth not only listen to God, they do what they are supposed to do, e.g., the sun rises and sets, seeds that are sown sprout, donkeys carry burdens. Heaven and earth do this without reward, without regard to what will happen to their children, without concern for reward and punishment. They do

דָּבָר אַחֵר **DAVAR AHER.** GIVE EAR, O HEAVENS, AND I WILL SPEAK; AND LET THE EARTH HEAR THE WORDS OF MY MOUTH. MAY MY TEACHING DROP AS THE RAIN, MY SPEECH DISTILL AS THE DEW, AS THE GENTLE RAIN UPON THE TENDER GRASS, AND AS THE SHOWERS UPON THE HERB. FOR I WILL PROCLAIM THE NAME OF THE ETERNAL. ASCRIBE GREATNESS TO OUR GOD! THE ROCK, GOD'S WORK IS PERFECT; FOR ALL GOD'S WAYS ARE JUSTICE... [Deut. 32.1-4].

Dear Shaye, This passage calls God a rock. I have never really understood how God is like a rock. Help me with that one. GRIS

Dear Joel, I don't think God really speaks...but these are the other ways God is like a rock:
1. A rock can build walls. *(Ah yes, my son, so you've already learned how religion can put walls between people...DH)*
2. A flint can light a fire.

not change from God's intention for them and neither should we.

At first God created the world with the upper realms for upper things, and the lower realms for the lower. But then Moses became a bridge: "AND MOSES WENT UP TO GOD" [Ex. 19.3] "AND GOD CAME DOWN UPON MOUNT SINAI" [ib. 20] God will redeem Israel only through bringing heaven to earth and earth to heaven: "OUT OF HEAVEN GOD MADE YOU TO HEAR THE VOICE, THAT GOD MIGHT TEACH YOU, AND ON EARTH GOD SHOWED YOU THE GREAT FIRE." [Deut. 4.36] [Mid.R. v,2]. Like Moses, we, who contain both heaven and earth, are a link between them. It is with the physical—our ears, eyes, and heart—that we apprehend that which is spiritual. We cannot imagine God without emblems of earth: God is a rock and God's words are rain. And without God, we cannot understand earth.

Torah is a bridge, too. It comes from heaven yet is made of skin, ink and human skill. "MY LESSON SHALL DROP LIKE RAIN, MY SAYING SHALL FLOW DOWN LIKE THE DEW—LIKE A DOWNPOUR ON THE HERB, LIKE A SHOWER ON THE GRASS" [Deut. 32.2]. Just as one rain falling on many trees gives to each a special savor in keeping with its species, so these words are one, yet within them are Tanakh, Mishnah, *halakhot* and *aggadot* [Sifre Devarim]. Once again we find a bridge, this time in the word.

Moses begins the Exodus out of Egypt with a word song, or musical poem [Ex.15.1-18], and ends the journey with the song in *Ha'azinu*. The Exodus song expresses gratitude for Israel's physical salvation, i.e., not drowning in the Red Sea, while the second poem sings of that which cannot be seen, the future. The last song reveals a leader less worried about his people's material well-being than with their spiritual

Synopsis: The song of Moses. The full circle from the Song at the Sea of Reeds to this final Song, Moses appeals to the universe for attention. He reviews history and takes from it the lessons to be learned and taught. He enjoins the people to take these words to heart. The parashah concludes with God telling Moses that he is to ascend Mount Nevo and to see the promised land from afar, and there, to be gathered to his people.

3. A rock can cover things (*I explained about wells in the Bible...DH*)
4. You can throw a rock at a bully who only wants to hurt people.
5. You can make a trap for a monster, bait it with the monster's favorite food at the bottom of the cliff, and roll a rock on him. (*This one is my favorite... DH*)
6. You can lean on it and it will always be there.
Shaye Horwitz , age 7

דָּבָר אַחֵר **DAVAR AHER.** "REMEMBER THE DAYS OF YORE, UNDERSTAND THE YEARS OF GENERATION AFTER GENERATION. ASK YOUR FATHER AND HE WILL RELATE IT TO YOU, AND YOUR ELDERS AND THEY WILL TELL YOU" [Deut. 32.7]. Part of the Rosh Ha-Shanah liturgy should include the words כָּל הַתְחָלוֹת קָשׁוֹת *kol hat-halot kashot, all beginnings are difficult,* to emphasize that if the new year is to be different than the old, the transition might be difficult, and as my

mother, ז״ל, used to say, "anything worthwhile is worth working for" (she was not a native English speaker, but still ended sentences with prepositions to show her level of Americanization). 5756 promises to be an especially new year for me and I am still very excited about it. **Avi Rivel <AvRivel@aol.com>**

journey, and he hopes for an Israel that will prevail in spirit as well as body. The people need their home, but without God, it means nothing.

If, as Marshall McLuhan suggests, the medium is the message, why does Moses sing the lesson? Maybe the words near the end of the parashah offer a clue: "AND MOSES CAME AND SPOKE ALL THE WORDS OF THIS SONG IN THE EARS OF THE PEOPLE, HE, AND HOSEA THE SON OF NUN. WHEN MOSES MADE AN END OF SPEAKING ALL THESE WORDS TO ALL ISRAEL, HE SAID UNTO THEM: 'SET YOUR HEART UNTO ALL THE WORDS I BEAR WITNESS WITH YOU TODAY, SO THAT YOU MAY CHARGE YOUR CHILDREN TO OBSERVE TO DO ALL THE WORDS OF THIS LAW'" [Deut. 32.44-46]. Like a poem, all the words, concentrated, associative, and mysterious, count.

Rashi describes the words of Torah as "mountains suspended upon a hair," because each word is so packed with meaning, connection and direction. Heaven is in each word, and no one word is more important than another. All of Torah is a song and not always plainly spoken. It is not merely allegory but invites, indeed requires, deeper inquiry and explanation. Moses warns that this is "NO VAIN TEACHING FOR YOU." If we don't get it, it's not because the teaching is empty, but that we are.

In *Hukkat*, God tells Moses to use words to bring forth water from a rock, but Moses loses patience and instead of speaking to the rock, he strikes it twice with a stick, and water gushes out [Num. 20.7-11]. The thirsty Israelites were happy but God was not, because the gesture was merely physical, while the word was the spirit. If the Israelites had seen that a rock, without eyes and ears, responded not to a blow but to the word, then they would have learned to know God's power made manifest through the word.

In *Ha'azinu*, why did Moses, who has been talking directly with the Israelites, gather them not to speak to them but to listen to him speak to heaven and earth? God created

Ha'azinu

האזינו השמים ואדברה יערף כמטר לקחי

heaven and earth to praise God, but for this one moment Moses silences them, commanding them to listen. For this one moment, all listen. Sometimes listening is the hardest thing. We live in a time where we are afraid to listen, afraid of what we may or may not hear. Will we hear love and justice or will we hear envy and hatred? How can we hear God? Like the Shema, *Ha'azinu* suggests that sometimes we need to sit quietly and listen; only then and there can we sense God's presence. While words are a bridge between heaven and earth, it seems that we have yet to find the right combination of letters and words. Perhaps when we can do that, we will be able to read both the white and black fires, or languages, of Torah. The parashah begins with the word "EAR." May we remember to use whatever earthly gifts we may possess to find, reach for, and plant heaven here.●

Rabbi Leonard Matanky

RABBI LEONARD MATANKY IS THE ASSISTANT SUPERINTENDENT OF THE ASSOCIATED TALMUD TORAHS OF CHICAGO, ILLINOIS, AND THE RABBI OF CONGREGATION K.I.N.S.

Ha'azinu

SHABBAT HOL HA-MOED SUKKOT 5756

Sukkot is a wonderful and exciting holiday. It is a week filled with family and joy, a holiday of extraordinary symbolism and significance. But have you ever tried to explain the holiday of Sukkot to a non-Jew? Have you ever tried to explain the meaning and importance of the many mitzvot and customs of this day? Well I did, just last week, when I met with an old friend of mine, a professor at a local university.

Yet, in spite of my best effort and intention, I don't think he believed me. In fact, by the time I was done describing the purchase of a lulav and an etrog and the building of a sukkah, I'm pretty sure that he thought that I was either pulling his leg, or a bona fide candidate for deep and serious psychological care.

"Let's see," he said. "You go to a Jewish bookstore and buy a branch of a palm tree, attach some leaves to it, hold it together with a fruit, called a citron-which looks and smells just like a lemon, but costs $75—and then march around the synagogue every day."

"That's right!" I said.

"And then you go home, eat outside in a sukkah, which is like a hut but without a roof, and this is all supposed to prove that God protects and cares for the Jewish people!?"

Thank God I didn't tell him about the procession of *hoshanot* or the annual "attack of the bees," or else he might never have spoken with me again!

But in truth, the more you consider the holiday of Sukkot, the more you have to concede that the meaning of so many of its symbols-unlike the symbols of any other holiday-is cloaked in mystery. Does anyone really know why God gave us the commandment of the etrog and lulav? Or why Sukkot is celebrated in the fall and not in the spring? And for that matter, why do we build sukkot-is it to commemorate, as Rabbi Eliezer suggested, the "clouds of glory" or as Rabbi Akiva said, to remember the buildings that the Jewish people built in the desert?

In fact, it seems as if the only thing that we do know and can agree upon is that the sukkah we eat in, and which is the focal point of this holiday, symbolizes God's care and protection of the Jewish people, as it is written in the Torah—"SO THAT YOUR GENERATIONS SHALL KNOW THAT I PLACED THE JEWS IN SUKKOT WHEN I TOOK THEM FROM EGYPT, I AM HA-SHEM YOUR GOD." [Lev. 23.43]

Maybe that is the reason the sukkah has been transformed not merely into an historical remembrance, but an expression of God's ultimate protection of the Jewish people. For whether it is within Psalms, where we read that God should hide us in a "sukkah" from verbal attacks [Psalms 31.21] or in the Talmud that describes the spiritual accomplishments of the Men of the Great Assembly as being as protective as a sukkah [Arachin 32b], it is the sukkah that is considered the epitome of God's protection.

But why? Why is it that a small, temporary structure, a building that requires little more than two walls plus a few more inches of a third, an edifice that even lacks a solid roof should serve as such a powerful symbol of protection? Why not choose something more permanent, more concrete to be the symbolic "fortress" of the Jewish people?

I'm sure there are a lot of reasons, but this week I want you to consider just two—both of which are contained in the very verse quoted above. The first is an explanation offered by the first Chief Rabbi of modern Israel, Rabbi Abraham Isaac Kook, while the second was suggested by my uncle, Rabbi Joe Lukinsky.

Asked Rabbi Kook: "Why is it that the commandment to build a sukkah ends with the words 'I AM HA-SHEM YOUR GOD?'" Answering his own question, Rabbi Kook explained that in essence these words are the key to understanding the entire mitzvah of the sukkah. For while a sukkah may appear outwardly flimsy, unfit even to be called a dwelling, it is through the strength of our acceptance of God and His Torah, that the sukkah is transformed into a fortress—in his words, a "*mivtzar haganah*!" This, he explained, is the message of a sukkah charged to all future generations: The fortress of the Jewish people, the strength of our nation and the strength of our homeland is dependent not upon the physical strength of its people, but upon their spiritual power. The words "I AM HA-SHEM YOUR GOD" have the ability to transform and empower even the smallest and weakest of nations to make them the mightiest of all people.

And then there is the second thought Rabbi Joe Lukinsky once shared with me. "Why is it," he asked, "that this verse described the sukkot as 'THE BUILDINGS THAT THE JEWS LIVED IN AS THEY WERE TAKEN FROM EGYPT?' Why not merely state that these were 'THE BUILDINGS THAT THEY LIVED IN IN THE DESERT?' Why the emphasis on their journey?" And the answer, he suggested, is that perhaps what the Torah was trying to teach us is that there are times when the journey, and the lessons learned through that journey, are just as important as the final destination itself. That the rela-

tionship we developed with God in the desert, the traditions that were begun and later transmitted, are precisely the reason for our strength as a people. It is the sukkah that appears so fragile which reminds us of who we are and how we began.

And if you consider these two messages together, if you consider the sukkah as a reminder of both our spiritual strength and the traditions through which it was developed, you begin to understand the power of a sukkah, the ability that this holiday has to shape and mold our lives and the reason that our Rabbis described this mitzvah as the equivalent of all of the other mitzvot combined.

So the next time that I have to explain what the holiday of Sukkot is all about, maybe I'll do it a little differently. Maybe instead of describing the holiday, I'll bring my professor friend over to our sukkah, show him what it means to be together on this holiday, to make the decorations together, the birds of tissue paper and egg shells that my grandmother taught us how to make. I'll tell him the stories of how Jews have fought for the opportunity to build a sukkah, whether it be in a field, a backyard, or even inside a tank during the Yom Kippur War. I'll give him the opportunity to see the beauty of the day, the dedication with which we observe the mitzvot and the traditions that we cherish. Shabbat Shalom and *Hag Sameah!*●

V'Zot Ha-Brakhah

Deuteronomy 33.1-34.12

Joel Lurie Grishaver

JOEL LURIE GRISHAVER IS THE CREATIVE CHAIRPERSON OF TORAH AURA PRODUCTIONS AND THE CO-EDITOR OF *LEARN TORAH WITH*....

Why Moses Can't Enter the Promised Land

These twin Divrei Torah emerged as a Shabbat dinner conversation between two friends.

THE COSMIC REWIND

ere is one basic, eternal question: "Is Judaism a line or a circle?"

THIS IS THE BLESSING WITH WHICH MOSES, MAN OF GOD, BLESSED B'NAI YISRAEL BEFORE HIS DEATH. HE SAID, "ADONAI CAME FROM SINAI AND SHONE LIKE SUNRISE...." IN GOD'S HANDS WAS אֵשׁ דָּת *EISH DAT*—THE "FIRE OF FAITH/KNOWLEDGE/TORAH" [DEUT. 33.1-2].

דָּבָר אַחֵר **DAVAR AHER.** "AND THIS IS THE BLESSING THAT MOSES, THE MAN OF GOD, BESTOWED UPON THE CHILDREN OF ISRAEL BEFORE HIS DEATH" [DEUT. 33.1]. *The Not-So-Simple Story of Simeon: my seven-year-old e-mail study buddy Shaye Horwitz asked me: "Why did Moses not bless Simeon just before he died?" I didn't know he didn't. It took two weeks of tracing an answer for him through the text and the midrash 'til I*

As *v'Zot ha-Brakhah* begins the end of the Torah, we are hurled against this incomprehensible word: *Ayshdat*. It goes from *alef* to *tav*, just as the Jewish year is going *tav* to *alef*. When Rashi hits the word אֵשׁ דָּת *EISH DAT*, he yells, "Stop the music!" Something deep and troubling is going on. He knows it. When something is troubling, Rashi knows that there is potential for deep learning. He says, "*Eish Dat* is a mystical truth, it alludes to the fire of the Torah that is written in black fire on white fire." And he says, "or perhaps the *Targum* is right, that the image is more tangible, following Exodus 18.19. *Eish dat* is the narrative truth that God gave us the Torah out of the Fire (at the top of Mt. Sinai)." In the end, Rashi says in essence, "Torah may be the exploding, contracting cycle of supernovas and black holes—or—Torah may be that which emerges from holocausts great and small." But the text rushes on; Moses is dying. The Torah is ending, yet the images are anything

found what I considered the whole story.

Dear Shaye, Boy that was a hard question. I am curious—how did you notice that Simeon had no blessing? Did you count? Or did you notice via a commentary? Neither I nor Stu Kelman, my Rabbi-friend who is the co-editor of *Learn Torah With...* (our international Torah Fax) ever knew

402—וְזֹאת הַבְּרָכָה

וזאת הברכה אשר ברך מ

but the Torah of a board and care facility. We are not going gently into that good night.

When I was twenty-something I watched Rabbi Joe Edleheit teach a bunch of high school kids called "Rashi's Rangers," a James Bond Torah Secret. Hidden in the last words of each book of the Torah is a secret message: "FROM EGYPT," "THEIR JOURNEYS," "SINAI," "JERICHO," "ISRAEL." Here is the spiritual road map of the Jewish people. I have often retaught that lesson. Now, however, I've learned that it is a lesson that is simultaneously true and untrue.

The end of the Torah feels like that moment when you're watching a TV show you've taped and you're just a few minutes before the end of the show, when all your viewing is about to make sense. Then the tape suddenly runs out. All of a sudden the recorder clicks into auto-rewind. The Torah does that to us. One minute we are Moses, standing at the edge of the Promised Land,

the next minute we are back at Adam and Eve. This is Möbius Torah—turn it and turn it again Torah—the Torah that is in eternal reruns on some cable channel. One minute we are FAT, THICK AND GROSS [Deut. 32.12]—perverse from years of sin and corruption. The next minute we are again NAKED AND UNASHAMED. [Gen. 2.25] The Torah is not only Alpha to Omega, but also, Omega to Alpha—that is one of its deepest truths.

If the Torah were a linear book, it would be a Shakespearean tragedy. Old Moses dies, victim of his pride and his anger; the *yetzer ha-ra* (the animal urges) that supercharged so much greatness couldn't find the right gear ratio to cruise with normal people. He is a soul that can't seem to get the idle right. His dream is painfully, after so much disappointment, left unfulfilled. In *Lamentations Rabbah*, the midrashic heart of the lament for the destruction of the Temple, God says, "Woe to a monarch who suc-

Synopsis: "This is the blessing with which Moses the man of God blessed the children of Israel prior to his death." (Deut. 33:1) What could be more appropriate than to conclude the Torah with a blessing for each of the tribes? Moses ascends Mount Nevo and dies. The people of Israel mourn him for 30 days. "And there never again was a prophet in Israel like Moses who knew God face to face" (Deut. 34:10).

that. It was the hardest and most interesting question you ever asked me so far. And, I got to do a lot of studying and learning before I came up with a good answer. One I liked. (By the way, what is your answer?)

Here is my best version of the answer….

Ibn Ezra says that Simeon got left out as a punishment for bad stuff done at

a place called Ba'al Peor . (We'll talk about that story, later.)

Rambam says that there must always be only twelve tribes. In these blessings, Joseph is counted as two tribes, Epharim and Manasseh (his sons) and so, one tribe has to be left out. Or else there would be thirteen. He explains that to keep the twelve balanced, Simeon is combined with

Judah—and so shares Judah's blessing. He says this is okay, because if you look ahead into the book of Joshua, we see in verse 19.2: "THE SECOND LOT CAME OUT FOR SIMEON, FOR THE TRIBE OF SIMEON, ACCORDING TO ITS FAMILIES; AND ITS INHERITANCE WAS IN THE MIDST OF THE INHERITANCE OF THE TRIBE OF JUDAH." Because, eventually, Simeon and Judah share land, it makes sense to share a blessing.

ceeded in youth, but failed in old age." It is a very powerful and painful image: God as Fredrich March in *A Star is Born*—the prodigy Who can't sustain a mature body of work. This is clearly an Image of the Divine in Whose form Moses feels created at this moment. In the sunset of Woodstock fantasies, in the decline of new deals, great societies, and new world orders—after inquisition and holocaust—and given most nights on CNN—we, too, often feel like we've been created in the image of a God Who succeeded in youth and failed in old age. It is easy to sing a chorus of "vanity of vanities." It is easy to wait for the Divine kiss on the edge of a dream that was already shredding and cracking long before the warranty ran out.

But, then you push the first valve down, and the Torah goes round and round. It is simple to explain this recycling of the scroll as the Torah of *t'shuvah*—our lives being washed clean by high holiday prayers and the coming of the rains of fall. It is true, but not sufficient.

We do sing *Hashiveynu*, we do ask God to renew our days as of old. We do wash away the old man Moses' makeup, the grandma Moses' makeup, and find Adam and Eve underneath. But, this isn't enough of a truth, either. Because when we take off our first-people masks, Moses' face is again revealed.

But, I think there is a deeper truth. Let's use a parable. Let's use "*The Sorcerer's Apprentice* in *Fantasia*. This is a story of *puer* (youth) and *senex* (the hoary head). This is the story of an heroic-adventuring child and it is the story of a wise, tired and bitter old man. Adam steals the Wizard's hat and wand and believes he can control the Power. Moses, over and over, struggles to clean up the flood waters that were left behind by the children who grab powers that they can't yet control. The story flashes from *tav* to *alef*, from the *Eish Dat*—a Buring Torah of Knowedge/Faith—back to *Eitz ha-Da'at*, The Tree of Knowledge. We go from Wizard to Adam, Mickey to

V'Zot Ha-Brakhah

I didn't like either answer. But I did find part of the truth in each answer, it made me go back and look at the whole story of Simeon.

Here is what I found:

(1) Simeon is Jacob's son. Leah, the wife whom Jacob liked second best, first gave birth to Reuben (God saw my pain) and then to Simeon (God hears my loneliness). Next come

Levi (God connects with me), and then Judah (I will thank God). Then she stops having kids and Rachel, the favorite wife, tries to have some sons on her side. Reuben, Simeon, Levi and Judah are "whole brothers" (same mother—same father). There are also two other full brothers: Issachar and Zebulun. The "Shabbat" (number 7) in the Jacob-Leah clan is the only daughter, "Dinah."

Moses. We cycle our inner selves, trapped in Xeno's paradox, getting only halfway closer to crossing the Jordan each year.

This is a moment where Judaism is a circle.We end, saying, "NEVER AGAIN WILL THERE ARISE IN ISRAEL A PROPHET LIKE MOSES [DEUT. 34.10], while we again

begin our journey in the garden. We are trapped in the cycle of the Dying and Rising Torah—endless big bang Torah, the Torah of Wilderness and Repentance, the Torah of supernova and black hole, waiting to emerge from the fire—waiting to understand enough to know Messiah.

Meanwhile, halfway each year is better than dying endlessly on the *Pisgah*. Meanwhile, we pray for the momentum to reach escape velocity—to create the vector, the line that takes Jewish history to the end. This year we want our Moses to finally enter his Promised Land—*Bereshit*.●

---

(2) Later on, Dinah has an unfortunate relationship with a local Canaanite, the son of Hamor, named Shekhem. Most commentators and the midrash think that he hurt her, but she still wanted to be with him. Jacob and the family were unhappy. They work out a deal with Hamor that every man in the entire city of Shekhem is to be circumcised and convert to Judaism, and then Shekhem may marry Dinah. On the third day after the big ceremony, Simeon and his brother Levi play "Navy Seals" and attack the city killing every man and destroying everything. Jacob is angry and says [Gen. 35.5] , "YOU HAVE BROUGHT TROUBLE ON ME BY MAKING ME ODIOUS TO THE INHABITANTS OF THE LAND, THE CANAANITES AND THE PERIZZITES; MY NUMBERS ARE FEW, AND IF THEY GATHER THEMSELVES AGAINST ME AND ATTACK ME, I SHALL BE DESTROYED, BOTH MY LAND AND MY HOUSEHOLD."

(3) Much later in the story, when Jacob is about to die, he gives Simeon and Levi a joint blessing. It reads: [Gen. 49.5-7] "SIMEON AND LEVI ARE BROTHERS; WEAPONS OF VIOLENCE ARE THEIR SWORDS. MAY MY SPIRIT NOT BE JOINED TO THEIR COMPANY; FOR IN THEIR ANGER THEY SLAY MEN...CURSED BE THEIR ANGER, FOR IT IS FIERCE; AND THEIR WRATH, FOR IT IS CRUEL! I

WILL DIVIDE THEM IN JACOB AND SCATTER THEM IN ISRAEL."

If you read carefully you can learn three things: (a) that Simeon and Levi have bad tempers which can get out of control, (b) when they are together, they are impossible to control, and [c] so that everybody can get along, God is going to separate them. This is a lot like a teacher splitting up two good friends who help each other get into too much trouble, and who can each control himself better when they are apart. This blessing is the key to the story, we know it comes true. Levi is split up and never becomes a tribe with land—they get to be priests, instead. And Simeon is split up and doesn't really become a tribe with land, either; instead, they become part of the kingly tribe of Judah and get to be part of the king's escort. Levi becomes the soldiers of God's Temple. Simeon becomes the soldiers of the king. Neither tribe is kept together as a unit. And, the two tribes are separated.

But that is not the end of the story!

(4) In the Joseph story, Simeon is the brother Joseph holds for ransom when the brothers go back to get Benjamin. In the midrash, we learn two things: (a) that Simeon was

among the brothers who bullied and was meanest to Joseph (who was number one son of the other and favorite wife), and (b) Simeon and Joseph made up and became friends while he was waiting in Egypt for the other brothers to return.

(5) The midrash tells us some stuff that was not in the Torah (directly). We learn that in Egypt, Simeon was pretty heroic. They kept their family and tribe together when many other tribes failed to do so. When it came to resisting the cruelty of Egypt, Simeon's strength and pride were an important part of Jewish survival.

(6) The worst story about Simeon (now a tribe and not just a brother) is the Ba'al Peor story. This is in Numbers. Almost ready to enter the land of Israel, the kids of Israel get in this trouble. They start dating and hanging out with Midianite (idol-worshiping) women. God and Moses get angry and say, "Just say no!" Most of Israel follows along with the new order except for Zimri and a bunch of other Simeonites. Zimri brings his date to the front of all Israel and in front of the Tabernacle. It is like a dare, and a guy named Phineas, from the tribe of Levi, grabs a spear and runs it through both Zimri and his

Michael Tolkin

MICHAEL TOLKIN WROTE AND DIRECTED *THE RAPTURE* AND *THE NEW AGE*. HIS NOVELS ARE *THE PLAYER* AND *AMONG THE DEAD*.

V'Zot Ha-Brakhah

DEATH OF MOSES

If the Auth-r were an almost-great writer, if he had pursued, from his first breath, the divine logic of his vision, but, like a mortal writer, had fallen too much in love with Moses, and after reading his first draft, had relented, just a little, from the rigor of his story, and in the end, while refusing to admit Moses to Canaan, he had just, for a second, realized his decree, what would suffer harm if we had the scene of Moses dying when he hears the sound of Joshua's trumpet?

And if the Auth-r had conceded to his greatest character his greatest desire, would the world have been so different if Moses, dying, had heard not just Gabriel's trumpet, but the sound of the tumbling walls, on a bluff overlooking the Jericho battle-field, on the Egyptian side of the river? Our rabbis would teach us: and in the death of Moses we learn that victory is guaranteed the faithful.

Now if the Auth-r, having broken the rigor of his original draft, had lowered His genius by only two more degrees, then Joshua, in defiance of the Lord's decree, would have carried the old man across the river, and set him in a tent, with a view of the battlefield.

"Lord," says Joshua, "you gave us Moses our great teacher and yet deny him the smallest taste of the first fruits of our labor."

"The first fruits belong to me.

But just this once...." And so the Auth-r, chipping away at the original plan, but still an Auth-r with a

date Cozbi (the Midianite lady). And, interestingly, God thanks Phineas for cooling God's anger!!!!!! (Strange!) Then comes a plague and a whole bunch of Israelites (especially from Simeon) die for messin' with the Moabites. (Tough story).

(7) That leads us to Moses leaving them out in the end. Here is what I think are the big lessons of every-thing.

It takes all kinds of people to make a family: including Simeon and Levi and the angry—sometimes out-of-control—but really brave brothers. They are the heroes, and heroes are hard to live with. They are defi-nitely not the peacemakers. They get out-of-control sometimes. God

great love of sadness, if not tragedy, starts to write, "And as Moses saw Joshua and his army capture Jericho, an angel of the Lord came into Moses' tent to take him away when…." When Moses said to the angel, "At least let me congratulate Joshua."

And if the Auth-r, in a resurgence of integrity, had conceded yet again, but reserved for himself some comment on the story invisible to the characters, then at this point he might have written, "And Joshua stopped at the tent. And Joshua entered the tent." This, so the rabbis would ask, "And why does it say, 'And Joshua stopped at the tent?' So Rashi teaches us, because Joshua stopped at the tent?" So Rashi teaches us, this is the indication of Joshua's reluctance to face his teacher, for fear that a deathbed rally might bring sufficient breath to the old man for one more book of laws.

And having given his beloved character everything he asked for, could he have denied him his last peroration? "Let me speak to the people one more time!" cried the teacher. So

in the middle of the city's main square, Moses gives his final lesson, starting with a second repetition of the story, and a few new laws, and a long blessing. Satisfied that he has had everything he asked for, and that his Auth-r is a merciful, an exceedingly merciful Auth-r, who concedes and teaches concession, Moses looks up at the sky and says, "Now, Lord, now." And why does Moses say "now" twice? For each smiting of the rock. And what does this teach us? Ah, well, now we're into deep Kabalah, and while I'd love to tell you, my Master bids me keep it secret.

He dies. The tribes surround his bed. They kneel in awe.

The Auth-r, when he rereads the revision, discovers that the new materials won't permit him one of the first draft's best images. At this point, carrying Moses to a hidden grave becomes a forced conceit. He could never trust Joshua to carry Moses away, and keep the grave's location a secret. No, coerced by his characters to give them what they want, the Auth-r writes the final

chapter of the **six** books of the Torah. Joshua calls for a state funeral, which lasts a month. This month becomes the Jews' most burdensome festival. During this month, the work begins on the grave.

The grave is the biggest problem, a greater challenge than the design of the ark. Here, the Auth-r withdraws, as the rabbis teach us, because he mourns Moses no less than do his chosen people, but also, as the rabbis teach us, to see what the people have learned.

Everyone contributes to the monument. They carry stones, they carry mortar, twelve tribes, three to a side, four sides, all the stones beautifully cut and shaped, because this grave is the great symbol of how the prince of Egypt triumphed over his birth. They build a pyramid.•

---

hates their anger. Jacob hates their anger. But, in a really cool part of Midrash Rabbah, one of the Rabbis says, "Jacob cursed their anger, he didn't curse them." So, to help them out, to maximize their potential, they get new jobs. Levi becomes the heroes of the Temple. Simeon becomes part of King David's Palace guard. (Levi is a little bit ahead of Simeon because they kept their cool

around the Midianite women, when Zimri and crew didn't.) But, this is the bottom bottom line. Anger is sometimes important. We need stubborn, hard-to-change-their-minds, real passionate Jews, too. The courage of Simeon, even though it is sometimes dangerous as uncontrolled anger, helped us to survive Egypt. There is a place in the Jewish people for every Jew. Basically, Simeon just got a new

Judean Lion's uniform—and got traded to the team that could really use him and his special skills.

Can't wait 'til next week's question. Meanwhile, look at Genesis 6.1-4 and tell me who the "Divine Beings" and the Nefilim actually were and what this teaches. 'Cause I have no idea.
Joel Grishaver
<gris@torahaura.com>

V'Zot Ha-Brakhah

דָּבָר אַחֵר **DAVAR AHER.** "Moses ascended from the plains of Moab, to Mount Nebo, to the summit of the cliff that faces Jericho, and Ha-shem showed him the entire land" [Deut. 34.1]. I have often wondered how Moses must have felt as he "ascended from the plains of Moab to the summit of the cliff of Mount Nebo that faces Jericho." What is it that Adonai wanted to show him, one last time, before his death? The Torah speaks about Adonai telling him one last time not to worry about his children, for they will be well-taken care of. As Moses and Adonai stood, looking down from this vantage point, there was something wonderful happening below them as their sight drifted from the barrier of the Jordan River into the distance. What thoughts were crossing Moses' mind as his children and grandchildren crossed into the promised land?

We are told that the Torah ends with the letter *lamed* and begins with the letter *bet*, demonstrating that we should serve God with all of our heart, *lev*. To this day, I waver like the lulav on Sukkot wondering whether Moses had a heavy heart or a light one as he overlooked the joy of his people as they finished their journey, returning to the land promised to them by Adonai. One of my colleagues, Rabbi Gloria Rubin, helped me to understand what was happening to Moses by offering this modern midrash: just as we are instructed to begin reading the Torah over again, immediately, on Simhat Torah, we can also imagine Moses standing on the mountaintop overlooking Eretz Yisrael. What he envisioned in those few brief moments with Adonai was the unfolding of Creation as Moses had recorded it in the Torah.

The two of them watched as a new world came into being, a new Garden of Eden, so perfect in many ways. Yet it required the help of Adonai's chosen people to maintain that world and to labor in it so that it continued to exist. So it is the tears of joy that are shed at the birth of a baby boy or a baby girl that Moses shed, as well as tears of sadness, for Moses knew in advance the trials and the tribulations that his family faced as they crossed the threshold back into the Garden that awaited them. **Steven J. Rubenstein, <RABBIOLI@aol.com>**

דָּבָר אַחֵר **DAVAR AHER.** "And Ha-shem said to him, 'This is the land which I swore to Abraham, to Isaac, and to Jacob, saying, 'I will give it to your offspring. I have let you see it with your own eyes, but you shall not cross over to there'" [Deut. 34.4]. Whether one may view time in a linear or cyclical construct, there are certain limitations to each view. The answer may be in the final Torah readings. A Midrash relates that Moses realized the only way he could continue to grow would be to enter the Land of Israel. When he makes 515 pleas but is still not allowed to enter Israel, Moses knows that there will be no life without growth and his days are numbered.

Although Judaism may favor a cyclical approach to seasons and life, we should not remain in a rut by making the same circle. We must continue to grow and change. As the Torah is a Tree of Life to those who grasp it, life, itself, replicates itself with a helix, both linear and cyclical. Time, as well, may be thought of as a helix. Other analogies may extend to a tightly woven helix as a community or the world as one, at peace, or an unwinding spool spinning out of control, or a helix cleaving and splitting going in disparate directions. This year, may we endeavor to work to make our world and community one, at peace. <Vitrealman@aol.com> *[Editor's Question: Does anyone understand the significance of 515 as the number of pleas in this Midrash? We don't.]*

דְּבָר אַחֵר **DAVAR AHER.** "AND HA-SHEM SAID TO HIM, 'THIS IS THE LAND WHICH I SWORE TO ABRAHAM, TO ISAAC, AND TO JACOB, SAYING, "I WILL GIVE IT TO YOUR OFFSPRING." I HAVE LET YOU SEE IT WITH YOUR OWN EYES, BUT YOU SHALL NOT CROSS OVER TO THERE.'" [DEUT. 34.4]. It would, of course, be easier if the folks who cite "a midrash" would be encouraged to specify a reference. This version (the number is different in other versions) is from a fragment published in *Otzar Midrashim* 2.376b. The gematria 515 is based on וָאֶתְחַנַּן *V'ET-HaNaN* "AND I PRAYED" [Deut 3.23]. **Rabbi Dennis Beck-Berman** <BeckBerman@aol.com>. *And we were afraid that this number was the Remez of an address in Brooklyn…. (Ed.)*

דְּבָר אַחֵר **DAVAR AHER.** On the new year: My father told me a wonderful midrash on this right before Rosh ha-Shanah. The difference

between the lunar and solar calendars is ten days per year. Ten days difference between our living on Jewish time and our living on "ordinary" time. It's as if the ten days of *t'shuvah* are those ten days, and they bridge the gap between our various selves and the worlds we live in. **Deb Gordon** <102551.500@compuserve.com>

דְּבָר אַחֲרוֹן **DAVAR AHARON.** Even though we skipped some, we've made it round the Torah the first time together (almost). Now, we get to do v'Zot ha-Brakhah and then back to Bereshit. So here is my end question, then we go back to Genesis again. How do you think that Moses spent his last day before he headed up the Pisgah to kiss God? I've been thinking about that one a lot. I am also looking forward to your last question. (Before I get your next first one). Shanah Tovah. GRIS.

Dear Joel Grishaver, I think Moses' last day was: (1) spent it saying goodbye to family and friends, (2) plotting with Joshua. **Shaye Horwitz, Age 7,** <RABBIDANNY@aol.com>

חֲזַק, חֲזַק, וְנִתְחַזֵּק

Hazak Hazak v'nit-Hazek

INDEX

INDEX

INDEX

Acknowledgments

We would like to thank our outstanding faculty and those who formed the community of learners who made **Learn Torah With...** *possible.*

We would also like to thank our proofreaders and copy editors:

> *Deborah Glass*
> *Elana Kelman*
> *Deborah Greenbaum*
> *Carolyn Moore-Mooso*
> *Rabbi Robert Ratner*

Other titles from Alef Design Group

For Adults

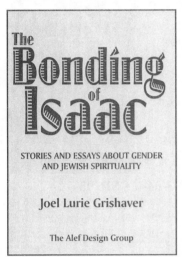

NEW! The Bonding of Isaac
Joel Lurie Grishaver

Issues of gender and spirituality are the subject of the new work by Joel Lurie Grishaver. Weaving together traditional Jewish texts with books, movies and other elements of popular culture, Mr. Grishaver considers the way men and women approach their own spiritual and relationship needs.

Is there another writer and thinker in the Jewish community like Joel Grishaver? I think not. This book is Grishaver unbound: wit, wisdom, lore, learning, midrash and memoir—the full range of his genius playing with and pondering core texts, core issues, bringing the Torah vitally alive. The Bonding of Isaac *is both in form and in content a unique book. Bravo, brother!*—PETER PITZELE, AUTHOR OF OUR FATHER'S WELLS: A PERSONAL ENCOUNTER WITH THE MYTHS OF GENESIS

Hardcover • Subject: Gender/Spirituality •
ISBN #1-881283-20-8 • $21.95

NEW! Tales of the Chutzper Rebbe
Rabbi Walter Rothschild

Illustrated by Paul Palnik

Lost in the forests and plains of Eastern Europe lies the little town of Chutzp. There they have never heard of Martin Buber or Elie Wiesel, yet somehow their lies and stories have an echo—a dark, reverse echo—of the Hasidic tales discovered and told by these masters. Like the *schlemiels* of Chelm, the Chutzper Hasidim somehow blunder their way through life, scattering scraps of Jewish tradition as they go. Whether in their travels, their work, their relationship to other Jews, to non-Jews, or even to God, the Chutsper Hasidim are simple, literal and to the point—even if they are not always sure what that point is...

This book will appeal most to those who know enough Hasidic stories and their backgrounds to appreciate and enjoy these mild parodies of the genre. A full glossary is provided of all Hebrew and Yiddish terms. The stories are improved—as are all stories—by telling them aloud.

Hardcover Edition • Subject: Humorous Stories •ISBN #1-881283-12-7 • $16.50

The Kosher Pig
And Other Curiosities of Modern Jewish Life
Rabbi Richard Israel/illustrations by Shan Wells

Richard Israel has been the only rabbi in Bombay, India, a beekeeper, a successful marathon runner, and the director of Hillel Jewish Student Centers on various college campuses. These diverse experiences give him a unique vantage point on the chaos which is modern Jewish life. He gets caught in the tension between being a traditional Jew and being a modern American...and suspects that, indeed, he may be neither.

Softcover • Subject: Jewish Life • ISBN #1-881283-15-1 • $14.95

40 Things You Can Do to Save the Jewish People
SOME REALLY PRACTICAL IDEAS FOR PARENTS WHO WANT TO RAISE "GOOD ENOUGH"
JEWISH KIDS TO INSURE THAT THE JEWISH PEOPLE LAST AT LEAST ANOTHER GENERATION

Joel Lurie Grishaver

An insightful book on Jewish parenting by a middle-aged divorced man without children, *40 Things* is based on the many failures and few successes of the author's friends' attempts to be perfect Jewish parents. It is a practical book about improving the odds which asks: "How much can we get away with and still raise fully Jewish children who will in turn raise other Jewish children?"

Softcover • Subject: Parenting/Education • ISBN #1-881283-04-6 • $16.95

Eight Great Dreidel Stories
Martin Gal

Hanukkah is not just for children. Every year Martin Gal writes a new Hanukkah story. Each year, he mails them to his friends as presents. The stories have nothing in common except that somewhere in each plot is a dreidel. These stories are for you to enjoy after the kids have gone to bed, or have grown up and left home. You deserve a present, too. These stories are the kind of Hanukkah stories they don't teach in Hebrew School.

Softcover • Subject: Hanukkah • ISBN #1-881283-10-0 • $13.95

Being a Blessing:
54 Ways You Can Help People Living with AIDS
Rabbi Harris R. Goldstein

This amazingly simple book by Rabbi Harris R. Goldstein leads us through the understanding and the actions needed to live up to the best of our intentions. Things as varied as "AIDS 101," how to visit a person living with AIDS, "people with AIDS Bill of Rights," and what it means to be created in God's image. The educational, the religious and the political aspects of the AIDS crisis are included—basic information on how to be a good person at a scary time.

Softcover • Subject: AIDS • ISBN #1-881283-08-9 • $13.95

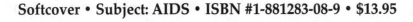

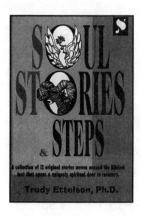

Soul Stories and Steps

Trudy Ettelson, Ph.D.

Jews have a long tradition of weaving their own stories between the line of the Biblical text. This embroidery of the Bible is called Midrash. In this collection of original stories, Trudy Ettelson weaves her own understanding of the Jewish tradition, not only around the Biblical text, but around the 12 Steps as well. Here is a spiritual book steeped in Jewish tradition, leading one along a path toward recovery.

Softcover • Subject: Spirituality • ISBN #1-881283-07-0 • $6.95

For Families

NEW! Stark's Amazing Jewish Family Cookbook
Written and Illustrated by Mark Stark

This cookbook is a collection of secret family recipes. It is a celebration of Jewish cooking for everyone who wishes to enjoy Jewish food. Everything is ready for even the most beginning of cooks. Each hand-drawn recipe shows the ingredients, the tools needed, and the steps used to make it. Recipes are listed by holiday, along with a description of each Jewish holiday. All recipes are coded for easy adherence to kashrut, the religious and dietary laws of the Jewish people. For those who want to discover the fun of creative Jewish cooking as well as the pride of accomplishment when they make something others enjoy, this book is a must.

Softcover • Family • Cooking/Jewish Life • ISBN #1-881283-19-4 • $26.50

Eight Nights, Eight Lights
Rabbi Kerry M. Olitzky

Courage. Gratitude. Sharing. Knowledge. Service. Understanding. Love. Hope. Eight nights. Eight lights. Eight family values. In this joyous and reflective work, Rabbi Kerry M. Olitzky provides families with a way of letting their Hanukkah celebrations affirm not only their Jewish identity, but the very Jewish values they wish to transmit to their children.

Softcover • Subject: Family/Hanukkah • ISBN #1-881283-09-7 • $8.95

For Children

NEW! Let's Talk About the Sabbath

Dorothy K. Kripke/Illustrated by Joy Nelkin Weider

Off the pen of a well respected Jewish children's author, *Let's Talk About the Sabbath* is a young person's guide to the Sabbath. From meeting the Queen of the Sabbath, to celebrating Havdallah, this book delights in the visions of a perfect Sabbath experience.

Beautifully written in poetry and prose, Ms. Kripke enchants readers with all the aspects of Sabbath, including candles and wine, Sabbath angels, study and prayer, Sabbath joy, and the farewell to this special day.

The full-color illustrations by Joy Nelkin Weider direct the eye to the beauty of the Sabbath.

Hardcover • Middle Reader • Subject: The Shabbat • ISBN # 1-881283-18-6 • $16.95.

NEW! Sing Time

Bruce H. Siegel/Illustrated by Joshua Siegel

A ten-year-old "master of the fast comeback" and connoisseur of rock and roll discovers in half an hour how a single teacher, a Cantor, can impact his life. This Cantor doesn't just sing songs, he shares the value of a single moment in time, and how music is the "calendar" of Jewish life. Cantor Jacobs steers our hero down a path he might never have taken otherwise, all because his dad decided that Jerry-the-Jerk (his older brother, Gerald) should have a bar mitzvah.

Softcover • Middle Reader • Subject: Jewish Connections • ISBN # 1-881283-14-3 • $5.95

Champion & Jewboy

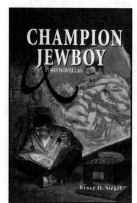

TWO NOVELLAS

Bruce H. Siegel/Illustrated by Spark

Two young adult novellas by Bruce H. Siegel are bound together in *Champion & Jewboy*. The first novella, *Champion*, follows a young boys discovery of his grandfather's hidden past as a boxer. The story reveals the anti-Semitic treatment the grandfather received in Russia as he tried to become an Olympic boxer.

The second novella, *Jewboy*, features a teenager convicted of vandalizing a synagogue who is transported through time to witness and participate in the most famous anti-Semitic event of the 20th century.

Softcover • Young Adult • Subject: Anti-Semitism, Self-Discovery • ISBN #1-881283-11-9 • $6.95

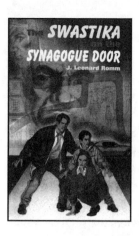

The Swastika on the Synagogue Door

J. Leonard Romm/illustrated by Spark

When a suburban synagogue on Long Island is attacked by anti-Semitic vandals, the hatred manifest in the spray paint forces the Lazarus kids to confront their own history, their own prejudice, and still find the guilty party.

This mystery for young adult readers takes them on an exciting roller-coaster through Jewish history and contemporary Jewish reality. The surprise ending is bound to get you, too.

Softcover • Young Adult • Anti-Semitism • ISBN #1-881283-05-4 • $6.95

The Grey Striped Shirt

Jacqueline Jules/Illustrated by Mike Cressy

Frannie is looking for Grandma's purple hat with the feather. By accident she discovers a grey striped shirt with a yellow star hidden in the back of the closet. Slowly, she begins asking her Grandparents questions. Slowly they begin to unfold the story of their Holocaust experience. This novel for middle readers gently reveals the truths about the Holocaust without reducing it to a horror show.

Softcover • Middle Reader • Subject: Holocaust • ISBN #1-881283-21-6 • $7.95

Dear Hope... Love, Grandma

Hilda Abramson Hurwitz & Hope R. Wasburn
Edited by Mara H. Wasburn

Eight-year-old Hope had a school project to become the summer pen pal of a senior citizen. When her assigned pen pal failed to write back, her mother suggested she write to her grandmother. A two-year correspondence resulted.

This book is a collection of letters in which Grandma reveals the stories of her childhood, the difficulties growing up in turn-of-the-century St. Louis, and some wonderful and joyous insights about human hearts.

**Hardcover • Middle Reader • Subject: Autobiography/Letters •
ISBN #1-881283-03-8 • $13.95**

Tanta Teva and the Magic Booth

Joel Lurie Grishaver/Illustrated by David Bleicher

It all started when Marc (with a "C") Zeiger ran away one night to get his parents to buy him a Virtual Reality hook-up (it's a long story). In the dark, lost in a part of the woods which couldn't possibly exist, he encounters Tanta Teva, a cleaning lady who is busy scrubbing graffiti off rocks in the forest. Together they visit young Joshua, David and Hillel. When Marc returns home, no one really believes the stories of where he'd been and who he'd met!

Softcover • Middle Reader • Subject: Fantasy • ISBN #1-881283-00-3 • $5.95

For Young Children

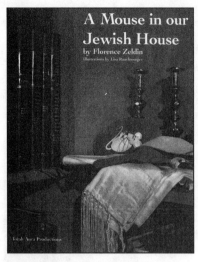

A Mouse in Our Jewish House
Florence Zeldin/Illustrated by Lisa Rauchwerger

This imaginative counting book by noted children's author Florence Zeldin combines the mastery of counting from one to twelve with the introduction of the basic celebrations of the Jewish year. A mouse named Archie Akhbar inhabits this book. Brought to life by the imaginative paper sculptures of Lisa Rauchwerger, Archie eats an escalating number of pieces of food on each subsequent Jewish holiday.

A counting book through the food of the Jewish holidays.

Hardcover • Picture Book • Subject: Jewish Holidays •
ISBN #0-933873-43-3 • $11.95

A Sense of Shabbat

Faige Kobre

In the sensuous photographs and simple text that make up this picture book, the taste, feel, sound, look and touch of the Jewish Sabbath all come alive. The Sabbath presented here is at once holy and wondrous, comfortable and familiar.

The joys of Shabbat stimulate the five senses.

Hardcover • Picture Book • Subject:
Sabbath • ISBN #0-933873-44-1 • $11.95

Alef Design Group

4423 Fruitland Avenue, Los Angeles, CA 90058
800-845-0662 • 213-582-1200
fax: 213-585-0327 • e-mail: <misrad@torahaura.com>

420

Order Information

_____ *Learn Torah With...5755 Torah Annual* (hc) $28.95 _____

_____ *The Bonding of Isaac* (hc) $21.95 _____

_____ *Tales of the Chutzper Rebbe* (hc) $16.50 _____

_____ *The Kosher Pig* (pbk) $14.95 _____

_____ *40 Things You Can Do to Save the Jewish People* (pbk) $16.95 _____

_____ *Eight Great Dreidle Stories* (pbk) $13.95 _____

_____ Being A Blessing (pbk) $13.95 _____

_____ Soul Stories and Steps (pbk) $6.95 _____

_____ Stark's Amazing Jewish Family Cookbook (pbk) $26.50 _____

_____ Eight Nights, Eight Lights (hc) $8.95 _____

_____ Let's Talk About the Sabbath (hc) $16.95 _____

_____ Sing Time (pbk) $5.95 _____

_____ Champion/Jewboy (pbk) $6.95 _____

_____ The Swastika on the Synagogue Door (pbk) $6.95 _____

_____ The Grey Striped Shirt (pbk) $7.95 _____

_____ Dear Hope...Love, Grandma (hc) $13.95 _____

_____ Tanta Teva and the Magic Booth (pbk) $5.95 _____

_____ A Mouse in the Jewish House (hc) $11.95 _____

_____ A Sense of Shabbat (hc) $11.95 _____

Shipping & Handling—$5.50 for the first book, $2.00 each additional book _____

California residents: Please add 8.25% sales tax _____

Total _____

Name _____

Address _____

Address _____

City _____

State/Zip _____

A check is enclosed for _____

Charge to my credit card:

   q VISA   q MASTERCARD   q AMEX

Name on card _____

Card # _____

Expiration Date _____

---

*Phone, fax, or mail to: **Alef Design Group*** •4423 Fruitland Avenue, Los Angeles, CA 90058
800-845-0662 • 213-582-1200 •fax: 213-585-0327 • e-mail: <misrad@torahaura.com>